Investment Funds

Jurisdictional comparisons   **Second edition 2013**

General Editor:
Sam Kay, Travers Smith LLP

General Editor
Sam Kay
Travers Smith LLP

Commercial Director
Katie Burrington

Commissioning Editor
Emily Kyriacou

Senior Editor
Bronwyn Hemus

Editorial Assistant
Magda Wika

Design and Production
Dawn McGovern

Published in September 2013 by The European Lawyer Reference Series,
100 Avenue Road, London NW3 3PF
part of Thomson Reuters (Professional) UK Limited
(Registered in England & Wales, Company No 1679046.
Registered Office and address for service:
Aldgate House, 33 Aldgate High Street, London EC3N 1DL)

A CIP catalogue record for this book is available from the British Library.

ISBN: 978-0414031265

Thomson Reuters and the Thomson Reuters logo are trade marks of Thomson Reuters. Crown copyright material is reproduced with the permission of the Controller of HMSO and the Queen's Printer for Scotland.

While all reasonable care has been taken to ensure the accuracy of the publication, the publishers cannot accept responsibility for any errors or omissions.
This publication is protected by international copyright law.
All rights reserved. No part of this publication may be reproduced or transmitted in any form or by any means, or stored in any retrieval system of any nature without prior written permission, except for permitted fair dealing under the Copyright, Designs and Patents Act 1988, or in accordance with the terms of a licence issued by the Copyright Licensing Agency in respect of photocopying and/or reprographic reproduction. Application for permission for other use of copyright material including permission to reproduce extracts in other published works shall be made to the publishers. Full acknowledgement of author, publisher and source must be given.

© 2013 Thomson Reuters (Professional) UK Limited

Investment Funds

Contents

Preface Sam Kay   Travers Smith LLP — iii
Introduction Mark O'Hare, Founder and CEO of Preqin Ltd — v
Foreword Margaret Chamberlain, Chair of the BVCA Regulatory Committee — ix
Overview Dörte Höppner, ECVA — xi
Australia Stephen Etkind, Andrew Yik, Henry Wong & Karen Payne   Minter Ellison Lawyers — 1
Brazil Alexei Bonamin, Ana Cláudia Akie Utumi & João Busin   TozziniFreire Advogados — 17
British Virgin Islands Tim Clipstone & Sophie Whitcombe   Maples and Calder — 35
Cayman Islands Paul Govier & Sophie Whitcombe   Maples and Calder — 51
Denmark Claus Bennetsen   Horten Advokatpartnerselskab — 67
Finland Marcus Möller, Antti Lehtimaja, Mirja Sikander & Pyry Somervuori   Krogerus — 81
Germany Uwe Bärenz & Dr Jens Steinmüller   P+P Pöllath + Partners — 95
Gibraltar Melo Triay, Robert Vasquez, Jay J. Gomez & Javier E. Triay   Triay & Triay — 105
Guernsey Gavin Farrell, James Haughton, Oliver Godwin & Mandy Andrade   Mourant Ozannes — 119
Hong Kong Susan Gordon & Mary Nieto   Deacons — 135
Ireland Nollaig Greene, Elaine Keane, Darragh Noone & Peter Maher   A&L Goodbody Solicitors — 151
Iceland Johann Magnus Johannsson & Gudmundur J Oddsson   LOGOS Legal Services — 163
Italy Paolo Iemma & Stefano Grilli   Gianni, Origoni, Grippo, Cappelli & Partners — 181
Japan Kazuhiro Yoshii, Ko Hanamizu, Anri Suzuki & Mariko Takashima   Anderson Mori & Tomotsune — 203
Jersey Niamh Lalor & Tim Morgan   Ogier — 223
Korea Eui Jong Chung, Tongeun Kim, Dongwook Kang & David Ahn Bae   Kim & Lee LLC — 241
Luxembourg Jacques Elvinger & Xavier Le Sourne   Elvinger, Hoss & Prussen — 253
Malta John Paul Zammit & Danièle Cop   Mamo TCV Advocates — 269
Mauritius Iqbal Rajahbalee, Shan Sonnagee & Bhavna Ramsurun   BLC Chambers — 285
The Netherlands Oscar van Angeren, Harm-Paul Plas & Sylvia Dikmans   Houthoff Buruma — 301
New Zealand Alasdair McBeth   DLA Phillips Fox — 313

Investment Funds

Portugal Diogo Coutinho de Gouveia, Filipe Santos Barata & Ana Paula Basílio 327
Gómez-Acebo & Pombo

Singapore Bill Jamieson, Amit Dhume & Manisha Rai   Colin Ng & Partners LLP 349

South Africa David Anderson, Francisco Khoza, Mogola Makola & Kirsten Kern 365
Bowman Gilfillan

Spain Fernando de las Cuevas, Valentina Rodríguez & Remedios García 381
Gómez-Acebo & Pombo

Sweden Niclas Rockborn & Olle Asplund   Gernandt & Danielsson 401

Switzerland Dr. Jasmin Ghandchi Schmid, LL.M.   Ghandchi Schmid Partners Ltd. 417

United Kingdom Sam Kay, Emily Clark & Phil Bartram   Travers Smith LLP 435

United States of America Jay Milkes, Sarah Davidoff & Michael Doherty 455
Ropes & Gray LLP

Contacts 471

Investment Funds

Preface

Sam Kay Travers Smith LLP

This book provides a global comparison of fundamental legal, tax and regulatory considerations relating to the establishment and operation of investment funds in a range of jurisdictions where the industry is active. Each chapter is written by leading legal advisers from the relevant jurisdiction, provided information on the structures typically used, the regulatory framework for those funds, any significant operational requirements, how the funds may be marketed, a summary of the tax treatment for both the fund itself and investors and customary or common terms.

A global comparison of investment funds is necessary because of the breadth and diversity of the market. As this book demonstrates, there are a multitude of different legal structures that are used and each jurisdiction applies its own legal and regulatory framework. But there is also a wide variety of asset classes that are captured within the market: from traditional long-only equity funds through to leveraged buyout funds and hedge funds. As a further example, in the last couple of years there has been a significant number of credit opportunity funds being raised as private institutions look to capitalise on the restructuring of the corporate balance sheet or fill the gap created by the larger retail banks imposing tougher lending criteria. Funds for different asset classes will have their own bespoke features and requirements.

There are a number of other reasons why a comprehensive global comparison is important:.

- The industry is becoming increasingly international, with funds being marketed to a wide investor base. Fund managers need to know how to offer their funds in a range of different jurisdictions and what rules apply. This book not only sets out the information needed, but also provides a network of leading experts from independent law firms around the world who can be called upon to provide advice.
- The regulatory environment in which investment funds operate has become more complex and the rate of change has accelerated over the last couple of years. An example is the recent introduction of the pan-European Alternative Investment Fund Managers Directive, which became directly applicable in the 28 members states of the European Union on 22 July 2013. We are grateful for the short section in this book explaining the Directive contributed by Margaret Chamberlain. Margaret is a partner at Travers Smith and has led a team that has been heavily involved for a number of years in negotiating the Directive on behalf of the funds industry with the politicians and regulators. Her insight is invaluable.
- The market is continually developing, becoming more sophisticated and challenging as different participants enter the fray with different

demands and requirements. In order to keep up with the pace of change, practitioners need to be up to date with the latest developments and be able to demonstrate thought leadership on structural and operational issues.

About this book

To try and provide a framework for each chapter, we have focused on two categorisations of 'investment funds': 'alternative investment funds' and 'retail funds'. There will obviously be overlaps between these two categories and some strategies or structures will not be adequately catered for (an obviously example being listed funds aimed at institutional investors). However, the suggested split is intended to be as follows:
1. Alternative Investment Funds cover the non-traditional private fund strategies such as private equity, venture capital, hedge funds and real estate.
2. Retail Funds cover the traditional mutual, authorised, regulated or registered funds that are commonly available to the public and, therefore, are not offered on a private placement basis. For this reason, retail funds have traditionally been more heavily regulated than other types of funds.

This book is intended to put the investment funds industry into its global context, to give some idea of its significance and, above all, to examine the key issues that are associated with the structuring and operation of investment funds. The chapters in this book have been written by some of the leading legal practitioners around the world and they have achieved the rare feat of providing an introduction to those not particularly familiar with the investment funds industry, whilst also providing points of interest and guidance to more seasoned experts. In addition to the section provided by Margaret Chamberlain that has already been referred to, we also have two further introductory sections: one from Dörte Höppner, the Secretary-General of the European venture capital and private equity industry group EVCA, and the second from Mark O'Hare of Preqin, the leading data and intelligence provider for the alternative asset industry. We thank each of them for contributing their invaluable and highly relevant industry comments.

Investment Funds

Introduction

Mark O'Hare, Founder and CEO of Preqin Ltd

REGULATION AND FUND TERMS & CONDITIONS – CONSIDERATIONS FOR ALTERNATIVE ASSETS FUNDS

Notwithstanding the challenging economic times, market conditions and prospects for the alternative assets industry remain robust and on a positive trajectory.

Preqin's latest Investor Outlook, completed during June to August 2013, surveyed the views and opinions of 450 institutional and private wealth investors in alternative assets, covering their views regarding private equity, infrastructure, real estate and hedge funds around the world. The findings were unequivocal, and point to continued growth for alternative assets over the coming years:

- significantly more investors are currently below their target allocations to alternatives (41 per cent to 59 per cent, depending on the individual asset class), than are above target (13 per cent to 24 per cent);
- a clear majority of investors (74 per cent to 93 per cent) feel that their alternative assets portfolios have met or exceeded their return expectations;
- significantly more investors plan to increase their allocations to alternatives over both the short term (next 12 months) and the longer term (one year plus) than are planning to decrease them; and
- the outlook is positive over all alternative assets, but most notably so in infrastructure and private equity.

Alternative assets is already a huge industry – $5.5 trillion of AUM globally invested by over 8,000 major institutional investors globally, with over 30,000 separate funds managed by more than 15,000 fund management organisations – and is clearly set to grow further as investors commit progressively larger sums in order to tap into the superior returns and diversification that alternatives can offer. The good news for law firms is clear: more investors, more funds, increased AUM all mean one thing – more work for lawyers. (For a free full copy of the survey's findings, please visit www.preqin.com.)

The most important considerations for investors in these funds are, of course, the fundamental and unchanging ones of opportunities, returns, risks, and the personal relationships and trust that play such a big role in any long-term and often illiquid investment. However, the investors that Preqin spoke with also highlighted Regulation and Terms and Conditions as increasingly important factors driving their interest and activity in investments in this area. Both of these are areas where lawyers are called on to advise their clients on either or both sides of the table, investor and fund manager.

Regulation is a constantly evolving backdrop to all relationships between investors and fund managers, and such has been the pace of new regulation that investors are understandably often unsure as to where they stand and cite this as high on their list of concerns. Life would be challenging enough if the regulatory trend were unidirectional, but the real challenge for investors and fund managers alike is that regulations often appear to move in opposing directions, with developments like AFMID tightening the regulatory screw, while others like the JOBS Act in the United States and developments in emerging economies are opening up more opportunities for investors and fund managers. It is little surprise therefore that investors in private equity funds cite regulation as one of their biggest concerns (see Fig. 2.6, taken from the survey.)

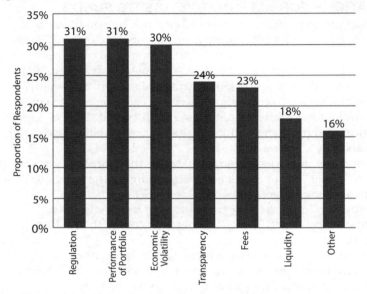

Interestingly, the investors polled by Preqin – the very people whom such regulation is presumably designed to help and protect – are distinctly lukewarm regarding the impact of recent regulatory developments on the industry and their interests. Fig. 1.9 opposite shows that a clear majority of the investors polled see more drawbacks than benefits in the new regulations.

Whilst regulators should clearly pay heed to the views of investors before proposing or enacting further regulations on the industry, the fact remains that the existing regulations are here to stay. Investors and fund managers alike need to keep up to speed with the constantly changing regulatory environment so that they can not only ensure that they comply with new rules as they emerge, but also that they are poised to take advantage of new opportunities as they open. Law firms are ideally placed to support their investor and fund manager clients in this increasingly vital area.

Terms and Conditions are often likened to a marriage contract, with the typical private equity fund lasting longer (10 to 12 years) than the average first marriage (around seven years). The LPA and the terms therein need to fairly reflect the interests of both investor and fund manager, and legislate for potential changes in circumstance over the fund's lifetime. This is another area where the parties to the LPA look to their legal advisors not only for practical execution of the agreement, but for sensitive and holistic advice as to how to formulate an agreement that respects and protects the interests of both sides to their mutual advantage.

In terms of how well the industry is doing at aligning the interests of

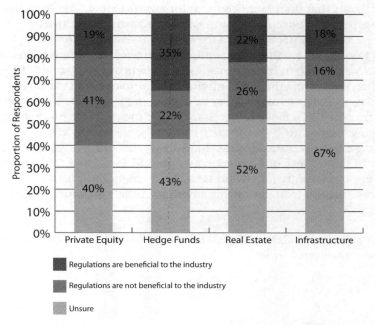

investors and fund managers, the assessment of the investors polled by Preqin would have to be "C+. OK but could try harder." Fig. 1.7 below demonstrates that, while a majority of investors feel that interests are at least

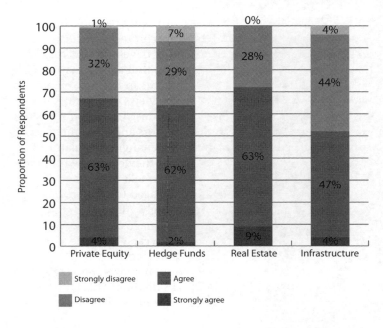

broadly aligned, the proportion who are not satisfied with current alignment (28 per cent to 46 per cent of investors, depending upon the type of fund concerned) suggests that there is much room for improvement. The situation appears to be especially concerning in infrastructure funds, where there is widespread investor dissatisfaction with fee levels.

Terms and Conditions are therefore another area where law firms can make a meaningful contribution to their clients' success in the marketplace. With more funds than ever competing for commitments from investors, the ability of a fund manager to offer terms that can be demonstrated to be best practice and investor-friendly can remove unnecessary impediments to the fundraising process, allowing the debate to focus where it truly should, on the ability of the fund manager to deliver superior risk-adjusted returns to his investors.

The increased importance of Regulation and of fund Terms and Conditions represent a huge opportunity for law firms to elevate themselves into a position of powerful and trusted strategic advisors for their investor and fund manager clients.

Mark O'Hare is Founder and CEO of Preqin Ltd., the global data provider in alternative assets. www.preqin.com

Investment Funds

Foreword

**Margaret Chamberlain,
Chair of the BVCA Regulatory Committee**

INTRODUCTION TO THE ALTERNATIVE INVESTMENT FUND MANAGERS DIRECTIVE

'...this is not the end. It is not even the beginning of the end. But it is, perhaps, the end of the beginning.' Winston Churchill

The Alternative Investment Fund Managers Directive (AIFMD), supplemented by its Level 2 Delegated Regulation and guidelines from the European Securities Markets Authority (ESMA), has ushered in a brave new world of regulation for many investment fund managers, including private equity firms and managers of hedge funds. It offers the lofty ideal of pan-European harmonisation of the regulatory and supervisory framework for the non-UCITS fund sector, together with the associated freedom to passport management and marketing activities on a cross-border basis. No passport is ever free, and for alternative investment fund managers (AIFMs) there will be significant costs and burdens; and in common with other Directives, the creation of freedoms within Europe can come at the price of newly-erected barriers to truly international business.

The AIFMD was developed in light of the dramatic developments in the financial world: Lehman Brothers had collapsed, the global markets were in meltdown and the Madoff scandal had exposed the vulnerability of European investors to fraud. A conviction was growing amongst European legislators and supervisors that even professional and institutional clients are not sophisticated enough to look after their own (and their clients') interests. The hedge fund management sector, in particular, had long been viewed with varying degrees of suspicion by some politicians; some even argued that (with their short selling strategies and use of leverage) they fanned the flames of the crisis, if not actually causing it. Against that backdrop, the development of the Directive was a deeply politicised process, with some in London declaring that it was all a barely-disguised attack on the United Kingdom, from where much of the alternative investment fund management in Europe takes place.

The legislation was all developed in a relatively short space of time. Much of the text was therefore drafted against tight deadlines, with little time for true consideration of the complexities involved, with limited cost-benefit analysis and often little or no transparency. The result has been, in the round, a tendency to homogenise as an industry sector what is in practice a highly heterogeneous collection of disparate fund structures and investment strategies.

Now that the 22 July 2013 transposition deadline has passed, firms will have to find practical ways to make the rules work. All of this is against a backdrop of continuing disagreement on key issues, for instance, as to when a fund is to be treated as 'closed-ended'. The Directive has a wide ranging impact and has implications for many non-EEA fund managers, as well as for those in the EEA. It will bring additional complexity and bureaucracy to fundraising by EEA and non-EEA fund managers.

Key requirements applicable to in-scope EEA fund managers include:
- the requirement to be fully compliant with the Directive by 22 July 2014 at the latest;
- a requirement to appoint, in respect of each fund, a depositary (the Directive also imposes obligations directly on the depositary);
- the obligation to meet regulatory capital requirements (together with the need to maintain professional indemnity insurance and/or maintain additional own funds to cover professional negligence liability);
- the imposition of conditions when delegating any of its functions, with particular restrictions when delegating the 'core' functions of portfolio management or risk management;
- remuneration rules, which could affect the design of incentives for certain key staff;
- organisational and conduct of business rules (including rules relating to conflicts of interest and risk and liquidity management) and high level organisational requirements (including those relating to resourcing, data protection, record-keeping and internal control mechanisms, such as personal account dealing). There are also detailed requirements regarding the establishment of procedures for the valuation of fund assets; and
- various obligations under the heading of 'transparency requirements', including the requirement to prepare and deliver annual reports, to make disclosures to investors both prior to investment and on an ongoing basis and to report to regulators.

The updated edition of this book therefore reflects, amongst other changes, the impact that AIFMD has so far had on non-UCITS investment funds. Of course, the AIFMD story is far from over. It remains to be seen whether the Directive will truly achieve the goal of harmonisation, and the introduction of a marketing passport for third country AIFMs and AIFs (alongside the phasing-out of the national private placement option) is not scheduled until late 2015 at the earliest.

What seems almost certain is that, in the not-too-distant future, the industry will face another round of consultations and negotiations as battle re-commences on 'AIFMD 2' ...

Margaret Chamberlain
Partner, Travers Smith LLP
(Margaret is also Chair of the Regulatory Committee of The City of London Law Society, a Member of the Council of the BVCA and Chair of the BVCA Regulatory Committee)
September 2013

Investment Funds

Overview

Dörte Höppner, ECVA

CHALLENGES AND OPPORTUNITIES

European private equity is facing a unique set of challenges and opportunities, thanks to the economic climate and a new regulatory landscape.

Even so, the asset class' abiding strengths – its competitiveness, adaptability, expertise and 'can-do' attitude – remain intact and will see the industry meet the challenges and seize the opportunities.

Despite emerging signs of improvement, the economic climate in Europe remains challenging and private equity is not immune to that.

The uncertainty generated by the banking crisis and the knock-on effect experienced in the euro area has understandably given some investors pause before investing in Europe.

But there are plenty of reasons for optimism. In 2012 alone, private equity invested in nearly 5,000 European businesses, a similar number to the previous year. Nearly half of those companies getting investment were private equity backed for the first time.

That's proof of private equity's continued commitment to and confidence in Europe, a confidence that should be shared by investors.

But as Henry Kravis once said: 'Look, don't congratulate us when we buy a company, congratulate us when we sell it. Because any fool can overpay and buy a company, as long as money will last to buy it.' So it is worthwhile to also look at exits.

More than 2,100 European companies were exited in 2012, representing former equity investments of EUR 22 billion. That's a similar amount to the year before and there are good reasons to believe that there will be an uptick in the future.

After all, Europe remains the world's largest single market with effective, stable, legal and political frameworks and plenty of superb companies brimming with growth potential.

Europe can also boast an established ecosystem of experienced general partners with the expertise to seek out the best opportunities.

By its nature, private equity can ride out and even benefit from downturns in the economic cycles. As an asset class, it has shown it can deliver strong, stable returns through recessions.

Based on cumulative returns data for fund vintages back to 1990, EVCA research shows that EU mid-cap firms (those raising between EUR 250 million and EUR 1 billion) generated an average IRR of 17.2 per cent.

And it is definitely time for investors to look again at European venture capital, which provides an excellent opportunity for those able to recognise it.

Europe now has seasoned venture capital managers with skills to match any Silicon Valley outfit and the knowledge to commercialise innovation on a global scale.

That combined with the rise of the serial entrepreneur and exciting start-up hubs in Europe points to a fascinating story of untapped potential and unexploited opportunity.

European private equity became subject to pan-European regulation for the first time in July this year.

The Alternative Investment Fund Managers Directive posed a unique set of challenges to the industry.

The EVCA was in the forefront of the battle to ensure the AIFMD did not hamstring the industry's ability to transform businesses and earn strong returns for its investors.

The final AIFMD, while it could have been more proportionate in some area, is much more appropriate than the earliest drafts suggested it would be and that is testament to our policy team's hard work.

But much still remains to be done. It's disappointing that after strenuous efforts from the industry to be prepared for AIFMD implementation, there is still some legal uncertainty.

About half of the EU member states have not finished their transposition and other details need to be finalised at a European level. National governments have also interpreted certain AIFMD provisions differently, which could prevent a level playing field.

The development of a true single market for private equity, with investors and private equity firms having much greater freedom to work together to find and finance investment opportunities all over Europe is a goal everyone should be pushing for.

The EVCA is engaging with European regulators and working closely with our national member associations but this goal won't be achieved unless AIFMD is transposed consistently and unless investor regulation such as Solvency II and the proposed revision to the IORP Directive is completed properly.

Our investor members want regulatory certainty, which they don't have at the moment, leaving them with unanswered questions. Fortunately, following a prolonged EVCA campaign, the European Commission has signaled it will shelve Solvency II style capital rules for workplace pensions.

The EVCA will continue to press for a similar recognition of the importance of institutional investors and private equity to Europe's economy in Solvency II. We can't be complacent as disproportionate capital adequacy rules have the potential to discourage investors from allocating capital to long-term opportunities like private equity funds.

The global economy needs investors who are patient and committed; who can provide the capital that companies need to grow and develop or can finance the infrastructure projects over the long-term.

While it is easy to understand why regulators want to use market prices to determine the value of an asset they equally have to find a way to take account of the characteristics of less liquid assets that create value over the long-term.

The EVCA is playing a leading role in explaining that long-term investments, such as private equity funds, deserve a different regulatory treatment to more liquid assets.

Making that argument successfully is both a challenge and an opportunity as we look forward to a future as an industry and an association.

It's an argument we can win by describing how private equity can provide smart capital for European companies that have the biggest growth potential. Private equity is also smart in the sense that it truly aligns the interests of fund managers and investors, something that makes the asset class unique in the sense that it could serve as an example of best practice for regulators.

Australia

Stephen Etkind, Andrew Yik, Henry Wong & Karen Payne
Minter Ellison Lawyers

1. MARKET OVERVIEW

Australia has one of the largest and fastest growing funds management sectors in the world. Its growth is underpinned by Australia's Government-mandated retirement scheme (superannuation).

Investment funds (also described as funds, managed funds or managed investment schemes) are typically established in Australia as a unit trust and often fall within the definition of a 'managed investment scheme' (MIS) under the Australian Corporations Act 2001 (Cth) (Corporations Act).

The Australian retail funds market is mature, with a high degree of regulation. Retail funds must be registered with the Australian corporate regulator, the Australian Securities and Investments Commission (ASIC).

Over the past year, following the global financial crisis, a clear trend has been an increase in regulation. For example, ASIC has:
- increased the financial requirements for Australian financial services licensees (AFS licensees) who operate funds; and
- prescribed disclosure requirements for funds that hold particular asset classes (such as unlisted property, hedge funds and infrastructure).

In addition, the retail fund industry will be affected by the introduction of the Future of Financial Advice reforms (FOFA) which includes changes to how advisors can recommend managed funds. There is also continuing development towards introducing an Asia Region Funds Passport.

More detail is set out in section 4 below.

The funds market is growing and is currently the fourth largest pool of funds under management in the world. At 31 March 2013, the managed funds industry had A$2,093.9 billion funds under management, an increase of A$69.4 billion (3 per cent) on the December quarter 2012 figure of A$2,024.5 billion (source: Australian Bureau of Statistics).

2. ALTERNATIVE INVESTMENT FUNDS
2.1 Common structures

Alternative investment funds are typically structured as unit trusts. While other legal vehicles can be used, such as a company or limited liability partnership, in practice there is a strong preference for the unit trust structure.

Alternative investment funds are available to both 'retail' and 'wholesale' clients in Australia. Wholesale clients generally include persons (eg, natural persons, bodies corporate or trusts) who:
- acquire interests in the fund of A$500,000 or more;
- are high net worth individuals (having net assets of A$2.5 million or

more, or having gross income of at least A$250,000 for each of the last two financial years, as certified by a qualified accountant and expectation of the same for the current financial year);
- are businesses that have more than 20 employees (or more than 100 if a manufacturer); or
- are professional investors (such as an Australian financial services licence holder, a superannuation/pension fund (with A$10 million or more of assets) or a bank).

A retail client is defined as a person who is not a wholesale client. The Australian Government has also released a discussion paper raising many options around amending and clarifying the wholesale/retail client distinction.

No distinction is generally made in the Corporations Act between different funds based on investment activities (eg, hedge, private equity and real estate funds are treated similarly, although ASIC has published policies as to how it will regulate these different asset classes). The majority of hedge funds in Australia are established as open-ended funds. Real estate and private equity funds that are invested in illiquid assets are commonly established as either open or closed-ended funds.

The main advantage of the unit trust structure is the tax efficiency (see section 2.5.). However, a unit trust structure is subject to different regulatory requirements (where they are required to be a MIS) in comparison to a company and therefore, the costs and resources involved in complying with those regulatory requirements may be higher. In addition, compliance with Australian trust law principles may make it more difficult to implement business decisions as trustees have a duty to act in the best interests of their members. On the other hand, the unit trust structure is well established and understood and the Corporations Act and tax laws do not easily accommodate other structures.

The liability of an investor in a unit trust is generally limited to the amount of their units and they should not be liable for the debts of the trustee relating to the unit trust. However, Australian case law is not definitive on this point and the Australian courts have not properly considered the matter.

Members in an alternative investment fund structured as unit trust are issued units, where each unit represents a beneficial interest in the fund's assets. The trustee of a registered MIS is called a 'responsible entity'.

Australian investment managers and/or advisers are typically structured as companies and are required to hold an Australian financial services licence (AFS licence) or an exemption to promote and manage the fund.

2.2. Regulatory framework

The Corporations Act is the primary source of legislation regulating alternative investment funds and investment managers in Australia. In addition, ASIC administers and enforces these laws which apply to activities such as:
- marketing and offers to investors of securities and other financial

products in Australia;
- establishing and operating funds; and
- the provision of financial services in Australia and the licensing of financial service providers (eg, investment managers/advisers and promoters).

Alternative investment funds that are not structured as a body corporate (eg, a unit trust) often fall within the definition of an MIS under the Corporations Act. A MIS is generally any arrangement where investors contribute money, to be pooled with other investors' contributions, to acquire benefits from the operation of the arrangement which is operated by a third party. MISs must be registered with ASIC if they are offered to retail clients, ie, same as for retail funds (see section 3.2.).

Although MISs offered to wholesale clients are not required to be registered, registration may have advantages from a distribution perspective within Australia since institutional investors (such as superannuation funds) may prefer to invest in registered funds which are subject to additional compliance and other obligations under the Corporations Act. Unregistered MISs are still required to have a trustee who either holds an AFS licence or can rely on an exemption from licensing. The trustee can either itself manage the assets of the fund or it can appoint an investment manager.

Foreign alternative investment funds can typically be offered to wholesale clients in Australia without much restriction (subject to the regulation of marketing activities by the investment manager/promoter). In practice, foreign funds (alternative investment or otherwise) are rarely offered directly to retail clients in Australia. This is because the fund must have an Australian compliant offer document. Further, if the foreign fund is not a body corporate, then the fund itself will need to be registered as a MIS, which is generally a very expensive and burdensome process for a foreign fund.

Investment managers and advisers are governed by the Corporations Act and regulated by ASIC as noted above.

Any person who provides a 'financial service' in Australia or to Australian persons will be required to hold an AFS licence covering the provision of the service unless an exemption applies.

Providing a 'financial service' includes, among other things, marketing a fund, arranging for a person to invest in a fund, issuing interests in a fund and providing investment management services to a fund.

There is no requirement for the investment manager to have a local resident. However as noted below, in practice an AFS licence applicant will typically have two to three persons located in Australia.

A foreign regulated manager or promoter relying on the exemption mentioned below will either need to be registered as a foreign company in Australia or appoint a local agent for receipt of service.

Where the manager or promoter of a fund is regulated by a foreign recognised regulator (such as the FCA (UK) and SEC (US)) it may apply to the ASIC to obtain an exemption to, among other things, provide investment manager services or promote funds in Australia provided this is only to wholesale clients.

Alternatively, the offshore manager or promoter could be appointed as a representative of an appropriate AFS licence holder in Australia to perform such functions.

If no exemptions apply or the manager/adviser wishes to obtain an AFS licence (eg, for market credibility) then a detailed licensing application and submission will need to be made to ASIC.

ASIC will only grant an AFS licence if the applicant can demonstrate skilled and experienced personnel and adequate organisational infrastructure (eg, compliance and risk management systems).

This will, in practice, generally necessitate the applicant having at least two to three persons in Australia (although this is not a strict rule), including persons with Australian legal and compliance experience and investment experience.

The applicant will be required to prepare documents of all its internal operations (eg, risk management and compliance) which is generally a lengthy and expensive process.

2.3. Operational requirements

There are generally speaking no legal restrictions on the types of activities or the types of investments for an alternative investment fund. However restrictions may be imposed under the fund's constitution or trust deed, which sets out the trustee's power to invest and/or borrow.

The trustee holds the property of the fund on trust for members, although in most cases the property will be held on the trustee's behalf by a separate custodian. Custodians are generally required to hold an AFS licence authorising them to provide custodial and depository services and to hold net tangible assets of the greater of A$10 million or 10 per cent of average revenue. ASIC have also recently introduced new financial requirements that will apply to trustees of unregistered MISs.

For registered MISs, a trustee/responsible entity will be subject to different financial requirements depending on whether the assets of the fund are held by a custodian (see section 3.3.). The custodian agreement is also required to contain certain matters as required by the responsible entity's AFS licence and ASIC policy.

Registered MISs are subject to a number of reporting requirements under the Corporations Act, including having to lodge audited annual financial reports with ASIC (see section 3.3.). Although, unregistered MISs are generally not subject to such reporting requirements, investors are typically provided with regular fund performance reports and audited annual financial reports.

A fund must generally only be offered to retail clients in Australia using a product disclosure statement (PDS). This is regardless of whether a private or public offer is made. The PDS must meet prescribed content requirements (see section 2.4.). Subject to a due diligence defence, there are potential criminal and civil liabilities for the issuer and other persons if the PDS is defective.

Exemptions to the requirement to provide a PDS include small-scale offerings and offers to wholesale clients, where a disclosure document may be used which does not have prescribed content (eg, private placement memorandum).

There are no restrictions on the use of side letters in Australia, except that a trustee is subject to general trustee duties and obligations, including acting in the best interests of members.

In Australia, it is an offence to acquire/dispose of or procure another person to acquire/dispose of securities or derivatives where that person possesses inside information.

Australia also has an anti-money laundering and counter-terrorism financing regime that imposes various obligations on 'reporting entities' (financial institutions or other persons, who provide 'designated services'). Key obligations include:
- having and complying with an anti-money laundering and counter-terrorism financing program which sets out customer identification procedures and also various compliance measures;
- carrying out procedures to verify a customer's identity; and
- reporting to the regulator (AUSTRAC) suspicious matters and certain transactions above a threshold.

The Australian Government has also implemented a ban on naked short selling and a disclosure regime in relation to covered short selling.

Naked short selling is where the seller, at the time of the sale, does not have (or reasonably believe they have) a presently exercisable and unconditional right to vest the product in the buyer. Naked short selling of a product is generally prohibited.

Covered short selling is where the seller, at the time of sale, has (or reasonably believes they have) a presently exercisable and unconditional right to vest the product in the buyer because of a securities lending arrangement entered into before that time. Covered short selling is subject to certain reporting requirements, including the reporting of short positions to ASIC.

2.4. Marketing the fund

The marketing, production and offering of marketing materials is governed by the Corporations Act (see section 2.2.).

The marketing of a fund in Australia (eg, by providing a fund offering document or making a recommendation about a fund) will be deemed to be providing financial service of 'financial product advice'. Generally, the marketing entity must either:
- hold an AFS licence with an authorisation to provide financial product advice and arrange for issue of interests in the fund; or
- rely on an appropriate licensing exemption (see section 2.2.).

There are no legislative restrictions on the persons or entities that an alternative investment fund can be marketed to provided that they have the appropriate AFS licence authorisation or exemption. For example, foreign regulated managers operating under the licensing exemption in section 2.2. can only market or promote funds to wholesale clients.

Retail clients can receive marketing information about Australian-domiciled funds, but only to the extent the fund can be offered in Australia as a registered MIS or under an exemption.

As noted in section 2.3., a fund must generally only be offered to retail clients in Australia using a PDS. The PDS must meet prescribed content requirements (see section 3.4.). There are also additional prescribed disclosure requirements (imposed by the regulator) for funds that hold particular asset classes (such as unlisted property, hedge funds and infrastructure) (see section 4 in relation to the new hedge funds disclosure requirements).

Offers to wholesale clients can be made using a disclosure document, which does not have prescribed content. While there are no prescribed content requirements for such disclosure documents, the Corporations Act does impose conduct-related sanctions in respect of misleading or deceptive conduct.

2.5. Taxation

Most Australian managed funds are structured as a unit style head trust with one or more unit style sub-trusts. Unit trusts are generally treated as 'tax transparent' entities or 'flow through' entities for tax purposes (that is, income tax is collected at the investor level and not at the fund level). Investors are generally taxed on their proportionate share of the 'taxable' income earned by the fund based on their proportionate entitlement to share in the trust income. This applies to:
- trust income that is distributed to, and/or reinvested by an investor; and
- trust income that an investor is entitled to but has not been distributed.

Tax losses incurred by a unit trust do not pass through to the investors. Instead, they remain at the fund level and can be carried forward and set off against future taxable income and gains if certain integrity tests are satisfied. Capital losses can only be set off against capital gains.

Public unit trusts that carry on or control a 'trading business' are taxed as companies. The company tax rate is currently 30 per cent. A prescriptive list of 'eligible' activities is included in the Tax Act, so that all other activity is deemed to be 'trading'. A trading business does not generally arise by reason of:
- investing or trading in debt and portfolio equity securities and derivatives; or
- investing in property primarily for the purpose of deriving rent.

Stapled entities are used in some sectors where there is a combination of passive (eligible) and active (trading) business activity. The trading activities are carried on by a company or public trading trust and other 'passive' investments are held by a transparent unit trust. The trading activities are generally taxed at the company tax rate at the fund level and the remaining investments qualify for flow through tax treatment. Stapled entities are commonly used in the REIT and infrastructure sectors and also (sometimes) in private equity funds.

If the unit trust qualifies as a managed investment trust (MIT) for tax purposes, the following concessions may be available for investors:
- The fund may elect for the capital gains tax (CGT) provisions to be the primary code for taxing gains and losses on the disposal of eligible assets including shares in a company, units in a trust and land (including an interest in land and a right to acquire or dispose of any of these assets). This election must be made in the first qualifying year. Otherwise the

fund is taxed on a deemed revenue account and no CGT discount or concession is available. This is intended to provide investor certainty on tax outcomes and consequences.
- A concessional rate of withholding tax applies to some distributions ('fund payments') made to non-resident investors who are tax resident in a jurisdiction that has an information exchange agreement with Australia (for example the Bahamas, British Virgin Islands, Cayman Islands, China, Japan, Singapore, the United Kingdom and the United States). The MIT withholding rate is set out below.

To qualify as an MIT and be eligible for the tax concessions noted above, a fund must satisfy various requirements, including:
- the fund must be an Australian resident trust (that is, the trustee of the trust must be an Australian resident or the central management and control of the trust must be in Australia);
- the fund must not be a trading trust or carrying on a trading business;
- investment management activities in respect of Australian assets of the fund should be carried out largely in Australia;
- the fund must be a managed investment scheme under the Corporations Act;
- the fund must be widely held (different rules apply for retail and wholesale funds to determine if the fund is widely held);
- the fund must not be closely held; and
- the fund must satisfy certain financial service licence requirements.

A number of the tax consequences outlined above are contingent on the fund being 'a fixed trust' for tax purposes. This term is not currently defined and recent case law suggests there is (technically) a risk that a fund will not qualify as a fixed trust unless the Australian Commissioner of Taxation exercises his discretion to treat the trust as 'fixed'. The Australian Government is currently reviewing the taxation arrangements for managed funds including the introduction of a more 'workable' definition of fixed trust.

Australia has a VAT-style tax regime known as the goods and services tax (GST) with a general rate of 10 per cent. This regime includes rules concerning the treatment of financial supplies which can limit the extent to which a fund can recoup GST paid by the fund.

A tax clearance procedure is available at the taxpayer's request in respect of the federal taxes due to the ATO (as described below). Because the ruling would typically relate to the tax consequences of a specific transaction and because it is not possible to predict how the fund will be managed or operated, it is not usual to obtain a ruling at the time the fund is established. It would be more usual to obtain a legal opinion which investors may review to confirm the tax treatment.

A private binding ruling can be obtained by a taxpayer or a class ruling can be obtained on behalf of a class of taxpayers (for example, all of the unitholders in the fund) in appropriate circumstances. Private rulings set out the Commissioner's opinion about how tax laws apply, including the following relevant taxes:
- income tax;

- fringe benefits tax;
- franking tax;
- withholding tax (generally for non-residents); and
- indirect taxes such as the GST.

The ATO provides written advice (in the form of a ruling) that provides full protection from any underpaid tax, penalties and interest in relation to an adjusted assessment. A private ruling only relates to the applicant taxpayer and cannot be relied on by another entity. The ruling will not provide full protection where the full facts are not provided at the time of application or if circumstances change.

Private rulings can also be obtained from each of the offices of state revenue in respect of stamp duties.

Resident investors
The tax treatment of income and capital gains for resident investors is generally as follows:

Income
The fund calculates its taxable income (including capital gains), which is generally taxed in the hands of the investors in proportion to their entitlement to receive distributions of 'trust' income. Any 'discount' capital gains distributed by the trust are eligible for discount tax treatment in the investor's calculation of their own taxable income. The taxable income can differ from the trust's net accounting income due to different treatment of income, gains and expenses for tax purposes compared with trust accounting.

The amount of trust income distributed can sometimes exceed the amount of taxable income. This excess is commonly called a 'tax-deferred distribution'. Any tax-deferred distribution will reduce the cost base of the units in the unit trust in the hands of the investors for CGT purposes. Once the cost base has been reduced to zero, any further tax-deferred distributions are taxed as capital gains of the investor. If the investor's share of taxable income exceeds their share of trust income, the investor is taxed on their full share of taxable income.

Capital gains on disposal or redemption of units
Resident investors are usually taxable on capital gains and losses made on disposal of their units. Capital gains can qualify for a CGT discount (a reduction of the gain by one-third for superannuation funds or one-half for individuals and trusts) if the units have been held in excess of 12 months.

Non-resident investors
The tax treatment for distributions made to non-resident investors depends on whether the unit trust is an MIT or not.

Unit trusts that are not MITs
The non-resident investor is subject to tax on their share of the income and capital gains of the unit trust (at their marginal rate of tax for individuals or 30 per cent for companies). However, the trustee is also subject to tax on the

same amounts (on behalf of the non-resident investor). The non-resident investor can claim a credit for any tax paid by the trustee on their share of taxable income. The non-resident investor is generally not subject to tax on capital gains unless they are gains on taxable Australian property (that is, generally direct and indirect interests in Australian real property and mining tenements). Final withholding taxes apply to some categories of income distributed to the non-resident investor, including:

Character of receipt	Withholding tax rate*
Interest	10%
Dividends	
Fully franked dividends (that is, dividends paid from profits that have been taxed in Australia) are not subject to any further withholding taxes	0%
Unfranked dividends (investor is resident in a tax treaty country) are generally subject to a reduced tax rate, typically	15%
Unfranked dividends (investors is resident in a non-treaty country)	30%

Unit trusts that are MITs

Foreign resident unitholders in the fund are generally subject to a final withholding tax on distributions from the fund. The rate of withholding tax depends on the character of the income component included in the distribution, which are broadly as follows:

Character of receipt	Withholding tax rate*
Interest	10%
Dividends	
Fully franked dividends (that is, dividends paid from profits that have been taxed in Australia) are not subject to any further withholding taxes	0%
Unfranked dividends (investor is resident in a tax treaty country) are generally subject to a reduced tax rate, typically	15%
Unfranked dividends (investors is resident in a non-treaty country)	30%
Capital gains	
Capital gains which do not relate to taxable Australian property	0%
Capital gains which relate to taxable Australian property (recipient is a resident of an information exchange country (IEC))	15%
Capital gains which relate to taxable Australian property (recipient is not a resident of an IEC)	30%
Other income that is Australian sourced	
Recipient is a resident of an information exchange agreement country	15%
Recipient is not a resident of an information exchange agreement country	30%
Foreign sourced income	0%

The responsible entity, as trustee, is responsible for remitting the withholding tax (where applicable) to the ATO.

Disposal or redemption of units by a non-resident investor

The tax position of gains and losses made by non-resident investors on disposal of their units varies, depending on the nature of their investment. Investments on capital account are generally not taxed unless the unit trust is 'land rich' and the investor has a non-portfolio unitholding. That is:
- more than 50 per cent of the market value of the fund is attributable to taxable Australian property; and
- the investor (including their associates) holds 10 per cent or more of the fund.

Investments in units held on revenue account (for example, units acquired by an investor for the purposes of short-term gain) can be taxable in Australia.

If units held by non-resident investors are used in carrying on a business through a permanent establishment in Australia, any gains or losses will be taxable in Australia. That is, the gain or loss will not qualify for a CGT exemption.

The Australian Government has removed the discount on capital gains earned after 8 May 2012 for non-residents on taxable Australian property. However, non-residents will still be entitled to a discount on capital gains accrued before 8 May 2012. This amendment was announced as part of the 2013 Federal Budget. The Act Tax Laws Amendment (2012 Measures No 2) Act received Royal Assent as 29 June 2013.

Stamp duty is imposed on a state-by-state basis in Australia. The rate of duty varies between states but may be as high as 7.25 per cent. Many funds are established in states with broad exemption from duty on the transfer of units. However, duty can apply on the transfer of units in real estate holding funds, particularly those that are unlisted.

There is generally no GST payable on the issue, redemption or transfer of units in a fund.

2.6. Customary or common terms

Real estate and private equity funds that are invested in illiquid assets commonly have a longer fund term (for example private equity funds typically have a fund life of around 10 years) but can also be offered as open-ended funds. Hedge funds commonly do not have a fixed fund term and are open-ended funds. All funds are subject to the 80-year rule against perpetuities.

The fund's constitution/trust deed will set out the circumstances in which the fund can be terminated, which commonly includes a provision allowing the members to terminate the fund. In addition, the Corporations Act specifies certain circumstances in which registered MISs can be terminated, for example by an extraordinary resolution of members (requiring 50 per cent of the total votes that may be cast) or by the responsible entity/trustee if the purpose of the fund has been accomplished or cannot be accomplished.

Restrictions can be placed on the issue, redemption and transfer of interests in alternative investment funds, provided they are consistent with the fund's constitution/trust deed and are clearly disclosed in the PDS/disclosure document. Real estate and private equity funds commonly offer limited or no redemption rights.

The Corporations Act also imposes constraints on the ability of a registered MIS to offer withdrawals to investors if the MIS is illiquid. No constraints apply to unregistered MISs, where the trust deed is paramount.

When implementing such restrictions for registered MISs, the responsible entity/trustee should bear in mind:

- its duty under the Corporations Act to treat members of the same class equally and members of other classes fairly;
- if the right to withdraw (if any) is exercised while the fund is liquid (that is, if liquid assets account for at least 80 per cent of the value of fund property), the redemption must be implemented in accordance with the fund's constitution; and
- if the right to withdraw (if any) is exercised while the fund is not liquid, the redemption must be implemented in accordance with the Corporations Act (which specifies when and how a withdrawal offer can be made and what must be disclosed in the withdrawal offer) and the fund's constitution.

Provisions around manager/adviser involvement are more common in hedge funds and private equity funds offered to institutional investors and are typically documented in the trust deed or negotiated by way of side letter agreements. For example, private equity fund trust deeds may contain key man provisions, restrictions on the ability to set up successor funds, and the ability for members to remove the manager for cause or no cause events.

Management fees and performance fees charged by Australian alternative fund managers are in quantums similar to the offshore market, although following the global financial crisis, the Australian investment fund market has seen a downward pressure on the fees paid. This is because Australian superannuation funds are themselves under political pressure to reduce their fee levels. In addition, there has been a push by some investors to invest into investment mandates rather than through a fund structure, which has resulted in lower fee structures.

In relation to performance fees/carried interest arrangements, there are a number of different fee structures used by Australian alternative fund managers, including performance fees with or without performance benchmarks, hurdle rates and high water marks and in respect of private equity funds, carried interest arrangements, with or without a catch-up, clawback and escrow arrangements.

Restrictions may be imposed under the fund's constitution or trust deed, which sets out the trustee's power to invest and/or borrow. For example, private equity fund trust deeds typically limit the investment period and impose certain borrowing and investment restrictions on the trustee and investment manager.

3. RETAIL FUNDS
3.1. Common structures
The structures used for retail funds are the same as for alternative investment funds (see section 2.1.).

Australia

3.2. Regulatory framework

The principal statutes, regulations and/or rules for retail funds are the same as for alternative investment funds (see section 2.2.).

A retail fund, as a public offer fund, is usually in the form of a MIS. A MIS is generally required to be registered under the Corporations Act with ASIC before it can be offered to investors if it has more than 20 members unless:
- the fund is offered only to 'wholesale clients'; or
- ASIC grants the operator of the MIS conditional relief from registration where the operator's home regulatory regime is sufficiently equivalent to the Australian regime and certain other requirements apply.

Other exemptions to registration may also apply, depending on specific factual circumstances, such as where a fund has less than 20 investors.

Registration has advantages from a distribution perspective within Australia since institutional investors such as superannuation funds may prefer to invest in registered funds which are subject to the compliance and other obligations under the Corporations Act.

Under the Corporations Act, a registered scheme requires:
- a responsible entity (ie, a trustee), which must satisfy various requirements, including holding an AFS licence;
- a constitution (ie, a trust deed); and
- a compliance plan.

The responsible entity of a registered scheme:
- is the entity that operates the scheme (and must perform the duties and functions conferred upon it by the constitution and the Corporations Act);
- holds the scheme property on trust for members (though in most cases the property will be held on the responsible entity's behalf by a separate custodian); and
- must be an Australian public company and hold an AFS licence authorising it to operate a registered MIS.

The principal statutes, regulations and/or rules that govern the investment manager or investment adviser are the same as for alternative investment funds (see section 2.2.).

The licensing of an investment manager or investment adviser are the same as for alternative investment funds. Additionally, the residency requirements for an investment manager or investment adviser are the same as for alternative investment funds (see section 2.2.).

An investment manager or adviser could be appointed as a representative of an AFS licence holder. The exemption for a foreign financial service provider regulated overseas is not available for retail funds.

The main steps involved in obtaining any necessary licences/authorisations for investment managers/advisers are the same as for alternative investment funds (see section 2.2).

3.3. Operational requirements

The restrictions on a retail fund are the same as for alternative investment funds (see section 2.3.).

The responsible entity of a registered scheme must:
- clearly identify and hold fund property separately; and
- hold fund property on trust for members of the fund. The responsible entity can appoint an agent to hold fund property separately from other property (that is, appoint a separate custodian while remaining responsible for the custodian's actions).

Responsible entities are also required to do all of the following:
- prepare a cash flow projection which covers a period of at least 12 months forward;
- if the assets of the fund are not held by a custodian, have net tangible assets (NTA) of A$10 million or 10 per cent of average responsible entity revenue;
- if all the assets of the fund are held by a custodian who meets the financial requirements, have NTA of:
  - A$150,000;
  - 0.5 per cent of the average value of fund property of registered schemes, and Investor Directed Portfolio Service (IDPS) property up to a maximum of A$5 million; or
  - 10 per cent of average responsible entity revenue;
- hold cash and cash equivalent to the greater of A$150,000 or 50 per cent of the required NTA and an amount of liquid assets equivalent to the required NTA;
- maintain a certain level of surplus liquid funds (SLF);
- there are extensive rules applicable to the:
  - calculations of NTA;
  - average responsible entity revenue; and
  - SLF amounts.

The responsible entity of a registered MIS must provide an audit report for each financial year that includes information about compliance with its financial requirements. Disclosure requirements are the same as for alternative investment funds (see section 2.3.).

There is no express prohibition on the use of side letters but for retail funds, unlike alternative investment funds, side letters are unusual in light of the obligation to treat all members of a class equally.

3.4. Marketing the fund

The offer of interests in a MIS to retail clients requires certain disclosure documents to be prepared in accordance with the content requirements mandated by law:

Product Disclosure Statement (PDS)
This document must be given to the retail client:
- at or before the time a recommendation is made to buy a financial product;
- when an offer is made to issue or arrange the issue of a financial product; or
- when a seller makes an offer to sell the product.

The PDS must contain sufficient information enabling a retail client to make an informed decision whether or not to purchase a financial product (for example, the fees payable, risks and benefits involved and characteristics of the financial product). Depending on the type of product, a PDS can be a:
- long-form PDS; or
- short-form PDS, which is limited to a maximum of eight pages. Only certain entities such as 'simple managed investment schemes' (which are funds that hold substantially all of their assets in highly liquid investments) can use a short-form PDS.

The content requirements for a PDS are largely prescribed, with additional disclosure mandated for certain asset classes (eg, infrastructure and unlisted property). Exemptions from the requirement to issue a PDS include small-scale offerings and offers to wholesale clients, provided another disclosure document with the prescribed content is provided, such as a private placement memorandum.

Financial Services Guide (FSG)
This document must be given to the retail client before a financial service is provided and must contain information to help the retail client make an informed decision whether to acquire a financial service. An FSG is not required if a PDS providing all sufficient information (see above) has already been given to a retail client.

Statement of Advice
This must be given to the retail client when or as soon as practicable after any 'personal advice' (that is, advice taking into account the individual client's specific objectives, financial situation and needs) is provided to a retail client. Most fund managers/product issuers do not provide personal advice.
The above obligations should be read in conjunction with ASIC published guidelines.

Marketing and marketing materials for a retail fund is the same as alternative investment funds (see section 2.4.).

3.5. Taxation
The taxation consequences for a retail fund are the same as alternative investment funds (see section 2.5.).

3.6. Customary or common terms
Retail funds are typically open-ended funds. The issues related to the term of a retail fund are the same as those of an alternative investment fund (see section 2.6.).

Additionally, the issues related to the liquidity of a retail fund are the same as those of an alternative investment fund (see section 2.6.).

The involvement if the manager/adviser in a retail fund is usually not as important as for an alternative investment fund. As such, a retail fund does not usually have key man provisions. That said, it is not uncommon for the manager or an associate of the manager to co-invest in a fund.

Retail funds usually allow the responsible entity/trustee to charge a management fee. Retail funds do not usually have the same fee structures as for alterative investment funds. In particular, for a registered MIS, the disclosure of fees and charges is in a mandated format, including a template table and example of fees and costs.

Restrictions on investment or borrowing can either be set out in the constitution/trust deed or specified in the PDS.

4. PROPOSED CHANGES AND DEVELOPMENTS

Future of Financial Advice reforms (FOFA)

The retail fund industry will be affected by the introduction of the FOFA reforms which aim to improve the trust and confidence of Australian retail investors in the financial planning sector by changing the way remuneration is structured for financial advisers. In particular, FOFA has banned conflicted remuneration structures such as commissions, rebates and percentage-based fees on geared products. Compliance with these new measures is voluntary until 1 July 2013.

Asia Region Funds Passport

There is also continuing development towards introducing an Asia Region Funds Passport. This would allow fund managers to operate and offer funds across the Asian region under a uniform framework. While retail funds remain common, there is increasing interest in establishing and offering wholesale fund vehicles which:
- can be more readily tailored to meet the requirements of investors; and
- do not have many of the disclosure and compliance issues associated with retail funds.

Significant Investor Visa

Australia has also recently introduced a new significant investor visa program that is available to individuals who are prepared to invest A$5 million into 'complying investments' in Australia for a minimum of four years. Eligible complying investments include regulated managed funds that invest in Australian cash, bonds, listed equities, real estate, infrastructure projects and agribusiness.

Hedge fund disclosure requirements

ASIC also recently released new disclosure requirements (RG 240) for hedge funds that are offered to retail clients. This is intended to improve investor awareness of the risks associated with hedge funds. RG 240 takes effect from 1 February 2014.

RG 240 sets out new benchmarks and disclosure principles that hedge funds have to apply and disclose. These new benchmarks and disclosure principles prescribe the:
- valuation of assets in the hedge fund;
- periodic reporting which must be provided to investors; and
- disclosure of certain information, such as the investment strategy, investment manager, fund structure, asset valuation, location and

custody.

Note that the hedge fund test that triggers the operation of RG 240 is broad, such that some conventional funds that would not normally be associated as a hedge fund are being classified as a hedge fund due to features such as a performance fee and use of borrowing and derivatives. There are continuing discussions with ASIC about the scope of the hedge fund test.

Investment Manager Regime (IMR)

Foreign fund managers of widely held funds have greater certainty for the purposes of reporting uncertain tax positions in relation to their Australian investments. The Australian Government passed tax laws, effective for 2011 and prior years, preventing the Commissioner of Taxation raising an assessment against a widely held foreign fund to tax profits or gains made on qualifying investments (generally portfolio style investments of less than 10 per cent).

Exposure draft legislation (Tax Laws Amendment (2013 Measures No.2) Bill 2013: Investment Manager Regime) has also been released for comment which (once passed) will mandate that all profits and gains (revenue and capital) made on portfolio securities (less than 10 per cent) by a foreign widely held fund will be exempt from tax in Australia.

Profits and gains (revenue and capital) from non-portfolio securities (10 per cent or more) will also be tax exempt unless:
- there is no relevant double tax agreement – the profits or gains are Australian 'sourced' income; or
- there is a double tax agreement – a permanent establishment in Australia that arises for reasons other than a resident agent who has authority to negotiate and conclude contracts.

The exemption for income and gains made in these circumstances is intended to provide certainty to IMR foreign funds and their foreign investors, in relation to their obligations to disclose Australian tax liabilities under US accounting standard ASC 740-10 (previously FIN48).

Brazil

Alexei Bonamin, Ana Cláudia Akie Utumi & João Busin
TozziniFreire Advogados

1. MARKET OVERVIEW
Retail funds
Retail funds can be divided into two different types: open-ended retail funds and closed-ended retail funds.

Rule 409 issued by the Brazilian Securities Commission (CVM) on 18 August 2004, as amended (CVM Rule 409/04) regulates all different types of Brazilian mutual retail funds, namely: (i) short-term funds; (ii) referenced funds; (iii) fixed income funds; (iv) equity funds; (v) foreign exchange funds; (vi) external debt funds; and (vii) multi-market funds. For the purpose of this publication, any type of fund not mentioned under such regulation shall be classified as an alternative investment fund.

Open-ended retail funds
On 31 March 2013, the Brazilian funds industry comprised of 10,798 (including open-ended retail funds), with a total net worth of about BRL2,386,604.64 trillion ($1 = BRL2.25 on 22 July 2013) according to the ANBIMA website (*Associação Brasileira das Entidades dos Mercados Financeiros e de Capitais*, the Brazilian self regulator of investment funds (ANBIMA)).

Closed-ended retail funds
The Brazilian fund industry concerning closed-ended retail funds is still at a development stage when compared to Brazilian open-ended retail funds.

One of the major hurdles for its growth is that Brazilian regulations do not allow investments to be redeemed at any time at the investor's discretion, meaning that redemption of shares is permitted only upon expiry of the duration of the fund or at the end of each series or class of shares, as described in the relevant fund's bylaws.

Alternative investment funds
For the purposes of this publication, alternative investment funds can be defined as those regulated by a specific regulation other than CVM Rule 409/04.

The most important types of alternative investment funds are private equity funds (*Fundo de Investimento em Participações* (FIP)), real estate funds (*Fundo de Investimento Imobiliário* (FII)), and receivables funds (*Fundo de Investimento em Direitos Creditórios* (FIDC)).

Private equity funds, real estate funds and receivables funds are governed respectively, by Rule 391, enacted by CVM on 16 July 2003, as amended (CVM Rule 391/03); Rule 472, enacted by CVM on 31 October 2008, as amended (CVM Rule 472/08); and Rule 356 enacted by CVM on 17 December 2001, as amended (CVM Rule 356/01). All of these funds are closed-ended funds according to these regulations, although, according to CVM Rule 356/01, receivables funds can also be formed as open-ended funds.

There are no general restrictions concerning the participation of financial institutions in investment funds imposed by Brazilian regulators due to the 2008 financial crisis. However, the National Monetary Council (CMN) Resolution 3,334, dated 22 December 2005, brings specific restrictions after the relevant financial institution becomes the fund's administrator and/or portfolio manager (CMN Resolution No.3,334/05). These restrictions are derived from a conflict of interest of the relevant financial institution when acting as administrator or portfolio manager of a certain fund, limiting, as an example, the acquisition of shares of the relevant fund.

Real estate funds have the fastest growth rate when compared to any other alternative investment fund. In 2012, they traded at BRL3,59 billion in 316,023 deals. The year before, the amount was close to BRL912,46 million with 77,075 deals made. The year 2012 ended with 93 real estate funds registered and authorised for negotiation with BM&F Bovespa's Stock Exchange or over-the-counter market (*www.bmfbovespa.com.br/en-us/home.aspx?idioma=en-us*). The real estate funds market is still very active.

According to the ANBIMA website, the current year's cumulative net funding (until April 2013) in respect to private equity funds and receivables funds is BRL4,409 billion and BRL3,892 billion, respectively.

2. ALTERNATIVE INVESTMENT FUNDS
2.1. Common structures
Under Brazilian legislation, investment funds are organised as a pool of assets jointly owned by the funds' shareholders under the structure of a co-property (condominium). There is no corporate structure behind pools of assets held by means of an investment fund structure. Therefore, investors in Brazilian investment funds are holders of shares that represent their co-investment in the assets that belong to the investment funds.

In this respect, investment funds do not provide limited liability to investors/shareholders. Thus, the shareholders of the investment fund will be liable for the debts and obligations of the respective investment fund unless the investment fund's administrator, and/or the portfolio manager be negligent, fraudulent or be involved in willful misconduct.

The advantages and disadvantages of using these structures is as follows:

Advantages
Because investment funds do not have a corporate structure, by and large, their portfolio transactions are not subject to taxation.

Disadvantages
Brazilian investment funds do not provide limited liability to their investors (shareholders).

Investment funds are organised as a pool of assets and investors participate as joint-owners of all investments comprising the joint-ownership of assets through the acquisition of shares, each of which corresponds to a notional fraction of all assets held by the relevant investment fund. As such, investment funds are not incorporated as legal entities (as companies, corporations, partnerships or trusts) despite the fact that they can assume the duties and obligations towards third parties, and they can sue and be sued.

The investors' interest in alternative investment funds are called 'quotas', which can be described as a share. The ownership of the fund's shares does not grant investors direct ownership of the fund's assets meaning that investors generally have rights over the whole fund's portfolio proportionally to the number of shares held by each investor.

Administrators are generally legal entities that comply with Rule 306, enacted by CVM on 5 May 1999 (CVM Rule 306/99), and are duly authorised by CVM to provide securities portfolio management services, according to Law 6,385, dated 7 December 1976 (Law 6,385/76).

Portfolio managers, which can either be a person or a legal entity, must also comply with CVM Rule 306/99 and be previously authorised by CVM (see section 2.2. below.)

2.2. Regulatory framework

The main regulations related to alternative investment funds are the following: (i) CVM Rule 391/03, CVM Rule 356/01, and CVM Rule 472/08, which, respectively, regulate the formation, operation and winding up of private equity funds, receivables funds and real estate funds; (ii) CMN Resolution No.3,334/05, as amended, which governs financial institutions when acting as a fund's administrator and portfolio manager; (iii) CMN Resolution No.2,907/01, dated 29 November 2001, which regulates receivables funds; (iv) Law 8,668/93, dated 25 June 1993; and (v) Law 6,385/76.

Private equity funds

Private equity funds are regulated by CVM Rule 391/03. Their purpose is to buy shares and convert securities (into shares) issued by listed or unlisted companies. Also, private equity funds must participate in the management of the company in which they invest, and can only be structured as a closed-ended fund. They are exclusively targeted at qualified investors (for any information regarding qualified investors, please see section 2.4. below).

A private equity fund's participation in the companies' decision making process may occur by holding controlling shares, by entering into any shareholder agreement or any procedure that ensures their effective influence in the management of the company's strategic policy.

In the case of investments on closely held corporations (unlisted corporations) the relevant bylaws must be adopted, to the extent necessary, in order to comply with the following corporate governance requirements and practices: (i) prohibition of the issuance of founders' shares (*partes beneficiárias*), as well as cancellation of any existing founders' shares; (ii) define a unified term of office for the entire board of directors; (iii) disclosure

Brazil

of (a) any agreement entered with related parties, (b) any shareholder agreement, (c) stock option programs or any issuer's security option program; (iv) if it decides to become a publicly held corporation it must undertake, before the fund, to adhere to the stock exchange or organised OTC market's special corporate governance segment; (v) adopt arbitration as the conflict/dispute resolution mechanism; and (vi) annually audit its financial statements by an independent auditor registered with CVM.

Also, private equity funds must allocate and maintain at least 90 per cent of its net worth in stock corporation shares or securities converted into shares.

Receivables funds

Receivables funds were created to facilitate securitisation transactions carried out in Brazil and are exclusively targeted at qualified investors.

The formation and operation of receivables funds in Brazil are primarily ruled by CVM Rule 356. Non-standardised receivables funds are also regulated by Rule No.444 of the CVM (CVM Rule 444/06).

The main differences between a receivables fund ruled by CVM Rule 356/01 and CVM Rule 444/06 is that the latter is capable of investing, inter alia, unpaid receivables, receivables arising from companies under judicial or extrajudicial recovery processes, future receivables with no defined amount, among others or any other asset not referred to under CVM Rule 356/01. The former is only allowed to invest in a wide range of receivables arising from financial, industrial, commercial, mortgage or real estate sectors with a defined amount.

Also, after 90 days of its commencement, any receivables fund must allocate at least 50 per cent of its net worth to receivables. At CVM's discretion, such period can be postponed for an additional 90 days if the fund's administrator has a justifiable reason to do so.

Recent modifications made by CVM Rule 531/13 on CVM Rule 356/01 have cleared up the custodian's role in the scope of receivables funds. Accordingly, custodians are responsible for, among other things, validating the receivable's underlying assets with the fund's eligible criteria, doing the custody and keeping in its records relevant documentation concerning the receivables portfolio and verifying on a semi-annual basis the documentation showing the connection between receivables represented by commercial, financial and services transactions and their respective underlying asset. This rule came to reinforce and determine the custodian's role in the scope of a receivables portfolio fund.

Real estate funds

Real estate funds are regulated by CVM Rule 472/08, and can only be structured as a closed-ended fund. They are targeted at any form of investor.

The purpose of a real estate fund is to acquire real estate, rights in connection with real estate, certain assets and securities issued by public listed corporations, performing real estate activities and securities registered with the CVM, such as:

- shares;

- debentures and warrants;
- shares of other real estate, private equity and receivables funds, provided that they are limited to a real estate-related activity; and
- other assets and securities set out in CVM Rule 472/08.

Where a real estate fund invests more than 5 per cent of its net worth in any of the above-mentioned securities, its relevant administrator or portfolio manager must be previously authorised by the CVM to manage the securities portfolio.

Alternative investment funds must be registered before the CVM prior to their operation.

The investment funds industry is regulated and supervised by the Monetary Council (*Conselho Monetário Nacional* (CMN)) and the CVM. The Brazilian Central Bank only regulates and supervises financial institutions when acting as administrator or portfolio manager, or as the case may be, service providers of the fund such as custodians.

According to CVM Rule 306/99, as amended, an administrator or portfolio manager (a financial or a non-financial legal entity) which intends to perform asset management activities must comply with all of the following requirements:

- be formed and have its principal place of business in Brazil;
- have as its corporate purpose the performance of asset management;
- be duly formed and enrolled with the National Legal Entities Registry of the Ministry of Finance (*Cadastro Nacional da Pessoal Jurídica do Ministério da Fazenda* (CNPJ));
- have a partner or an officer with an individual authorisation from CVM to act as a portfolio manager and be responsible for the asset management activity of the legal entity; and
- have a securities research and analysis department (the services of this department can be outsourced to a third party duly authorised by the CVM).

The main documents to be filed prior to authorisation of such funds, in some cases, can be very similar. Nevertheless, each fund has its own specific list of documents.

Generally speaking, the following documents must be filed by the relevant administrator prior to the operation of a fund: (i) the fund's formation document which is obtained through a resolution by the fund's administrator; (ii) the fund's bylaws; (iii) registration forms concerning the fund's administrator, portfolio manager and other providers of services retained by the fund; (iv) disclosure of any documents used for the distribution of shares; and (v) the prospectus, as the case may be.

2.3. Operational requirements

Private equity funds must allocate at least 90 per cent of their net worth to shares and/or convertible securities (into shares) issued by listed or unlisted corporations. Thus, under CVM Rule 391/03, private equity funds are not allowed to invest in limited liability companies, but they are allowed to invest in stock corporations.

As mentioned above, real estate funds are only allowed to acquire real estate, rights in connection with real estate, certain assets and securities issued by public listed corporations, performing real estate activities and securities registered with the CVM, such as shares, debentures and warrants, shares of other real estate, private equity and receivables funds provided that they are limited to a real estate-related activity.

A receivables fund may acquire receivables from the same debtor up to the limit of 20 per cent of the fund's net worth. Also, after 90 days from the beginning of its activities, the fund must have at least 50 per cent of its net worth invested in receivables.

CVM Rule 89/88 provides for the authorisation by CVM to render services in connection with the custody of securities. CVM Rule 310/99 describes all obligations and duties related to the custody of securities by any given custodian or any financial institution hired by such custodian to act so (sub-custodian).

For recent modifications regarding the custodian's activity in the scope of receivables funds, please see section 2.2. above.

Alternative investment funds' administrators must periodically provide documents and information to CVM on a monthly, semi-annual and annual basis.

Each form of alternative investment fund described in this chapter has its own list of required documents and information to comply with.
The most common information among these three types of alternative investment funds are:
- the fund's net worth and the number of shares issued;
- the fund's portfolio composition and diversification;
- balance sheet;
- profile of investment; and
- financial statements.

Alternative investment funds must inform CVM and immediately disclose any material act or fact that relates to the operation of the funds or the assets comprising their portfolio by letter to all shareholders. Doing so will allow all shareholders or prospective investors to access information that may reasonably influence the share price or the investors' decision to buy, sell or keep these shares.

In the case of public purchase of shares, the fund's administrator must provide the investor with the relevant prospectus before the investor's effective investment in the fund, with exception of a public offering with limited underwriting efforts.

Public offerings in Brazil are regulated by Rule 400, enacted by the CVM on 29 December 2003, as amended (CVM Rule 400/03), and the public offerings with limited underwriting efforts are regulated by Rule 476, enacted by CVM on 16 January 2009, as amended (CVM Rule 476/09). When shares are available for public purchase, these shares must be registered before the CVM, unless exempt from registration in accordance with CVM Rule 476/09.

Alternative investment funds cannot leverage through borrowing.

Private equity funds and receivables funds must have their respective assets valued and priced according to provisions described under their relevant bylaws.

Real estate funds shall have their respective assets valued by a technical report drawn up within 60 days after the end of the first semester and 90 days after the end of the fiscal year, and priced by market value.

2.4. Marketing the fund

CVM Rule 400/03 governs the public offering of securities in both primary and secondary markets. Accordingly, any information disclosed or any marketing material provided shall comply with the most recent prospectus provided to the CVM.

The use of any wording for any public marketing material must be previously approved by the CVM which can, at its sole discretion and at any time, request corrections, amendments or even the termination of the relevant advertisement.

Although not considered marketing material, any fund's supporting documentation shall be sent to the CVM prior to its utilisation.

The marketing of investment funds in Brazil and the distribution of their shares are restricted to institutions duly authorised by the CVM to operate in the securities distribution system which comprises, inter alia, securities dealers, distributors, securities brokers and independent agents acting as intermediaries for the purposes of trading of securities on stock exchanges or OTC markets. If the administrator of an investment fund is not a member of the securities distribution system, the administrator is required to enter into a distribution agreement with a third party to perform the distribution of the investment funds' shares. Members of the Brazilian securities distribution system are authorised by the CVM to distribute securities within Brazil.

Except for real estate funds, which can generally be marketed to the market at large, private equity funds and receivables funds shall only be marketed to qualified investors. According to CVM Rule 409/04, the qualified investors are financial institutions, pension funds, insurance entities, individuals or legal entities with investments in the financial and capital markets in excess of BRL300,000, and investment funds directed at qualified investors and asset managers and dealers.

Alternative investment funds exclusively targeted at qualified investors may only sell their shares in the secondary market if the purchaser is also a qualified investor.

In relation to the public offering of alternative investment fund shares, CVM Rule 400/03 establishes that marketing materials should not contain any dishonest or conflicting information, should be written in a clear and accessible way, and should highlight all risks involved.

The marketing material should state that it is in fact made for marketing purposes and should contain the phrase, 'read the prospectus before accepting the offer' (*leia o prospecto antes de aceitar a proposta*).

People involved in the fundraising process must be authorised to act in that capacity by the CVM. (Please see section 2.4. above.)

2.5. Taxation

In accordance with Brazilian legislation, generally, investment funds are deemed to be a condominium and not a standard legal entity. This does not mean that a fund is treated as a tax transparent entity, but, in general, its portfolio is exempt from Brazilian taxes (such as corporate income tax or social contributions) until income is distributed to its shareholders.

In general, investment funds are exempt from withholding tax (WHT) on any income obtained from their investments, except for real estate funds, which are subject to WHT on income derived from fixed or variable financial investments.

There are some cases in which real estate funds may be treated as a corporation for tax purposes, and are thus subject to corporate taxes. This treatment generally occurs in cases where the real estate fund does not observe its investment characteristics or restrictions.

The tax treatment for resident investors and the tax treatment for non-resident investors is set out below.

Private equity funds

Any gains obtained upon sale or redemption of shares of private equity funds, by resident investors, are generally subject to withholding tax at a 15 per cent rate. However, where a private equity fund does not hold a portfolio comprising at least 67 per cent of stocks of corporations, convertible debentures or subscription bonuses, it will be treated as fixed income investment and thus subject to income tax at rates varying from 22.5 per cent to 15 per cent, depending on the term of the investment.

Non-resident investors are generally subject to the same taxation as resident investors. However, non-resident investors that invest in shares of a private equity fund in accordance with the CMN Resolution No.2,689/00 may be subject to withholding tax at a zero per cent rate in case such investor, alone or along with related parties: (i) does not hold 40 per cent or more of shares of the fund; (ii) does not hold interests in the funds that grants such investor 40 per cent or more of the fund's income; and (iii) is not resident in a jurisdiction that taxes income at a maximum rate of less than 20 per cent.

Receivables funds

Resident investors are generally subject to the payment of withholding tax on the gains obtained as of the redemption of the funds' shares, at rates varying according to the characteristics of the fund and the term of the investment.

Investment funds with an average investment period of more than 365 days are considered long-term investment funds and funds that have an average investment period of 365 days are considered short-term investment funds.

Gains obtained in short-term investment funds are subject to withholding tax at a rate of 22.5 per cent if the redemption or sale of shares occurs up to 181 days after the acquisition date. The rate will be 20 per cent in any other case.

Gains obtained in long-term investment funds are subject to withholding tax at a rate of 22.5 per cent if the redemption or sale of shares occurs up to 181 days after the acquisition date. The rate will be 20 per cent for sales or redemptions that occur between 181 and 360 days; 17.5 per cent for sales or redemptions that occur between 361 and 720 days; and 15 per cent for sales or redemptions that occur more than 720 days after the shares are acquired.

The gains obtained in the sale or redemption of such shares by individuals will not be included in the calculation basis for purposes of the income tax adjustment. In the case of institutional investors, the income tax amounts withheld as the sale or redemption of the shares will be considered as an anticipation of the entity's final tax liability.

Non-resident investors are generally subject to the same taxation as resident investors. However, non-resident investors that invest in receivables funds in accordance with the CMN Resolution No.2,689/00 may be subject to withholding tax at a rate of 15 per cent, if such investor is not resident in a jurisdiction that taxes income at a maximum rate of less than 20 per cent.

Non-resident investors that are not resident in a jurisdiction that taxes income at a maximum rate of less than 20 per cent may benefit from a zero rate on income derived from receivables funds destined to the financing of infrastructure, technology, research and development projects, if the following requisites are observed: (i) the term of the fund is of at least six years; (ii) the redemption of shares is forbidden in the first two years of the fund; (iii) it is forbidden for the debtor or the lessor of the credits to acquire the funds' shares; (iv) the payments occur with a minimum term of 180 days from each other; (v) the shares are negotiated in a stock exchange or over-the-counter; and (vi) at least 85 per cent of the assets of the fund must be invested in credit rights and the remaining amount is invested in federal bonds.

Real estate funds
Both resident and non-resident investors are subject to payment of withholding tax at a 20 per cent rate on any distributions made by real estate funds. Upon redemption of shares of the fund, any gain realised will be subject to withholding tax at a 20 per cent rate.

Individual investors are exempt from withholding tax in case of real estate funds that are exclusively negotiated in a stock exchange or over-the-counter and have more than 50 investors. In order to be eligible for such treatment, the investor must not hold more than 10 per cent of the shares of the fund or interests in the funds that grants more than 10 per cent of the fund's income. Such exemption is granted for both resident and non-resident investors.

The acquisition of shares of investment funds in Brazil will generally be subject to the tax on transactions with bonds and securities (commonly known as IOF/Bonds) if the investment in such shares lasts less than 30 days. Investments that last longer than 30 days will not be taxed.

Non-resident investors may also be subject to foreign exchange tax (known as IOF/FX) on the inflow of funds into Brazil for the acquisition of a funds' shares. The current tax rate is zero however this is due to be changed to 25 per cent by presidential decree.

2.6. Customary or common terms
The term of a fund is dependent on its bylaws. Early termination of an

investment fund is stipulated in the bylaws. However, the decision to terminate early has to be approved at a shareholder's meeting and a copy of the minutes must be filed with the CVM to be deemed effective.

According to CVM Rule 356/01, the administrator can place restrictions on the issuance and redemption of shares provided that such provisions are described in the fund's bylaws.

The fund's administrator can decide to issue further shares or stop the issuance of shares provided this action applies to all investors. Additionally, in certain specific illiquidity circumstances, fund managers can suspend redemption to protect the best interests of investors. Likewise, this treatment must apply to all investors.

Shares of open-ended alternative investment funds cannot be traded on the secondary market. Investors can only exit the investment by redeeming their shares in accordance with the terms and procedures set out in the fund's bylaws.

Shares of closed-ended funds can be listed for trading on the secondary market and/or stock exchange. Intermediaries trading shares targeted exclusively at qualified investors must ensure that the purchasers in the secondary market are also considered qualified investors.

Furthermore, redemption of shares in both real estate funds and private equity funds is not possible.

Individuals cannot be appointed as an administrator of the alternative investment funds described in this chapter.

The fund's administrator is allowed to acquire shares of its own alternative investment funds provided that he/she acts in his/her own name and without conflict of interest as described under the relevant bylaws or applicable legislation.

Replacement or removal of the fund's administrator or portfolio manager shall be approved at a shareholder's meeting following the procedures described under the bylaws.

The fund's bylaws will stipulate the administrator's remuneration with regards to the amount and when the remuneration is paid. The administration fee shall be sufficient to remunerate both the administrator and all service providers of the investment fund. In case the administration fee is not enough to remunerate the service providers of the fund, the administrator is responsible for meeting such payments. Additionally, the bylaws will determine whether the fund will pay a performance fee to the portfolio manager.

The administration and performance fees are usually established as carried interest, through which the administrator will receive a share of the net assets annually accounted for in the private equity fund. From the amount established for the administration and performance fees, the administrator shall deduct the portfolio manager's fee and the remuneration of other service providers, unless otherwise determined in the bylaw.

Alternative investment funds exclusively targeted at qualified investors have a greater flexibility to charge performance fees.

The alternative fund's bylaws will define the investment period of the

Brazil

fund. Also, such term may be shortened or extended by the shareholders.

Investment must also comply with the fund's investment policy. In case this does not occur the administrator or the portfolio manager will be liable for any losses suffered by the fund.

Investment funds are not covered by any form of deposit insurance. Finally, alternative investment funds cannot leverage through borrowing.

3. RETAIL FUNDS
3.1. Common structures

As mentioned in section 2.1. above, considering that investment funds are a collection of assets jointly owned by investors under the structure of a sui generis condominium and provided that they do not constitute an independent legal entity from its shareholders, retail investment funds do not provide limited liability to them.

CVM Rule 409/04 provides for concentration limits for the retail fund's portfolio. Such concentration limits may vary according to the class of the fund (for different classes of retail fund please refer to section 3.3. below) and refer to:
- the type of asset or security (ie, debentures, shares, derivatives, bonds, funds shares); and
- the issuer of the relevant assets and securities (ie, financial institutions, investment funds, private companies, federal government and individuals).

Concentration limits by issuer

For the purposes of ICVM 409, 'issuer' shall mean any individual, legal entity, investment fund or segregated or independent pool of assets directly or indirectly responsible for the payment of an asset or security.

In addition to the specific provisions relating to each class of fund, retail investment funds must comply with the following concentration limits by issuer:
- up to 20 per cent of the fund's net worth for securities/assets issued by financial institutions;
- up to 10 per cent of the fund's net worth for securities/assets issued by publicly-held companies;
- up to 10 per cent of the fund's net worth for securities/assets issued by investment funds;
- up to 5 per cent of the fund's net worth for securities/assets issued by individuals or legal entities that are not a publicly-held companies or financial institutions authorised to operate by the Central Bank of Brazil; and
- no limits apply for securities/assets issued by the Brazilian Federal Government.

Furthermore, a limit of 20 per cent of the fund's net worth applies to assets/securities issued by the fund administrator, portfolio manager and/or their affiliates, provided that the fund bylaws shall provide for a maximum limit for the investment by the fund in shares of investment funds administered by the fund administrator, portfolio manager or their affiliates.

Finally, as a general rule, a retail investment fund may not hold shares issued by its administrator, except if the fund's investment policy is to follow certain market indexes of the shares issued by the administrator or its affiliates is a component. In the latter case, the fund may invest in such shares up to the proportion of their participation in the composition of the relevant market index.

Concentration limits by financial asset
In addition to the specific provisions relating to their class and to the limit by issuer, retail funds must comply with the following concentration limits by financial asset:
- up to 20 per cent of the fund's net worth may be composed of the following assets:
- shares of investment funds with the purpose to invest in investment funds;
- shares of real estate investment funds;
- shares of receivables funds and shares of investment funds having the purpose to invest in shares of receivables funds;
- shares of index funds traded in stock exchanges or in the organised over-the-counter market;
- real estate receivables certificates;
- other assets expressly provided for by ICVM 409; and
- repo transactions where the fund undertakes repurchases the underlying asset;
- no concentration limit applies for investments in the following assets:
- bonds issued by the Brazilian Federal Government and repo transactions backed by such bonds;
- gold, when traded by means of transactions carried in futures and commodities exchange;
- any security, contracts and transactions constituting direct or indirect obligations of financial institutions;
- securities registered with the CVM and distributed through a public offer; and
- derivative transactions which are not referenced to the assets specified above.

3.2. Regulatory framework
The main regulations related to retail investment funds are the following:
- CVM Rule 409, as amended, which rules the formation, operation and winding up of retail funds;
- Rule 438 enacted by CVM on 12 July 2006 (CVM Rule 438/06), as amended, which consolidated the retail investment funds' accounting rules;
- CMN Resolution 3,568, dated 29 May 2008, as amended, which addresses the foreign exchange controls applicable to investment funds investing abroad, among other things;

- CMN Resolution No.3,334/05, as amended, which rules financial institutions when acting as fund's administrators and portfolio manager; and
- Law 6,385/76, which regulates the Brazilian capital markets and created the CVM.

The details of the main steps involved in obtaining any necessary licences/authorisations are as follows:

Open-ended retail funds
Registration is obtained automatically upon the filing of certain documents with the CVM and is deemed effective as of the date of filing. The filing of documentation is done electronically through the CVM's website.

The following documents must be electronically presented for the registration to be obtained:
- bylaws;
- information on the registration of the bylaws before the registrar of title and deeds;
- offering memorandum or prospectus (if required);
- statement of the administrator confirming that the relevant agreements of the investment fund have been executed;
- name of independent auditor;
- registration before tax authorities (CNPJ); and
- form containing the required information on the investment fund, as provided by the CVM.

Although, registration with the CVM is automatic, the CVM is responsible for verifying the content of the documents and it can request additional information.

The formation of a fund occurs through the manager's resolution, which must also approve the fund's bylaws with the following minimum requirements: (i) the fund's investment policy; (ii) management fee; (iii) target investors; (iv) tax treatment; (v) the fund's investment abroad; (vi) concentration limits; and (vii) use of derivatives.

Closed-ended retail funds
Closed-ended retail funds must also register with the CVM. Their registration is not automatic, and requires the presentation of the required documents and depends on prior analysis by the CVM.
The documents required to form a closed-ended retail fund are quite similar to open-ended retail funds.

3.3. Operational requirements
Currently CVM Rule 409/04 divides retail investment funds into different categories based on the assets they are designated to acquire:
- Short-term fund: short-term funds are only allowed to invest in bonds: (i) issued by the federal government; or (i) issued by private companies. In each case, bonds must be indexed to pre-fixed interest rates, SELIC rates or another interest rate, or price index, with a maximum life (term

until maturity) of 375 days. The fund's portfolio must have an average maturity of less than 60 days. Short-term funds can only invest in derivatives for hedging purposes. Repo transactions backed by federal government bonds are admitted. Issuers of private securities within a short-term fund must be rated as low credit risk or equivalent, as certified by a rating agency located in Brazil.
- Referenced fund: the referenced funds' name shall indicate the performance indexer to which the fund is referenced. These funds must comply with the following requirements: (i) not less than 80 per cent of the fund's net worth must be represented, individual or cumulatively; by (a) securities issued by the National Treasury and/or by the Central Bank of Brazil, and (b) fixed income securities issued by entities rated as low credit risk by a rating agency located in Brazil; (ii) not less than 95 per cent of the fund's net worth must be represented by assets that follow, directly or indirectly, the variation of the performance indexer to which the fund is referenced; and (iii) derivative transactions must be limited to the hedging of positions held by the fund, subject to the amounts thereof.
- Fixed income fund: fixed income funds are designed to hold assets indexed to local interest rates, price indexes or both. At least 80 per cent of the fund's net worth must be represented by assets relating to, directly or synthesised through derivative transactions, the interest rate or price index to which the fund is exposed.
- Equity fund: equity funds' must have not less than 67 per cent of their net worth represented by: (i) shares; (ii) subscription bonuses or receipts; (iii) certificates of deposit of shares; (iv) shares of equity and index funds; (v) Brazilian Depositary Receipts classified as level II and III; in each case traded in stock exchanges or in the organised over-the-counter market.
- Foreign exchange fund: foreign exchange funds are designed to hold assets indexed to the fluctuation of foreign currency prices or of the exchange coupon. Therefore, at least 80 per cent of the fund's net worth must be represented by assets relating to, directly or synthesised through derivative transactions, the foreign exchange indicator to which the fund is exposed.
- External debt fund: an external debt fund must invest at least 80 per cent of its net worth in securities representing the Brazilian external debt, provided that such securities are held in custody by Euroclear or LuxClear: Central Securities Depositary of Luxembourg (CEDEL). The remaining 20 per cent may be invested in credit instruments traded in the international market. These funds may enter into derivative transactions for hedging purposes, provided that: (i) the transactions are conducted in organised markets abroad, in which case no limitations apply; or (ii) in case the derivative transactions are contracted in the Brazilian market, such transactions are referenced to securities representing the Brazilian external debt and are limited to 10 per cent of the fund's net worth.
- Multi-market fund: multi-market funds may invest in assets subject to different indexers and risks, with no obligation to concentrate on any

particular index or risk adopted by the above-mentioned classes.

Additionally, as expressly set forth in CVM Rule 409/04, depending on the retail fund classification, its respective portfolio may be composed of the following assets:
- sovereign bonds issued by the Brazilian Federal Government;
- derivative transactions;
- shares, debentures, subscription bonus, their coupons, rights, subscription receipts and split certificates, securities deposit certificates; investment funds shares, promissory notes, and any other securities (except for the ones described in the equity funds point), which issuance or trading have been approved or registered with the CVM;
- securities or contracts of collective investment, registered with the CVM and publicly offered, that grant participation rights, partnership or remuneration, including resulting from rendering services, which revenue arise from the enterpriser or third parties effort;
- deposit certificates or receipts issued in the foreign market backed by securities issued by publicly-held Brazilian companies;
- gold, as financial asset, when traded in accordance with general accepted international standards;
- any security, contracts and transactions constituting direct or indirect obligations of financial institutions authorised to operate by the Central Bank of Brazil; and
- warrants, commercial purchase and sale agreements for future delivery of goods and products and/or future services providing, certificates representing these agreements and any other credits, certificates, transactions and agreements expressly provided for in the fund bylaws.

According to CVM Rule 409/04, in both open-ended and closed-ended retail funds, investors must be periodically provided with the following information by the relevant fund's administrator: (i) on a daily basis: share price information and the fund's net asset value; (ii) on a monthly basis: the investments profile, monthly balance sheet and portfolio composition and diversification.

The above documents must also be provided to CVM in the same timeframes.

Each class of retail fund (please see section 3.3. above) will determine the investment risk involved according to their respective investment policy and investment restrictions, which generally refers to:
- the percentage of the net worth of the fund that should be invested in a determined type of securities;
- the possibility of the fund to enter in transaction with derivatives; and
- the term of the fund.

However, administrators must: (i) adopt policies, practices and compliance rules to turn the liquidity of all assets of the fund compatible with: (a) the redemption periods provided in the relevant fund's bylaws, and (b) the execution of all obligations undertaken by the fund; and (ii) submit the fund's assets portfolio to periodical stress scenario tests.

Valuation and pricing of assets of any retail investment fund shall follow

Brazil

all instructions described under CVM Rule 438/06, which consolidates the retail investment funds' accounting rules. Basically, retail investment funds' assets must be accounted according to their acquisition price and adjusted on a daily basis to their market value.

Retail investment funds cannot leverage through borrowing.

3.4. Marketing the fund
According to CVM Rule 409/04, marketing material shall not conflict with the fund's bylaws and/or prospectus, it must be written in a moderate language, it must be identified as a marketing material and it must mention the prospectus' existence.

3.5. Taxation
Resident investors are generally subject to withholding tax on the gains from the funds' shares, at rates which vary according to the characteristics of the fund and the term of the investment.

Gains obtained in short-term investment funds are subject to withholding tax at a 22.5 per cent rate if the redemption or sale of shares occurs up to 181 days after the acquisition date; the rate will be 20 per cent in any other cases.

Gains obtained in long-term investment funds are subject to income tax withholding at a 22.5 per cent rate if the redemption or sale of shares occurs up to 181 days after the acquisition date; the rate will be 20 per cent for sales or redemptions that occur between one 181 and 360 days; 17.5 per cent for sales or redemptions that occur between 361 and 720 days; and 15 per cent for sales or redemptions that occur more than 720 days after the shares are acquired.

The gains obtained in the sale or redemption of such shares by individuals will not be included in the calculation basis for purposes of the income tax adjustment. In case of institutional investors, the income tax amounts withheld as of the sale or redemption of shares will be considered as an anticipation of the entity's final tax liability.

Non-resident investors are generally subject to the same taxation as resident investors. However, non-resident investors that invest in retail funds in accordance with the CMN Resolution No.2,689/00 may be subject to withholding tax at a 15 per cent rate when the investor is not resident in a jurisdiction that taxes income at a maximum rate of less than 20 per cent.

3.6. Customary or common terms
The term of retail investment funds shall be by their respective bylaws.

The decision to terminate the fund early has to be approved by the shareholders at a shareholder's meeting and a copy of the minutes must be filed with the CVM for it to be effective.

Open-ended retail funds
According to CVM Rule 409/04 and the fund's bylaws, the administrator of open-ended retail funds can restrict the issuance and redemption of interests.

The fund's administrator is also able to decide on the issuance of new shares or to stop the issuance of shares provided this action applies to all investors. In certain circumstances relating to illiquidity, fund managers can suspend redemption to protect the best interests of investors provided this treatment is equal to all investors.

Open-ended retail funds' shares cannot be traded in the secondary market and investors can only exit their respective investment by redeeming their shares in accordance with the terms and procedures set out in the fund's bylaws.

Closed-ended retail funds

Issuance of new shares in the scope of closed-ended retail funds must be approved by the shareholders at a shareholder's meeting. Additionally, timing regarding redemption of interest may only be changed by the fund's administrator if it is approved by investors following directions of the fund's bylaws.

Shares of closed-ended funds can be listed in the secondary market or stock exchange for trading purposes. Also, intermediaries trading fund's shares targeted exclusively at qualified investors must ensure that the relevant purchasers of secondary market are also considered qualified investors.

Retail investment fund's administrators are entitled to a management fee which is a fixed rate and is related to a percentage of the fund's annual net worth.

Insofar as performance fee is granted, it shall comply with the following requirements: (i) it must be linked to a reference parameter duly compatible to the investment policy of the fund and the fund's portfolio; (ii) the fee may not be linked to any percentage less than 100 per cent; (iii) it has a minimum semi-annual charge period; and (iv) it shall only be charged after all expenses have been paid by the fund, including the management fee.

Both, the administrator and the performance fee must be described in the bylaws together with their respective forms of calculation.

On the other hand, retail funds exclusively targeted at qualified investors have a greater autonomy to charge performance fees according to their respective bylaws.

4. PROPOSED CHANGES AND DEVELOPMENTS

CVM intends to start public discussions regarding the review of CVM Rule 89/88 which provides for the authorisation by the CVM for companies to render services in connection with the custody of securities.

Another regulation that is under public discussions is CVM Rule 306/99 which deals with asset management activities.

British Virgin Islands

Tim Clipstone & Sophie Whitcombe **Maples and Calder**

1. MARKET OVERVIEW

The British Virgin Islands (BVI) has been a popular jurisdiction of choice in which to incorporate or establish investment funds since the late 1980s and early 1990s when George Soros first established and/or promoted a number of highly publicised funds in the jurisdiction. Since then the territory has developed a solid investment funds industry.

Historically, the BVI was seen as a fairly low cost option, offering extremely flexible corporate laws together with an appropriate level of regulation suitable for the type of business the jurisdiction wanted to attract, namely the open-ended hedge fund business aimed at institutional and professional/high net worth investors. In addition, because of the competitiveness of the fee regime, the jurisdiction has in the past attracted, and continues to attract, a substantial number of start-up managers looking to establish their first funds.

The BVI has also been a popular jurisdiction in which to establish closed-ended funds where, once again, the suitable degree of regulation, flexible corporate laws and competitive professional fees and government applied charges have made it an ideal jurisdiction in which to establish such entities. However, as these types of structures are unregulated and therefore not approved by any regulatory bodies in the BVI, there are no official statistics available to verify how many of these vehicles currently exist.

Some of the major attractions of the BVI as a domicile for investment funds are the following:
- the BVI legal system is a common law system, primarily based on principles of English law and with the final court of appeal being the Judicial Committee of the Privy Council in London;
- the BVI is recognised as being politically stable, due to its status as a British Overseas Territory and its long history as a financial centre that has not suffered political upheaval;
- favourable tax regime;
- no exchange controls;
- modern insolvency law based on English legislation;
- robust and healthy compliance culture which complies with international anti-money laundering, anti-terrorist financing and other financial regulatory standards;
- established judiciary with an independent commercial court;
- professional infrastructure and reputation: the BVI is well known for its established and experienced financial services sector represented by global service providers;
- no requirement to have fund audits signed off by an accounting firm

located in the BVI; and
- no requirement for functionaries of the fund (investment managers, advisers, brokers, administrators, etc.) to be located in the BVI.

The primary legislation in respect of the regulation of investment funds in the BVI is the Securities and Investment Business Act 2010 (as amended) (SIBA), which came into force on 17 May 2010 and is administered and enforced by the BVI Financial Services Commission (the Commission). SIBA provides, among other things, a legislative regime which regulates securities and investment business in the BVI.

Responsibility for the regulation of mutual funds, mutual fund administrators, mutual fund managers, custodians and other persons carrying on investment business rests with the Commission.

Wide-ranging powers are given to the Commission to cancel fund certificates of recognition or registration and the Commission may also direct any person to whom SIBA applies to furnish such information, or provide access to any records, books or other documents, as it deems necessary.

Ancillary legislation, such as the Mutual Funds Regulations 2010 (the Regulations) and the Public Funds Code 2010 (the Code), has also been introduced to supplement the provisions of SIBA and, together with SIBA, have replaced the now repealed Mutual Funds Act 1996 (the Former Act). The Regulations and the Code are considered further in sections 3 and 4 of this chapter.

SIBA provides for the licensing, regulation and supervision of open-ended mutual funds through the registration of public mutual funds and the recognition of professional and private mutual funds.

SIBA defines a mutual fund as a company incorporated, a partnership formed, a unit trust organised or other similar body formed or organised under the laws of the BVI or the laws of any other country (but excludes any company or other body, partnership or unit trust which is of a type or description designated by the Regulations as not being a mutual fund) which:
- collects and pools investor funds for the purpose of collective investment; and
- issues fund interests (defined as the rights or interests, however described, of investors in a mutual fund with regard to the property of the fund, but does not include a debt) that entitle the holder to receive on demand or within a specified period after demand an amount computed by reference to the value of a proportionate interest in the whole or in a part of the net assets of the company or other body, partnership or unit trust, as the case may be.

This includes:
- an umbrella fund whose fund interests are split into a number of different class funds or sub-funds; and
- a fund which has a single investor which is a mutual fund not registered or recognised under SIBA.

SIBA applies to the following:
- mutual funds which are formed under the laws of the BVI;
- mutual funds formed under the laws of a jurisdiction other than the BVI

but which carry on business in the BVI through a branch operation or representative office;
- foreign mutual funds which solicit the purchase of their shares to individual persons who are BVI residents or citizens and individuals who are physically present in the BVI;
- mutual fund administrators, managers and custodians which are formed under the laws of the BVI (including BVI business companies); and
- foreign mutual fund management or administrative entities which carry on their business in the BVI, for example, through a branch operation or representative office.

SIBA does not apply to a closed-ended fund.

Under SIBA, a mutual fund must be registered as a 'public fund', recognised as a 'professional fund' or a 'private fund' or be a 'recognised foreign fund', and unregistered or unrecognised funds must not carry on business or hold themselves out as carrying on business as a mutual fund in or from within the BVI.

In addition to any government registration fees, mutual funds are required to pay an annual mutual fund fee (currently $1,000 for a private or professional fund and $1,500 for a public fund).

Existing fund administrators and fund managers which were, immediately before 17 May 2010, licensed as a fund administrator and/or a fund manager under the Former Act, are deemed to be licensed under SIBA as a fund administrator and/or a fund manager, as the case may be, with effect from 17 May 2010.

A BVI business company acting as a fund manager, a fund administrator or a custodian to a mutual fund established in the BVI is required under SIBA to be licensed by the Commission.

Once the Commission has licensed a fund manager, fund administrator, custodian, or any other person carrying on investment business in or from within the BVI, the licensee's obligations are, among other things, as follows:
- directors and senior officers of the licensee must not be appointed without the prior written approval of the Commission;
- the Commission must be notified of the actual appointment, resignation or removal of a director or senior officer or such person otherwise ceasing to act in such capacity for any reason whatsoever, in each case within 14 days of the occurrence of the event;
- any disposal or acquisition of a 'significant interest' (as defined in SIBA) in a licensee must be approved in writing by the Commission and the licensee may not cause, permit or acquiesce to any sale, transfer, charge or other disposition without the prior written approval of the Commission;
- the Commission must approve in writing any issue or allotment of any shares or any other reorganisation of the share capital of a corporate licensee that results in a person acquiring a significant interest in the licensee or a person who already owns or holds a significant interest in the licensee increasing or decreasing the size of that interest; and
- pay the prescribed annual licence fee (currently $1,500) on or before 31

March in each year. There are penalties for late payment.

In December 2012, the Investment Business (Approved Managers) Regulations 2012 (Manager Regulations) came into force. The Manager Regulations provide a new, less onerous, regime for the regulation of persons acting as investment advisers or investment managers to the entities prescribed in the Manager Regulations, which include private and professional mutual funds (see section 3.1. below) and closed-ended funds. A person approved under the Manager Regulations (an approved investment manager) must also ensure that its assets under management do not exceed the thresholds provided for in the Manager Regulations. An approved investment manager is subject to less regulatory obligations as it is not required to appoint a compliance officer, to maintain a compliance procedures manual or to submit audited financial statements (although it is still required to submit financial statements to the Commission within six months of its financial year end). Many of the provisions of SIBA will, however, still apply to an approved investment manager.

2. CLOSED-ENDED FUNDS
2.1. Common structures

Although the limited partnership is typically used for closed-ended venture capital and private equity funds with a limited number of investors, there are three main structures available to establish closed-ended funds. There is no significant regulatory or other reason for preferring one vehicle or structure over another and the decision will usually be driven by administrative issues, regulatory and taxation implications. The general features of each type of structure are set out below.

Limited partnership

The limited partnership concept is similar to that which applies in the United States except that a BVI limited partnership constitutes a contractual relationship between the partners and is not a separate legal personality distinct from its partners. The limited partnership must act through its general partner which contracts for and on behalf of the limited partnership. Limited partnership structures are popular with United States promoters and their advisers.

Company

Companies are almost always incorporated with limited liability, although it is possible to incorporate companies with unlimited liability or with liability limited by guarantee. The liability of a shareholder of a limited liability company is limited to the amount paid up or agreed to be paid up on the shares subscribed for by that shareholder.

Shares of the same class in a company rank equally with each other. However, by appropriate amendment of the memorandum and articles of association (constitutional documents) of a BVI company, it is possible to create separate share classes (or separate sub classes or series within the same share class). This may be necessary if, for example, performance fees payable to an investment manager are to be calculated differently in certain circumstances or if certain categories of investors are not permitted to participate in certain assets or classes of assets held by the company.

Unit trust
The concept of a unit trust is that subscribers contribute funds to a trustee, which holds those funds as custodian while they are managed by the investment manager for the benefit of the subscribers, known as unit holders. Each unit holder is entitled to a pro-rata share of the trust's assets.

Unit trusts are often used in preference to companies for investors in jurisdictions where participation in a unit trust is more acceptable or attractive than owning shares in a company for regulatory compliance or appropriate tax treatment.

Unit holders in an exempted trust such as a unit trust must not include persons resident or domiciled in the BVI.

2.2. Regulatory framework
SIBA only regulates open-ended funds which come within the definition of 'mutual funds'. Closed-ended funds do not fall within the definition of 'mutual fund' or 'fund' under SIBA and are therefore not regulated by SIBA. Any person who acts as a functionary to a BVI closed-ended fund is only subject to SIBA (in its capacity as a licensee under SIBA) if the person is carrying on its business in the BVI or is a BVI incorporated company.

2.3. Operational requirements
(i) Regulatory requirements under SIBA
Since closed-ended funds are not regulated by the Commission under SIBA, the regulatory reporting or filing requirements set out in SIBA do not apply to such funds.

(ii) Anti-money laundering requirements
As closed-ended funds are not licensed or registered in the BVI, no specific provisions of the Anti-Money Laundering and Terrorist Financing Code of Practice 2008 (AML Code) and Anti-Money Laundering Regulations 2008 (AML Regulations) currently apply to such funds (please refer to section 3.3(vi)). However, any functionary to a closed-ended fund will be subject to the AML Code and AML Regulations if the functionary is a BVI business company or it carries on business in the BVI as it will then be deemed to be a relevant person (as defined in the AML Regulations).

(iii) Other requirements:
- Holding of assets: there is no requirement for the appointment of a depository or a custodian.
- Risk: there are no requirements relating to risk.
- Valuation and pricing of assets: there are no requirements relating to the valuation and pricing of assets.
- Transparency: while investors have the right to certain information

relating to the fund (such as its constitutional documents), there is no requirement for accounts or reports to be made available to investors. All BVI companies and partnerships must keep or cause to be kept proper books of account sufficient to show the financial position of the company or partnership with reasonable accuracy. Such books of account must be kept for at least five years.
- Short selling: there are no restrictions on short selling.

2.4. Marketing the fund

Although there are no requirements to carry out promotion or marketing activities of a fund from within the BVI or by an entity established or, in the case of a foreign company, registered in the BVI, any such entity that does carry out marketing or promotion of a BVI fund must be licensed under SIBA in order to be able to do so.

There are no restrictions as to whom the fund may be marketed except that:
- other than as far as is necessary in order to carry on its business outside the BVI, an international limited partnership may not undertake business with persons resident in the BVI; and
- unit holders in an exempted trust must not include persons resident or domiciled in the BVI.

2.5. Taxation

There are no BVI income, corporation, capital gains or withholding taxes or death duties that are applied directly to BVI funds.

2.6. Customary or common terms

- Term of the fund: where a closed-ended fund is structured as a limited partnership, the term of the fund will depend upon the investment strategy and type of investments held by the fund; this is often between seven and ten years, with an option to extend for one- or two-year rollover periods.
- Liquidity of interests: by definition, a closed-ended fund does not allow for redemptions of interests at the option of the investor.
- Manager/operator involvement: there is no legal requirement for the manager or operators of the fund to invest their own money in the fund, although in practice this is quite common.
- Remuneration arrangements: the most common level of management fee paid to managers is between 1 per cent and 2 per cent and, where funds are structured as limited partnerships, 'waterfall' arrangements are applied by which distributions/profits will be allocated first to the limited partners until the capital amount contributed by the limited partners has been repaid. Thereafter, a preferred return may be paid to the limited partners (often around 8 per cent) and the manager will be paid a percentage of the remaining profits.
- Investment and borrowing restrictions: there are no statutory restrictions on borrowing and most funds permit the use of leverage either as part of the investment strategy or as an administrative tool.

- Reporting obligations: there are no statutory reporting obligations to any regulatory authorities or reporting obligations to investors. However, it is often the case that the fund will state in its offering document that it will make financial reports available to investors on an annual basis.

3. HEDGE FUNDS
3.1. Common structures

As set out at section 2.1., the three structures available for hedge funds (referred to in the BVI as mutual funds) are the limited partnership, the company and the unit trust. The majority of BVI domiciled hedge funds are formed as companies.

Where different investors in a mutual fund are pursuing materially different investment strategies, some protection against third party creditors referable to a particular portfolio of assets can be afforded by the use of a segregated portfolio company. A segregated portfolio company is still a single legal entity but with separate segregated portfolios. Such portfolios cannot contract with each other or acquire shares in each other, but the legislative intent is that third parties who contract with the company acting on behalf of a particular portfolio will have recourse limited only to the assets of that portfolio.

There are three available categories of mutual funds under SIBA:

Private fund

A private fund is defined in SIBA as a mutual fund the constitutional documents of which specify: (a) that it will have no more than 50 investors; or (b) that the making of an invitation to subscribe for or purchase fund interests issued by the mutual fund is to be made on a private basis only. SIBA provides that, for the purposes of the definition of private fund, an invitation to subscribe for or purchase fund interests issued by a mutual fund on a private basis includes an invitation which is made: (i) to specified persons (however described) and is not calculated to result in fund interests becoming available to other persons or to a large number of persons; or (ii) by reason of a private or business connection between the person making the invitation and the investor.

Professional fund

A professional fund is defined in SIBA as a mutual fund the constitutional documents of which specify that the fund interests shall only be issued to professional investors and the initial investment by each investor in the fund (other than a small category of exempted investors) is not less than such sum as may be prescribed in the Regulations (currently $100,000 or its equivalent in any other currency). A professional investor is defined in SIBA as a person: (a) whose ordinary business involves, whether for that person's own account or the account of others, the acquisition or disposal of property of the same kind as the property, or a substantial part of the property, of the fund; or (b) who has signed a declaration that they, whether individually or jointly with their spouse, have a net worth in excess of $1,000,000 or its equivalent in any other currency and that they consent to being treated as a professional investor.

Public fund

A public fund is a mutual fund which is neither a private nor a professional fund. While it is not a requirement of BVI law for a public fund to be a retail fund, given the fact that there is no statutory initial minimum investment and that public funds are subject to a greater degree of oversight, this is often the case. The characteristics and criterion for a public fund are as set out in section 4 of this chapter.

3.2. Regulatory framework

As set out at section 1.2., the primary legislation in respect of BVI mutual funds is SIBA. The following are requirements for private and professional funds:

(i) The Regulations provide that no offer or invitation shall be made to an investor or potential investor to purchase or subscribe for fund interests in a private or professional fund unless the investor or potential investor is provided with the prescribed investment warning which must be included in a prominent place in the fund's offering document. Where a private or professional fund does not issue an offering document, the investment warning must be provided to each investor in a separate document.

(ii) The investment warning must clearly indicate that:
- the fund has been established as a private or professional fund (as the case may be);
- in the case of a private fund, that the fund is suitable for private investors only and that either: (i) the fund is limited to 50 investors; or (ii) any invitation to subscribe for fund interests shall be made on a 'private basis' only;
- in the case of a professional fund, that the fund is suitable for professional investors, and with respect to each investor, a minimum initial investment of $100,000 (or such larger sum as may apply with respect to the fund) is required;
- the fund is not subject to supervision by the Commission or by a regulator outside the BVI and that the requirements considered necessary for the protection of investors that apply to public funds do not apply to private or professional funds;
- an investor in a private or professional fund is solely responsible for determining whether the fund is suitable for their investment needs; and
- by reason of the above, investment in a private or professional fund may present a greater risk to an investor than investment in a public fund.

(iii) No person should be accepted as an investor in a private or professional fund unless that person has provided a written acknowledgement that they have received, understood and accepted the prescribed investment

warning.
(iv) The confidentiality of private and professional funds is preserved by prohibiting the Commission from disclosing any material filed with it, except in very limited circumstances, for instance, where disclosure may be made pursuant to a court order or on request by a foreign regulatory authority approved by the Commission.
(v) A private fund and a professional fund must at all times have at least two directors, at least one of whom must be an individual. Where a private fund or a professional fund breaches the requirement to have at least two directors, the fund must notify the Commission in writing immediately.
(vi) A private fund and a professional fund must at all times have a fund manager, a fund administrator and a custodian. The custodian of a private fund or a professional fund must be a person who is functionally independent from the fund manager and the fund administrator.
(vii) The Commission may, on written application made by or on behalf of a private or professional fund, exempt the fund from the requirement to appoint a custodian or a fund manager. No exemption is available in respect of the requirement to have a fund administrator.
(viii) Private funds are required to be recognised before commencing business.
(ix) Professional funds are granted a 21-day grace period in which such a fund can commence business without being recognised, provided that the application for recognition as a professional fund is submitted to the Commission within 14 days of the fund's commencement of business.
(x) No person should be appointed as a functionary of a private or professional fund unless at least seven days' prior notification of the proposed appointment has been given to the Commission. Notice must also be given to the Commission within seven days of a functionary resigning, having its appointment terminated or otherwise ceasing to act as a functionary of the fund.
(xi) A BVI private or professional fund must notify the Commission within 14 days of the appointment of a director, authorised representative or auditor, or of a director, authorised representative or auditor ceasing to hold office, any change in the fund's place of business, any amendment to its constitutional or offering documents, or issuance of a new offering document.

3.3. Operational requirements

(i) Pursuant to section 56A of the Financial Services Commission Act 2001, the Commission in November 2009 introduced the Financial Services (Prudential and Statistical Returns) Order 2009 which requires all BVI recognised or registered mutual funds to file an annual prudential or statistical return with the Commission by 30 June. The return relates to information in respect of the calendar year immediately preceding the year of submission. The purpose of the return is to provide information to measure and develop the BVI funds industry, to safeguard the interests of the BVI financial services industry and the reputation of the BVI. Each mutual fund must report on the following:

- basic prudential and governance information, which includes information on the fund's BVI registered agent and its functionaries; and
- summary financial information for the relevant reporting period, which includes the beginning net asset value (NAV), total subscriptions, total redemptions, net income/loss, dividends/distributions, ending NAV and year end gross assets.

(ii) The mutual fund must also inform the Commission if it has changed its registered office or its principal office or (in the case of a unit trust) if there has been a change in the trust company acting as its trustee.

(iii) The fund must also comply with any special conditions which SIBA has imposed in respect of its recognition or registration as a mutual fund.

(iv) Auditors
A BVI private or professional fund must appoint an auditor (who does not need to be located in the BVI) and prepare financial statements which must be submitted to the Commission within six months of the end of the financial year to which they relate (unless granted a specific exemption by the Commission). The deadline for submission of audited financial statements can, on application, be extended for a period of not more than 15 months following the financial year to which they relate.

(v) Local service providers
There are only two statutory requirements as to the use of local service providers: the registered office/registered agent and the authorised representative of a mutual fund must both be resident in the BVI.

The registered office/agent maintains certain statutory records and registers at its office in the BVI and acts as agent for service of process for the fund.

The functions of the authorised representative as prescribed by SIBA are as follows:

- to act as the main intermediary between the BVI mutual fund that it represents and the Commission;
- to accept service of notices and other documents on behalf of the fund;
- to keep in the authorised representative's office in the BVI such records, or copies of such records, as may be prescribed in the Regulations;
- to submit all documents required to be submitted to the Commission by the fund; and
- to pay all fees required to be paid to the Commission by the fund.

(vi) Anti-money laundering
The BVI has adopted a 'risk-based' approach to anti-money laundering and compliance (BVI AML Regime). In order to comply with the AML Regulations, the AML Code and other legal and regulatory requirements in the BVI, recognised/registered BVI funds and/or service providers to BVI funds to which the AML function has been properly delegated are required to verify the identity of all investors and to update such verification information supplied from time to time.

In particular, the BVI AML Regime applies specific requirements to funds and service providers in the BVI that conduct 'relevant business' in or from within the BVI, such entities being referred to as 'relevant persons'. Relevant business essentially includes business activities for which licensing by or registration with the Commission is required, a full description of such activities being listed within the definition of relevant business in the AML Regulations and include carrying on business as a mutual fund or providing services as manager or administrator of a mutual fund.

The BVI AML Regime requires a recognised/registered fund (being a relevant person) to conduct a risk profiling and assessment in relation to each subscriber to the fund in order to determine the suitability of accepting any subscription proceeds and to determine the extent of any due diligence required. Thus, subscribers will be assessed as low risk, ordinary risk and high risk in order to meet the minimum standards for each type of investor.

Any investor being a person or entity from a 'BVI recognised jurisdiction' (ie, a jurisdiction on a list of jurisdictions published by the Commission that are recognised as having in place an anti-money laundering regime equivalent to that in the BVI) is likely to be considered low risk unless circumstances exist which indicate that they may be in a higher risk category, such as: (i) a politically exposed person; (ii) a person located in a country considered or identified as being high risk or that has sanctions, embargos or other restrictions imposed on it; or (iii) a business activity, ownership structure, anticipated, or volume or type of transaction that is complex or unusual, having regard to the risk profile of the applicant for business or customer, or where the business activity involves an unusual pattern of transactions or does not demonstrate any apparent or visible economic or lawful purpose.

The provisions of the AML Regulations and the AML Code, as set out above, apply to any investment business licensee and to any recognised/registered mutual fund. The majority of BVI recognised/registered mutual funds delegate the maintenance of their AML procedures to a third party, often its administrator, based in a BVI recognised jurisdiction.

(vii) Other requirements:
- (i) Risk: a mutual fund's offering document must contain such information as is necessary to enable a prospective investor in the fund to make an informed decision about whether to subscribe for or purchase equity interests.
- (ii) Valuation and pricing: a mutual fund must have an administrator. Generally, the administrator will, under the terms of its appointment, be responsible for the calculation of net asset value.
- (iii) Holding of assets: a mutual fund must have a custodian, unless the Commission has granted an exemption.
- (iv) Transparency: while investors have the right to certain information relating to the fund (such as its constitutional documents), there is no requirement for accounts or reports to be available to investors. All BVI companies and partnerships must keep or cause to be kept proper books of account sufficient to show the financial position of the company or partnership with reasonable accuracy. Such books of account must be kept for at least five years.
- (v) Short selling: there are no restrictions on short selling.

Further requirements imposed on public funds are set out in section 4.3.

3.4. Marketing the fund
The same provisions as are set out at section 2.4. apply equally here.

3.5. Taxation
The same provisions as are set out at section 2.5. apply equally here.

3.6. Customary or common terms
- Term of the fund: the majority of BVI hedge funds are formed as companies and generally do not have a fixed life.
- Liquidity of interests: the frequency of days upon which the investors can redeem from the fund will often depend upon the type of investment strategy employed by the fund. Usually, redemption days will be on a monthly or quarterly basis but they can be more or less frequent. A fund's constitutional and offering documents can be drafted to allow the fund to impose a 'gate' on redemptions (a provision which limits the volume of redemptions, on any redemption day), hard lock-ups (ie, periods during which no redemptions are permitted) and/or soft lock-ups (ie, periods during which redemptions are permitted upon payment of a fee).
- Manager/operator involvement: there is no requirement for the manager or operator of the fund to invest their own money in the fund although it is often the case that they will do so.
- Remuneration arrangements: while, traditionally, BVI hedge funds have operated a 'two and twenty' fee structure (ie, a 2 per cent management fee and a 20 per cent performance fee), more recently, the trend has been towards lower fees, particularly management fees. While the majority of funds still have a 20 per cent performance fee, in recent years a significant number of funds have been formed with lower or alternative performance fee structures. In respect of the performance fee the majority of funds have a classic high water mark although some operate an adjusted or resetting high water mark or hurdle rate. Performance fee clawback is not common.
- Investment and borrowing restrictions: unless the fund's constitutional offering documents state otherwise, there are no restrictions on borrowing under BVI law, and no restrictions on how the portfolio of assets of the fund are typically held. Most new funds permit the use of leverage and appoint at least one prime broker and custodian.
- Reporting obligations: mutual funds are required to file audited accounts with the Commission annually. Although there are no reporting requirements as regards investors, most funds state in their offering memoranda that audited financial statements will be sent to investors every year.

4. RETAIL FUNDS
4.1. Common structures
Most BVI retail funds are formed as companies and will be registered under SIBA as public funds.

4.2. Regulatory framework
As set out at section 1.2., the primary legislation in respect of BVI mutual

funds is SIBA. The following are requirements for public funds.

A mutual fund will be registered by the Commission as a public fund provided that the Commission is satisfied that:
- the fund is a BVI business company or, in the case of a unit trust, a unit trust that is governed by the trust laws of the BVI and has a trustee based in the BVI; under SIBA, a public fund cannot be structured as a limited partnership;
- the fund satisfies the requirements of SIBA and the Code;
- the fund will, on registration, be in compliance with SIBA and any practice directions issued by the Commission which are applicable to the fund;
- the fund's functionaries satisfy the Commission's 'fit and proper' criteria;
- the fund has, or on registration will have, an independent custodian;
- the fund's name is not undesirable or misleading; and
- registering the fund is not against the public interest.

Public funds are required to be registered under SIBA before commencing business and, in addition, mutual fund administrators, mutual fund managers, mutual fund custodians, investment advisers and other persons carrying on investment business (as defined in SIBA) are required to be licensed before commencing business.

Ongoing requirements:
- a public fund must at all times have a manager, an administrator and a custodian (unless exempted by the Commission from the requirement to appoint a custodian);
- a functionary of a public fund must be functionally independent from every other functionary of the fund;
- where the company acting as custodian to the public fund is the same as the company acting as the fund manager or fund administrator, the fund in question can request the approval of the Commission for the company to act as custodian where that company has systems and controls that ensure that the persons fulfilling the custodial role are functionally independent from the persons fulfilling the fund management or fund administration roles;
- a public fund must appoint an auditor who is approved by the Commission, maintain adequate accounting records, prepare audited financial statements which must be submitted to the Commission within six months of the end of the financial year to which they relate, and keep such accounting records and financial statements available for examination by the Commission, any other authorised person and all investors;
- a public fund must at all times have at least two directors. Only individuals can serve as directors of public funds; and
- where the required information disclosed in the prospectus of a public fund ceases to be accurate the public fund must publish an amendment to the prospectus within 14 days of the change occurring.

4.3. Operational requirements
See sections 3.3(i), (iii), (iv) and (v) above.

A BVI public fund must notify the Commission within 14 days of any of the appointment of a director, authorised representative or auditor, or of a director, authorised representative or auditor ceasing to hold office, any change in the fund's place of business or any change in the place where the fund's financial and other records are kept. Any amendment to its constitutional or offering documents or issue of any new offering document must be notified to the Commission 21 days prior to the proposed date of issue of the amendment or new offering document.

A public fund must also comply with any special conditions which SIBA has imposed in respect of its licensing as a mutual fund.

Under the Code, a public fund must at all times carry on business in accordance with the following four principles:

- integrity;
- management and control: a public fund must take reasonable care to organise and control its affairs effectively, taking into account the nature, scale, complexity and diversity of its business and the risks it faces;
- investors' interests: a public fund must have due regard for the interests of its investors and treat them fairly. A public fund must also make appropriate arrangements to protect the fund's property and take all reasonable steps to identify and manage conflicts of interests; and
- relationship with the Commission: a public fund must deal with the Commission in an open and co-operative manner.

The Code provides that a prospectus issued by a public fund must not contain any matter that is unfairly prejudicial to investors generally or to any class of investors, or conflicts with SIBA, the Regulations or the Code. Any prospectus must provide full and accurate disclosure of all such information as investors would reasonably require and reasonably expect to find for the purpose of making an informed investment decision and must contain the information and matters set out in Schedule 1 of the Code, which are as follows:

- certain particulars of the manager, the administrator, the custodian, the prime broker, the investment adviser, the directors and other relevant persons associated with the fund;
- the constitution and objectives of the fund;
- the characteristics of fund interests in the fund;
- the characteristics of the fund;
- details of the valuation of fund property and fund interests;
- details of fees associated with investment in the fund and any other payments which may lawfully be made out of fund property;
- details of distribution of income;
- details regarding the issue and redemption of fund interests;
- details of umbrella funds; and
- other general information.

If a public fund issues a prospectus that contains any misrepresentation relating to any of the disclosures required under SIBA, a person who purchased any fund interests on the basis of the prospectus is deemed to have relied upon the misrepresentation and may elect to exercise a right of action for the rescission of the purchase, or for damages.

The Code also provides that a public fund must take reasonable care to maintain a clear and appropriate apportionment of significant responsibilities between its governing body and the functionaries so that:
- the separation of responsibility is clear; and
- the business and affairs of the fund can be adequately monitored and controlled by the governing body.

A public fund that is a BVI business company must have an adequate number of directors who:
- are capable of exercising independent judgment;
- have sufficient knowledge, skills, experience and understanding of the fund's business to ensure that the governing body is able to fulfil its responsibilities; and
- have sufficient time and commitment to undertake their duties diligently.

Among other things, the Code requires a public fund to establish proper policies and procedures for the operation of a public fund, the segregation and safekeeping of fund property, the issue and redemption of fund interests, the valuation and pricing of fund assets, the maintenance of the independence and separation of the fund's functionaries, the preparation and publishing of NAV reports, proper disclosure to investors and the maintenance of proper records. The Code also provides a list of events affecting the fund and its structure which must be notified to the Commission.

Other requirements

Generally, the provisions set out in section 2.3(iii) will apply in respect of closed-ended retail funds and the provisions set out in section 3.3(ii) will apply in respect of regulated open-ended retail funds.

4.4. Marketing the fund
The same provisions as are set out at section 2.4. apply equally here.

4.5. Taxation
The same provisions as are set out at section 2.5. apply equally here.

4.6. Customary or common terms
- Term of the fund: the majority of BVI retail funds are formed as companies, incorporated with an unlimited life.
- Liquidity of interests: given the often less sophisticated nature of the investor in a public fund, such funds generally have greater liquidity than hedge funds.
- Manager/operator involvement: there is no requirement for the manager or operators of the fund to invest their own money in the fund, although it is often the case that they will do so.
- Remuneration arrangements: public funds generally have similar fee structures to hedge funds, although they tend to have a lower management fee and sometimes no performance fee.

- Investment and borrowing restrictions: the use of leverage as a material tool in the investment strategy is less common than for hedge funds.
- Reporting obligations: BVI public funds are required to file audited accounts with the Commission annually and, in order to comply with the Code, the prospectus should state the nature and frequency of the distribution of financial reports to investors.

5. PROPOSED CHANGES AND DEVELOPMENTS

In light of the recent introduction of SIBA and related ancillary legislation regulating the incorporation, establishment and ongoing operations of mutual funds and the conduct of investment business in the BVI, it is not anticipated that there will be any material legislative developments in the foreseeable future, other than further ancillary legislation to clarify and expand on the existing provisions of SIBA.

In August 2009, BVI was promoted to the OECD 'white list', which lists jurisdictions that have committed to the OECD's international agreed exchange of tax information standards. As at 31 May 2013, BVI has signed 24 tax information exchange agreements. This recognition by the OECD adds to earlier recognition of BVI's adherence to international standards by the IMF, International Organisation of Securities Commission (IOSCO) (of which the Commission is a member) and the Caribbean Financial Action Task Force (CFATF).

The Commission has also entered into a model Memorandum of Understanding (MoU) with the European Securities and Markets Authority (ESMA) which, once executed by the Commission and the relevant EU member states, will ensure that BVI funds can continue to be marketed in the European Union once the Alternative Investment Fund Management Directive comes into force on 22 July 2013.

Cayman Islands

Paul Govier & Sophie Whitcombe **Maples and Calder**

1. MARKET OVERVIEW

The Cayman Islands (Cayman) is the leading offshore jurisdiction for mutual funds of all kinds: closed and open-ended corporate funds, unit trusts and limited partnerships. In particular, it has become the global domicile of choice for the establishment of alternative investment funds such as hedge funds and private equity funds. It has been estimated that approximately 80 per cent of the world's hedge funds are established in Cayman.

As at 31 December 2012, the number of active regulated funds was 10,841, with over 1,500 being formed in 2012. There are, in addition, a significant number of unregistered funds that fall under available exemptions. There are 12,988 limited partnerships established in Cayman, the majority of which are generally closed-ended private equity funds, with 2,037 being established in 2012.

There are a variety of reasons for the popularity of Cayman for the establishment of investment funds. Principally, it is because Cayman inherited the English common law legal system and, in consultation with industry, tailored and adapted it through legislation so that it provided a prudent, effective and flexible framework. That framework has been developed over decades with the participation of stakeholders including institutions, fund managers, fund service providers, governmental and quasi-governmental bodies and investors. Supporting that framework is a local industry with unparalleled experience in the establishment and maintenance of alternative investment funds; a government who prioritises the finance industry in legislation; and an experienced judiciary. Particular advantages include:

- speed and simplicity of establishing Cayman entities;
- relatively low cost of doing so, particularly in the context of typical transaction sizes;
- flexible and practical business statutes;
- clear and certain insolvency law which provides appropriate protection to creditors;
- robust and healthy compliance culture;
- English-based legal system, established judiciary and absence of political or sovereign concerns;
- professional infrastructure and reputation: Cayman is well known for its established and experienced financial services sector and substantial capacity;
- compliance with international anti-money laundering, anti-terrorist financing and other financial regulatory standards; and
- significant number of international tax information exchange agreements and Organisation for Economic Co-operation and Development (OECD) 'white list' status.

Because Cayman does not have securities regulation (or the commensurate expense and bureaucratic burdens) of the type required to enable its mutual funds easily to be sold directly to retail investors in places such as Europe, funds established in Cayman have tended to be for sophisticated or institutional investors, able, where necessary, to take advantage of appropriate exemptions in relevant jurisdictions. More recently, however, retail funds have been established in Cayman, particularly by US promoters, which are sold, where permitted, on a retail or semi-retail basis, for example to Latin American, Middle Eastern and Far Eastern investors. Nevertheless, retail funds still only account for a small fraction of Cayman funds.

2. PRIVATE FUNDS – CLOSED-ENDED
2.1 Common structures

The choice of structure is usually determined by the requirements of the fund manager or investors, with regard to factors including tax, regulatory requirements, familiarity or preference for one structure over another and market practice.

There are three main structures available for Cayman investment funds:

Limited partnership
The limited partnership is the most popular type of structure for closed-ended funds.

A limited partnership is a partnership which has at least one general partner (who is liable for all debts and obligations of the partnership) and one limited partner (who, subject to certain exceptions, is liable for the debts and obligations of the partnership only to the extent set out in the partnership agreement).

Cayman exempted limited partnerships are governed by the Exempted Limited Partnership Law (2012 Revision) (ELP Law), which maintains the English common law principle that a partnership, including an exempted limited partnership, is not a separate legal person and conducts its business through its general partner. In all practical respects, however, the administrative ease and flexibility of the corporate form is provided, with the result that a limited partner of an exempted limited partnership stands in most respects (but notably not in respect of confidentiality) in a similar position to a shareholder in a Cayman exempted company.

At least one general partner must be an individual resident in Cayman, a company incorporated in Cayman or, if a foreign company, registered as such pursuant to Part IX of the Companies Law (2012 Revision) (Companies Law) or, if a partnership, an exempted limited partnership.

The limited partnership is usually used in the offshore context for private equity funds with a limited number of investors.

Company
The company (in particular, the exempted company) is the more common vehicle for open-ended funds, however, it is often used in the context of listed corporate funds.

The principal statute relating to company law in Cayman is the Companies

Law, which is substantially derived from the UK Companies Act 1948.

Companies are almost always incorporated with limited liability, although it is possible to incorporate companies with unlimited liability or with liability by guarantee. The liability of a shareholder of a company incorporated with limited liability is limited to the amount paid up and agreed to be paid up on the shares taken by that shareholder.

Shares may be issued in separate share classes (or separate series within the same class) with different currencies and different rights and fractional shares may be issued.

The vast majority of Cayman companies issue shares of a stated par value (although no par value shares are permitted). Cayman legislation permits amounts standing to the credit of a company's share premium account to be used for dividends or other distributions, subject to the company being solvent, even if no profits are available.

Shares in a Cayman company may be redeemed or repurchased from capital, subject to the company being able to pay its debts as they fall due in the ordinary course of business. It is this feature that makes the company so popular for open-ended funds (see below).

Unit trust

The unit trust (in particular, the exempted unit trust) has been a popular vehicle for many years, particularly for funds marketed in Asia. Cayman trust law essentially follows English trust law and employs the substantial body of English case law on the subject. The Trusts Law (2011 Revision) (the Trusts Law) is based on the (English) Trustee Act 1925 together with some provisions of the Trustee Investments Act 1961 and now incorporates the Trusts (Amendment) (Immediate Effect and Reserved Powers) Law 1998.

A trust is established by a declaration of trust and a trust deed under which a trustee holds legal title to the underlying property on trust for the beneficiaries, who are the beneficial owners of such property.

The concept of a unit trust is that subscribers contribute funds which are held by a trustee (effectively as custodian, although a separate custodian may be appointed by the trustee) while they are managed by the investment manager for the benefit of the subscribers, known as unit holders. Each unit holder is entitled to a pro-rata share of the trust's assets.

Unit trusts are often used (in place of companies) for investors in jurisdictions where participations in a unit trust are more acceptable or attractive than shares in a company. There may, for example, be less regulation of an offering of units in a trust rather than shares in a company, in jurisdictions that do not recognise the trust concept. Thus, some jurisdictions do not regard unit trusts as 'securities' for the purposes of their domestic securities laws. Occasionally, units may result in a more favourable tax treatment for the investor.

2.2 Regulatory framework
(a) Mutual Funds Law

The primary legislation in respect of the regulation of investment funds in

Cayman is the Mutual Funds Law (2012 Revision) (Mutual Funds Law), which is administered by the Cayman Islands Monetary Authority (CIMA). The Mutual Funds Law only applies to open-ended funds (ie, funds which issue equity interests redeemable at the option of the investor); it does not regulate closed-ended funds.

(b) Ancillary legislation
Ancillary legislation which may apply to investment funds (depending on the type of fund in question) includes:
- Companies Law (which governs the constitution, incorporation, management and winding up of companies);
- ELP Law (which governs the constitution, establishment, management and dissolution of exempted limited partnerships);
- Partnership Law (2011 Revision) (which governs the nature, management and dissolution of partnerships and limited partnerships);
- Trusts Law (which governs the administration of trusts and sets out the law relating to trustees);
- Banks and Trust Companies Law (2009 Revision) (which governs banks and trust companies and banking practices);
- Securities Investment Business Law (2011 Revision) (SIB Law) (which governs entities or persons carrying out securities investment business); and
- Proceeds of Crime Law 2008 and the Money Laundering Regulations (2010 Revision) (ML Regulations) (which together form the main framework for the anti-money laundering and anti-terrorist financing regime).

(c) SIB Law
The SIB Law regulates 'securities investment business' as defined in the SIB Law. Any entity established in Cayman or registered in Cayman (in the case of a foreign company) conducting securities investment business must be licensed by CIMA, unless it is exempt from holding a licence in which case it may still be subject to registration under the SIB Law (which means that it is required to make an annual filing with CIMA).

Securities investment business includes:
- dealing in securities (defined to include most forms of shares and stock, debt instruments, options, futures, contracts for differences and derivatives) as an agent or a principal (but only where the person dealing holds himself out as dealing in securities at prices determined generally and continuously, or holds himself out as engaging in the business of underwriting securities or regularly solicits members of the public to induce them to buy or sell or subscribe for securities and the dealing that results from that solicitation);
- making arrangements in relation to securities with a view to another person dealing in securities or a person who participates in the arrangements dealing in securities;
- managing securities belonging to another person on a discretionary basis; or
- advising in relation to securities (but only if the advice is given to

someone in their capacity as investor or potential investor and the advice is on the merits of that person buying, selling, subscribing for or underwriting a particular security or exercising any right conferred by a security to buy, sell, subscribe for or underwrite a security).

Under the SIB Law, a person carrying on securities investment business may be exempt from the requirement to obtain a licence, however they are still subject to certain provisions of the SIB Law as a result of carrying on securities investment business, including, in the case of certain exemptions, registering with CIMA as an 'excluded person'.

An 'excluded person' includes:
- a company carrying on securities investment business exclusively for one or more companies within the same group;
- a person whose registered office in Cayman is provided by a Cayman licensee, carrying on securities investment business exclusively for a sophisticated or high net worth person (as defined in the SIB Law) or a company, partnership or trust of which the shareholders, limited partners or unit holders are all sophisticated or high net worth persons;
- a person who is regulated by a recognised overseas regulatory authority in the country or territory (other than Cayman) in which the securities investment business is being conducted;
- a person participating in a joint enterprise with another person (or, if a company, any company within the same group of companies) where the securities investment business is carried on for the purposes of or in connection with that joint enterprise; or
- a person carrying on securities investment business only in the course of acting in any of the following capacities: director; partner (limited and general); liquidator; trustee in bankruptcy; receiver; executor or administrator; and, as long as certain conditions are met, a trustee.

In practice this means that a fund manager established or operating in Cayman will have to consider its status under the SIB Law and is likely either to have to rely on a specific exemption or to obtain a licence.

2.3 Operational requirements
(a) Regulatory requirements under the Mutual Funds Law
Since, as set out above, closed-ended funds do not fall within the definition of a 'mutual fund' and are not regulated by CIMA under the Mutual Funds Law, the regulatory reporting or filing requirements and audit requirements set out in the Mutual Funds Law do not apply to such funds.

(b) Anti-money laundering requirements
Cayman has for some time enacted legislation that meets and exceeds best practice international standards for preventing and detecting money laundering and combating terrorist financing. The ML Regulations, first enacted in 2000, are the primary legislation in this regard, which apply to anyone carrying out 'relevant financial business in or from the Cayman Islands'. 'Relevant financial business' is defined in the ML Regulations and includes the business of a regulated mutual fund (as defined under the Mutual

Funds Law) but does not specifically include a fund unless it is regulated by CIMA. Whether or not a closed-ended fund is carrying out relevant financial business and is subject to the ML Regulations will therefore turn on the actual business carried out by the fund.

In respect of any management entity established in Cayman, the ML Regulations would apply to any such entity conducting securities investment business, whether they are licensed or an excluded person under the SIB Law.

Anti-money laundering procedures to be maintained under the ML Regulations include reporting suspicious activity and the appointment of a money laundering reporting officer (MLRO). Other procedures include client identification and verification (ie, know your client (KYC)/due diligence), record keeping, internal controls and communication and training and awareness (to the extent the person is staffed) (AML Procedures).

An entity subject to the ML Regulations essentially has two options in relation to maintaining the AML Procedures. It can either choose to maintain the AML Procedures itself in accordance with the laws of Cayman or it can delegate the maintenance of the AML Procedures to a suitable party. If it elects to maintain the AML Procedures itself, it is likely it will need to adopt and follow a Cayman compliant anti-money laundering manual.

Alternatively, the entity can delegate the maintenance of its AML Procedures to another appropriate person, subject to certain disclosure conditions being met. Where the delegate is subject to the anti-money laundering regime (ie, is obliged by law to maintain similar AML Procedures) in a jurisdiction listed under the Third Schedule of the ML Regulations (regarded as having equivalent anti-money laundering legislation to Cayman), the delegate can maintain the AML Procedures on behalf of the entity in accordance with its own jurisdiction's anti-money laundering requirements, which will be regarded by CIMA as compliance with the ML Regulations. Identification and due diligence requirements will then be determined by whatever rules apply in the delegate's jurisdiction and the MLRO is likely to be the MLRO of the delegate.

(c) Other requirements
- Holding of assets: there is no requirement for the appointment of a depository or a custodian.
- Risk: there are no requirements relating to risk.
- Valuation and pricing of assets: there are no requirements relating to the valuation and pricing of assets.
- Insider dealing and market abuse: creating a false or misleading market in listed securities and insider dealing in listed securities are offences under the SIB Law.
- Transparency: the ELP Law provides that, subject to any express or implied term of the limited partnership agreement, each limited partner is entitled to receive from the general partner true and full information regarding the state of the business and financial condition of the exempted limited partnership.

In respect of companies, while investors have the right to certain information relating to the fund (for example the memorandum and articles of association of a fund that is an exempted company), there is no requirement for accounts or reports to be available to investors.

All Cayman companies and partnerships must keep or cause to be kept proper books of account including, where applicable: material underlying documentation including contracts and invoices, in relation to all sums of money received and expended and matters in relation to which the receipt of expenditure takes place; all sales and purchases of goods; and assets and liabilities. Such books of account must be kept for at least five years.
- Short selling: there are no restrictions on short selling.

2.4 Marketing the fund

Any entity established in Cayman or registered in Cayman (in the case of a foreign company) or that has established a place of business in Cayman from which marketing of the fund is undertaken must either be licensed or an 'excluded person' under the SIB Law in order to market a fund.

There are no restrictions regarding to whom the fund may be marketed except that:
- no public offering of interests in the fund may be made in Cayman by an exempted company that is not listed on the Cayman Islands Stock Exchange;
- an exempted limited partnership may not do business with the public of Cayman, save as may be necessary for carrying on its business exterior to Cayman; and
- unit holders in an exempted trust must not include persons resident or domiciled in Cayman.

2.5 Taxation

Cayman has no direct taxes of any kind. There are no income, corporation, capital gains, withholding taxes or death duties. Under the terms of relevant legislation it is possible for all the types of fund vehicle – the company, the unit trust and the limited partnership – to register with and apply to the Government of Cayman for a written undertaking that they will not be subject to various descriptions of direct taxation, for a minimum period, which in the case of a company is usually 20 years, and in the case of the unit trust and limited partnership, 50 years.

2.6 Customary or common terms

- Term of the fund: where the private fund is structured as a limited partnership (as is most commonly the case), the term of the fund will very much depend upon the investment strategy and type of investments held by the fund, but will usually be in the region of seven to ten years, sometimes with extension periods of a year or so.
- Liquidity of interests: by definition, a closed-ended fund does not allow for redemptions of interests at the request of the investor.
- Manager/operator involvement: there is no requirement for the manager or operators of the fund to invest their own money in the fund, although in practice this is quite common.

- Remuneration arrangements: generally speaking, 'waterfall' or 'cascade' arrangements will apply to funds formed as limited partnerships. Under such arrangements, distributions will be allocated first to the limited partners until the amount drawn-down has been repaid; then a preferred return will be paid to the limited partners of a rate which is usually 8 per cent; then the manager will share in the remaining profits (such a share generally being somewhere between 10 and 20 per cent). Managers are generally also paid a management fee in the region of 2 per cent.
- Investment and borrowing restrictions: there are no restrictions on borrowing under Cayman law and most new funds permit the use of leverage. The type and extent of investment restrictions will largely depend on the type of investor in the fund.
- Reporting obligations: where a fund is closed-ended there are no statutory reporting obligations in respect of any regulatory authorities. As set out at section 2.3(c), in respect of exempted limited partnerships the ELP Law provides that, subject to any express or implied term of the limited partnership agreement, each limited partner is entitled to receive from the general partner true and full information regarding the state of the business and financial condition of the exempted limited partnership. Most limited partnership agreements will contain terms overriding this statutory provision. However, most funds set out in their offering memoranda that financial statements will be sent to investors every year.

3. HEDGE FUNDS
3.1 Common structures
As set out at section 2.1., the three main structures are the limited partnership, the company and the unit trust. The large majority of Cayman hedge funds are formed as companies although this is generally due to factors in the domicile of the manager or its investors, not Cayman law.

3.2 Regulatory framework
Mutual Funds Law
As set out at section 2.2., the primary legislation in respect of Cayman investment funds is the Mutual Funds Law, which regulates mutual funds and mutual fund administrators. Responsibility for such regulation is vested in CIMA.

The aim of the Mutual Funds Law is to provide a regulatory framework that is sufficiently flexible to allow managers to invest capital that has been raised in the most efficient manner, while at the same time providing appropriate safeguards and protection for investors and prudent regulation designed to guard against systemic risk or other undesirable public policy outcomes. For that reason, the Mutual Funds Law does not generally take a prescriptive or codified approach to the regulation of investment funds. Rather, it takes a 'principles-based' approach based on ensuring that investors receive full and fair disclosure in relation to the activities of the relevant fund; that investors and the regulator receive independent confirmation of relevant information from approved auditors and administrators; and that it is supported by extremely broad supervisory and enforcement powers conferred on CIMA. The

Cayman Islands

Mutual Funds Law reflects the commercial reality in that it recognises that very little of the investment funds' substantive day to day activities occur within Cayman. It therefore does not seek to duplicate regulation that would be applicable to an investment manager, prime broker, custodian or administrator operating in another jurisdiction which has its own rules and regulations and operates entirely extraterritorially to Cayman. The objective of the Mutual Funds Law is to ensure that the fund structure itself is appropriately established and fairly described so that investors can decide whether or not to invest in it based on an accurate and complete disclosure of its investment objectives, risks, service providers and all other material information.

A mutual fund is any company, unit trust or partnership which issues equity interests redeemable at the option of the investor, the purpose or effect of which is the pooling of investor funds with the aim of spreading the investment risks and enabling investors to receive profits or gains from investments.

Mutual funds and mutual fund administrators are required to be licensed before commencing business, although certain exemptions from regulation under the Mutual Funds Law are contained in section 4(4) of the Mutual Funds Law. These exemptions cover mutual funds:

- where the equity interests are held by not more than 15 investors the majority of whom are capable of appointing or removing the 'operator' of the fund (ie, directors, the trustee or the general partner of the fund, as the case may be); and
- which are not incorporated or established in Cayman and which make invitations to the public in Cayman to subscribe for equity interests therein through a person licensed under the SIB Law, provided that the fund in question must be either: (i) listed on a stock exchange recognised for the purpose by CIMA; or (ii) regulated in a category and by a regulator recognised for the purpose by CIMA.

The reasoning behind the exemptions is that mutual funds need not be regulated by CIMA if either:

- the number of investors is conveniently small and those investors may control the appointment and removal of managers or operators of the mutual fund, ie, control of the mutual fund rests with those investors; or
- appropriate regulation is already in place.

In all cases, there is no look through to beneficial ownership; the term investor is defined to mean the investor of record. Thus, if all the equity interests are issued as a matter of record to, say, a single institutional nominee or custodian for the underlying investors, the mutual fund will fall outside the scope of the Mutual Funds Law.

There are three available forms of regulation under the Mutual Funds Law:

Licensed mutual fund

The first route is to apply to CIMA for a licence for the mutual fund that may be issued at CIMA's discretion and is most commonly used in respect of retail funds. It is necessary to file with CIMA an offering document together with the prescribed statutory form (MF3) and to pay an application fee (currently $4,268). If CIMA considers that each promoter is of sound reputation, the administration of the mutual fund will be undertaken by persons who have sufficient expertise and who are fit and proper to be directors (or, as the case may be, managers or officers in their respective positions), and that the business of the fund will be carried out in a proper way, then the licence will be granted. This route will be appropriate for mutual funds which are promoted by well-known and reputable institutions and which do not propose to appoint any Cayman mutual fund administrator.

Administered mutual fund
The second route is for the mutual fund to designate its principal office in Cayman at the office of a licensed mutual fund administrator. In this case, an offering document together with the prescribed statutory form (MF2) must be filed with CIMA together with an application fee (currently $4,268). The administrator and the fund must also complete a prescribed statutory form (MF2A). There is no requirement for the mutual fund itself to obtain a licence. Instead, the mutual fund administrator is required to be satisfied that each promoter is of sound reputation, the administration of the mutual fund will be undertaken by persons who have sufficient expertise to administer the mutual fund and are of sound reputation and that the business of the mutual fund and the offer of equity interests will be carried out in a proper way. The administrator must report to CIMA if it has reason to believe that a fund for which it provides the principal office is acting in breach of the Mutual Funds Law or may be insolvent or is otherwise acting in a manner prejudicial to its creditors or investors.

Section 4(3) mutual fund
The third category of regulated mutual fund, which is by far the most common type of regulation for Cayman hedge funds, exists pursuant to section 4(3) of the Mutual Funds Law and is of application either:
- where the minimum investment per investor is at least $100,000; or
- where the equity interests are listed on a recognised stock exchange.

For a section 4(3) fund, there is no requirement for licensing or the provision of a principal office by a mutual fund administrator in Cayman; rather the section 4(3) mutual fund simply registers with CIMA by filing an offering document together with the prescribed statutory form (MF1) and the application fee (currently $4,268).

The Mutual Funds Law now requires all 'master funds' (as defined in the Mutual Funds Law) to be registered with CIMA as a regulated mutual fund pursuant to section 4(3) of the Mutual Funds Law. A master fund registers with CIMA by filing the prescribed statutory form (MF4) and the application fee (currently $3,050). A master fund is not required to have an offering document but if it does have one then this should be filed with CIMA also.

Every regulated mutual fund must issue an offering document (unless exempted by CIMA), which must describe the equity interests in all material respects and contain such other information as is necessary to enable a prospective investor to make an informed decision as to whether or not to invest. In addition, the pre-existing statutory obligations with regard to proper disclosure of all material matters continue in effect. There is no specific power in CIMA to dictate the substance or form of the offering document. Rather, section 4(6)(b) of the Mutual Funds Law states generally that the offering document should 'contain such other information as is necessary to enable a prospective investor in the mutual fund to make an informed decision as to whether or not to subscribe for or purchase the equity interest'. However, CIMA occasionally issues policy statements with respect to the content of offering documents and has provided checklists of information it would require offering documents of certain types of funds to contain. For example, it would expect offering documents of section 4(3) funds to contain, among other matters: risk factors; details of the operators of the fund, principals of the management entities and the service providers; subscription and redemption policies; and net asset value calculation policies.

Every regulated mutual fund must file, with its initial application, a written consent from each of the administrator and the auditor to its appointment. The auditor must be located in Cayman and must be approved by CIMA. Further obligations in respect of the audit requirements of the fund are set out below.

Ancillary legislation
The provisions in respect of ancillary legislation as set out at section 2.2(b) apply equally here.

SIB Law
The provisions of the SIB Law as set out at section 2.2(c) apply equally here.

3.3 Operational requirements
(a) Regulatory requirements under the Mutual Funds Law
Once CIMA has registered the mutual fund, its obligations are as follows:
- CIMA has implemented its electronic reporting system for all funds registered with CIMA in Cayman. CIMA has released on its website the electronic Fund Annual Return (FAR) form and has opened the internet portal through which funds' local auditors must submit the requested returns. The FAR form must be submitted annually through the fund's auditor, although the operators of the fund remain responsible for the accuracy of the contents of the FAR form.
- The mutual fund must file with CIMA a copy of its current offering memorandum or prescribed details relating thereto. The Mutual Funds Law provides in the case of a continuing offering of securities that a mutual fund is deemed not to be in compliance with the relevant provisions of the Mutual Funds Law if there are any material changes in the information contained in the offering memorandum or in the prescribed details filed with CIMA. Accordingly, there is an obligation in the case of a continuing offering of securities to amend the offering document or the prescribed details (as the case may be) and file the amended document or details with CIMA within 21 days of the promoter or operator becoming aware of the material changes.
- The fund must also inform CIMA if it has changed its registered office

or its principal office or (in the case of a unit trust) if there has been a change in the trust company acting as its trustee.
- The fund must have its accounts audited annually and send a copy of those accounts to CIMA within six months of the end of the relevant financial year.
- The fund is required to pay the prescribed annual registration fee (currently $4,268).
- The fund must also comply with any special conditions which CIMA has imposed in respect of its licensing as a mutual fund.

(b) Anti-money laundering

The provisions of the ML Regulations, as set out at section 2.3(b), apply equally here in respect of any management entity established in Cayman and would also apply in respect of any regulated mutual fund.

The majority of Cayman regulated mutual funds delegate the maintenance of their AML Procedures, often to an administrator based in a jurisdiction listed under the Third Schedule of the ML Regulations (regarded as having equivalent anti-money laundering legislation to Cayman). Further details of the rules relating to such delegation are set out at section 2.3(b).

(c) Other requirements
- Risk: under the Mutual Funds Law, a fund's offering document must describe the equity interests in all material respects and contain such other information as is necessary to enable a prospective investor in the fund to make an informed decision about whether to subscribe for or purchase equity interests.
- Valuation and pricing: most regulated mutual funds appoint an administrator who must provide a letter to CIMA setting out the nature and extent of their role. Generally speaking, the administrator would, under the terms of their appointment, be responsible for the calculation of net asset value. Regulated mutual funds must also have an auditor and the audit requirements for a regulated mutual fund are listed under section 3.3(a).
- Holding of assets: there is no requirement for the appointment of a depository or a custodian.
- Insider dealing and market abuse: creating a false or misleading market in listed securities and insider dealing in listed securities are offences under the SIB Law.
- Transparency: the provisions set out at section 2.3(c) relating to transparency apply equally here.
- Short selling: there are no restrictions on short selling.

Further obligations in respect of licensed mutual funds (or retail funds) are set out in section 4.3.

3.4 Marketing the fund
The same provisions as set out at section 2.4. apply equally here.

3.5 Taxation
The same provisions as set out at section 2.5. apply equally here.

3.6 Customary or common terms
- Term of the fund: as set out above, the large majority of Cayman hedge funds are formed as companies and generally do not have a fixed life.
- Liquidity of interests: the frequency with which the investors can redeem from the fund will depend upon the type of investment strategy employed by the fund. Often, redemption days will be on a monthly or quarterly basis but they can be more or less frequent. Fairly often, a fund's constitutional and offering documents will allow them to employ a gate on redemptions (ie, a device which limits the volume of redemptions on any redemption day), usually at fund level or, less often, at investor level. Hard lock-ups (ie, periods during which no redemptions are permitted) are relatively unusual among new funds although soft lock-ups (ie, periods during which redemptions are permitted upon payment of a fee) are more common.
- Manager/operator involvement: there is no requirement for the manager or operators of the fund to invest their own money in the fund although it is often the case that they will do so.
- Remuneration arrangements: while, traditionally, Cayman hedge funds have operated a 'two and twenty' fee structure (ie, a 2 per cent management fee and a 20 per cent performance fee), more recently, the trend has been towards lower fees, particularly management fees. In the last year, a large number of hedge funds were formed with a management fee of less than 2 per cent. While the majority of funds still have a 20 per cent performance fee, in the last couple of years a significant number of funds have been formed with lower or alternative performance fee structures. In respect of the performance fee, the majority of funds have a classic high water mark although some operate an adjusted or resetting high water mark or hurdle rate. Performance fee clawback is rare.
- Investment and borrowing restrictions: there are no restrictions on borrowing under Cayman law and most new funds permit the use of leverage. There are no restrictions on how the portfolio of assets of the fund is typically held and the vast majority of new funds appoint at least one prime broker and custodian and often more. However, the Mutual Funds Law provides that the fund's offering document must contain such information as is necessary to enable a prospective investor to make an informed decision as to whether or not to subscribe for or purchase the equity interest and such information would generally be disclosed to prospective investors therein.
- Reporting obligations: as set out at section 3.3(a), regulated mutual funds are required to file audited accounts with CIMA annually. Although there are no reporting requirements as regards investors, most funds set out in their offering memoranda that audited financial statements will be sent to investors every year.

4. RETAIL FUNDS
4.1 Common structures
As set out at section 2.1., the three main structures are the limited partnership, the company and the unit trust. The majority of Cayman retail funds are formed as companies.

4.2 Regulatory framework
Mutual Funds Law
Retail funds which are closed-ended would not fall within the definition of a 'mutual fund' and would therefore not be regulated by CIMA under the Mutual Funds Law.

In respect of retail funds which are open-ended, except where they are exempt from regulation under section 4(4) of the Mutual Funds Law (further details of which are set out at section 3.2.), they must be registered as a mutual fund under the Mutual Funds Law. Details of each type of regulated fund and an outline of the regulations that apply thereto are set out at section 3.2. In most cases, open-ended retail funds will be registered as licensed mutual funds (ie, they must apply to CIMA for a licence).

The Retail Mutual Funds (Japan) Regulations (2007 Revision) (Retail Mutual Funds (Japan) Regulations) provides a regulatory regime for Cayman mutual funds that are sold to the public in Japan.

In addition, CIMA has issued further rules to enhance the regulation of the retail funds sector. These rules include the rule on the contents of offering documents, the rule on the calculation of asset values and the rule on the segregation of assets for licensed funds. The rules (which do not apply to funds registered under the Retail Mutual Funds (Japan) Regulations) are intended to ensure that prospective retail investors are able to make informed investment decisions and enhance the overall protection of investors and investors' assets in the licensed funds. Further details of these rules are set out in section 4.3.

Ancillary legislation
The provisions in respect of ancillary legislation as set out at section 2.2(b) apply equally here.

SIB Law
The provisions of the SIB Law, as set out at section 2.2(c), apply equally here.

4.3 Operational requirements
Regulatory requirements under the Mutual Funds Law
In respect of closed-ended retail funds, the regulatory reporting or filing requirements and audit requirements set out in the Mutual Funds Law do not apply.

In respect of regulated open-ended retail funds, the provisions set out in section 3.3(a) will apply. In addition, the rule on the contents of offering documents sets out the minimum information that must be included in an offering document for a licensed fund.

Money laundering regulations
The provisions set out at section 2.3(b) in respect of the ML Regulations apply equally here.

Additional requirements
Generally, the provisions set out in section 2.3(c) will apply in respect of closed-ended retail funds and the provisions set out in section 3.3(c) will

apply in respect of regulated open-ended retail funds.

In addition, the following provisions will apply in respect of regulated open-ended retail funds:
- Valuation and pricing: under the rule on the calculation of asset values, licensees must establish, implement and maintain a net asset value (NAV) calculation policy and must outline the scope of such a policy. This rule mandates that the policy be 'fair, reliable, of high quality and verifiable'.
- Holding of assets: the rule on the segregation of assets for licensed funds calls for a licensed fund's portfolio to be segregated and accounted for separately from any assets of any service provider. Also, licensed funds must ensure that service providers do not use the portfolio to finance their own or any other operations in any way. Another requirement is that licensed funds ensure, by contract, that service providers who hold or manage the portfolio are regulated by CIMA or by a recognised overseas authority or by another regulator approved by CIMA.

4.4 Marketing the fund
The same provisions as set out at section 2.4. apply equally here.

4.5 Taxation
The same provisions as set out at section 2.5. apply equally here.

4.6 Customary or common terms
- Term of the fund: the large majority of Cayman retail funds are formed as companies and generally do not have a fixed life.
- Liquidity of interests: retail funds generally have greater liquidity than hedge funds.
- Manager/operator involvement: there is no requirement for the manager or operators of the fund to invest their own money in the fund although it is often the case that they will do so.
- Remuneration arrangements: in comparison to hedge funds, retail funds tend to have a lower management fee and no performance fee.
- Investment and borrowing restrictions: the use of leverage is less common than for hedge funds. There are rules in connection with the holding of assets by licensed mutual funds, which are set out under section 4.3.
- Reporting obligations: licensed mutual funds are required to file audited accounts with CIMA annually. Although, in respect of companies, there are no reporting requirements as regards investors, most funds set out in their offering memoranda that audited financial statements will be sent to investors every year. Under the rule on the contents of offering documents, licensed funds' offering memoranda must state the nature and frequency of financial reports' distribution to investors.

5. PROPOSED CHANGES AND DEVELOPMENTS
The law in Cayman relating to companies, trusts and limited partnerships, investment funds and all business and finance related matters are constantly monitored and updated. The Companies Law and the ELP Law were

last updated in 2012, the SIB Law was last updated in 2011 and the ML Regulations in 2010.

In light of the circumstances which affected the global financial sector in recent years, CIMA has undertaken a review of all sectors regulated by CIMA and has consulted international bodies including the International Monetary Fund (IMF). The review is ongoing and although there are no specific changes yet planned, areas which CIMA has covered in its review include ways of increasing transparency and risk management.

At the OECD Global Forum meeting on 30 September 2010, the OECD recognised that Cayman's legal and regulatory regime complies with international standards for transparency and exchange of tax information. In August 2009, Cayman was promoted to the OECD 'white list', which lists jurisdictions that have committed to the OECD's international agreed exchange of tax information standards. As at 31 March 2013, Cayman has signed 31 tax information exchange agreements and was awaiting signature on a further four agreements. This recognition by the OECD adds to earlier recognition of Cayman's adherence to international standards by the IMF, International Organisation of Securities Commission (IOSCO) (of which CIMA is a member) and the Caribbean Financial Action Task Force (CFATF).

CIMA has also entered into a model Memorandum of Understanding (MoU) with the European Securities and Markets Authority (ESMA) which, once executed by CIMA and the relevant EU member states, will ensure that Cayman Islands funds can continue to be marketed in the European Union once the Alternative Investment Fund Management Directive comes into force on 22 July 2013.

CIMA is currently engaged in an industry consultation process in relation to certain proposals to enhance the Cayman Islands corporate governance regulatory framework. Whilst it is too early to state what the outcome of the consultation will be, current proposals include, but are not limited to, the creation of a public database that provides limited information regulated entities and some form of registration process for directors of regulated entities. It is expected that the proposals put forward will evolve during the consultation process and amendments to current legislation and guidance will be required in order to make the relevant changes to the Cayman Islands' current corporate governance regime.

Denmark

Denmark

Claus Bennetsen **Horten Advokatpartnerselskab**

1. MARKET OVERVIEW

The Danish funds market is dominated by two large groups of players. First, there are the pension funds most often structured as life insurance companies which offer either pooled savings arranged by the pension funds or more segregated arrangements in the form of unit-link schemes. The pension funds are very large customers in the funds business with an estimated EUR 450 billion under management in total. Foreign fund managers play a significant role in this market both through funds' shares and segregated mandates.

The second group is the retail banks which all operate substantial UCITS schemes that are distributed through the individual bank's retail network and in some cases through groups of retail banks' retail networks. There is very little cross-distribution between the various groups and only recently has a growing awareness of foreign products arisen in the retail market on such products as index tracking funds and exchange traded funds (ETFs) as well as foreign actively managed funds, being valid supplements to the local offerings. Primarily, the banks' customers will purchase the UCITS shares for their individual tax-incentivised pension account in the banks and for their general securities savings outside the pension system. While pension accounts are tax neutral to foreign funds, heavy tax discrimination against foreign funds occurs in respect of other securities savings.

Due to the implementation of the Alternative Investment Fund Managers Directive (AIFMD), an estimated EUR 70 billion under management is shifting from the national to the EU regulation scheme. If and how the implementation of AIFMD will change the structure and outlook of the Danish investment funds market is yet to be seen.

2. ALTERNATIVE INVESTMENT FUNDS

By Alternative Investment Funds (AIFs) we presuppose; any collective investment undertaking, which raises capital from a number of investors, with a view to investing it in accordance with a defined investment policy for the benefit of those investors, and which does not require authorisation as a Danish UCITS in accordance with the Danish Investment Associations Act (DIA).

2.1. Common structures

Neither the legal structure, nor the assets in which the company invests, are material in the assessment of whether the company is covered under the AIF-regime. A typical AIF will be a capital fund (private equity fund), venture capital fund or a hedge fund. However, limited partnerships (K/S'es) owning real estate or a wind farm, may also qualify as AIFs. A specific assessment of each company is necessary in order to determine whether the company is subject to the Danish AIF-regulation.

Closed-ended AIFs
Closed-ended funds virtually do not exist in Denmark. However, closed-ended AIFs could be established as limited liability companies (A/S, ApS), limited partnerships (K/S), limited partnership companies (P/S) or capital associations with restricted redemption rights.

Open-ended AIFs
Open-ended AIFs would be established as limited partnerships (K/S), limited partnership companies (P/S) or capital associations/funds. P/S and K/S are transparent companies, which means that taxation takes place with each investor in the limited partnership based on the particular investor's share. This allows for a tax loss/deduction to be set off in the investors' personal income. Unlike K/S'es which are largely not regulated by statutory law, P/S companies are subject to the procedures and requirements in the Danish Companies Act (DCA).

Alternative investment fund managers and advisers
In Denmark, there is no explicit distinction between managers and advisers with respect to legal structures. Danish licensed Alternative Investment Fund Managers (AIFMs) must be structured as legal persons according to the DCA, ie, as limited liability companies or limited partnership companies. Limited partnership companies will often be preferable due to tax transparency as described above.

EU-AIFMs are allowed to manage AIFs either directly or through a branch in Denmark. If the AIFMs want to establish a branch, the DCA applies and requires the branch to be registered with the Danish Business Authority (DBA). Otherwise, the AIFMD simply requires the EU-AIFMs to be legal persons.

Third-Country (TC)-AIFMs, which have Denmark as their member state of reference, must be limited liability companies.

2.2. Regulatory framework
Alternative investment funds
The principal legislation governing both closed-ended and open-ended AIFs is the Danish Alternative Investment Fund Managers Act (AIFMA) which implements AIFMD. AIFMA governs the AIFMs and self-managing AIFs, and it provides some structural guidelines on the establishment and operation of capital associations. AIFMs are subject to supervision by the Danish Financial Supervisory Authority (DFSA) whereas AIFs are not, unless the AIFs are self-managing.

The DFSA has issued a number of government orders in addition to the general Executive Order on Alternative Investment Funds namely on registration in the DFSA's register of assessment experts, on marketing of third-country AIFs in Denmark, on marketing towards retail investors, on remuneration policies and disclosure requirements regarding remuneration of AIFMs, and on the form and content of documents containing key investor information regarding AIFs.

Furthermore the DFSA has issued guidance on application for authorisation or registration as AIFM and guidance on AIFs' custodians.

As regards the establishment and operation of closed-ended AIFs structured as limited liability companies and limited partnership companies, the DCA applies besides the AIFMA. Furthermore, closed-ended funds will typically also be governed by the Prospectus Directive, implemented in the Danish Securities Trading Act (STA). Danish capital associations (eg, professional, special or restricted associations or hedge funds) are required to be registered with the DBA. Such capital associations, which meet the conditions for being AIFs, are required to be licensed or registered with the DFSA if they are self-managing AIFs only.

Alternative investment funds managers
As regards AIFMs, depending on the volume of assets under management, licensing or registration is a prerequisite for managing AIFs. AIFMs must be registered when they have assets under management below EUR 100 million or below EUR 500 million where the assets under management are unleveraged and no redemption rights exist within a five-year period. AIFMs below these thresholds can apply for registration as managers of European Venture Capital Funds (EuVECA-funds) or managers of European Social Entrepreneurship Funds (EuSEF-funds). AIFMs with assets under management exceeding this threshold are required to be licensed. An extended authorisation is required to provide investment advisory services.

As regards EU-AIFMs, which intend to manage EU/EEA-AIFs in Denmark, no licensing or registration is required with the DFSA, provided that the AIFMs are authorised by the competent authorities in their home member state to manage the particular type of AIFs. Such EU-AIFMs may initiate management of the particular AIFs in Denmark, when the AIFMs have received a notification from their competent authorities stating that the required information has been forwarded to the DFSA for either direct managing or managing through a branch.

TC-AIFMs must be licensed to manage AIFs in accordance with their member state of reference. If Denmark is the member state of reference, a license must be obtained from the DFSA and the AIFMs will be governed by AIFMA. TC-AIFMs applying for license to manage AIFs in Denmark must ensure that: (i) appropriate co-operation agreements exist between the DFSA and the competent authorities in the home states of the AIFs; (ii) the third country, in which the TC-AIFM has its registered office, is not registered as a non-cooperative country; (iii) the third country has an agreement with Denmark, which complies with the standards in section 26 of the OECD Model Tax Convention; and (iv) the supervisory functions of the DFSA as provided in AIFMA are not restricted by any TC-regulation, administrative provisions or practices. Additionally, TC-AIFMs applying for license to manage AIFs in Denmark are required to have a legal representative, established in Denmark, who possesses the competencies and resources to ensure that the AIFM complies with AIFMA.

2.3. Operational requirements

In principle, AIFs are not restricted as to the types of activities that they can perform. However, activities which require a license such as eg, discretionary portfolio management, would not be permitted. If an AIFM is licensed to perform discretionary portfolio management, it is not permitted to invest all or part of the client's portfolio in units or shares of the AIFs it manages, unless approved by the client. AIFs are generally not restricted in its investment activities. However, the DFSA may lay down further rules on what securitisation positions can be included in an AIF's portfolio.

Disclosure and reporting

Unless the AIFs are self-managing, AIFMA does not require any public disclosures from the AIFs. Instead, it is the AIFMs that are responsible for the public disclosures. AIFMs are obliged to disclose to the AIF-investors, on a regular basis, information regarding leverage and, specifically, information on the percentage share of illiquid assets, new arrangements for controlling the AIF's liquidity and the AIF's current risk profile and risk controlling systems. Furthermore, AIFMs must inform AIF-investors and other relevant parties on potential conflicts of interest and publish on their website any supervisor reactions/statements issued to them by the DFSA. The DBA may upon an evaluation of the specific AIFM stipulate an extended disclosure duty.

Under AIFMA, only AIFMs and self-managing AIFs are required to hand in annual reports. The reporting provisions require that an annual report is made available no later than six months following the end of the financial year. The annual report must be prepared in accordance with the accounting rules and standards in the AIFs' home state and must be audited by an authorised auditor. Further, AIFMs are obliged on a regular basis to file with the DFSA reports containing information on the AIFMs' most important markets and the instruments used in the portfolio management as well as information on substantial risk exposures and concentrations for each AIF managed. At the end of each quarter, the AIFMs shall, on request, submit to the DFSA a list of the AIFs under management.

For each AIF, AIFMs must submit information covering inter alia the current risk profile and market risk controlling systems, specifications on important asset categories in which the AIF has invested, the results of the proper stress tests, new arrangements for controlling liquidity and the percentage share of illiquid assets. Further, AIFMs must make available to the DFSA certain information in the event an AIF acquires control over a non-listed company or wishes to use substantive leverage.

Specific requirements

AIFMs to be licensed must select a depositary in compliance with AIFMA for each AIF under management. Additionally, each AIF and the AIFMs are required to have a certified auditor and the AIFMs must organise their business in order to be able to identify conflicts of interests. Moreover, AIFMs must prepare suitable policies and procedures to handle conflicts of interest in the event organisational structures and preparations are insufficient. The management of AIFMs must set up management target quotas for the underrepresented sex and AIFMs, which has securities traded at a regulated exchange or which have total assets exceeding DKK500 million throughout two successive financial years, must establish a corporate policy with a view to increasing the share of the underrepresented sex in the management team.

AIFMs must ensure that each AIF under management has valuation procedures for pricing of the funds' assets and liabilities. In addition, AIFMs must ensure that each AIF under management is valued at least once a year and that its equity value is calculated. AIFMs are obliged to set up in writing a maximum level of leverage for each AIF under management and to establish a risk management function controlling the AIFs and running appropriate stress-tests. For each leveraged open-ended AIF under management, AIFMs must set up an appropriate liquidity management system and monitoring procedures.

Generally, the use of side letters is not restricted in Denmark. AIFMA, however, requires that no AIF-investor is given preferential treatment, unless such treatment is disclosed in the relevant AIF's articles of association or fund provisions.

2.4. Marketing the fund

In addition to AIFMA, the Executive Order on Marketing of third-country AIFs in Denmark and the Danish Marketing Practices Act regulate the marketing of units or shares in AIFs.

Marketing of AIFs is allowed only towards professional investors. However, the DFSA may grant permission to AIFMs licensed by the DFSA or to EU-AIFMs licensed according to rules implementing the AIFMD to market one or more AIFs towards retail investors. AIFMs, which are simply registered, cannot obtain a license to market towards retail investors. At this stage, neither can TC-AIFMs.

EU-AIFMs, licensed to manage AIFs in accordance with AIFMD, hold a marketing passport and may as a consequence initiate the marketing of EU-AIFs towards professional investors in Denmark, as soon as the AIFMs have received a notice from their competent authorities declaring that a notification letter and a statement have been submitted to the DFSA. Marketing of TC-AIFs initiated prior to 22 July 2013 of AIFs which were in existence prior to this date may be continued for a transitional period of one year without obtaining a license from the DFSA. Marketing of TC-AIFs initiated post 22 July 2013 or marketing of AIFs which were not in existence prior to this date requires the AIFM to be licensed by the DFSA in accordance with the Executive Order on Marketing of Third-Country AIFs in Denmark.

EU-AIFMs, which are simply registered with their competent authorities and hence are not licensed to manage AIFs, are not entitled to market units or shares in Denmark, whether towards professional or retail investors, unless specific authorisation is granted by the DFSA according to AIFMA.

From 2015, TC-AIFMs will be allowed to hold a marketing passport from EU member states as managers of AIFs. Then the AIFMs may initiate marketing in Denmark when the AIFMs have been notified by the competent authorities in the member state of reference, that a complete application and a statement have been submitted to the DFSA. As regards marketing of TC-AIFs, some more stringent requirements must be met as emphasised above, eg, appropriate cooperation agreements must exist between the DFSA and the competent authorities of the TC-AIFs home state. Until 2015, TC-AIFMs may only market AIFs in Denmark according to the Danish private placement rules.

TC-AIFMs, which do not hold a marketing passport, may obtain an authorisation by the DFSA to market units or shares in the AIFs managed towards Danish professional investors, depending on the AIFs being EU- or TC-AIFs. When marketing TC-AIFs, the executive order must be complied with. The conditions to be met by TC-AIFMs in order to obtain a marketing authorisation are set forth in AIFMA and include requirements on annual reports, investor information, disclosures to the DFSA and co-ordination agreements between the DFSA and the competent authorities in the AIFMs' home state.

Marketing material

The requirements on content of marketing materials are found in AIFMA, which loyally implements AIFMD. Key items are information on the AIF's investment strategy and objectives, asset investment specifications, the AIF's historical performance, fees and costs, leverage permitted, identification of the AIFM, custodian, auditor and other service providers, etc. Requirements on content may be stricter when units or shares are marketed towards retail investors, eg, some key investor information may be provided. Further, we notice that in case of an overlap between AIFMA requirements and requirements flowing from the prospectus directive, only the information not included in the prospectus needs to be published.

Pension funds and intermediaries

As described above, AIFs can be marketed only to professional investors unless special permission is granted by the DFSA. As mentioned, pension funds are very active in the Danish investment funds market and may invest in AIFs in accordance with the Danish Financial Business Act (FBA). The FBA lays down investment ratio limitations and requirements regarding the articles of association of the capital associations, in which pension funds are allowed to invest. The FBA largely mirrors the rules of the third Life Insurance Directive (Directive 2002/83/EC of the European Parliament and of the Council of 5 November 2002 concerning life assurance).

Restrictions on the use of intermediaries to assist in the fundraising process are limited to authorisation requirements. Intermediaries handling the brokering of any securities are subject to having a brokerage license either in Denmark or validly passported into Denmark from another EU/EEA country. Furthermore, acting as an introducer also requires a brokerage license.

2.5. Taxation
AIFM and AIF tax treatment
Resident AIFMs and AIFs, as well as non-resident AIFMs and AIFs having their effective management in Denmark or carrying out business activities through a permanent establishment in Denmark, are taxed in accordance with the Danish Corporation Tax Act at a flat corporate tax rate of 25 per cent (expected to decrease to 22 per cent.). However, the effective rate is less, as business expenses and depreciation are tax deductible.

Open-ended funds that comply with a complex system may avoid taxation of funds distributed. No foreign funds currently comply.

Branches of foreign companies located in Denmark are taxed on trading income and capital gains arising on disposal of trading assets situated in Denmark at a flat corporate tax rate of 25 per cent. Thus, branches are generally subject to double taxation – both in Denmark and abroad – unless avoided by double taxation agreements. Representation offices are not subject to taxation and shall not be registered for corporate purposes as long as they are not actually trading.

Investor tax treatment
An important distinction in relation to taxation is whether the fund is structured as a taxed or a tax transparent entity. Partnerships are transparent for tax purposes, meaning that only the partners are subject to tax and consequently that tax loss/deduction is set off in the investors' personal income.

Resident investors in taxed funds will be taxed on gains at realisation at rates of 15.3 per cent for pension funds (whether managed by life insurance companies or individually), 25 per cent for companies (expected to drop to 22 per cent) and 43.5 per cent for individuals (dropping to 42 per cent in 2014). Non-resident investors will be taxed in their home country on gains while dividends may be subject to a withholding tax of 27 per cent, which is often reduced or eliminated in double taxation treaties resident as well as non-resident investors in tax transparent funds will be taxed in Denmark on an ongoing basis on the type of income (capital gains, dividends, financial instrument gains, etc.) that the fund generates and at the rates indicated above.

In general, Danish companies can pay dividends to other foreign companies free of withholding taxes, if the shares in the distributing company qualify as subsidiary shares or group shares and the foreign company is domiciled in an EU/EAA-country or another state with which Denmark has concluded a double taxation agreement, and the receiving company is able to claim a reduction or elimination of the taxation on dividends under a tax treaty or under the EU Parent Subsidiary Directive (Council Directive 2003/123/EC of 22 December 2003 amending Directive 90/435/EEC on the common system of taxation applicable in the case of parent companies and subsidiaries of different member states). If the shares in the distributing company qualify as portfolio shares and the receiving company is domiciled in a country with which Denmark has an agreement under which the countries are obliged to share information regarding the taxation, the withholding tax is 15 per cent. Otherwise, dividends are subject to a 27 per cent withholding tax.

As regards capital gains on shares for corporate shareholders taxable in Denmark, taxes are exempted provided the shares are group shares or subsidiary shares. Other capital gains for corporate shareholders taxable in Denmark are taxed at the corporate tax rate of 25 per cent. Foreign shareholders not taxable in Denmark, are not taxed on capital gains in Denmark. For shares not traded on a regulated market the taxpayer may however opt for taxation on a realisation basis.

Other tax issues
Denmark has an extensive network of double taxation agreements and the Danish transfer pricing legislation is in accordance with the OECD guidelines. Denmark levies no capital duties, share transfer taxes, nor wealth taxes (except on real property).

It is neither necessary nor advisable to obtain a tax ruling from the Danish Tax Administration (SKAT) or the Danish Tax Assessment Council. Nonetheless, if desired, a binding ruling from the tax authorities may be obtained against a fee.

2.6. Customary or common terms
With respect to remuneration, AIFMA stipulates that the variable remuneration component for the AIFMs' management is limited to 50 per cent of the fixed base salary of the employee in question. This is in accordance with the Danish legislation on variable remuneration standards for financial institutions.

3. RETAIL FUNDS
3.1. Common structures
Retail funds are commonly structured as investment associations (UCITS) and not as limited companies. Danish UCITS are structured as investment associations, SIKAVs or security funds, which, after the implementation of AIFMD, are the main retail fund structures in Denmark not categorised as AIFs. However, AIFs governed by AIFMA may, upon special authorisation from the DFSA, be marketed to retail investors in Denmark, provided that the AIFM is licensed under AIFMD. It is worth noting that, at present, it is not possible for TC-AIFMs to obtain permission to market AIFs towards retail investors in Denmark.

The investors' liability will normally be limited to the extent of their contribution to the fund, meaning that investors' liability is limited to the amount invested. The investors' interest in the investment association is called unit certificates.

3.2. Regulatory framework
Following the implementation of AIFMD in Denmark, the regulation of retail funds not covered by AIFMA is found in the DIA and the Executive Order on Marketing in Denmark of Foreign Investment Institutes. Both domestic UCITS and the marketing in Denmark of foreign UCITS are governed by DIA.

Denmark

Prior to initiating their businesses, Danish UCITS are required to be licensed by the DFSA. Furthermore, due to placement restriction rules, a separate authorisation is needed to become a feeder fund.

Foreign UCITS can apply by the application form and procedures laid down in Regulation No.584/2010 implementing the UCITS Directive. Nonetheless, foreign UCITS are required to have a representative located in Denmark when marketing is addressed to retail investors. The representative must possess a license as a securities trader from the DFSA.

Closed-ended funds are exempted from the license requirements within DIA by virtue of the executive order which aligns the Danish legislation with the Prospectus Directive. Closed-ended funds are covered by the Prospectus Directive and the AIFM regime.

Notification of foreign UCITS investment institutes covered by the UCITS Directive

The notification procedure has been simplified with the executive order based on the UCITS IV rules. The UCITS fund merely has to provide a notification of its intention to market its shares in Denmark. This notice must be given to the FSA in the UCITS' home state which will then contact the DFSA. More common notifications, such as termination of share-classes, may be sent directly to the DFSA. Any marketing activity in Denmark by the fund will trigger the requirement of notification. Thus there are no exemptions for a small number of investors or approaching professional investors only.

The notification procedure is implemented from the UCITS IV Directive. A foreign UCITS intending to market its shares directly or indirectly in Denmark should specify the types of investors, whom the UCITS will approach, such as retail investors or professional investors. This is a very important distinction to be aware of, because it determines whether or not the UCITS needs a Danish information representative. If the UCITS markets itself directly to retail investors, it will be required to have a Danish information representative. A Danish paying agent is not required.

When a UCITS wishes to notify the DFSA of its intention to market its shares in Denmark, it must provide, in the prospectus or in a supplement thereto, information on the Danish information representative of the UCITS, if one is required by reason of the fact that retail investors are approached.

3.3. Operational requirements

Danish UCITS are prohibited from providing loans or guarantees to third parties, and from borrowing, unless special permission is granted by the DFSA.

Furthermore, Danish UCITS cannot restrict redemption, except where the equity value cannot be set for the time being. As a consequence hereof, the principal rule is that Danish UCITS shall redeem upon investor request. In respect of feeder-master structures, some additional rules apply with respect to permitted redemption restrictions.

The fiscal year of Danish UCITS must follow the calendar year. The mandatory audited annual report must be handed in to the DFSA in two copies without unjustified delay after the final board approval and no later than four months after the end of the fiscal year.

The external auditor(s) and the internal fund officer, who is responsible for the auditing, shall immediately provide to the DFSA information of critical importance for the Danish UCITS' status as going concern.

Management

The board of directors must comply with the fit and proper requirements and the board members must possess adequate experience with the type of association in question. The experience requirement implies inter alia that the members of the board of directors must be experienced with and have an understanding of the risks involved in the activities of an investment association.

The board of directors is required to set up management target quotas for the underrepresented sex and to prepare a corporate policy with a view to increase the share of the underrepresented sex in the management team. The latter requirement only applies for investment associations and SIKAVs which have total assets exceeding DKK500 million throughout two following fiscal years.

Delegation

The association cannot delegate the performance of core tasks, which are defined in the Executive Order on Core Tasks in Investment Associations as being:
- investment decisions;
- supervision of and calculation of net asset value (NAV), issue price and redemptions price;
- supervision of the investment association's compliance with law;
- supervision of the daily accounting; and
- supervision of periodic reports to the DFSA.

The rules on delegation are derived from the UCITS Directive. A key element is that the board of directors of an association must make the decision to delegate certain tasks to a third party; this cannot be done by the daily management. In addition, the board determines the boundaries of these delegation agreements, because the board is responsible for an efficient and proper financial management of the association.

A decision to delegate tasks to third parties requires the delegation to contribute to more efficient and less expensive services to the association. An investment association cannot delegate one and all of its management functions to third parties, with the result that the investment association becomes an 'empty shell'.

Delegation of tasks is possible to companies, which are under supervision of the Danish or a foreign FSA. However, delegation must not prevent effective supervision of the investment association or cause the association to be managed contrary to the interests of its investors. In addition, this implies that delegation of tasks must never result in ambiguity about who is responsible for performing a given task.

An association must ensure that the companies, to which tasks are delegated, are properly qualified and capable of performing those tasks. The board of directors must approve the agreement on delegation. Thus, the board remains responsible for the tasks, and must ensure that the quality of the performance is not being compromised by the delegation.

Under certain conditions, the regulation allows the funds to delegate specific tasks in order to achieve a more efficient operation. The purpose of this provision is to ensure that the regulated investment funds do not circumvent the supervision by the DFSA through delegation of all of their key elements.

It has been practice that associations delegate some of their tasks to others. Primarily, the delegated tasks are related to the marketing of units in the associations, certain functions related to IT, and tasks relating to investment management.

Pursuant to DIA, all decisions regarding an association's investments must be made by the daily management or by employees authorised by the management. Investment decisions cannot be delegated; such decisions must be made within the investment instructions issued by the board of directors of the investment association or by the board of directors itself.

An investment association's management may only under observance of restrictive measures and limitations, provide a third party with a specific mandate for the performance of portfolio management. Such mandate must be given only for a limited part of the portfolio, when invested in a geographically distant market or in special securities, and the third party must have a special expertise related to the particular investments.

An association may receive investment advice from others to the extent that the advisers are subject to financial supervision. Such advice is not considered to come within the meaning of delegation, as the final responsibility for the investments remains with the board of directors of the association.

The custodian's obligations towards an association are not affected by the fact that the association has delegated tasks to third parties. This implies inter alia that an investment association is never able to delegate the responsibility of ensuring that all management tasks are carried out properly, and that the custodian bank continues to fulfill its tasks.

No later than eight days after the signing of a delegation agreement, the investment association must inform the DFSA, of the content and conditions of the agreement.

3.4. Marketing the fund

The marketing material and the offering are governed by the DIA and the executive order. These legislative acts are all part of the implementation of the UCITS Directive in Denmark and thereby in line with the EU regulation on UCITS funds. As mentioned in the above, notification must be given to the DFSA through the home state's supervisory authority, before any marketing activity whatsoever of foreign UCITS is commenced into Denmark.

A local representative should be appointed, when marketing foreign UCITS in Denmark to retail investors as described above. The representative must hold a securities trading (MiFID) license in Denmark. However, there are no restrictions as regards to whom, the UCITS funds can be marketed, whether retail or professional investors.

Furthermore, any other intermediary or placement agent utilised should either hold a MiFID license in Denmark or have passported its MiFID license into Denmark from another EU country prior to commencing marketing of the UCITS fund. If the UCITS fund is marketed through a unit-link product in a pension scheme, the pension fund should hold a MiFID equivalent license as well.

General marketing practice
Investment associations must operate in accordance with the principles of good faith and fair dealing, including fair business practice within the area of investment associations.

The good conduct rules are set out in an executive order which provides as a general principle that an investment association must act honestly and loyally to its customers. An association must not use misleading or false statements or omit essential information where this may significantly distort the behaviour of customers in the market. Marketing, which by form or approach exposes the customers to an improper influence and thereby affects their economic behaviour, is not allowed. Furthermore, all facts stated in the marketing plan must be documented upon request.

These regulatory rules are examples of rules which can and will be enforced against foreign funds marketed in Denmark, because the provisions are justified in the public interest, including consumer protection and hence above the principle of home country control otherwise applying.

The DFSA supervises compliance with the above-mentioned rules.

3.5. Taxation
Resident investment associations, as well as non-resident investment associations having their effective management in Denmark or carrying out business activities through a permanent establishment in Denmark, are taxed in accordance with the Danish Corporation Tax Act at a flat corporate tax rate of 25 per cent (expected to decrease to 22 per cent.). However, the effective rate is less, as business expenses and depreciation are tax deductible.

Investor tax treatment
Resident investors in taxed investment associations (UCITS) will be taxed on gains and dividends at rates of 15.3 per cent for pension funds at realisation (whether managed by life insurance companies or individually), 25 per cent for companies using the stock method (expected to drop to 22 per cent) and without qualifications as to what instruments the investment association has invested in.

Non-resident investors will be taxed in their home country on gains while dividends may be subject to a withholding tax of 27 per cent, which is often reduced or eliminated in double taxation treaties. Foreign investors not taxable in Denmark, are not taxed on gains in Denmark.

For corporate investors, the taxable income including dividend income and gains on investment certificates are taxed using the stock method which works as follows. A gain or loss is calculated as the difference between the value at the end of an income year and the value at the beginning of that income year. If unit certificates are acquired during the income year, the gain or loss is calculated as the difference between the value at the end of the income year and the purchase price of the investment certificates. If unit certificates are sold during the income year, the gain or loss is calculated as the difference between the sale value of the investment certificates and the value at the beginning of that income year. If unit certificates are acquired and disposed of in the same income year, the gain or loss is calculated as the difference between sale price and purchase price.

Personal investors who invest 'free funds' directly, including through a distributor
Under the Personal Tax Act individual retail investors investing outside pension schemes will be taxed on gains from investment in investment association units (certificates) as capital income or stock income depending on the association's investment strategy.

Gains or losses realised on units in distributing UCITS with minimum taxation investing in stocks will be taxed as stock income whereas realised gains or losses on units in UCITS investing in bonds (less than 50 per cent stock instruments in portfolio) will be taxed as capital income.

Gains and losses on units in accumulating UCITS, ie, funds that reinvest the dividends instead of distributing them among its investors, will be taxed on an annual basis in accordance with the stock approach, meaning that gains (and losses) are determined as the difference between the value of the investment certificate by the end of an income year and the value at the beginning of the income year.

Dividends or part hereof received from investment association are similarly taxed as capital income or stock income *pro rata* depending on how the dividend's yield is composed by yields from stock or/and non-stock instruments.

Gains, losses and dividends from non-stock investment associations are included in the calculation of the taxable income and taxed jointly as capital income. Personal stock income are, including gains, losses and dividends from stock investment associations, however not taxed as part of the taxable income but handled separately. Consequently, stock losses can only be deducted in positive stock income.

Positive capital income is taxed at approximately 43.5 per cent for individuals (dropping to 42 per cent. in 2014). Capital losses are deductible with a net value of approximately 33 per cent. The tax rate on positive stock income is 27 per cent on amounts up to DKK48,300 and 42 per cent on anything above (2013).

Other tax issues
Denmark has an extensive network of double taxation agreements and the Danish transfer pricing legislation is in accordance with the OECD guidelines. Denmark levies no capital duties, share transfer taxes or wealth taxes (except

Denmark

on real property).

It is neither necessary nor advisable to obtain a tax ruling from the Danish Tax Administration (SKAT) or the Danish Tax Assessment Council. Nonetheless, if desired, a binding ruling from the tax authorities may be obtained against a fee.

Simplified personal tax rules on dividends from investment associations are set to come into force January 2014.

3.6. Customary or common terms

The Danish players in the market are dominated by standard products, while foreign players show a combination of more basic products and tailor-made products to suit in particular their larger pension fund customers.

4. PROPOSED CHANGES AND DEVELOPMENTS

No reforms are proposed at present. However, the Danish Minister of Business and Growth and the DFSA is authorised to lay down further rules and guidelines relating to AIFMA.

The Danish implementation acts of the AIFMD came into force 22 July 2013. A large set of executive orders have been adopted subsequent to the implementation and more delegated legislation must be expected.

In respect of UCITS rules, no local Danish initiatives are expected in the near future other than further EU legislation.

Finland

Marcus Möller, Antti Lehtimaja, Mirja Sikander &
Pyry Somervuori **Krogerus**

1. MARKET OVERVIEW

The investment funds market in Finland can basically be divided into two different types of investment funds: mutual funds and private closed-ended funds. The mutual funds category can further be divided into two different categories, namely UCITS funds and non-UCITS funds, the non-UCITS funds category covering a wide variety of funds and including also hedge funds. The vast majority of the assets held by Finnish mutual funds are held by UCITS funds. Non-UCITS funds account for a smaller portion and, within this category, hedge funds represent an even smaller share.

According to a survey of the Federation of Finnish Financial Services, the aggregate amount of assets invested in mutual funds registered in Finland was EUR 69.7 billion as of 30 April 2013, which means that the Finnish mutual fund market has again reached its peak level of late 2007 and early 2008 after the dip in late 2008 when the aggregate amount of assets plummeted to EUR 40 billion following the start of the financial crisis.

Private closed-ended funds are a viable part of Finland's alternative investments market and private closed-ended funds are used for investments in a multitude of asset classes such as venture capital, growth capital, buyout, mezzanine finance and real estate. According to a survey of the Finnish Venture Capital Association (FVCA), Finnish venture capital and private equity managers had EUR 5.6 billion worth of assets under management at the end of 2012. In addition, there are numerous real estate and other funds structured as private closed-ended funds.

The year 2012 was reasonably active in terms of funds raised to private closed-ended funds managed by member firms of the FVCA, and the aggregate amount of funds raised increased to EUR 467 million, the highest amount since 2008. Generally, fundraising is still at a lower level in comparison to the years 2005 through 2007, the 2007 vintage topping the chart with EUR 989 million in funds raised. The fundraisings of 2012 include eg, CapMan successfully closing their tenth buyout fund in November 2012 with first closing aggregate commitments at EUR 152 million. As for the first half of 2013, the market has seen some notable successful fundraisings such as Pohjola Property Investment raising EUR 100 million at first closing to their real estate debt and secondaries fund.

2. ALTERNATIVE INVESTMENT FUNDS
2.1. Common structures

In Finland private closed-ended funds are typically formed as limited partnerships. Pursuant to Finnish law, a limited partnership gains separate legal personality as of the execution of its limited partnership agreement. However, in its memorandum published in April 2013 (the Memorandum), the Finnish Ministry of Justice has proposed that a limited partnership would gain separate legal personality upon registration of the partnership agreement with the Finnish Trade Register. A Finnish limited partnership must have a general partner that has unlimited liability for the partnership's liabilities and one or several limited partners that are liable for the partnership's liabilities up to the amount of their capital commitments as set out in the limited partnership agreement of the partnership.

Unless otherwise agreed upon in the limited partnership agreement, the transfer of a limited partner's interest in the partnership requires the consent of all partners. However, this requirement is typically relaxed in the limited partnership agreement so that only the consent of the general partner is required for the transfer of a limited partner's interest. Certificates or similar documents representing partnership interests are generally not issued.

In Finland, hedge funds are typically structured as mutual funds regulated by the Mutual Funds Act (48/1999). Funds regulated by the Mutual Funds Act (48/1999) are all open-ended funds and thus hedge funds established in Finland are typically open-ended non-UCITS mutual funds. Therefore the text on hedge funds below only discusses hedge funds structured as such non-UCITS mutual funds.

The term of a hedge fund structured as a mutual fund is not predetermined and the term of each fund is thus indefinite. A mutual fund does not have corporate legal personality under Finnish law, but is merely a pool of assets raised from investors and invested in accordance with the fund rules. Investors in a mutual fund are called unit holders. The unit holders own the mutual fund in proportion to their holding of units. Units of a mutual fund are either yield units or growth units. Holders of yield units are entitled to annual distribution of profits whereas holders of growth units do not receive annual profit distributions as the annual profit in respect of their units is capitalised for the benefit of the holders of such units.

The structure described above has in practice proved to be generally suitable for private closed-ended funds. As discussed in further detail in section 2.5. below, a Finnish limited partnership is a flow-through entity in taxation and the income of the fund is thus in general subject to taxation only as income of the partners. Finnish limited partnerships are subject to certain mandatory provisions of the Partnerships Act (389/1988), but the partners are generally able to agree rather freely on most of the terms and conditions governing the fund.

Clear benefits of using a mutual fund structure for a hedge fund have been the liberal marketing regime and the tax treatment that applies to mutual funds. Further benefits include the flexibility associated with the fact that the number of units available to be issued is unrestricted, which entails that mutual funds can be structured as very flexible in accepting new subscriptions and executing redemptions. However, this flexibility is somewhat limited by the requirements imposed by the Mutual Funds Act (48/1999) that a mutual fund must have a minimum of 50 unit holders (and an aggregate minimum of EUR 2 million of assets). If this level is not reached within six months from the establishment of the fund, or not maintained thereafter, the fund has to be either terminated or merged into another fund. One of the most significant disadvantages associated with the mutual fund structure for a hedge fund is the lack of flexibility associated with the fact that mutual funds are regulated vehicles that do not permit such bespoke arrangements that can be accomplished eg, in a limited partnership structure where the manager and the investors can negotiate and agree on the terms and conditions applicable to the fund.

The liability of a limited partner of a Finnish limited partnership generally cannot exceed the amount of such limited partner's unfunded capital commitment. As the distribution provisions of private equity funds are typically intended to regulate the distribution of cash flows, in the absence of any relevant case law it remains unclear whether and to what extent any distributions to such limited partner should be taken into account in determining the unfunded commitment of such limited partner. If a pro rata cancellation of capital commitments, or parts thereof, is desirable eg, in cases where the general partner is entitled to cancel unfunded commitments, then such cancellation should be registered with the Finnish Trade Register in order to effect a corresponding change to the liability of limited partners.

As a general rule, limited partners of a Finnish limited partnership are not entitled to manage the fund's activities, unless otherwise agreed upon in the limited partnership agreement. As the general rule is non-mandatory and Finnish law does not contain express provisions on losing limited liability status due to taking part in the management of the partnership, the limited partners of a Finnish limited partnership may generally be given such powers to engage in the activities of the partnership as is deemed commercially desirable.

An interest in a Finnish limited partnership is called a partnership interest, whereas an interest in a mutual fund is called a unit.

A Finnish private fund formed as a limited partnership is represented by its general partner which is usually formed as a Finnish limited liability company. In most cases, the general partner entity does not employ any personnel and the management and/or advisory services in relation to the fund are provided by a separate management and/or advisory company. The management and/or advisory company is usually formed as a Finnish limited liability company and, at the time of writing this article, should be formed so if such an entity is an alternative investment fund manager regulated under the Draft Finnish Act on Alternative Investment Fund Managers published on 25 June 2013 (the Draft AIFM Act).

2.2. Regulatory framework

Private closed-ended funds have generally been considered to fall outside the scope of Finnish securities market regulation. However, such funds are subject to certain mandatory provisions of the Partnerships Act (389/1988), eg, a provision allowing each partner to give notice of termination of the partnership's limited partnership agreement as of the tenth anniversary of such partner's adherence to the partnership as well as mandatory rules on the clawback obligation of a limited partner. The Ministry of Justice's Memorandum proposes that the foregoing right of a partner to give notice of termination of the partnership's limited partnership agreement be abolished in respect of such partners that are legal persons.

The single most important act of legislation regulating hedge funds, fund management companies and custodians in Finland is the Mutual Funds Act (48/1999). Investment managers and investment advisers are further regulated by the Investment Services Act (746/2012).

The Directive on Alternative Investment Fund Managers (AIFMD) and the Finnish implementing measures in relation thereto impose a significant additional regulatory burden on managers falling under the scope thereof.

If a private closed-ended fund has an investment adviser in Finland, then an obligation to register pursuant to the Investment Services Act (746/2012) may under certain conditions apply to such investment adviser. In any case such obligation will not apply to the investment adviser if it belongs to the same group of companies as the general partner and refrains from providing services to clients not belonging to the same group of companies as the investment adviser. If the investment adviser is under the obligation to register, then it must apply for authorisation from the FIN-FSA. Receiving such an authorisation requires, inter alia, meeting minimum capital and reliability requirements as well as requirements relating to internal control and risk management. In a like manner to that set out in respect of alternative investment fund managers and MiFID regulated entities in Article 6 of the AIFMD, the Draft AIFM Act provides such restrictions on the activities an alternative investment fund manager may engage in which in practice are anticipated to exclude investment firms regulated under the Investment Services Act (746/2012) from the group of investment advisers and fund managers that will seek authorisation or registration under the Draft AIFM Act.

Before the implementation of UCITS IV into the Mutual Funds Act (48/1999), only a limited liability company incorporated in Finland was to be granted an authorisation to act as the fund management company of a hedge fund structured as a mutual fund. However, the implementation of a fund management company incorporated in the European Economic Area has been able to establish, with the permission of the FIN-FSA, a hedge fund in Finland and act as its fund management company. The board of directors of a Finnish fund management company has to comprise at least three members and at least one-third of the members of the board of directors have to be elected by the unit holders. The minimum share capital of the fund management company is EUR 125,000. In addition to the minimum share capital, the fund management company must have further proprietary assets in the minimum amount of 0.02 per cent of the amount by which the aggregate value of the mutual funds managed by it exceeds EUR 250 million. However, the aggregate proprietary assets of the fund management company need not exceed EUR 10 million.

The FIN-FSA is the main supervisory body of the Finnish financial markets.

Mutual funds, fund management companies, alternative investment fund managers, custodians, investment managers and investment advisers all need to be authorised by or registered with the FIN-FSA. A Finnish hedge fund that is structured as a mutual fund becomes authorised upon the FIN-FSA approving its fund rules, following which the fund management company may commence its marketing and accept subscriptions for fund units.

2.3. Operational requirements

The AIFMD and the Finnish implementing measures in relation thereto impose significant operational requirements on Finnish fund managers of private closed-ended funds as well as hedge funds structured as mutual funds. As Finnish alternative investment fund managers often employ a relatively small number of staff (eg, from 5 to 15), especially the provisions on organisational and administrative arrangements for preventing conflicts of interest (Article 14 of the AIFMD and section 7:6 of the Draft AIFM Act respectively) and the separation of the risk management function (Article 15 of the AIFMD and section 8:2 of the Draft AIFM Act) are anticipated to impose a serious burden on the Finnish manager community and may require some managers to implement changes to their current company structures. Further, at the time of writing this article, the lack of service providers carrying out the depositary functions set out in the AIFMD and Draft AIFM Act may prove a challenge for the Finnish fund industry.

In addition, the Draft AIFM Act introduces a new placement regime applicable to all alternative investment funds that are offered in Finland. The operational requirements of the regime provide that the manager shall comply with the information on how funds are to be invested that has been given to the investors pursuant to the disclosure obligation set out in Article 23 of the AIFMD and section 12:4 of the Draft AIFM Act, respectively. Further, according to section 12:8 of the Draft AIFM Act, the manager shall know its customers and identify ultimate beneficiaries or persons acting on behalf of the customer, have sufficient risk management systems for assessing the risks caused by its customers and comply with the reporting obligations relating to suspicious transactions and suspected terrorist financing in accordance with the Act on Preventing and Clearing Money Laundering and Terrorist Financing (503/2008) that eg, requires the alternative investment fund manager to have internal guidelines on anti-money laundering and to perform customer due diligence measures prior to establishing new customer relationships. In respect of non-EU managers and EU managers managing non-EU alternative investment funds, the foregoing imposes additional requirements in comparison to the requirements set out in Article 36 and Article 42 of the AIFMD.

In addition, funds, general partners and investment advisers are subject to generally applicable requirements such as the obligation to file a company's annual financial statements with the Finnish Trade Register.

The assets of a hedge fund structured as a mutual fund are held by its custodian. Such assets need to be held in a reliable manner and segregated from the custodian's assets and the assets of other mutual funds and clients of the custodian.

The fund management company of a hedge fund is required to publish an annual, a semi-annual and a quarterly report on each fund it manages. The annual report must be published and filed with the FIN-FSA within three months from the end of the financial period whereas the semi-annual and quarterly reports must be published and filed within two months from the end of the relevant reporting period. Further, the fund management company has to publish and file with the FIN-FSA the prospectus and simplified prospectus of each fund as well as all changes made to these documents. All changes made to the fund rules have to be approved by the FIN-FSA prior to the entry into force of such changes.

The fund management company of a hedge fund is obliged to treat all unit holders of the same fund equally. This means that all unit holders must receive the same information concerning the fund and have the same rights to have their units redeemed. Finnish mutual funds may have several unit classes with each class having different minimum investment amounts and different overall fee structures. However, the fund rules need to clearly set out the fund's fee structure in a manner that permits every unit holder or prospective unit holder to assess the fees.

If the number of unit holders or the value of the hedge fund's assets has fallen below the required minimum level and such minimum level is not reached within 90 days, the fund management company must interrupt the redemption of fund units. If redemptions are interrupted, all marketing materials of the fund must during such interruption include a statement detailing the exceptional situation of the fund.

The FIN-FSA may also grant the fund management company permission to temporarily interrupt the issue of fund units if so required by the interests of the unit holders. Further, the FIN-FSA may order the issuance and/or redemption of units to be halted, if this is necessary in order to protect the trust in the securities or real estate markets, to safeguard the interests of unit holders or for another especially significant reason.

Each alternative investment fund manager is required to maintain an insider register of the holdings and trading of certain employees and connected parties, and certain holdings of such persons are also subject to public disclosure requirements. Fund management companies are also subject to the insider dealing and market abuse rules of Directive 2003/6/EC (ie, the Market Abuse Directive) as implemented by eg, the Securities Market Act (2012/746).

2.4. Marketing the fund

The AIFMD and the Finnish implementing measures in relation thereto will impose significant restrictions on the marketing of alternative investment funds to prospective investors. In addition, the Draft AIFM Act introduces a new private placement regime. The marketing restrictions of the regime provide that, in addition to the restrictions set out in Article 36 and Article 42 of the AIFMD, the following rules set out in sections 12:2 and 12:3 of the Draft AIFM Act apply in the marketing of alternative investment funds in

Finland:
- good practice in the securities market as set out in section 1:2 of the Securities Market Act (746/2012) shall be complied with. This restriction also expressly applies in situations involving reverse solicitation; and
- no marketing shall be conducted by giving false or misleading information. If any information material to investors is found to be false or misleading following its disclosure, such false or misleading information shall be rectified or complemented without delay. This restriction also expressly applies in situations involving reverse solicitation.

In respect of a non-EU alternative investment fund manager, marketing a non-EU alternative investment fund in Finland to professional investors by way of private placement, such marketing shall also be subject to the condition that an agreement ensuring efficient exchange of information in tax matters fully equivalent to the requirements set out in Article 26 of the OECD Model Tax Convention on Income and on Capital shall be in place between Finland and the third country where the non-EU alternative investment fund is established.

In addition to the foregoing, the marketing by an EU alternative investment fund manager of a non-EU alternative investment fund in Finland to professional investors by way of private placement is subject to the condition that that the alternative investment fund manager shall submit a notification to the FIN-FSA in a manner equivalent to that set out in Article 31 of the AIFMD.

An obligation to publish a prospectus (and certain other marketing restrictions) may apply, unless the alternative investment fund interests are offered: (i) solely to qualified investors, as defined in the Securities Market Act (2012/746); (ii) in each relevant EEA jurisdiction to less than 150 investors not being deemed qualified investors; (iii) to be acquired for a consideration of at least EUR 100,000 per investor or with regard to an offer or in portions of at least EUR 100,000 in nominal value or counter-value; (iv) in the EEA so that the aggregate consideration is less than EUR 1,500,000 calculated over a 12-month period; or (v) in the EEA so that the aggregate consideration is less than EUR 5,000,000 calculated over a 12-month period, provided that the fund interests are sought to be admitted to multilateral trading in Finland and a company prospectus in compliance with the rules of the operator of the trading system is available to the investors throughout the offering period; and (vi) transferable certificates or evidences of interest are not issued and may not be issued pursuant to the limited partnership agreement governing the fund. Private closed-ended funds have generally been structured so that the obligation to publish a prospectus and certain other marketing restrictions have not been applicable to such funds.

The units of a hedge fund structured as a Finnish mutual fund may be marketed to the general public in Finland. As such units under Finnish law are considered to be securities, the general prohibition against marketing of securities by giving false or misleading information or by using methods that are contrary to good practice or otherwise unfair still applies to the marketing

Finland

of such units.

The Draft AIFM Act provides that when marketing alternative investment funds to retail investors in Finland, the Finnish Consumer Protection Act (38/1978) shall be applicable. According to the Finnish Consumer Protection Act (38/1978) no conduct that is inappropriate or otherwise unfair shall be allowed in marketing. Further, marketing is regarded as being against good practice when it is clearly in opposition to generally accepted values. In addition, aggressive marketing, including harassment and coercion, is prohibited. The relevant provisions of the Finnish Consumer Protection Act (38/1978) are broadly based on the Unfair Commercial Practices Directive (2005/29/EC).

The marketing of alternative investment funds under the Draft AIFM Act has been limited to relatively well-known company forms. The alternative investment funds that are marketed to retail investors must be limited companies, limited partnerships, non-UCITS funds regulated under the Mutual Funds Act (48/1999), registered associations, cooperatives, or foreign equivalents regulated under the AIFMD. Each alternative investment fund marketed to retail investors in Finland must be based in an EEA member state.

Alternative investment funds formed as limited partnerships may be marketed to retail investors only if the profit-sharing of the fund has been limited in the partnership agreement, with appropriate sanctions. This restriction relates to the fact that under the Partnerships Act (389/1988) a general partner of a limited partnership may withdraw funds from the partnership, unless otherwise agreed upon in the partnership agreement. As Finnish private closed-ended funds formed as limited partnerships typically employ detailed provisions on distribution of cash flows, this restriction is not anticipated to restrict the marketing of private closed-ended funds to retail investors.

Furthermore, under the Draft AIFM Act, alternative investment fund managers shall create in respect of each alternative fund marketed to retail investors, a document containing information that is material to the investors (key information prospectus). The Draft AIFM Act sets out specific regulations as regards the content of the key information prospectus as well as specific language requirements. Retail investors must be provided with identifying information concerning the alternative investment fund, a short description of investment targets and policy, return history and, if necessary, expected returns, expenses and related fees, the investment's risk-reward profile and appropriate instructions and warnings on the risks concerning the relevant alternative investment fund.

The key information prospectus shall, among other things, be appropriate, concise and clear, understandable to retail investors and written in standard language. The FIN-FSA may exempt an alternative investment fund manager from the responsibility to create such a prospectus.

The marketing of hedge funds structured as mutual funds is regulated under the Mutual Funds Act (48/1999).

2.5. Taxation

A Finnish limited partnership is treated as 'semi-transparent' for Finnish income tax purposes. This means that the taxable income of the fund itself is calculated based on Finnish tax laws but it is, after deducting possible losses carried forward from previous years, taxed in the hands of its partners based on the partners' entitlement to the partnership's income. In relation to dividend income, the transparency of the fund is even more apparent, as the partners are entitled to a deduction corresponding to the dividend taxation level in their own taxation should they have received these dividends directly.

The partnership income of corporate limited partners is generally taxed at the rate of 24.5 per cent. However, dividend income received by the partnership may be subject to a lower effective tax rate of approximately 18.4 per cent (75 per cent out of 24.5 per cent) or 0 per cent in the hands of the limited partner due to the more apparent transparency of the limited partnership in respect of dividend income. Many domestic institutional investors in Finnish closed-ended private funds are tax-exempt or are in practise in a zero tax position due to the possibility of making certain tax deductible reservations.

The limited partner income of private individuals is divided into a capital income portion taxed at the flat rate of 30 per cent (and 32 per cent to the extent annual capital income exceeds EUR 50,000) and into an earned income portion taxed at a progressive rate up to approximately 54 per cent. The division is based on the net asset value of the partnership. Capital gains derived from a sale of shares that are part of the fixed assets of the partnership (eg, target shares of portfolio companies' of closed-ended private equity or venture capital funds) are treated as capital income regardless of the net asset value of the partnership. Generally only 70 per cent of the dividend income received by the partnership is taxable in the hands of the limited partner.

Non-resident limited partners of the partnership are generally taxed as having a permanent establishment in Finland. Their share of the partnership's income is thus taxed at the rate of 24.5 per cent (assuming that they are corporates). Qualifying non-resident investors in limited partnerships that carry on private equity investment activities are taxed as if they had invested directly in the assets held by the partnership. Therefore, only dividends received by the partnership from Finnish resident portfolio companies or real estate related income (rental income or capital gains) from the partnership's investments in Finnish real estate are taxed in Finland. In that case, the tax is withheld by the partnership from payments to the qualifying investor. A non-resident investor needs to be entitled to the benefits of a tax treaty between Finland and the domicile country of such investor to be considered a qualifying investor. The general dividend withholding tax rate for corporate investors is 24.5 per cent but there are exemptions available from this both in tax treaties and in domestic law for certain EU resident corporations. Real estate related income is taxed at the rate of 24.5 per cent (assuming that the qualifying investors are corporates). Based on Finnish case law, closed-ended private funds investing in private equity funds (ie, funds-of-funds) or real estate are generally deemed to carry on private equity investment activities for Finnish tax purposes.

Although hedge funds structured as mutual funds do not have corporate legal personality under Finnish law, they are for Finnish tax purposes treated as corporations and thus opaque rather than transparent. However, based on a special exemption they are exempt from income tax. Further, from a Finnish point of view, mutual funds are generally deemed to be entitled to tax treaty benefits relating to any foreign source income they may receive.

Any distributions or capital gains from the sale of units in mutual funds are taxed as regular taxable income (at the flat rate of 24.5 per cent) of corporate investors and as capital income of private individuals that is taxed at the flat rate of 30 per cent (32 per cent to the extent investors' annual capital income exceeds EUR 50,000).

The exchange of a yield unit to a growth unit of the same mutual fund, or vice versa, is not deemed to be a transfer for tax purposes, and does thus not cause capital gain taxation. However, the exchange of a fund unit to a fund unit of another fund is deemed to be a taxable transfer, even if both mutual funds were managed by the same fund management company, and in such case a capital gain or loss is deemed to occur. This is the case even if no cash were received by the investor in the exchange, but the redemption price of the fund units would be used in full to pay for the subscription of units in another fund.

As mutual funds are deemed to be tax treaty subjects, non-resident investors may claim tax treaty benefits relating to the distributions they receive from the fund. From a Finnish point of view distributions are not for tax treaty purposes deemed to be dividends, but are considered as 'other income' so most tax treaties do not allow Finland to tax the distributions.

As regards the contemplated changes to the above tax rules that are expected to take effect as of 2014, please see section 4 below.

2.6. Customary or common terms

Regarding private closed-ended alternative investment funds, the term of the fund often continues until the tenth anniversary of its first closing. Such term may also expire earlier or later and limited partnership agreements typically provide for early termination upon realisation of all investments or the removal of the general partner (provided that no replacement general partner is elected).

The investment period may terminate eg, on the fifth anniversary of the fund's first closing. However, the inclusion of provisions on early termination of the investment period is customary, and such early termination is usually triggered eg, when a substantial amount of commitments have been drawn down. Following the expiration of the investment period uncalled capital commitments may in most cases be drawn down for the purpose of covering operational expenses, funding follow-on investments and/or investments in relation to which the fund prior to the expiration of the investment period has executed a letter of intent, term sheet or binding agreement.

The inclusion of a minimum commitment size in the limited partnership agreement is customary, and the relative size of the minimum commitment varies by the commercial targets and fundraising prospects of the manager. Limited partner interests are typically not transferable without the prior consent of the general partner and the assumption by the transferee of all obligations of the transferring limited partner.

The commitment of the key investment professionals to the fund is usually secured by a number of provisions of the limited partnership agreement. Such key investment professionals are regularly required to make and maintain a firm commitment to invest also part of their personal wealth in the fund eg, through the general partner. Further, if key investment professionals cease to devote substantially all of their business time to the fund, and if such a key man event is not remedied to the satisfaction of the limited partners, typically certain adverse consequences are triggered (eg, a termination of the investment period or even a removal of the general partner).

The general partner commonly charges a management fee (eg, 2 per cent) calculated on the basis of aggregate commitments to the fund (up to the expiration of the investment period) and the aggregate acquisition cost of the fund's unrealised investments (as of the expiration of the investment period). Board member remuneration, transaction fees and similar fees paid by portfolio companies to the manager or its representatives are commonly offset against management fees payable by the fund.

The distribution waterfall provision setting out the partners' entitlement to proceeds distributed by the fund is customarily crafted on the basis of a whole-of-fund approach rather than on a deal-by-deal basis. Distribution waterfalls often provide for a carried interest at 20 per cent payable to the general partner following the payment of the preferred return to limited partners (at eg, 8 per cent per annum).

Limited partners are customarily protected by specific clawback clauses requiring the general partner to repay to the partnership any excess distributions received by the general partner and such clawback clauses may also provide for an escrow arrangement in respect of part of the distributions received by the general partner or a requirement on the general partner to provide some form of security for its obligation to make such repayments.

A Finnish private closed-ended fund is under the obligation to file the fund's annual financial statements with the Finnish Trade Register and its tax return to the Finnish Tax Administration. With respect to contractual reporting obligations to limited partners, general partners are typically required to prepare quarterly reports to the limited partners. The content of such reports varies, yet in most cases the report contains updated valuation information on the assets of the fund. Finnish venture capital and buyout funds frequently apply the International Private Equity and Venture Capital Valuation Guidelines.

Typically the fees payable by unit holders of a hedge fund structured as a mutual fund are: (i) a subscription fee; (ii) a redemption fee; (iii) a management fee (which also covers the fees payable to the custodian and any separate investment manager); and (iv) a performance fee based on the success of the fund. Fee levels vary depending on eg, the fund's investment strategies and the fixed costs of the fund management company.

Whereas UCITS-compliant mutual funds have daily liquidity, non-UCITS funds such as hedge funds do not have to comply with this requirement. However, according to the FIN-FSA, in order for a hedge fund (or other non-UCITS fund) to be considered as an open-ended mutual fund under the Mutual Funds Act (48/1999), the fund must permit redemptions and subscriptions at intervals no longer than every three months.

Finnish hedge funds structured as mutual funds do not typically use redemption gate provisions, but the fund rules may impose certain restrictions on liquidity and the fund management company may temporarily interrupt the redemption of the units in a mutual fund in situations referred to in the fund rules.

3. RETAIL FUNDS
3.1. Common structures
Finnish retail funds are typically structured as open-ended mutual funds under the Mutual Funds Act (48/1999), and thus much of what is set out above in respect of hedge funds also applies to the retail funds discussed in this section. Retail funds investing in real estate could also be structured as real estate funds under the Real Estate Funds Act (1173/1997). However, as these structures are not commonly used, real estate funds structured in accordance with the Real Estate Funds Act (1173/1997) will not be discussed further in this section.

As stated in section 1 above, mutual funds can be either UCITS compliant or non-UCITS compliant and both of these fund types can be used for retail funds. In fact, a UCITS fund must be open for all investors, who are willing to invest the minimum subscription amount in the fund and thus a UCITS fund cannot restrict its investor target group in its fund rules. However, a non-UCITS fund can restrict the scope of eligible investors in its fund rules.

As discussed in section 2.1. above in respect of hedge funds structured as mutual funds, a mutual fund does not have corporate legal personality under Finnish law and its term is not predetermined. Similarly, what has been set out in section 2.1. above in respect of fund units and the establishment process applies to all mutual funds, and the benefits and disadvantages discussed in respect of hedge funds structured as mutual funds are also broadly the same in respect of all mutual funds.

3.2. Regulatory framework
The regulatory framework discussed in section 2.2. above in respect of hedge funds structured as mutual funds applies to all mutual funds (including retail funds).

3.3. Operational requirements
The operational requirements discussed in section 2.3. above in respect of hedge funds structured as mutual funds in many respects apply as such to all mutual funds (including retail funds). However, there are a few notable exceptions that mainly relate to retail funds structured as UCITS funds.

UCITS funds are prohibited from engaging in short selling and the assets of a UCITS fund may not be invested in precious metals or certificates entitling to precious metals. Further, the fund management company may not use the assets of a UCITS fund to make available loans or provide guarantees or other collateral to secure the obligations of third parties. The fund management company may also not invest the assets of the UCITS funds it manages in the shares of another fund management company. As regards reporting requirements, UCITS funds are exempt from the requirement to publish quarterly reports.

3.4. Marketing the fund
The marketing of mutual funds (including retail funds) is discussed in section 2.4. above.

3.5. Taxation
The taxation of mutual funds (including retail funds) is discussed in section 2.5. above.

3.6. Customary or common terms
The information set out in section 2.6. is generally applicable to all mutual funds (including retail funds).

4. PROPOSED CHANGES AND DEVELOPMENTS
The key development for the Finnish market of closed-ended private funds currently is the entry into force and national implementation of the AIFMD, which imposes significant new regulation of the industry. At the time of writing this article, the Finnish national implementation of the AIFMD is expected to be delayed by several months from the 22 July 2013 deadline set out in the AIFMD. This could have adverse consequences to fund managers currently conducting or contemplating cross-border fundraisings. The AIFMD also affects the managers of many mutual funds, namely the managers of all non-UCITS funds (including hedge funds) that fall within the scope of application of the AIFMD.

In May 2013, the Finnish Government announced its intention to propose to the Parliament later during year 2013 that the Finnish corporate income tax rate be decreased from 24.5 per cent to 20 per cent and that the threshold between 30 per cent capital income tax rate and 32 per cent capital income tax rate be decreased from EUR 50,000 to EUR 40,000. The intention is to have these rates apply as of the beginning of the year 2014. Should these changes be enacted, this would have a corresponding effect on the rates discussed above in section 2.5.

Germany

Uwe Bärenz & Dr Jens Steinmüller **P+P Pöllath + Partners**

1. MARKET OVERVIEW

The German investment funds market has grown almost continuously during the last three decades. This applies to both investment funds, which are only suitable for certain kinds of (institutional) investors (specialised funds), as well as undertakings for collective investment in transferable securities (UCITS), and alternative investment funds (AIF), which are also suitable for retail investors (retail funds). Germany has a well-developed market for investment funds, both UCITS and AIF, whether in the form of specialised funds or retail funds. Nevertheless, a significant portion of the German investor base uses fund vehicles in other jurisdictions or a combination of German and foreign vehicles. Therefore, the German investment fund market is characterised by diverse cross-border constellations, involving onshore jurisdictions such as Luxembourg, the United Kingdom, and the United States, as well as certain offshore jurisdictions such as the Cayman Islands and the Channel Islands.

Whereas collective investment schemes were originally used as instruments of risk diversification for the retail market, they have also become essential for the portfolios of large institutional investors. Many institutional investors previously had a conservative investment approach in the past. The ongoing difficult situation in the financial markets, however, is causing an increasing number of them to participate in riskier investments, including shares in AIF. Many of these institutional investors (eg, banks and financial institutions, other investment funds, insurance companies and pension funds) are subject to regulation. Therefore, sponsors of AIF must often consider not only the regulatory framework that applies to them and the funds they manage, but also the regulatory requirements of potential institutional investors. Investor regulations have often been challenging for sponsors, managers and distributors of AIF. However, the increasing appetite for alternative investments has also stimulated the regulators to provide rules, under which these types of investments become feasible for these investor groups.

2. ALTERNATIVE INVESTMENT FUNDS

The following discussion regarding AIF exclusively refers to specialised AIF as specified in the German Capital Investment Act (*Kapitalanlagegesetzbuch* (GCIA)). The GCIA is the main piece of legislation containing the transposition of AIFMD into German law. Under the GCIA, basically all investment funds that do not qualify as UCITS are considered AIF. Specialised AIF (*Spezial-AIF*) comprise AIF in which only professional or semi-professional investors may invest, whereas all other AIF are considered to be retail AIF (*Publikums-AIF*). To qualify as a specialised AIF, in addition to certain other requirements, a fund may only accept investors (other than professional investors, ie, certain institutional investors and investors which could be classified as deemed professional clients under MiFID) that commit to investing at least EUR 200,000 to such a fund. For retail funds (including retail AIF and UCITS) please refer to section 3 below.

2.1. Common structures
Until 22 July 2013, AIF could be established as regulated or – mainly – unregulated vehicles. Under the new GCIA, all AIF are subject to mandatory requirements regarding the legal structure:
(i) An open-ended fund can only be established as:
- a contractual fund (*Sondervermögen*);
- an investment company with variable capital (*Investmentaktiengesellschaft mit variablem Kapital*); or
- an open-ended investment partnership (*offene Investmentkommanditgesellschaft*).

(ii) A closed-ended fund has to be set up as either:
- an investment company with fixed capital (*Investmentaktiengesellschaft mit fixem Kapital*); or
- a closed-ended investment partnership (*geschlossene Investmentkommanditgesellschaft*).

As for regulated open-ended funds, the typical structure in Germany until now has been the contractual fund. Contractual funds are managed by a management company on the basis of certain terms and conditions (*Vertragsbedingungen*). Assets of a contractual fund are either solely owned by the management company, in which the investors are comparable to trustors, or are co-owned by the investors, whereby such investors do not have the power to dispose of such assets. In any case, the assets of the fund have to be held separately from the investment company's assets. German law also provides a statutory type of open-ended investment funds called investment companies with variable capital established as stock corporations. In general, these corporations issue two types of shares: investor shares (*Anlageaktien*) and sponsor shares (*Unternehmensaktien*). Investors holding investor shares participate in the fund's assets without being entitled to attend shareholders' meetings or to vote, whereas sponsor shares convey such rights to their holders. The open-ended investment limited partnership is a new investment vehicle under German law that exclusively addresses certain institutional investors seeking to invest through a regulated open-ended vehicle that is internationally recognised as tax-transparent.

The most common vehicle for closed-ended alternative investment funds in Germany thus far has been a German limited partnership; the general partner is typically a company with limited liability (GmbH & Co KG). Investors can participate as limited partners holding limited partnership interests. Limited partnerships offer a cost-efficient and tax neutral approach of structuring private funds. Limited partners can be admitted comparably easily. Carried interest can be structured to be tax efficient, ie, in such a way that 40 per cent of the carried interest can be tax-exempt. Under the German Commercial

Code (*Handelsgesetzbuch* (HGB)), a partnership has its own legal personality. Limited partners are only liable for partnership debts up to the amount of their capital contribution registered with the commercial registry. The general partner is liable for the partnership debts without limitation. In cases in which the general partner is a corporation, the shareholders of the corporation are not liable for the general partner's liabilities. Under the new law, these funds can be set up under the new regime that applies to closed-ended investment limited partnerships. The German market has also seen closed-ended funds established on the basis of corporate vehicles. The rules concerning investment companies with fixed capital provide the regulatory format for this option.

2.2. Regulatory framework

As of 22 July 2013, the GCIA provides a comprehensive regulatory framework for virtually all investment funds, including AIF and their managers. The terms of AIF need to be filed with BaFin, and basically all AIF are subject to supervision by BaFin.

The recent legislation has significantly broadened the scope of the license requirement for managers of AIF (AIFM). Under the GCIA, AIFM in general will be required to have a license as a capital investment management company (*Kapitalverwaltungsgesellschaft* (CIMC)). Advisors to AIF are not subject to regulation under the GCIA, but must have a MiFID licence if they offer advice on financial instruments. Recent legislation has broadened the scope of the term 'financial instruments', which historically did not cover the interests of most closed-ended funds.

Certain regulatory requirements under applicable investment fund legislation depend on whether an AIF and/or an AIFM qualifies as a domestic, EU or third country entity.

An AIFM does not need a license if it does not manage any retail funds or only manages closed-ended funds and directly and indirectly has capital under management of less than EUR 500 million (only if no retail funds are managed, no leverage is employed and investors do not have any redemption rights in the first five years from the date of the first investment) or (in all other cases) EUR 100 million (including assets acquired with borrowed funds). Even in cases in which a manager does not need a licence, the manager is still subject to reduced regulation under the GCIA, including an obligation to register as CIMC. In principle, all AIFM have to file an application for a license or for registration, respectively, before 22 July 2014. Managers may manage funds in accordance with the GCIA without having been granted a license, if they have filed an application or (by 21 July 2014) bindingly declare their intention to do so. AIFM that only manage closed-ended funds, which do not make any additional investments after 21 July 2013, will be allowed to continue without authorisation. In addition, an AIFM may also continue to manage closed-ended AIF without authorisation, if such AIFM only manages closed-ended AIF, the subscription period of which expired prior to 21 July 2011 and the terms of which expire by 22 July 2016 at the latest.

Details of the authorisation processes differ from each other depending on whether authorisation is sought for an AIFM or an adviser. However, both authorisation as an AIFM and as an adviser require an application, which must be filed with BaFin together with a business plan, further documents and information. Decisions must be rendered within six months.

2.3. Operational requirements

AIFM's activities are restricted with respect to the AIF managed by them. Restrictions partly depend on the type of AIF and, in part, are generally applicable to AIFM. The latter includes obligations with respect to potential conflicts of interest, proper management of risks and liquidity management.

Specialised AIF can be established as:
- general open-ended specialised AIF (*allgemeine offene inländische Spezial-AIF*);
- hedge funds (*Hedgefonds*);
- open-ended specialised AIF with fixed investment terms (*offene inländische Spezial-AIF mit festen Anlagebedingungen*); or
- closed-ended specialised AIF (*geschlossene inländische Spezial-AIF*).

General open-ended specialised AIF are usually flexible as to the assets in which they may invest, as long as they adhere to the principle of risk diversification and the assets can be valued. Furthermore, open-ended AIF have to redeem their fund units at least once in a one-year period, and the structure of the portfolio must be created in accordance with such requirement. General open-ended specialised AIF may not acquire control of a target company that is not listed on an organised market.

According to German law, the main characteristic of a hedge fund is that it can either employ leverage to a considerable extent or short selling.

Open-ended specialised AIF with fixed investment terms are basically the successors of a fund type that has been used extensively by many institutional investors, including insurance companies and pension funds looking for a flexible investment vehicle for relatively liquid assets. These vehicles can be used to acquire shares of both single AIF and fund of funds AIF. However, investment limits apply to shares which are not listed on an organised market.

Closed-ended specialised AIF are relatively flexible in what they may invest in from a regulatory point of view. Nevertheless, funds acquiring a controlling position in a portfolio company (typically private equity funds) have to comply with certain transparency requirements.

2.4. Marketing the fund

Until recently, private placements of most AIF were not subject to substantial regulatory restrictions. Under the German private placement regime, it was possible to market both German and foreign funds without the need to register or publish marketing materials, if the selected investor group was either experienced or committed to investing at least EUR 200,000. Under the GCIA, there is no longer such a private placement regime.

Marketing of specialised AIF to professional and/or semi-professional investors is subject to certain procedural requirements, depending on whether the marketing is a purely domestic or a cross-border issue involving other EU jurisdictions or third countries. Before a domestic management company may start marketing a domestic AIF or an EU AIF, it must notify BaFin accordingly.

Marketing of domestic AIF or EU AIF by EU management companies is subject to the passport procedure provided by the AIFMD. As of July 2015 (at the earliest), a non-EU management company may apply for a marketing passport, which would allow it to market its funds to professional investors throughout the EU without relying on national private placement regimes. In order to hold a marketing passport, a non-EU fund manager would need to apply for AIFM authorisation and comply in full with the AIFMD (which includes, among other things, appointment of a depositary, independent valuation, minimum capital, compliance with remuneration guidelines and implementation of certain organisational requirements). For the interim period until the EU introduces the above marketing passport for non-EU management companies (ie, until at least July 2015), non-EU fund management companies that market activities in Germany to professional and semi-professional investors are subject to certain requirements under German domestic law. As a procedural requirement prior to any marketing, the management company must notify BaFin of the intended marketing and seek BaFin's approval. Once the marketing passport has been introduced, only the AIFMD marketing passport regime will be available to non-EU fund management companies marketing in Germany. The domestic rules mentioned above will no longer apply and the non-EU management company must obtain an AIFMD marketing passport and be fully compliant with the AIFMD requirements in order to be able to distribute its funds to professional and semi-professional investors in Germany. The German legislator has not made use of its option to apply both procedures for a transitional period ending in 2018, as provided by the AIFMD.

Whereas there are no specific prospectus and key investor information (*wesentliche Anlegerinformationen* (KID)) requirements for AIF, to the extent that they are marketed to professional and semi-professional investors, the GCIA requires disclosure of certain information regarding the respective AIF in such cases.

Depending on the type of investor, certain regulatory requirements might have to be considered, which shall apply in addition to the investment fund regulations. For example, insurance companies and pension funds are subject to certain restrictions pursuant to the Investment Ordinance (*Anlageverordnung*) regarding the investments of their assets. AIFM establishing AIF for the German market should carefully consider these restrictions in order to ensure that their fund products are suitable for the German institutional investors' market.

2.5. TAXATION
The tax treatment of AIF and their investors under German law is currently undergoing substantial changes. On 16 May 2013, the German Act on the Adaption of Investment Fund Taxation in Connection with the AIFMD (*AIFM-Steuer-Anpassungsgesetz* (AIFM Tax Adaption Act)) was passed by the German Federal Parliament (*Bundestag*). This bill provides for significant changes of the taxation of funds and their investors for both existing and new structures.

The scope of the AIFM Tax Adaption Act comprises all kinds of investment undertakings regulated by the GCIA, ie, all AIF and UCITS. Nevertheless, the bill does not intend to implement a single tax regime for all such investment undertakings, but creates categories of funds solely for tax purposes which shall be subject to different tax regimes.

German and non-German private equity funds and other closed-end AIF such as mezzanine, infrastructure and real estate funds, as well as certain open-ended funds which do not comply with the German product regulation for tax purposes, are to be treated as so-called *Investitionsgesellschaften*. The tax treatment of these non-qualifying companies depends on their legal format, ie, whether they have been established as partnerships or corporations. It is important to note that funds of the contractual type (such as a Luxembourg *fonds commun de placement* or a German *Sondervermögen*) are to be treated like corporations under that regime. As for non-qualifying partnerships (eg, German GmbH & Co KG, limited partnerships), the general rules of taxation remain applicable, ie, there are no changes to the taxation rules currently in force. Non-qualifying AIF set up as corporations (eg, German stock corporations, Luxembourg SCA/SA SICAV, Irish PLC) are subject to a new tax regime. Domestic AIF are subject to German corporate income tax, as well as German local trade tax under that regime. For foreign corporate AIF, the German tax treatment of the fund vehicle depends on to what extent the AIF has German source income.

Certain open-ended AIF (those that meet the new product regulation requirements for tax purposes and are thus treated as qualifying investment funds) are subject to a specific semi-tax transparency regime. Under this regime, in principle, AIF are treated as corporate income tax subjects, but they benefit from a personal tax exemption.

Compensation paid to managers and advisors of AIF (such as management/advisory fees, as well as performance fees) are generally subject to German income tax and German trade tax, as the case may be. Under certain conditions, 40 per cent of carried interest paid by a fund that qualifies solely as an asset management vehicle rather than a business entity is tax free.

Taxation of investors in AIF depends, inter alia, on whether the shares in the fund are units of a qualifying or a non-qualifying AIF. If the fund is a qualifying AIF, taxation of investors is based on the principle of restricted transparency, ie, investors are subject to German income tax on certain distributions, as well as retained income of the fund and capital gains upon a transfer of fund units. Investors in non-qualifying AIF are, in principle, taxed in accordance with the fund vehicle's legal structure. Resident investors are taxed on their worldwide income, including income from AIF, whereas non-resident investors are only taxable in Germany with regard to their German source income as determined in accordance with German domestic law and further qualified by applicable treaty law.

In cases in which a fund is structured as a partnership that is neither engaged in trade or business nor constitutes a deemed business entity, the fund vehicle itself is tax transparent, ie, it is not subject to German income tax or local trade tax and the allocable share of the partnership's income is taxed at the level of the investors, which are taxable in Germany in accordance with the general rules of German income tax law.

Whether a partnership is engaged in a trade or business is an inherently factual issue depending on all facts and circumstances. Courts and tax authorities have developed certain criteria for different types of investments (such as private equity, real estate or securities) that can serve as indicators of business or non-business activity, as the case may be.

Even if a partnership is not engaged in trade or business, it can still be a business partnership according to the deemed business concept. Under this concept, a limited partnership is deemed to be in business regardless of the nature of its activities, and solely due to its legal structure, if its general partner is a corporation and only the corporate general partner or persons who are not partners are authorised to manage the affairs of the limited partnership. A limited partnership, however, is not deemed to be in business if at least one of its general partners is not a corporation or management authority has been vested under the partnership agreement in a limited partner acting in that capacity. In order to avoid a deemed business designation of a limited partnership, it is usually necessary to also vest management rights in a limited partner (the 'designated limited partner').

Investors of non-qualifying AIF treated as corporations do not qualify for the so-called partial income taxation and/or the tax exemption for dividends and capital gains, unless the income of the AIF is subject to tax (in sufficient degree) at the AIF level.

2.6. Customary or common terms

The terms of AIF primarily depend on the investment strategy of each respective AIF. For example, AIF in developed fund jurisdictions use similar fund terms, eg, most commonly 10 years with one or more possible one-year extensions for private equity funds or between 20 and 30 years for infrastructure funds. Usually, the fund term is divided into an investment and a divestment period. During the investment period, which usually ends either when half of the fund term has elapsed or the committed capital has been invested, the fund is allowed to draw capital from investors and acquire portfolio assets in accordance with the fund's investment strategy. After the investment period, investments are mainly limited to follow-on investments (ie, investments in portfolio companies in which the fund already holds a share).

In order to align the sponsors' and the investors' interests, an obligatory management team capital commitment to the fund of between 1 and 2 per cent of the aggregate capital commitments is customary.

Remuneration arrangements normally include fixed compensation (often referred to as a management fee) and variable compensation (carried interest). During the investment period, the fixed compensation is normally calculated as a percentage of the aggregate capital commitments of the fund. At the end of the investment period, it is reduced either by applying the same percentage on the amount of invested capital or by reducing the applicable percentage. Whereas this compensation drop-down is an internationally recognised standard in the private equity world, terms used in German funds can exhibit specific features due to the value added tax (VAT) treatment of management fees under German law. It has become a standard feature of certain AIF that the management fee forms part of the allocable share of the fund's gain and thus is free of VAT. The German tax authorities have challenged this concept

Germany

on the grounds that a management fee that is paid irrespective of the fund's gain or loss was, for VAT purposes, a fee owed for services rendered by the management company to the fund. Accordingly, German fund terms should either contain provisions whereby the management fee is structured as a genuine part of the fund's gain, which is only owed if the fund generates sufficient gain, or which determine whether the fund or the management company has to bear the VAT burden.

Terms of German funds can be distinguished according to the specific market segment to which they belong to rather than to the law to which they are subject. However, funds established as partnerships and marketed in Germany (irrespective of whether they are established under German law or any other law) must be subject to certain restrictions regarding their investment strategy in order to be treated as non-business entities under German income tax law. Under an administrative pronouncement on the taxation of venture capital and private equity funds issued by the German Federal Ministry of Finance in 2003, certain criteria must be observed, which generally indicate that a private equity fund is not engaged in business activities from a German tax perspective. The following criteria are an extract of the criteria set forth in the administrative pronouncement:

- Investments are generally financed with equity rather than debt. However, funds using government subsidies structured as a loan, as well as short-term loans against outstanding capital calls, used to bridge the notice period for capital contributions are permitted.
- In general, funds must not provide collateral for indebtedness of portfolio companies. As an exception, providing collateral is permitted if the portfolio company's indebtedness is connected with the unpaid balance of the investors' capital commitments to the fund.
- The partnership may not 'trade' with investments. Proceeds realised by a fund upon the sale or other disposition of investments shall not be reinvested, but shall be distributed. As exceptions to this general concept, proceeds up to the amount of which management fees and other expenses have been funded out of capital contributions can be reinvested in investments, and proceeds up to an amount of 20 per cent of the total committed capital of a fund can be reinvested in portfolio companies in which the partnership already holds an investment (follow-on investments).
- Investments should be held 'long-term', ie, for a 'weighted' average holding period of three to five years.
- A fund and its agents or representatives should not engage in the day-to-day management of the portfolio companies. This does not affect the possibility of monitoring the investments through the exercise of shareholder rights, including the right to appoint members of the board of directors of the portfolio companies as non-executive directors. As a rule, the definition of a catalogue of management actions requiring board approval is permitted, unless the catalogue has the effect that the management board of the portfolio company does not retain an actual scope to exercise entrepreneurial discretion.

3. RETAIL FUNDS

3.1. Common structures

Open-ended retail funds may, in general, be organised as contractual funds or as investment companies with variable capital, whereas open-ended investment limited partnerships cannot be used for retail funds. Closed-ended retail funds may be organised as investment companies with fixed capital or closed-ended investment limited partnerships. Whereas investors in specialised AIF established as closed-ended investment limited partnerships must become limited partners, investors in a retail closed-ended investment limited partnership can also participate as trustors with a trustee limited partner (*Treuhandkommanditist*) actually holding a limited partner interest.

3.2. Regulatory framework

As for specialised funds, the main source of regulatory legislation that applies to retail funds is the GCIA. As a general rule, the terms of retail funds need to be approved by BaFin and managers of retail funds must obtain a license from BaFin. Managers of retail funds may be exempt from the license requirement if the assets under management do not exceed EUR 100 million.

3.3. Operational requirements

Under the GCIA, only certain types of investment funds subject to restrictions regarding their investment policy can be established, managed and distributed in Germany, if the shares in such funds are to be acquired by retail investors (ie, all investors that do not qualify as professional investors or semi-professional investors).

Types of open-ended retail funds include UCITS, the rules for which have been harmonised within the European Union since 1985, as well as the following types of retail AIF:
- mixed investment funds (*gemischte Investmentvermögen*);
- other investment funds (*sonstige Investmentvermögen*);
- funds of hedge funds (*Dach-Hedgefonds*); and
- open-ended real estate funds (*Immobilien-Sondervermögen*).

Whereas the aforementioned types of open-ended real estate funds are subject in principle to similar rules as the corresponding types under the prior investment funds legislation, certain substantial conditions have changed. Among the more significant changes is the fact that participation in businesses that do not qualify as securities are no longer eligible for 'other investment funds'. This is crucial since other investment funds have so far been one of the broadly available types of open-ended investment funds that can allocate at least a small portion of their portfolio to shares of closed-ended funds. However, from a regulatory point of view, it should still be possible for 'other investment funds' to invest in closed-ended AIF, the shares of which qualify as securities.

As for closed-ended funds, the GCIA provides a uniform set of rules for all retail funds (*geschlossene inländische Publikums* (AIF)). This type of fund can acquire certain types of assets, including real assets (as further specified in the law, including real estate, ships, planes, renewable energy facilities, railway vehicles, electric vehicles, containers and infrastructure for the

Germany

aforementioned assets), participation in certain PPP infrastructure projects, certain participations (including those in non-listed businesses), units in other retail AIF or specialised closed-ended AIF. Closed-ended retail AIF must invest in accordance with the principle of risk diversification, except in cases in which no retail investors invest that do not invest at least EUR 20,000 in the fund (in addition to further requirements). However, this exception does not apply to private equity funds.

3.4. Marketing the fund
As the AIFMD does not provide an EU passport for distribution to retail investors, retail funds can only be provided with a passport within the EU to the extent that they are UCITS. The marketing of AIF to retail investors is subject to domestic notification with BaFin. Under the draft GCIA, marketing material, including the prospectus and KID, is required for AIF that are marketed to retail investors. The material needs to be filed with BaFin before marketing activities may begin.

3.5. Taxation
The AIFM Tax Adaption Act provides uniform rules for all UCITS and AIF, both specialised and retail AIF. Whereas the rules described above for (specialised) AIF also apply to retail funds, it seems to be an accurate expectation that the portion of open-ended retail funds qualifying for 'investment fund' taxation under the revised German Investment Funds Tax Act will be larger than for specialised AIF. Closed-ended funds, however, will always be treated as non-qualifying funds, their tax treatment thus solely depends on each fund vehicle's legal format.

3.6. Customary or common terms
There is a large spectrum of possible terms of retail funds, depending on the type of investments pursued by the fund and the legal and regulatory form of the fund. GCIA provides minimum requirements applicable to all fund types and more specific rules for each fund type.

4. PROPOSED CHANGES AND DEVELOPEMENTS
Whereas the AIFMD is still in the process of being transposed to domestic law in each affected jurisdiction, and whereas legislators, regulators, tax authorities and market participants have to substantiate, digest and/or implement the new framework driven by AIFMD and corresponding outstanding level 2 measures, the next reforms, such as UCITS V and VI, are just around the corner. Moreover, notwithstanding the reform introduced through the AIFM Tax Adjustment Act, the German system of investment fund taxation is still under review. Whereas no further significant changes should be expected before the elections for the German federal parliament, there are plans on the side of both the political world and the tax administration to introduce a major reform which would basically further limit the tax transparency of investment funds for German income tax purposes.

Gibraltar

Melo Triay, Robert Vasquez, Jay J. Gomez & Javier E. Triay
Triay & Triay

1. MARKET OVERVIEW

Gibraltar is a British Overseas Territory located at the southernmost tip of Spain, with a legal system which is widely based on that of England and Wales, implementing all EU directives (such as the UCITS and the AIFM directives) by virtue of its EU membership since 1973.

Gibraltar is self-governing with parliamentary elections held every four years. The elected parliament assumes responsibility for all aspects of running the territory including taxation, health, education and policing. Gibraltar is self financing and the UK's remit is limited to defence and foreign policy. However, as a British Dependant Overseas Territory, Gibraltar maintains very strong links with the United Kingdom and whilst most of the population is bilingual, the business language is English, the currency is sterling and schools operate to UK standards and curriculum.

The current Government was elected into power in December 2011, with a firm manifesto commitment to drive forward the financial services sector. In particular the Government pledged to work with the professionals in the finance industry to make Gibraltar one of Europe's premier jurisdictions for the establishment of fund managers and funds.

Unlike most other EU jurisdictions, Gibraltar's economy has continued to expand, with a record budget surplus and a GDP growth of 7.8 per cent being recorded in 2013, GDP per capita at £41,138 (up from 9th to 4th in the world on the IMF 2012 chart), net debt down from £303 million to £291 million and cash reserves quadrupled in 12 months.

Primarily as a result of its good regulation, transparency, an approachable regulator and high quality service providers, Gibraltar has historically been very well recognised in the online gaming and insurance industries and as a global finance centre since the 1990s. However, Gibraltar was not, until 2005, known as a funds jurisdiction. The birth of the Experienced Investor Fund (EIF) Regulations in 2005 coupled with an efficient tax regime and good regulation within the EU framework has positioned Gibraltar as the finance centre of choice for those looking to re-domicile, or establish, a fund within a European jurisdiction. Gibraltar now has a solid position within the investment funds arena, whilst maintaining competitiveness amongst the more traditional EU jurisdictions.

The Gibraltar Financial Services Commission (FSC) regulates Gibraltar's finance sector, including the investment funds industry. The size of the jurisdiction enables the FSC to understand and supervise the finance industry in a pragmatic manner in the fulfilment of its responsibilities to protect the public, reduce systematic risk and protect the reputation of Gibraltar. In its 2012 annual report the FSC reiterated that its aim is to enable that regulation is delivered in a way which is conducive to and encourages financial services business in Gibraltar. In 2001 the IMF noted that Gibraltar's regulator, the FSC, 'carries out its duties diligently and has an intimate knowledge of institutions under its supervision. The results of our assessments indicated that supervision is generally effective and thorough and that Gibraltar ranks as a well-developed supervisor.' The IMF again endorsed Gibraltar's robust regulatory environment and anti-money laundering regime in 2007, concluding that the 'Gibraltar authorities are concerned with protecting the reputation and integrity of Gibraltar as a financial centre, and are cognizant of the importance of adopting and applying international regulatory standards and best supervisory practices. Gibraltar has a good reputation internationally for co-operation and information sharing.' Since these reports the FSC has continued to adhere to international standards in the provision of financial services regulation in an effective and efficient manner in order to protect the public from financial loss and enhance Gibraltar's reputation as a quality finance centre.

In order to cater for Gibraltar's attractiveness as a jurisdiction, since 1996, foreign companies have been able to move their seat of registration to Gibraltar, allowing for the uninterrupted continuity of asset ownership without triggering any exit charges. The process offers a swift, inexpensive and efficient re-domiciliation. The trouble-free re-domiciliation process and close relationship with the regulator that a small jurisdiction can offer, makes Gibraltar the perfect EU setting for funds wishing to re-domicile into the EU and become AIFMD compliant whilst benefiting from the Mediterranean lifestyle.

2. ALTERNATIVE INVESTMENT FUNDS
2.1. Common structures
Following the success of the Experienced Investor Fund Regulations in 2005, the laws governing the establishment of Experienced Investor Funds (EIF) were amended in April 2012. The amendments sought to address the issues which had led to the 2008 financial crisis (which in any event only minimally affected Gibraltar) and thus now requires funds to provide more expansive details on the fund's activities, processes, subscriptions, redemptions and restrictions.

EIFs and private schemes (also known as private funds) are the structures of choice when setting up Gibraltar alternative investment funds. Both the EIF and the private scheme are collective investment schemes which sit outside of the retail environment. In the case of the EIF, it is targeted at investors with sufficient experience, knowledge and understanding of the investments they choose to make and its associated risks. In the case of a private scheme, it is perhaps perceived as the entry-level fund into the industry and is often used when, for example, an investor is backed by a few close friends, a fund is required for the pooling of employee investments, as a feeder system or in particular where an investor has some initial seed capital and is keen to establish a trading record within a collective investment scheme at an absolute minimum expense ratio.

Gibraltar

Historically, these types of funds were frequently established in offshore jurisdictions such as the British Virgin Islands, the Cayman Islands and Mauritius. These jurisdictions were perceived to offer relatively less burdensome supervision as well as offshore tax advantages. The financial crisis has accelerated the enforcement of international cooperation in the cross jurisdictional supervision of investment products for the protection of consumers and the ever growing requirements for fiscal transparency. As a result the perceived advantages of going offshore have disappeared and most fund managers are now seeking to establish themselves within the EU. Additionally the implementation of AIFMD which will provide those domiciled and authorised in the EU with various advantages over the non-EU domiciled investment funds and managers has had its impact too.

2.2. Regulatory framework and operational requirements
Experienced Investor Funds and Private Schemes

An EIF is a collective investment scheme which is established under the Financial Services (Collective Investment Schemes) Act 2011 (the CIS Act) and the Financial (Experienced Investor Funds) Regulations 2012 (the EIF Regulations), and is regulated by the FSC.

A Private Scheme is a collective investment scheme established under the CIS Act and the Financial Services (Collective Investment Schemes) Regulations 2011 which up until now has not been regulated by the FSC but with the advent of the AIFMD now falls within the realms of such legislation as further explained below.

EIFs and Private Schemes can be established using a variety of legal entities – a private limited liability company, a public limited liability company, a protected cell company (PCC), a limited partnership, a unit trust and any form of legal entity established in any EEA state. The most commonly used vehicle is the PCC incorporated under the Protected Cell Companies Act 2001 or the private limited liability company incorporated under the Companies Act 1930. It is however worth noting that a Gibraltar private limited liability company established as an EIF is not restricted to a maximum of fifty participants. The use of the PCC as a Private Scheme is limited and its use, for this purpose, should be explored first with the Gibraltar Finance Centre Director.

A PCC is a company which can segregate its assets and liabilities into cells which are statutorily protected and are remote from each other in the event of insolvency. This provides a useful vehicle for the segregation of assets and liabilities of a sub-fund from other sub-funds under the umbrella of an EIF or Private Scheme. This has become an increasingly popular entity offering investors the opportunity to split their investment between different strategies whilst complying with any relevant overall minimum investment thresholds. It also assists with the marketing of related funds under a single banner and provides a fast and cost effective way of launching new independent funds once the general structure is in place.

Under Gibraltar law the assets and liabilities of a cell of a company compliant with the PCC Act will be protected against those of another cell. Whilst such segregation is recognised under the law of Gibraltar, it may not be recognised in other jurisdictions in which the fund's assets, or the assets of a cell of the fund, may be located. Therefore, it is important to form separate special purpose vehicles below each cell of a PCC to ensure segregation of any assets and liabilities held by any cell outside of Gibraltar.

There has been recent interest in the use of the Gibraltar limited partnership as a vehicle for the establishment of EIFs. This is primarily as a result of their commercial flexibility and tax transparency. Whilst a Gibraltar limited partnership is comparable to the UK equivalent, there are some key differences. The Gibraltar limited partnership has perpetual succession and separate legal personality.

Although a unit trust is not considered as having separate legal personality, there has also been interest recently in its use as a vehicle for Gibraltar funds as a result of the tax transparency of the trust vehicle. This tax transparency enables investors to take advantage of fiscal arrangements between their jurisdiction of residence and the jurisdiction of the investments.

The 2005 experienced investor fund regulations permitted an exceptionally fast and user-friendly form of establishing and authorising EIFs under the deemed authorisation route, where once a qualifying entity fulfilled certain requirements and resolved to become an EIF, it was deemed to be authorised by the FSC and could commence to undertake investment activities. This format was left unchanged under the EIF Regulations and now provides an efficient and unique route to market for small self-managed EIFs in accordance with AIFMD.

Private Schemes are also exceptionally fast to set-up and can commence investment activity upon resolving to operate as a Private Scheme although the provisions of the AIFMD will apply. The Private Scheme is a versatile structure for the purposes of small, self-managed funds. Following a year of trading as a Private Scheme it would be possible to remarket and convert a Private Scheme to an EIF and make it available to a wider investor pool that would require the higher form of regulatory supervision that is provided by an EIF. The use of the Private Scheme in Gibraltar in this way highlights the flexibility of the Rock's investment fund industry and its ability to find solutions to fit the needs of all investment opportunities.

Gibraltar implemented the AIFMD on 22 July 2013 by virtue of the Financial Services (Alternative Investment Fund Managers) Regulations 2013 (the AIFM Regulations). Most EIFs and Private Schemes in Gibraltar are self-managed and fall, and will continue to fall, within the *de minimus* thresholds under the AIFMD. Therefore unless those small AIFMs decide to opt into the AIFMD and obtain full AIFM authorisation, they will continue to be able to launch as an EIF and a Private Scheme as aforementioned and commence investment activity almost immediately. This provided of course that they notify the FSC as a small AIFM under the AIFM Regulations (in the case of EIFs, apart from the notification under the EIF Regulations).

On the other hand and again bearing in mind that most EIFs are self-managed, the EIF Regulations also provide an alternative route of authorisation for entities wishing to be registered with the FSC before launch. This route will be particularly effective for entities being in-scope AIFMs or small AIFMs wishing to opt in and obtain authorisation under the AIFM Regulations.

2.3. Marketing the fund

Investment in EIFs is open to anyone who fulfils the qualification requirements of the definition of experienced investor as set out in the EIF Regulations. There are no qualification requirements for investment in Private Schemes albeit that Private Schemes cannot be listed on a stock exchange and are not permitted to have more than 50 participants.

Where an EIF or Private Scheme is set up in the form of a private limited liability company or PCC, the investor will subscribe for shares in the fund and limited liability therefore applies. Typically those shares will take the form of Participating Shares which ordinarily give the investor very limited voting rights. Those limited rights usually relate to fundamental changes to the fund's objective/strategy or investment restrictions. The investor, therefore, has no say on the day-to-day management of the fund's investments. Management of the fund is typically vested in the fund manager or if internally managed, the board of directors, who will control the ordinary shares of the fund. It is however worth noting that ordinarily the ordinary shares carry no rights to participate in any profits of the fund.

In the case of an EIF or Private Scheme set up as a unit trust the vehicle is created by trust deed between the manager of the fund and the trustee of the scheme. Thus the trust deed is the constituting document of the unit trust and is the agreement that the trustee will hold all the assets of the fund on terms of the trust deed. The underlying value of the assets is always directly represented by the total number of units multiplied by the unit price less the cost (Net Asset Value).

Where a limited partnership is utilised as the vehicle of choice for the EIF or Private Scheme, an investor would typically participate as a limited partner, whereas the general partner would usually be a Gibraltar limited liability company with responsibility for managing the investments of the fund.

An experienced investor includes:
- an investor who has a current aggregate of EUR 100,000 invested in one or more EIFs;
- an investor who invests a minimum of EUR 50,000 in an EIF and who has been advised by a professional advisor to invest in the EIF;
- an investor whose ordinary business or professional activity includes, acquiring, underwriting, managing, holding or disposing of investments, whether as principal or agent, or the giving of advice concerning investments;
- an investor who has net assets in excess of EUR 1,000,000 (or in the case of an individual together with his/her spouse, excluding that person's principal place of residence);
- an investor who is a professional client, as defined under the Financial Services (Markets in Financial Instruments) Act 2006; or
- an investor in an EIF that has re-domiciled to Gibraltar where the FSC has permitted the inclusion of such investor either in respect of a specific

EIF or generally in respect of funds or categories of funds from a certain jurisdiction.

It should however be noted that an EIF or Private Scheme which is in-scope for the purposes of the AIFM Regulations or which wishes to opt in to AIFMD or an EIF or Private Scheme which is managed by an EU AIFM will be bound by the requirement under AIFM that it markets the units or shares in the fund to professional investors (as defined under the Financial Services (Markets in Financial Instruments) Act 2006) only. However, there is no restriction in Gibraltar on the marketing of units or shares of a fund (whether marketed on a domestic or cross border basis) to retail investors (ie, investors not being professional investors) provided of course that for the purposes of an EIF, the retail investor falls within the remit of the EIF Regulations and the units or shares are promoted on the basis of private placement. In relation to Private Schemes, it is also important to note that there are specific restrictions on its promotion:

- to an identifiable category of people to whom it is directly offered by the offeror or its appointed agent;
- the members of that category have sufficient information to reasonably evaluate the offer;
- the number of people to whom the offer is made is not more than fifty; and
- that the scheme will remain as a Private Scheme for at least one year from the date that the offer was made.

There is no requirement for the promoters of an EIF or a Private Scheme to be licensed. EIFs and Private Schemes can either be managed by a third party fund manager (the AIFM Regulations would apply) or internally managed by the fund's board of directors. Directors who manage a Private Scheme do not require any specific personal licensing. An EIF is required to have two Gibraltar resident licensed directors (EIF Directors) being licensed under the Financial Services (Investment and Fiduciary Services) Act 1989. The role of the EIF Directors is to ensure that the fund is managed in accordance with the EIF Regulations and assist in anchoring the management and control of the fund in Gibraltar.

With regards to externally managed EIFs/Private Schemes or those which are internally managed (by virtue of an investment director with responsibility for investment decisions) typically the preferred vehicle for such investment manager/director is the private limited liability company incorporated in accordance with the Companies Act 1930. Depending on the services provided by such external manager to the EIF or Private Scheme, they may require licensing under the CIS Act and/or the Financial Services (Markets in Financial Instruments) Act 2006 and/or the Financial Services (Investment and Fiduciary Services) Act 1989 or the AIFM Regulations. Applications for licensing are made to the FSC as the supervisory and regulatory body under the Acts. The FSC's service level standards provide that they will attempt to acknowledge and raise any initial queries to a complete application no later than 8 weeks from its receipt and subject to prompt receipt of all required information, to determine a complete application no later than 18 weeks after its receipt. Application time periods will vary but typically are in the region of three months from submission of a complete application but this is dependent on the quality of the application, the entity and individuals behind the entity having appropriate backgrounds and experience, the initial application clearly explaining all processes (ie, business plan, procedures manuals, etc) and any concerns/queries raised by the FSC being dealt with in a timely manner.

With regards to the internally managed EIF/Private Scheme, an investment director of such a fund would not typically require licensing on the basis that the activities it undertakes in relation to such fund are not being provided by way of business to third parties. Under the AIFM Regulations, an internally managed fund may however require licensing if it does not fall within the *de minimus* thresholds of the AIFM Regulations.

Whilst under the EIF Regulations the requirement that all EIFs must have an administrator still stands, the restriction on EIF administrators being authorised by the FSC and having a physical presence in Gibraltar has been altered. This change allows an administrator that is established in the EEA or in a jurisdiction that is in the opinion of the FSC regulated under equivalent provisions to Gibraltar. An administrator permitted to undertake business in Gibraltar but not being authorised by the FSC and not having a physical presence in Gibraltar must appoint an agent for service in Gibraltar. Primarily the purpose of this change is to allow for significantly larger funds to re-domicile to Gibraltar (ie, into the EU) whilst their administrator may remain in another jurisdiction.

EIF and Private Schemes are extremely flexible structures, particularly because they are not restricted on the types of activity or investments they choose to make, provided they are clearly identified within the offer document. Notwithstanding this, the FSC has in the past expressed concern in relation to EIFs looking to operate within, for example, the pay-day-lending industry and the negative impact that could have on Gibraltar as a financial services jurisdiction. Therefore where an EIF is not going to operate a vanilla strategy, it is worth discussing any potential plans with the FSC before commencing investment activities.

Small self-managed EIFs and Private Schemes, ie, internally managed funds not being in-scope for the purposes of authorisation under the AIFM Regulations, are not required to comply with the requirements of the AIFM Regulations, such as the depositary requirement. However, all EIFs are required to appoint a depositary under the EIF Regulations except where the EIF is closed ended or where the FSC makes a determination to that effect. Therefore a small self-managed EIF which is closed ended may appoint a banker for cash transactions. Whilst an open ended small self-managed EIF (which has not opted into the AIFMD) is required to appoint a depositary, the depositary will not be subject to the obligations under the AIFM Regulations. Conversely, in-scope EIFs and Private Schemes for the purposes of the AIFM Regulations or small internally managed EIFs and Private Schemes which opt in to the AIFMD regime require a depositary as per the AIFM Regulations and the depositary is required to be situated within the same jurisdiction as the fund, ie, Gibraltar. However, in order to ensure a smooth transition for such funds, the AIFM Regulations provide that they may utilise depositaries in other EU member states until 22 July 2017.

An EIF is required to undergo an annual audit by an auditor approved under the Financial Services (Auditors) Act. It is then required to submit its audited accounts to the FSC within six months of its year-end, together with a form containing the fund's general compliance and statistical information. EIFs are also required to notify the FSC of any regulatory breaches and of material changes to the EIF within twenty business days. EIFs and Private Schemes established as corporate entities are required to file an annual return and accounts (which typically takes the form of an abridged balance sheet provided the entity qualifies as a small company under the Companies (Accounts) Act 1999) each year at Companies House. EIFs and Private Schemes subject to the AIFM Regulations will be required to comply with the reporting obligations therein.

An EIF is required to produce an offer document (also known as a private placement memorandum or PPM). The PPM must contain such information as would reasonably be required and expected by participants, and potential participants, and their professional advisors for the purposes of making an informed judgement about the merits of participating in the EIF and the extent of the risks of participating in the EIF. Such requirements are set out in the EIF Regulations and include, *inter alia*, an explanation of the structure and details of the EIF, the names and addresses of the individuals involved, details of existing and/or potential conflicts of interest, details of the investment objective and strategy, including the EIF's approach to borrowing and gearing, the term of the fund, redemption interests and the maximum liquidity of the fund, details of every person who undertakes any activity in relation to the fund and the scope of those activities, the remuneration of each of those parties, including performance fees where applicable, etc. Whilst there are no requirements as to the content of a Private Scheme's offer document, generally they contain the same provisions as that of an EIF. Furthermore, EIFs and Private Schemes subject to the AIFM Regulations will be required to comply with the requirements therein, including, *inter alia*, delegation, operation conditions such as remuneration, risk management, liquidity management, etc.

Provided a self-managed EIF or Private Scheme (which falls within *de minimus* thresholds of the AIFM Regulations) complies with the laws of each jurisdiction in which it promotes the shares or units of the fund, it may for the time being continue to do so on the basis of private placement. However, it is envisaged that with time it will become harder to promote funds via private placement. Internally managed small EIFs may be promoted by the board of directors of the fund or by promoters appointed by the fund provided that they are marketed in accordance with the laws of each jurisdiction and only to experienced investors.

Inscope AIFMs and EIFs/Private Schemes managed by AIFMs will be able to promote or in the case of Private Funds, only via a private placement, the shares or units of the fund within the EU by virtue of the passporting provisions under the AIFM Regulations. As aforementioned they may be marketed to professional investors (as defined within the Financial Services (Markets in Financial Instruments) Act 2006) within the EU.

2.4. Taxation

Perhaps one of the factors that make Gibraltar an attractive jurisdiction within Europe is its low corporate and personal tax regimes in comparison to other EU jurisdictions. On 1 January 2011 the Income Tax Act 2010 (the IT Act) came into force. The IT Act ended the distinction between offshore and onshore business. On 24 June 2013 it was announced that the European Council of Economic and Finance Ministers of the 27 EU Members States (ECOFIN) endorsed Gibraltar's Income Tax Act 2010 as being compliant with the EU Code of Conduct for business taxation. This is the first time that Gibraltar's tax system has been fully endorsed by both ECOFIN and the Code of Conduct Group (which is a group formed of the tax authorities of the 27 EU member states and chaired by the EU commission). These approvals mark a major milestone in the transformation of Gibraltar as a mainstream and compliant tax jurisdiction.

Firstly, there is no capital gains tax, wealth tax, inheritance tax, VAT or estate duty in Gibraltar. The only relevant tax, income tax is levied on a territorial source basis under the 'accrued in' or 'derived from' Gibraltar principle. Whilst Gibraltar does not at the moment have any bilateral double tax treaties in place with other countries, Her Majesty's Government of Gibraltar has recently confirmed that it is actively looking to enter into double taxation treaties.

In general, all companies are taxed on profits accruing in or derived from Gibraltar, thereby preserving the territorial basis of taxation. In the case of companies licensed and regulated under Gibraltar law, the activities which give rise to profits are deemed to take place in Gibraltar (with the exception of profits generated by overseas branches or permanent establishments). Furthermore, a company is considered to be ordinarily resident in Gibraltar if the management and control of the company is exercised from Gibraltar. From 1 January 2011, companies are generally chargeable on taxable profits at the rate of 10 per cent. This is an attractive rate of corporation tax for alternative investment fund managers looking to relocate within the EU who could immediately benefit from the 10 per cent rate upon coming to Gibraltar.

The question of a fund's liability to pay tax in Gibraltar can be confirmed with the Commissioner of Income Tax in advance. It is therefore almost always advisable to obtain such confirmation before the commencement of investment activities. Generally a properly structured fund that does not have income accruing in or deriving from Gibraltar will not have a liability to pay tax.

There is no charge to tax on the receipt by a Gibraltar company of dividends from any other company regardless of its place of incorporation. It is also important to note that Gibraltar funds can benefit from the Parent Subsidiary Directive (PSD). The PSD provides for no withholding tax on dividends payable by a subsidiary in an EU Member State to a Gibraltar parent company. This is particularly advantageous when used in the context of EU investments or when an EU special purpose vehicle is utilised by a Gibraltar fund.

Personal taxation is also comparably low to other EU jurisdictions. Individuals are also taxed on income accrued in or derived from or received in Gibraltar. Gibraltar has a dual tax system under which a taxpayer is free to elect between an allowances based system and a gross income based system. The Commissioner of Income Tax will automatically tax the individual on the basis of the system that produces the most beneficial rate for the tax payer. Rates under the gross income based system are split between gross income of less than GBP 25,000 and gross income exceeding that amount. The rate on income under the GBP 25,000 is 6 per cent on the first GBP 10,000, 20 per cent between GBP 10,001 to GBP 17,000 and 28 per cent on the balance. The rates on gross income exceeding GBP 25,000 start at 16 per cent and peak at 28 per cent. The rates start to reduce for gross income exceeding GBP 105,000 up to a minimum of 5 per cent for income exceeding GBP 1 million. On the other hand, the allowance based system has a reduced rate of 15 per cent for the first GBP 4,000, a rate of 24 per cent for the next GBP 12,000 and the remainder of the taxable income at 40 per cent. Although it should be noted that under the allowance based system the rates are charged on income after deduction of allowances.

High Executives Possessing Specialist Skills (or HEPSS) is a status designed for individuals who will promote and sustain economic activity of particular economic value to Gibraltar. It is therefore available, upon application to the Gibraltar Finance Centre Director, to employees of fund managers, who will earn more than GBP 100,000 per annum. The effect of HEPSS status is to limit the tax payable by such employees to under GBP 30,000 per annum.

Finally, with regards to the Gibraltar tax treatment of investors in an EIF, it is worth noting that there is no transfer tax in Gibraltar, there is no withholding tax on dividends paid, however where a company declares a dividend in favour of a Gibraltar resident individual or company, it must submit a return of dividends and a redemption of a participation in a Gibraltar fund, if there is a gain, it is treated as a capital gain and there is no capital gains tax in Gibraltar. Note however, that an individual investor may be subject to taxation under the laws of his/her jurisdiction of residence or citizenship.

Undoubtedly, the fast evolving EU financial services industry, the requirement to remain compliant and the need to adhere to foreign legislation such as the United States Foreign Account Tax Compliance Act (FATCA) and FATCA-type legislation requires establishment within a well established and tax transparent EU jurisdiction. It is worth noting that the Government of Gibraltar has already made a stern commitment to entering into FATCA and FATCA-type inter-governmental exchange agreements which will overcome the local legal impediments associated with compliance of the same. Coupled with a low corporate tax rate, low personal taxation, the ability for funds to become tax exempt, efficient EU regulation and a Mediterranean lifestyle, it is understandable why so many entities and individuals are deciding to make Gibraltar their jurisdiction of choice within the EU.

3. RETAIL FUNDS
3.1. Common structures
As may have been explained within other chapters, undertakings for collective investment in transferable securities (or UCITS) are open-ended collective investment schemes which comply with Directive 2009/65/EC (or UCITS IV).

The UCITS IV directive recast and replaced Directive 85/611/EEC (or UCITS I) and made significant changes to the UCITS regime. The aim of UCITS I was to create a single market for open-ended retail investment funds, while ensuring a high level of protection for those retail investors. As a result of UCITS I Member States implemented harmonised rules regulating the authorisation, supervision, structure and activities of funds incorporated in Member States, along with harmonised rules about the information they were required to make available to retail investors. However, certain perceived problems with UCITS I led to the adoption of two further directives and finally UCITS IV.

3.2. Regulatory framework
As detailed above under the heading of Alternative Investment Funds, the CIS Act regulates the establishment, promotion and operation of collective investment schemes in Gibraltar. Additionally, by virtue of the CIS Act, UCITS IV has been transposed into Gibraltar law together with other subsidiary legislation governing the operation and administrative provisions of UCITS IV. Gibraltar is thus fully up to date in the transposition of the Directives.

As is evident from the Alternative Investment Funds section of this chapter, whilst Gibraltar has experienced an exponential growth in the alternatives fund industry and there are a fair number of EU recognised UCITS schemes passporting into the jurisdiction, that growth has not been seen in the establishment/set-up of UCITS and/or UCITS management companies. In light of this, we limit ourselves to the main principles of UCITS IV and the benefits of establishing within the jurisdiction rather than the practicalities.

3.3. Operational requirements and marketing the fund
A Gibraltar UCITS can be established as a Gibraltar company, a Gibraltar unit trust comprising a trustee as an independent manager or as a contractual fund. A Gibraltar company is a corporate body established by constitutional documents and includes a protected cell company (please see section 2). A contractual fund is an unincorporated body established by a management company whereby the investors in the fund agree to participate and share in the assets of the fund under an investment contract. It should be noted that as a contractual fund the structure will not have separate legal personality and is therefore tax transparent. The choice of vehicles may therefore be determined by the need for tax transparency and whether investors will be able to benefit from investing in a particular vehicle in their jurisdiction of residence.

A Gibraltar UCITS structured as a company can opt to be internally managed by its board of directors. Conversely, a Gibraltar UCITS structured as a common fund must appoint an authorised UCITS management company. It is however worth noting that both forms of UCITS funds will need to appoint a Gibraltar licensed UCITS depositary.

One of the key aspects of the UCITS regime is the ability of a UCITS fund authorised in one Member State (its home Member State) to be marketed in any other Member State (the host Member State), ie, the marketing passport. A Gibraltar UCITS is therefore able to market itself in another Member State once having undergone the simplified notification procedure with the FSC in Gibraltar who will then notify the relevant jurisdictions.

Investor disclosure under UCITS IV was also altered to introduce the concept of the key investor information document (or KII or KIID). The KIID replaces the old simplified prospectus requirement contained within past UCITS legislation and is intended to provide a shorter, more concise form of disclosure that contains all the required information for investors to make an informed decision. Details of the requirements in relation to KIIDs can be found within the Financial Services (Collective Investment Schemes) (Key Investor Information) Regulations 2011.

As explained for Alternative Investment Funds and for the same reasons, Gibraltar investment funds may not be subject to tax in Gibraltar. This can be confirmed with the Commissioner of Income Tax in advance. It is therefore almost always advisable to obtain such confirmation before the commencement of investment activities.

UCITS IV also introduced the management company passport that allows UCITS management companies established in one Member State to operate a fund established in another. This right can be exercised by the management company either through the freedom to provide cross-border services or through the establishment of a branch. In order to facilitate the day-to-day functioning of such passporting right, UCITS IV harmonised the rules relating to management companies' organisational requirements, conflicts of interests procedures, conduct of business and risk management. Therefore these rules apply to all management companies, irrespective of whether they are exercising their passporting rights or not.

The decision whether or not to utilise a UCITS management company will also be determined by the capital requirements under the CIS Regulations. Whilst under the CIS Regulations a UCITS which has not appointed a management company must have an initial capital of EUR 300,000, a UCITS management company must have an initial capital of EUR 125,000 taking into account that where the value of the portfolio exceeds EUR 250 million, the management company is required to provide an additional amount of its own funds which is equal to 0.02 per cent of the amount by which the value of the portfolios of the management company exceeds the EUR 250 million but the required total of initial capital and the additional amount shall not, however, exceed EUR 10 million.

3.4. Taxation
The same tax principles would apply to UCITS management companies,

their employees and officers as to those of AIFMs (please see the Alternative Investment Funds section for further details, particularly the 10 per cent corporation tax and HEPSS status).

Finally, UCITS IV, *inter alia*, introduced the ability for a UCITS to operate as a feeder fund, ie, that a UCITS can invest the majority of its assets in another UCITS (the master fund) provided it complies with UCITS IV. UCITS feeders can therefore be used to facilitate tax efficiency and can facilitate better local distribution channels.

With the investment funds industry already being well versed in the set-up of Alternative Investment Funds and the funds industry already forming a substantial part of Gibraltar's flourishing economy, it is expected that UCITS and UCITS managers will be attracted into Gibraltar in search of a safe, secure, low-tax European jurisdiction. Gibraltar is definitely open for business.

3.5. Customary or common terms
There are none beyond those commonly used in the UK.

4. PROPOSED CHANGES AND DEVELOPMENTS
In 2012 the experienced investor fund legislation was altered to take account of the incoming AIFMD and therefore there are no drastic proposals or alterations planned for the investment funds industry. There has however been talk within the industry of amending the experienced investor fund legislation to allow for further efficiency in light of AIFMD but these proposals are still at the conceptual stage.

Guernsey

Gavin Farrell, James Haughton, Oliver Godwin
& Mandy Andrade **Mourant Ozannes**

1. MARKET OVERVIEW

The formation and operation of investment funds in Guernsey is regulated by the Guernsey Financial Services Commission (GFSC) pursuant to the Protection of Investors (Bailiwick of Guernsey) Law 1987, as amended (POI Law) and certain rules and regulations made pursuant to the POI Law. The criteria for granting an authorisation or registration of a fund and the manner in which that fund will be subject to regulatory oversight will depend on whether the fund is open or closed-ended and the type of investor targeted. The GFSC also regulates the approval, or licensing, of fund service providers in Guernsey.

Guernsey's fund industry has grown successfully and substantially over the last three decades. This has enabled Guernsey to establish a sophisticated infrastructure to promote the establishment of investment funds, which means Guernsey remains at the forefront of offshore fund centres. The growth of the investment funds industry in Guernsey is attributable in part to the policies of the Guernsey authorities and the diversity and flexibility of the regulatory and legal system. Growth is also attributable to the high-quality services available in Guernsey in relation to fund management, administration and custody. The POI Law set up a modern statutory structure for the regulation and administration of collective investment schemes in Guernsey and provides a framework for investor protection whilst retaining flexibility to adapt quickly to changing market conditions.

The GFSC quarterly statistical review to 31 March 2013 reveals that the net asset values of funds under management and administration in Guernsey totals £296.5 billion, an increase of 9.8 per cent on the previous year. Within these totals, open-ended funds increased by £3.8 billion over the quarter to £54.1 billion. The closed-ended sector increased to £137 billion, an increase of 10.6 per cent since 31 March 2012. Non-Guernsey schemes, for which some aspect of management, administration or custody is carried out in Guernsey, increased to £105.4 billion.

It is also possible to list Guernsey funds on most exchanges including the Channel Island Stock Exchange and the London Stock Exchange (LSE) markets. A report published by Guernsey Finance as of 31 December 2012, states that Guernsey is the leading jurisdiction for company listings on the LSE and that there are considerably more Guernsey companies listed on the LSE markets than any of its close competitors. There are a total of 122 Guernsey entities listed on the LSE markets in comparison with Jersey where there are only 86 entities, Isle of Man where there are 52 entities and the

Cayman Islands where there are only 46 entities listed.

2. ALTERNATIVE INVESTMENT FUNDS
2.1 Common structures

Guernsey alternative investment funds can be structured using a variety of different vehicles including limited partnerships, limited liability companies, protected cell companies, incorporated cell companies or unit trusts.

The choice of vehicle for a Guernsey fund will usually be driven by a number of considerations including the nature of the underlying assets, taxation, market practice and investor requirements and expectations. The vehicles most often used for alternative investment funds are corporate vehicles, and limited partnerships, depending on the type of transaction and investor requirements or expectations. A summary of the main alternative investment fund vehicles used in Guernsey is set out below.

Companies

All Guernsey companies are incorporated under the Companies (Guernsey) Law 2008 (Companies Law), and are subject to that law and to their memorandum and articles of incorporation. Investors in a company will be issued shares, the terms of which will be contained in the company's memorandum and articles of incorporation. Subject to the Law and the articles, the liability of a member of a company is limited to the amount (if any), for the time being, unpaid on the shares held by the member.

All Guernsey companies have separate legal personality and are capable of suing and being sued in their own capacity. Management and control is vested in the board of directors, although investment management may be delegated to a management company. The Companies Law was implemented on 1 July 2008 with the intention of providing a flexible, competitive and leading framework for the operation of companies in Guernsey.

Protected cell companies (PCCs) and incorporated cell companies (ICCs)

PCCs and ICCs are types of companies that can be incorporated under the Companies Law. A PCC is a single legal entity made up of a core and a number of protected cells. The assets of each individual cell are only available to the creditors of that particular cell. An ICC has cells like a PCC, but in an ICC, each individual cell is an incorporated company with a separate legal personality. The incorporated cells are not subsidiaries of the ICC and cannot bind the ICC but must contract in their own individual names. Investors in a PCC or an ICC will receive shares issued in respect of a cell.

Some of the benefits of establishing a fund as a PCC or an ICC include:
- the ring-fencing of various assets of the various cells to avoid contagion;
- cost savings in areas of corporate governance and company administration;
- faster regulatory consent for new cells; and
- a variety of investment strategies in one corporate entity.

PCCs and ICCs are commonly used for funds with managers wishing to establish a number of sub-funds that have many similar or different features, including terms, investments or target investors.

Unit trusts
A unit trust is constituted by an instrument of trust, usually between the manager and the trustee and is subject to the Trusts (Guernsey) Law 2007. The assets of a unit trust are held by its trustee and are managed by the manager. Typically the manager will be a Guernsey special purpose vehicle or a subsidiary of an international fund management group which will undertake promotion of the fund. A unit trust is not a separate legal entity in itself but is based on the concept of a trustee who has legal title to the assets and who holds them on trust for the benefit of the unit holders. Investors hold units in the trust, with each unit representing an undivided fractional interest in the trust property. Compared to companies, unit trusts have more flexibility in regulating their own affairs as they see fit, within the confines of the applicable fund rules.

Limited partnerships
Limited partnerships are established under the Limited Partnerships (Guernsey) Law 1995, as amended (Limited Partnerships Law). A Guernsey limited partnership is not a legal entity in its own right (unless it elects to have legal personality and to be a body corporate) and is managed by a general partner who will ordinarily have unlimited liability for the debts of the partnership. The limited partners are issued with limited partnership interests and are not liable over and above the amounts which they have agreed to contribute to the capital of the partnership, provided that it does not do anything that would constitute conduct or management of the partnership's business.

Limited partnerships appear to be the vehicle of choice for closed-ended private equity funds. One of the main advantages of using a limited partnership is that it can be structured in a flexible manner. The main operative provisions of a limited partnership will be contained in a limited partnership agreement, which can be drafted to cater for the investment objectives of the fund and the requirements of the investors. A Guernsey limited partnership is fiscally transparent and is not assessable to Guernsey income tax. As a matter of Guernsey tax law, limited partnerships remain tax transparent whether they have elected legal personality or not.

Foundations
The Foundations (Guernsey) Law 2012 (Foundations Law) came into force with effect from 7 January 2013. A Guernsey foundation has some of the characteristics of a company (such as separate legal personality) and some of the characteristics of a trust (such as the ability to hold assets for the benefit of others). A Guernsey foundation has: a constitution made up of a charter and set of rules; a council to administer the foundation; a founder to provide the initial endowment; and, depending on the terms of the foundation, a guardian.

It is anticipated that foundations in Guernsey will principally appeal to clients from civil law jurisdictions that are uncomfortable or unfamiliar with trusts. The flexibility that is afforded by the foundations law will permit foundations to be used for a myriad of purposes ranging from the traditional private client wealth structures to commercial and finance transactions, such as being utilised by funds as orphan vehicles.

Conclusion
Guernsey's flexible regulatory regime lends itself to the establishment of alternative investment funds. It is, therefore, suitable for the establishment of hedge funds, although funds of hedge funds seem to have proved to be the most popular. Such funds tend to be established as Class B or Class Q open-ended authorised funds as non-retail open-ended structures. However, a hedge fund could also, subject to the structuring requirements, be established as a Guernsey closed-ended scheme.

Class B funds are not usually for sale to the general public and are typically established for marketing to institutions or high net worth individuals. Class Q funds are restricted to qualifying professional investors, as defined below.

2.2 Regulatory framework
The principal regulatory body responsible for regulating funds in Guernsey is the GFSC. The principal legislation governing funds in Guernsey is the POI Law. The POI Law divides Guernsey funds into two categories:
- authorised collective investment schemes (authorised funds) which can be split into the following categories:
  - closed-ended authorised funds, subject to the requirements of the Authorised Closed-Ended Investment Scheme Rules 2008 (closed-ended authorised rules);
  - Class A authorised funds, which are discussed later in the context of retail funds;
  - Class B authorised funds, subject to the requirements of The Collective Investment Schemes (Class B) Rules 1990 (Class B rules);
  - Class Q authorised funds, subject to the requirements of The Collective Investment Schemes (Qualifying Investor) Rules 1998 (Class Q rules), and
- registered collective investment schemes (each a registered fund), subject to the requirements of the Registered Collective Investment Scheme Rules 2008 (registered rules), and the Prospectus Rules 2008 (prospectus rules).

Both open-ended and closed-ended funds may be either authorised funds or registered funds. The principal difference between authorised funds and registered funds is the approval process and its timing. The administrator of a proposed authorised fund will seek a declaration of 'authorisation' from the GFSC. The application comprises a three-stage process involving the analysis of the fund documentation and principal parties by the GFSC. For registered funds, there is a fast-track application process under which the GFSC relies on the administrator's due diligence and warranties on the promoter (being the entity that introduced the fund to Guernsey and being responsible for its success, being usually the investment manager or adviser, the 'promoter') and the principal documents thereby reducing the GFSC's response time.

Funds may not be promoted directly in Guernsey although they may be offered to regulated entities in Guernsey or promoted by entities appropriately licensed under the POI Law.

Authorised funds
Closed-ended funds
Closed-ended authorised funds are subject to continuing supervision by the GFSC and the requirements of the closed-ended authorised rules. Any offer document circulated by a closed-ended authorised fund needs to contain the mandatory disclosures in the closed-ended authorised rules, which are not onerous and are market practice. The closed-ended authorised rules also contain requirements for other matters such as administration and custodian duties, related party transactions and notification obligations.

In seeking a declaration of 'authorisation' from the GFSC, the administrator must submit the appropriate forms, together with signed or certified copies of the fund's offering document and material contracts, the application fee and such other information as the GFSC may require. Applications are undertaken in three stages (outline, interim and final) and usually take between six and eight weeks. As part of the process the GFSC will review the principal documents and forms and may revert with any comments or queries. Once the points raised by the GFSC have been addressed, final form copies of the offering document and all other documentation constituting or relating to the fund are submitted. Final consent is then usually granted within 48 hours.

Open-ended funds
Class B funds
The Class B rules, made under the POI Law regulate Class B open-ended authorised funds. The Class B rules do not contain specific prescribed investment restrictions other than that the scheme property must be invested with the aim of spreading risk. There is further flexibility in that the GFSC may grant derogations from the Class B rules if it is satisfied that investor protection will not be compromised. No minimum subscription levels are prescribed. Minimum prospectus disclosure requirements apply but these are not particularly unusual or onerous.

The procedure to follow in seeking 'authorisation' from the GFSC for a Class B fund is undertaken in three stages (outline, interim and final) as describe above for authorised funds.

Class Q funds
The Class Q rules, made under the POI Law regulate Class Q open-ended authorised funds. Class Q schemes are restricted to qualifying professional investors, namely: a government local authority; public authority; trustee of a trust with net assets exceeding £2 million; company or limited partnership if it, its parent or subsidiary have net assets exceeding £2 million; or an individual who with their spouse has a minimum net worth of £500,000 or a

minimum investment per investor of $100,000. The requirements in respect of Class Q funds are similar to but less onerous than those for a Class B fund. Considerable flexibility is permitted in respect of this type of fund.

Again, the property of the scheme must be subject to a spread of risk and the criteria for this must be disclosed in the scheme's information particulars. Documentation requirements and procedure to follow when seeking authorisation from the GFSC are similar to Class B.

Qualifying investor fund (QIF)

Promoters of all authorised funds which will only be offered to professional or experienced investors, knowledgeable employees or persons willing to invest a minimum of $100,000, may take advantage of the fast-track QIF. The GFSC has released guidelines in respect of the QIF regime. An application under the QIF regime must be supported by the Guernsey administrator who must certify to the GFSC that it has performed due diligence on the promoter and the procedures for offering the scheme, including procedures for effectively restricting the offer and transfer of securities to qualifying investors, and that the requisite disclosures are made in the offering document of the fund. A QIF application is processed in three working days.

Registered funds

Registered funds, whether open or closed-ended, are subject to the registered rules and the prospectus rules, issued by GFSC. The former set out such matters as administration and custodian duties (optional for closed-ended funds) and notification requirements. The latter sets out information for inclusion in the offering document of any registered fund. Overall, the regulatory regime applying to closed-ended registered funds is similar to that applying to closed-ended authorised funds.

Registered fund applications are fast-track applications like the QIF applications described above and the GFSC relies solely on warranties supplied by the administrator on the promoter and the fund documentation. Therefore, the administrator should become involved at the earliest possible stage in order to allow it to conduct sufficient due diligence to be able to give the necessary warranties. The GFSC attaches great importance to these warranties and expects applicants to be able to demonstrate that they have documentary evidence to support the warranties. Apart from the application form, the documents that need to be submitted to the GFSC for a registered fund application are identical to those required for authorised funds. Registered funds may not be offered directly to the public in Guernsey. The 'public' for this purpose is defined as meaning any person not regulated under any of Guernsey's financial services regulatory laws.

Regulation of service providers

The GFSC also regulates Guernsey service providers to funds such as administrators, custodians and managers. The POI Law requires any person who carries out 'controlled investment business' in or from within Guernsey to obtain a licence from the GFSC. Controlled investment business includes activities such as administration, custody and administration in relation to funds. Accordingly, service providers such as administrators, custodians and investment managers/advisers (if based in Guernsey) will need to be appropriately licensed. In addition, management entities set up in Guernsey specifically to manage funds, such as the general partner of a private equity fund, will generally require a POI licence.

Often, the promoter, usually being the ultimate investment manager or adviser to a fund, is a UK entity regulated by the Financial Services Authority. Provided that the promoter does not conduct its activities in Guernsey, it should not require a licence.

The QIF and registered fund regimes are complemented by a fast-track licence application process where a Guernsey-based manager or general partner is required. The GFSC will fast-track the licence application, again with reliance on the administrator certification, within 10 business days of receipt.

2.3 Operational requirements
Designated manager
All Guernsey funds, whether closed-ended or open-ended, will require a Guernsey regulated fund administrator (designated manager), which must be licensed under the POI Law and operate, and have a place of business, in Guernsey.

Custodian
Closed-ended authorised funds and registered funds may (but are not required to) appoint a custodian. In the absence of a formal custodian, as part of the application process, the GFSC must be advised as to the arrangements for safe custody of the fund's assets. The closed-ended authorised rules and registered rules both allow for the designated manager to provide safekeeping facilities to a closed-ended fund. Where it is wished to appoint a custodian/trustee, such custodian may be domiciled outside Guernsey provided provisions are in place to ensure the assets of the closed-ended authorised fund are adequately safeguarded.

The Class B rules require the appointment of a designated custodian that is incorporated and licensed in Guernsey. The role of the designated trustee/custodian includes oversight over the designated manager. However, full separation is not required and such persons may be entities in the same group, although they may not have directors in common.

Class Q schemes, are also required to appoint a designated custodian. However, there is no oversight role for the custodian over the designated manager.

Principal manager
In relation to a Class B scheme, a 'principal manager' may also be appointed but this is now optional. A principal manager is normally a special purpose vehicle established in Guernsey by a promoter and licensed under the POI Law to have overall responsibility for management and administration of the

fund and to then delegate such functions.

Notification requirements

The closed-ended authorised rules list certain instances when immediate notifications are required to be made to the GFSC in instances where there are material changes proposed to the fund or its service providers or on the occurrence of significant events affecting the fund. The registered rules also provide certain more limited notification requirements although the designated manager must notify the GFSC in writing if there has been any change to the information contained in the application form submitted for registration of a registered fund. There are also periodic notification requirements. These include annual reports and financial statements, which the designated manager must submit to the GFSC no later than six months following the end of the annual accounting period of the fund. There is also statistical information which must be submitted by the designated manager on behalf of the fund for each quarter.

The Class B rules require that annual and interim reports and accounts must be filed with the GFSC and sent to shareholders within the specified time frames of six and four months respectively following the relevant financial period end. Statistical returns must be made on a quarterly basis to the GFSC.

In relation to a Class B fund, prior GFSC approval is required in respect of certain material changes, eg, change of investment, borrowing or hedging powers or change of manager. The Class B fund prospectus must be updated at least annually, or sooner in the case of a material change, and filed with the GFSC and the custodian before shares may be offered to investors.

Flexible approach to authorisation policy

The GFSC has issued guidance adopting a flexible approach aimed specifically towards hedge funds and prime broker and custody arrangements. This would allow a prime broker regulated in an acceptable jurisdiction and having substantial net worth to be appointed as the designated trustee/custodian. In practice the GFSC has also been willing to discuss other arrangements for custody and the safeguarding of assets in circumstances where a prime broker is to be appointed. In any event full disclosure of the arrangements and associated risks must be disclosed in the fund prospectus.

The GFSC's flexible approach to hedge funds and prime broker and custody arrangements described above in connection with Class B funds applies equally to Class Q.

Outsourcing

Subject to any restriction in the principal documents or any directions of the directors, a designated manager may outsource its functions provided any such outsourcing arrangement is in accordance with the GFSC's guidance notes on outsourcing (outsourcing guidance). The outsourcing guidance applies where functions are outsourced either to entities within the same group or to third party service providers, both within and outside Guernsey.

A designated manager cannot, however, outsource any function where it would not retain the expertise (skills and knowledge) to oversee the function. A designated manager must retain the competence and ability to be able to ensure that the delegate complies with the relevant regulatory requirements and any changes in the requirements. It is important to note that although the designated manager can outsource its functions it cannot outsource its responsibility for the performance of those functions. This means that GFSC regards the ultimate responsibility and accountability for the outsourced functions as remaining with the designated manager, including its board of directors and senior management.

The GFSC would expect to be advised at an early stage of any proposals to outsource. However, whilst it is expected that licensees communicate with the GFSC in respect of any proposals to outsource functions, it is not necessary to seek the GFSC's formal approval, or confirmation that it has no objection to such proposals.

COB rules
The Licensees (Conduct of Business) Rules 2009 (COB rules), apply to all entities licensed under the POI Law. The COB rules cover the Guernsey-based general partners or managers of funds but not funds themselves. They set out overriding principles which all licensees are expected to observe in carrying out their investment business. These are: (i) integrity; (ii) skill, care and diligence; (iii) conflicts of interest; (iv) information about customers; (v) information for customers; (vi) customer assets; (vii) market practice; (viii) financial resources; (ix) internal organisation; and (x) relations with the GFSC.

The board of a licensee must ensure that there are effective and appropriate policies, procedures and controls in place to enable the board to meet its obligations under the POI Law and the COB rules. This includes evaluating and recording the assessment of its compliance with 'Guidance on Corporate Governance in the Finance Sector in Guernsey' and retaining responsibility for outsourcing any of its functions.

The licensee has effective responsibility for compliance with the POI Law and the COB rules.

Risk
The applicable fund rules require clear disclosures of all material risks to the fund and investors, in order to enable the investor to make an informed decision as to whether or not to invest.

Borrowing restrictions
The applicable rules do not specifically impose borrowing restrictions but do require that details of the borrowing powers be disclosed in the fund documentation and in certain instances disclosure of any amounts of current borrowing or indebtedness.

Valuation and pricing
The applicable fund rules do not prescribe a method of valuation or pricing.

However, the fund documentation must disclose the valuation policy.

Insider dealing
The Company Securities (Insider Dealing) (Bailiwick of Guernsey) Law 1996 (Insider Dealing Law) is the Guernsey equivalent of the insider dealing provisions contained in the Criminal Justice Act 1993 in England and Wales.

Market abuse
Section 41(A) of the POI Law creates an offence of 'market abuse', being behaviour (whether by one person alone or by two or more persons jointly or in concert) which occurs in relation to qualifying investments traded on an applicable market and which is likely to be regarded by a regular user of that market who is aware of the behaviour as a failure on the part of the person(s) concerned to observe the standard of behaviour reasonably expected of a person in his or their position in relation to the market.

Short selling
There are no applicable regulations relating to short selling.

Money laundering
Anti-money laundering legislation such as the Criminal Justice Proceeds of Crime (Bailiwick of Guernsey) Law 1999, and the Criminal Justice (Proceeds of Crime) (Financial Services Businesses) (Bailiwick of Guernsey) Regulations 2007 (criminal justice regulations) require licensees to identify and verify the identity of investors in funds and obtain suitable records proving such identity. A licensee must, in accordance with the criminal justice regulations, appoint a money laundering officer (MRLO). The MRLO is responsible for ensuring that the licensee complies with the anti-money laundering laws and regulations in place in Guernsey.

2.4 Marketing the fund
Guernsey funds may be marketed without restriction in or from within Guernsey, including to private investors, provided that the person doing so is licensed under the POI Law to carry on the restricted activity of 'promotion'. Any marketing other than in Guernsey has to be carried out in accordance with applicable laws in the relevant jurisdiction. As regards marketing other than in Guernsey, the GFSC has negotiated with certain other jurisdictions their recognition of Guernsey Class B schemes.

If any marketing is to be carried out in or from within Guernsey by a person other than an appropriately licensed local person, that person would either need to apply for a licence under the POI Law or it would be necessary seek to rely on certain limited exemptions available.

A prospectus to be circulated in Guernsey containing an offer to the public in respect of unlisted securities must be registered with the GFSC. It must also meet the disclosure requirements set out in the prospectus rules.

Guernsey regulations do not prevent the issue of red herring offering documents prior to the grant of authorisation or the registration of a fund, providing that appropriate language describing the status of the document is included on the cover sheet. It should be noted that no monies may be raised until authorisation has been granted or the fund has been registered, as appropriate.

For marketing considerations under the EU Alternative Investment Fund Managers Directive (AIFMD), refer to Part 4 – AIFMD.

2.5 Taxation
Companies
The States of Guernsey abolished exempt status for the majority of companies with effect from 1 January 2008 and introduced a zero rate of tax for companies carrying on all but a few specified types of Guernsey-based business. However, the Administrator of Income Tax continues to allow open-ended and closed-ended funds established as companies to apply for exempt status and consequently, be treated as non-resident for tax purposes. An annual tax-exempt fee of £600 is payable. Payment of dividends or distributions by an exempt fund out of non-Guernsey-sourced income are regarded by the administrator as having their source outside Guernsey and are, therefore, payable without deduction of tax in Guernsey. A non-Guernsey resident shareholder will not be liable to Guernsey income tax unless they are carrying on business from a permanent establishment situated in Guernsey (in which case, distributions would only be taxable if they form part of the profit of the business in question).

Alternatively, if the fund chooses not to apply for tax-exempt status, it will be treated as resident in Guernsey for tax purposes and its income will be taxable, albeit at the rate of 0 per cent.

Unit trusts
The Administrator of Income Tax allows open-ended and closed-ended funds established as unit trusts to apply for exempt status on the same conditions that apply to companies.

Limited partnerships
A Guernsey limited partnership is transparent for the purposes of Guernsey tax and will not itself be liable to tax in Guernsey. Accordingly, the profits and losses of a fund established as a limited partnership will be attributed to investors according to their proportionate share.

Investors in a Guernsey limited partnership, other than residents of Guernsey, are not subject to tax in Guernsey in respect of the income of the limited partnership to the extent that any part of the investors' income is not derived from Guernsey-source income (other than bank interest). Guernsey-source income includes profits from a business carried on in Guernsey but excludes profits from international activities carried on outside of Guernsey. No deductions will be made in respect of tax and no withholding tax is payable in Guernsey in respect of investors interests in a limited partnership.

General

Guernsey

Guernsey authorities do not levy capital gains taxes (other than a dwellings profit tax on real estate, which is currently suspended), inheritance taxes, gift taxes or estate duties (other than small probate charges), nor is there any value added tax on the provision of goods or services. No stamp duty is payable in Guernsey on the issue or transfer of shares, units or interest in a fund.

EU Savings Tax Directive
Guernsey has introduced measures that are equivalent to the EU Savings Tax Directive. However, the States of Guernsey have issued guidance stating that only Class A authorised funds established in Guernsey are within the scope of the directive. Closed-ended funds, therefore, currently fall outside the scope of the directive and paying agents are not required to operate the measures on distribution to major shareholders of such funds. Amendments to the EU Savings Tax Directive are currently being considered and it is possible that Guernsey will introduce equivalent amending measures. This could lead to changes that may affect Guernsey funds.

2.6 Customary or common terms
The regulatory framework and applicable rules are non-prescriptive, allowing great flexibility.

There are no required customary or common terms under Guernsey law or regulation.

3. RETAIL FUNDS
3.1 Common structures
The only truly retail scheme in Guernsey is the Class A authorised open-ended fund. However, a Class B scheme, because of the flexibility discussed above under section 2, could be structured and classed as retail.

A Class A scheme established under the Collective Investment Schemes (Class A) Rules 2002, as amended (2002 Class A rules) is recognised under section 270 of the UK Financial Services and Markets Act 2000 by means of a designation order as being equivalent to a UK-authorised UCITS scheme. New and updated Collective Investment Schemes (Class A) Rules 2008 (2008 Class A rules), are expected to be so-recognised and will replace the 2002 Class A rules in the near future.

Class A funds' common structures are as above, corporate or unit trust schemes being the most usual. It must be noted, however, that the current UK designation order referred to above does not extend to Class A schemes that have been established as PCCs. This position is expected to change once the new designation order is made.

The 2002 Class A rules provide for a Class A scheme to be established as a 'securities fund', a 'money market fund', a 'fund of funds', a 'futures and options fund', a 'property fund', a 'warrant fund', a 'feeder fund' (although it must be noted that such a fund would not be recognised under the UK designation order referred to above) and an 'umbrella fund'.

3.2 Regulatory framework

The principal funds legislation that applies is the POI Law and the rules that may govern Class A funds (Class A rules) are:
- the 2002 Class A rules; or
- the 2008 Class A rules.

As noted above, it is Class A funds established under the 2002 Class A rules that are currently designated in the United Kingdom and therefore eligible upon completion of the registration formalities for marketing to the public in the United Kingdom.

A Class A fund is subject to a higher level of regulation than a Class B fund. The principal difference is that the Class A rules are more prescriptive on matters such as investment and borrowing powers. A scheme which is declared to be a Class A scheme is bound to comply with all of the Class A rules without exception.

3.3 Operational requirements

There continues to be a requirement for a designated manager and a designated custodian (as custodian of the Class A fund) both of whom must be registered and regulated in Guernsey. Full separation is required between such persons. They may not be entities in the same group.

3.4 Marketing the fund

The position is as described above in connection with the other types of funds.

Guernsey Class A schemes are recognised in certain countries.

3.5 Taxation

The position is as described above in connection with alternative investment funds.

3.6 Customary or common terms

The regulatory framework and applicable rules are non-prescriptive, allowing great flexibility. This also means that there are no customary or common terms or standard type Class A funds.

4. PROPOSED CHANGES AND DEVELOPMENTS

Fund regulatory regime

Proposals are currently under discussion between the GFSC and the Guernsey fund industry concerning reviews of the Class B rules and Class A rules.

In relation to Class A schemes the UK Treasury has issued, as part of its second consultation on the AIFMD, proposed changes to sections 270 and 272 of the Financial Services and Markets Act 2000 (FSMA). These are the sections of FSMA that permit non-UK schemes to be recognised as UCITS equivalent for marketing to retail investors in the United Kingdom. Currently, Guernsey Class A schemes achieve recognition via section 270, which involves UK approval of the Guernsey regulations, ie, the Class A rules whereas section 272 permits recognition on a scheme by scheme basis.

The proposal is that schemes recognised under sections 270 and 272 will be combined into a modified new section 272 regime and that the section 270 regime will fall away.

Under the proposed transitional arrangements all section 270 registered schemes will be treated from 22 July 2013 as schemes recognised under section 272. The operator of the relevant scheme will have until 21 July 2014 to provide confirmation to the Financial Conduct Authority as to whether the scheme is compliant with the requirements for UK retail schemes under the amended section 272 procedure.

AIFMD

The question needs to be asked about the potential effect and impact of AIFMD. Following full implementation of the AIFMD in July 2013, Guernsey managers of Guernsey alternative funds are able to continue marketing those funds to professional investors in EU member states pursuant to the national private placement regimes of the relevant member states. The ability to do so hinges upon the GFSC having entered into 27 regulatory co-operation agreements with the regulator in each relevant member state and Guernsey remaining a co-operative jurisdiction as by assessed the Financial Action Task Force (FATF). There are now additional disclosure and reporting obligations the manager will have to comply with under the AIFMD. These national private placement regimes are expected to remain available to non-EU funds until 2018/19.

From 2015, Guernsey managers should also be able to market their Guernsey funds throughout the EU on the basis of an EU-wide 'passport', into those EU member states with which Guernsey has entered into a tax information exchange agreement. Guernsey has already entered into such agreements with prominent member states, including the United Kingdom, Germany, France, Sweden, the Netherlands, Ireland, Norway and Denmark. The availability of this passport will depend, however, upon the manager being authorised and fully regulated under the AIFMD via an EU member state regulator 'of reference'. Full AIFMD compliance will be exacting and will involve, among other things, the appointment of a duly qualified credit institution as depositary (custodian) of the fund's assets.

From 2018/19, if EU marketing of Guernsey funds via national private placement regimes is curtailed, marketing pursuant to the AIFMD passport in full compliance with the AIFMD's authorisation requirements will be the only means of actively marketing Guernsey funds to EU investors.

From 2013, full AIFMD compliance will be required by all EU managers of EU-domiciled alternative funds targeting professional investors worldwide. It should be noted that the AIFMD does not regulate the marketing of Guernsey funds to investors outside the EU nor passive marketing, whereby investors invest in a fund on their own initiative.

As of 22 July 2013, The AIFMD (Marketing Regulations) 2013, apply to Guernsey alternative investment fund managers (AIFMs) actively marketing alternative investment funds to professional investors in the European Economic Area (EEA). Those regulations arise under the AIFMD and under new local rules in Guernsey to be adopted to accommodate the implementation of AIFMD.

Going forward, it is anticipated that Guernsey will offer a dual funds regime: one where Guernsey managers can opt in to complying with Guernsey's rules reflecting the requirements of AIFMD for certain EU marketed funds (an entirely optional arrangement at the behest of the Guernsey manager); and the second being Guernsey's current regulatory regime that will continue unchanged (subject to the marketing rules mentioned above) for all Guernsey managers not wishing to opt in and for non-EU business.

Under the new regulations, in order for an AIFM not to be considered a letter box entity and therefore no longer be considered to be the AIFM, it must not delegate substantially more tasks than it performs and must retain sufficient expertise and resources to oversee delegated tasks. Therefore, on the assumption that most Guernsey based AIFMs will delegate the portfolio management back to the onshore advisor, the AIFM needs to retain an appropriate physical presence in Guernsey in relation to risk management and overseeing its delegated tasks.

Companies Law

After a period of extensive consultation, the Companies Law is to be amended to remove problems that have arisen in practice, simplify certain procedures and provide clarity so as to maintain Guernsey's overall competitiveness.

One proposed change welcomed by those who offer fund incubator platforms based on cells of PCC's is the extension of the conversion provisions of the companies law to allow conversion of a cell of a PCC into a stand-alone company. This will allow continuity for cells which reach a critical mass of investment and then spin off as a limited company.

Further, in relation to PCCs, it is proposed that the Companies Law be amended to allow the directors of a PCC to prepare individual accounts for cells instead of consolidated accounts as currently.

Currently all companies with a share capital are required as part of their annual validation to provide detailed information regarding the company's shares as at 31 December of the previous year. Given that such data is not required for the purpose of any of Guernsey's States and is only accurate for the 31 December preceding the annual validation, this requirement is being repealed, relieving funds of a costly administrative burden.

The prescriptive provisions of the Companies Law relating to the issue of shares and the five-year authority therefore will be repealed. Directors will have a general power to issue shares to the extent permitted by the company's articles of incorporation or by ordinary resolution.

At present there is no time limit on the recovery from members of distributions made at a time when immediately after the distribution the company did not satisfy the solvency test or made without compliance with the procedure set down by the Companies Law. It is proposed that a time limit of two years is introduced to provide some certainty. It is also proposed that a 'whitewash' provision be introduced in respect of directors' personal liability under this section. This is expected to provide that no recovery from a director can be made where the company would have passed the solvency test at the time the distribution was made and would pass it at the time recovery is contemplated. This change increases certainty for directors and shareholders whilst providing appropriate protection to creditors.

A new category of 'small company' is to be introduced with legislation to relax certain requirements of the Companies Law in relation to such companies, such as the requirements relating to the content of notices of member resolutions. Small companies will be defined by reference to the number of members, so the relaxation of certain administrative procedures will be of particular relevance to funds utilising single-member special purpose vehicles to hold investments.

The draft amendments to the Companies Law are expected towards the end of this year. The amendments will make the companies law more user friendly, maintaining Guernsey's competitive advantage in the funds sector.

Limited partnerships

Certain changes are proposed to the Limited Partnerships Law including relaxing restrictions on the names that can be used by a limited partnership, allowing a limited partnership to convert between incorporated and unincorporated status and permitting amalgamations and migrations. If all the proposed changes are approved this will provide further flexibility in the use of limited partnerships.

Limited liability partnerships

For those wishing to establish a physical presence to conduct business in Guernsey, for reasons of AIFMD or otherwise, the four main structures that are currently available are: a company; a conventional partnership; a limited partnership; or a sole trader. Guernsey is intending to introduce legislation to enable the formation of a new structure to the jurisdiction, the limited liability partnership (LLP). The Guernsey LLP will offer the flexibility of a partnership with the advantages of some limited liability for members.

Being straightforward to form and maintain, having separate legal personality and having no minimum capital contribution requirements, the Guernsey LLP is intended to be internationally competitive. Those who provide professional services to investment funds now have an increased choice as to how they wish to structure their business in Guernsey.

Hong Kong

Susan Gordon & Mary Nieto **Deacons**

1. MARKET OVERVIEW

Hong Kong has for more than 20 years maintained a system which allows both domestic and overseas collective investment schemes to be authorised for public sale, as well as having a defined system to permit private placements of funds not authorised for public sale.

According to the Securities and Futures Commission (SFC), Hong Kong's securities regulator, the combined fund management business of Hong Kong achieved a record high of HK$12,587 billion at the end of 2012, representing a year-on-year growth of 39.3 per cent from 2011. On a trailing three-year average basis (2010-2012), the combined fund management business continued on an uptrend and amounted to HK$10,572 billion. There has been overall growth in different types of fund management business activities, attributable to various market players in Hong Kong during the year.

Hong Kong's robust financial regime, sound legal system and strong professional infrastructure has, over the years, attracted the major international fund management houses to establish offices in the city. Hong Kong attracts international investors as a platform for investing in the Asia Pacific region, with a particular focus on mainland China. Given the Asia Pacific region emerged relatively unscathed from the last financial turmoil, Hong Kong has benefited from significant inflow of investment capital. Hong Kong also serves as a gateway for mainland investors to invest in overseas markets and acts as a platform for mainland firms to gain exposure to global financial practices, with an increasing number of People's Republic of China (PRC)-related institutions establishing operations in Hong Kong.

Closed-ended private funds market

According to data published by Hong Kong's Trade Development Council, Hong Kong is the second largest private equity centre in Asia, trailing the Chinese mainland, and managing about 18 per cent of the total capital pool in the region. As at the end of 2011, the Asian Venture Capital Journal noted there were 355 Hong Kong-based private equity funds with capital under management amounting to more than $68 billion.

Hedge funds market

Hong Kong was one of the first jurisdictions in the world to authorise hedge funds for distribution to the public, with the first hedge funds being authorised in late November 2002. As at the end of May 2013, there were five retail hedge funds.

Authorised hedge funds enjoy certain advantages over unauthorised funds:

primarily authorisation permits advertising and sale to the public in Hong Kong. Unauthorised funds can only be marketed on a private placement basis or to professional investors. Although the SFC does not regulate hedge funds unless they are authorised for sale to the public, hedge fund managers carrying on business in Hong Kong must obtain an SFC asset management licence.

According to a recent SFC survey, Hong Kong's hedge fund industry continues to register growth: the number of hedge funds managed by SFC-licensed hedge fund managers increased from 538 in 2010 to 676 as of 30 September 2012. The total hedge fund assets under management (AUM) in Hong Kong expanded from $63.2 billion in 2010 to $87.1 billion as of 30 September 2012, an increase of 37.8 per cent. A significant portion of the AUM growth can be attributed to foreign hedge fund managers that relocated their headquarters to Hong Kong, spun off as local managers, or merged with local managers. Overseas institutional investors made up a majority of the investor base.

Retail funds market
During May 2013, there were 1,847 authorised retail unit trusts and mutual funds in Hong Kong, of which 1,324 were classified by the SFC as undertakings for collective investment in transferable securities (UCITS) funds established and managed outside Hong Kong.

The renminbi (RMB) product offering continues to expand in Hong Kong. In August 2010, the SFC authorised the first investment fund denominated in RMB, which invests in RMB fixed income assets. This was the first RMB fund offered outside mainland China. In 2011, the PRC authorities announced the Renminbi Qualified Foreign Institutional Investor (RQFII) pilot scheme that allows Hong Kong subsidiaries of qualified fund managers and securities companies to use RMB raised in Hong Kong to invest in mainland securities markets. The successful launch of the RQFII scheme not only marks another major milestone in the process of internationalisation of the RMB, but also confirms the strategic significance of Hong Kong for the mainland's financial reforms – bringing Hong Kong one step closer to becoming an offshore RMB centre. As of May 2013, the SFC authorised more than 20 RQFII funds, including four RQFII exchange traded funds (ETFs). For the first time, Hong Kong retail investors can directly use RMB to invest in the mainland equity and bond (in particular, the interbank bond) markets and have access to daily liquidity. The four RQFII ETFs can be traded in both RMB and HKD on the Stock Exchange of Hong Kong.

UCITS funds offered in Hong Kong may now offer RMB-denominated share classes on a private placement basis or to professionals only.

2. PRIVATE FUNDS – CLOSED-ENDED
2.1. Common structures
A majority of private funds in Hong Kong, including closed-ended structures, are domiciled offshore in a tax neutral jurisdiction such as the Cayman Islands, managed by offshore managers which in turn delegate the investment management functions to Hong Kong based investment advisers.

2.2. Regulatory framework

While funds themselves are not regulated in Hong Kong except when sold to the public, the managers of the funds are regulated. The SFC seeks to ensure that fund managers are fit and proper and adequately resourced. Managers must be licensed by the SFC before they can carry on business in Hong Kong.

The main statutes governing the offering of securities for sale in Hong Kong are the Securities and Futures Ordinance (SFO) and the Companies Ordinance (CO), the latter of which is relevant where the securities being offered are issued by a corporate vehicle. The SFO covers offers of securities (see section 2.4.) and the licensing framework for industry participants.

Licensing

As at 1 June 2013, there are 10 types of regulated activities stipulated by the SFO. A fund management company in Hong Kong and its investment personnel to whom a fund's discretionary portfolio management functions are delegated should normally be licensed under the SFO for type 9 regulated activity (asset management) and, depending on the business structure, type 4 regulated activity (advising on securities).

A licensed entity must have at least two responsible officers to supervise each type of regulated activity it undertakes. At least one must be resident in Hong Kong and at least one must be an executive director of the licensed entity. Responsible officers must fulfil the competence requirements under the SFO and be approved by the SFC.

All employees or representatives who undertake regulated activity must be licensed as representatives of the licensed entity. The qualifications for licensed representatives are lower than for responsible officers. All licensed representatives must pass a local regulatory framework exam.

The SFC has issued a code of conduct which applies to all licensed persons. The Fund Manager Code of Conduct, also issued by the SFC, applies to persons licensed for type 9 activity when managing a fund. In addition, every licensed entity must prepare a compliance manual which is tailored to the business of the licensed entity, with which its staff must comply.

When applying for a licence, a large amount of information regarding the applicant entity's group structure, its directors and substantial shareholders (both direct and indirect) must be provided to the SFC. Any changes to this information must also be notified to the SFC.

There are extensive reporting requirements in relation to changes affecting the licensed entity or its representatives. Entities must comply with the financial resources requirements. Monthly financial resources returns must be filed by a type 1 (dealing in securities) licensee, and a semi-annual return is required to be filed by type 9 licensees who do not hold client assets. In addition, an annual business risk management questionnaire must be completed and filed with the SFC by every licensed entity.

2.3. Operational requirements
Money laundering

In Hong Kong, legislation dealing with money laundering and terrorist financing includes: the Anti-Money Laundering and Counter-Terrorist Financing (Financial Institutions) Ordinance (AMLO), the Drug Trafficking (Recovery of Proceeds) Ordinance (DTROP), the Organized and Serious Crimes Ordinance (OSCO) and the United Nations (Anti-Terrorism Measures) Ordinance (UNATMO).

The AMLO, which came into effect on 1 April 2012, imposes on financial institutions requirements regarding customer due diligence and record-keeping whereas the DTROP, OSCO and UNATMO require reporting of suspicious transactions regarding money laundering or terrorist financing.

The SFC's guideline on anti-money laundering and counter-terrorist financing provides practical guidance to assist licensed corporations and their senior management in designing and implementing their own anti-money laundering and counter-terrorist financing policies, procedures and controls so as to meet the AMLO and other relevant legal and regulatory requirements.

Short selling
Covered short sales are permitted on designated securities. Hong Kong has retained the uptick rule, under which stocks cannot be shorted below the most recently traded price, and short sales must be declared when orders are placed. Hong Kong's disclosure of interests regime for listed securities requires persons with a long position of 5 per cent or more also to disclose short positions of 1 per cent or more. In addition to this transactional reporting regime, the Securities and Futures (Short Position Reporting) Rules came into effect in June 2012 which requires weekly positional reporting requirements for short positions reaching 0.02 per cent of the relevant company's issued share capital or HK$30 million, whichever is lower.

2.4. Marketing the fund
Hong Kong's securities legislation is aimed at preventing the unauthorised offer of securities and investment arrangements to the public. Unlike authorised funds which allow advertising and sale to the public in Hong Kong, unauthorised funds can only be marketed on a private basis or to professional investors, as described below.

Unauthorised private funds can be marketed to professional investors, including:
- SFC licensees;
- banks;
- insurance companies;
- collective investment schemes and their operators;
- governments;
- trust companies having trust assets of at least HK$40 million;
- corporations and partnerships having either a portfolio of at least HK$8 million or assets of at least HK$40 million; and
- individuals having a portfolio of at least HK$8 million.

Unauthorised private funds can also be marketed to up to 50 persons who do not qualify as professional investors.

Unauthorised private funds issued by corporate vehicles may also offer

shares in relation to which in Hong Kong:
- the total consideration payable does not exceed HK$5 million or its equivalent in another currency; or
- the minimum subscription per investor is not less than HK$500,000 or its equivalent in another currency.

In each case, the offering document must include a statutory prescribed warning statement.

An offer to persons who are outside Hong Kong does not constitute an 'offer' and can be disregarded in determining whether a relevant exclusion applies.

Marketing private funds (whether local or foreign) constitutes type 1 regulated activity (dealing in securities). Anyone carrying on a business in a regulated activity must be licensed accordingly by the SFC. Managers holding a licence for type 9 regulated activity (asset management) may promote the funds which they manage as this should fall within an incidental exemption. A licence for type 1 regulated activity is required for a manager who promotes third party funds which are not under his management.

An overseas corporation or individual carrying on a business outside Hong Kong which in Hong Kong constitutes a regulated activity may also apply for a temporary licence to carry on the same business in Hong Kong. This provision may be useful for fund managers intending to make intermittent visits to Hong Kong to undertake marketing activities.

However, such temporary licences are not available for a type 9 regulated activity, and licence holders are prohibited from holding any client assets in the course of conducting the regulated activities.

Subject to certain exemptions, section 174 of the SFO prohibits cold calling. That is, a licensee or its representatives may not make an offer to a person to enter into an agreement to provide financial products or services, nor induce or attempt to induce a person to enter into such an agreement, during or as a consequence of an unsolicited call.

Fund promoters should also be aware of changes to the Personal Data (Privacy) Ordinance relating to direct marketing which came into effect on 1 April 2013.

2.5. Taxation
At the fund level
Unauthorised domestic funds carrying on a business in Hong Kong are subject to Hong Kong profits tax in respect of their Hong Kong sourced revenue profits. Such resident funds are required to file annual profits tax returns with the Inland Revenue in Hong Kong. The rate of profits tax in Hong Kong for individuals and corporations for 2012/2013 are 15 per cent and 16.5 per cent respectively.

However, unauthorised foreign funds being distributed in Hong Kong may be eligible for profits tax exemption under amendments which were introduced in March 2006 by the Revenue (Profits Tax Exemption for Offshore Funds) Ordinance. Pursuant to the amendments, profits derived by an offshore non-resident private fund from six types of specified transactions carried out through or arranged by a specified person (for example, an asset management company or broker licensed by the SFC) are exempt from Hong Kong profits tax provided that certain conditions are met. To qualify for the exemption, the fund would, among other things, need to be able to demonstrate that its central management and control is not in Hong Kong.

Profits sourced outside Hong Kong and capital gains (which are not revenue in nature) are not taxable for Hong Kong profits tax purposes. There are no withholding taxes on interest, dividends and capital gains arising from investments held in Hong Kong.

Stamp duty (at the rate of 0.2 per cent) is payable on transfers of Hong Kong registered stock, subject to some exceptions.

At the investor level
Investors carrying on trade or business in Hong Kong are subject to tax on distributions and gains (which are not capital profits) arising from the sale of shares or units in a fund that arise from that business and that have a Hong Kong source.

Distributions from corporate funds in the form of dividends are not taxable at the hands of investors, and distributions from a non-Hong Kong resident fund may be treated as offshore sourced. Profits from the disposal of an interest in a fund may be treated as having a Hong Kong source if the fund is listed on the Hong Kong Stock Exchange or the investor negotiates and/or concludes the acquisition or disposal of the interest in the fund in Hong Kong.

2.6. Customary or common terms
Term of the fund – a life span of 10 to 12 years is most common for a closed-ended private equity vehicle, often with limited extensions to the term permitted to provide for an orderly winding up of the fund.
Liquidity of interests – closed-ended private equity funds normally prohibit redemption of interests and provide for any transfer of interests to be subject to prior approval by the general partner.
Manager/operator involvement – for closed-ended private equity funds, typical key main provisions can be found in the fund agreement.
Remuneration arrangements – the management fee of a closed-ended private equity fund will typically range from 1.5 per cent to 2.5 per cent of the committed capital, and a performance fee in the form of carried interest is usually received by general partners at 20 per cent of the fund's net profits, with standard clawback provisions for overpayment.
Investor and borrowing restrictions – the fund agreement for a closed-ended private equity fund may contain provisions on various limits on investments that the private fund may make, by, for example, prohibiting more than a specified portion of the fund's capital commitments (often between 15 per cent and 25 per cent) from being invested in any one portfolio company, prohibiting hostile transactions, limiting certain foreign investments, and restricting borrowing (for example to a specified percentage of the fund's net asset value (NAV)).

Commitment period/investment period – for private equity funds, the fund agreement will typically provide for an investment period of three to five years, after which time new investments will not be made.
Reporting obligations – provisions are commonly contained in the fund agreement requiring the fund to provide periodic financial, tax and other information to investors. For reporting obligations to the licensing regulator, see section 2.2.

3. HEDGE FUNDS
3.1. Common structures
The structure commonly adopted for a new Hong Kong hedge fund involves the establishment of a fund in an offshore jurisdiction such as the Cayman Islands (normally an open-ended investment company), an investment management company also located offshore, and a Hong Kong investment management or investment advisory company. The fund would normally appoint the Cayman investment management company as fund manager, which then obtains investment management or advisory services from the Hong Kong company. The Hong Kong investment management company will need to be licensed for type 9 regulated activity by the SFC.

In the event that significant subscriptions are anticipated from US taxable investors, a more complex master-feeder structure may be considered. An alternative to the master-feeder structure is for a standalone fund to prepare passive foreign investment company reports to give to its US taxable investors for their use when filing their tax returns with US tax authorities.

3.2. Regulatory framework
Although a small number of hedge funds have been authorised for public distribution, interest in the vast majority of hedge funds in Hong Kong is offered on a private basis or only to professional investors.

Both domestic and overseas retail funds in Hong Kong must be authorised by the SFC if they are intended to be offered to the public. Retail funds are regulated principally under the SFO and its subsidiary legislation. In addition, the SFC has issued codes and guidelines which set out the principles and requirements that need to be complied with for the authorisation of funds. The main guidelines for authorisation of funds for sale to the public are set out in the SFC Handbook for Unit Trusts and Mutual Funds, Investment-Linked Assurance Schemes and Unlisted Structured Investment Products (handbook), in particular the sections covering the Code on Unit Trusts and Mutual Funds (code).

For an overview of the SFC's fund authorisation process, see section 4.2.

Private hedge funds are not regulated by the SFC, and hence are not subject to the code. The managers of retail and private hedge funds are nevertheless subject to the SFC's licensing requirements – see section 2.2.

3.3. Operational requirements
Please refer to section 2.3.

3.4. Marketing the fund
Marketing retail hedge funds
Hedge funds (whether foreign or local) authorised by the SFC can be advertised and marketed to the public, subject to a minimum subscription of $50,000, or for funds of hedge funds, $10,000. No minimum investment is required for 100 per cent capital guaranteed funds.

Advertisements and other invitations to invest in the fund must comply with the handbook and the SFC's advertising guidelines applicable to collective investment schemes authorised under the product codes.

Marketing private hedge funds
Please refer to section 2.4.

3.5. Taxation
At the fund level – retail funds
Retail hedge funds authorised by the SFC are exempt from Hong Kong profits tax and there is no requirement for such funds to file Hong Kong profits tax returns.

At the fund level – private funds
Please refer to section 2.5.

At the investor level
Please refer to section 2.5.

3.6. Customary or common terms
Term of the fund – standard market terms apply.
Liquidity of interests – provisions commonly impose restrictions on transfers to persons whose holding of interests in the fund would be illegal or which could result in regulatory, pecuniary, legal, taxation, or material administrative disadvantage for the fund or its unit holders or shareholders generally.
Remuneration arrangements – in accordance with standard market terms, the hedge fund manager will typically receive a management fee equal to 2 per cent per annum based on the NAV of the fund and a performance fee equal to 20 per cent of the fund's profits. Where an investment adviser is appointed in Hong Kong, the manager will typically pay the investment advisory fee to the investment adviser on a cost plus 5 or 10 per cent basis.
Reporting obligations – for private funds, provisions are commonly contained in the funds agreement requiring the fund to provide periodic financial, tax and other information to investors. For reporting obligations to the licensing regulator, see section 2.2.

4. RETAIL FUNDS
4.1. Common structures
Locally established open-ended retail funds are usually unit trusts constituted under bilateral trust deeds, under which the trustee and manager are parties. Hong Kong company law does not currently provide for companies with

variable capital. Accordingly, open-ended retail funds structured as companies are domiciled offshore.

Generally, retail funds in Hong Kong are open-ended funds. The SFC will authorise closed-ended retail funds only if they are listed and therefore subject to the Hong Kong Stock Exchange Listing Rules. The principal market for closed-ended retail funds is in real estate investment trusts (REITs), which must comply with the SFC's Code on Real Estate Investment Trusts (REIT code).

4.2. Regulatory framework

Retail funds are regulated principally under the SFO and its subsidiary legislation, together with codes and guidelines issued by the SFC, and in particular, the code.

The current version of the code came into effect on 25 June 2010. The code sets out the detailed conditions for the authorisation of open-ended unit trusts, mutual funds and other similar open-ended collective investment schemes. It contains specific authorisation criteria applicable to futures and options funds, guaranteed funds, index funds, hedge funds, structured funds and funds that invest in financial derivative instruments, in addition to those for the more traditional equity, bond, money market and warrant funds and funds of funds.

Authorisation process

The authorisation process for funds has two parts: the first dealing with the key operators of the fund, and the second dealing with the fund itself. The key operators are the manager (including its delegates with discretionary management functions), the fund trustee (where the fund is in the form of a unit trust) or custodian (for mutual fund corporations).

Manager

The manager of an authorised fund must be approved by the SFC to manage public funds in Hong Kong. This is notwithstanding that the manager is already licensed and regulated by its home regulator. Generally, the SFC will only approve a manager which is regulated in an acceptable inspection regime (AIR) such as Australia, France, Germany, Ireland, Hong Kong, Luxembourg, United Kingdom and the United States. Malaysia is regarded as an AIR jurisdiction only in respect of certain Islamic funds and Taiwan is regarded as an AIR jurisdiction only in respect of certain ETFs.

Delegation of discretionary investment management functions to an affiliate of the manager in a non-AIR jurisdiction is permissible provided that the affiliate is subject to a system of internal controls and compliance similar to those of the manager and demonstrates compliance with the requirements of the code. Non-affiliate delegation to a non-AIR manager will be considered by the SFC on a case-by-case basis.

In order to approve a manager to manage public funds, the SFC needs to be satisfied that the manager is engaged primarily in the business of fund management, is appropriately regulated, has sufficient experience managing public funds and has appropriately qualified personnel (that is, at least two key personnel with at least five years' investment experience managing public funds). In addition, the manager must have paid-up capital and reserves of HK$1 million or equivalent (approximately $130,000).

There is no requirement for a manager of an authorised fund in Hong Kong which carries out asset management activity outside of Hong Kong to be licensed by the SFC or to have an office in Hong Kong. If the manager does not have a place of business in Hong Kong, the fund will be required to appoint a representative in Hong Kong. The Hong Kong representative acts as a contact point for Hong Kong investors in the fund, thus the manager is encouraged to appoint a Hong Kong representative within the manager group of companies. The representative must be an entity licensed or registered under the SFO or a trust company under the trust ordinance which is an affiliate of a Hong Kong authorised financial institution.

Trustee/custodian

Funds seeking authorisation by the SFC which are established as trusts must have a trustee acceptable to the SFC, while mutual fund corporations must have an acceptable custodian. The trustee or custodian must be a bank licensed in Hong Kong, a trust company which is a subsidiary of such a bank, or a trust company under the Trustee Ordinance. In addition, a banking institution or trust company incorporated outside Hong Kong which is acceptable to the SFC may also be appointed as trustee or custodian of an authorised fund in Hong Kong.

The trustee or custodian must be independently audited and have an issued paid-up capital and non-distributable capital reserves of HK$10 million or its equivalent. However, if it is a wholly owned subsidiary of a substantial financial institution, its issued paid-up capital and non-distributable capital reserves can be less than HK$10 million if an acceptable letter of comfort in the prescribed form from its holding company is submitted.

An acceptable trustee or custodian should either be subject to regulatory supervision on an ongoing basis, or appoint an independent auditor to provide a periodic review of its internal controls and systems on terms of reference agreed with the SFC, and file the report with the SFC.

Products

The SFC's review of the fund itself falls under two broad categories: plain vanilla equity/bond funds; and specialised schemes such as fund of funds, money market funds, warrant funds, futures and options funds, guaranteed funds, index funds, hedge funds, index tracking exchange traded funds, structured funds and funds that invest in financial derivative instruments (FDIs). Each of these funds is required to comply with the specific requirements of the code, particularly on investment limitations and prohibitions.

The SFC recognises that some funds such as UCITS already comply in substance with certain provisions of the code by virtue of prior authorisation in certain recognised jurisdictions. Currently, the list of recognised jurisdictions includes Australia, France, Germany, Guernsey, Ireland, Isle of Man, Jersey, Luxembourg, Malaysia (in respect of Islamic collective investment schemes only), Taiwan (in respect of ETFs only), the United Kingdom and the United States.

Application for authorisation of recognised jurisdiction schemes should be reviewed on the basis that the scheme's structural and operational requirements and core investment restrictions already comply in substance with the code. In practice, the perceived advantages of recognised jurisdiction schemes are limited as the SFC reserves the right to require compliance with the code as a condition of authorisation.

The SFC has adopted a pragmatic approach to the authorisation of UCITS funds in Hong Kong, including a procedure to facilitate the processing of such funds. The authorisation process of UCITS funds which use expanded investment powers, including those using FDIs for investment purposes, has been simplified: the risk management and control process (RMP) of the fund manager is no longer required to be submitted to the SFC. Instead, an applicant must submit to the SFC a written confirmation from the fund or its manager that there are suitable risk management and control systems which are commensurate with the fund's risk profile, together with evidence of approval of the RMP by the home regulator or written confirmation that the RMP has been filed with the home regulator and the home regulator has no further comments on it.

Structured funds may be authorised by the SFC under chapter 8.8 of the code. A structured fund is defined as a passively managed scheme which seeks to achieve its investment objective by investing substantially in FDIs. Non-UCITS funds that acquire FDIs for investment purposes may seek authorisation under chapter 8.9 of the code.

Documentation requirements
The fund's constitutive documents (such as the trust deed for unit trusts and the articles of association for a mutual fund) are required to be submitted to the SFC for review. The code contains details of the particular information required to be provided in the constitutive documents. In theory, the requirement to reflect the code's terms in the constitutive documents may be waived for recognised jurisdiction funds, but in practice the SFC frequently requires that these be addressed.

The code requires the fund's offering document to be issued in Hong Kong in both English and Chinese. The offering document must always be accompanied by the fund's most recent audited annual report and accounts (once issued) and, if more recent, its semi-annual report.

Product summaries in the form of a product key facts statement (KFS) must also be prepared. The KFS is similar to the key investor information document for UCITS. The KFS shall be deemed to form a part of the offering document of the fund unless otherwise approved by the SFC. The SFC may on an exceptional basis allow the KFS not to be deemed to form part of the offering document for certain foreign schemes, on the basis of overriding legal requirements of the home jurisdiction.

An application for authorisation of funds must also be accompanied by a duly completed and signed application form and information checklist together with certain confirmations and undertakings to the SFC.

Authorisation of hedge funds

In addition to complying with the standard requirements for authorisation under the code, chapter 8.7 of the code also specifies various criteria that a retail hedge fund and its operators must fulfil (the hedge fund guidelines). For the manager, this includes:
- Professional expertise – the management company must have sufficient resources including at least two key personnel with relevant experience. For a single strategy fund, 'relevant experience' means at least five years' general experience in managing hedge funds, with at least two years in the particular strategy of that hedge fund. For funds of hedge funds, it means five years' general hedge fund management experience and two years' experience as a fund of hedge funds manager.
- AUM – the investment manager (not its corporate group) must have at least $100 million in hedge fund assets under management.
- Monitoring and compliance – the management company must have in place suitable internal controls and risk management systems commensurate with the company's business and risk profile, including a clear risk management policy and written control procedures.

The SFC has been applying these requirements strictly and requires detailed and specific information demonstrating compliance.

In the case of a fund of hedge funds, while the manager of the fund of hedge funds needs to fulfil the criteria set out above, the managers of the underlying funds (which do not need to be authorised) do not. The only requirement is that 90 per cent of the underlying funds in which a fund of hedge funds invests must have key personnel with at least two years' hedge fund management experience. However, the fund of hedge funds' manager will have to submit a detailed compliance plan to satisfy the SFC on how it proposes to monitor the activities of the underlying fund managers on an ongoing basis.

The hedge fund guidelines also set out various requirements that the fund itself must fulfil, including:
- Limited liability – the liability of holders must be limited to their investment in the hedge fund. Where the fund is structured as an umbrella fund, there must be legally enforceable provisions to ring-fence the assets and liabilities between the sub-funds.
- Investment and borrowing restrictions – there must be a set of clearly defined investment and borrowing parameters disclosed.
- Reporting requirements – an authorised hedge fund will be required to issue annual, semi-annual and quarterly reports to investors. The SFC has issued guidelines on hedge fund reporting requirements that set out the required contents of these reports.
- Prime broker – where a hedge fund uses a prime broker, the hedge fund guidelines set out various requirements to which the prime broker must

adhere. One issue for most prime brokers has been the limit on the value of the assets which may be charged to the prime broker to secure the fund's indebtedness.
- Independent trustee/custodian – the fund must have an independent trustee or custodian.

4.3. Operational requirements
Reporting requirements
For all retail funds, annual reports and accounts containing the information stipulated in the code must be published and distributed to holders within four months of the end of the scheme's financial year, and interim reports within two months of the end of the period they cover. As an alternative to the distribution of printed financial reports, holders may be notified of where such reports, in printed and electronic forms, can be obtained within the relevant time frame.

The fund's latest available offer and redemption prices or NAV must be published at least once a month in an English language and a Chinese language daily newspaper in Hong Kong (assuming the offering document is published in both languages).

Financial reports of the fund must be filed with the SFC. On request by the SFC, the manager or its Hong Kong representative must supply all information relevant to the scheme's financial reports and accounts.

The SFC should also be notified as soon as possible of any change to the data originally provided in the fund's application for authorisation.

Investment and borrowing restrictions
Open-ended retail funds
Chapter 7 of the code prescribes restrictions on borrowings and the type, spread and exposure of investments for equity and bond funds. Further, chapter 8 prescribes different restrictions for different types of specialised schemes.

Closed-ended retail funds
Specific requirements applicable to REITs are set out in the REIT code. REITs and other Hong Kong listed funds are subject to listing rules and must inform investors, in a timely and transparent manner, of any material information concerning the issuer. For REITs, the only permissible investment is generally income-generating real estate. REITs cannot invest in vacant land or engage in property development, and investments in uncompleted units in a building are subject to 10 per cent of the REIT's NAV.

Money laundering and short selling
Please refer to section 2.3.

4.4. Marketing the fund
Retail funds which have been authorised by the SFC can be advertised and marketed to the general public. Advertisements and other invitations to

invest in the fund must comply with the advertising guidelines applicable to collective investment schemes authorised under the product codes.

Generally, the person marketing the retail fund in Hong Kong must be licensed by the SFC for type 1 regulated activity (dealing in securities). Managers holding a licence for type 9 regulated activity (asset management) may promote the funds which they manage as this should fall within an incidental exemption.

Fund promoters should also be aware of changes to the Personal Data (Privacy) Ordinance relating to direct marketing which came into effect on 1 April 2013.

4.5. Taxation
At the fund level
Please refer to section 3.5.; see also section 2.5.

Resident investors
Please refer to section 2.5.

4.6. Customary or common terms
Term of the fund – unlimited for all retail funds.
Liquidity of interests – common restrictions for open-ended retail funds include:
- imposing a requirement for prior notice on applications for the subscription or redemption of interests;
- imposing a redemption gate, that is, redeeming no more than a specified percentage of the interests on a particular dealing day, with all excess applications for redemption being dealt with on subsequent redemption dealing days;
- prohibiting the issue or transfer of interests to any person whose holding would be illegal or which may result in regulatory, pecuniary, legal, taxation or material administrative disadvantage for the fund or its unit holders or shareholders generally; and
- declaring a suspension of the calculation of the NAV of the fund, and therefore, the issue and redemption of shares or units, on the occurrence of certain specified events.

The above restrictions also apply to closed-ended retail funds, except that issues of units by a REIT must usually be offered to existing holders' pro-rata to their existing holdings prior to it being allotted or issued to other persons. Also, interests in closed-ended funds are not redeemable at the option of the investor. REITs can purchase their own units on the Hong Kong Stock Exchange subject to requirements similar to those applicable to listed companies under the listing rules.

Investment/borrowing restrictions
For REITs, the various investment and borrowing restrictions are set out in the REIT code. Common provisions in the constitutive documents may include, for example, that the REIT may only invest in income-generating real estate;

that investments in uncompleted units in a building are subject to 10 per cent of its NAV; or that aggregate borrowings of the REIT shall not at any time exceed 45 per cent of the total gross asset value of the scheme.

For open-ended retail funds, the investment limitations on borrowings and the type, spread and exposure of investment for equity and bond funds are set out in chapter 7 of the code. For example, a common provision is that the value of a fund's holding of securities issued by any single issuer may not exceed 10 per cent of its total NAV. Closed-ended retail funds are expected to comply with the same investment and borrowing restrictions.

5. PROPOSED CHANGES AND DEVELOPMENTS
Enhanced disclosures
The SFC remains vigilant of any possible contagion effect resulting from overseas developments. It has issued circulars to fund managers regarding enhanced disclosure on the proposed Indian taxation legislation and investments of more than 10 per cent of the fund's NAV in securities issued and/or guaranteed by a single sovereign issuer which is below investment grade.

The SFC has recently imposed new disclosure requirements for authorised funds that may distribute dividends out of capital. These funds are required to disclose the specific risks relating to such distribution policy and make available the compositions of the dividends (ie, the relative amounts paid out of income and capital) for the last 12 months with effect from 8 November 2012.

Market developments
The SFC and the China Securities Regulatory Commission (CSRC) are working together towards a mutual recognition status for fund products sold in Hong Kong and mainland China. In due course, it is hoped China will be added to the SFC's list of mutually recognised jurisdictions. This will be an exciting breakthrough in creating new business opportunities for both Hong Kong and mainland fund management companies. At the same time, mutual recognition will also open up a new gateway for international players, prompting them to set up operations and funds in Hong Kong.

Further, to facilitate the development of the mutual funds industry in Hong Kong, the government has initiated discussions on a legal framework for locally domiciled open-ended or variable capital investment companies.

Regulation of electronic trading
The SFC released consultation conclusions on the regulation of electronic trading in March 2013. The rules will affect SFC-regulated asset managers that use third party trading algorithms, such as broker-provided trading algorithms or use their own or their group's internally-developed trading algorithms. Under the rules, an asset manager is responsible for the settlement and financial obligations of orders sent to the market through its electronic trading system and for implementing policies, procedures and controls to

supervise those orders. The rules are likely to lead to more formality around, and a need to devote more resources to, the documentation, testing and use of internal and third party electronic trading systems and related controls. The rules will come into effect on 1 January 2014.

Iceland

Johann Magnus Johannsson & Gudmundur J Oddsson
LOGOS Legal Services

1. MARKET OVERVIEW

Shortly after the collapse of the Icelandic banking system in the fall of 2008, work was commenced on reviewing and amending legislation governing the Icelandic funds market. The legislation in force at the time had been enacted in 2003 and had been aimed at increasing the competitiveness of Icelandic funds and the protection of investors in a funds market that had emerged in the preceding decade. The funds market had continued to grow until the collapse.

Once concluded, in 2011, the review produced a new act on funds, Act no.128/2011 on Undertakings for Collective Investment in Transferable Securities, Investment Funds and Professional Investor Funds (Funds Act). This act currently forms the backbone of the legal framework regulating the Icelandic funds market.

It was a primary objective of the new legislation to enact provisions considered necessary due to the effect of the collapse of Iceland's three major banks on its financial markets and economy.

Another objective underlying the enactment of the Funds Act was to bring the framework in line with developments on the UCITS front in Europe. European initiatives have been a major catalyst for change to the legislation on funds in Iceland and the legislator has responded to comments from the European Surveillance Authority to ensure the adequacy of implementation. To a limited extent rules have been implemented into regulations as opposed to legislative acts.

Under the Funds Act there are three types of funds:
- UCITS approved by the Icelandic Financial Supervisory Authority (IFSA) and authorised to operate in the European Economic Area (EEA) that are established and operated by a management company which issues interests that are redeemable at the investors' demand from the funds' assets;
- investor funds approved by the IFSA, but not authorised to market its products in the EEA, that issue interests; and
- institutional investor funds for collective investment, that do not accept funds from the members of the public and issue redeemable interests or shares. Generally UCITS and investor funds would fall within the category of 'Retail Funds' but institutional investor funds, by comparison, would be considered 'Alternative Investment Funds'.

Some of the changes introduced by the Funds Act had the effect of restricting the participation by financial institutions in funds. For example increased demands were made on the independence of management companies and their directors, limits on investing in related parties were tightened and the investment policy for investment funds was narrowed. Not all of the amendments were directly or indirectly aimed at making the regulation of fund markets more rigid, for example avenues for withdrawing the authorisation issued to a management company were simplified and streamlined.

At the end of 2012, 10 management companies were supervised by the IFSA, an increase of one company from the previous year. The companies operated a total of 56 UCITS and fund divisions and 28 investment funds and fund divisions. At year-end 2012, total assets of UCITS and investment funds amounted to ISK328 billion or roughly EUR 2 billion. Broken down, assets of UCITS were just over ISK255 billion (EUR 1.6 billion) and assets of investment funds just over ISK71 billion (EUR 440 million).

The Icelandic funds market continues to grow. Last year saw a rise in the assets of UCITS and investment funds by over ISK28 billion or 9.5 per cent. UCITS increased by almost ISK 7 billion during the year, or by 2.7 per cent, while investment funds grew by over ISK21 billion or by 43.1 per cent. The increase in investment funds can be attributed to a large extent to the increase in investments in equities. The great majority of assets of UCITS and investment funds (around 73 per cent) are invested in bonds issued by or guaranteed by the Icelandic state. The remainder is in equities, deposits and UCITS.

At year-end 2012, 47 institutional investor funds were in operation and their total assets amounted to ISK288 billion (EUR 1.8 billion). This was the first year that the IFSA supervised institutional investor funds so no numbers exist from previous years for comparison.

2. ALTERNATIVE INVESTMENT FUNDS
2.1. Common structures
In Iceland institutional investor funds are the main type of funds that would qualify as alternative investment funds. They can be set up either as open-ended funds that issue redeemable interests or as closed-ended funds that issue shares. In both cases, the liability of investors is limited to their contribution to the alternative investment fund.

Seeing as management companies are restricted from acquiring shares with voting rights which enable them to significantly influence the management of the shares' issuer, under Act no.161/2002 on Financial Undertakings (Financial Undertakings Act), they cannot set up or operate a closed-ended fund.

Other entities are generally not subject to the same restriction on operating a fund that issues shares as opposed to interests. Closed-ended funds are typically incorporated as partnerships limited by shares, for tax reasons, or public limited liability companies under Act no.2/1995 on Public Limited Liability Companies.

In many respects, management companies licensed by the IFSA operate alternative investment funds within a more robust legal framework than other entities. Different mechanisms apply to the operation of open-ended and closed-ended funds in terms of the process for issuing new interests and shares. Tax considerations are liable to limit investment opportunities feasible for closed-ended funds and open-ended funds have more investment flexibility.

Management companies licensed to operate funds by the IFSA must be incorporated as public limited liability companies. There are limited restrictions on what types of other entities can operate alternative investment funds.

2.2. Regulatory framework
Until 2011, alternative investment funds were effectively unsupervised. The fact that the investors, that these funds are marketed to, do not generally enjoy any investor protection was considered to outweigh the inherent risk in investing in alternative investment funds on account of effectively non-existent restrictions on permitted investments.

Alternative investment funds were brought under the Funds Act's scope of application on the basis that they should be the subject of, at least, minimal supervision and registration with the IFSA. It is noted in legislative preparatory works that these new requirements are not very burdensome and that more is gained than lost by the IFSA being informed about the establishment and operations of these funds.

The IFSA supervises the activities of alternative investment funds in accordance with the Funds Act and regulations issued under it. The IFSA may demand access to all documents and information from the parties covered by the Funds Act. If the IFSA considers the activities of regulated entities to violate provisions of the Funds Act (or rules or regulations issued under it), or is otherwise abnormal, it can provide a reasonable period for improvements unless the violations are serious.

If the IFSA believes that activities under the Funds Act are conducted without the required licenses or authorisations it may request documents and information from the parties concerned or regulated entities to determine whether the alleged violations have occurred. In addition, the IFSA is allowed to make public the names of entities that are considered to have offered services without the required authorisation.

The regulatory framework for investment managers of alternative investment managers is primarily set out in the Funds Act and the Financial Undertakings Act. The IFSA supervises the activities of management companies of alternative investment funds, in accordance with the Funds Act and regulations issued under it. The IFSA may demand access to all documents and information from the parties covered by the Funds Act. If the IFSA considers the activities of regulated entities to violate provisions of the Funds Act (or rules or regulations issued under it), or is otherwise abnormal, it can provide a reasonable period for improvements unless the violations are serious.

Investment managers operating an alternative investment fund must have passed an examination in securities trading in accordance with the Financial Undertakings Act. The same act sets out additional eligibility criteria which must be met by an investment manager who is a management company's general manager.

These additional criteria require managers of management companies to be competent to manage their own affairs and have an untarnished reputation. In addition they may not have been declared bankrupt within the previous five years or, in the preceding ten years, have been sentenced before a court of law for any criminal act in connection with the conduct of business. Managers of management companies must be resident in a member state of the EEA but the IFSA may grant an exemption from this requirement.

2.3. Operational requirements

Although their investment strategy is unrestricted by the Funds Act, alternative investment funds are required to approve their own investment strategy and rules, both of which must always be available to investors. Alternative investment funds are bound by their investment strategy and their rules must identify the nature and causes of possible conflicts of interest.

Since November 2008 foreign exchange restrictions have been in effect in Iceland. Cross-border capital movements are restricted under Act no.87/1992 on Foreign Exchange (Foreign Exchange Act). Among other things, the Foreign Exchange Act generally prohibits Icelandic investors from investing in securities, unit shares of UCITS and/or investment funds, money market instruments or other transferable financial instruments in foreign currency. The prohibition applies to both legal and natural persons, but the Foreign Exchange Act sets out limited exceptions, such as for reinvestment, and there is a process by which companies, who have more than 80 per cent of their revenue and 80 per cent of expenses abroad, may apply for an exemption.

A custodian or depository does not have to be engaged by an investment manager. Where alternative investment funds are managed by a management company it must operate a surveillance system that allows it to monitor and assess risk of individual assets and portfolios of its funds at any time.

The IFSA must be notified of the operations of an alternative investment fund within one month of the fund's establishment. The notice to the IFSA must be accompanied by the rules of the alternative investment fund, its investment strategy and information on its fund manager or its general manager, where the fund manager is a legal entity. In order to enable the IFSA to carry out its supervisory functions, it must be notified of any subsequent changes to these matters.

Information about an alternative investment fund's assets must be set out in its annual and semi-annual financial statements, which must always be available to investors. Alternative investment funds are required to provide the IFSA with a report breaking down the investments of funds they operate in the form acceptable to the IFSA.

Act no.108/2007 on Securities Trading (Securities Trading Act) requires a prospectus to be published in connection with the public offering of interests or shares in funds that do not accept funds from members of the public. Alternative investment funds fall under the scope of the relevant provisions. But there are certain private placement exemptions and the offering of interests or shares in an alternative investment fund is exempt from the requirement, to publish a prospectus, where they are offered exclusively to institutional investors.

Operations of alternative investment funds must reflect proper and sound business practices and promote the overriding objectives of market credibility and the interests of investors. Provisions of the Securities Trading Act on insider dealing and market abuse may be relevant to transactions involving interests or shares in an alternative investment fund. Legislation on measures against money laundering and terrorist financing may also have to be taken into account.

2.4. Marketing the fund
Production and offering of marketing materials for alternative investment funds is governed by the Funds Act. The act defines the term 'marketing' as an offer or promotion by advertising or other presentation, of the purchase of units or shares, in UCITS or other funds for collective investments.

Marketing of alternative investment funds must be authorised by the IFSA. Foreign alternative investment funds must notify the IFSA in advance of their intention to market their interests or shares in Iceland and provide it with information about: (i) the fund's home state; (ii) the identity and address of the fund manager; (iii) whether the fund is subject to supervision; and (iv) other information deemed necessary by the IFSA.

Alternative investment funds may not be marketed or promoted to the general public. For these purposes, the general public includes anyone who is not an institutional investor within the meaning of the Securities Trading Act. Institutional investors include:
- legal entities licensed to operate or engage in regulated activities in the financial markets, or which are authorised in another state in the EEA and which have a passport to provide the relevant investment services on a cross-border basis into Iceland;
- large undertakings meeting certain criteria;
- national and regional governments, central banks and international organisations;
- other institutional investors whose main activity is to invest in financial instruments; and
- individuals resident in Iceland as professional clients who request in writing to a financial undertaking to be treated as professional clients.

Marketing of alternative investment funds must be consistent with proper and sound business practices. Apart from this general obligation the Funds Act sets out no specific content requirements for materials marketing alternative investment funds.

2.5. Taxation
The taxation of the income of alternative investment funds has to be addressed in three separate parts: (i) taxation of the management companies; (ii) taxation of the funds themselves; and (iii) the taxation of the investors who own the interests or shares in the funds.

Although the income of alternative investment funds is not beneficially owned by the management company it is treated as the income of the management company provided that the fund is a non-taxable fund. If the management company bore no costs it would be liable for tax on the income. But management companies' eventual liability to pay out all of the income to the holders of the interests is classified as an interest liability under Icelandic law. Interest from debt is deductible from a management company's income which means that management companies are generally not liable for tax on the fund's net income.

Open-ended alternative investment funds are generally treated as tax transparent under the Icelandic tax code on the basis that they do not conduct business. To the extent that an open-ended alternative investment fund makes no net gain from its activities, ie, in circumstances where all its income is matched by corresponding liabilities, it is very unlikely that the fund would be considered to conduct business according to Icelandic law. In order to be able to rely on the exemption, the fund should not enter into other business areas than holding and trading of financial instruments and it should not employ any people. It should merely hold and trade securities and enter into a contract with the management company which should conduct the necessary activities for this purpose on behalf of the fund. Otherwise the risk of the fund being engaged in business or the holders of the interests possibly having a permanent establishment in Iceland arises.

Closed-ended alternative investment funds in the form of public limited liability companies are generally liable for income tax. However, if they invest only in shares a full deduction against dividends or capital gains can be obtained in accordance with legislation on income tax. Other income is liable to be subject to income tax. A closed-ended fund in the form of a partnership limited by shares will not be liable for any tax, but the shareholders will be taxed proportionally.

Lastly, the investors' income from interests in open-ended funds is classified as interest income upon realisation by redemption or sale. However, if the investors hold shares in a closed-ended fund their income would be classified as dividend or capital gains. For domestic individuals the current tax rate for financial income is 20 per cent. Domestic companies effectively do not pay tax on dividends or capital gains, but are subject to 20 per cent tax on interest income. The taxation on foreign investors varies and depends on type of income, type of legal persons and the availability of double taxation protection.

In some cases it may be advisable to obtain an advance tax ruling prior to establishing alternative investment funds.

2.6. Customary or common terms
Given the lack of publicly available information on alternative investment funds, it is difficult to provide details on any terms considered customary or common to such funds.

3. RETAIL FUNDS
3.1. Common structures
UCITS and investor funds are the main type of funds that would qualify as

retail funds in Iceland. Both types can be set up as open-ended funds that issue interests, but neither can take the form of closed-ended funds that issue shares. Retail funds are not separate legal entities and are operated by a management company which must be a public limited liability company licensed and regulated by the IFSA. The liability of investors in retail funds is limited to their contribution for interests in the fund. Delivery of interests may only take place on payment of the contribution.

Flexibility on the structuring of UCITS and investor funds is very limited. The main differences between the two types are that investor funds are not permitted to market themselves within the EEA and they enjoy considerably greater investment freedom. In addition, interests in UCITS are generally redeemable at the investors' request but interests in investor funds are redeemable in accordance with the funds' rules.

Public limited liability companies are the principal legal vehicles used to set up retail funds. Management companies licensed to operate funds by the IFSA must be incorporated as public limited liability companies.

3.2. Regulatory framework

Retail funds fall under the Funds Act's scope of application. Their structure, operations and purpose is comparable in many respects and many of the same provisions of the Funds Act apply to both types of retail funds.

The IFSA supervises the activities of retail funds in accordance with the Funds Act and regulations issued under it. The IFSA may demand access to all documents and information from the parties covered by the Funds Act. If the IFSA considers the activities of regulated entities to violate provisions of the Funds Act (or rules or regulations issued under it), or is otherwise abnormal, it can provide a reasonable period for improvements unless the violations are serious.

If the IFSA believes that activities under the Funds Act are conducted without the required licenses or authorisations it may request documents and information from the parties concerned or regulated entities to determine whether the alleged violations have occurred. In addition, the IFSA is allowed to make public the names of entities that are considered to have offered services without the required authorisation.

The regulatory framework for investment managers is primarily set out in the Funds Act and the Financial Undertakings Act. Management companies have to be approved by the IFSA and no other entities may be licensed to operate funds. In addition to the operation of UCITS and other funds for collective investment a management company may carry out: (i) portfolio management; (ii) investment advice; and (iii) custody and management of financial instruments in collective investment.

In order to be able to obtain a license, a management company must meet certain minimum requirements under the Financial Undertakings Act, for example, on share capital and equity ratios. A number of requirements under the Funds Act are meant to ensure that the management company and its directors are independent of custodians of funds. Management companies can delegate their tasks on receiving approval from the IFSA, but are responsible for ensuring that the third party is qualified and authorised to carry out the delegated tasks. Delegating tasks does not affect the liability of management companies to investors.

The IFSA supervises the activities of management companies of retail funds, in accordance with the Funds Act and regulations issued under it. The IFSA may demand access to all documents and information from the parties covered by the Funds Act. If the IFSA considers the activities of regulated entities to violate provisions of the Funds Act (or rules or regulations issued under it), or is otherwise abnormal, it can provide a reasonable period for improvements unless the violations are serious.

Investment managers operating an alternative investment fund must have passed an examination in securities trading in accordance with the Financial Undertakings Act and meet additional eligibility criteria set out in the act.

These additional criteria require managers of management companies to be competent to manage their own affairs and have an untarnished reputation. In addition they may not have been declared bankrupt within the previous five years or, in the preceding 10 years, have been sentenced before a court of law for any criminal act in connection with the conduct of business. Managers of management companies must be resident in a member state of the EEA but the IFSA may grant an exemption from this requirement.

Applications for the approval of retail funds must be made to the IFSA in writing and accompanied by the following documents:
- the latest fund rules;
- its prospectus;
- the key investor information document;
- information about the fund's management; and
- other relevant information.

The IFSA is permitted to implement more detailed rules on disclosure of information. If the IFSA requires additional documents or further information it must bring this to the attention of the management company as soon as possible or within one month of receiving the application. As soon as possible after, and no later than two months after, an application adequately meeting the IFSA's requirements has been filed the IFSA must notify the management company whether it approves the application. A decision to reject an application must be reasoned.

3.3. Operational requirements

Compared to alternative investment funds retail funds are subject to much tighter restrictions on the types of activity and the types of investments they can make. A number of restrictions on the investments that can be made by UCITS funds are detailed in the Funds Act. The provisions are applicable for investment funds with certain exceptions.

Restrictions on cross-border capital movements in effect under the Foreign Exchange generally prohibit investors resident in Iceland, including retail funds, from investing in securities, unit shares of UCITS and/or investment funds, money market instruments or other transferable financial instruments in foreign currency. Certain exemptions may apply.

A custodian or depository approved by the IFSA must be entrusted with the custody of a retail fund in accordance with the Funds Act. Commercial banks, savings banks, credit undertakings, securities companies and branches of comparable foreign entities that operate in Iceland can be approved as custodians. Management companies cannot transfer their funds to a new custodian without IFSA approval. Custodians are permitted to delegate their tasks to a limited extent, but that does not affect their liability to management companies or investors.

Assets of retails funds have to be kept separate from the custodian's assets. The custodian is responsible for: (i) ensuring that the sale, issue, repurchase, redemption and annulment of redeemable interests is in accordance with legislation and the rules of the relevant entity; (ii) ensuring that the redemption value of redeemable interests is calculated in accordance with legislation and the rules of the relevant entity; (iii) putting into effect instructions from the management company unless they are contrary to legislation or the relevant entity's articles; (iv) ensuring that in transactions with fund assets the remuneration for them is paid within reasonable time limits; and (v) ensuring that a fund's income is disposed of in accordance with legislation and the fund's rules.

Retail funds are required to provide the IFSA with a report breaking down the investments of funds they operate in the form acceptable to the IFSA. They must prepare annual and semi-annual financial statements that must be accessible to the public and published on the websites of management companies. The same applies to rules of retail funds, their prospectuses and key investor information document.

A retail fund's management company is required, under the Funds Act, to issue a prospectus and key investor information document for the fund. The prospectus has to contain the information necessary to enable investors to evaluate the advantages of investing in the funds. The key investor information document must summarise the main points from the prospectus. If the management company amends or updates the prospectus or key investor information document it must resubmit them to the IFSA.

The offering of interests or shares in a retail fund is exempt from the Securities Trading Act's requirement to publish a prospectus in connection with the public offering of interests.

With limited exemptions UCITS may not extend loans or act as guarantors. Short-term credit in order to meet redemption of unit shares is the only type of borrowing permitted to UCITS. Such credit must not exceed the equivalent of 10 per cent of the asset of the UCITS or its individual divisions. Investor funds are subject to the same lending and borrowing restrictions with the exception that they are permitted to borrow, short term, up to 25 per cent of the value of the fund.

UCITS are not permitted to sell financial instruments that they do not hold, but for investor funds the short selling restriction extends only to unlisted securities.

Provisions of the Securities Trading Act on insider dealing and market abuse may be relevant to transactions involving interests or shares in a retail fund. Legislation on measures against money laundering and terrorist financing may also have to be taken into account.

3.4. Marketing the fund
Production and offering of marketing materials for retail funds is governed by the Funds Act and the marketing of retail funds must be authorised by the IFSA.

Foreign UCITS may be marketed in Iceland provided that the regulator in its home state has given notification to the IFSA under the UCITS Directive. Foreign investor funds can be marketed to the public if they are registered with the IFSA. However, the IFSA imposes certain eligibility criteria for registration, such as a requirement that the funds be adequately regulated in their home state.

Foreign UCITS
For marketing of UCITS in Iceland, whose home state is a member of the EEA, a notification has to be submitted to the UCITS home member state regulator who then transmits this to the IFSA. The following documents must accompany the notification:
- the latest fund rules or its instruments of incorporation;
- its prospectus;
- the key investor information document;
- latest annual and any subsequent semi-annual financial statements (if available);
- description of the proposed marketing activity (including details of the entity which will handle sales and redemptions on behalf of the fund in addition to the target group of investors); and
- information on the proposed measures of the fund to ensure investors' rights with respect to profits, redemption of shares and the information which the fund is obliged to disclose.

In addition, the IFSA may request additional documentation in line with Icelandic law requirements. Certain information, including the key investor information document, must be translated into Icelandic, unless otherwise agreed with the IFSA.

Under the UCITS IV passporting process, the home member state regulator has 10 working days from receiving notification from the UCITS to transmit the notification to the IFSA. UCITS may be marketed in Iceland five working days after the IFSA has received notification from the UCITS home member state regulator.

In the event of a change in the UCITS' marketing arrangements or a change in the share classes to be marketed in Iceland the UCITS is required to notify the Icelandic regulator before implementing the change.

Foreign Non-UCITS
For the marketing of investor funds, who cannot passport into Iceland on the basis of UCITS, an application for authorisation must be filed with the Icelandic regulator. The following documents need to accompany the

application:
- the latest fund rules or its instruments of incorporation;
- its prospectus;
- the key investor information document;
- audited annual financial statements of the preceding year, and semi-annual financial statements;
- a declaration by the fund's home state regulator that the fund and its management company are appropriately licensed and regulated in that state;
- a declaration by the fund's home state regulator that it would be willing to authorise a similar Icelandic fund to be distributed in the respective state – certain exceptions apply; and
- any other information which the fund is obliged to publish in its home state.

Marketing of alternative investment funds must be consistent with proper and sound business practices. In particular, any marketing materials and other promotion of retail funds must present correct and detailed information about the operations of the funds. For example, they must include information about: (i) whether the fund is a UCITS or investor fund; (ii) the name of the management company; (iii) the risks undertaken by the fund; and (iv) the prospectus and key investor information document and where it can be accessed.

This information shall be accessible on the management company's website which shall also publish information about the ten largest issuers that the fund invests in, as well as information about the proportion of investment in each entity. This information shall be updated at least once every six weeks.

3.5. Taxation
The taxation of the income of retail funds has to be addressed in three separate parts: (i) taxation of the management companies; (ii) taxation of the funds themselves; and (iii) the taxation of the investors who own the interests in the funds.

Although the income of retail funds is not beneficially owned by the management company it is treated as the income of the management company provided that the fund is a non-taxable fund. If the management company bore no costs it would be liable for tax on the income. But management companies' eventual liability to pay out all of the income to the holders of the interests is classified as an interest liability under Icelandic law. Interest from debt is deductible from a management company's income which means that management companies are generally not liable for tax on the fund's net income.

Retail funds are generally treated as tax transparent under the Icelandic tax code on the basis that they do not conduct business. To the extent that a retail fund makes no net gain from its activities, ie, in circumstances where all its income is matched by corresponding liabilities, it is very unlikely that the fund would be considered to conduct business according to Icelandic law.

In order to be able to rely on the exemption, the fund should not enter into other business areas than holding and trading of financial instruments and it should not employ any people. It should merely hold and trade securities and enter into a contract with the management company which should conduct the necessary activities for this purpose on behalf of the fund. Otherwise the risk of the fund being engaged in business or the holders of the interests possibly having a permanent establishment in Iceland arises.

Lastly, the investors' income from interests in retail funds is classified as interest income upon realisation by redemption or sale. For domestic companies and individuals the current tax rate on interest income is 20 per cent. The taxation on foreign investors varies and depends on type of income, type of legal persons and the availability of double taxation protection.

In some cases it may be advisable to obtain an advance tax ruling prior to establishing retail funds.

3.6. Customary or common terms
Terms of retail funds show a combination of bespoke and standard terms that vary depending on the funds' investment strategies.

4. PROPOSED CHANGES AND DEVELOPMENTS
The Funds Act was most recently amended in the spring of 2013 to implement the European Parliament and Council Directive 2009/65/EC on UCITS. Preparations for implementing the European Parliament and Council Directive 2011/61/EU on Alternative Investment Fund Managers (AIFMD) are still in the early stages as it has not yet been incorporated into the EEA Agreement. Once the AIFMD forms part of the EEA Agreement Iceland will be required to transpose it into domestic law.

Ireland

Nollaig Greene, Elaine Keane, Darragh Noone & Peter Maher
A&L Goodbody Solicitors

1. MARKET OVERVIEW

The Irish investment funds market is founded on Ireland's position as a leading global centre for domiciling and servicing investment funds. Ireland is the world's largest hedge fund administration centre and fastest growing UCITS centre. UCITS have grown 600 per cent since 2000 with 25 per cent growth since the start of 2012. UCITS are aimed at the retail market and, because they may avail of the EU cross-border passport, are far more popular, although this may change with the advent of the Alternative Investment Fund Managers Directive (AIFMD), which also provides for an EU cross-border passport.

Assets serviced by the Irish funds industry stand at over EUR 2.3 trillion or $3 trillion as at March 2013. The Irish funds industry has grown every year for 23 years (the exception being 2008 when there was a small fall). Ireland has developed an effective and robust regulatory framework and it operates a favourable tax environment which delivers the best tax outcome for the investor. Almost all of the world's major fund service providers have a presence in Ireland. Ireland is a member of the EU, Eurozone, OECD, FATF and IOSCO and is an internationally recognised jurisdiction. Ireland does not operate banking secrecy and was the only international funds centre to appear on the original OECD white list of countries that are in compliance with internationally agreed tax standards. Irish funds are distributed worldwide.

With a continuously expanding tax treaty network approaching 70 countries, Ireland has one of the most developed and favourable tax treaty networks in the world.

Ireland has signed bilateral Memoranda of Understanding with 24 jurisdictions including China, Dubai, Hong Kong, Isle of Man, Jersey, South Africa, Switzerland, Taiwan, UAE and USA and cooperates with all EU member states.

(All data is from the Irish Funds Industry Association.)

The Central Bank of Ireland (Central Bank) is responsible for the authorisation and ongoing supervision of investment funds in Ireland.

An investment fund may list its shares or units on the Irish Stock Exchange, in which case the Irish Stock Exchange will supervise compliance with its listing rules and continuing obligations.

The last year has seen a significant increase in regulation which includes increasing financial requirements for many financial institutions participating in investment funds, as well as increasing focus on conflicts of interest and corporate governance in general which impacts where financial institutions are participating in investment funds.

Ireland

The funds market in Ireland has been active in the past year, particularly because the Irish economy has shown signs of tackling the economic challenges which became evident because of the 2008 financial crisis. In addition to this, the perception is that the property market has hit bottom and so provides significant opportunity for growth.

2. ALTERNATIVE INVESTMENT FUNDS
2.1. Common structures
Unregulated funds
Private unregulated funds in Ireland typically take the form of limited partnerships established pursuant to the Limited Partnerships Act 1907. These are suitable for private placement only. The partnership will comprise one or more general partners (who manage the business and have unlimited joint and several liability for the debts and obligations of the partnership) and one or more limited partners. The liability of each limited partner will be limited to their contribution provided that it does not take part in the management and that the partnership has no more than 20 members (except in limited circumstances). In practice, this number can be increased where investors invest in a nominee company which invests as a limited partner. The general partner will typically be a limited company also. The general partner will commonly obtain an indemnity from the partnership in its favour.

It is generally accepted that the general partner of a limited partnership is not providing investment services to third parties (but to its partners) and so does not require to be authorised to provide investment services. Because such structures are unregulated, they do not involve promoter approval, administration or custodian services, investment or borrowing restrictions, and so on. General partners will need to consider their position under the AIFMD regime in the light of their particular circumstances.

Regulated funds
From 22 July 2013 (implementation date for AIFMD), new regulated alternative investment funds (AIFs) fall into the retail investor alternative investment fund (RIAIF) category (detailed under the 'Retail Funds' section below) or the qualifying investor alternative investment fund category (QIAIF).

QIAIFs may be established as:
- unit trusts;
- investment companies with variable share capital;
- common contractual funds; or
- investment limited partnerships.

Investment companies
Part XIII of the Companies Act 1990 (as amended) provides for the incorporation of non-UCITS open ended investment companies with variable capital and closed-ended investment companies with variable capital whose sole object is the collective investment of their funds in property with the aim of spreading investment risk and giving their members the benefit of the results of the management of their funds. Before such an investment

company can raise capital by providing facilities for the direct or indirect participation by the public in the profit and income of the company, it must have been designated by the Central Bank as a designated company. A variable capital company (VCC) may be self-managed and not employ a management company unlike the other vehicles or it may appoint a management company.

The VCC is the most common vehicle chosen for AIFs. It is a public limited company whose share capital does not have a par value but is equal to the net asset value of the VCC at any time. It has a separate legal personality established by its incorporation with memoranda and articles of association as its constitutional document and can enter into contracts itself. The VCC's day-to-day management and control is carried out by a board of directors, which generally delegates many functions to service providers. A VCC may be open-ended or closed-ended.

Unit trusts

A unit trust fund is defined by the Unit Trusts Act 1990 (the principal legislation governing unit trusts in Ireland) as any arrangement made for the purpose, or having the effect, of providing facilities for the participation by the public, as beneficiaries under a trust, in profits or income arising from the acquisition, holding, management or disposal of securities or any other property whatsoever.

Unit trusts may be closed-ended or open-ended. A unit trust is not a separate legal entity. It is created by a trust deed entered into between the trustee and the management company. Because of this, a unit trust must have a management company and does not enter into contracts in its own name. Instead, the management company or trustee enters into contracts on behalf of the unit trust. The trustee is registered as the legal owner of assets on behalf of the trust.

Investors hold units which represent a beneficial interest in the assets of the unit trust. Unit trusts may be single funds or umbrella funds.

Common Contractual Funds (CCFs)

Many multi-national pension schemes seek to achieve economies of scale and efficiency of operation by pooling pension fund assets into one entity. For such pooling to successfully take place, it is imperative that the pooling vehicle is tax transparent (ie, that the income and gains of such vehicle are treated as arising or occurring to the unitholders or investors and not to the vehicle itself) in order to ensure that the tax status of the pension schemes is not prejudiced, and that the efficiencies of a pooling vehicle are not negatived by detrimental tax treatment. CCFs are established under The Investment Funds, Companies and Miscellaneous Provisions Act 2005. Under Irish law, CCFs are tax transparent vehicles which may be established for such purpose. CCFs have the following characteristics:

- they are pooling vehicles established under the laws of contract namely by a deed of constitution to which a management company and custodian will be party;

- they are not body corporates and have no legal personality of their own;
- participants otherwise known as unitholders in CCFs hold co-ownership rights in the property and assets of the CCF represented by units;
- the liability of unitholders is limited to the amount contributed or agreed to be contributed for units;
- the deed of constitution may be drafted to provide that income is distributed on an annual basis so as not to prejudice the tax transparency of the vehicle in certain jurisdictions; and
- the custodian is a party to the deed of constitution to specifically acknowledge its terms and the obligations at law of a custodian. The custodian is not a trustee and its obligations will be more precisely defined in a separate custodian agreement.

Investment limited partnerships

The Investment Limited Partnerships Act 1994 permits the creation of a limited partnership structure as a regulated investment vehicle. As a tax transparent vehicle it has many uses and is particularly suitable as an investment vehicle for investment in US securities with US advisers. The Finance Act 2013 restored the tax transparent nature of investment limited partnerships.

The tax issues relevant to the different structures are set out in section 2.5.

VCCs are the most popular legal structure used for investment funds in Ireland because investors are familiar with the corporate structure. While VCCs may choose to appoint a manager (which must be authorised) they may also choose to operate as self-managed investment companies (SMICs). VCCs have their own legal personality and ultimate management authority resides with the board of directors, two of whom must be Irish resident. VCCs issue shares to investors and these shares do not represent a legal or beneficial interest in the VCCs assets. VCCs must hold an annual general meeting of shareholders and obtain shareholder approval to change their memorandum and articles of association.

Unit trusts are contractual arrangements (created by trust deed) made between the management company and the trustee. Unit trusts must have a management company. This is the most significant difference, in practice, between a unit trust and a VCC. Unit trusts do not have their own legal personality. Ultimate management authority rests with the management company. Unit trusts are not required to hold annual investor meetings. Changes can be made to the trust deed without having to obtain prior investor approval if both the management company and trustee certify that such changes do not prejudice the interests of investors.

CCFs are used to achieve tax transparency in the pooling of multi-national pension fund assets. CCFs do not hold investor meetings and units are redeemable but not transferable.

Investment limited partnerships are particularly suitable as an investment vehicle for investment in US securities with US advisers.

Participants interests in VCCs are called shares, participants interests in unit trusts, CCFs and investment limited partnerships are called units.

Ireland

Since July 2005, Irish VCCs established as umbrella funds (where sub-funds are established under a common structure, such as a VCC but are treated as separate funds with separate pools of assets, investment objectives and policies and investors) enjoy segregated liability between sub-funds. Unit trusts established as umbrella funds are generally set up with segregated liability between sub-funds. CCFs enjoy segregated liability between sub-funds under statute.

Investment managers and/or investment advisors of Irish authorised AIFs are generally established as limited liability companies and, if EU based, generally hold a MiFID authorisation.

2.2. Regulatory framework

The legislation underlying the different AIF vehicles is set out in section 2.1. above. In addition, the AIFMD and related regulation is relevant as is the Irish regulation implementing the AIFMD regime. Also, the Central Bank has issued its AIF Rulebook and a Q&A document. The Central Bank issues a markets update as necessary and this informs interested parties of recent policy developments.

Other than private, unregulated funds (detailed in section 2.1. above), AIFs must be authorised by the Central Bank.

For regulatory purposes, the Central Bank requires an application to be made to it to permit an entity to be investment manager of an Irish authorised fund before the application for authorisation of the fund can be made. The investment manager of an Irish authorised fund is not required to be Irish but must be deemed acceptable by the Central Bank. Where the investment manager is located in Ireland, it must hold an authorisation under MiFID. Applications in respect of EU investment managers (who are generally authorised under MiFID) are fast tracked. For non-Irish non-MiFID investment managers, the Central Bank must be satisfied that the firm is authorised and subject to ongoing supervision in its home state.

Where an investment adviser to an Irish authorised fund has discretionary powers, the Central Bank treats it as an investment manager and the entity must be cleared by the Central Bank. Where an investment adviser with no discretionary powers is being appointed, the Central Bank imposes notification requirements.

Irish authorised funds must have two Irish resident directors and an Irish custodian/trustee.

The various parties to the QIAIF which may include the management company, directors, trustee or custodian and other service providers must be approved or deemed acceptable by the Central Bank before the application for authorisation can be made. A QIAIF has a minimum subscription and only qualifying investors may invest in a QIAIF (see below).

A QIAIF can be authorised on the day after its documentation is filed with the Central Bank. The documentation must include a fully completed Central Bank application form, a dated prospectus (which may include supplements), a constitutional document and original counterparts of the material contracts (such as custodian agreement, administration agreement, management agreement, prime broker agreement, investment management agreement, distribution agreement). The documentation must reflect the necessary authorisation requirements which are detailed in the Central Bank application forms.

2.3. Operational requirements

The investment restrictions of a QIAIF are set out in section 2.6. below.

QIAIFs must appoint a depositary (also currently referred to as a custodian or trustee). The depositary must meet the requirements of AIFMD and:
- have appropriate expertise and experience to carry out its functions;
- have sufficient resources to effectively conduct its business;
- organise and control its internal affairs in a reasonable manner with proper records and adequate arrangements for ensuring that employees are suitable, adequately trained and properly supervised; and
- hold a minimum capital requirement.

AIFMD imposes regulatory reporting requirements as regards main instruments traded, main markets, principal exposures, concentrations, liquidity, risk and requires the filing of monthly and quarterly returns as well as semi-annual and annual reports.

Specific detailed information must be disclosed to investors under a variety of headings (including remuneration) in accordance with AIFMD, before they invest. Periodic disclosures must also be made to investors.

Under AIFMD, the use of side letters is not restricted but investors must be given details of any preferential treatment (or right to preferential treatment) received by an investor (such as by way of a side letter) before they invest.

Funds are subject to a wide variety of regulation (a great deal of which is EU-based with some Irish nuances) on risk (AIFMD), borrowing restrictions (AIFMD); valuation and pricing of the assets held by the fund (AIFMD); insider dealing and market abuse (MAD); transparency (AIFMD); money laundering (AML); and short selling.

Closed-ended investment companies may be required to issue a prospectus under the Prospectus Directive regime in tandem with obtaining Central Bank authorisation unless (in essence) minimum subscription limits are met or the fund is offered to less than 100 investors per EU state.

2.4. Marketing the fund

The production and offering of marketing materials is governed by the same legislation which governs the authorisation of funds (such as Part XIII of the Companies Act 1990, Unit Trusts Act 1990, Prospectus Directive). A fund which is not availing of the AIFMD passport, which is situated in another jurisdiction and which proposes to market its units in Ireland, must make application to the Central Bank in writing, enclosing various documentation and must comply with marketing requirements.

The following services are regulated by the Central Bank under the MiFID regime:
- receiving and transmitting orders;
- executing orders; and

- providing investment advice.

Other than the fund itself and its management company, any entity engaging on a professional basis in Ireland in marketing activities which involve the services listed above requires authorisation under MiFID.

A QIAIF has a minimum subscription of EUR 100,000 (or its equivalent in another currency). The minimum subscription may be spread among various sub-funds of an umbrella QIF. Only a qualifying investor may invest in a QIF, being:
- an investor who is a professional client within the meaning of Annex II of Directive 2004/39/EC (Markets in Financial Instruments Directive); or
- an investor who receives an appraisal from an EU credit institution, a MiFID firm or a UCITS management company that the investor has the appropriate expertise, experience and knowledge to adequately understand the investment in the fund; or
- an investor who certifies that they are an informed investor by providing the following:
  - confirmation (in writing) that the investor has such knowledge of, and experience in, financial and business matters as would enable the investor to properly evaluate the merits and risks of the prospective investment; or
  - confirmation (in writing) that the investor's business involves, whether for its own account or the account of others, the management, acquisition or disposal of property of the same kind as the property of the fund.

Within the EU, QIAIFs may be marketed to professional investors as defined in the AIFMD, subject to certain filings. Where the member state in question permits, under the laws of that member state, AIFs to be sold to other categories of investors and this permission encompasses investors set out above, they may also be marketed to that category of investor.

The private unregulated funds referred to in section 2.1. above may only be sold by private placement, when approved by the Central Bank.

The marketing materials must satisfy the Central Bank requirements. There are no additional requirements on marketing to public bodies such as government pension funds, other than as prescribed in respect of the investor bodies themselves.

There are no restrictions on the use of intermediaries to assist in the fund-raising process (other than conflict of interest requirements).

2.5. Taxation
Taxation of funds
An Irish fund is not subject to tax on its income and gains. Unless an investor in an Irish fund is resident or ordinarily resident in Ireland, generally there is no tax payable in Ireland in respect of any payments received from the fund by the investor.

Irish regulated funds however they are constituted (whether for example as a variable capital company or a unit trust) are not subject to tax on their income and gains but instead operate an exit tax regime.

VAT

A fund will be required to register for Irish VAT in certain circumstances, for example, where in receipt of services from abroad for which it is obliged to self-account. Registration may also be relevant where the fund is seeking to recover VAT charged to it (although a fund does not necessarily have to register for VAT in order to reclaim VAT suffered), or where an Irish VAT registration number is needed in order for a foreign service provider not to charge foreign VAT on the service. VAT registration does not in itself entitle a fund to recover VAT charged to it. VAT recovery is available either to the extent the fund is engaged in activities which are subject to VAT or is engaged in exempt financial services outside the EU. Based on current practice the latter is considered to apply where a fund has non-EU assets or has non-EU investors. VAT therefore is not necessarily a cost to a fund.

VAT will be chargeable on certain services supplied to a fund eg, legal services provided to the fund. However, there are exemptions for certain services. The principal exemption is for investment management services and applies to discretionary investment management services, administration services and marketing services.

Taxation of CCFs

CCFs are intended to facilitate the obtaining of relief from withholding tax in jurisdictions where investments are held. For Irish tax purposes, the income and gains on CCFs are treated as accruing directly to the investors and therefore, there is no exposure to Irish tax for investors outside the scope of Irish tax. A CCF is tax transparent under Irish law so as to facilitate the CCF investor in obtaining relief under the terms of a double tax treaty between their home jurisdiction and the jurisdiction where the withholding is suffered, effectively ignoring the existence of the Irish CCF. The CCF itself is not liable to tax in Ireland on its income or gains.

Taxation of an Investment Limited Partnership (ILP)

An ILP is a partnership which has as its principal business the investment of its funds in property. The ILP must have at least one general and one limited partner. The Finance Act 2013 has restored the original tax transparency of the ILP. Prior to that an ILP was grouped with other regulated funds such as unit trusts and variable capital companies as an investment undertaking and treated as opaque for tax purposes. An ILP is no longer defined as an investment undertaking but is treated separately as a tax transparent vehicle akin to a CCF.

Double tax relief

Whether the benefits of a double tax agreement can be availed of by an Irish fund is determined under normal treaty principles. Usually, a double tax agreement with Ireland will provide that for a fund to be able to avail of the treaty provisions, it must be resident in Ireland for tax purposes. In practice, if a confirmation of the Irish residence of a fund is requested from the Irish Revenue Commissioners, they will normally issue a letter, where they are satisfied that the fund concerned is resident in Ireland, that the fund is so resident but will note that the fund is only liable to tax in Ireland to the extent that it has Irish resident investors. As to whether this would be sufficient for the foreign tax authority to grant treaty relief is obviously dependent on the practice of the foreign tax authority.

Taxation of a management company
Subject to certain conditions, it is possible to establish a management company which will be liable to corporation tax on its fee income in respect of the management of funds at the tax rate of 12.5 per cent.

A management company is entitled to the benefit of the Irish double tax treaties. This is of benefit in repatriating profits from the management company to a foreign parent if the relevant treaty has the effect of preserving the benefit of the low rate of Irish tax in the hands of the parent, and may also be of benefit in ensuring that the management company is not subject to tax in a foreign jurisdiction (which has a relevant double tax treaty) unless it carries on business in that jurisdiction through a permanent establishment.

EU Savings Directive
The EU Savings Directive may be relevant in the context of Irish funds which are UCITS, or deemed UCITS, where there are investments in underlying debt securities. The Directive requires the reporting of, or in the case of Austria and Luxembourg the withholding of, interest paid cross-border to EU resident individual beneficial owners.

An exit tax charge should only arise in respect of certain Irish resident or ordinarily resident investors on the happening of certain chargeable events. (Note: In order for non-Irish resident investors to avoid a charge to exit tax, an appropriate declaration is generally required to be provided to the fund in advance of the chargeable event). A chargeable event arises for example on a payment of any kind to an investor, whether an income distribution or a full or partial redemption, on a transfer of units, and on a rolling eight-year deemed disposal at market value. In certain circumstances a fund may elect not to operate the exit tax on such a deemed chargeable event, in which case it is obliged to report certain investor details to the Irish Revenue Commissioners and the tax liability arises on the investor on a self-assessment basis.

Similarly there are a number of categories of Irish resident investor that are entitled to an exemption from this exit tax including:
- pension schemes;
- insurance companies;
- other funds;
- charities;
- approved retirement funds, approved minimum retirement funds, special savings incentive accounts and PRSAs; and
- credit unions.

If there are Irish taxable investors on the occasion of any chargeable event the fund must operate an exit tax deducting the tax due from payments to the relevant investor, or where there is no such payment by appropriating and cancelling the relevant number of units necessary to pay the tax. The rate of exit tax is 33 per cent where the chargeable event is an income distribution, and on any other chargeable event is 36 per cent of any gain realised by the investor, or in the case of the eight-year chargeable rolling event any deemed gain. However in the case of a company holding units in a fund, and where the appropriate declaration has been made to the fund the rate of exit tax is 25 per cent in all cases. The rate of tax is increased to 56 per cent if, under the terms of an investment in a fund, the investor (being an individual) or certain persons associated with the investor have an ability to influence the selection of the assets of the fund.

Transfers of units/shares in a fund will generally not be liable to Irish stamp duty. Generally gifts/inheritances of units/shares between non-Irish residents will not be liable to gift or inheritance tax provided certain conditions are met.

2.6. Customary or common terms

QIAIFs may be established as open-ended (at least quarterly redemption and other conditions), limited liquidity (less than quarterly redemption and other conditions) or closed-ended and must make this clear. The life of the fund will vary depending on its purpose.

The Central Bank does not impose rules on how liquidity is managed other than to require clear disclosure in the prospectus. Funds operate a variety of restrictions on the issue and redemption of units or shares, depending on the nature of the fund. Funds are not required to provide investors with the right to transfer shares or units, unless they are listed on the Irish Stock Exchange.

QIAIFs may purchase assets and place these in side pockets with no limit placed on the amount of assets that can be side pocketed. A QIAIF which avails of this flexibility must classify itself as 'open-ended with limited liquidity' or 'closed-ended'.

There is no requirement for the management company/adviser to invest its own money in the fund, nor are there requirements for key individuals to be involved in the management of the fund, nor are any key main provisions typically included in the fund arrangements. Investors do not have the direct ability to remove the management company/adviser of the fund although investors may be able to change the directors of the fund (if the fund is structured as a company).

For AIFMs, AIFMD remuneration requirements must be complied with and these requirements will become clearer over time. The Central Bank does not impose rules on how remuneration is typically structured other than that it must be clearly disclosed. The management company's remuneration cannot be increased without investor approval and the calculation of performance fees must be verified by a suitable independent party, such as an auditor.

QIAIF investment restrictions are as follows:
- QIAIFs may not raise capital from the public through the issue of debt securities (this does not operate to prevent the issue of notes by QIAIFS, on a private basis, to a lending institution to facilitate financing arrangements provided that details of the note are provided in the

Ireland

prospectus).
- QIAIFs may not grant loans or act as a guarantor on behalf of third parties (but QIAIFs may acquire debt securities, securities which are not fully paid and may enter into bridge financing arrangements in certain circumstances).
- QIAIFs may not (and its manager may not) acquire any shares carrying voting rights which would enable it to exercise significant influence over the management of an issuing body (other than as disclosed for venture capital, development capital or private equity QIAIFs or in respect of investments in other investment funds).
- QIAIFs may only invest in units of an investment fund managed by its management company or AIFM or by an associated or related company of either of these, where the management company of the investment fund in which the investment is being made has waived the preliminary/ initial/ redemption charge which it would normally charge.
- QIAIFs must ensure that the calculation of performance fees is verified by the depositary or a competent person appointed by the AIFM and approved for the purpose by the depositary. QIAIFs with a minimum subscription requirement of EUR 500,000 may invest more than 50 per cent in a single unregulated scheme, subject to certain disclosure requirements.
- QIAIFs must have detailed procedures in place to cover a variety of issues which include liquidity management, risk, conflicts of interest, recordkeeping, remuneration and reporting process.
- Under AIFMD, AIFM must set reasonable leverage limits for each AIF. The AIF leverage may be capped by the AIFM's regulator. The amount of leverage employed must be reported to regulators regularly.

3. RETAIL FUNDS
3.1. Common structures
From a regulatory perspective, the most popular structure for retail funds in Ireland are UCITS. All UCITS, however structured, must comply with UCITS investment and borrowing restrictions, authorisation processes and operating conditions (such as two redemption dates per month) and must have an Irish based trustee/custodian. Retail funds may also be established as Retail Investor Alternative Investment Funds (RIAIFs).

The different retail investment fund vehicles, whether a UCITS or a RIAIF (which mirror the vehicles used for AIFs as detailed above) are:
- unit trusts;
- investment companies with variable share capital; and
- common contractual funds.

RIAIFs may be structured as investment limited partnerships. Technically UCITS may also be established as companies with fixed capital but these are not used in practice.

The advantages and disadvantages of the structures are detailed in section 2.1. above as regards the vehicle used. As regards the choice between a UCITS or a RIAIF, UCITS enjoy an EU marketing passport (subject to filings and

Ireland

complying with local marketing requirements) whereas the RIAIF enjoys slightly more flexibility in respect of its investment restrictions and leverage but no EU wide marketing passport.

3.2. Regulatory framework

UCITS are authorised under the UCITS regime (the UCITS Directive, Regulations, ESMA materials, implementing Irish regulations, Central Bank UCITS Notices, Guidance Notes and policy). RIAIFs are authorised under the legislation underlying the particular vehicle used, ie Part XIII of the Companies Act 1990 (as amended), Unit Trusts Act 1990, The Investment Funds, Companies and Miscellaneous Provisions Act 2005 and the Investment Limited Partnerships Act 1994 as detailed in section 2.1. above.

In addition the Central Bank has issued its AIF Rulebook and a Q&A to further clarify its requirements. The Central Bank also issues a Markets Update which informs interested parties of recent policy developments.

The funds themselves must be authorised by the Central Bank.

The principal statutes regulating the funds are detailed in section 2.1. above. In addition to this, details relating to the investment manager are outlined in section 2.1.

There are no exemptions from the regulatory regime.

The various parties to the RIAIF or UCITS (which may include the management company, directors, trustee or custodian and other service providers) must be approved or deemed acceptable by the Central Bank.

The fund documentation must be approved by the Central Bank and must comply with its detailed requirements. This will include a fully completed Central Bank application form, a dated prospectus (which may include supplements), a constitutional document, and original counterparts of the material contracts (such as custodian agreement, administration agreement, management agreement, investment management agreement, distribution agreement). For a UCITS, it will also include a business plan, risk management process and Key Investor Information Document (KIID).

3.3. Operational requirements

RIAIFs are more limited in terms of investment restrictions and eligible assets than QIAIFs, UCITS are more limited again (see section 3.6. below).

All Irish regulated funds must appoint a custodian/trustee to safe-keep the assets of the fund. That entity must itself be authorised.

All Irish authorised funds make regular filings with the Central Bank on a monthly, quarterly and annual basis.

UCITS and RIAIFs are subject to significant reporting and disclosure obligations which are aligned with requirements under the UCITS regime and the AIFMD regime respectively.

The use of side letters is not restricted provided that all investors are treated equally by the fund in the case of a UCITS and fairly in the case of a RIAIF.

Funds are subject to a wide variety of regulation (a great deal of which is EU-based with some Irish nuances) on risk, borrowing restrictions, transparency, valuation and pricing of the assets held by the fund (UCITS and

AIFMD); insider dealing and market abuse (MAD); money laundering (AML); and short selling.

Closed-ended investment companies may be required to issue a prospectus under the Prospectus Directive regime in tandem with obtaining Central Bank authorisation unless (in essence) minimum subscription limits are met or the fund is offered to less than 100 investors per EU state.

3.4. Marketing the fund
The issues are as detailed for AIFs above except that UCITS funds may be marketed under the EU passport, anywhere in the EU, subject to registration and compliance with local marketing rules.

There are no restrictions concerning to whom a retail fund may be marketed (save as set out in the fund documentation). The key content requirements and required authorisations for marketing materials is set out in section 2.4. above.

There are no restrictions on the use of intermediaries to assist in the fund-raising process.

3.5. Taxation
The tax treatment for retail funds is as set out in section 2.5. above.

3.6. Customary or common terms
UCITS must have two dealing days in every month and do not set a life term. For RIAIFs, the issues are as detailed for AIFs above.

For UCITS, there will not be any restrictions on liquidity of interests. Typically, investors will not be able to transfer or assign their interests in unit trusts or CCFs but will be able to transfer shares in VCCs. For RIAIFs, the issues are as detailed for AIFs above.

The Central Bank does not impose rules on how remuneration is typically structured other than that it must be clearly disclosed, the management company's remuneration cannot be increased without investor approval and the calculation of performance fees must be verified.

UCITS and RIAIFs must have detailed procedures in place to cover a variety of issues which include liquidity management, risk, conflicts of interest, recordkeeping and reporting processes.

Permitted investments
Investments of a UCITS are confined to:
- transferable securities and money market instruments which are listed on a stock exchange or other regulated market;
- recently issued transferable securities which will be admitted to official listing on a stock exchange or other regulated market within a year;
- money market instruments, as defined in the UCITS Notices, other than those dealt on a regulated market;
- units of UCITS;
- units of non-UCITS as set out in Central Bank Guidance ;
- deposits with credit institutions as prescribed in the UCITS Notices; and
- financial derivative instruments (FDIs) as prescribed in the UCITS Notices.

Ireland

Investment restrictions
The following investment restrictions apply to UCITS:
- A UCITS cannot invest more than 10 per cent of net assets in transferable securities and money market instruments other than those referred to above (permitted investments).
- A UCITS cannot invest more than 10 per cent of net assets in recently issued transferable securities which will be admitted to official listing on a stock exchange or other market within a year.
- A UCITS cannot invest more than 10 per cent of net assets in transferable securities or money market instruments issued by the same body provided that the total value of transferable securities and money market instruments held in the issuing bodies in each of which it invests more than 5 per cent must be less than 40 per cent. This limit of 10 per cent is raised to 35 per cent if the transferable securities or money market instruments are issued or guaranteed by a member state or its local authorities, or by a non-member state or public international body of which one or more member states are members.
- A UCITS cannot invest more than 20 per cent of net assets in deposits made with the same credit institution. Deposits with certain institutions, held as ancillary liquidity, must not exceed 10 per cent of net assets. This limit can be raised to 20 per cent in the case of deposits made with the trustee or custodian.
- The risk exposure of a UCITS to a counterparty to an OTC derivative cannot exceed 5 per cent of net assets. This limit is raised to 10 per cent if the counterparty is a certain type of credit institution.
- A combination of two or more of the following issued by, or made or undertaken with, the same body cannot exceed 20 per cent of net assets: investments in transferable securities or money market instruments; deposits; and/or risk exposures arising from OTC derivatives transactions.
- A UCITS fund can invest 100 per cent of its net assets in transferable securities and money market instruments issued or guaranteed by: an EU member state, its local authorities or agencies; an Organisation for Economic Co-operation and Development (OECD) member state; or public international bodies of which one or more EU member states are members.
- A UCITS cannot invest more than 20 per cent of net assets in any one collective investment scheme (CIS). Investment in non-UCITS cannot, in aggregate, exceed 30 per cent of net assets. A UCITS cannot invest in a CIS, which can itself invest more than 10 per cent of net assets in other schemes.
- A UCITS can invest up to 20 per cent of net assets in shares and/or debt securities issued by the same body where the investment policy of the fund is to replicate an index which satisfies the criteria set out in the UCITS Notices and is recognised by the Central Bank. This 20 per cent limit can be raised to 35 per cent, and applied to a single issuer, where this is justified by exceptional market conditions.
- An investment company, or a management company acting in

connection with all of the CIS it manages, cannot acquire any shares carrying voting rights which would enable it to exercise significant influence over the management of an issuing body.
- UCITS are generally restricted from acquiring more than: 10 per cent of the non-voting shares of any single issuing body; 10 per cent of the debt securities of any single issuing body; 25 per cent of the units of any single CIS; 10 per cent of the money market instruments of any single issuing body.
- A UCITS cannot carry out uncovered sales of: transferable securities; money market instruments; units of CIS; or FDIs.
- A UCITS's global exposure (as prescribed in the UCITS Notices) relating to derivatives must not exceed its total net asset value.
- A UCITS can borrow up to 10 per cent of its net asset value provided such borrowing is on a temporary basis. A UCITS can charge its assets as security for such borrowings.

Examples of some of the alternative investment strategies being employed within UCITS include:
- equity long/short funds;
- 130/30 funds;
- hedge fund or commodities index products;
- fund of funds/fund of hedge funds;
- managed futures/commodity trading products;
- absolute return funds; and
- tactical asset allocation funds.

The following investment restrictions apply to RIAIFs. RIAIFs:
- may not (and its manager may not) acquire any shares carrying voting rights which would enable it to exercise significant influence over the management of an issuing body (this requirement does not apply to investments in other investment funds and is also disapplied for RIAIFs which are venture capital, development capital or private equity RIAIFs provided its prospectus indicates its intention regarding the exercise of legal and management control over underlying investments);
- may not grant loans or act as a guarantor on behalf of third parties (this is without prejudice to the right of a RIAIF to acquire debt securities and will not prevent RIAIFs from acquiring securities which are not fully paid);
- may not raise capital from the public through the issue of debt securities;
- may only track or gain an exposure to an index where the index complies with certain conditions;
- may not invest more than 20 per cent of its net assets in securities which are not traded in or dealt on a regulated market which operates regularly and is recognised and open to the public;
- in general, the RIAIF may not invest more than 20 per cent of its net assets in securities issued by the same institution. For RIAIFs whose investment policy is to replicate an index, this limit is increased to 35 per cent in the case of a single issuer where this is justified by exceptional market conditions, for example in regulated markets where certain transferable securities or money market instruments are highly dominant

or other exceptional market conditions;
- in general, a RIAIF may not hold more than 20 per cent of any class of security issued by any single issuer. This requirement does not apply to investments in other open-ended investment funds;
- may only invest up to 100 per cent of its net assets in transferable securities issued or guaranteed by any state, its constituent states, its local authorities, or public international bodies of which one or more states are members with the prior approval of the Central Bank;
- may not keep on deposit more than 10 per cent of its net assets with any one institution; this limit is increased to 30 per cent of net assets for deposits with or securities evidencing deposits issued by or securities guaranteed by certain institutions;
- in general, may only invest in open-ended investment funds provided the underlying investment funds are regulated investment funds;
- in general, may not invest more than 30 per cent of net assets in any one open-ended investment fund;
- where a RIAIF invests more than 30 per cent of net assets in other investment funds it must ensure that the investment funds in which it invests are prohibited from investing more than 30 per cent of net assets in other investment funds. Any such investments must not be made for the purpose of duplicating management and/or investment management fees;
- may not invest more than 20 per cent of net assets in unregulated open-ended investment funds;
- may only invest in units of an investment fund managed by its management company or AIFM or by an associated or related company of either of these where the management company of the investment fund in which the investment is being made has waived the preliminary/ initial/redemption charge which it would normally charge;
- must ensure that any commission or other fee received by the management company or AIFM must be paid into the property of the RIAIF;
- may not have a risk exposure to a counterparty in an OTC derivative transaction which exceeds the following:
- where the counterparty is a relevant institution, 10 per cent of the RIAIF's net assets, or
- in any other case, 5 per cent of the RIAIFs net assets;
- must ensure that its global exposure relating to FDIs does not exceed the total net asset value of its portfolio. When a transferable security or money market instrument contains an embedded derivative, the latter shall be taken into account;
- may only: (i) borrow; and (ii) secure such borrowing on the assets of the RIAIF where permitted by its constitutional document;
- may not borrow, or have at any given time, borrowings exceeding 25 per cent of its net assets. The RIAIF shall not offset credit balances (eg, cash) against borrowings when determining the percentage of borrowings outstanding;
- where the RIAIF engages in transactions in FDIs, whether such

transactions are for investment purposes or for hedging purposes, it must comply with specific requirements;
- in terms of warehousing, the RIAIF may only acquire assets pursuant to a warehousing arrangement where the use of such arrangements is fully disclosed in its prospectus, including details of any fee payable in relation to such arrangements and that the RIAIF will pay no more than current market value for these assets;
- may establish side pocket share classes into which assets which have become illiquid or difficult to value may be placed provided that the ability to establish these share classes has been provided for in the RIAIF's constitutional document and has been disclosed to investors in advance; and
- physical short selling will be permitted in RIAIFs and RIAIFs may gain exposure to any commodity through derivatives. RIAIFs will also be permitted to invest directly in gold. Direct investment in other commodities may be permitted.

4. PROPOSED CHANGES AND DEVELOPMENTS

At EU and global level, we see many proposals which will reform or impact the investment funds market and these will impact on Ireland. These include UCITS V and VI, PRIPs, money market funds, FATCA, AML reform, EMIR, European Long-Term Investment Funds, European Social Entrepreneurship Funds, European Venture Capital Funds and so on.

In Ireland, the Minister for Finance has approved, in principle, the development of legislative proposals for a new corporate structure (an ICAV) which will be more suited to the funds industry as it will remove the need for compliance with various requirements under Irish company law which serve no real purpose where investment vehicles are concerned, resulting in a reduced administrative burden and reduced costs. One of the primary advantages of the ICAV will be to provide for a corporate entity that meets US check-the-box taxation rules.

The Central Bank is consulting on the circumstances in which QIAIFs may engage in lending activities (eg, investing in loans on the primary market). It is also consulting on streamlining its authorisation process and other improvements.

Italy

Paolo Iemma & Stefano Grilli*
Gianni, Origoni, Grippo, Cappelli & Partners

INTRODUCTION

For consistency with the other chapters in this book, we have described the Italian regime applicable to mutual funds according to the 'retail' versus 'alternative' funds classification.

However, current Italian rules are not structured around such a classification. Rather, they distinguish between open-ended and closed-ended funds; different rules apply to open-ended funds, depending on whether they are 'EU harmonised' or not; special rules also apply, *inter alia*, to: (i) closed-ended funds directed at professional investors only; (ii) hedge funds; and (iii) real estate funds.

By way of example, non-harmonised open-ended funds may be categorised both as alternative funds or retail funds, depending on their target investors.

1. MARKET OVERVIEW

According to the 2012 annual report published by the Bank of Italy, net disinvestments from open-ended funds were 50 per cent less than in 2011 (EUR 14 billion in 2012 against EUR 34 billion in 2011). The net collection of foreign funds offered in Italy increased from 1 billion in 2011 to 15 billion in 2012, with a general increase of the overall assets of funds marketed in Italy by approximately 10 per cent, equalling EUR 457 billion.

Net divestments mainly affected non-harmonised funds and, in particular, speculative funds. Investments in fixed income funds (in particular funds investing in corporate bonds, emerging markets bonds and Italian sovereign bonds) have been significant, due to low interest rates paid on short-term assets and the uncertainty associated with equity markets.

The net collection of real estate closed-ended funds (defined as new investments flow net of redemptions) fell from EUR 4.7 billion to EUR 2.7 billion, whilst the net collection of closed-ended funds (mainly private equity funds) has been equal to EUR 781 million.

The average yield of Italian harmonised open-ended funds, net of fees, has turned positive again (from -3.2 per cent in 2011 to 8.2 per cent in 2012), reflecting a positive trend of financial markets in the second half of the year.

The impact of the total fees on the average net assets value of harmonised open-ended funds went up for the first time from 2009 (1.7 per cent in 2011 *vis-à-vis* 1.8 per cent in 2012), as a consequence of the higher incentive fees applied by fund managers.

---

* The Authors would like to thank Marco Zaccagnini and Alessandro Del Guerra (Regulatory aspects) and Fabio Chiarenza and Marco Busia (Tax aspects).

The market share of investment funds promoted by Italian groups calculated on the overall assets of funds placed in Italy further turned down from 73 per cent to 71 per cent. As of the end of 2012, Italian groups were managing approximately 7 per cent of the assets of European open-ended funds. Among the investment funds placed in Italy an even more significant market share is represented by foreign funds (from 63 per cent in 2011 to 67 per cent in 2012), most of them incorporated in Luxembourg.

2. ALTERNATIVE INVESTMENT FUNDS
2.1. Common structures
Under current common practice, alternative investment funds may be divided among the following common structures: non-harmonised open-ended funds (*fondi aperti non armonizzati*), reserved funds (*fondi riservati a investitori qualificati*) which may be either open-ended or closed-ended (the latter also including reserved real estate funds) and speculative (hedge) funds (*fondi speculativi*).

Another form of alternative investment fund is also represented by non-harmonised SICAVs (*società di investimento a capitale variabile non armonizzate*) which, under Italian law, must be mandatorily incorporated as an open-ended structure and are subject to certain provisions commonly applicable to Italian companies limited by shares (*società per azioni*). Whilst the generality of the investment funds provides for the issuance of units representing the assets of the fund, the SICAV is the only UCITS under Italian law which – being a company limited by shares – issues shares. Nevertheless, due to the very limited diffusion of this kind of UCITS in the Italian market (the mandatory open-ended structure prevents the manager from investing in illiquid assets), the following analysis will be only focused on 'proper' investment funds, as described above.

Non-harmonised open-ended funds (reserved)
Non-harmonised open-ended funds (*fondi aperti non armonizzati*) are open-ended funds which may invest in certain liquid assets (see section 2.3., 'Non-harmonised open-ended funds (reserved)' for more details) and do not comply with the requirements set forth by Directive 2009/65/EC. Under Italian law they may be considered as alternative investment funds when they are only offered to qualified investors (see below 'Reserved open-ended and closed-ended funds') but this category of fund may also be addressed to retail investors (see for the relevant discipline, section 3.3., 'Non-harmonised open-ended funds (retail))'. For the purposes of this Part 2, they will be treated with the relevant applicable discipline when the subscription of their units is only reserved to qualified investors.

Reserved open-ended and closed-ended funds
As anticipated, reserved funds may be either reserved open-ended funds (*fondi aperti riservati a investitori qualificati*) and reserved closed-ended funds (*fondi chiusi riservati a investitori qualificati*).

Reserved open-ended funds substantially coincide with non-harmonised open-ended funds when the latter are reserved to qualified investors and, therefore, see section 2.3., 'Non-harmonised open-ended funds (reserved)' for the relevant discipline.

Reserved closed-ended funds may invest in both liquid and illiquid instruments set out by the Ministerial Decree No.228 of 1999. Their units may only be subscribed or purchased by qualified investors and the investors may not redeem the units at any time but only at maturity. As being reserved to qualified investors, reserved closed-ended funds may derogate, if so provided by the rules of the fund, to risks concentration limits and prudential rules set forth by the Bank of Italy with respect to retail closed-ended funds (excluding the limits to financial leverage). Among the reserved closed-ended funds, an important sub-category is represented by the reserved real estate funds (*fondi immobiliari riservati*), which mainly invest in real estate properties and rights, stakes in real estate companies and parts of other Italian and foreign real estate funds. Real estate funds are subject to a peculiar discipline which is described below under section 2.3., 'Reserved open-ended and closed-ended funds'. Reserved closed-ended funds represent also the category according to which investment funds operating in the fields of private equity and venture capital are commonly set up in the Italian market.

Speculative (hedge) funds
Speculative (hedge) funds (*fondi speculativi*) may invest in any assets provided for by the relevant rules of the fund. Their peculiarity is that such kind of funds may derogate to all risk concentration limits and prudential rules set forth by the Bank of Italy, including the limits to financial leverage which may be exceeded up to the limits set forth by the rules of the fund. A speculative fund may be established either as an open-ended fund, a closed-ended fund or a real estate fund. The definition as a 'speculative fund' entails the application to the relevant fund of specific operational requirements which are better described below under section 2.3., 'Speculative (hedge) funds'.

2.2. Regulatory framework
Regulatory provisions applying to SGRs and alternative investment funds
In Italy, alternative investment funds are governed by the following laws and regulations:
- Legislative Decree No.58 of 24 February 1998 as amended (the Consolidated Financial Law) which is the main legislation on the regulation of financial markets;
- Ministerial Decree No.228 of 24 May 1999 as amended, regarding the general criteria which investment funds have to comply with;
- the Bank of Italy regulation on collective portfolio management adopted on 8 May 2012 (as amended on 8 May 2013) which sets forth, *inter alia*, the regulatory framework for the corporate organisation and operations of the SGRs (including the authorisation regime and the patrimonial requirements), the minimum information which must be included in the rules of the fund, provisions concerning the prudential regulations which investment funds must comply with, the discipline of the offer, in Italy

and abroad, both of Italian and foreign investment funds;
- the joint regulation issued by the Bank of Italy and Consob on 29 October 2007, as amended, on the organisation of financial intermediaries;
- the Consob regulation No.16190 of 29 October 2007, as amended, regulating the way in which investment service and collective portfolio management must be carried out *vis-à-vis* the investors;
- the Consob regulation No.11971 of 14 May 1999, as amended, concerning the issuers of securities; and
- the Ministerial Decrees No.468 and 469 of 11 November 1998 which regulate, respectively, the experience and integrity requirements which must be met by directors, statutory auditors and general managers of SGRs and the integrity requirements which must be met by any of the shareholders of SGRs and SICAVs.

Licensing requirements for alternative investment funds

Alternative investment funds categorised as reserved funds and/or speculative funds (such as non-harmonised open-ended funds reserved to qualified investors, reserved closed-ended investment funds, reserved real estate funds, speculative open-ended, closed-ended or real estate funds) are not subject to any approval of the relevant rules by the Bank of Italy nor to clearance in case of amendments to the rules. Therefore, the SGR is only obliged to submit to the Bank of Italy the rules of the fund approved by its competent bodies together with the minute of the relevant meeting of the corporate bodies within 10 days from such approval.

The investment manager

All the investment funds in Italy must be managed by an investment manager which, under Italian law, may only be established as a company limited by shares (*società per azioni*) and is defined as '*società di gestione del risparmio*, (SGR)'. SGRs operate under the supervision of the Bank of Italy with respect to the risk management, asset stability and sound and prudent management of the company and under the control of Consob with respect to the transparency and correctness of the conducts. SGRs must be endowed with a minimum corporate capital equal to EUR 1 million but Bank of Italy admits the minimum corporate capital to be set at EUR 120,000 under certain circumstances.

In the case of SICAVs, the same may be directly managed by its board of directors (internally managed SICAVs) or, otherwise, a management proxy may be attributed to a SGR which will be therefore responsible for the investment activities of the SICAV (externally managed SICAVs).

Licensing requirements for the SGR

SGRs' activity is subject to the prior authorisation of the Bank of Italy (after consultation with Consob). The clearance process starts with the application containing the details of the SGR together with the annexes set out in the Bank of Italy regulation adopted on 8 May 2012, as amended (such as, by way of example, the by-laws, the indication that the minimum capital has been fully paid-in, the program of activity and the report concerning the organisational structure, the list of the shareholders which must comply with the integrity requirements set forth by the Ministerial Decree No.469 of 11 November 1998).

The Bank of Italy will assess the compliance with the sound and prudent management requirements and the other conditions provided by law, including the adherence of the SGR to an officially recognised indemnity and investor protection system (that is, on a very general basis, a fund set up to compensate the investors from damages arising out of the carrying out of investment services and activities when the relevant intermediary goes bankrupt).

Where the clearance is granted, the SGR is further enrolled in the special register held by the Bank of Italy.

Due to the particular nature of speculative funds, in case a SGR not managing speculative funds subsequently intends to set up and manage one or more speculative funds, it must update its operational models, by enhancing and strengthening its internal control, risk management and compliance functions.

The license will be declared forfeited by the Bank of Italy if: (i) the SGR does not commence its activity within one year from the release of the authorisation by the Bank of Italy; or (ii) if the SGR suspends its activity for a period exceeding six months (eg, as it liquidated, or assigned the management of, the managed funds and did not apply for the setting up of any new investment funds).

As better detailed under succeeding section 4, the licensing requirements for investment managers managing and offering parts of alternative investment funds in Italy will be significantly amended under the new provisions of the Directive 2011/61/EU (the Alternative Investment Funds Directive, (AIFMD)) once it will be effectively transposed in Italy.

2.3. Operational requirements
Requirements applicable to the generality of investment funds
As a general rule, all the investment funds in Italy are compelled to appoint a bank acting as depository and custodian which is entrusted, among others, to keep and protect the assets and cash of the fund (with the obvious exception of the real estate properties, other real estate rights and commodities which cannot be safely kept), manage the payments due from and to the investors, keep and update the certificates in the name of the investors representing the units of the fund held by each of them, check the legitimacy of operations of issuance and redemption of the units of the fund and the allocation of the fund's income and, if so expressly entrusted by the SGR, calculate the net asset value of the fund. The role of custodian and depository may be exercised by an Italian bank or an Italian branch of an EU bank, having a net asset at least equal to EUR 100 million and specifically authorised by the Bank of Italy to carry out the activity of custodian and depository. A further authorisation is also required in order to allow the depositary bank to carry out the calculation of the net asset value of investment funds.

As far as reporting requirements are concerned, the SGR, in addition to its own financial statements, must: (i) prepare and keep a journal of the fund in which the transactions involving the management of the fund as well as the operations of issuance and redemption of units must be recorded on a daily basis; (ii) prepare the annual report of the fund within 60 days' from the earlier between the end of any financial year and the date on which any distribution is made in favour of the investors to be published within the subsequent 30 days; and (iii) prepare the semi-annual report of the fund within 30 days from the end of the relevant half-year to be published within the subsequent 30 days. The SGR may, when it is required by specific needs related to the structure or the purpose of the fund, extend of a further 30-day period the term for the preparation and publication of the annual report and the semi-annual report, expressly stating the reasons grounding any such extension. All those documents must be kept at disposal of the investors (who may extract copies for free) at the registered office of the SGR and the depositary bank, even though reserved and speculative funds may set out, in the relevant rules of the funds, different ways to publish any such documents. Real estate funds must also publish information concerning: (i) the appraisals made by the independent experts; (ii) the deeds of contribution, purchase or sale of assets; (iii) the lending obtained for the redemption of the units; and (iv) the group which the financial intermediary entrusted with the assessment of the consistency and profitability of the contributions belongs to (see below paragraph 'Reserved open-ended and closed-ended funds' for further details).

In the provision of the asset management activity, SGRs must also comply with all the requirements set out by Consob regulation No.16190 of 29 October 2007 as amended. Accordingly, SGRs are compelled to carry out their management services with diligence, accuracy and transparency, in the interest of the investors and market integrity, ensuring that the activity is carried out independently and in compliance with the targets, the investment policies and the specific risks of the managed funds. The Consob regulation provides several rules which apply both generally to the provision of the asset management activity (with specific provisions applying to closed-ended funds, such as the obligation to draft and update an asset, economic and financial plan consistent with the term of the fund and the market conditions) and specifically with respect to: (i) the best execution rule in the transmission and execution of orders on behalf of the managed funds; (ii) the funds' orders management criteria; (iii) limitations and policies concerning the inducements; (iv) orders reporting to investors and phone orders recording obligations; (v) criteria for marketing and promotional communications (which must be clearly identified as such and must always be correct, accurate and non-misleading); (vi) in case of SGRs marketing their own funds, information requirements to investors in respect of the SGR and the services provided, the safe-keeping of the financial instruments and the cash held by the fund, the financial instruments commonly negotiated, the costs and expenses to be borne by the investors, the clients' profiling; and (vii) in case of SGRs marketing their own funds, the obligation to carry out the appropriateness assessment.

Italy

Non-harmonised open-ended funds (reserved)
Non-harmonised open-ended funds may invest in a number of liquid financial instruments which are generally indicated by the Ministerial Decree No.228 of 1999 as amended (securities listed or unlisted on any regulated market and bank deposits) and further detailed by the Bank of Italy regulation adopted on 8 May 2012 as amended (listed equity and debt instruments such as shares and bonds, unlisted money market instruments, listed and OTC derivatives instruments, parts of harmonised and non-harmonised open-ended funds, parts of closed-ended funds, bank deposits and financial indices, all of them provided that they comply with the requirements set forth by the Bank of Italy). Non-harmonised open-ended funds may also invest up to 20 per cent of its assets in Italian and foreign speculative funds (such percentage is increased to 30 per cent, under certain conditions, if the fund is also reserved to qualified investors).

Non-harmonised open-ended funds reserved to qualified investors are not subject to any limits to investments and risk diversification provided for by the Bank of Italy in respect of non-harmonised open-ended funds addressed to retail investors (see below section 3.3., 'Non-harmonised open-ended funds (retail)') with the exception of the limits to the use of financial leverage. In particular, they are prevented from using financial leverage (borrowings may only be assumed up to 10 per cent of the fund's overall value and for a term not exceeding six months to the extent they are aimed at facing temporary liquidity shortfalls). Non-harmonised open-ended funds (regardless of the fact that they are 'reserved' or 'retail' funds) are also prevented from short selling with the exception of short selling on physical settled and cash settled derivatives (eg, short selling on physical settled derivatives is only allowed if the fund holds the underlying commodity for the whole term of the derivative, whilst short selling on cash settled derivatives is only allowed to the extent that the fund has sufficient assets to cover the payment obligations arising out of the short selling itself) as well as from granting borrowings, investing in financial instruments issued by the managing SGR, acquiring precious metals or certificates representing precious metals, investing in assets directly or indirectly assigned or contributed by a shareholder, a director, a general manager or a statutory auditor of the SGR or companies belonging to the SGR's group.

In addition, if the non-harmonised open-ended fund is also a speculative fund, all the limits above may be exceeded, so that the fund may have recourse to indebtedness under the terms and within the limits autonomously set forth by the relevant rules of the fund.

The net asset value of the fund (and, therefore, the fund's units' value) must be calculated and published at least on a monthly basis.

Reserved open-ended and closed-ended funds
As far as reserved open-ended funds are concerned, please see the above paragraph.

Reserved closed-ended funds may invest in financial instruments, parts of Italian and foreign closed-ended funds meeting certain requirements indicated by the Bank of Italy, harmonised and non-harmonised funds, receivables, other commodities marketed and having a value which may be calculated at least on a semi-annual basis, bank deposits, Italian and foreign speculative funds. They also may invest in real estate properties, real estate rights, stakes in real estate companies and parts of real estate funds (in these cases the fund is commonly recognised as a real estate fund). Moreover, real estate funds must invest at least two thirds of their overall net assets value in real estate properties, real estate rights, stakes in real estate companies and parts of real estate funds. Such threshold may be reduced to 51 per cent of the net assets value if at least 20 per cent of the net assets value of the fund is also invested in securities issued in the context of real estate securitisation transactions.

Reserved closed-ended funds are not subject to any limits to investments and risk diversification provided for by the Bank of Italy in respect of retail closed-ended funds (see below section 3.3., 'Retail closed-ended funds') with the exception of the limits to the use of financial leverage. In particular, reserved closed-ended funds may assume borrowings up to 10 per cent of the overall net asset value of the fund. Reserved real estate funds may assume borrowings up to 60 per cent of the value of the real estate assets, real estate rights, stakes in real estate companies and parts of other real estate funds held in its own portfolio and up to 20 per cent of the value of the other assets held.

The net asset value of the fund (and, therefore, the fund's units' value) must be calculated and published at least on a semi-annual basis.

Units of reserved funds may never be placed, redeemed or resold, directly or in the context of the placement of securities, to investors other than qualified investors.

Unless they are real estate funds (see below), reserved closed-ended funds are also prevented from investing in assets directly or indirectly assigned or contributed by a shareholder, a director, a general manager or a statutory auditor of the SGR or companies belonging to the SGR's group.

Particular provisions apply if the reserved closed-ended fund is also a real estate fund. In such a case, the units may also be subscribed by virtue of contribution of the real estate assets in the fund. In such a case, the fund shall: (i) obtain an appraisal by an independent expert appointed by the SGR certifying the value of the asset to be contributed and bearing a date not elder than 30 days before the date of contribution; and (ii) obtain the assessment of a financial intermediary with respect to the consistency and profitability of the contribution *vis-à-vis* the investment policy of the fund. Real estate funds may also be invested in assets directly or indirectly assigned or contributed by a shareholder, a director, a general manager or a statutory auditor of the SGR or companies belonging to the SGR's group provided that: (i) the units issued against the contribution are held by the investor and locked-up for an amount not lower than 30 per cent of the value of the subscription for a period of at least two years; (ii) the financial intermediary above indicated does not belong to the group of the investor who contributed the asset; and (iii) the resolution of the SGR's board of directors approving the transaction indicates the interest of the fund and the investors in the execution of the transaction and must be approved with the consent of the board of the statutory auditors.

Closed-ended funds (irrespective of being reserved or not) are also subject to a peculiar discipline concerning the voice rights of the investors. Indeed, investors in closed-ended funds are vested with the right to express their binding vote in the context of a special meeting on the following subjects: (i) amendment to the management policies of the fund; (ii) replacement of the managing SGR; and (iii) application for the listing of the fund's units on a regulated market. The rules of the fund of reserved closed-ended funds may also set out further attributions to the unitholders' meeting to the extent they do not concern investment decisions, which are mandatorily attributed to the exclusive competence of the SGR. When the law or the rules of the fund provide that a specific matter must be approved by the unitholders' meeting, the SGR may not act on such a matter without the approval of the meeting.

Speculative (hedge) funds
As anticipated above, speculative funds may be set up as open-ended or closed-ended funds (including real estate funds) as well as reserved funds.

Their nature of 'speculative funds' implies several consequences. First, speculative funds may invest in all the assets which are provided for by the relevant rules of the fund, without any particular limitations. Furthermore, speculative funds are not subject to any limitations in investments, to risk diversification or to other prudential provisions, including the use of financial leverage. All such limits are indicated in the rules of the fund and may be freely and autonomously determined by the SGR.

The high degree of risk related to this kind of fund pushed the Italian lawmaker to provide specific limitations with respect to the subscription of their units. In particular, the units of a speculative fund must have a par value of at least EUR 500,000 and under no circumstances can such units be subsequently fractioned. Accordingly, no subscriptions lower than EUR 500,000 may be accepted by the SGR. In addition, the units may not be offered to the public.

2.4. Marketing the fund
The marketing of an alternative investment fund must be made in compliance with the provisions set forth by the Consolidated Financial Law as well as with the rules set forth by Consob regulation No.16190 of 29 October 2007, as amended (concerning the transparency and correctness in the provision of investment services and activities).

As alternative investment funds are usually not addressed to retail investors, the marketing of the relevant units will not be, on a general basis, subject to the duty to publish a prospectus approved by Consob. As a matter of fact, the relevant offering should be carried out under the exemptions provided for by the Consolidated Financial Law and the Consob regulation No.11971 of 14 May 1999, as amended. By way of example, no prospectus is required for an offering of units of an investment fund if, *inter alia*, the units are offered to qualified investors, or the offer is addressed to a number of investors not higher than 150, or the par value of each unit is at least equal to EUR 100,000.

As illustrated below in section 4, the marketing rules applicable to alternative investment funds will be deeply revised following the transposition in Italy of the AIFMD with the introduction of specific provisions (such as the passport) regulating the offering to professional investors of parts of Italian, EU and non-EU alternative investment funds by Italian SGRs and other EU and non-EU investment managers. However, as of the date of this contribution, the AIMFD has still not be implemented in Italy and the transposition will expectedly occur in the national legal framework with a significant delay *vis-à-vis* the deadline which is set on 22 July 2013.

2.5. Taxation
Italian tax treatment of open-ended and closed-ended investment funds
Italian taxation levied at the level of the fund
A new tax regime for investment funds (other than real estate funds) was enacted in Italy with effect from 1 July 2011 aiming at (i) aligning the tax treatment of Italian investment funds with that of foreign 'harmonised' funds and (ii) removing tax discriminations between investments in Italian funds vs. investments in certain type of foreign funds.

Under the new regime, Italian investment funds are no longer subject to 12.5 per cent tax on the management results and the taxation has been shifted at the investors' level, where they are generally taxed on a cash basis (ie, on proceeds' distributions by same fund).

The new tax regime applies to both open-ended and closed-end investment funds, also including certain open-end funds based in Luxemburg, proportionally to their units placed in Italy, (so-called 'Luxemburg historical funds').

Italian investment funds are neither subject to the Italian income taxes (IRES) – though they have been included, together with Luxembourgian historical funds placed in Italy, in the list of entities liable to IRES, nor to regional tax on productive activities (IRAP).

Furthermore, the main categories of income realised by Italian investment funds are not subject to ordinary Italian withholding taxes. In particular, Italian withholding taxes do not apply to, *inter alia*: (i) dividends and capital gains from shareholdings; (ii) interest and similar proceeds from governmental bonds and bonds issued by banks and listed companies; (iii) interest and similar proceeds from current bank accounts (provided that the amount deposited in not higher than 5 per cent of the average value of the investments of the fund); (iv) income from repo and stock landing transactions; and (v) income from participations in other Italian investment funds (including real estate funds) and from foreign investment funds.

When applicable, withholding taxes are levied as final payment and no tax credit is granted to the relevant funds.

Italian taxation levied at the level of the investors of real estate investment funds
As anticipated, effective from 1 July 2011, taxation no longer applies at the fund's level, being instead levied directly on the investors.

In particular, the new rules provide for that a 20 per cent withholding tax

applies on:
- periodic distributions received by investors (the taxable base consisting in the proceeds actually distributed); and
- the redemption, liquidation or sale of the units: in this case the taxable base is equal to the difference between the value of the redemption, liquidation or sale of the units and the weighted average cost of subscription or acquisition of the units, (these items to be determined on the basis of the net asset value provided by the management company).

The withholding tax is applied as final payment or an advance payment depending on the different categories of investors and, in particular:
- as a final payment, in case of individuals who are Italian tax resident not holding the fund units in connection with a business activity;
- as an advance payment, in case of: (i) Italian tax resident individuals who hold the fund units in connection with a business activity; (ii) commercial entities (eg, limited liability companies, joint stock companies); and (iii) permanent establishment in Italy of non-resident entities, if the units are attributable to the same permanent establishment;
- the relevant proceeds is included in the taxable basis for personal tax (IRPEF) and IRES purposes (IRPEF is levied at progressive rates up to 43 per cent plus local surcharges, whilst IRES is generally levied at a rate of 27.5 per cent), depending on the type of investors. Moreover, certain type of investors (eg, banks and insurance companies) may also be subject to IRAP, at the rates (eg, 4.25 per cent is the standard rate for banks and insurance companies) which may vary in each region; and
- as a final payment, in case of non-resident investors with no Italian permanent establishment to which the units are attributable.

However, a withholding tax exemption is granted to certain non-resident investors (so-called 'qualified investors'), ie:
- investors resident in states that allow an adequate exchange of information with the Italian tax authorities (so-called 'white-list' countries), as currently listed under Ministerial Decree 4 September 1996;
- 'institutional investors' established in white-list countries, even if not subject to taxation in their states; and
- international bodies and organisations established in accordance with international agreements ratified by Italy, as well as central banks or other organisations managing the official reserves of the state.

In addition, the 20 per cent withholding tax is not levied with respect to proceeds from the funds realised by Italian real estate funds, certain pension schemes, Italian investment funds and Luxemburg historical funds placed in Italy.

From a procedural perspective, the withholding tax at hands has to be applied:
- by the management company;(as for Luxembourgian historical funds placed in Italy, the withholding tax has to be applied by the Italian intermediaries in charge of the placement);
- in case of units traded on regulated markets, by the Italian intermediaries in charge of the trading of the fund units; and
- in case of fund units held in centralised depositary system, by Italian

intermediaries – with which the units are deposited – adhering (directly or indirectly) to a centralised depositary system managed by authorised companies, or by non-resident intermediaries adhering to the same system or to foreign centralised depositary systems that participate to the above system.

The mentioned reform substantially aligned, in the hands of Italian investors, the tax treatment of investments in foreign funds with that of investments in Italian funds. In particular, proceeds arising from foreign investment funds investing in transferable securities are subject to the same tax regime outlined above in respect of proceeds arising from Italian investment funds (ie, ordinarily, the application of the 20 per cent withholding tax), provided that such foreign funds qualify:

(i) either as 'harmonised' funds (ie, compliant with the UCITS Directive) and are established in a EU or EEA 'white-list' state; or
(ii) or as 'non-harmonised' funds (ie, non-compliant with the UCITS Directive), but are established in a EU or EEA 'white-list' state and are subject in that state to regulatory supervision.

On the contrary, proceeds arising from foreign investment funds investing in transferable securities other than those listed above, will not be subject to the ordinary 20 per cent withholding.

The reform also addresses – although only partially – the applicability of tax treaty benefits to funds. In particular, they expressly state that foreign investments under letters. (i) and (ii) above may benefit from the double taxation conventions executed with Italy in respect of Italian-source income, but: (i) only for that part of the income proportionally referable to fund units held by persons resident in the other tax treaty country; and (ii) provided that the country of residence of the foreign fund grants, on a reciprocal basis, similar treaty benefits to Italian investment funds.

Taxation of the management company
Italian management company is subject to IRES according to ordinary rules. The management fees charged by the SGR to the fund are VAT exempt.

Tax regime of Italian real estate investment funds
Italian taxation levied at the level of the fund
Italian real estate investment funds are not subject to IRES nor to IRAP. Accordingly, income derived from the ownership, the management (rental) and the transfer (capital gain) of the immovable property is not taxed at the level of the real estate investment funds.

In general, proceeds received by the real estate investment funds are not subject to withholding or substitutive taxes. However, withholding or substitutive taxes may be levied with respect to certain income. For instance, interest on bonds issued by non-listed companies are subject to a final withholding in the hands of the real estate investment funds.

Moreover, real estate investment funds are subject to Municipal Real Property Tax (*Imposta Municipale Unica* (IMU)).

Real estate investment funds do not qualify for VAT purposes. On the other hand, their management company is liable for the VAT liabilities deriving from the transactions carried out by the real estate investment funds managed by the same. Such management company is also responsible for the VAT compliance duties of real estate investment funds. The VAT liabilities of such funds is determined separately from that of their management company and from that of any other fund managed by the same management company.

Italian taxation levied at the level of the investors of real estate investment funds

Investors are subjected to a different tax regime according to: (i) their subjective qualification; and to (ii) their percentage of participation held in the funds.

Proceeds paid by the real estate investment funds to Italian resident individuals not holding the units of the funds in connection with entrepreneurial activities are subject to a 20 per cent final withholding tax.

Capital gains realised by such investors are subject to a 20 per cent substitutive tax.

Proceeds paid by the real estate investment funds to: (i) Italian resident legal/individual persons holding the units of such funds in connection with entrepreneurial activities; and (ii) permanent establishment of non-Italian resident entities which the units of the funds are effectively connected, are subject to a 20 per cent provisional withholding tax.

The gross amount of the proceeds distributed by the real estate investment funds is computed in the income taxable basis of the relevant investor. Capital gains realised by such investors are computed in their income taxable basis and they are taxed accordingly. In such a case substitutive tax on capital gains does not apply.

Proceeds paid by the real estate investment funds to non-Italian resident investors (having no permanent establishment in Italy) are subject to a 20 per cent final withholding tax. The withholding's rate may be reduced by the applicable double taxation treaty (if any).

Capital gains realised by such non-Italian resident investors are: (i) not taxable in Italy in case the units of the real estate investment funds are listed; or (ii) subject to a 20 per cent substitutive tax if the units of such funds are not listed and if such units are held in Italy. In this latter case, domestic law provides for an exemption from the 20 per cent substitutive tax for capital gains realised by non-Italian resident investors that are resident in (or qualify as institutional investors established in) a white listed countries. Moreover, exemption from Italian taxation may arise from the application of double taxation treaty provisions (if any).

In particular, investors that own a percentage of participation in the real estate investment funds which is higher than 5 per cent – taking into consideration also the units indirectly held, *inter alia*, through subsidiaries or through investor's family member – are subjected, for income tax purposes, to a so called 'transparency tax regime'. This means that, for each fiscal year, such investors are taxed proportionally to their percentage of participation held in the real estate investment funds, regardless to the actual perception of the proceeds. Please note that, with regard of the sale of the units of the real estate investment funds, such tax treatment does not apply with respect to capital gains realised by investors that own a percentage of participation in the real estate investment funds which is higher than 5 per cent.

Transparency tax regime does not apply (regardless of the percentage of participation held in the real estate investment funds) with respect to certain participants of such funds called 'qualified investors'.

According to Article 32(3) Law Decree No.78/2010, the qualified investors are the following:
- Italian state and other governmental or public entities;
- collective investment schemes;
- pension schemes and social security funds mandatory;
- insurance companies, limited to investments to cover the technical reserves;
- banks and other financial intermediaries subject to prudential supervision;
- foreign entities corresponding to any of the above categories, incorporated in countries or territories that allow an exchange of information aimed at identifying the beneficial owners of income or of the outcome of the management activity and that are included in the decree of Ministry of Finance referred to in Article 168-bis, paragraph 1, of Tax Code No.917/86;
- private entities resident in Italy pursuing only the purposes specified in Article 1, paragraph 1, letter c-bis) of Legislative Decree 153/1999, as well as companies resident in Italy pursuing only mutual purposes; and
- vehicles set up in a corporate or contractual form, participated for more than 50 per cent from subjects indicated in the previous letters.

Proceeds paid by the real estate investment funds to qualified investors are, in general, subjected to a 20 per cent withholding tax.

Moreover, 20 per cent withholding tax is not levied with respect to proceeds paid by the real estate investment funds to: (i) collective investment schemes (OICR) established in Italy; and (ii) pension schemes.

As written above, 20 per cent withholding tax may apply with respect to proceeds paid by the real estate investment funds to non-resident investors. Besides, certain non-resident investors are exempt from the withholding (*inter alia* pension funds and collective investment funds established in countries or territories that allow the exchange of information between tax authorities).

2.6. Customary or common terms
Term
Under Italian law, the generality of the investment funds (ie, not only the alternative investment funds) shall have a term consistent with the specific kind of investments carried out and, in any case, it cannot exceed the term of the SGR which established such funds. With respect to closed-ended funds, the term may not exceed 50 years.

The term of the fund may be extended, if the relevant rules of the fund expressly provide so. The rules of the fund may put the decision to extend the term on the SGR itself or, in case of closed-ended funds, on the unitholders' meeting. Closed-ended funds (including real estate funds), due to the possible illiquidity of the assets in which they are invested, may also benefit from a further maximum three-year period of extension (so called 'grace period') which may be used by the SGR to dismiss the assets. The right of the SGR to make recourse to the grace period must be expressly provided in the rules of the fund and the SGR shall inform Bank of Italy and Consob thereof, pointing out the reasons grounding such decision.

The fund may be liquidated before its term when the rules of the funds so provide. In the market practice the advanced liquidation of the fund may be usually resolved by the SGR or, in the case of closed-ended funds, also by the unitholders' meeting and, on a general basis, it follows the anticipated achievement of the full dismissal of the assets or the impossibility to continue to carry out the investment activity. In 2012, the lawmaker introduced a regulated advanced liquidation proceeding for investment funds. It is a complex process which may be activated before the competent court either by the SGR or by the creditors of the fund when the assets of the fund are insufficient to allow the fund to meet its obligations and when there are no reasonable perspectives that such a distressed situation may be overcome.

Liquidity of interests
As far as the liquidity of the units of Italian investment funds is concerned, all the investment funds may be categorised between open-ended and closed-ended funds. In this respect, the units of an open-ended investment fund may be subscribed and redeemed by the investors at any time. According to Italian law, the SGR has the duty to redeem the units of the fund within 15 days from the receipt of the investor's request.

Closed-ended investment funds instead may not be subscribed or redeemed at any time by the investors. The investment fund may be subscribed during the initial subscription period, which may not exceed a term of 24 months from the approval of the rules of the fund and may be redeemed only at maturity. Advanced units redemption in closed-ended funds is only allowed to the extent that the SGR decides to open new subscription periods throughout the term of the fund (such right must be expressly provided in the rules of the fund). Accordingly, investors in closed-ended funds may usually liquidate their investment only by selling their units to third parties.

Management involvement
The directors, general managers and statutory auditors of the SGR must meet the experience and integrity requirements set forth by Ministerial Decree No.468 of 11 November 1998. If such requirements are not met, the interested party may not be appointed and, if appointed, is declared forfeited. Under certain circumstances, the concerned person may be suspended without being definitively revoked (eg, in case of non-definitive conviction for certain criminal offences: the revocation will become final if the concerned person is definitively convicted). When the SGR employs key managers for the management of the fund (especially in case of private equity funds) it is common that the rules of the fund provide for specific key man clauses under which the investments of the fund must be suspended in case of such key managers leave the office,

with the consequent anticipated closure of the investment period if such key manager are not replaced within a certain period of time.

In addition, as detailed above, in the case of closed-ended funds, the unitholders' meeting is empowered by operation of law of the right to replace the SGR. It is customary, in case of reserved and speculative closed-ended funds, that the rules of the fund provide for a lock-up period during which the SGR may not be replaced and, if replaced before the expiry of the lock-up period, for an indemnification right in its favour.

Remuneration arrangements
With respect to alternative investment funds, the remuneration due to the SGR is not subject to particular mandatory provisions. In the common practice, the fund pays a management fee calculated as a percentage over the net asset value of the fund and, in certain cases, also a subscription fee. Certain reserved closed-ended funds (especially private equity funds) also provide, in accordance with the international common practice, the payment of carried interests in favour of the key managers of the SGR. In such a case, carried interests are usually payable upon the investors having received the reimbursement of the invested capital increased of a determined hurdle rate. Escrow or claw-back mechanisms can also be provided in order to ensure that carried interests are not perceived by the key managers until the investors have not reached the expected yield.

3. RETAIL FUNDS
3.1. Common structures
In the Italian market, retail funds may be divided into non-harmonised open-ended funds (*fondi aperti non armonizzati*), harmonised open-ended funds (*fondi aperti armonizzati*) and retail closed-ended funds (*fondi chiusi non riservati*) which are addressed to the general public (this category also includes retail real estate funds).

As already seen for alternative investment funds, another form of retail investment fund is represented by harmonised SICAVs (*società di investimento a capitale variabile armonizzate*) which are incorporated as an open-ended structure and is compliant with the requirements set forth by Directive 2009/65/EC. Despite being more common than non-harmonised SICAVs, harmonised SICAVs still do not represent a significant market share in Italy and, therefore, they will not be treated in this analysis.

Non-harmonised open-ended funds (retail)
As anticipated under section 2.1. above, non-harmonised open-ended funds (*fondi aperti non armonizzati*) are open-ended funds which may invest in certain liquid assets and do not comply with the requirements set forth by Directive 2009/65/EC. They will be treated under this section with the relevant discipline applying when the subscription of their units may be carried out by the generality of retail investors but please remind that this kind of fund may also be considered as alternative investment funds, if they are reserved to qualified investors (see section 2.3., 'Non-harmonised open-ended funds (reserved)' for the relevant legal framework).

Harmonised open-ended funds
Harmonised open-ended funds (*fondi aperti armonizzati*) are open-ended funds which comply with the requirements set forth by Directive 2009/65/EC and may invest in certain liquid assets (see section 3.3., 'Harmonised open-ended funds' for more details). According to the Directive 2009/65/EC, they are offered to retail investors.

Retail closed-ended funds
Retail closed-ended funds (*fondi chiusi non riservati*) may invest in both liquid and illiquid instruments set out by the Ministerial Decree No.228 of 1999. There is no difference in this respect between retail closed-ended investment funds and reserved closed-ended investment funds with the important exception that retail closed-ended funds are subject to the observance of the risks concentration limits and prudential rules set forth by the Bank of Italy. Also retail closed-ended funds may be qualified as real estate funds when they mainly invest in real estate properties and rights, stakes in real estate companies and parts of other Italian and foreign real estate funds.

3.2. Regulatory framework
Regulatory provisions applying to SGRs and retail funds
See section 2.2., 'Regulatory provisions applying to SGRs and alternative investment funds'.

Licensing requirements for retail funds
Investment funds targeting retail investors are subject, under a licensing standpoint, to the supervision of the Bank of Italy which is entrusted, *inter alia*, with the powers to approve the rules of the fund and any relevant changes thereof. In case of: (i) rules of open-ended funds drafted in accordance with the form of simplified rules (*regolamento semplificato*); and (ii) rules of investment funds drafted with limited variations from the rules of other operative investment funds established by the same SGR, the relevant rules of the fund are deemed to be approved by the Bank of Italy 'in via generale' (meaning that no formal approval will be released by the Bank of Italy as the SGR is only obliged to submit the text of the rules of the fund approved by its competent corporate bodies within 10 days from such approval together with the minute of the relevant meeting of the corporate bodies attesting certain circumstances).

The investment manager
See section 2.2., 'The investment manager'.

Licensing requirements for the SGR
See section 2.2., 'Licensing requirements for the SGR'.

3.3. Operational requirements
Requirements applicable to the generality of investment funds
See section 2.3., 'Requirements applicable to the generality of investment funds'.

Non-harmonised open-ended funds (retail)

Non-harmonised open-ended funds addressed to retail investors may invest in the same liquid financial instruments indicated in section 2.3., 'Non-harmonised open-ended funds (reserved)'.

In contrast to non-harmonised open-ended funds reserved to qualified investors, non-harmonised open-ended funds addressed to retail investors cannot derogate to prudential provisions set forth by the Bank of Italy. Therefore, they are subject to strict restrictions in investing the assets in securities issued by the same issuer as well as in bank deposits and derivative instruments (the total exposure *vis-à-vis* the same issuer, irrespective of the kind of securities held, may not exceed 20 per cent of the fund's assets).

In addition, they are subject to peculiar limits in holding both securities bearing and not bearing voting rights and are prevented from using financial leverage (borrowings may only be assumed up to 10 per cent of the fund's overall value and for a term not exceeding six months to the extent they are aimed at facing temporary liquidity shortfalls). Non-harmonised open-ended funds (regardless of the fact that they are 'reserved' or 'retail' funds) are also prevented from short selling with the exception of short selling on physical settled and cash settled derivatives (eg, short selling on physical settled derivatives is only allowed if the fund holds the underlying commodity for the whole term of the derivative, whilst short selling on cash settled derivatives is only allowed to the extent that the fund has sufficient assets to cover the payment obligations arising out of the short selling itself) as well as from granting borrowings, investing in financial instruments issued by the managing SGR, acquiring precious metals or certificates representing precious metals, investing in assets directly or indirectly assigned or contributed by a shareholder, a director, a general manager or a statutory auditor of the SGR or companies belonging to the SGR's group.

The net asset value of the fund (and, therefore, the fund's units' value) must be calculated and published at least on a monthly basis.

In addition to the reporting requirements set out in previous section 2.3., 'Requirements applicable to the generality of investment funds' this kind of funds (as retail open-ended funds) are also required to prepare a prospectus detailing the units' value and the net asset value of the fund, on the same dates on which the units are issued or redeemed to be publish the day immediately after on a newspaper.

Harmonised open-ended funds

Harmonised open-ended funds may invest in the same assets already detailed for non-harmonised open-ended funds in preceding section 2.3., 'Non-harmonised open-ended funds (reserved)' with the difference that harmonised open-ended funds are prevented from investing in parts of Italian or foreign speculative (hedge) funds.

Harmonised open-ended funds are subject to the same severe investment and risk limitations (including the prohibition to have recourse to financial leverage) already described with respect to non-harmonised open-ended funds under preceding paragraph 'Non-harmonised open-ended funds (retail)'.

The net asset value of the fund (and, therefore, the fund's units' value) must be calculated and published at least on a weekly basis.

In addition to the reporting requirements set out in previous section 2.3., 'Requirements applicable to the generality of investment funds' this kind of funds (as retail open-ended funds) are also required to prepare a prospectus detailing the units' value and the net asset value of the fund, on the same dates on which the units are issued or redeemed to be publish the day immediately after on a newspaper.

Retail closed-ended funds

Retail closed-ended funds may invest in the same assets already described in respect of reserved closed-ended funds under section 2.3., 'Reserved open-ended and closed-ended funds'.

Differently from reserved closed-ended funds, retail closed-ended funds are subject to several limits to investments and risk diversification requirements. In particular, this kind of fund is prevented from carrying out short selling, investing in securities issued by the managing SGR and investing in assets directly or indirectly assigned or contributed by a shareholder, a director, a general manager or a statutory auditor of the SGR or companies belonging to the SGR's group but it can grant borrowings and acquire precious metals and certificates representing precious metals. In addition, retail closed-ended funds are subject to limits in investing in securities (eg, the total exposure *vis-à-vis* the same issuer cannot exceed 20 per cent of the total assets value) and bank deposits, real estate assets and stakes in real estate companies exercising building activity (eg, fund's assets cannot be invested in a single real estate in an amount exceeding 33 per cent), receivables and financial instruments endowed with voting rights. Retail closed end funds are also subject to the same limits in using financial leverage already described under section 2.3., 'Reserved open-ended and closed-ended funds'.

If the retail closed-ended fund is also a real estate fund, in case of subscription of units by virtue of contribution of assets, the fund shall, in addition to the duties described under section 2.3., 'Reserved open-ended and closed-ended funds', meet the following requirements: (i) the value of the single asset must not exceed 10 per cent of the fund's value, the total value of transactions carried out with SGR's shareholders must not exceed 40 per cent of the fund's value and the total value of transactions carried out with SGR's shareholders and other entities belonging to the SGR's group must not exceed 60 per cent of the fund's value; (ii) after the first issuance of units, the value of the single asset and, in any case, the total value of transactions carried out with SGR's shareholders and other entities belonging to the SGR's group may not exceed, on a yearly basis, 10 per cent of the fund's value; and (iii) the acquired or sold assets must be appraised by an independent expert. Retail closed-ended funds are also endowed of the unitholders' meeting (already seen with respect to reserved closed-ended funds), which may resolve exclusively upon: (i) amendment to the management policies of the fund; (ii) replacement of the managing SGR; and (iii) application for the listing of the fund's units on a regulated market.

3.4. Marketing the fund
The marketing of a retail fund must be made in compliance with the provisions set forth by the Consolidated Financial Law as well as with the rules set forth by Consob regulation No.16190 of 29 October 2007, as amended (concerning the transparency and correctness in the provision of investment services and activities).

Harmonised open-ended funds may also be managed and marketed by other EU harmonised fund managers under the passport provisions set out by Directive 2009/65/EC in accordance with the principles commonly applied in the whole European Union.

As being addressed to the public, the marketing of the units of a retail fund is always subject to the duty to publish a prospectus approved by Consob, unless an exemption applies (see section 2.4.).

3.5. Taxation
See section 2.5., 'Italian tax treatment of open-ended and closed-ended investment funds'.

3.6. Customary or common terms
Term
See section 2.6., 'Term'.

Liquidity of interests
See section 2.6., 'Liquidity of interests'. In addition, retail closed-ended funds are obliged to request the admission of the units to listing on a regulated market (typically the Market in Investment Vehicle (MIV), organised and managed by Borsa Italiana) when the minimum subscription amount per investor is lower than EUR 25,000 by and no later than 24 months after the closure of the subscription period. The provision is aimed at providing the retail investors with an easier way out from the fund, taking into account that, as a closed-ended fund, the units may not be redeemed before the maturity of the fund.

Management involvement
The directors, general managers and statutory auditors of the SGR must meet the experience and integrity requirements already described under section 2.6., 'Management involvement'.

In addition, as detailed above, in the case of closed-ended funds, the unitholders' meeting is empowered by operation of law of the right to replace the SGR but lock-up periods (see section 2.6., 'Management involvement') are not customarily provided in the case of retail funds.

Furthermore, all SGRs managing retail closed-ended funds are obliged to subscribe to units of the fund for an amount at least equal to 2 per cent of the initial assets under management for any single fund and for any subsequent units' issuance. If the net asset value of the relevant fund exceeds EUR 150 million, the above percentage is reduced, for the quota exceeding such threshold, to 1 per cent.

Italy

Remuneration arrangements
With respect to retail open-ended investment funds, the remuneration due to the SGR is subject to the specific mandatory provisions set out by the Bank of Italy. In particular, the management fee due to the SGR must always refer to the net asset value of the fund. It is also possible to provide an incentive fee but, in such a case, the incentive fee must be referred to a clear determined and objective index (the incentive fee will be due if the yield is higher than the reference index) or to a target yield or, residually, to the absolute high watermark of the units' value.

Retail closed-ended funds may freely provide the calculation basis for the fees due to the SGR but the management fee must be related to the traded value of the assets or, where a traded value is unavailable, to the historical cost of the assets.

4. PROPOSED CHANGES AND DEVELOPMENTS
As anticipated, the transposition of the AIFMD will entail significant changes to the legal framework for alternative investment funds even though the Italian lawmaker will likely adopt a one-year grandfathering period under which the current provisions will continue to apply, thus exempting certain operators from applying the AIFMD requirements.

Besides the significant amendments to marketing regulations, where the introduction of the passport for alternative investment funds addressed to professional investors will imply a huge opening of the market where also other EU and non-EU managers will be allowed to manage and market in Italy their alternative investment funds by virtue of the passport or, to the extent applicable, the private placement regime, other important changes will occur.

In general, and with no claim of being exhaustive, the licensing requirements for the SGRs will be amended in order to take into account the different authorisations to manage alternative funds under the AIFMD and harmonised funds under the Directive 2009/65/EC. New provisions detailing a different level of accountability will be provided with respect to depositories as well as specific disclosure requirements in relation to the financial leverage used in the management of the funds. Moreover, it is very possible that the Italian lawmaker will re-arrange the above described categories of investment funds, including the current reserved and speculative funds in the broader category of 'alternative investment fund'.

Notwithstanding certain rules that apply in Italy immediately as of 22 July 2013 (ie, the provisions set out by the implementing EU Regulations, such as the EU Regulation No.231/2013), a full and comprehensive impact over the Italian market will be assessable only once the AIFMD will be fully implemented together with the necessary amendments to the Ministerial Decree No.228 of 1999 and Consob and Bank of Italy regulations which, as of the date of this contribution, are expected to be adopted between late 2013 and the beginning of 2014.

Japan

Kazuhiro Yoshii, Ko Hanamizu, Anri Suzuki & Mariko Takashima
Anderson Mori & Tomotsune

1. MARKET OVERVIEW

Although it has no express definition under Japanese law, the term 'investment funds' can be tentatively defined to encompass any structures in which investors commit monetary resources to managers or schemes for collective investment, with such managers or schemes investing the resources in specified assets (eg, securities), and with any resulting proceeds being received by the investors. Mechanisms of this kind are common in Japan, as they are in western countries. Investment targets vary among investment funds in Japan as they do elsewhere, and include securities, real estate and derivatives, among others.

A report published by Japan's principal securities regulatory entity, the Financial Services Agency of Japan (FSA), entitled Results of Monitoring of Funds sets forth information regarding investment funds in Japan as of 28 March 2012, broken down by vehicle type (though it does not includes alternative investment funds that employs other types of schemes), as set forth below.

Sales of Monitored Funds (from April 2011 to March 2012)

	Number of transactions in Japan	Amount sold in Japan (JPY100 million)	Hedge Funds	
			Number of transactions in Japan	Amount sold in Japan (JPY100 million)
Contractual type domestic investment funds	18,534	590,032	63	4,036
Investment company type domestic investment funds	30	1,785	-	-
Contractual type and investment company type foreign investment funds	946	39,382	74	699
Collective investment schemes	2,310	11,659	107	219
Total	21,820	642,858	244	4,954

(Note) Numbers of transactions above may differ from actual numbers, due to the fact that several distributors may engage in sales of the same fund.
(Note) Please see section 2.1 and section 3.1 'Hedge funds' for explanations of each type of investment funds referred to in above.

Management of Monitored Funds (as of 31 March 2012)

	Number of funds managed in Japan	Amount managed in Japan (JPY100 million)	Hedge Funds	
			Number of funds managed in Japan	Amount managed in Japan (JPY100 million)
Contractual type domestic investment funds	8,870	1,407,675	170	9,161
Investment company type domestic investment funds	48	90,831	-	-
Contractual type and investment company type foreign investment funds	712	212,259	70	18,420
Collective investment schemes	4,692	175,699	165	497
Total	14,322	1,886,464	405	28,078

(Note) Information regarding management of contractual type and investment company type foreign investment funds has been provided by Japanese agents of such funds (or Japanese distributors where no agents exist).
(Note) Please see section 2.1 and section 3.1 'Hedge funds' for explanations of each type of investment funds referred to in above.

2. RETAIL FUNDS
2.1. Common structures

Investment funds intended to be distributed to retail investors in Japan are generally structured as investment trusts (*Toshi-Shintaku*) established under Japanese law (domestic investment funds, or DIFs) or investment trusts established under the laws of foreign countries (foreign investment funds, or FIFs). Distribution of retail funds is typically carried out by public offering. Each structure is summarised below. For both DIFs and FIFs, investors may lose their investment but their risks are limited to such extent.

DIFs

DIFs are subdivided into two types, generally referred to as contractual type funds (*Keiyaku-Gata*) and investment company type funds (*Kaisha-Gata*). DIFs are regulated primarily by the Act on Investment Trusts and Investment Corporations of Japan (Act No.198 of 1951, as amended (ITIC Act)).

Contractual type

In the case of contractual type domestic investment funds (CTDIFs), a settlor and a trustee execute a trust agreement, and multiple investors purchase beneficial interests in the trust. (Typically, each beneficial interest is represented by a security and provides identical rights.)

CTDIFs are further subdivided into two types, namely investment trusts managed based on instructions from settlor and investment trusts managed without instructions from settlor. The former is the prevalent form in Japan. Investment trusts managed based on instructions from settlor refers to investment trusts: (i) the trust assets of which are invested in specific targets, in accordance with instructions from the settlor; (ii) which are established under the ITIC Act; and (iii) the purpose of which contemplates that beneficial interests will be held by multiple investors (Article 2, section 1 of the ITIC Act). Investment trusts managed based on instructions from settlor are generally structured as follows:

- the settlor and the trustee execute a trust agreement consistent with an underlying trust deed previously filed with the commissioner of the FSA, and thereby establish a trust. The settlor must be a company registered as an investment management business operator under the Financial Instruments and Exchange Act of Japan (Act No.25 of 1948, as amended (FIEA));
- the settlor designates a distributor, which handles distribution of securities representing the beneficial interests to investors in Japan; and
- the settlor, or an investment adviser designated by the settlor, provides investment instructions to the trustee.

Investment company type

In the case of investment company type domestic investment funds (ICTDIFs), an investment company is established in accordance with the ITIC Act, and investors purchase units. The investment company executes an investment management agreement with an investment manager under which it delegates investment management authority in respect of the assets contributed by investors. The investment manager must be a company registered as an investment management business operator under the FIEA. The investment company's assets are held in custody by a custodian under a custodian agreement between the custodian and the investment company. In addition, the investment company delegates its administrative functions to an administrator pursuant to an administrative services agreement.

FIFs

Under the ITIC Act, investment funds established outside Japan which have similar structures to DIFs are categorised as FIFs (Article 2, sections 22 and 23 of the ITIC Act). These will generally include, among others, unit trusts and mutual funds established under the laws of the Cayman Islands, as well as *fonds commun de placement* (FCPs) and *societe d'investissement a capital variable* (SICAVs) established under the laws of Luxembourg. FIFs are also subdivided into two types, generally referred to as contractual type funds (CTFIFs) and investment company type funds (ICTFIFs). They are also regulated primarily by the ITIC Act.

2.2. Regulatory framework

DIFs and FIFs are subject to regulation under the ITIC Act. In addition, requirements under the FIEA and related regulations may be applicable to investment fund interests of any type in Japan, and may also be applicable to investment managers and distributors.

Filing under the ITIC Act
In the case of CTDIFs, the ITIC Act will require the settlor to file the trust deed and an accompanying notification with the competent local finance bureau (LFB) prior to the execution of the trust agreement (Article 4). The contents of this notification will include: basic information concerning the fund (legal nature, parties concerned, trust period, etc.), and information concerning target investments, investment policy, etc. Required attachments to the notification will be a consent letter from the relevant trustee, as well as a draft of the trust deed. The notification will not be available for public inspection.

In the case of ICTDIFs, the ITIC Act will require the founders to file a notification regarding establishment of the investment company with the competent LFB (Article 69). In addition, the investment company will be required to register with the competent LFB prior to commencement of asset management (Article 187).

In the case of any FIF of which beneficial interests (in the case of contractual type) or units (in the case of investment company type) will be distributed in Japan, the ITIC Act will require the issuer of the investment fund to file a notification with the commissioner of the FSA (Articles 58 and 220 of the ITIC Act). The contents of the notification will include: information concerning the beneficial interests or units to be distributed; basic information concerning the fund; and information concerning target investments, investment policy, fees, etc. Required attachments to the notification will include a power of attorney, legal opinion, trust deed, etc.

Requirements for public offering
In addition, in the case of public offering, the FIEA requires the issuer to file an SRS with the competent LFB prior to any marketing and sale.

The SRS is required to contain the following: (i) financial information concerning the relevant fund and the management company; (ii) information concerning performance of the fund, including net asset value and rate of return; and (iii) information concerning the status of fund investments, risk factors, taxes, etc. This information is not required in the notification under the ITIC Act. Once filed, the SRS will be available for public inspection for a certain period.

The issuer must also prepare and deliver or cause to be delivered to the offerees, on or prior to their purchase of beneficial interests or units, a prospectus in Japanese summarising the contents of the SRS.

Sale of units through public offering in Japan may not commence until the SRS comes into effect. (As a general rule, SRSs come into effect 15 days following their filing dates.)

Requirements for private placement
In the case of private placements, there is no requirement to file an SRS or to prepare or deliver a prospectus.

There are basically three types of private placements under the Japanese regulatory regime: (i) small number private placements; (ii) professional private placements; and (iii) professional investor private placements. Typically regimes (i) and (ii) above are used for private placement of DIFs and FIFs.

Small number private placements refer to private placements in which solicitation is directed to 49 or fewer persons (excluding qualified institutional investors (QIIs), as defined under the FIEA) (see Article 2, section 3(2)(c) of the FIEA). Professional private placements refer to private placements in which solicitation is directed only to QIIs (see Article 2, section 3(2)(a) of the FIEA).

In order to use any private placement exemption, requirements under the FIEA must be satisfied, including that: (i) a resale restriction must be imposed, such as (in the case of professional private placements) a restriction under which purchasers are prohibited from reselling such securities to third parties other than QIIs; and (ii) any person who engages in marketing and sales for the private placement must give notice to offerees of certain matters specified by the FIEA.

Registration of investment management companies

Any entity wishing to engage in the management of assets of a DIF must first register to engage in investment management business pursuant to Article 29 of the FIEA.

In the case of FIFs, the investment management functions are generally assigned to investment managers outside Japan pursuant to legal and market practices in the jurisdictions where such FIFs are established. In such cases, there is no requirement under the FIEA to register the relevant investment manager. In the case of FIFs for which an investment manager located in Japan is designated, the investment manager must be registered as an investment management business operator.

In order to register as an investment management business operator, the applicant: (i) must be a Japanese *kabushiki kaisha* (with the board of directors or committee systems as specified under the Corporation Act of Japan) or its foreign equivalent; (ii) must have paid in capital of JPY50 million; and (iii) must have net asset of JPY50 million, respectively. In addition, certain other requirements including the requirements for its directors and employees must be satisfied (eg, they must have appropriate experiences in relevant business). No local office is required.

On 1 April 2012, a 2011 amendment to the FIEA became effective and a new category of licence named 'investment management business for qualified investors' was introduced, under which certain registration requirements will be eased. Under this license, target investors will be limited to 'qualified investors,' which includes QIIs, certain pension funds and others as specified in the FIEA, and the maximum value of assets will also be limited.

2.3. Operational requirements
Regulations for the types of investments

The ITIC Act requires CTDIFs and ICTDIFs to invest their assets primarily in 'specified assets' as defined under the ITIC Act. The scope of specified assets has been expanded several times, and it currently includes securities, rights with respect to derivatives transactions, real estate, monetary claims, commodities and commodity investment transactions. ICTDIFs that primarily invest in real estate and certain interests relevant to real estate are so called J-REIT, which are described in detail in section 3.

Regulations concerning trustee and custodian
The trustee of CTDIFs must be a licensed trust company under the Trust Business Law (Act No.154 of 2004, as amended) or other financial organisation licensed to engage in ancillary trust business under the Act on Provision, etc. of Trust Business by Financial Institutions (Act No.43 of 1943, as amended) (collectively, 'trust company etc.').

A company that may act as a custodian of ICTDIFs is also limited to: (i) trust company etc.; (ii) a financial instruments business operator that engage in securities custody business as defined under the FIEA; or (iii) an entity that has sufficient financial and personnel basis to engage in custody of certain assets including real estates.

Reporting and disclosure requirements, etc.
Preparation and delivery of investment management reports
On an annual basis, the settlor of a CTDIF and issuer of beneficial interests of a CTFIF must prepare and deliver investment management reports setting forth information regarding fund performance to the known holders of beneficial interests or unit holders as at the end of each fiscal year (Articles 14 and 59 of the ITIC Act). An investment manager of an ICTDIF which is registered as an investment management business operator must also periodically prepare and deliver investment management reports to known investors (Article 42–7 of the FIEA). The reports must also be filed with the commissioner of the FSA.

Filing of annual securities report, etc.
DIFs and FIFs which file SRSs in connection with public offerings in Japan will become subject to ongoing reporting requirements under the FIEA, which will apply for as long as they continue to exist. Reporting requirements will include the filing of annual and semi-annual securities reports, as well as extraordinary reports if necessary. All such reports will be made publicly available for legally prescribed periods.

Operational requirement for investment manager
Registered investment management business operators are subject to ongoing obligations under the FIEA including: (i) preparation and maintenance of prescribed books and records; and (ii) preparation of business reports and filing them with the competent LFB (Articles 47 and 47–2 of the FIEA).

Side letters
Execution of side letters may be restricted if it intends to differentiate a fee arrangement for such beneficial interests or units from that for other

beneficial interests or units, because the ITIC Acts require each beneficial interest and unit provides identical rights.

Other operational regulations
The other major operational regulations for DIFs and FIFs are summarised below.

Insider trading
Persons who are in a position to have access to material information of a publicly-traded company which has an effect on investment decisions for securities are prohibited from conducting transactions of securities or derivative transactions before the material information which he/she came to know in his/her position is publicised (Article 166 of the FIEA).

Restriction on short selling
Naked short selling of securities is prohibited in principle, and certain short selling that exceeds the amount prescribed under the FIEA is subject to reporting obligations to the financial instruments exchange (Article 162 of the FIEA). These were initially introduced as a temporary legislation in October 2008 following the collapse of Lehman Brothers; however on 7 March 2013, the FSA released a Plan for Integrated Revision of Regulations for Short Selling and suggested to introduce further tighter restrictions as permanent rules.

Act on Prevention of Transfer of Criminal Proceeds
In order to prevent money-laundering and terrorism financing, certain business operators including a registered financial instruments business operator are required to conduct a know-your-customer procedure when they enter into transactions, and to provide a report of suspicious transactions if applicable (Articles 4 and 8 of the Act on Prevention of Transfer of Criminal Proceeds (Act No.22 of 2007, as amended)).

2.4. Marketing the fund
Registration requirements for distribution
Any entity wishing to act as a distributor in Japan of beneficial interests or units of a DIF must be registered as a type 1 financial instruments business operator (Article 3 of the ITIC Act). The settlor of CTDIFs and the investment manager of ICTDIFs may themselves undertake the sale of beneficial interests or units to investors in Japan, provided that they must register as type 2 financial instruments business operators prior to commencing the sale (Article 28, section 2(1) of the FIEA, Article 196, section 2 of the ICIT Act).

In the case of sales in Japan of units of FIFs through distributors, the distributors are subject to the same regulations. Please note that foreign securities companies which are not registered as type 1 financial instruments' business operators may not engage in the sale in Japan of investment fund units except in very limited circumstances.

Prospectus and other marketing materials

For distribution of beneficial interests or units in DIFs and FIFs through public offering in Japan, delivery of prospectuses to investors is required on or prior to purchase. Marketing materials that are to be used for offering must not include false or misleading indication. No licences or authorisations are required for prospectuses and marketing materials.

2.5. Taxation

The following summary addresses the current general structure of Japanese taxation. Tax treatment at both fund and investor levels may be subject to additional variations not discussed below, depending upon the circumstances of the relevant fund or investor. Furthermore, timing issues with respect to fund income may affect taxation at both fund and investor levels, depending upon relevant circumstances.

Taxation at investment fund level
CTDIFs

In the case of beneficial interests in CTDIFs publicly offered in Japan, no taxation will be imposed at the trust level if certain requirements are fulfilled, eg, the inclusion of certain prescribed language in trust deeds, due filing of registration statements, etc.

In the case of beneficial interests in CTDIFs privately placed in Japan, if such a CTDIF qualifies as a securities investment trust as defined under Japanese tax law to include investment funds the scope of investment of which contemplates investing a majority of total trust assets in securities, there is no taxation at the trust level. In the case of CTDIFs other than securities investment trusts to be privately placed in Japan, taxation is generally imposed at the trust level; and in such cases, taxation at the investor level will also be imposed, as discussed below, resulting in double taxation. Japanese tax law recognises, however, that such trusts in practice are merely vehicles for investment funds; accordingly, if the relevant trust fulfils certain requirements (eg, more than 90 per cent of surplus available for dividend are distributed to investors), profit distributions to investors may be accounted for by the trust as a deductible expense. This effectively eliminates double taxation on the amounts of the profit distributions.

ICTDIFs

Under Japanese tax law, investment companies established as vehicles for DIFs are deemed domestic Japanese corporations and are treated as such. Accordingly, in principle, taxation will be imposed at both the investment company level and the investor level. As in the case above, however, Japanese tax law recognises that such investment companies are merely vehicles for investment funds; accordingly, if the relevant investment company fulfils certain requirements (eg, more than 90 per cent of surplus available for dividend are distributed to investors), dividends paid to investors may be accounted for by the trust as a deductible expense. This effectively eliminates double taxation on the amounts of the dividends.

CTFIFs
In the case of CTFIFs, as defined under the ITIC Act, there is no corporate income taxation at the level of the fund itself, although dividends, interest and certain other passive income received may be subject to withholding tax in Japan.

ICTFIFs
In the case of ICTFIFs, as defined under the ITIC Act, if the relevant foreign investment company has income from any Japanese source, such as interest from Japanese government or corporate bonds, or dividends from Japanese companies, such income will be subject to taxation.

Taxation at investor level
Taxation at investor level is listed below. Please note that with respect to the tax rates marked with an asterisk(*), a special reconstruction income tax of 2.1 per cent will be added from 1 January 2013 to 31 December 2037. The funds from this tax will be utilised to cover reconstruction expenses as a result of the earthquake on 11 March 2011.

CTDIFs
(i) Taxation of Japanese residents
In the case of CTDIFs, the scope of investment of which is limited to public and corporate bonds only (bond investment trusts), profit distributions will be treated under Japanese tax law as interest income, and will be subject to income tax withholding at a rate of 15 per cent* and local tax withholding at a rate of 5 per cent. The interest income will be taxable separately from other income, and the withholding will constitute the only required taxation.

In the case of publicly offered CTDIFs which qualify as securities investment trusts other than bond investment trusts (equity investment trusts), profit distributions will be treated as dividend income, and currently will be subject to income tax withholding at a rate of 7 per cent* and local tax withholding at a rate of 3 per cent (the taxation rate will be each 15 per cent* and 5 per cent from 1 January 2014); the withholding constituting the only required taxation. In response to the termination of reduced tax rate on dividends and capital gains from publicly traded equities (including publicly offered equity investment trusts), 'Japanese ISA (individual savings account)' will be introduced from 1 January 2014, through which individuals will be able to open tax-free investment accounts subject to contribution limits of JPY1 million per year concerning dividends and capital gains from the above securities.

In other cases (including the case of privately placed CTDIFs), profit distributions will be treated under Japanese tax law as dividend income, and will be subject to income tax withholding at a rate of 20 per cent* and no local withholding tax. In principle, such income will be subject to comprehensive taxation, including income tax at applicable progressive rates. The tax withheld may be credited against the income tax.

(ii) Taxation of domestic corporations

In the case of bond investment trusts, profit distributions will be treated as interest income, and will be subject to income tax withholding at a rate of 15 per cent and local tax withholding at a rate of 5 per cent*. On or after 1 January 2016, local withholding tax will be abolished and only income tax withholding at a rate of 15 per cent* will be imposed.

In the case of publicly offered CTDIFs which qualify as equity investment trusts, profit distributions will be treated as dividend income, and will be subject to income tax withholding at a rate of 7 per cent* (the taxation rate will be 15 per cent* from 1 January 2014) and no local tax.

In other cases, withholding tax will be the same as the taxation of Japanese residents mentioned above.

In addition, the recipient corporation will be required to include the profit distributions in its income subject to corporate tax and to file a corporate tax return. The tax withheld may be credited against the corporate tax.

ICTDIFs
(i) Taxation of Japanese residents

Since ICTDIFs are treated as corporations, dividends from ICTDIFs will be treated under Japanese tax law as dividend income.

In the case of publicly offered: (a) open-ended ICTDIFs, and (b) listed closed-ended ICTDIFs, dividends will be subject to income tax at a rate of 7 per cent* and local tax at a rate of 3 per cent (the taxation rate will be each 15 per cent* and 5 per cent from 1 January 2014). In both cases, such withholding will constitute the only required taxation. (Investors in publicly offered units, however, will have the option of filing tax returns with respect to profit distributions, even though tax withholding has taken place. This may be beneficial to investors which have other losses on sales of listed shares or publicly offered securities, because such losses in some circumstances may offset the income from the relevant profit distributions, entitling them to refunds of tax withheld.) On or after 1 January 2016, losses derived from the sale of certain bonds can also be offset against dividends income, interest income from certain bonds and other gains derived from the sale of listed shares, publicly offered securities and bonds under certain requirements.

In other cases, dividends will be subject to income tax withholding at a rate of 20 per cent and no local withholding tax. In principle, such income will be subject to comprehensive taxation, including income tax at applicable progressive rates. The tax withheld may be credited against the income tax.

(ii) Taxation of domestic corporations

Withholding tax will be the same as the taxation of Japanese residents mentioned above. In addition, the recipient corporation will be required to include the dividends in its income subject to corporate tax and to file a corporate tax return. The tax withheld may be credited against the corporate tax.

CTFIFs

In the case of: (a) privately placed CTFIFs, and (b) publicly offered CTFIFs which qualify as bond investment trusts, CTFIFs are generally treated identically for tax purposes to their domestic equivalents (ie, investment trusts). If Japanese residents or domestic corporations receive profit distributions through Japanese domestic payment handling agents, such profit distributions will be subject to withholding tax.

In the case of publicly offered CTFIFs other than bond investment trusts, profit distributions will be treated as dividend income. If Japanese residents or domestic corporations receive profit distributions through Japanese domestic payment handling agents, the profit distributions will be subject to withholding tax. Withholding tax will be comprised of income tax withholding at a rate of 7 per cent* and local tax withholding at a rate of 3 per cent (the taxation rate will be each 15 per cent* and 5 per cent from 1 January 2014) in the case of Japanese residents, and of income tax withholding of 7 per cent* (the taxation rate will be 15 per cent* from 1 January 2014) and no local tax withholding in the case of domestic corporations. While Japanese residents will not be required to file income tax returns with respect to such profit distributions, Japanese corporations will be required to file corporate tax returns.

ICTFIFs

Dividends from ICTFIFs will be treated identically to dividends from foreign stock companies. In the case of privately placed ICTFIFs, if Japanese residents or domestic corporations receive dividends through Japanese domestic payment handling agents, the dividends will be subject to income tax withholding at a rate of 20 per cent* and no local tax withholding. The investor in addition will be required to include the profit distributions in its income subject to corporate or income tax and to file a corporate or income tax return (as applicable). The tax withheld may be credited against the corporate tax.

In the case of publicly offered ICTFIFs, withholding tax will be comprised of income tax withholding at a rate of 7 per cent* and local tax withholding at a rate of 3 per cent (the taxation rate will be each 15 per cent* and 5 per cent from 1 January 2014) in the case of Japanese residents, and of income tax withholding of 7 per cent* (the taxation rate will be 15 per cent* from 1 January 2014) and no local tax withholding in the case of domestic corporations. While Japanese residents will not be required to file income tax returns with respect to such dividends, Japanese corporations will be required to file corporate tax returns.

Taxation of non-residents

Income tax will be imposed on non-Japanese residents and foreign corporations (and a corporation tax, in the case of foreign companies) only with respect to income categorised as domestic source income. The scope of domestic source income subject to Japanese taxation depends on whether it has a permanent establishment (PE) in Japan.

In the case of a non-resident or a foreign corporation who does not have a permanent establishment in Japan, dividends from publicly offered CTDIFs other than bond investment trusts will be subject to income tax withholding at a rate of 7 per cent* (the taxation rate will be 15 per cent* from 1 January 2014) and no local tax withholding. Dividends from FIFs will not generally be subject to Japanese taxation.

Other taxation may be applicable if an applicable tax treaty otherwise provides.

Taxation of capital gains
In the case of CTDIFs, capital gains will realise where: (i) beneficial interests are redeemed due to the termination of the trust; (ii) an investor requests for redemption to the settlor (*kaiyaku*); or (iii) an investor transfers its beneficial interests to the distributor (*kaitori-seikyu*). In the case of publicly offered CTDIFs which qualify as equity investment trusts, capital gains arising from either (i), (ii) and (iii) will be treated as transfer income, and currently will be subject to income tax at a rate of 7 per cent* and local tax at a rate of 3 per cent (the taxation rate will be each 15 per cent* and 5 per cent from 1 January 2014) by filing an income tax return. In the case of CTDIFs that qualify as bond investment trusts, capital gains arising from (i) and (ii) will be treated as interest income, and will be subject to income tax withholding at a rate of 15 per cent* and local tax withholding at a rate of 5 per cent; while capital gains arising from (iii) will not be subject to Japanese taxation. On or after 1 January 2016, capital gains arising from (i), (ii) and (iii) will be subject to Japanese taxation, comprising of 15 per cent* income tax and 5 per cent local tax.

2.6. Customary or common terms
With respect to DIFs, a Japanese self-regulatory association called the Investment Trusts Association, Japan (ITA) has been established. Although membership is voluntary, virtually all settlors, investment managers and trustees for DIFs are members of the ITA. Members are subject to ITA-established regulations, which include limitations on securities included among investment assets and on permissible investment instructions by settlors. FIFs are not subject to regulation by the ITA.

With respect to public offerings of beneficial interests or units of FIFs, the regulations of the Japan Securities Dealers Association (JSDA) will apply. Although membership in the JSDA is not mandatory for securities companies operating in Japan, as a practical matter, membership is necessary to engage in the securities business. Accordingly, all securities companies handling public offerings of units of FIFs in Japan will be subject to JSDA regulations. Regulations include certain standards applicable to units of FIFs, eg, minimum assets, restrictions on short selling and borrowing, and prohibition on obtaining effective management control over any entity. As a practical matter, units of a FIF not fulfilling these standards may not be distributed in Japan. Please note that such selection standards are applicable only to open-ended FIFs, not to closed-ended funds.

3. ALTERNATIVE INVESTMENT FUNDS
3.1. Common structures
Major investment funds that employ alternative investment strategies in

Japan are hedge funds, private equity and real estate funds.

Hedge funds
There is no express definition of the term 'hedge fund' in Japanese law or regulation. Generally, however, according to the FSA Report, funds having the following characteristics tend to be referred to as hedge funds:
- investment targets include a variety of financial instruments;
- compared with other types of investment funds, they use more financial engineering, conduct more short selling transactions for which the underlying assets are investment targets, and invest in more derivative transactions characterised by complex structures and a variety of risks; and
- they seek absolute return through hedging risks.

Information published by one securities industry source indicates that the majority of hedge funds in Japan use investment fund legal structures, with FIF structures (eg, unit trusts and limited partnerships established in offshore centres, such as the Cayman Islands) being particularly prevalent. DIF and schemes as categorised as collective investment schemes (CIS) as defined under the FIEA have also been used to establish hedge funds.

Collective investment schemes
Investment structures which do not constitute DIFs or FIFs to be regulated by the ITIC Act, but in which the investment vehicle: (i) receives contributions from investors; (ii) conducts investment business using such contributions; and (iii) distributes the profits from such investment business to investors are generally considered to constitute collective investment schemes (CISs) in Japan. A variety of vehicles are potentially usable in CISs, including, among others, partnerships under the Civil Code of Japan (Act No.89 of 1896, as amended (Civil Code)), silent partnerships and investment limited partnerships. Similar structures implemented through foreign entities are also used as CISs in Japan.

Partnership (*Kumiai*) under the Civil Code of Japan
A partnership is established pursuant to a partnership agreement under the Civil Code, under which each of the partners agrees to make a contribution to a joint business to be operated using such contributions (Article 665 of the Civil Code). Partnerships under the Civil Code are not subject to mandatory statutory audit, and no statutory limitation is imposed on the investment targets of partnerships, which provides this vehicle with substantial structural flexibility.

Partnerships, however, do not constitute separate legal entities under the Civil Code; accordingly all members are liable for all partnership obligations. In the event that a partnership suffers a loss, this loss will be shared among all members. The imposition of full and direct liability upon all members (including managing partners) of investment funds established in the form of partnerships under the Civil Code, without benefit of any legal limitation on liability, constitutes a weak point in the use of this vehicle.

Silent partnership (*Tokumei Kumiai*)
A silent partnership is established pursuant to one or more two-party silent partnership agreements under the Commercial Code of Japan (Act No.48 of 1899, as amended (Commercial Code)), under which one party (the silent partner) agrees to contribute assets to a business operated by the other party (the manager), with profits generated from the business to be distributed to all silent partners (Article 535 of the Commercial Code). All assets contributed by the silent partners become the property of the manager, and the silent partners retain no interests. Under the silent partnership mechanism, silent partners are subject only to loss of their investments, while the manager is subject to unlimited liability. Disclosure of the content of each silent partnership agreement is not required, and the identities of silent partners may also be kept secret. The resulting anonymity and flexibility has made this vehicle popular and widely used in transactions targeting retail investors. Large institutional investors, however, may avoid this vehicle due to the impossibility of determining the content of partnership agreements executed by other silent partners.

Investment limited partnership (*Toshi Zigyo Yugen Sekinin Kumiai*) (investment LP)
An investment limited partnership is established pursuant to a limited partnership agreement for investment under the Investment Limited Partnership Act of Japan (Act No.90 of 1998, as amended (Investment LP Act)). Under Article 3 of this Act, each of the parties agrees to make financial contributions and to jointly carry out a particular business from among a list of permitted businesses specified in the Investment LP Act. Participants in investment LPs are subdivided into general partners and limited partners, and the general partners assume responsibility for management of the investment LP. Each of the general partners is subject to joint and several liability with respect to all partnership obligations, while limited partners are subject only to loss of their investments.

Private equity funds
A variety of entities are used as vehicles for private equity funds, but CIS schemes are most commonly used.

Real estate funds
Legal vehicles that are commonly used for real estate investment funds in Japan are a J-REIT, which is a kind of DIF, a *Tokutei Mokuteki Kaisha* (TMK) and *Godo Kaisha* (GK). Each scheme is summarised below.

J-REITs
A J-REIT is an investment trust (CTDIF) or an investment corporation (ICTDIF) that primarily invests its assets in real estate or real estate-related interests (such as lease interest) established under the ITIC Act. Generally in a J-REIT scheme, an investment company is established as an investment vehicle that invests funds gathered from investors in real estate-related assets

and distributes income from such investment to investors in the form of dividends. An investment corporation issues its equity securities called 'units' to investors, and such units meeting certain criteria for listing can be listed and traded on a stock exchange. Currently the major stock exchange on which J-REITs are listed is the Tokyo Stock Exchange.

A J-REIT can also be formed as a CTDIF, but there are currently no CTDIF-type J-REIT listed on the stock exchange.

TMK schemes
A TMK is a specified purpose company established under the Act on Securitisation of Assets of Japan (Act No.105 of 1998, as amended (Securitisation Act)) that will purchase real estate as part of securitisation transactions. A TMK receives funds from investors and uses the funds to purchase real estate, real estate beneficiary interests in trust or other assets specified in its asset liquidation plan. Proceeds obtained from the management of real estate will be distributed to the investors. In real property transactions using a TMK, the acquisition of underlying real property is funded primarily by loans, bonds and preferred equity securities issued by the TMK.

GK-TK schemes
A GK is a limited liability company established under the Companies Act in Japan (Act No.86 of 2005, as amended (Companies Act)). Under this scheme, a silent partnership (*tokumei kumiai*) agreement is typically entered into by and between a GK as the manager of a silent partnership and a silent partner. A GK receives funds from silent partners and uses the funds to purchase real estate beneficiary interests in trust, and distribute proceeds obtained from the management to silent partners. The acquisition of beneficiary interests in trust is funded primarily by non-recourse loans and contributions by silent partners.

These three are so-called real estate securitisation schemes, both of which are structured to avoid double taxation (see section 3.6.) and to ensure bankruptcy remoteness. In case of J-REITs, an investment corporation may only engage in investment management activities related to its real estate investment business (see section 3.3., 'Regulations for the types of activity and investments'), which consequently minimises bankruptcy risk of the investment corporation.

3.2. Regulatory framework
DIFs and FIFs
See section 2.2.

CISs (including GK-TK schemes)
Any entity wishing to act as the manager of a CIS, eg, the general partner of an investment LP, a manager of a silent partnership (to which a GK under a GK-TK scheme falls in) and any entity wishing to act as an equivalent general partner for a limited partnership in a foreign jurisdiction must first register to engage in investment management business pursuant to Article 29 of the FIEA with respect to its investment management. An exception to this requirement

exists in the case of investment managers for funds targeting professional investors (ie, CISs targeting QIIs and having 49 or fewer investors who are not QIIs), for which the registration requirement is eliminated. Investment managers for such funds, however, are required to file a prior notification with the commissioner of the FSA (Article 63, section 2 of the FIEA).

Interests in CISs are generally not subject to the disclosure requirement under the FIEA, with some exceptions.

J-REITs

See the first three subsections under section 2.2. J-REITs are subject to notification and registration requirements under the ITIC Act and requirements for public offering or private placement under the FIEA. When units of J-REITs are to be listed on a stock exchange in Japan, criteria under the listing rules must also be satisfied, eg, the total net assets shall be JPY1 billion or more (in the case of the Tokyo Stock Exchange).

As described in section 2.2., 'Registration of investment management companies', an investment manager for a J-REIT must be a registered investment management business operator.

In the case of an investment company which mainly invests in real estate (ie, a J-REIT), the investment manager must in addition: (i) obtain license as a real estate broker under the Building Lots and Buildings Transaction Business Act (Act No.176 of 1952); and (ii) obtain approval by the Minister of Land, Infrastructure and Transportation for conducting intermediary or agency services with respect to real estate transactions pursuant to the same Act.

TMKs

Before commencement of its business, a TMK must file a notification with the LFB. An asset liquidation plan which provides basic matters concerning asset securitisation business of the TMK (eg, issuance of preferred equity securities and contents of specified assets) must be attached to the notification (Articles 4 and 5 of the Securitisation Act).

Preferred equity securities are subject to the filing requirement under the FIEA. See section 2.2. above.

If a TMK directly acquires actual real estate (ie, as a hard asset), the asset manager who engages to manage TMK's assets must obtain a license and approval under the Building Lots and Buildings Transaction Business Act as well (see section 3.2., 'J-REITs').

If a TMK purchases real estate beneficiary interests in trust, activities of asset managers would be subject to the license requirement under the FIEA as an investment management business operator or an investment advisory and agency business operator, depending on the scope of its business.

3.3. Operational requirements
Regulations for the types of activity and investments
J-REITs

An investment company may not engage in businesses other than asset management, and the scope of the asset management is limited to certain acts as listed in the ITIC Act (eg, acquisition and/or transfer of real estate relating to the specified assets).

With respect to the investments, at least 50 per cent of the total assets of an investment company must be invested in specified assets as referred to in section 2.3., 'Regulations for the types of investments'. To have units listed on the Tokyo Stock Exchange, there are additional requirements such as that real estate (inclusive of certain limited categories of real estate-related asset classes) must make up at least 70 per cent of the total assets under management.

TMKs

TMKs are prohibited from engaging in businesses other than those related to asset securitisation conducted pursuant to an asset liquidation plan and other incidental businesses (Article 195, section 1 of the Securitisation Act). Assets that TMKs shall acquire are limited to 'specified assets' as defined under the Securitisation Act (the contents of which are different from those of the 'specified assets' under the ITIC Act) and as listed in the asset liquidation plan.

Regulations concerning trustee and custodian
J-REITs

The investment company's assets must be held in custody by a custodian which is a licensed trust company or certain other prescribed type of companies. See section 2.3., 'Regulations concerning trustee and custodian'.

TMKs

TMK must entrust management and disposition of specified assets to trust company, etc. (Article 200 of the Securitisation Act).

Reporting and disclosure requirements etc.
J-REITs

Requirements under the ITIC Act and the FIEA for ICTDIFs apply equally here. See section 2.3., 'Reporting and disclosure requirements, etc.' If a J-REIT will be listed on the Tokyo Stock Exchange, it will also be subject to disclosure requirements under the rules of the exchange.

TMKs

Preferred equity securities of a TMK which file SRSs in connection with public offerings in Japan will also be subject to ongoing reporting requirements under the FIEA. See section 2.3., 'Reporting and disclosure requirements, etc.'

An investment manager/asset manager registered under the FIEA is subject to ongoing obligations under the same Act. See section 2.3., 'Reporting and disclosure requirements, etc.'

Other operational regulations

The information in section 2.3., 'Other operational regulations' applies equally here.

3.4. Marketing the fund
Registration requirements for distributor
DIFs (including J-REITs) and FIFs
See section 2.4., 'Registration requirements for distribution'.

TMKs
Any entity wishing to act as a distributor in Japan of preferred equity securities of a TMK must be, in principal, registered as a type 1 financial instruments business operator under the FIEA. The originator may, however, handle the offering of preferred equity securities without the registration through filing a notification to the LFB (Article 208 of the Securitisation Act). If the originator has not made such filing, directors and employees of a TMK may themselves conducts the offering of preferred equity securities to investors in Japan without the registration under the FIEA (Article 207 of the Securitisation Act).

CISs (including GK-TK schemes)
Any entity wishing to act as a distributor in Japan of interests in CISs must be registered as a type 2 financial instruments business operator. If solicitation is made by the investment fund itself, the fund's manager must be registered as a type 2 financial instruments business operator; provided that in the case of private placements targeting professional investors as described above, the fund will not be required to register, but only to file a prior notification with the FSA (Article 63, section 2 of the FIEA).

Prospectus and other marketing materials
The information in section 2.4., 'Prospectus and other marketing materials', applies equally here.

3.5. Taxation
As referred to in section 3.1., 'Real estate funds', major schemes for real estate funds are structured to avoid double taxation. In the case of a J-REIT, if it fulfils certain requirements (eg, more than 90 per cent of the distributable profit are distributed as dividend), dividends paid to investors may be accounted for by the trust as a deductible expense. Taxes for acquisition and holding of real estate will be imposed additionally (eg, real estate acquisition tax, registration license tax and fixed assets tax).

At investors' level, dividends and capital gains from J-REITs paid to Japanese residents will be subject to income tax at a rate of 7 per cent* and local tax at a rate of 3 per cent (the taxation rate will be each 15 per cent* and 5 per cent from 1 January 2014). See section 2.5., 'Taxation at investor level'.

3.6. Customary or common terms
In addition to the points raised in section 2.6., the following should be noted:
An investment manager's fees for hedge funds are typically structured either as management fees or as performance fees. As noted, the former arrangement typically contemplates that the investment manager will

receive a fee based on the total assets of the relevant fund, without regard to performance. Performance fee arrangements, by contrast, contemplate that management compensation will be determined based upon the performance of the relevant fund. Information published by one securities industry source indicates that average management fees amount to 1.0–1.5 per cent of fund assets per annum, while average performance fees amount to 10–20 per cent of fund performance per annum.

It is customary for hedge funds operating in Japan that the investment manager itself will invest in the relevant fund, as implicit assurance that the investment manager will avoid unreasonably risky deployments of investors' assets.

With respect to listed J-REITs, the listing rules require the investment manager to be a member of the ITA. The investment manager will be subject to ITA's regulations including the rules concerning real estate investment trust and real estate investment corporation, under which specific operational rules for J-REITs are provided.

4. PROPOSED CHANGES AND DEVELOPMENTS

An amendment to the FIEA was passed in June 2013, under which substantial revisions in J-REIT regulations will come into effect with the goal of further expanding the utilisation of J-REITs. Such revisions will include: (i) enabling J-REITs to raise funds through rights offerings and to acquire their own units; (ii) permitting J-REITs to acquire overseas real estate indirectly through special purpose companies, in addition to direct acquisition; and (iii) making units of listed investment corporations subject to insider trading regulations. These amendments will become effective no later than 18 June 2014 (in the case of (ii) and (iii) above) and 18 December 2014 (in the case of (i) above).

Although not included in the amendment mentioned above, the Final Report by the Working Group on Review of Investment Trust and Investment Corporation Regulation of the FSA dated 12 December 2012 suggested further revisions in investment trust and investment corporation regulations. These suggestions included development of quantitative regulations for diversification of credit risk related to investment assets under the management of investment trusts (both DIFs and FIFs), reflecting the increasing complexity of investment trust products distributed to investors who may not have sufficient investment expertise. We anticipate that this report may lead to further amendments in the future.

Jersey

Niamh Lalor & Tim Morgan **Ogier**

1. MARKET OVERVIEW
Jersey is a leading global centre for the establishment of funds and has been at the forefront of international developments that have attracted international sponsors, fund managers, advisors and professional investors. One of the key features of Jersey's fund industry is the flexibility and range of structures and corresponding regulatory and commercial approaches.

Jersey offers a full range of fund vehicles from private funds through to retail offerings and alternative investment funds – in particular private equity, real estate, mezzanine, infrastructure and hedge funds.

The Alternative Investment Fund Managers Directive (AIFMD) came into force in July 2013, and brings with it additional regulatory obligations for managers of EU funds or funds marketing to investors in the EU. Although such obligations do not affect Jersey based funds per se (the regulatory regime for Jersey funds falling outside the scope of the AIFMD remains entirely unaltered), they will have an impact on funds or fund managers based in Jersey wishing to market funds to professional investors in the EU.

2. ALTERNATIVE INVESTMENT FUNDS
2.1. Common structures
The regulatory regime in Jersey has developed a number of different products to cater for market needs and the expectation of investors in relation to the establishment of alternative investment funds. An example of this is the development of unregulated fund products that are targeted either at investors who can demonstrate sufficient wealth to cope with an unregulated fund product or that are listed on a regulated exchange. In tandem with such new products, the Jersey funds regime has streamlined the process for authorisation and registration of Jersey-based fund service providers to Jersey and non-Jersey funds.

As a result, there are a number of regulatory options for the establishment of an alternative investment fund, including very private schemes, Control of Borrowing Order funds (COBO-only funds) and closed-ended expert and eligible investor funds described below.

Private funds that are offered to fewer than 15 investors are referred to as 'very private schemes'. Very private schemes are unregulated, other than the need to obtain consent to the establishment of the fund vehicle.

Private funds that are offered to 50 or fewer investors are referred to as 'COBO-only funds' under the Control of Borrowing (Jersey) Order 1958 (COBO Order). Private Placement Funds are a streamlined category of COBO-only funds that have been specifically designed for the professional and institutional investor market.

Expert funds are a category of funds targeted at expert investors which can be established within a matter of days on the basis of a self-certification approach without the requirement for any formal regulatory review of the fund or its Promoter.

Eligible investor unregulated funds have a still higher minimum investment level than expert funds and are targeted at institutions and professional investors who can demonstrate sufficient net worth or experience to be able to bear the risk of investing in an unregulated product.

Jersey-domiciled investment funds may be structured as limited liability companies (including incorporated cell companies or protected cell companies), limited partnerships or unit trusts. Recent enhancements to Jersey's existing companies law have further developed the flexibility for corporate funds – for example, the abolition of the prohibition on the giving of financial assistance by a Jersey company for the acquisition of its own shares. There is now greater flexibility around the sources from which a Jersey company can make distributions and share redemption payments. The provisions relating to statements of solvency made by directors who approve redemptions or distributions have been simplified.

The principal legal vehicle used for the investment manager or adviser to such a fund will vary, depending on the form of the fund, but is likely to be a separate company (in the case of a corporate fund), a general partner company (in the case of a limited partnership) or a trustee or separate management company (in the case of a unit trust). There is a familiarity with structures such as limited partnerships acting as general partners and Jersey separate/incorporated limited partnerships which are usually used in certain structures.

2.2. Regulatory framework
Very private structures
A fund vehicle which is established for a small number of co-investors (up to a maximum of 15 offerees to subscribe for interests in the vehicle in total over the duration of the fund) or for a single purpose and where there is no formal offering of securities is regarded as a 'very private' structure. Typically, such 'very private' structures are closed-ended and do not have a third-party investment manager/adviser. Such funds are regulated under COBO and can be established within a short period, usually within a few days upon disclosure only of the identity of the proposed investor(s) to the Jersey Financial Services Commission (Commission). This type of structure is appropriate for single investor vehicles, as well as for joint ventures and co-investment structures either as corporate bodies, limited partnerships or unit trusts.

COBO-only funds
A Jersey investment vehicle (whether a company, limited partnership or unit trust) will be treated as a 'COBO-only' fund or private placement fund if it falls outside the scope of regulation as a collective investment fund (see below) and it has either (i) an offer document; or (ii) it has no offer document

but some or all of the following characteristics:
- more than 15 (but fewer than 50) offerees to subscribe for interests in the fund over its lifetime (excluding 'red-herring' recipients of information); and/or
- a third-party investment manager/adviser; and/or
- investors being unconnected persons; and/or
- being open-ended.

Such COBO-only funds are governed principally by the Control of Borrowing (Jersey) Law 1947 (referred to as the COBO Law and together with the COBO Order, the COBO Laws), which provides for the supervision in Jersey of the raising of money, the issue of securities and the circulation of offers for subscription, sale or exchange of securities. Subordinate legislation made pursuant to this law (namely, the COBO Order) gives the Commission control, amongst other things, over the raising of investment capital.

The issue of shares, interests or units in a COBO-only fund and the circulation of private placement memoranda/prospectuses and sales literature in relation to such a fund is not permitted to take place unless a COBO consent has been obtained from the Commission.

The Commission will exercise regulation both through a preliminary review of the 'Promoter' behind the scheme (under its promoter policy) as well as a review of the private placement memorandum prior to the issue of a COBO consent. When considering an application for consent, the COBO Laws require the Commission to have regard to the need to protect the integrity of Jersey in commercial and financial matters and the best economic interests of Jersey.

Private Placement Funds (PPFs) are exempt from the promoter test. A key attraction with the PPF is that it has a highly flexible structure and there are no prescribed investment restrictions, concentration limits or leverage restraints. Regulatory consents for a PPF can be obtained within a matter of days and the PPF is subject only to light-touch ongoing regulatory control.

Expert funds

To be an expert fund, the fund must be a collective investment fund and have obtained a certificate under the Collective Investment Funds (Jersey) Law 1988 (CIF Law). The fund must also comply with the Jersey Expert Fund Guide (EFG) published by the Commission.

The main regulatory requirements applicable to an expert fund are set out in the EFG and include, among others, the following:
- the fund company, general partner or trustee (as the case may be) must have at least two Jersey resident directors with appropriate expertise and the fund itself must be a Jersey company or have a Jersey general partner (if it is a Jersey limited partnership) or a Jersey trustee or manager (if a unit trust);
- each investor must sign an investment warning and fall within one of the categories set out in the EFG to be an 'expert investor';
- the investment adviser, which may be an entity based outside of Jersey, must satisfy the requirements as set out in the EFG (typically it must

be established in an Organisation for Economic Co-operation and
  Development (OECD) or equivalent country and be regulated there);
- an expert fund must treat one of its service providers (typically a Jersey
  administrator but can be an investment manager) as a monitoring
  functionary. The monitoring functionary must be registered to provide
  fund services business in Jersey, have at least two Jersey resident directors
  with appropriate experience together with staff and a physical presence
  in Jersey. The monitoring functionary will be required to monitor the
  compliance of the investment adviser with any investment or borrowing
  restrictions set out in the offer document and must have access to
  appropriate records of the investment adviser to enable it to carry out
  such monitoring function;
- an expert fund must appoint an auditor;
- if the fund is open-ended, then custodial arrangements must be sourced
  from a separate custodian or trustee with staff and a physical presence in
  Jersey (although this can be waived in certain circumstances);
- the offer document must contain certain specified information set
  out in the EFG and the Collective Investment Funds (Certified Funds)
  (Prospectuses) (Jersey) Order 2012 (the CFPO). The offer documents must
  include all information that investors would reasonably require to enable
  them to make an informed judgement about an investment in the expert
  fund; and
- there are no restrictions imposed upon the level of borrowing or gearing
  adopted by an expert fund, provided that the approach to borrowing
  or gearing is clearly disclosed in the offer document. However, the
  Commission expects to be given full details of any risk posed by
  borrowings where the fund is permitted to borrow in excess of 200 per
  cent of its net asset value and how such risks are to be managed by the
  fund in the expert fund application to the Commission.

If an expert fund does not comply in all respects with the EFG, it is
possible to obtain derogations from the Commission in relation to such non-
compliance.

An application form setting out the key features of an expert fund,
including a confirmation from the investment adviser that it satisfies the
requirements of the EFG must be submitted with supporting documentary
evidence, namely, the latest draft of the offer document, a fund structure
chart, the investment adviser's confirmation and completed personal
questionnaires in respect of directors and principal persons of the expert
fund. The monitoring functionary must countersign the investment advisor's
confirmation, having carried out its own general due diligence against the
investment adviser, stating that it has no reason to believe the investment
adviser's confirmation to be incorrect. These must be submitted to the
Commission, together with the prescribed application fee as set out on
the Commission's website. Although the Commission will check that the
application form has been appropriately completed, it will not generally carry
out any detailed regulatory review of the expert fund offer document.

The requisite consents to the establishment of an expert fund will be issued within three working days of receipt of an application, provided the requirements of the EFG are complied with or any derogation from such requirements is agreed with the Commission prior to the submission of the expert fund application.

Where Jersey service providers are appointed to an expert fund then they must be licensed to hold a registration certificate to conduct fund services business under the Financial Services (Jersey) Law 1988 (FSJ Law). (For more detail in relation to the regulation of fund services providers, please see section 3.2 below).

Eligible investor funds

An unregulated eligible investor fund is a scheme or arrangement established in Jersey and in which only 'eligible investors' may invest.

Such funds are exempted from regulation as 'collective investment funds' in Jersey by virtue of an enabling order made under the CIF Law, namely the Collective Investment Funds (Unregulated Funds) (Jersey) Order 2008 (as amended) (referred to as the Unregulated Funds Order).

The definition of 'eligible investor' is set out in detail in the Unregulated Funds Order and includes an entity who, whether through the initial offering or by subsequent acquisition, makes a minimum initial investment or commitment of $1,000,000 (or currency equivalent) in the unregulated fund or if an individual investor has a net worth, or joint net worth with that person's spouse, greater than $10,000,000 (or currency equivalent) excluding that person's principal place of residence. An 'eligible investor' also includes both any entity that is a functionary to the unregulated eligible investor fund or an associate of a functionary to the unregulated eligible investor fund and professional investors.

Eligible investor unregulated funds may be structured as open- or closed-ended. Regulated funds that have already been established in Jersey are not permitted to convert to unregulated funds. Transfers of interests in an unregulated eligible investor fund will only be possible to other eligible investors with restrictions to ensure that any non-eligible investor does not become a registered holder of an interest.

The offer and/or listing document of an unregulated eligible investor fund needs to contain a prominent statement that the fund is unregulated, together with a form of prescribed investment warning.

Where Jersey service providers are appointed to an unregulated fund then they must, in general (there are limited exceptions), be licensed to hold a registration certificate to conduct fund services business under the FSJ Law. (For more detail in relation to the regulation of fund services providers, please see section 3.2 below.)

Other than a general partner of a Jersey limited partnership or the Jersey corporate trustee or manager of a unit trust and the registered office provider (generally a regulated administrator), there is no requirement for Jersey service providers to be appointed as functionaries to an unregulated fund and these may be selected on a global basis to provide the best service to fund structures. In contrast to expert funds and listed funds (see below), Jersey resident directors are not required to be appointed to the board of the fund vehicle (or the general partner or trustee if the fund is a limited partnership or unit trust).

Although the unregulated fund is regarded as an unregulated fund product in Jersey, it is still necessary for the fund vehicle to hold a COBO consent to issue shares, partnership interests or units in Jersey.

Subject to the structure of an unregulated fund complying with the Unregulated Funds Order, there is no regulatory review or oversight of the terms of offer or ongoing operations of an unregulated fund.

An unregulated eligible investor fund is required to file a notice (Unregulated Fund notice or UF1) with the Commission once established. An unregulated fund may be offered to investors immediately following the filing of this prescribed notice provided that the interests offered in the unregulated fund are within the consent issued to the unregulated fund vehicle under the COBO Order.

2.3. Operational requirements
Very private schemes
There are no ongoing operational or licensing requirements in relation to very private vehicles, other than compliance with general corporate, limited partnership or unit trust requirements applicable to all companies, limited partnership and unit trusts (as applicable). The structure can be operated with absolute flexibility (as permitted by its constitutional documents) and there are no disclosure or filing requirements.

COBO-only funds
Ongoing regulation of a COBO-only fund is exercised through the requirement for the fund to comply with the relevant conditions set out in the COBO consent.

Expert funds
Once the Commission has issued a registration certificate under the CIF Law in respect of the expert fund, then the fund vehicle must comply with the conditions set out in that registration certificate and continue to comply with the EFG and the Codes of Practice for Funds (the Fund Codes). In addition, any service provider to the fund vehicle (including any general partner, trustee and any manager) must comply with the Codes of Practice for Fund Services Business (the FSB Codes and, together with the Fund Codes, the Codes) and the Commission's 'Policy Statement: Licensing Policy in respect of those activities that require registration under the Financial Services (Jersey) Law 1998' (Licensing Policy).

The annual fees payable for a certificate holder under the CIF Law and fund services business license holders under the FSJ Law are set out on the Commission's website.

Eligible investor funds
If the Jersey-based service provider to the fund is required to hold a fund

services business registration under the FSJ Law, then such license holder will continue to be required to comply with the conditions contained in such certificate, the FSB Codes and the Licensing Policy. There are currently no application or annual license fees payable by an unregulated fund. The annual fees for Jersey-based license holders under the FSJ Law are set out on the Commission's website.

2.4. Marketing the fund
Very private schemes
Very private vehicles may not be offered to more than 15 investors.

COBO-only Funds
COBO-only funds may not be offered to more than 50 investors.

Expert Funds
Expert funds may only be offered to 'expert investors' (as defined in the EFG). There is no limit on the number of investors that may be admitted.

Any distributor appointed by the expert fund that is either a Jersey entity or carries on its business from Jersey must be licensed under the FSJ Law.

Eligible investor funds
Eligible investor funds may only be offered to 'eligible investors' (as defined in the Unregulated Funds Order). There is no limit on the number of investors that may be admitted.

Any distributor appointed by the eligible fund that is either a Jersey entity or carries on its business from Jersey must be licensed under the FSJ Law.

2.5. Marketing the Fund in the EEA – AIFMD requirements
To enable fund managers based in Jersey to market Jersey based funds to professional investors in EEA Member states either by using the existing private placement rules (until at least 2018), or by virtue of an EU-wide marketing passport from such time as marketing passports become available, Jersey has implemented a regulatory infrastructure to comply with the AIFMD. The infrastructure consists of the Jersey Alternative Investment Funds (Jersey) Regulations 2012 (effective from 22 July 2013) (the Regulations), the AIF codes of practice (the AIF Codes), and various amendments to existing codes of practice already in force. Pursuant to the Regulations, a Jersey fund that wishes to market into the EEA needs to obtain a certificate (an AIF Certificate), unless an exemption applies. The AIF Codes incorporate the AIFMD requirements for private placement (such as disclosure, reporting and transparency). From 22 July 2013, the regulatory position for Jersey based alternative investment funds wishing to market into the EU will be as follows:

Very private schemes
Very private schemes will be subject to the AIF Regulations (and as such will need to obtain an AIF Certificate), and will need to comply with the AIF Codes. The Commission will require further information to accompany the

application for an AIF Certificate (beyond that already provided to them by a very private scheme).

COBO-only Funds
COBO-only Funds will need to obtain an AIF Certificate, comply with the AIF Regulations, and the AIF Codes.

Expert Funds
Pursuant to the Regulations, a fund that already holds a registration certificate under the CIF Law will be exempt from the requirement to hold an AIF Certificate, provided that it submits written notification to the Commission of its intention to market in the EEA. A Jersey Expert Fund wishing to benefit from this exemption will need to make such notification to the Commission. The applicability of the AIF Codes to the fund in question will be reflected by the addition of a condition on the certificate granted to that Expert Fund under the CIF Law.

Eligible investor funds
The Commission has introduced a new certified type of 'Jersey Eligible Investor Fund' to which eligible investor funds may convert. Such new Jersey EIFs would be regulated under the CIF Law (with certain dispensations to the current licensing and authorisation regime), would be issued with a certificate under the CIF Law and be subject to the existing Codes applicable to funds, together with the AIF Codes.

2.6. Taxation
The principal Jersey income tax statute is the Income Tax (Jersey) Law 1961 (as amended) (Income Tax Law) which determines the rate of Jersey income tax payable by Jersey investment vehicles.

Under current Jersey law, there are no capital gains, capital transfer, gift, wealth or inheritance taxes or any death or estate duties (other than as set out below). No stamp duty is levied in Jersey on the issue, conversion, redemption or transfer of shares (except in relation to Jersey companies whose articles of association confer a right of occupation of land in Jersey), limited partnership interests or unit trust units. Generally, stamp duty is only levied in Jersey on certain court documents and certain documents relating to Jersey real property.

On the death of a private individual investor (whether or not such individual was domiciled in Jersey), duty at a rate of up to 0.75 per cent is payable on the registration of any Jersey probate or letters of administration which may be required in order to transfer, convert, redeem or make payments in respect of, Jersey shares, limited partnership interests or unit trust units held by the estate of such deceased individual sole shareholder.

Companies
All Jersey companies, (save for those that are tax resident outside Jersey in a jurisdiction where the highest rate of corporate income tax in that jurisdiction is 20 per cent or higher), and non-Jersey companies managed and controlled in Jersey, will be chargeable to Jersey income tax.

The general rate of Jersey corporate income tax is 0 per cent subject to the limited exceptions set out below:
- certain specified domestic Jersey utility companies shall be chargeable to Jersey income tax at a rate of 20 per cent (comprising the Jersey gas, water, electricity, postal and telecoms utilities);
- income derived from leasing or ownership of Jersey land will continue to be chargeable to Jersey income tax at a rate of 20 per cent; and
- certain 'financial services companies' shall be chargeable to Jersey income tax at a rate of 10 per cent.

For these purposes, 'financial services companies' are Jersey companies that are regulated in Jersey as banks; as fund administrators or custodians; or are registered to carry out trust company business or investment business. Such administrators, custodians or registered persons will only be chargeable to Jersey income tax at the 10 per cent rate if they carry on that business through a permanent establishment in Jersey.

Permanent establishment entails a physical presence in Jersey or a place of management of the company. The fact that the directors of a company regularly meet in Jersey will not, of itself, make their meeting place a permanent establishment. Nor will the exercise of clerical functions such as invoicing operations, management and administration services or the entering into of contracts in respect of a company's international business (to include, for example, swap financing and loan funding agreements) at the address of the company's registered office amount to carrying on business through a permanent establishment in Jersey for these purposes.

Investment funds are subject to 0 per cent tax rate on their income or profits in Jersey. In addition, on December 2010 a law was brought into force in Jersey such that arrangements for the collective investment of capital acquired by means of an offer for units for subscription, sale or exchange (including investment funds as well as any subsequent investment holding companies) can be certified as exempt from income tax in Jersey by the Comptroller of Taxes in Jersey. In order to obtain such certification, it is necessary for the participant to register with the Comptroller of Taxes in Jersey by 31 March each year in respect of the preceding year of assessment and pay an annual fee of £500.

Jersey income tax for shareholders

Shareholders in a Jersey company who are not Jersey tax resident are not subject to taxation in Jersey in respect of any income or gains arising in respect of such shares held by them.

Jersey tax resident shareholders will be liable to Jersey income tax at a rate of 20 per cent (subject to the application of allowances and reliefs relevant to their own personal tax status).

Jersey companies chargeable to corporate income tax at the 0 per cent rate are not obliged or entitled to deduct withholding tax on dividends.

Jersey limited partnerships

Jersey limited partnerships established under the Limited Partnerships (Jersey)

Law 1994 (as amended) are tax transparent. The limited partnership is not itself chargeable in respect of Jersey income tax, income is treated as accruing directly to the limited partners.

Jersey resident partners are therefore chargeable to Jersey income tax on their apportioned share of the income arising to the limited partnership. Non-Jersey resident partners are chargeable to Jersey income tax only in respect of Jersey source income (excluding Jersey bank account interest). Jersey source income refers to the income profits of a trade carried on in Jersey. It does not include capital profits, interest paid on limited partners' loans to the limited partnership or income profits from investment activities outside Jersey.

Jersey unit trusts
By longstanding published concession, the trustees of Jersey unit trusts are not chargeable to Jersey income tax in respect of non-Jersey source income (and Jersey bank account interest) arising for the benefit of non-Jersey resident unit holders. This concession applies automatically where all unit holders are non-Jersey resident and no withholding on account of Jersey tax will occur.

Jersey resident unit holders will be chargeable to Jersey income tax in respect of relevant distributions made to them. Therefore, where some unit holders are Jersey resident and some are non-Jersey resident, formal application for full exemption will be made to the Comptroller of Taxes in Jersey, the trustee will undertake to the Comptroller of Taxes in Jersey to deduct and account for Jersey income tax in respect of distributions to Jersey residents. In certain circumstances, an anti-avoidance notice may need to be given to Jersey-resident potential investors.

2.7. Customary or common terms
Private funds are generally closed-ended and have a limited term, though the number of years varies depending on the asset class.

Generally the terms of a Jersey fund will mirror those in the global fund market and will vary by industry – for example, there is greater use of investor side letters in private equity funds than hedge funds.

3. RETAIL FUNDS
3.1. Common structures
The broad range of regulatory products available for Jersey has resulted in great flexibility in structuring options for retail funds. The most commonly used structures are open-ended unclassified funds, listed funds and recognised funds.

3.2. Regulatory framework
Open-ended unclassified funds
The CIF Law distinguishes between 'recognised funds' and 'unclassified funds'. Broadly, the term 'unclassified funds' includes all regulated funds which are not Recognised Funds (as described below).

An unclassified fund may have a corporate structure (including cells), or be a unit trust or limited partnership.

To the extent that a fund is to be offered to more than 50 investors or is to be listed and the fund is not able to fall under the expedited regulatory approach offered under either the EFG or the Listed Fund Guide (LFG) published by the Commission, a collective investment fund may be regulated as an unclassified fund. In this situation the Commission will regulate the fund in accordance with its policy (as referred to below), which will need to include compliance by the Promoter of the fund with the Commission's promoter policy. This will include an evaluation of the track record, experience and reputation of the Promoter of the fund as well as of the financial resources and spread of ownership of the Promoter.

The application of the regulatory guidelines to an unclassified fund will primarily depend upon the minimum investment level of the fund and whether the fund is open-ended or closed-ended. An 'open-ended' fund is generally one that is open for redemptions and subscriptions at the option of the investor.

If the fund is to be open-ended, the Commission's Open-Ended Unclassified Collective Investment Funds Guide will apply. This guide sets out the documentary and structural requirements in relation to the fund, suggests investment and borrowing restrictions for different categories of fund (mostly restricted to 10 per cent of the net asset value of the fund) and is particularly aimed at retail funds marketed to unsophisticated investors. The Commission will also have regard to the CFPO in defining what is an acceptable standard of information in the offering document in relation to a 'collective investment fund' that is an open-ended company or open-ended unit trust.

No investment or borrowing restrictions are prescribed for closed-ended unclassified funds. However, the Commission will, for a retail fund, have regard to the guide as a benchmark and, as a condition to the registration certificate granted to the fund under the CIF Law, will require that any change in the investment or borrowing restrictions receives prior written consent from the Commission.

An open-ended and an unclassified fund will require a Jersey-resident manager and custodian. For a closed-ended fund, no separate custodian is required. The fund will be required to comply with the Fund Codes.

All Jersey fund service providers to an unclassified fund must be registered in Jersey under the FSJ Law and will have to comply with the FSB Codes and Licensing Policy as referred to above.

Listed funds

There are two types of vehicles available for a listed product – a fund established under the CIF Law and governed by the LFG and an unregulated exchange-traded fund established in accordance with the Unregulated Funds Order.

The LFG provides a fast track process for the establishment of closed-ended corporate funds that are listed on recognised stock exchanges or markets. The

Listed Fund's fast track approval process is very similar to the Jersey expert funds application process.

To be a listed fund, the fund must be a collective investment fund and have been issued with a registration certificate under the CIF Law. The fund must be closed-ended, listed on a recognised stock exchange or market (including, amongst others, the main list of the London Stock Exchange, Alternative Investment Market, Specialist Fund Market, Euronext and the Channel Islands Stock Exchange) and must comply with the LFG.

A listed fund will be subject to a light degree of regulation. In particular the promoter of a listed fund will not be subject to any regulatory review or approval. There will be no requirement to adopt any prescribed investment or borrowing restrictions or risk diversification strategy, there is no required minimum subscription and a listed fund may be offered to any category of investors including retail investors. Similar to expert funds, although no investment or borrowing restrictions are prescribed, the Commission expects to be given full details of any risk posed by borrowings where the fund is permitted to borrow in excess of 200 per cent of its net asset value and how such risks are to be managed by the fund.

The main regulatory requirements in respect of a listed fund are set out in the LFG and are generally similar to those referred to above in respect of an expert fund. The main differences are that there are no equivalent 'expert investor' restrictions, there are additional criteria that need to be fulfilled in respect of the investment adviser to the listed fund and there is no requirement for a listed fund to appoint a Jersey custodian.

If a listed fund does not comply in all respects with the LFG, it is possible to obtain derogations from the Commission in relation to such non-compliance.

An unregulated exchange-traded fund is a scheme or arrangement established in Jersey, which is a closed-ended fund and which is listed on a stock exchange or market or which is applying for its shares or units to be granted such a listing.

Unregulated funds are exempted from regulation as 'collective investment funds' in Jersey by virtue of the Unregulated Funds Order.

The offer and/or listing document of an unregulated exchange-traded fund needs to contain a prominent statement that the fund is unregulated, together with a form of prescribed investment warning.

Where Jersey service providers are appointed to an unregulated fund then they must, in general (there are limited exceptions), be licensed to hold a registration certificate to conduct fund services business under the FSJ Law.

Other than a general partner of a Jersey limited partnership or the Jersey corporate trustee or manager of a unit trust, there is no requirement for Jersey service providers to be appointed as functionaries to an unregulated fund and these may be selected on a global basis to provide the best service to fund structures. In contrast to expert funds and listed funds, Jersey resident directors are not required to be appointed to the board of the fund vehicle.

Recognised funds
Recognised funds are authorised as collective investment funds and as

well as complying with the CIF Law they must comply with the Collective Investment Funds (Recognised Funds) (Rules) (Jersey) Order 2003 (as amended).

The Collective Investment Funds (Recognised Funds) (Rules) (Jersey) Order 2003 (as amended) was introduced to give investors protection which is at least equivalent to that given to investors under the Financial Services and Markets Act 2000 in the United Kingdom. As a result, any fund which has a permit from the Commission may seek authorisation under the Financial Services and Markets Act 2000 to market directly to the 'retail' public in the UK. Recognised funds may also be marketed to the public (subject to local requirements) in a number of other territories, including Australia, Belgium, Hong Kong, the Netherlands and South Africa.

Recognised funds are more highly regulated and provide investors with access to a statutory compensation scheme should the custodian, manager or trustee of the fund become insolvent or unable to or likely to become unable to satisfy claims in respect of any description of civil liability incurred in connection with the fund. The legislation prescribes detailed requirements as to the fund's structure and operation and the contents of any prospectus.

Each service provider established or incorporated in Jersey who provides services to a Recognised fund is required to hold a functionary permit under the CIF Law.

Regulation of fund service providers in Jersey
Fund service providers based in Jersey are regulated under the FSJ Law. The FSJ Law sets out specific classes of regulation under various types of financial services that can be provided. One category of such financial service business is 'fund services business'. Under the FSJ Law, a person carries on 'fund services business' if the person is:
- a manager, manager of a managed entity, administrator, registrar, investment manager or investment adviser;
- a distributor, subscription agent, redemption agent, premium-receiving agent, policy proceeds-paying agent, purchase agent or repurchase agent;
- a trustee, custodian or depositary; or
- a member (except a limited partner) of a partnership, including a partnership constituted under the law of a country or territory outside Jersey,

in relation to an unclassified fund (including Jersey expert funds and listed funds but excluding COBO-only funds and very private structures) or an unregulated fund.

Regulation of fund services business under the FSJ Law applies to fund services provided to Jersey unregulated funds and unclassified funds (including Jersey expert funds and listed funds but excluding COBO-only funds and very private structures) where the business is carried on in or from within Jersey or by a Jersey company anywhere in the world. Fund services business provided from Jersey to non-Jersey domiciled funds are equally subject to regulation under the terms of the FSJ Law.

The regulation entails the registration of that fund services business for the provision of one or more class of fund services business. The relevant classes are listed within the FSJ Law and generally include principal functions which are provided to fund structures. Once registered for fund services business, the subordinate legislation to the FSJ Law provides an exemption from the requirement for a registered entity to obtain additional class registrations if the activities covered by the fund services business registration would also give rise to the need to be registered for 'trust company business' or 'investment business' as those terms are defined in the FSJ Law.

Once registered for a specific class of fund services business, the Jersey-based service provider can provide similar services to both Jersey-domiciled and non-Jersey-domiciled funds. In the case of the latter, it must notify details of the non-Jersey-domiciled fund(s) to the Commission. Under the current regulatory regime, once the third-party service provider is registered to carry out fund services business, then upon notification, it can act for any number of 'collective investment funds', subject to the payment of an increasing annual fee correlated to the number of funds to which it provides services.

When considering whether to grant a registration certificate under the FSJ Law to a Jersey-based service provider, the Commission will have regard to the Licensing Policy and the FSB Codes and the contents of a business plan that needs to be submitted to the Commission in respect of the Jersey-based service provider.

The Licensing Policy provides guidelines on the 'fit and proper' assessment carried out by the Commission. The Licensing Policy is available on the Commission's website. Except as otherwise stated in the Licensing Policy, the Licensing Policy sets out continuing obligations on the registered person and needs to be read alongside the Codes.

The FSB Codes set out the principles and standards of conduct expected of persons registered under the FSJ Law for carrying on fund services business activities. They consist of seven fundamental principles, each of which is further described, explained and delimited in the accompanying text set out alongside each of these fundamental principles in the FSB Codes. The FSB Codes are available on the Commission's website.

The business plan of the Jersey-based service provider that needs to be submitted to the Commission is required to state, among other things: (i) the proposed fund services business activity of the service provider and the rationale for the service provider undertaking such business; (ii) a description of the types of funds for which the service provider proposes to act and types of investors within those funds; (iii) the level of anticipated involvement the service provider will have with the funds it proposes to act for ie, daily, weekly, monthly; (iv) the paid-up share capital of the service provider; (v) the projected revenues/fees and expenses to be incurred in respect of the proposed activities of the service provider; and (vi) the role of the 'principal persons' (as such term is defined in the CIF Law) and their proposed activities for the service provider, ie, how the service provider will operate in practice, who, on the board of directors of the service provider will be responsible for monitoring and overseeing such activities of the service provider and the

Jersey

roles of administrator in assisting the service provider to comply with the core principles of the Codes.

Entities that are managed or administered by a Jersey-based fund services business license holder under the FSJ Law are permitted only to comply with the seven fundamental principles of the FSB Codes (rather than all of the FSB Codes in full) if they provide fund services to an expert fund, related expert fund or materially equivalent funds.

A Jersey based manager of an EU Fund will be required to be registered for the conduct of 'AIF services business'. This is a new category of financial services business under the FSJ Law. An exemption applies if the Jersey AIFM is already registered for the conduct of fund services business or, in relation to a Recognized Fund, is the holder of a permit under the CIF Law (and its classes of business include at least the same functions as AIF services business). A Jersey based manager registered for AIF services business will need to comply with the AIF Codes either in their entirety or, in the period running until 2018, with those parts which set out the minimum requirements of the AIFMD.

3.3. Operational requirements
Open-ended unclassified funds

Once the Commission has issued a registration certificate under the CIF Law in respect of an unclassified fund, then the fund vehicle must comply with the conditions set out in that registration certificate and continue to comply with the Fund Codes. Service providers to the fund must comply with the FSB Codes and the Licensing Policy.

Listed funds

Once the Commission has issued a registration certificate under the CIF Law in respect of a listed fund established in accordance with the LFG, then the fund vehicle must comply with the conditions set out in that registration certificate and continue to comply with the LFG and the Fund Codes. Service providers to the fund must comply with the FSB Codes and the Licensing Policy.

An exchange-traded unregulated fund needs to comply with any conditions set out in its COBO consent and the rules of the relevant stock exchange.

Recognised funds

Recognised funds are authorised as collective investment funds and as well as complying with the CIF Law they must comply with the Collective Investment Funds (Recognised Funds) (Rules) (Jersey) Order 2003 (as amended).

Each service provider established or incorporated in Jersey who provides services to a recognised fund is required to hold a functionary permit under the CIF Law.

3.4. Marketing the fund
Open-ended unclassified funds

There is no limit on the number of investors that may be admitted.

Any distributor appointed by the expert fund that is either a Jersey entity

Jersey

or carries on its business from Jersey must be licensed under the FSJ Law.

Listed funds
There is no limit on the number of investors that may be admitted.
Any distributor appointed by the expert fund that is either a Jersey entity or carries on its business from Jersey must be licensed under the FSJ Law.

Recognised funds
Providing a fund complies, a recognised fund will be granted a permit under the CIF Law by the Commission and may then seek authorisation under the Financial Services and Markets Act 2000 to market directly to the 'retail' public in the UK.

3.5. Marketing the fund in the EU – AIFMD requirements
As each of the types of fund discussed in this section 3 holds a certificate or permit under the CIF Law, it will be able to rely on the exemption to the Regulations enabling it to access markets in the EEA provided that it submits a written notification to the Commission. The certificate or permit issued under the CIF Law to any fund that has submitted such written notification will be updated by the addition of a condition to reflect the applicability of the AIF Codes.

3.6. Taxation
See section 2.5 above.

3.7. Customary or common terms
Generally the terms of a Jersey fund will mirror those in the global fund market and will vary by industry.

4. PROPOSED CHANGES AND DEVELOPMENTS
The Alternative Investment Fund Managers Directive (AIFMD)
From July 2013 onwards, managers of EU funds need to comply fully with the AIFMD in order to market to investors in the European Union. The AIFMD brings with it additional regulatory obligations in relation to depository requirements, capital adequacy, leverage restrictions, valuations and manager remuneration restrictions.

However, fund managers based in eligible 'Third Countries' (such as Jersey) are able to continue to market Third Country funds to professional investors in EU member states by using the existing private placement rules, subject to continuing to meet the following conditions:
- A supervisory co-operation agreement remaining in place between the regulator of the EU member state in which the fund is to be marketed and the Commission.
(Building on the positive relationship built up between the Commission and The European Securities and Markets Authority (ESMA), on 22 May 2013 Jersey announced the entering into of co-operation agreements with the regulators of the EEA member states co-ordinated by ESMA, which

enables Jersey funds to be marketed in the EU from July 2013.)
- The Jersey fund complying with certain transparency and reporting requirements set out in the AIFMD.
(Jersey satisfies this condition by enabling Jersey funds to opt into new codes (AIF Codes). The AIF Codes contain a number of requirements, but managers privately placing their funds will be required to comply only with those elements of the AIFMD necessary for private placement and not the more detailed provisions relating to full passporting).
- Jersey remaining off the Financial Action Task Force blacklist.

FATCA
FATCA is intended to create a new information reporting and withholding regime for payments made to certain Foreign Financial Institutions (FFIs) and other 'foreign' persons. The definition of FFI is very broad and includes funds.

Approximately 50 countries, including the UK Crown Dependencies, are now in the process of negotiating Intergovernmental Agreements (IGAs) with the US, and, in part, these are intended to overcome the legal barriers to FATCA compliance, and simplify some of the requirements.

The UK government approached the Crown Dependencies and the Overseas Territories to discuss a mechanism for applying FATCA-type principles more widely to an exchange of information with the UK. As part of its commitment to combat global tax evasion, the States of Jersey has accordingly announced its intention to sign an agreement with the UK aimed at furthering tax transparency. The 'UK FATCA' agreement includes an alternative reporting arrangement for UK residents who are categorised as non-domiciled for tax purposes and a disclosure facility that will allow eligible investors with assets in Jersey to disclose their tax arrangements prior to information on their accounts being automatically exchanged.

The finalisation of UK FATCA will allow Jersey to move forward with finalising an IGA with the US on FATCA.

Korea

Eui Jong Chung, Tongeun Kim, Dongwook Kang & David Ahn
Bae, Kim & Lee LLC

1. MARKET OVERVIEW

In Korea, the asset management industry is highly regulated across all investment space, traditional and alternative. The method of offering, retail or private placement, does not determine whether a fund is an alternative or a traditional investment fund. However, because funds offered by private placement ('private funds') generally benefit from a relatively small restrictive set of regulations on portfolio diversification, use of derivatives and leverage, regulatory reporting, etc., private placement has been a common feature of alternative investment funds. (We note that 'collective investment' is the legal term used under Korean law to refer to asset management, funds management or other similar activities involving the management and operation of pooled investments. For this chapter, we have used 'asset management' to refer to all such activities, reflecting common usage in the industry.)

The primary body of law regulating asset management business in Korea is the Financial Investment Services and Capital Markets Act (FSCMA). Introduced in February 2009, FSCMA consolidates all bodies of law governing the capital markets in Korea other than banking and insurance. However, owing to historical reasons, certain types of investments also remain regulated under various other laws including investments in social infrastructure, offshore resource development, shipping, real estate and venture capital. The primary regulator of the financial industry is the Financial Services Commission (FSC). Many of the supervisory affairs of the FSC have been delegated to the Financial Supervisory Service (FSS), an enforcement arm of the FSC, including fund registration and reporting of fund establishment, regular and ad-hoc regulatory reporting, securities registration statement filing, processing of license application, etc.

Under FSCMA, funds are categorised into the following five types depending on their underlying investment theme:
- securities fund;
- real estate fund;
- special assets fund;
- mixed-purpose fund; and
- short-term financial instruments (MMF).

Funds can be offered to both 'retail investors' and/or 'professional investors' via 'public offering' and/or 'private placement.'

Professional investors are mostly financial institutions and government organisations including insurance companies, pension funds, banks and securities companies. Retail investors are general investors who are not a professional investor.

The key distinction between a public offering and a private placement is in the number of persons to which the offering is made. If the number is limited to less than 50 (excluding professional investors), the offering is deemed a private placement.

An overview of the various fund categories in both the alternative and traditional investment space in Korea is provided below.

	Asset class	Categorisation (FSCMA)	Offering type Retail/Private
Traditional	Equity	Securities	Both
	Fixed income	Securities	Both
	Money market	MMF	Both
Alternative	Derivative	Securities	Both
	Special assets	Special assets	Both
	Commodities	Special assets	Both
	Real estate	Real estate	Both
	Hedge	Mixed purpose	Private
	Private equity	Private equity	Private

Private equity funds (PEF) are treated as a separate category of funds altogether and must be offered exclusively on a private placement basis. The key difference between a PEF and other types of funds including hedge funds is that a form of asset management license is not required to establish a PEF. However, a PEF must be registered with the FSC. From 29 August 2013, the general partner of a PEF must also be registered with the FSC. For PEFs already registered as of 29 August 2013, it is anticipated that administrative guidance/grandfathering will be available to facilitate GP registration and smooth implementation of the new registration regime.

Rules permitting the establishment of PEFs were introduced into law in December 2004 in order to foster growth of merger and acquisition (M&A) activities within Korean borders. (Relevant law at the time was the Indirect Investment Asset Management Business Act.) Under such policy direction, PEFs have historically been used as a conduit for M&A, leveraged buyouts or acquisition of significant equity stakes with controlling influence in target companies.

Hedge funds are new to Korea. In September 2011, rules were introduced to FSCMA permitting the establishment of Korean domiciled hedge funds and the commencement of prime brokerage services by financial institutions meeting certain standards of capital and operational adequacy. The first batch of 'Korean style' hedge funds has launched toward the end of 2011. Most of this first-batch adopts 'equity long/short' investment style using a small degree of leverage. The Korean hedge fund market is still at a nascent stage of development and the more complex strategies are yet to be offered.

The following is an overview of the Korean funds market by fund category and assets under management (AUM) in KRW as at 1 July 2013.

Equity	Mixed equity	Mixed bond	Bond	MMF	Derivatives	Fund of funds	Real estate	Commodities	Special asset	PEF
147	13.7	27.2	292	71.4	37.25	14.6	21.62	0	23.3	2.5

The figures in the table are an approximation. Source: Korea Financial Investment Association (KOFIA) website. Capital Markets Statistics: total figure of AUM by AMC as at 1 July 2013.

Traditional space
In the traditional space, retail funds generally cater to the needs of retail investors (ie, mothers and fathers) and private funds to professional investors. By and large, private funds have been a substitute for the discretionary investment mandate (commonly, 'segregate account') for professional investors with a large number of such funds being a single-investor fund. Recognising that such market practice does not accord with the concept of collective investment, the FSC will soon introduce certain legislative changes to address such an anomaly by requiring that a fund must have at least two investors, to be effective from 1 January 2015.

Alternative space
In the alternative space, private funds generally cater to the needs of professional investors and high net worth individuals (HNWI) in such areas as private equity, infrastructure, natural resources, real estate, shipping, distressed assets, venture capital, hedge funds, etc.

Although not common, retail funds with alternative investment themes do exist, but against the headwind of the credit crunch in 2008, have proven to be an operational nightmare.

2. PRIVATE FUNDS
2.1. Common structures
FSCMA recognises and regulates the following forms of legal entities as investment vehicles for funds:
- trust (*shintak*);
- company (*hoesa*);
- limited liability company (*yoohanhoesa*);
- incorporated limited partnership (*hapjahoesa*); and
- association (*johap*).

We note that an incorporated limited partnership is a type of company under Korean law. Other entity forms exist and certain variant forms of entities listed herein have been introduced to FSCMA in 2013.

Other than for PEFs, there is no restriction on what form a fund may take. However, the more common forms of private funds are trusts and companies. PEFs are required by law to be in the form of a limited partnership. Hedge funds take the form of a trust largely due to historical reasons.

Salient features of the more common entity forms are provided below:

Trust
- Asset management company (AMC) executes a trust agreement with a trustee duly authorised to operate a trust (trustee), which typically is a bank or securities company.
- Investors receive trust units evidencing pro-rata entitlement to the net assets of the trust.
- AMC has the responsibility and discretion to manage and operate the fund in accordance with the funds' investment objectives.
- Trustee keeps custody of fund assets and is obligated to execute the AMC's instructions for the acquisition and/or disposal of fund assets.
- Although not obligated to do so, AMCs customarily delegate fund accounting and net asset value (NAV) calculation duties to an administrative services entity (Administrator).

Company
- AMC incorporates a company in which investors are shareholders.
- As shareholders, investors are entitled to the net assets of the company pro-rata to the number of shares held.
- The company is governed by a charter document such as articles of incorporation (AOI).
- AMC sits on the company board of directors as executive director with the responsibility and discretion to manage and operate the investment objectives of the company.
- The company is required by law to appoint a trustee and administrator for the same purposes and in the same functional capacity as those of a trust type fund.

Incorporated limited partnership
- AMC incorporates a limited partnership with one GP and one LP.
- GP must be an AMC and there cannot be more than one GP.
- LP's liability to a third party creditor of the partnership is limited to the LP's capital contribution.
- GP's liability to a third party creditor of the partnership is unlimited.
- LPs and GP can agree on different rates and priority of distribution of partnership gains. This is the key differentiating feature of a limited partnership.
- All operational aspects of a limited partnership are by and large the same as a company type or trust type fund in all material respects including the roles and responsibilities and the respective functional capacities of the AMC, trustee and administrator.

Private equity fund
- PEF must take the form of a limited partnership.
- Members of a PEF consist of GPs with unlimited liability and LPs with limited liability to third party creditors of the partnership.

- To incorporate a PEF, at least one GP and one LP are required, but the total number of GPs and LPs may not exceed 49.
- There can be multiple GPs. However, if there are two or more GPs, the managing partner (MP) must be appointed from among the GPs. If there is only one GP, it will act as the de facto MP.
- The MP is responsible for the management and operation of the PEF.
- Other aspects are the same as described in 'Limited partnership' section above.

Association
Funds may be set up in the form of an association.
- An association operates on capital contributed by its members.
- There are ordinary members and an executive member.
- Ordinary members receive membership interest pro-rata to their capital contribution.
- Ordinary members' liability is limited to their respective capital contribution.
- The executive member manages and operates the fund.
- The executive member has unlimited liability *vis-à-vis* third party creditors.

2.2. Regulatory framework
Asset management license
In order to engage in asset management business in Korea, a form of license is required. The licensing regime under FSCMA for asset management business comprises the following three authorisation units and their respective components:

	Authorisation unit	Component
1	Business activity	Collective investment, broker, dealer, or trust
2	Financial investment product in the case of collective investment	All or any one or more of the 5 fund categories (securities, real estate, special assets, mixed-purpose, and MMF)
3	Target investor group	Professional and/or retail

An applicant can choose a specific component for each of the three authorisation units and become licensed for a specific business activity, product type and investor group. For example, an asset management license to specialise in real estate funds offered only to professional investors would comprise the following components in each authorisation unit: (i) collective investment; (ii) real estate funds; and (iii) professional investors. In comparison, a comprehensive/unrestricted license would comprise: (i) collective investment; (ii) all fund types; and (ii) all investor groups.

Varying levels of regulatory capital is required depending on the desired activity, product type and target investor group.

In order to obtain an AMC license, the applicant must satisfy the FSC, among other things, that it has adequate capital, a feasible business plan, necessary infrastructure, adequate personnel including qualified investment professionals, adequate conflict of interest management framework, and is of good order and standing.

Fund registration
- Both retail and private funds must be registered with the FSC prior to the offering.
- Although a form of license is not required to incorporate and manage a PEF, a PEF must be registered with the FSC within two weeks of incorporation. From 29 August 2013, GPs are required to be registered with the FSC. In order to register, a GP must satisfy certain adequacy standards of capital, senior management, investment professional, and conflicts of interest framework, etc.
- Hedge funds are not required to be registered, however a report must be filed with the FSC within one month of establishment.

Offshore fund registration
- Funds domiciled offshore can be registered in Korea for distribution in Korea. Distribution of offshore funds must be through an authorised distributor – generally banks, securities companies and insurance companies but not asset management companies. If the offshore fund is to be privately placed in Korea, depending on the type of target investors, the fund may be registered with the FSC for placement either to: (i) professional investors only, or (ii) all investor types. If the offshore fund is to be publicly offered in Korea, a securities registration statement must be filed with the FSC.
- Registered funds can be packaged into a Korean domiciled fund of funds (FOF) that invests only into the registered fund, similar to a master-feeder structure.
- Registration requirements are clear and prescriptive. Both the AMC and the fund must satisfy certain requirements. Broadly, in the case of registration for public offering, the AMC must have a certain level of AUM, retain sufficient high quality capital, be of good order and standing and appoint a liaison contact in Korea, etc. The fund must be domiciled in an OECD country or in Hong Kong or Singapore, have a reasonable fee structure by international standards, be redeemable, etc.

Qualification standards for investment professionals
For all types of funds, retail, private, PEFs or hedge, investment professionals must satisfy certain standards of professional qualification and these requirements are stipulated as part of registration requirements of a fund or license requirements for an AMC.

2.3. Operational requirements
Investment restrictions
Under FSCMA, there are various rules which impose certain limits and restrictions on investment regulating portfolio diversification, excessive

exposure, etc. Generally, retail funds in the traditional investment space are subject to the full spectrum of such limits and restrictions including on:
- acquiring in excess of 10 per cent of a single issue;
- investing in excess of 10 per cent of a fund's AUM into a single issue;
- investing in excess of 20 per cent of the total AUM across all funds under an AMC's management into a single issue;
- taking on counterparty risk exposure in an OTC derivatives contract in excess of 10 per cent of a fund's AUM; and
- taking on risk exposure to the underlying asset of a listed derivative in excess of 10 per cent of a fund's AUM.

FSCMA exempts private funds from most of these limits and restrictions (including all of the above) making private funds a feasible structure for alternative investment opportunities, which often require sizable investment in a single asset.

In addition, FSCMA makes certain specific provisions to permit or exemptions required for alternative investments for both private and retails funds. For example, real estate funds can invest 100 per cent of their assets into real estate related assets including real estate operating companies, securitised interests on real estate, etc. In respect of certain stocks, bonds, securitised interests issued under a specific law such as Special Purpose Companies for Mortgage Backed Bond Act, Private Investment in Social Infrastructure Act, etc., FSCMA makes specific provisions enabling a fund to invest 100 per cent of the fund's assets in such stocks, bonds or interests.

Under FSCMA, PEFs are subject to its own set of investment restrictions. PEFs can only take on equity stake equal to or greater than 10 per cent of a target company or invest in a way that gives the PEF *de facto* controlling influence (eg, by having the right to appoint directors or otherwise) in a target company.

Hedge funds are generally exempt from most investment limits and restrictions except that its total risk exposure on derivative transactions cannot exceed 400 per cent of its net assets.

Depository or custodian for asset protection
For both private and retail funds, custody of fund assets is required to be entrusted to a duly authorised trustee. However, such requirement does not apply for a PEF.

Reporting and securities registration statement
Client reporting
For retail funds, AMCs are required to provide investors with a report of fund performance on a quarterly basis. However, for private funds, PEFs and hedge funds, such a requirement does not exist. Regardless, AMCs often choose to provide regular reports of fund performance to clients for relationship management purposes.

PEFs are required to provide LPs with statement of financial affairs together with an explanation on the operation and investment of the PEF on a semi-annual basis.

Reporting to regulator
For retail funds, AMCs are required to provide reports on various financial, operational and investment related matters (including changes to registration status) of the fund and the AMC on both a regular and an ad hoc basis. For private funds, PEFs and hedge funds, such reporting requirements are relatively more lenient, less burdensome or non-existent under various exemptions.

Securities registration statement
For retail funds, AMCs are required to file a securities registration statement (SRS) with the FSC and provide an investment prospectus (containing the same information as the SRS) to the investors. The requirement to file an SRS does not exist for private funds, PEFs or hedge funds. However, it is common practice for private funds, PEFs and hedge funds to provide some form of investment proposal eg, a private placement memorandum or abbreviated form of the investment prospectus when soliciting investment from investors.

Public disclosure
For retail funds, AMCs are required to publicly disclose various material matters related to funds such as change of investment professional, change of investment prospectus or proposal, results of meetings of beneficiaries, deferral of redemption and reasons for such deferral, etc. Private funds, PEFs and hedge funds are not subject to such public disclosure obligations.

Borrowing restriction
Retail and private funds are subject to certain borrowing restrictions. Generally, these funds can borrow only up to 10 per cent of the funds' total assets and such borrowing can only be made for purposes limited to dealing with sudden liquidity shortage upon: (i) investors making a large size redemption request; or (ii) investors exercising a large size put-back option.

There are certain exceptions to the borrowing restriction under FSCMA, eg, real estate funds borrowing money to buy land on a collateralised basis.

A PEF can borrow money or provide guarantee up to 10 per cent of its equity capital. If a special purpose company (SPC) is incorporated by a PEF for investment purposes, such SPC can borrow money or provide a guarantee up to 300 per cent of its equity capital.

A hedge fund can borrow money up to 400 per cent of its total assets and provide a guarantee up to 50 per cent of its total assets.

Price sensitive information, insider trading, market misconduct, etc.
AMCs and their staff are subject to rules on insider trading and the use of non-public price sensitive information. These rules prohibit a person, who is an insider of a corporation and is in possession of non-public price sensitive information or who receives such information from an insider of a corporation (ie, a 'tippee'), from using or causing others to use such information.

Market misconduct rules regulate transactions executed through listed securities and derivatives markets (ie, the Korea Exchange, KRX) as well as general dealings in financial investment products between any two parties. Related to listed market transactions, price manipulation, collusive trading, false price indication, price fixing, spreading rumors, etc., are prohibited. Related to dealings between two parties, falsifying, misrepresenting and deceiving for the purpose of making a gain from dealing in financial investment products is prohibited. Violation of these prohibitions can result in civil liability, including disgorgement of profits, as well as criminal penalties.

Money laundering
All persons employed in the financial services industry as well as financial institutions are subject to certain surveillance and reporting obligations related to money laundering or illegal activities.

Short sale
Short sale of securities is prohibited with certain exceptions. Covered short sale in certain prescribed circumstances and contexts where settlement is deemed warranted (eg, through pre-arranged borrowing) is permitted.

Closed-ended funds
Funds, private or retail, can be offered as an open-ended fund or closed-ended fund. Given that redemption is not possible for a closed-ended fund, a closed-ended fund must have a fixed term of existence and unless a way to liquidate the investment is provided under its charter document, a closed-ended retail fund must be listed for trading in the secondary market ie, the KRX.

2.4. Marketing the fund
Only authorised distributors are permitted to distribute funds – generally, banks, securities companies and insurance companies. Although an AMC is permitted to distribute its own funds (ie, not third party AMC's funds), market practice is for AMCs to always use authorised distributors because of the additional operational, administrative and compliance burden that accompanies being a distributor. Prior to registration, a fund cannot be distributed or advertised by the distributor.

2.5. Taxation
Tax treatment of income from fund investment is different for each type of fund vehicle.

Trust funds
For trust funds, there is no tax imposed at the fund level. Distribution made by a fund is taxed as dividend income of the fund investor. However, this treatment is afforded to funds that satisfy certain criteria. Failing to meet such criteria will result in tax being imposed in accordance with the nature of the underlying income of the fund such as interest, capital gain, dividend, and business profit.

Company funds
For company funds, profit from investment is subject to corporate income tax at the company level. Dividends distributed to investors are taxed again as dividend income of the investors. However, relief from double taxation is available if 90 per cent or more of the company profit is distributed in a given tax year.

Limited partnership
Partnership funds may elect to receive a 'pass-through' treatment for tax purposes. If so elected, partnership income from investment will be taxed to the investors in accordance with the nature of the underlying partnership income such as interest, dividend, capital gain or business profit.

PEF
A PEF can elect to be treated as a 'pass-through' entity for tax purposes. If so elected, tax will not be imposed at the PEF level but be imposed at the investor level in accordance with the nature of the underlying income. In order for a 'pass-through' treatment, certain conditions related to beneficial ownership of the PEF must be satisfied.

For investors, individual tax consequences may differ depending on the vehicle type, pass-through election, tax residency status, tax presence in Korea, investors' entity form, nature of investment income, etc. Depending on these factors, tax may be collected by way of withholding or direct assessment against the taxable entity and the applicable tax rate may be different as well.

2.6. Customary or common terms
Term
There is no restriction or requirement on the term of existence of a fund, private or retail. However, closed-ended funds must have a fixed term of existence and unless a way to liquidate the investment is provided under its charter document, a closed-ended retail fund must be listed for trading in the KRX. For PEFs, the term of existence may not exceed 15 years.

Liquidation of interests
For retail and private funds, it is not customary for investors to transfer their interest to a third party. Usually, such transfer is prohibited in the applicable charter document – trust deed, articles of incorporation, etc. However, investors generally can, by unanimous consent or agreement, dissolve a fund. Charter documents customarily provide investors with such power to dissolve the fund.

Redemption is a customary way of liquidating fund interest. However, for closed-end funds which are listed for trading in the KRX, there is a secondary market in which fund interests can be bought and sold in any given trading day.

An LP's interest in a PEF can be transferred to a third party with the unanimous consent of all GPs. However, a GP's interest in a PEF can only be transferred to a third party with the unanimous consent of all partners of the PEF if such ability to transfer is stipulated in the articles of incorporation of the PEF.

Management fee and performance fee
Generally, management fees are charged at a rate of AUM for all types of funds.
Retail funds are prohibited from charging performance based fees.
Private funds, PEFs and hedge funds can charge performance based fees.
Generally, for PEFs, performance based fee is charged in the form of 'carried interests' (subject to claw-back), and for hedge funds, as incentive fee at a rate of realised profits above a certain 'hurdle rate' or 'high-watermark.'

3. HEDGE FUNDS
Newly introduced to the Korean funds market in late 2011, hedge funds are regulated to a certain extent under the FSCMA.

Distinguishing features of hedge funds include: (i) target investors; (ii) permission to use higher leverage and derivatives than private funds; and (iii) access to a prime broker.

Target investors – qualification requirements
Hedge funds may be offered to, and invested by, only certain types of professional investors and individuals investing KRW500 million or more (ie, HNWI) per fund. Hedge funds can only be offered on a private placement basis. Distributors of hedge funds have the obligation to perform a suitability check on prospective investors.

Leverage and derivatives
As already outlined in previous sections:
- a hedge fund can borrow money up to 400 per cent of its total assets and provide a guarantee up to 50 per cent of its total assets;
- a hedge fund can take on total risk exposure on derivative transactions up to 400 per cent of its net assets; and
- AMCs are required to file quarterly reports with the FSC on the status of transactions related to derivatives, leverage, guarantee and collateral related to hedge funds.

Prime broker
Hedge funds can appoint a prime broker for a broad range of services and transactions including trust and custody, broker of securities, trade execution and settlement, securities lending and borrowing, credit line, distribution of funds, provision of financial advice, hedge counterparty, ie, for OTC derivative transactions, etc.

Only certain financial institutions with an adequate capital base (ie, at least KRW3 trillion) can provide prime brokerage services. There are also adequacy standards applying to risk management, internal control, professional personnel, infrastructure, conflict of interest management, etc., of a prime broker.

4. RETAIL FUNDS
As already discussed in previous sections, retail funds are offered by way of public offering. Key differences between a retail fund and a private fund are that: (i) a securities registration statement must be filed with the FSC prior to

offering of a private fund; and (ii) operational requirements, particularly those related to regulatory reporting, public disclosure and investment restrictions, etc., are much more stringent for retail funds than for private funds. Please refer to section 2 for details. All points in section 2 apply to retail funds.

Securities Registration Statement (SRS)
SRS for a retail fund is prescriptive. Details required to be provided on an SRS for filing with the FSC include the following aspects:
- investment objective, policy and strategy;
- management fee, distribution fee and fund related expenses;
- investment capital;
- financials;
- AMC and investment professional;
- management and operational matters;
- subscription and redemption procedures;
- distribution and taxation;
- trustee and administrator;
- delegation of functions;
- governance;
- corporate/fund history;
- investment performance;
- benchmark index for performance measurement; and
- other matters necessary for the protection of investors.

SRS is publicly disclosed for general viewing by investors for three years.

5. RECENT DEVELOPMENTS
FSCMA is up for a legislative revision soon. There are certain pending measures that are due to be introduced. In relation to the funds industry, such measures include the following:

As of 29 August 2013:
- GP of a PEF must be registered. Certain registration criteria must be satisfied for registration; and
- in principle, distributors of funds must provide investors with a summary form investment prospectus. If an investor requests a comprehensive version of the prospectus, it must be provided.

As of 1 January 2015, a fund must have at least two investors.

Luxembourg

Jacques Elvinger & Xavier Le Sourne
Elvinger, Hoss & Prussen

1. MARKET OVERVIEW

Luxembourg is one of the most experienced and dynamic global investment fund centres. The first Luxembourg investment fund was incorporated in 1959 under the contractual form and Luxembourg counts today more than 3,800 undertakings for collective investments (UCIs). It has been very active in the latest developments of the European UCI industry, in particular during the implementation phase of Directive 2011/61/EU on Alternative Investment Fund Managers (AIFM Directive).

The Luxembourg legal and regulatory system offers sponsors and promoters three different regimes for incorporating their UCIs, namely:
- Part I of the Law of 17 December 2010 on UCIs (2010 Law), which repealed the former Law of 20 December 2002 on UCIs, as amended (2002 Law);
- Part II of the 2010 Law; and
- the Law of 13 February 2007 on specialised investment funds (SIF Law).

The label 'Part II Funds' originates from the 2002 Law, which drew a distinction between the investment funds compliant with the undertakings for collective investment in transferable securities (UCITS) Directives (originally Directive 85/611/EEC, repealed by Directive 2009/65/EC) and the investment funds that were regulated under Part II of the 2002 Law. It is therefore common to define the Part II Funds by comparison with the UCITS (subject to Part I of the 2010 Law), it being noted that only UCITS benefit from the retail European distribution passport throughout the European Economic Area (EEA, ie, the EU and Norway, Iceland and Liechtenstein), whereas other UCIs may under certain conditions set forth in the AIFM Directive benefit from a marketing passport to professional investors.

Investment funds can be subject to different legal regimes as set forth above and be incorporated under numerous legal forms, including public limited liability companies (société anonyme – SA), corporate partnerships by shares (société en commandite par actions – SCA) or private limited liability companies (société à responsabilité limitée – SARL). The implementation of the AIFM Directive has been the occasion for the Luxembourg fund industry to develop a new form of investment vehicle, namely the Special Limited Partnership (the SLP), in French the société en commandite spécial, whose main features are also worth analysing in this outline.

The industry has been growing constantly since 2008. The table below – taken from the Luxembourg Commission for the Supervision of the Financial Sector (Commission de Surveillance du Secteur Financier (CSSF)) Activity

Report (2012) – presents the evolution over the last (full) five years for all three Luxembourg types of UCIs described above:

	Part I		Part II		SIFs	
	Number	Net assets (in bn EUR)	Number	Net assets (in bn EUR)	Number	Net assets (in bn EUR)
2008	1,826	1,169.4	708	259.8	837	130.5
2009	1,843	1,465.7	649	221.2	971	154.1
2010	1,846	1,762.7	629	222.2	1,192	214.1
2011	1,870	1,655.5	601	201.7	1,374	239.3
2012	1,801	1,913.1	555	193.8	1,487	276.9

Part I of the 2010 Law deals with UCITS regulated pursuant to Directive 2009/65/EC of 13 July 2009 (UCITS Directive). The exclusive object of UCITS is the investment in transferable securities and/or other eligible liquid financial assets referred to in Article 41(1) of the 2010 Law, namely money market instruments, units of UCITS (including within the same UCITS) and some other UCIs, deposits with credit institutions and financial derivative instruments.

Where the acronym UCITS refers to regulated European branded retail funds, the Commission through the AIFM Directive submits the managers of alternative investment funds (AIFs) to similar organisational and transparency requirements.

The term AIF, as used in the AIFM Directive, refers to collective investment undertakings, which do not qualify as UCITS and, which raise capital from a number of investors with a view to investing it in accordance with a defined investment strategy for the benefit of those investors.

The AIFM Directive introduces a marketing passport to professional investors throughout the EEA subject to compliance with all conditions set forth in the AIFM Directive.

Part II of the 2010 Law deals with UCIs that can be placed with the public but whose principal object may depart from investments in eligible assets within the meaning of Part I, or which are excluded from Part I in the light of either the investment policy (eg, real estate) pursued by them or in the light of the rules applicable to the marketing of their units.

The SIF regime is applicable to UCIs whose securities are restricted to one or several well-informed investors and whose constitutive documents submit them to the SIF regime. They may qualify as AIFs subject to certain criteria listed under section 2. This vehicle offers greater flexibility in terms of corporate structure and investment rules.

With regard to the involvement and contribution of Luxembourg to the private equity industry, the Law of 15 June 2004 regarding investment companies in risk capital (2004 Law) added to the range of Luxembourg products the so-called investment company in risk capital (société d'investissement en capital à risque – SICAR). The SICAR has been conceived as a customised vehicle for sponsors involved in private equity and venture capital. The SICAR offers a favourable tax treatment, which is further described in section 2.5. and should largely benefit from the creation of the Luxembourg SLP. The SICAR may qualify as an AIF and may also prove to be a dedicated structure for those managers willing to contribute to the development of the European venture capital industry and use the newly created EuVECA label provided for under Regulation (EU) 345/2013 on European venture capital funds (the EuVECA Regulation).

All Luxembourg UCIs and SICARs are subject to the authorisation and ongoing supervision of the CSSF. This is not the case with certain other entities such as the société de participations financières (SOPARFI) which may nevertheless qualify as AIFs and then be regulated at the level of its manager.

2. ALTERNATIVE INVESTMENT FUNDS

Because of their retail distribution features and investment strategies, Part II Funds qualify de jure as AIFs. Other structures, whether regulated or not such as SOPARFIs, SIFs or SICARs, may fall outside the scope of this definition.

2.1. Common structures

The definition given to AIF in the Directive is broad. It captures all non-UCITS regardless of their asset class, eg, hedge funds, real estate funds, infrastructure funds, private equity and venture capital funds and regardless of their legal form and regulatory regime, if any.

Non-regulated vehicles

Private investment vehicles can be set up under Luxembourg law in the form of SOPARFIs. The introduction of a marketing passport to EU professional investors makes anachronistic the former disadvantage of this type of company, whose units could not be placed beyond a small circle of investors. The structure itself remains nevertheless outside the scope of supervision of the CSSF and does not benefit from the taxation regime that applies to UCIs or SICARs (see section 2.5. below).

SOPARFIs are most commonly incorporated in Luxembourg as SA, SCA or SARL. Their structuration already benefits from the introduction into the Law of 10 August 1915 on commercial companies (the 1915 Law) of the SLP.

Part II Funds

Part II Funds qualify as AIF under the AIFM Law.

Part II Funds may be set up as FCPs, SICAVs or SICAFs. This section merely focuses on these common forms of investment structures. To some identified extent, they also apply to the other types of AIFs.

The FCP structure is based on three components: the FCP itself, the management company, that may also act as the AIFM and the depositary. It is a contractual-type fund which is, in terms of structure, similar to an English unit trust or a US mutual fund.

The FCP is not a legal entity but is defined as an undivided collection of transferable securities and other assets made up of the collective investments of investors who are entitled to participate equally in the profits and assets by virtue of their investment. Due to the FCP not being organised as a company, the individual investor is by definition not a shareholder but is commonly referred to as a unitholder. Unlike investors in an investment company (as explained below), unitholders in an FCP are entitled to vote only if and to the extent that the management regulations provide for such a possibility.

If the management company also bears the AIFM licence, it will provide investment management (ie, portfolio and risk management) to the FCP. The management company shall otherwise and where required have to appoint an external AIFM as further analysed under sections 2.2. and 3.1.

The Part II SICAV is set up under the legal form of an SA. Depending on the management structure of the SICAV, its board of directors will have the alternative either to qualify as an internally managed AIFM or appoint an external AIFM as further analysed under section 2.2. The board of directors, appointed from time to time by the shareholders, will in the first instance be in charge of the investment management function or appoint an external AIFM, which will take the responsibility therefor, in both scenarios with the possibil¬ity of delegating portfolio management or advisory functions to local or foreign experts and administration to local service providers. In this structure, the shareholders are convened at least once a year to an annual general meeting to approve the accounts and to appoint or reappoint, as appropriate, the directors of the UCI.

The SICAF is a third route which may be of interest in certain circumstances. A SICAF may be incorporated under the form of an SA but also – as opposed to a SICAV – an SCA. The SCA may prove to ease the control of a promoter on its vehicle. This type of company has indeed two categories of shareholders: the limited shareholders (associés commanditaires) who hold negotiable shares and at least one unlimited shareholder (associé commandité commonly referred to as the general partner) who is indefinitely and jointly liable for all the obligations of the SCA. The general partner is then incorporated in the form of a SARL with a minimal capital (EUR 12,500), thereby in fact limiting the indefinite joint liability of the general partner. It would also be conceivable to incorporate a SICAF in the form of a SARL but the shares in such a company could then neither be publicly offered nor admitted to trading on a stock exchange.

As for the differences between a SICAV and a SICAF, the capital of a SICAF is fixed and does not change automatically with the variations of the net assets as applicable for the SICAV. SIFs and SICARs can also benefit from this feature, as opposed to SOPARFIs. The capital of a SICAF is set forth in the articles of incorporation and the general meeting can increase or reduce the capital or give the board of directors this prerogative within the limits of the authorised capital. It must be noted that the shares in a SICAV must be issued at the net asset value (NAV). This requirement to issue at NAV does not apply to the issue of shares in a SICAF, which can be issued at nominal or par value.

SIFs and SICARs – Preliminary common statement
Whereas units issued by Part II Funds can be placed within the public, other AIFs such as SIFs or SICARs issue securities which may only be held by well-informed investors. Well-informed investors include institutional investors,

professional investors and any other (individual or corporate) investor who: (i) confirms in writing his/its adherence to the status of well-informed investor; and (ii) either invests a minimum of EUR 125,000 or has been subject to assessment by a credit institution, an investment firm or a UCITS management company confirming its knowledge in adequately appraising the considered investment.

SIFs

SIFs, like Part II Funds, are collective investment vehicles subject to the principle of risk-spreading.

SIFs can be incorporated under the form of FCPs or the corporate form, including SICAVs, which may be established under various legal forms (commonly SCA or SA). The new SLP will also be an alternative to these corporate structures.

In a nutshell, the SLP is a partnership, that does not constitute a legal person separate from that of its investors, entered into by one or more general partners (GP) with unlimited and joint and several liability for all the SLP's obligations, with one or more limited partners (LPs) contributing only a specific amount pursuant to the provisions of the limited partnership agreement (LPA).

The SLP may be used by regulated and non-regulated entities whether qualifying as AIFs or not. Thus, regulated investment vehicles such as SIFs may adopt the legal form of the SLP with the inherent structural and tax advantages, which this new type of investment vehicle will offer.

SICARs

SICARs commonly adopt the corporate form of SA or SCA. A SICAR will also have the alternative of the SLP for sponsors willing to offer their investors fully tax transparent structures.

A SICAR may be structured with a fixed or a variable capital.

Multiple class structures

Part II Funds, SIFs and SICARs – as opposed to SOPARFIs – can be set up with multiple compartments (umbrella structure).

Each compartment is legally linked to a specific portfolio of investments that is segregated from the portfolio of investments of the other compartments. Pursuant to this 'ring-fencing' principle, although the umbrella structure constitutes one single legal entity, the assets of a compartment are exclusively available to satisfy the rights of investors in relation to that compartment and the rights of creditors whose claims have arisen in connection with the operation of that compartment, unless a clause included in the constitutional documents of the investment entity provides otherwise.

Different classes of securities can be created within such types of AIFs or even within a compartment thereof. Such classes may have different characteristics, notably as regards the fee structure, the type of targeted investors or the distribution policy.

2.2. Regulatory framework
AIFM Regulatory framework
The AIFM is the legal person whose regular business is to manage one or more AIF, and which provides at least portfolio and risk management functions to such AIFs.

Managers who manage AIF assets which do not exceed EUR 100 million or EUR 500 million (when the portfolio of AIF consists of AIF that are not leveraged and have no redemption rights exercisable during a period of five years following the date of the initial investment in each AIF) are exempt from complying with the full scope of the AIFM Directive and benefit from a lighter registration regime. These managers are required to register with their national regulators and report to them on the AIF they manage on a regular basis. They will not however be allowed to manage AIFs whose total assets are above these thresholds (Full Scope AIFs), which must appoint a fully licensed AIFM.

The investment management function is identified in the AIFM Directive as the key function to be performed by the AIFM and includes portfolio management and risk management. AIFM may also perform administrative and marketing functions as well as activities related to the assets of the AIF.

The AIFM Directive makes a distinction between internally managed AIF and externally managed AIF:
- internal AIFMs refers to a structure where the legal form of the AIF permits an internal management (eg, an SA) and where the AIF's governing body (eg, the board of directors) has chosen not to appoint an external AIFM. They are prohibited from engaging in activities other than the internal management of that AIF.
- external AIFMs must engage solely in the investment management of AIF and the performance of additional functions mentioned above (ie, administration, marketing and activities related to the assets of the AIF). External AIFM may however extend their licence to be allowed also to manage UCITS (subject to authorisation under the UCITS Directive). They may also and in addition to the management of the AIF(s), be authorised to provide discretionary management and non-core services (including investment advice).

AIF Regulatory framework
Depending on whether the AIF benefits from an exemption, or from a grandfathering clause, or falls under the registration regime of the AIFM Directive, the authorisation procedure may require the introduction of a file with information on the AIFM (including on the persons conducting the business and the delegation arrangements), and on the AIF(s) itself.

Material shall also have to be produced in relation to a regulated AIF, including a prospectus or any forms of issuing document describing *inter alia* the investment policy and the different service providers. Luxembourg laws already request sponsors of regulated AIFs to provide investors with transparent and adequate information and to keep the essential elements of the document up to date. In this regard and many other disclosure requirements under the AIFM Directive, Luxembourg regulated AIFs already comply with most of the transparency obligations set forth in the AIFM Directive.

2.3. Operational requirements
Common operational requirements
Many of the ongoing obligations imposed on AIFs under the AIFM Directive are familiar to the Luxembourg fund industry, either because the AIFs already comply therewith under the relevant law or because they derive from the UCITS regime. They include minimum capital requirements, delegation rules or the obligation for any Full Scope AIF or any Luxembourg regulated AIF to have a depositary.

The required share capital of the AIFM varies depending on whether the AIFM is internal or external. Internally managed AIF must have an initial share capital of EUR 300,000. This amount is reduced to EUR 125,000 for an externally appointed AIFM.

Additional own funds may be required, including where the value of the portfolios of an externally appointed AIFM exceeds EUR 250 million.

An independent depositary must be appointed for any regulated or Full Scope AIF. Its functions and liabilities are extensive and include cash monitoring, safe-keeping of assets of the AIF and supervision of transaction and assets of the AIF.

In relation to certain types of funds (essentially private equity, venture capital and real estate funds) which have no redemption rights exercisable during a period of five years from the date of the initial investments, Luxembourg has pragmatically levied the option offered under the AIFM Directive that the depositary can be an entity other than a credit institution or an investment firm which has applied the new licence of 'professional depositary of assets other than financial instruments'.

The delegation of some of the AIFM's functions is permitted, subject to prior notification to the regulator and appropriate disclosure. The AIFM may not, however, become a letter-box entity. The delegation of portfolio management or risk management: (i) can be given only to authorised and registered firms for the purpose of asset management; and (ii) the cooperation between authorities must be ensured. Where condition under (i) cannot be met, the prior approval of the authorities of the home member state of the AIFM must be obtained. Sub-delegation is permitted subject to similar conditions.

Other rules of conduct apply to AIFM, including the obligation to set up remuneration policies that are consistent with effective risk management and do not encourage inconsistent risk taking. Organisational arrangements must also be taken in order to identify, prevent, manage and monitor conflicts of interest as well as structure the risk management function that must be functionally and hierarchically separated from the operating units, including from the portfolio management function.

Additional operational requirements in relation with SICARs
The SICAR benefits from an attractive tax regime described in section 2.5, which can only benefit those vehicles whose purpose is to invest their assets

in securities representing 'risk capital'.

Compliance of the proposed investment policies with the SICAR Law is assessed on a case-by-case basis by the CSSF. The concept of risk capital is defined by the SICAR Law as 'the direct or indirect contribution of assets to entities in view of their launch, development or listing on a stock exchange'. The parliamentary documents of the SICAR Law clearly state that this definition is only indicative. A comprehensive definition was deemed undesirable though so as to avoid the SICAR Law lagging behind the market. As per the SICAR Circular the concept of 'risk capital' generally hinges on two cumulative elements, namely a high risk and an intention to develop the target entities (portfolio companies). The SICAR Circular lists a series of elements that should be considered in order for the sponsor of the SICAR to confirm to the CSSF in a written statement the reasons that make the investment policy acceptable, such as the number and the nature of the target entities, their maturity level, the SICAR's development projects and the envisaged duration of holding.

2.4. Marketing the fund
Passport
The AIFM Directive regulates the marketing of AIF. It introduces a passport for the marketing of AIF to professional investors in the EU. The passport will initially only be available to EU AIFMs managing EU AIFs. The passport will only be available to non-EU AIFMs and non-EU AIFs as from July 2015.

There is no EU passport for the distribution of AIF to retail investors in the AIFM Directive, although the member states may allow AIFM to market to retail investors in their territory units or shares of AIF managed in accordance with the Directive. Luxembourg has opted to introduce this flexibility into the AIFM Law.

Private placement
The AIFM Directive lays down the conditions subject to which AIFMs may market the units of AIFs to professional investors in the EU. The marketing shall only be allowed insofar as the Luxembourg AIFM complies with the AIFM Directive. The marketing occurs with a passport. Private placement rules shall therefore no longer be acceptable, save for the marketing – with a few additional AIFMD requirements – of AIFs by AIFMs that cannot benefit from the passport, such as those established outside the EU or falling below the thresholds as referred to under section 2.2.

The dual regime should nevertheless last until 2018, at which point the EU authorities shall decide on the possible end of national private placement regimes.

Reverse Solicitation
The marketing is defined under the AIFM Directive as a direct or indirect offering or placement, which is made on the initiative of the AIFM or on behalf of the AIFM, of units or shares of an AIF it manages or with investors domiciled or with a registered office in the European Union. Based on this

definition, the solicitation made by an investor to subscribe for units in an AIF received by its AIFM should therefore fall outside the scope of the marketing and not require any notification to be made by the AIFM in order to register the AIF for commercialisation in a different member state. Burden of proof should rely with the AIFM, which would need to show positively that the communications were exclusively initiated by the investor. This may prove to be complicated where the AIF has been notified for marketing to professional investors in the relevant member state.

2.5. Taxation
SOPARFIs
The overall combined rate of corporation taxes is 29.22 per cent in Luxembourg City. Corporation taxes include a: (i) 21 per cent corporate income tax (impôt sur le revenu des collectivités) on which a 7 per cent solidarity surcharge (contribution au fonds pour l'emploi) is added on top, leading to an effective corporate income tax rate of 22.47 per cent; plus (ii) a municipal business tax (impôt commercial communal). The municipal business tax rate varies from one municipality to another. In Luxembourg City, the municipal business tax is 6.75 per cent.

Entities whose assets consist of more than 90 per cent in financial assets, transferable securities and bank deposits, receivables held against related parties or shares or units in tax transparent entities are subject to a minimum flat rate of EUR 3,000 (EUR 3,210 including the 7 per cent solidarity surcharge).

Other entities which have their registered office or their central administration in Luxembourg and which are not subject to the above minimum flat rate are subject to a minimum tax which is determined on the basis of the total assets in the balance sheet of the tax year concerned. This minimum tax ranges from EUR 500 to EUR 20,000 (plus the 7 per cent solidarity surcharge). The EUR 20,000 minimum tax is due for a balance sheet exceeding EUR 20 million. The net value of assets generating or potentially generating income, which is only taxable in a state other than Luxembourg by virtue of a double tax treaty (real estate for example), shall be disregarded for the purpose of computing the minimum tax.

The minimum taxation is not a final tax but an advance tax payment on the corporate tax due in the future. This minimum tax, however, is not refundable.

SOPARFIs are also liable to an annual 0.5 per cent net wealth tax in Luxembourg (impôt sur la fortune) on their unitary value (ie, taxable assets minus liabilities financing such taxable assets) as at 1 January of each year.

Part II Funds
According to Article 174(1) of the 2010 Law, Part II Funds existing under the laws of Luxembourg pay a subscription tax (taxe d'abonnement) at the rate of 0.05 per cent per annum on their total net assets at the end of each quarter except as stated below. According to Article 174(2) of the 2010 Law, a reduced rate of 0.01 per cent per annum is applicable for Luxembourg investment funds whose exclusive object is the collective investment in money market

instruments and the placing of deposits with credit institutions, or in deposits with credit institutions, or whose individual compartments in an umbrella structure or individual classes of units are reserved to one or more institutional investors.

Article 175 of the 2010 Law also provides for tax exemptions applicable under certain conditions to money market instruments, institutions for occupational retirement pensions or similar investment vehicles as well as to microfinance institutions and exchange traded funds (ETFs).

UCIs set up under the 2010 Law are not subject to any Luxembourg ordinary income, capital gain, estate or inheritance taxes payable by the UCI or its non-Luxembourg resident shareholders or beneficiary unitholders in respect of their shares or units in the UCI.

Dividends and interests received by either type of investment fund on its portfolio may be subject to withholding taxes in the countries of origin of those dividends.

SIFs

SIFs are subject to an annual subscription tax (taxe d'abonnement) at a rate of 0.01 per cent based on the basis of the total net assets valued at the end of each calendar quarter. The SIF is not subject to any corporate income tax, municipal business tax or net wealth tax.

Concerning double tax treaties, withholding taxes deducted at source from income received by the SIF on its investments are normally not recoverable. However, SIFs under the corporate form (disregarding whether they qualify as SICAVs or SICAFs) may benefit from certain double taxation treaties. A SIF under the contractual form may also create a subsidiary in order to benefit from a double taxation treaty.

SICARs

The SICAR is liable to corporate income tax and municipal business tax. Any income arising from securities held by a SICAR, as well as any income arising from the sale, contribution or liquidation thereof shall be exempt from its tax base.

However, no corporate income tax and municipal business tax is due on income deriving from the SICAR's investments in risk capital. Debt funding to subsidiaries of the SICAR must, however, be structured as securities as opposed to a simple loan instrument.

The SICAR is not liable to any net worth tax.

With regard to the investors, there is no withholding tax on dividend distributions and interest payments made by a SICAR except, to the extent applicable, under the Savings Directive.

AIFM

Luxembourg offers a tax regime that is comparable in terms of end-tax figure to the other main EU jurisdictions. An AIFM is prima facie subject to the same overall combined rate of corporation tax as a SOPARFI, ie, in Luxembourg City 29.22 per cent.

Taxable profits are calculated by determining the difference between the AIFM's net assets at the beginning and at the end of a given accounting year, adjusted for capital paid in or withdrawn, dividends, and similar distributions of profits. Taxable profits are generally based on the accounting profits. The tax balance sheet generally corresponds to the commercial balance sheet unless tax valuation rules require otherwise. Profits are taxed on an accrual basis.

It is common practice for the AIFM to determine the fees it charges to the AIF it manages on the basis of the costs and expenses it bears to manage the AIF, to which it adds its own profit margin. In practice, the Luxembourg tax authorities accept this 'cost plus method' to determine the profits, and may confirm their approval of the margin determination mechanism. It is however recommended that the profit margin of the AIF be determined on the basis of a transfer pricing report that complies with OECD standards.

2.6. Customary or common terms
SOPARFIs
SOPARFIs are commercial companies that are not subject to any governance rules other than those set forth in the Law of 10 August 1915 on commercial companies (the 1915 Law). SOPARFIs hold financial participations in any type of underlying assets, including one sole underlying, whether listed or non-listed as well as in investment funds, real estate, infrastructure, etc.

Part II Funds
Part II Funds qualify as UCIs, the principle object of which is the investment in securities other than transferable securities and to all investment funds which are excluded from Part I of the 2010 Law. Part II Funds are subject to the risk diversification and investment limits set forth in CSSF Circular 91/75. Part II Funds may not in principle:
- invest more than 10 per cent of their assets in securities which are not listed on a stock exchange or dealt in on another regulated market;
- acquire more than 10 per cent of the securities of the same kind issued by the same issuing body;
- invest more than 10 per cent of their net assets in securities issued by the same issuing body; and
- borrow more than 25 per cent of their net assets.

The CSSF may produce adapted guidelines for particular types of AIFs or investment strategies such as hedge funds (Circular 02/80), real estate or more recently infrastructure investments (which, subject to regulatory confirmation, would be entitled to a 30 per cent diversification calculated on the total assets of the Part II Fund).

SIFs
SIFs must also comply with risk-spreading requirements. Such requirements have been detailed in Circular 07/309 relating to risk-spreading in the context of SIFs (SIF Circular).

As a matter of principle, a SIF may not invest more than 30 per cent of its assets or commitments to subscribe in securities of the same nature issued by the same issuer (or hold more than 30 per cent thereof in a cash deposit with the same banking institution). This restriction does not apply to sovereign securities and target UCIs that are subject to risk-spreading requirements at least comparable with those applicable to a SIF.

The CSSF may also adapt the diversification rules on a case-by-case basis, depending on a particular project or a type of investment strategy (including infrastructure-related type, which may, subject to the same reserve as outlined above for Part II Funds, may benefit from a 75 per cent diversification limit calculated on the total assets of the SIF).

In light of the virtually unlimited types of assets in which a SIF can invest, including artworks, hedge funds, real estate, infrastructure or private equity, it was considered important to provide for flexible valuation rules. For that reason, the SIF Law provides that, unless otherwise stipulated in the constitutive documents, the assets of a SIF must be valued at 'fair value'.

Furthermore, SIFs are not required to calculate and publish the asset value per share on a regular basis (although some type of determination of total net assets will have to be performed on a quarterly basis for the purpose of assessing the amount of taxe d'abonnement to be payable on a quarterly basis as discussed above).

SICARs

The SICAR Law does not require any risk-spreading (ie, the SICAR may hold only securities of one single issuer) and does not impose any investment rules or restrictions as regards the targeted jurisdictions, industries or currencies. The SICAR Circular provides that, in principle, all financing modes are eligible.

In addition, there is no prohibition on having a majority stake in an entity or being the sole owner.

As regards the functioning rules of a SICAR and its dividend policy, there are no restrictions on repayments and distribution of dividends. The assets of a SICAR must also be valued by reference to the fair value.

3. RETAIL FUNDS

For the purpose of the developments below, retail funds shall be understood as investment funds whose shares or units may be placed with any person, legal or natural, and which do not impose any specific requirements in terms of minimum investments or ongoing shareholding.

3.1. Common structures

Luxembourg investment funds that may be placed with retail investors can be set up under the form of UCITS or Part II Funds. The main legal forms available are described above and include FCPs and SICAV incorporated under the legal form of an SA. Following the entry into force of the AIFM Law, a particular focus should be made on their respective managers.

In combination with these provisions, different regulatory regimes will indeed be available to managers established in Luxembourg and providing collective portfolio management services to retail funds.

Luxembourg

- UCITS management companies; UCITS management companies, as regards their authorisation and permitted activities, remain governed by the UCITS laws. No UCITS management company shall engage in activities other than the management of UCITS with the exception of the additional management of other UCIs. The AIFM Law does not have an impact on these, except for the 'super licence' described below.
- AIFM; This is the licence introduced by the AIFM Directive, which must be obtained by a manager managing and/or acting as management company to one or more Part II Funds and which cannot benefit from the registration regime set forth in the AIFM Directive (or other Full Scope AIFs). Managers managing and/or acting as management company to AIFs with assets below the thresholds set out under section 2.2 can opt in to this regime to have the benefit of the marketing passport which the AIFM Directive confers to AIFM.
- UCITS management companies also authorised as AIFM; This is the 'super licence' permitting a manager to manage and act as management company to both types of retail funds, ie, UCITS and Part II Funds (and any other Full Scope AIFs).
- Other management companies; This is to some extent the equivalent of the former non-UCITS management companies under Chapter 16 of the UCI Law but with extended types of activities under the new Article 125-1 of the 2010 Law. These management companies may, in summary: (i) act as manager or management company to any type of investment vehicle which does not qualify as AIF; (ii) act as management company to one or more FCP, SICAV or SICAF that are Full Scope AIF, provided it has designated, on behalf of that Full Scope AIF, a fully authorised AIFM; or (iii) act as manager or management company to AIFs the aggregate assets of which are less than the above thresholds introduced by the AIFM Directive.

These management companies may however not provide the services under (i) without also providing the services under (ii) or (iii), unless the investment vehicles referred to under (i) are eg, SIFs or SICARs that do not qualify as AIFs (ie, not falling within the scope of the AIF definition set forth under section 1). This restriction aims at avoiding that a management company authorised by the CSSF would solely manage non-regulated investment vehicles such as SOPARFIs.

3.2. Regulatory framework

The main duty of the CSSF consists of the supervision of the UCITS and their compliance with the law and their respective constitutive documents, including their contractual documents, such as the offering prospectus. The set-up of a Luxembourg UCITS requires the approval of the CSSF. The same applies to Part II Funds as detailed above.

An application has to be filed with the CSSF for the registration of the fund on the official list of UCI, which shall comprise *inter alia* material attesting to the professional repute of the directors/managers, the risk management process as well as the constitutive documents of the UCI (articles of incorporation or management regulations, offering prospectus and UCITS Key Investor Information Document).

A UCITS will have the choice between appointing a Luxembourg UCITS management company or being created as a self-managed investment company. In the first case, the application must indicate the name of the management company. In the second case, the application must contain information on the human and technical resources at the disposal of the investment company and describe the manner in which the management, administration and distribution functions will be monitored according to Circular 12/546.

3.3. Operational requirements

There are specific substance requirements in relation to UCITS management companies in particular as regards capital requirements, management and infrastructure as provided for under Circular 12/546, which has also integrated Circular 11/508 regarding applicable organisational requirements, principles to deal with conflicts of interest, applicable rules of conduct, risk management and the right to provide services on a cross-border basis.

A substantial part of Circular 12/546 is therefore dedicated to the arrangements regarding the central administration and internal governance of UCITS management companies and self-managed SICAV. Circular 12/546 reiterates that the central administration must be established in Luxembourg and specifies that it does not only consist of an 'administrative centre', but also of a 'decision-making centre'. As a matter of illustration, it is now required to have at least two conducting officers being permanently based in Luxembourg. The Circular also contains certain interesting precisions regarding premises, operating staff, delegation and incompatibilities affecting the persons in charge of the compliance function, the internal audit and the risk management.

Any change to the constitutive documents and any change of director or main service providers to a Luxembourg UCITS requires prior CSSF approval.

3.4. Marketing the fund

The UCITS Directive provides for specific arrangements in order to ease the cross-border distribution of UCITS-compliant investment funds.

The notification procedure set out in the UCITS Directive has made the European passport for UCITS more effective, by the introduction of an efficient 'authority-to-authority' communication procedure for the cross-border marketing of UCITS or sub-funds within the EU.

The CSSF has also enacted Circular 11/509 relating to the new notification procedures to be followed by a UCITS governed by Luxembourg law wishing to market its units in another member state of the EU and by a UCITS of another member state of the EU wishing to market its units in Luxembourg.

3.5. Taxation

According to Article 174(1) of the 2010 Law, investment funds existing under the laws of Luxembourg pay a subscription tax at the rate of 0.05 per cent per annum on their total net assets at the end of each quarter except as stated below.

The same reduced rate of 0.01 per cent per annum and exemptions of subscription tax provided for under Article 174 and 175 of the 2010 Law and developed under section 2.5, apply to retail funds covered in this section.

3.6. Customary or common terms

UCITS may only invest in transferable securities, units of other investment funds, deposits with credit institutions, financial derivative instruments and money market instruments. The transferable securities (meaning securities, bonds and similar securities or instruments) and the money market instruments need to be listed on a stock exchange or dealt in on another regulated market, except that up to 10 per cent of the assets of the UCITS may be invested in non-listed transferable securities.

UCITS must comply with specific diversification and concentration limits specified in Part I of the 2010 Law, which reflect the restrictions imposed by the UCITS Directive. A UCITS may indeed not invest more than 10 per cent of its net assets in securities of the same issuer (diversification limit) and may not acquire more than 10 per cent of the securities issued by a single issuer (concentration limit).

4. PROPOSED CHANGES AND DEVELOPMENTS

AIFs

The alternative investment fund industry is entering into a phase of adaptation to the AIFM Directive. The Luxembourg government, in close collaboration with the CSSF, has used the opportunity of implementing the AIFM Directive to introduce some new flexibility such as the SLP or an attractive carried interest regime for certain managers.

Luxembourg is also currently working on the adaptation of the SICAR and SIF Laws to adapt them to the new requirements of the EuVECA Regulation and of Regulation 346/2013 on European social entrepreneurship funds (EuSEF), which introduce a marketing passport to AIFM managing venture capital funds or social entrepreneurship funds and whose assets under management do not exceed the thresholds set forth under section 2.2. above.

UCITS

The UCITS industry is now focused on the proposal for a Directive amending the UCITS Directive (already known as UCITS V) and which aims at addressing discrepancies between member states (and existing European rules such as the AIFM Directive) in respect of depositary duties and liability and remuneration policy.

As for the depositary regime, the current proposal mostly pastes the provisions of the AIFM Directive, although it does not permit any contractual discharge of liability in the case of loss of assets, which remains permitted under certain strict conditions set forth under Article 21 of the AIFM Directive.

It also seems that the remuneration policy regime that has been adopted in the Parliament's report of July 2013 excludes the caps on performance fees and bonuses. Confirmation on this latter issue will have to be closely supervised in light of the upcoming tripartite discussions between the Council, the Commission and the Parliament. This will be another key issue in the future development of the UCITS brand within the European Union and far beyond.

Malta

John Paul Zammit & Danièle Cop **Mamo TCV Advocates**

This chapter is intended to give a brief introduction to and highlight some of the salient features of the regime governing investment funds and their service providers in Malta, and does not purport to give an exhaustive overview of the legal and regulatory provisions applicable to such entities under Maltese law.

At the time of writing of this chapter most of the amendments to the local rules and regulations required for the implementation of the Alternative Investment Fund Managers Directive (AIFMD) were not published yet. Where relevant, an indication of the expected changes to the Maltese regulatory regime is given, on the basis of consultation procedures conducted by the local regulator, the Malta Financial Services Authority (MFSA).

1. MARKET OVERVIEW

The number of investment funds established in Malta has grown steadily over the years, especially after Malta joined the European Union in 2004. The success story of the Professional Investor Fund (PIF) regime has put Malta on the map as a jurisdiction of choice for alternative investment funds. According to figures published by the MFSA, there were 587 funds (including sub-funds) domiciled in Malta at the end of 2012, representing an increase of over 5 per cent from the previous year; the number of licensed PIFs went up from 442 in 2011 to 478 in 2012.

In recent years, there has also been a growing interest in Malta as a domicile for fund management companies, in particular managers of alternative investment funds.

Malta's single regulator for the financial services industry, the MFSA, is committed to maintaining a flexible yet robust regulatory framework and seeks to secure Malta's competitive position amongst other European jurisdictions by regularly reviewing and updating the existing laws, rules and policies, and by implementing European legislation in an optimal way, in consultation with local practitioners and service providers.

The MFSA's responsibilities include the regulation and supervision of investment funds, referred to as Collective Investment Schemes (CISs) in Malta, fund managers, investment advisers, fund administrators and custodians of collective investment schemes on the basis of the Investment Services Act (Chapter 370 of the Laws of Malta) (ISA).

As a rule, CISs carrying on activities in or from Malta require a CIS licence granted by the MFSA, but exemptions from the licensing requirement may be obtained, for instance, in the case of certain arrangements entered into for commercial purposes and employee participation schemes. For regulatory purposes, a distinction is made between:

- PIFs, comprising CISs (open-ended or closed-ended) available only to eligible investors. Hedge funds, funds of (hedge) funds, venture capital funds, private equity funds, and immovable property funds, would be typical examples of investment funds set up as PIFs in Malta;
- retail CISs, namely CISs available to the general public, comprising UCITS and retail non-UCITS schemes; and
- private CISs in which no more than 15 individuals are allowed to participate and which satisfy a number of other conditions; these do not require a licence but are subject to recognition by the MFSA (in view of their limited use, private CISs will not be discussed further in this chapter).

It is expected that when the relevant provisions of the AIFMD are transposed into Maltese law (by 22 July 2013), an additional category of investment funds will be created, namely alternative investment funds (AIFs) managed by alternative investment fund managers or internally managed AIFs authorised under AIFMD, for which the MFSA will adopt a dedicated rulebook.

2. ALTERNATIVE INVESTMENT FUNDS
2.1. Common structures

Currently, open-ended and closed-ended alternative investment funds (including, hedge funds, private equity and real estate funds) typically fall within the PIF regime; nevertheless, a number UCITS that adopt hedge fund-style strategies have been established (see section 3 below). In general, a PIF may be set up as:

- an investment company with variable share capital (SICAV), which can be either a private or a public limited liability company;
- an investment company with fixed share capital (INVCO);
- a partnership *en commandite* or limited partnership (LP);
- a unit trust; or
- a common contractual fund.

To date, virtually all PIFs established in Malta, whether open or closed-ended, are organised as SICAVs. A SICAV may be set up either as a multi-class (single fund) company or a multi-fund (umbrella) company with one or more sub-funds, whereby one class or a group of classes of shares constitutes a distinct sub-fund of the company. Furthermore, an umbrella company may elect to have the assets and liabilities of each sub-fund treated for all intents and purposes of law as a patrimony separate from the assets and liabilities of each of the other sub-funds of the company. In cases where such an election is made, save for the proportion of the liabilities of the company which are stated to be attributable to one or more sub-funds, the liabilities incurred in respect of each sub-fund will be paid out of the assets forming part of its patrimony and the creditors in respect thereof will have no claim or right of action against the assets of the other sub-fund/s or of the company.

CISs, including PIFs, in the form of a SICAV, may be organised as 'self-managed' funds, ie, funds that do not appoint an external manager.

The Companies Act (SICAV Incorporated Cell Companies) Regulations (Legal Notice 559 of 2010) make it possible for a SICAV to be constituted as an incorporated cell company (ICC). The ICC may establish one or more funds as incorporated cells, each cell being a limited liability company (SICAV or INVCO) with separate legal personality (unlike the sub-funds of a multi-fund SICAV, which may have their assets and liabilities treated as a separate patrimony but do not have legal personality separate from that of the SICAV). Furthermore, it is possible to set up a Recognised Incorporated Cell Company (RICC); the RICC is constituted as a limited liability company, which may establish incorporated cells in the form of SICAVs or INVCOs, and which purports to provide such incorporated cells with administrative services, in accordance with the Companies Act (Recognised Incorporated Cell Companies) Regulations (Legal Notice 119 of 2012). The RICC is required to obtain recognition from the MFSA for the provision of administrative services, while each incorporated cell must obtain a CIS licence. The rules on ICCs and RICCs are designed particularly to accommodate fund platforms. The RICC structure presents certain advantages compared to the ICC, including the fact that the RICC itself must not be licensed as a collective investment scheme, and that the incorporated cells of an RICC may be constituted as umbrella companies, with their own segregated sub-funds.

So far, the LP has rarely been used as a vehicle for investment funds. An LP has its obligations guaranteed by the unlimited and joint and several liability of one or more general partners (vested with the administration and representation of the LP), and by the liability limited to the amount (if any) unpaid on the contribution of one or more limited partners. Under Maltese law, the LP has legal personality separate from that of its partners. For LPs qualifying as CISs, it is possible to choose whether or not to divide the LP's capital into shares. Such LPs may be constituted (with the written approval of the MFSA) either as 'multi-class partnerships', the capital of which is (or is capable of being) represented by different classes of units or shares (as the case may be) not constituting any distinct sub-fund, or as a 'multi-fund partnership' or 'umbrella partnership', the capital of which is (or is capable of being) represented by different classes of units or shares with each class or group of classes of units or shares constituting a distinct sub-fund of the LP. An umbrella partnership may elect to have the assets and liabilities of each sub-fund comprised in it treated for all intents and purposes of law, as a patrimony separate from the assets and liabilities of (and ring-fenced from the creditors of) each other sub-fund of such partnership. Furthermore, an LP which has its capital divided into shares may be constituted with variable share capital, in which case the relevant rules of the Companies Act governing SICAVs would apply mutatis mutandis.

Although Maltese law has been amended over the years to offer flexibility in structuring LPs as a vehicle for CISs (for instance, whether or not the LP's capital is divided into shares may be a critical factor for foreign tax authorities in determining whether the vehicle is transparent or opaque for tax purposes), the use of LPs has not picked up yet. However, the MFSA has indicated that amendments to the Companies Act will be proposed with a view to making the LP structure more appealing, especially as a vehicle for private equity funds.

Fund managers, investment advisers and fund administrator are generally established in Malta in the form of limited liability companies (which may be public or private).

2.2. Regulatory framework
Key statutes, regulations and rules
The ISA and subsidiary legislation issued thereunder (regulations published by Legal Notice) purport to regulate CISs and investment services providers carrying on activities in or from Malta, including fund managers, investment advisers, fund administrators and custodians of CISs. The MFSA administers the ISA, and is empowered to issue Investment Services Rules under the ISA and related regulations; most licensing and ongoing regulatory requirements are laid down in the MFSA's Investment Services Rules.

Fund managers and investment advisers established in Malta need to obtain the appropriate investment services licence from the MFSA. While the rules governing fund managers will change with the transposition of the AIFMD, it is expected that fund managers falling below the thresholds set out in Article 3(2) AIFMD (so-called '*de minimis* licence holders') will still be required to obtain a licence from the MFSA (rather than mere registration), but will be subject to less onerous licensing and ongoing requirements than fund managers authorised under the AIFMD as implemented locally.

Fund administrators established in Malta are required to obtain a recognition certificate issued by the MFSA under the ISA.

Custodians of collective investment schemes established in Malta also need to be in possession of the appropriate investment services licence granted by the MFSA under the ISA.

Categories of PIFs
A distinction is made between three categories of PIFs according to the type of investors they are allowed to target: PIFs may be promoted to 'experienced investors', 'qualifying investors' or 'extraordinary investors', each as defined in the Investment Services Rules for Professional Investor Funds (PIF rules) issued by the MFSA. The investor eligibility criteria can be summarised as follows:
- 'Experienced investors' are persons having the expertise, experience and knowledge to be in a position to make their own investment decisions and understand the risks involved. The investors must state how they satisfy this criterion, either by confirming that they have relevant working experience (having worked in the financial sector for at least one year, in a professional position of a person who has been active in type of investments concerned); or have reasonable experience in the acquisition or disposal of funds of similar nature or risk profile or property of the same kind as the kind of property to which the fund relates; or have carried out investment transactions of significant size at a certain frequency; or by providing any other appropriate justification. Persons qualifying as 'professional clients' in terms of the Markets in Financial Instruments Directive (MiFID) automatically qualify as experienced

investors. The manager or sales agent or any third party selling units of the fund is bound to take reasonable steps to ensure that the investor has sufficient knowledge and understanding of the risks involved in investing in the fund.
- The term 'qualifying investor' essentially covers entities or individuals whose net assets exceed EUR 750,000/$750,000; individuals who have (or entities the management of which has) reasonable experience in the acquisition or disposal of funds of a similar nature or risk profile or property similar to that in which the fund invests; senior employees or directors of the fund's service providers; relations or close friends of the promoter (maximum 10 persons per PIF); entities with a minimum of EUR 3.75 million/$3.75 million under discretionary management, investing on their own account; PIFs promoted to qualifying or extraordinary investors; and investment vehicles wholly owned by persons or entities satisfying any of the foregoing conditions.
- 'Extraordinary investors' are entities or individuals with net assets exceeding EUR 7.5 million/$7.5 million; senior employees or directors of service providers to the PIF; PIFs targeting extraordinary investors; and investment vehicles wholly owned by persons or entities satisfying any of the aforementioned conditions.

Different minimum investment requirements apply for each category of PIFs: experienced investors are required to invest (and to continue to hold) at least EUR 10,000/$10,000, qualifying investors EUR 75,000/$75,000, and extraordinary investors EUR 750,000/$750,000 (or an amount in another currency equivalent to the amount in Euro).

It appears that, when the AIFMD is implemented, the PIF regime will be retained for *de minimis* licence holders and third country fund managers wishing to set up alternative investment funds in Malta (ie, fund managers which do not require authorisation under AIFMD), and that the PIF rules will also continue to apply to *de minimis* self-managed AIFs. Furthermore, it is envisaged that fund managers authorised under AIFMD will be able to manage not only AIFs, but also PIFs established in Malta, provided that they ensure compliance with the relevant provisions of the AIFMD as implemented in the relevant jurisdiction.

Licensing of PIFs
A CIS, including a PIF, requires a CIS licence granted by the MFSA under the ISA, in order to issue or create any units or to carry on any activity in or from within Malta or otherwise for it to use Malta as a base (ie, where a CIS formed in accordance with or existing under the laws of Malta carries on any activity in or from within a place outside Malta). The licensing requirement does not, however, preclude the CIS from taking such steps as may be necessary for its establishment and for securing its authorisation by the MFSA.

It appears that a CIS licence will in principle also be required for Maltese AIFs, once the AIFMD is implemented.

Essentially, the application procedure for a CIS licence involves the following three stages:

- Preparatory stage: it is recommended that the promoters arrange a preliminary meeting with representatives of the MFSA to describe their proposal. Following the submission of the draft application form together with supporting documentation, the MFSA will review the documentation and revert with its comments. The MFSA will also carry out the 'fit and proper' checks on the persons involved at this stage. The MFSA will consider the nature of the proposed PIF and a decision will be made regarding the applicable licence conditions (standard licence conditions for PIFs are set out in the PIF rules).
- Pre-licensing stage: as soon as the MFSA's review has been completed, revised documents have been submitted where necessary and the draft licence conditions have been agreed upon, the MFSA will issue its 'in principle' approval for the issue of the licence. Once the applicant finalises any outstanding matters (which would usually include the establishment of the chosen structure), the licence will be issued.
- Post-licensing/pre-commencement of business stage: the applicant may be required to satisfy a number of post-licensing matters prior or post commencement of business.

Service providers

PIFs are at liberty to appoint such service providers as they may deem necessary (eg, an investment manager, an investment advisor, a fund administrator, a custodian and/or one or more prime brokers). The appointment of a custodian, however, is compulsory in the case of PIFs targeting experienced investors; apart from the safekeeping of the fund's assets, the custodian of PIFs targeting experienced investors is responsible for monitoring the extent to which the investment manager abides by the investment, leverage and borrowing powers and restrictions applicable to the fund.

The PIF's service providers do not necessarily have to be established in Malta, but they should, as a rule, be established and regulated in a 'recognised jurisdiction' (including the EU and EEA member states as well as countries that are signatories to a multilateral or bilateral memorandum of understanding with the MFSA covering the relevant sector). The MFSA may nevertheless accept service providers not established in a recognised jurisdiction, if the service provider is a subsidiary of a firm that is regulated in a recognised jurisdiction and that retains control over its subsidiary and undertakes to provide all the necessary information to the MFSA, or in cases where the MFSA considers that the service provider is subject to regulation equivalent to local regulation.

If all the appointed services providers are based outside Malta and the PIF has not appointed a local resident director (in the case of a PIF set up as an investment company), a local general partner (in the case of a PIF set up as an LP) or a local trustee (in the case of a PIF set up as a unit trust/common contractual fund), then a local representative would need to be appointed.

Foreign investment managers, investment advisers and custodians servicing Maltese PIFs, are exempt from the requirement to obtain an investment services licence, or in the case of fund administrators, recognition, from the MFSA in terms of the ISA (subject to a determination in writing by the MFSA that the exemption applies).

If a Maltese PIF, organised as a SICAV, does not appoint an external investment manager, the board of directors retains full responsibility for the investment management of the PIF's assets (and would ordinarily be expected to appoint an investment committee) and the PIF would be subject to the supplementary licence conditions for self-managed funds.

PIFs are required to appoint a (local) auditor approved by the MFSA.

An important change under the AIFMD regime will be that pursuant to the AIFMD, a single depositary (custodian) must be appointed for each AIF, essentially with the duty to properly monitor the AIF's cash flows, to perform safe-keeping functions in respect of the AIF's assets and to carry out a monitoring function. As a rule, the custodian will need to be established in the same country as the AIF; however, the MFSA will allow credit institutions established in another Member State to be appointed as a custodian until 22 July 2017.

It appears that investment funds governed by the dedicated AIF rulebook (AIFs), expected to be adopted as part of the implementation of the AIFMD in Malta, will per definition be managed by a Maltese or EU AIFM which is authorised under the AIFMD or, in the case of self-managed AIFs, be authorised themselves as an AIFM.

2.3. Operational requirements

The operational requirements to which PIFs are subject mainly derive from the PIF rules. The PIF rules include the standard licence conditions normally imposed on PIFs, which cover, amongst other things: requirements related to the PIF's service providers, the compliance officer, the money laundering reporting officer, the PIF's investment objections, policies and restrictions, the offering document, promotion, reporting and record-keeping obligations, as well as supplementary conditions regarding PIFs formed as investment companies or LPs, the use of special purpose vehicles, self-managed funds, and draw-downs on investors' committed funds.

PIFs are required to publish an 'offering document' (PIFs promoted to extraordinary investors may choose to publish a brief 'marketing document' instead), which must be offered to investors free of charge before they become committed to investing in the fund. The offering document/ marketing document must contain sufficient information for investors to make an informed judgement about the investment proposed to them and is required to contain at least the information listed in the PIF rules. The offering document and any amendments thereto must be submitted to and agreed with the MFSA before publication (except in the case of PIFs targeting extraordinary investors, which are required to submit the offering document/ marketing document and any amendments thereto to the MFSA within five business days from publication; nevertheless, any amendments that relate to the creation of a new class of units or to any other matter that requires the MFSA's approval in terms of the PIF rules must be submitted to the MFSA for approval before publication). Unless offered on a private placement basis, closed-ended PIFs may be subject to the prospectus requirements derived from the EU Prospectus Directive.

The following ongoing requirements prescribed by the PIF rules are particularly worth noting:

Safekeeping of assets
The PIF is required to have adequate arrangements in place for the safekeeping of its assets. To this effect, PIFs may appoint a custodian (or prime broker/s) or establish other safekeeping arrangements (except in the case of PIFs targeting experienced investors, where the appointment of a custodian is compulsory). Funds, such as private equity funds and venture capital funds, would typically resort to the latter option if they invest in assets that do not necessitate the use of a custodian bank and can be physically kept safe by a third party (eg, documents of title or certificates of shares in unlisted companies). Such safekeeping arrangements must be described in the offering document/marketing documents and are subject to the MFSA's approval.

As noted above, AIFs will be subject to the strict depositary regime introduced by the AIFMD.

Investment, borrowing and leverage restrictions
PIFs targeting qualifying or extraordinary investors are not subject to any investment or borrowing/leverage restrictions, other than those that may be self-imposed in terms of the offering documentation and the leverage restrictions applicable to open-ended immovable property funds available to qualifying investors. In the case of PIFs offered to experienced investors, however, a number of restrictions apply, mainly in the form of diversification requirements, limits on single-issuer exposure, and a general restriction on borrowing for investment purposes (and leverage through derivatives) set at 100 per cent of the fund's net asset value (NAV). PIFs promoted to experienced investors that invest directly or indirectly in immovable property are subject to certain supplementary conditions in this regard.

Draw-downs
PIFs targeting qualifying or extraordinary investors established as SICAVs may enter into written agreements with investors to effect draw-downs on investors' committed funds, subject to the relevant provisions of the Companies Act (Investment Companies with Variable Share Capital) Regulations (Legal Notice 241 of 2006, as amended) relating to the issue of shares at a discount, and certain supplementary conditions set out in the PIF rules.

Finally, it is worth mentioning that PIFs are in principle allowed to enter into side letters in accordance with the relevant provisions of the PIF rules. Also, PIFs are allowed to create and use side pockets if this is provided for in the offering document; the MFSA has issued specific guidance notes on this matter.

2.4. Marketing the fund
PIFs may only be marketed to experienced, qualifying or extraordinary investors, as the case may be. The promotion of the PIF is subject to the rules concerning 'investment advertisements' (or marketing communications)

prescribed by Article 11 of the ISA and the applicable investment services rules for investment services providers issued by the MFSA.

Publicity comprising an invitation to purchase shares or units in the PIF must be approved by the PIF's compliance officer, and any promotional material issued by the PIF must indicate that an offering document/marketing document exists and the places where it, and any documents updating it, may be obtained.

The PIF rules also state that a PIF may only be promoted in jurisdictions outside Malta if it satisfies the relevant rules of such jurisdictions.

Foreign funds which are actively marketed in Malta, are in principle subject to the licensing requirement for CISs under the ISA (see section 3.4. below).

AIFs will benefit from the passport regime created under the AIFMD for the marketing of AIFs managed by managers authorised under the AIFMD, to professional investors throughout the European Union.

2.5. Taxation

For tax purposes, a distinction is made between prescribed and non-prescribed funds. Essentially, a fund in a locally based CIS that has assets situated in Malta constituting at least 85 per cent of its total asset value is classified as a prescribed fund; other licensed funds, including funds in an overseas-based CIS, are non-prescribed funds.

In the case of prescribed funds, the CIS qualifies for exemption from tax on income 'other than income from immovable property situated in Malta and investment income' earned by the prescribed fund. The withholding tax on local investment income is 15 per cent for bank interest and 10 per cent for other investment income.

Non-prescribed funds (in practice, most PIFs, which typically invest outside Malta) are exempt from tax on income and capital gains realised on their investments and also enjoy a blanket stamp duty exemption on their transactions.

Foreign investors are not subject to Maltese tax on income or capital gains when they dispose of their investment or when they receive a dividend or other income from the fund. Such investors would also be entitled to benefit from the stamp duty exemption obtained for the fund in connection with the acquisition or disposal of their units in the fund.

Malta is generally regarded as a tax-efficient location in respect of fee and participation income or gains (including carried interest through participation shares or otherwise in the fund) that the investment manager may receive from the fund, particularly when the manager establishes its own operations in Malta but also when it remains established in, and provides the management services from, another jurisdiction. This is mainly due to the fact that Maltese law offers flexibility to structure participation income/carried interest in a variety of ways (whether as dividends, capital gains or bonus shares), which when coupled with the various tax benefits afforded by Maltese domestic tax laws can offer substantial opportunities for tax planning.

Furthermore, tax incentives are available for highly qualified persons (HQPs) holding an 'eligible office', that is, employment with companies licensed and/or recognised by the MFSA (eg, investment management companies, fund administrators and credit institutions) in certain positions, including the following: (i) chief executive officer, chief risk officer, chief financial officer, chief operations officer, chief technology officer, chief commercial officer; (ii) portfolio manager, chief investment officer, senior trader/trader, senior analyst (including structuring professional), actuarial professional, head of research and development; (iii) head of marketing, head of investor relations. HQPs have the option to be taxed at a reduced rate of 15 per cent (as opposed to the normally applicable progressive rate of tax, which could go up to 35 per cent) on their income arising in Malta, subject to a number of conditions being satisfied.

2.6. Customary and common terms

Closed-ended private funds licensed as PIFs in Malta enjoy the benefits of a flexible regulatory framework and, for corporate structures, company law that has been modelled on UK law, which permits the creation of different classes of shares with different rights attached to them (eg, in terms of voting powers and participation in profits) in various permutations.

PIFs are not subject to any specific rules on the lifespan of the fund, liquidity of interests, remuneration arrangements and frequency of valuations and reporting to investors, and are basically free to establish their own terms in this respect. Such terms would normally need to be disclosed in the offering document and may need to be included in the fund's constitutional documents, as may be required under Maltese law or pursuant to policies that the MFSA may adopt (but are not necessarily made public) from time to time. However, as explained above, certain investment, leverage and borrowing restrictions apply to PIFs promoted to experienced investors (and open-ended property funds licensed as PIFs available to qualifying investors). Also, regard should be had for the reporting requirements vis-à-vis the MFSA and other competent authorities, and the duty of investment companies to act honestly, fairly and with integrity (including action to be taken where any conflict of interests may arise) as prescribed by the PIF rules.

3. RETAIL FUNDS

3.1. Common structures

Retail CISs (whether UCITS or non-UCITS schemes) may be set up in Malta as:
- a SICAV;
- an LP;
- a unit trust; or
- a common contractual fund.

So far, practically all retail CISs established in Malta take the form of a SICAV (see also section 2.1. above). Whilst UCITS are by definition open-ended, Maltese non-UCITS schemes may be either open-ended or closed-ended, and they may also be set up as an INVCO.

The ICC and RICC (see section 2.1. above) may also be used to structure retail CISs.

Retail CISs may be managed by an external fund manager or (if they take the form of a SICAV) be self-managed.

3.2. Regulatory framework
Key statutes, regulations and rules
Retail CISs are regulated and supervised by the MFSA on the basis of the ISA and subsidiary legislation issued thereunder. The bulk of the regulatory requirements applicable to retail CISs is contained in the Investment Services Rules for Retail Collective Investment Schemes (RCIS rules) issued by the MFSA under the ISA. The laws, regulations and rules governing retail CISs include provisions transposing the UCITS Directive 2009/65/EC (UCITS IV).

The regulatory regime for retail CISs caters for four main categories:
- Maltese non-UCITS schemes;
- Maltese UCITS;
- overseas-based non-UCITS schemes; and
- European UCITS.

Maltese UCITS and non-UCITS schemes (ie, those formed in accordance with or existing under the laws of Malta), as well as overseas-based non-UCITS schemes marketed in Malta require a CIS licence issued by the MFSA, whilst European UCITS marketed in Malta are exempt from the licensing requirement provided that they follow the prescribed passporting procedure, in accordance with the UCITS Directive.

Maltese non-UCITS schemes do not currently benefit from any passport rights that would allow them to market their units in other EU/EEA states without the need to obtain such authorisation as may be required under the national laws of such states. Maltese non-UCITS schemes are, therefore, predominantly used for retail products offered to the Maltese market.

It appears that when the AIFMD is implemented, retail non-UCITS schemes that qualify as AIFs (ie, whose manager is authorised under AIFMD or self-managed AIFs authorised as an AIFM) will be allowed to be marketed in the EU, at least to professional investors, subject to the relevant rules on passporting under AIFMD. It is expected that the MFSA will allow AIFs to be marketed to retail investors in Malta in certain circumstances and subject to supplementary licence conditions.

For an overview of the application procedure for a CIS licence, kindly refer to section 2.2. above.

Services providers
Maltese UCITS and non-UCITS schemes are required to appoint an investment manager unless they are set up as a self-managed (SICAV) structure, in which case they are subject to certain supplementary licence conditions (including minimum initial capital requirements and the requirement to appoint a director resident in Malta). A Maltese UCITS may appoint a Maltese UCITS management company or an EU/EEA UCITS management company passporting into Malta. Maltese non-UCITS schemes ordinarily appoint a local fund manager, but the MFSA may exceptionally allow the appointment of a foreign manager established in a recognised jurisdiction or otherwise, if the MFSA is satisfied that the manager is subject to regulation of an equal and comparable level in the jurisdiction concerned.

The appointment of a sub-manager (which may be established outside

Malta), is subject to the MFSA's approval in the case of Maltese UCITS which appoint a Maltese UCITS management company, and non-UCITS schemes. A UCITS management company is, subject to certain conditions, allowed to delegate its functions (which include investment management, as well as administration and marketing) to third parties, if and to the extent that (amongst other conditions) the management company has duly notified the competent authority of its home member state of such delegation; the competent authority will then notify the home member state of the relevant UCITS (including the MFSA in the case of a Maltese UCITS).

Maltese retail funds are in principle required to appoint a custodian (depositary), which must be established in Malta and be in possession of a Category 4 Investment Services Licence issued by the MFSA in terms of the ISA.

The appointment of an investment advisor and/or a fund administrator, by the CIS or the investment manager, is optional, but subject the MFSA's approval. If no fund administrator is appointed, the administration function is considered to be the responsibility of the investment manager. If a Maltese non-UCITS scheme (or its investment manager) chooses to appoint a fund administrator, such administrator should be based in Malta and be recognised in terms of the ISA (although, in exceptional circumstances, a foreign administrator regulated in a recognised jurisdiction may be appointed). Fund administration services in relation to a Maltese UCITS may be carried out by the investment manager or be delegated to a fund administrator; if the fund administrator is based in Malta (which is not required) it should be in possession of a fund administration recognition certificate.

The investment advisor may be established in or outside Malta. It is understood that the investment advisor would not have any discretion with respect to the investment of the CIS's assets (discretionary management of assets being the responsibility of the investment manager).

Maltese retail funds have to appoint a (local) auditor approved by the MFSA.

Once the AIFMD is implemented and if a Maltese retail non-UCITS scheme qualifies as an AIF, the relevant rules regarding service providers, including the fund manager (AIFM) and custodian (depositary) will apply (see section 2, 'service providers' above).

3.3. Operational requirements
As far as Maltese UCITS are concerned, the operational requirements are laid down, primarily, in the RCIS rules and reflect the relevant provisions of the UCITS Directive. It is worth noting that in Malta most options and discretions available to the member states under the UCITS Directive were exercised.

The ongoing requirements applicable to Maltese retail CISs are set out mainly in the RCIS rules. These include (without limitation) rules regarding the following:

Safekeeping of assets
The role of the custodian is the safekeeping of the CIS's assets and to carry out a monitoring function over the activities of the investment manager. Under Maltese law, specific rules regarding the custody of assets of a CIS, including

on the liability of the custodian and the delegation of safekeeping functions, are set out in the Investment Services Act (Control of Assets) Regulations (Legal Notice 240 of 1998, as amended).

Officers
Maltese CISs are required to appoint a compliance officer, and a money laundering reporting officer. The appointment and replacement of such officers must be approved by the MFSA.

Investment, borrowing and leverage restrictions
Maltese retail funds are subject to stringent investment, borrowing and leverage restrictions, and Maltese UCITS may only invest in certain types of eligible assets in line with the UCITS Directive. Supplementary licence conditions apply to retail fund of funds and to master-feeder fund structures.

A risk management process adapted to the fund's risk profile must be in place for Maltese UCITS, and details of the risk management process must be notified to the MFSA in advance.

Prospectus requirements
Maltese retail funds are required to publish a prospectus that contains at least the information prescribed by the RCIS rules and must be kept up to date. Whilst Maltese UCITS are also required to publish a key investor information document, open-ended Maltese non-UCITS schemes have the option to do so. Closed-ended Maltese non-UCITS schemes would in principle need to draw up and issue the prospectus in accordance with the provisions of Maltese law transposing the prospectus directive.

The prospectus and any changes thereto must be approved by the MFSA before being published.

The use of side letters is not allowed in respect of retail funds.

Regular reporting
Maltese retail funds are required to submit half-yearly and (audited) annual reports to the MFSA, and such other information, returns and reports as the MFSA may request from time to time, as well as statistical returns required by the Central Bank of Malta. The half-yearly and annual reports must be published and submitted to the MFSA within two and four months respectively of the end of the period concerned. Maltese UCITS are also obliged to submit, together with the annual report, a report on their derivative positions.

The issue, sale, repurchase or redemption price (NAV) of the units of a Maltese retail fund must be made public each time such units are issued, sold, repurchased or redeemed, and at least twice a month. The MFSA may, however, permit the fund to reduce this frequency to once a month on condition that such derogation does not prejudice the interests of unit holders.

3.4. Marketing the fund
The promotion of Maltese retail funds is subject to Article 11 of the ISA

concerning 'investment advertisements' and the applicable requirements set out in the investment services rules for investment services providers, which establish the disclosure requirements for information to clients, including marketing communications, pursuant to the MiFID.

All investment advertisements issued directly by the CIS must be approved by its compliance officer and all promotional material issued directly by the CIS needs to indicate that a full prospectus exists and the places where it, and any documents updating it, may be obtained.

The fund may only be promoted in jurisdictions outside Malta if it satisfies the relevant rules of such jurisdictions. However, Maltese UCITS have the right to market their units in other EU/EEA states, provided that they follow the prescribed passporting procedure pursuant to the UCITS Directive.

European UCITS that intend to actively market or promote their units in Malta, either directly or through intermediaries, would need to exercise their passport right under the UCITS Directive. In such a scenario they would be exempt from the licensing requirement under the ISA. Overseas-based non-UCITS schemes may only be actively marketed or promoted, whether directly or indirectly through intermediaries, if they are in possession of a CIS licence. For clarity's sake, the MFSA has provided an indication of the scenarios that would constitute marketing or promotion of foreign CISs in Malta; this would capture, for instance:
- issuing 'investment advertisements' as defined under the ISA in Malta;
- organising seminars or meetings in Malta aimed at the general public or class or classes of investors to promote the CIS;
- the use of a circular or mailshot or other medium of communication to promote the CIS in Malta;
- placing documentation in a location accessible to the public or uploading documents or information regarding the CIS on a local distributor's internet site which targets mainly investors in Malta; and
- direct or indirect promotion of the CIS by means of press releases.

The MFSA has also clarified that the following instances would not be considered to amount to marketing:
- the sale of the CIS to persons in Malta exclusively on a one-to-one basis; or
- the provision of information (including marketing material) solely upon the request of an investor in Malta; or
- CISs that are available for linking to unit-linked policies that are themselves marketed in Malta, without the CIS being marketed in its own right.

Under the AIFMD, the marketing of Maltese retail non-UCITS schemes qualifying as AIFs, at least to professional investors, should in principle be possible in accordance with the relevant rules on passporting for the marketing of AIFs.

3.5. Taxation
Kindly refer to section 2.5.

3.6. Customary or common terms

The terms and conditions under which the shares or units in the retail fund are issued would need to be disclosed in the prospectus, and would be subject to the provisions included in the fund's constitutional documents. Such terms and conditions would need to be in line with the laws and rules to which the fund is subject, in particular the standard licence conditions set out in the RCIS Rules (eg, regarding investment objective, policy and restrictions; frequency of dealings and publication of the fund's NAV; distribution of income; the method of calculation of exposure to financial derivative instruments and the use of (reverse) repurchase agreements and securities borrowing/lending by Maltese UCITS).

Regard should also be had for the MFSA's policies, which may not always be published. For instance, it appears that the MFSA would generally expect, as a matter of policy, that investors holding shares in a SICAV licensed as a retail fund, would be given certain voting rights.

As regards remuneration arrangements, fees based on performance determined by reference to the growth in the NAV over a given period may only be adopted in respect of a retail fund subject to the conditions and restrictions established by the Investment Services Act (Performance Fees) Regulations (Legal Notice 239 of 2006). One of the essential requirements for performance fees is that such fees must be subject to a high watermark or other permitted benchmark.

4. PROPOSED CHANGES AND DEVELOPMENTS

A very important development for the Maltese fund industry is, of course, the implementation and transposition of the AIFMD into Maltese law as from the 22 July 2013. Although the AIFMD is said to regulate the managers of investment funds (other than UCITS), it will clearly have a bearing on the current regime for funds in Malta, in particular PIFs (including private closed-ended funds and hedge funds) and non-UCITS retail funds. However, at the time of writing, most of the final implementing measures had not been published yet, and some of the concrete effects and consequences of the AIFMD remain unclear. Nevertheless, the introduction of harmonised rules for fund managers and the right of EU/EEA AIFMs authorised under the AIFMD to manage and market EU/EEA alternative investment funds throughout the EU/EEA, is expected to offer an incentive for managers targeting European investors to set up shop in 'friendly' EU jurisdictions such as Malta.

Finally, it is worth noting that a review of the rules governing LPs laid down in the Companies Act is being carried out, with the intention to introduce the amendments necessary to accommodate private equity funds typically using the LP structure.

Mauritius

Iqbal Rajahbalee, Shan Sonnagee & Bhavna Ramsurun
BLC Chambers

1. MARKET OVERVIEW

Mauritius is considered a leading international financial services centre and a gateway for investment in many Asian and African countries. It has in the past year further consolidated its position as a hub for financial transactions by introducing innovative vehicles, structuring and financing products. Mauritius is a recognised jurisdiction for global investment funds. According to the Financial Services Commission (FSC) statistics, as of June 2013, there were 894 global funds (including both open-ended and closed-ended funds). They consist mainly of private equity funds and qualified funds meant for professional investors, which benefit from the Mauritius network of tax treaties to invest in African and Asian countries.

The domestic (or onshore) fund industry is widely perceived to be under-tapped, comprising only 35 funds as at 30 April 2013. Global and specialised investment funds are authorised to trade on the Stock Exchange of Mauritius.

The Listing Rules of the Stock Exchange of Mauritius allow for the listing of global and specialised investment funds to trade on its two platforms, the Official Market and the Development and Enterprise Market. As at May 2013, 22 global and specialised investment funds are listed.

Mauritius contains both retail funds and alternative investment funds (which are non-retail funds). Alternative investment funds can be classified as expert funds or professional collective investment schemes under the laws of Mauritius and they are available only to sophisticated and expert investors and high net worth individuals. Alternative investment funds are exempted from the strict regulations which apply to retail funds and they comprise of private closed-ended funds, hedge funds and real estate funds. There is no specifically constraining regime applying to hedge funds in Mauritius, and the terminology 'hedge fund' is not used to designate any category of investment funds. However, they are usually offered to professional investors or high net worth individuals. For that reason, they can apply to be categorised either as expert funds or professional collective investment schemes.

Retail funds can be offered to the public and are regulated as open-ended (collective investment schemes) or closed-ended funds. Open-ended retail funds allow their participants to exit the fund at their request, at a price corresponding to the net asset value of those investments (less any applicable fees and commissions). This obligation does not exist with closed-ended retail funds. Such funds are characterised principally by the fact that the investors do not have control over exiting the funds and they are subject to fewer regulations than open-ended retail funds.

2. ALTERNATIVE INVESTMENT FUNDS
2.1. Common structures
Alternative investment funds are usually set up as companies, trusts or limited partnerships. Companies are the most common structures used for private funds that are closed-ended. To date, only a few limited partnerships under the Limited Partnership Act 2011 have been formed. It is therefore not a tried and tested vehicle and we expect some teething issues with regulators which have been used to dealing with companies until the use of the partnership becomes more widespread. Another vehicle which can be used is a Société en Commandite, which is a French form of a partnership.

Companies
There are various types of companies. Public and private companies are incorporated under the Companies Act 2001. Participants are issued with shares of the company. A private company is limited to 25 shareholders and cannot offer shares to the public.
Companies have the following advantages:
- the limited liability principle means that investors enjoy liability only up to the extent of their investment;
- the statutory rules of filing and reporting ensure transparency and accountability;
- the governing body (board) is responsible to investors for their decisions under the doctrine of fiduciary responsibility; and
- the flexible rules of the Mauritius company legislation allow a company to be used in the same manner as a limited partnership. For example, the articles of its constitution can be drafted as an agreement reflecting the general partner/limited partner relationship, and can provide for capital calls, capital commitments, return of proceeds and the waterfall of distribution (in accordance with the 80/20 split between returns to investors and carried interest). All of these inherent features of partnership fund structures can be replicated within Mauritian companies.

Companies have the following disadvantages:
- their corporate formalities are an additional compliance cost;
- they are not tax transparent: a company is one legal person and is treated as one taxable unit, and investors are not taxed in Mauritius at their level;
- the distribution of income is subject to the company remaining solvent; and
- company migration (that is, where a company relocates to another jurisdiction), and corporate restructuring, merger and termination, require corporate formalities.

Protected cell companies
A company may also be set up as a protected cell company, which is subject to the Protected Cell Companies Act 1999 as well as the Companies Act 2001. Participants in a protected cell company are issued with shares in the relevant cell in which they invest. Segregation of assets and liabilities can be

achieved by the use of a protected cell company. In particular, protected cell companies are often structured to meet the objectives of investment such as providing for investor returns from specific cells, distinct separation of non-cellular assets and cellular assets and restricting liability arising from one cell to that cell only.

As a matter of compliance, the creation of each cell would usually require the approval of the FSC. The board of directors has the responsibility of keeping cellular assets separate and separately identifiable from non-cellular assets and is also required to maintain this level of distinction from cell to cell.

Limited partnerships

Limited partnerships are new vehicles that can now be used to structure investment funds in Mauritius. This is a form of partnership governed by the Limited Partnership Act 2011. A limited partnership can be set up with or without legal personality and will have at least one general partner and one or more limited partners. The general partner is responsible for the management of the limited partnership and has unlimited liability for the debts and obligations of the partnership. The liability of the limited partner is limited to the maximum amount of its commitment provided that such limited partner takes no part in the management of the partnership. The limited partner will be treated as a general partner and be liable to the debts of the partnership to the extent the limited partner is involved in the management of the partnership. Participants' interests are referred to as partnership interests.

Limited partnerships have the following advantages:
- it offers the benefits of relative flexibility of the vehicle, the mitigation of fiduciary risks, the ability to account for profits and losses at limited partner level and tax transparency;
- in terms of tax, a limited partnership may elect to be tax transparent and as such, only partners who are tax-resident in Mauritius are liable to pay tax on their share of profits; and
- the limited partners have limited liability in the limited partnership.

Limited partnerships have the following disadvantages:
- the general partners are jointly and severally liable for the debts of the partnership (where it has legal personality) and personally liable to third parties (where the partnership has no legal personality); and
- only a limited partnership which has elected to be tax opaque can avail itself of the benefits of the different tax treaties to which Mauritius is a party.

Trusts

Trusts are created under the Trusts Act 2001 and participants are issued with units in the trust.

Trusts have the following advantages:
- they are easy to set up: the creation of a trust does not require any registration or incorporation;
- they require no corporate filings;
- a trust can be structured as a 'non-resident' trust, which is not liable to tax in Mauritius;

- trustees are subject to fiduciary duties; and
- migration, restructuring and termination are relatively simple to accomplish.

Trusts have the following disadvantages:
- the lack of formality and reporting requirements make a trust less transparent than a company or a limited partnership; and
- they do not have corporate personality.

Sociétés
Sociétés are set up under the provision of the Mauritius Civil Code or Commercial Code. The participants' interests are referred to as *parts sociales*.

Sociétés have the following advantages:
- they are fiscally transparent;
- the liability of the general partner can be limited; and
- it is possible to structure the sociétés so that they are not liable to tax in Mauritius.

Sociétés have the following disadvantages:
- they are based on a form of French partnership law, which has not evolved to accommodate modern fund structures; and
- French legal concepts and terminology may not be understood by all investors.

Investment manager and investment adviser
A fund in Mauritius can be managed by an investment manager licensed by the FSC or by its board of directors as a self-managed scheme subject to the approval of the FSC. The legal vehicle of an investment manager must be a body corporate.

There are two types of investment adviser in Mauritius, namely the restricted and unrestricted investment adviser. An investment adviser can be either a body corporate.

2.2. Regulatory framework
Prior to 2007, the funds market in Mauritius was largely regulated by best practices and licensing conditions. There was no consolidation of the relevant legal provisions and funds were loosely referred to as authorised mutual funds, private equity funds and unit trusts.

In 2007, in a bid to ensure fund regulation is comprehensive, precise and in line with international standards, the Government of Mauritius introduced a regulatory framework. The legal framework applicable to any fund, fund manager and adviser includes the:
- Financial Services Act 2007;
- Securities Act 2005;
- Securities (Collective Investment Schemes and Closed-ended Funds) Regulations 2008;
- Securities (Licensing) Rules 2007;
- Securities (Disclosure Obligations of Reporting Issuers) Rules 2007;
- Financial Services (Consolidated Licensing and Fees) Rules 2008 (in

relation to licence fees);
- Financial Intelligence and Anti-Money Laundering Act 2002 (in relation to anti-money laundering provisions);
- Companies Act 2001 (for funds structured as companies);
- Protected Cell Companies Act 1999 (for funds structured as protected cell companies);
- Trust Act 2001 (for funds structured as trusts); and
- Limited Partnerships Act 2011 (for funds structured as limited partnerships).

The regulatory bodies that govern funds in Mauritius are the FSC, which is the regulator for all non-banking financial services activities and the Registrar of Companies, the regulator in relation to all corporate and partnership matters.

All funds must obtain authorisation to operate from the FSC and the authorisation process is as follows:

(i) A prescribed application form must be sent to the FSC. This must be accompanied by the following documents:
- the proposed offering document;
- the governing documents of the proposed fund (constitution, trust deed or partnership agreement, whichever is applicable);
- copies of major agreements to be put in place (for example, investment management agreement, custody agreement, administration agreement, shareholders' agreement and any advisory agreements as may be applicable);
- know-your-customer documentation on promoters, beneficial owners and proposed directors;
- 'fit and proper' person questionnaire; and
- the prescribed first annual registration and processing fees.

(ii) Once the FSC is satisfied that the fund meets the legal and regulatory requirements, the fund entity can be incorporated.

A fund, constituted as a company and where it is not self-managed by its board of directors, must appoint a fund manager duly licensed by the FSC to manage the fund or in some cases may also appoint a foreign investment manager.

A distinction is made between foreign and offshore funds. A foreign fund is a fund established in a foreign jurisdiction. The FSC has the power to recognise such a fund and permit it to operate in Mauritius if it is satisfied that the fund is regulated in its country of domicile, and the FSC has in place an adequate agreement for co-operation with the regulator in the foreign jurisdiction. An offshore fund, referred to as a 'global fund', is a fund which is managed in Mauritius, but raises subscriptions from non-resident investors and makes the majority of its investments in countries other than Mauritius. An offshore fund must also apply for a category one global business licence (GBL1), to take advantage of certain corporate flexibilities and fiscal incentives.

Local requirements
A fund issued with a GBL1 is subject to certain local requirements. It must be managed and controlled from Mauritius and must at all times be

administered by a management company (management company) licensed by the FSC. There is no legal definition of management and control but in determining whether the entity will be managed and controlled in Mauritius, the FSC will inter alia have regards whether the GBL1:
(i) constituted as a company:
- will have or have at least two directors of sufficient calibre to exercise independent mind and judgment, resident in Mauritius;
- will maintain or maintains at all times its principal bank account in Mauritius;
- will keep and maintain, at all times, its accounting records at its registered office in Mauritius;
- will prepare or proposes to prepare its statutory financial statements and causes or proposes to have such financial statements to be audited in Mauritius; and
- provides for meetings of directors to include at least two directors from Mauritius.
(ii) constituted as a limited partnership:
- will have at least one partner of the limited partnership resident in Mauritius, where the partner is a natural person; or incorporated, formed or registered under the laws of Mauritius, where the partner is not a natural person;
- will maintain or maintains at all times its principal bank account in Mauritius;
- will keep and maintain, at all times, its accounting records at its registered office in Mauritius; and
- will prepare or propose to prepare its statutory financial statements and causes or proposes to have such financial statements to be audited in Mauritius.

Exemptions
Alternative investment funds that are categorised as 'expert funds' (which has to be an open-ended fund) or 'professional CIS' (which can be both open-ended and closed-ended) are exempted from certain regulations. The following are some examples:
- the requirement to have a prospectus in the prescribed form; the offering memorandum can be customised subject to a few mandatory disclosure requirements;
- the minimum funding requirements;
- investment and borrowing restrictions;
- the requirement to prepare and file management reports and annual reports;
- the requirement to conduct daily valuations; and
- the requirement to publish, weekly, the prices of interests in the collective investment scheme.

An expert fund is only available to: (i) an investor which makes initial investments for its own account of no less than $100,000; or (ii) a sophisticated investor, as defined in the Securities Act 2005 (or any similarly defined investor in the securities legislation of another country).

A professional CIS is only available to: (i) a sophisticated investor (as defined below), or (ii) by way of a private placement where, in practice, the subscription amount is generally not less than $100,000.

A sophisticated investor is defined under the Securities Act 2005 as including:
- the Government of Mauritius;
- a statutory authority, or an agency established by an enactment for a public purpose;
- a company, all the shares in which are owned by the Government of Mauritius, a statutory authority or an agency established by an enactment for a public purpose;
- the government of a foreign country, or an agency of that government;
- a bank;
- a fund manager;
- an insurer;
- an investment adviser;
- an investment dealer; and
- a person declared by the FSC to be a sophisticated investor.

Investment managers and investment advisers

An investment manager licensed by the FSC must:
- be incorporated or registered as a body corporate and have its place of business in Mauritius;
- be engaged principally in the business of managing funds;
- have directors, officers and beneficial owners who meet the fit and proper test;
- have appropriately qualified staff;
- maintain at all times a minimum stated capital of at least MUR1 million (or an equivalent amount in a different currency);
- establish and document their rules of internal control to ensure that they are legally compliant and are sufficiently supervised; and
- have in place a code of ethics and a code of conduct which are binding on their officers, advisers and employees.

An exception applies to offshore funds which can be managed by a foreign manager once the manager has been approved by the FSC. The latter will grant approval where it is satisfied that the proposed manager is regulated as an investment manager in the jurisdiction where the fund is regulated. The governing documents of the foreign investment manager, and evidence of its regulated status, must be submitted to the FSC for approval.

An unrestricted investment adviser is licensed and authorised by the FSC for managing, under a mandate, portfolios of securities on a discretionary basis and providing professional advice on securities transactions through written material or any other means. Such investment adviser may make investment decisions on behalf of their clients which include the most appropriate securities to buy or sell consistent to each client's objectives and guidelines and also as a duty of loyalty, care and righteousness to act in the best interest of its clients.

On the other hand a restricted investment adviser is a company or an individual licensed and authorised by the FSC only to give advice in securities dealings in the best interest of its clients' through written material or any other means. Such licensed investment adviser may solicit any person to enter into securities transactions from or within Mauritius.

2.3. Operational requirements

Certain alternative investment funds are exempt from the requirement to appoint a custodian. The portfolio of assets is held in the name of the fund itself. However, an alternative investment fund holding a GBL1 from the FSC shall have a local cash custodian, ie, a banker in Mauritius.

Alternative investment funds are exempted from the investment and borrowing restrictions as set out in section 3.6. below that are imposed on a retail fund.

The following areas are covered by specific requirements imposed by regulation:

- Risk: there is no regulation specifically concerning exempt fund risk. However, the prospectus or offering memorandum of the exempt fund must disclose all material risks to potential investors.
- Valuation and pricing: an exempt fund is free to specify the method and frequency of its valuations.
- Insider dealing and market abuse: the Securities Act 2005 contains a chapter on market abuses. This chapter creates the offences of insider dealing, false trading, market rigging, fraud and deceptive conduct involving securities. The prohibition on insider dealing is a general prohibition applicable to any person who uses insider information to: (i) deal in the securities of a reporting issuer; (ii) procure, or advise another person to deal in, the securities of a reporting issuer; or (iii) disclose insider information otherwise than in the course of that person's lawful occupation. A reporting issuer is an entity which has made a public offer of its securities. The offence attracts both a criminal sanction of up to 10 years' imprisonment and a fine. The fine levied is either three times the amount of the profits earned as a result of the offence, or MUR500,000, whichever is the greater sum. A person who has committed an act of insider dealing may also be sued for damages by the FSC, irrespective of the criminal liability.
- Transparency: exempt funds have reduced filing requirements. Exempt funds only need to file annual audited financial statements which shall be in accordance with the International Financial Reporting Standards (IFRS) with the FSC (save for an exempt fund constituted as an open-ended professional collective investment scheme, in which case, it will also have to file quarterly reports).
- Money laundering: all funds must comply with the Financial Intelligence and Anti-Money Laundering Act 2002, a law inspired by Financial Action Task Force (FATF) principles. Funds must carry out customer due diligence (CDD) in accordance with a code prescribed by the FSC. This includes

verifying the identity of investors and being satisfied that the source of funds is lawful. For corporate investors, the fund must obtain copies of incorporation documents and CDD information on the beneficial investor(s). Reduced or enhanced CDD may be applied depending on the profile of the investors, whether they are regulated institutions, and their country of domicile. There is no difference in the obligations of both retail and exempt funds under the anti-money laundering laws.
- Short selling: there is no legal requirement for such disclosure with an exempt fund.

2.4. Marketing the fund

The production and offering of marketing materials is governed by the Securities Act 2005 and the rules and regulations made thereunder.

Offerings are made either by a licensed investment intermediary (such as an investment dealer, investment adviser or distributor of financial products, licensed by the FSC) or the fund manager, using the fund's prospectus. There are no separate rules for marketing or offering different kinds of funds.

Shares or interests in alternative investment funds which are authorised as professional CIS or expert funds may only be offered to specific types of investors and are subject to the exemptions as described in section 2.2. above.

2.5. Taxation

Funds

Funds in Mauritius, incorporated as a company, are subject to a flat rate of corporate income tax of 15 per cent on its business profits. However, a fund is also entitled to foreign tax credit for any foreign tax paid on the same source of income. Foreign tax includes underlying tax paid provided that the Mauritian entity owns not less than 5 per cent of the share capital of the entity paying the income. No foreign tax credit is allowed in respect of foreign tax unless written evidence showing the amount of foreign tax which has been charged is capable of being produced to the competent authorities. Funds holding a GBL1 are entitled to an automatic tax credit of 80 per cent, therefore making them liable to a maximum effective rate of tax of 3 per cent.

A fund set up as a limited partnership and holding a GBL1 may opt to be taxed as a company (where the tax treatment will be as mentioned above) or as fiscally transparent where profits and losses are attributed to the partners who are taxed according to their share of such profits (or losses) in the partnership. In such a case, partners who are not resident in Mauritius, and assuming that the partnership only received foreign source income, would not be liable to tax in Mauritius.

There is no capital gains and transfer tax in Mauritius. Any capital gains realised by a Mauritius tax resident will not be subject to tax in Mauritius. There is also no withholding tax on dividends in Mauritius.

Any person who derives income in Mauritius may apply to the Mauritius Revenue Authority for a ruling on that income. It is not necessary to obtain a tax ruling prior to the establishment of a fund. A ruling may be obtained at any stage for the sake of clarity on the tax treatment of any income derived in

Mauritius.

Mauritius has further strengthened its position in the international financial services arena with the introduction of the Special Purpose Fund (SPF) which will attract promoters using Mauritius as a platform for investment funds in countries having no tax treaties with Mauritius. A SPF is a fund (either a collective investment scheme or a closed-ended fund) which is not resident in Mauritius for tax purposes and it will not hold any global business licence.

The FSC may approve a fund as a SPF if:
- it conducts investment solely in countries which do not have tax arrangements with Mauritius;
- it invests mainly in securities whose returns will be exempted from taxation; or
- its investors are pension schemes or other persons entitled to tax exemptions.

Resident investors
Resident investors are subject to a 15 per cent tax on their taxable income, which excludes capital gains.

Non-resident investors
No tax liability is imposed on any non-resident investor. Withholding taxes on dividends are not payable by a non-resident investor in a Mauritian fund.

2.6. Customary or common terms
Private funds – closed-ended
- Term of fund: private funds which are authorised as closed-ended funds are typically set up with limited life and such funds normally have a life span of about 10 to 12 years.
- Liquidity of assets: restrictions on transfer may be imposed in the constitutive documents of the fund. In such types of fund, shares or interests cannot be resold to the public. Holders of shares or interests in the fund do not have the possibilities to exit the fund at their option.
- Manager/operator involvement: it is common to have key persons who should devote a substantial amount of their business time to the affairs of the fund. Where a key person is replaced, the approval of participants is usually required; further, in the event of the person ceasing to be a key person, the operation of the fund may be suspended. Furthermore, in a fund constituted as a company, it is common for the investment manager to hold a class of shares with all voting rights but no economic rights. Otherwise, in a limited partnership, the manager can be a limited partner.
- Remuneration arrangements: managers are paid management fees and performance fees out of the assets of the fund. Further, a manager may be attributed a class of shares or interests in the limited partnership for the purposes of carried interest. In such arrangements, a clawback provision is also provided so that in the event the investors do not receive their entitled distributions, the manager will not be entitled to receive a

portion of the carried interest payment.
- Investment and borrowing restrictions: private funds authorised as closed-ended funds are not subject to investment and borrowing restrictions as per the applicable laws. However, the constitutive documents may provide such restrictions on a case by case basis.
- Reporting obligations: see section 2.3.

Hedge funds
- Term of fund: the life of such funds may be limited or unlimited.
- Liquidity of assets: funds which are organised as expert funds or professional CIS may contain certain restrictions on transfer; such restrictions vary from fund to fund. However, there are restrictions imposed by law for certain exempt funds; for instance, shares or interests in a professional CIS cannot be resold to the public, and an expert fund may only provide for issue of shares or interests to persons who are sophisticated investors or expert investors as defined in section 2.2.
- Manager/operator involvement: there is generally no requirement for an investment manager to invest its own money. An investment manager can hold nominal shares that have voting rights but no economic rights in a company and in a limited partnership, it can be a limited partner by a making a capital contribution. The approval of participants and the FSC are required prior to the replacement of the investment manager.
- Remuneration arrangements: managers normally receive management fees and performance fees out of the assets of the fund.
- Investment and borrowing restrictions: hedge funds are not subject to investment and borrowing restrictions.
- Reporting obligations: see section 3.3.

3. RETAIL FUNDS
3.1. Common structures
Retail funds (open-ended or closed-ended) are usually set up as companies, protected cell companies, trusts, sociétés or limited partnerships (see section 2.1. for an analysis on each legal vehicle).

3.2. Regulatory framework
See section 2.2., which also applies to retail funds (open-ended or closed-ended).

3.3. Operational requirements
Retail funds (open-ended)
An open-ended retail fund must appoint a custodian licensed by the FSC to safeguard the assets of the fund. Only banks and trust companies that are subsidiaries of banks are eligible for a custodian licence. Custodians must:
- maintain a minimum stated 'unimpaired' capital of MUR10 million (or an equivalent amount). 'Unimpaired' means that the assets of the minimum capital must not be encumbered, and that if a loss is sustained, it must inject funds to ensure that this minimum capital requirement is

Mauritius

maintained; and
- be independent from the manager of the fund.

An open-ended retail fund must both file with the FSC and send to participants:
- quarterly unaudited financial statements prepared in accordance with the IFRS, which contain matters prescribed by Securities (Collective Investment Schemes and Closed-ended Funds) Regulations 2008 (the CIS Regulations), no later than 45 days after the end of each quarter;
- quarterly management reports, which include performance reports of the fund in the form, and the containing matters, prescribed by the CIS Regulations; and
- annual reports, including annual audited financial statements, no later than 90 days after the fund's balance sheet date.

For domestic retail funds, the quarterly reports and annual reports must also be made public.

The following areas are covered by specific requirements imposed by the CIS Regulations:
- Risk: where the prospectus or offering memorandum of the open-ended retail fund is departing, for example, from the investment restrictions (as set out in section 3.6.), it will have to describe the nature of the risks, including minimum exposure to stock market, sensitivity to rate of interest risk, exposure to currency risk, concentration risk, derivative risk, foreign investment risk and illiquid securities risk.
- Valuation and pricing: a retail fund must conduct a valuation on a daily basis (or at such other intervals as are agreed with the FSC).
- Insider dealing and market abuse: see section 2.3.
- Transparency: see reporting requirements above.
- Money laundering: see section 2.3.
- Short selling: there are no rules that specifically address short selling. For retail funds, short sales (and any collateral for such purposes) must be disclosed in the financial statements.

Retail funds (closed-ended)

Closed-ended retail funds are exempt from the requirement to appoint a custodian. The portfolio of assets is held in the name of the fund itself. However, a closed-ended retail fund which is listed is deemed to be a collective investment scheme and therefore must meet the same conditions as an open-ended retail fund with respect to custodians (see above, retail funds (open-ended)).

A closed-ended retail fund must file with the FSC and in the case of funds not holding a GBL1, make public:
- a comparative quarterly financial statement prepared in accordance with IFRS, no later than 45 days after the end of each quarter; and
- an annual report, including audited comparative financial statements prepared in accordance with IFRS, no later than 90 days after the fund's balance sheet date.

The following areas are covered by specific requirements imposed by regulation:

Mauritius

- Risk: the prospectus or offering memorandum of the closed-ended retail fund must disclose all material risks to potential investors.
- Valuation and pricing: a closed-ended retail fund is free to specify the method and frequency of its valuations.
- Insider dealing and market abuse: see section 2.3.
- Transparency: see reporting requirements above.
- Money laundering: see section 2.3.
- Short selling: there are no rules that specifically address short selling. For retail funds, short sales (and any collateral for such purposes) must be disclosed in the financial statements.

3.4. Marketing the fund

For open-ended and closed-ended retail funds, offerings are made either by a licensed investment intermediary (such as an investment dealer, investment adviser or distributor of financial products, licensed by the FSC) or the fund manager, using the fund's prospectus. There are no separate rules for marketing or offering different kinds of funds. However, different obligations can arise which depend on the manner in which the offering is made. For example, there are different obligations for private placement offers and public offers, and for instances where an offer is made to a specific category of investors, such as sophisticated or institutional investors. In the case of a public offering, the fund is subject to an additional disclosure requirement (to the FSC) as a reporting issuer. The fund must register itself as a reporting issuer and file a prospectus (the regulations specify both the form and content required for the prospectus). Reporting issuers must file quarterly financial statements, and must notify the FSC of any material changes to their affairs. They must also declare how many of their shares or interests are held (directly or indirectly) by their holding companies, subsidiaries, officers, and persons holding or controlling more than 5 per cent of the securities of the reporting issuer (referred to as insiders). The disclosure requirements extend to securities of the reporting issuer held by any associates of such insiders. Further, any changes to such interests have to be similarly reported.

Open-ended and closed-ended retail funds can be offered to the public, and they are required to provide a prospectus. There are no differences between how local or foreign funds are marketed, as they must both have licensed intermediaries. However, the FSC will expect a disclaimer statement for foreign funds, which is broadly to the effect that the recognition of foreign funds does not imply that the regulator is vouching for the merits of investing in the scheme. Once authorised, there are no restrictions on the categories of persons to whom retail funds can be marketed.

3.5. Taxation
Funds
Retail funds (open-ended and closed-ended) are taxed in the same way as detailed in section 2.5.

Mauritius

Resident investors
See section 2.5.

Non-resident investors
See section 2.5.

3.6. Customary or common terms
Retail funds (open-ended)
- Term of fund: open-ended funds normally have unlimited life.
- Liquidity of assets: shares or interests in such funds are normally freely transferrable to the extent that restrictions are not imposed in the fund's constitutive documents. Redemption of shares or return on contribution is effected at the prevailing net asset value subject to the fund meeting the solvency test.
- Manager/operator involvement: there is generally no requirement for an investment manager to invest its own money. It is customary to see an investment manager holding nominal shares that have voting rights but no economic rights in a company and in a limited partnership, it can be a limited partner by a making a capital contribution. The approval of participants and the FSC are required prior to the replacement of the investment manager.
- Remuneration arrangements: managers normally receive management fees and performance fees out of the assets of the fund.
- Investment and borrowing restrictions: an open-ended retail fund has a number of investment restrictions. It cannot:
  (i) invest more than 5 per cent of its net assets in the security of an issuer unless it is a debt security issued by the Government of Mauritius or the government of any other country;
  (ii) purchase a security of an issuer where, immediately after the purchase, it would hold more than 10 per cent of a class of securities of that issuer;
  (iii) purchase real estate;
  (iv) purchase a mortgage;
  (v) purchase a security for the purpose of exercising control or management over the issuer of that security;
  (vi) have more than 10 per cent of its net assets in illiquid assets;
  (vii) purchase or sell derivatives, except where the FSC has authorised that fund as a 'specialised fund';
  (viii) buy or sell any physical commodity, including precious metals, except where the FSC has authorised that fund as a 'specialised fund';
  (ix) engage in the business of underwriting or marketing the securities of any other issuer;
  (x) guarantee the securities or obligations of another person;
  (xi) purchase or sell securities not traded through market facilities unless the transaction price is negotiated at arm's length;
  (xii) subscribe to securities offered by a company in formation; or
  (xiii) invest in aggregate more than 5 per cent of its net asset value in the

shares of other collective investment schemes or acquire more than 10 per cent of the shares of any single collective investment scheme, unless it is authorised as a feeder fund on such terms as the FSC may determine.

An open-ended retail fund can only borrow money or create a charge over its assets when either:
(i) the transaction is only a temporary measure to accommodate a request for the redemption of securities of that fund, and the outstanding amount of all borrowings does not exceed 5 per cent of the fund; or
(ii) the charge secures a claim for fees and expenses incurred for services rendered while redeeming those securities.

These investment and borrowing restrictions can be lifted on an application to the FSC, and the FSC will lift them where it is satisfied that the fund has sufficient justification to borrow or make the investment. Before the FSC lifts the restrictions, it can impose any additional conditions that it considers appropriate to protect investors.

Reporting obligations – see section 3.3. (retail funds (open-ended)).

Retail funds (closed-ended)
- Term of fund: closed-ended funds are typically set up with limited life and such funds normally have a life span of 10 to 12 years.
- Liquidity of assets: restrictions on transfer may be imposed in the constitutive documents of the fund; otherwise there are no restrictions on transfer imposed by law. Holders of shares or interests in the fund do not have the possibilities to exit the fund at their option.
- Manager/operator involvement: in a fund constituted as a company, it is common for the investment manager to hold a class of shares with all voting rights but no economic rights. The manager can be a limited partner in a limited partnership.
- Remuneration arrangements: managers normally receive management fees and performance fees out of the assets of the fund.
- Investment and borrowing restrictions: retail funds (closed-ended) are not subject to investment and borrowing restrictions.
- Reporting obligations: see section 3.3. (retail funds (closed-ended)).

4. PROPOSED CHANGES AND DEVELOPMENTS
EU Alternative Investment Fund Management Directive (AIFMD)
The FSC has on 17 July 2013 officially signed a Memorandum of Understanding (MoU) with the European Securities and Markets Authority (ESMA). The MoU reaffirms the FSC's commitment to the highest standards in international engagement and information sharing, in particular, non-EU alternative investment funds will need to comply with the transparency provisions of the directive, providing for reporting to the competent EU regulators and disclosure obligations to investors, and also with certain anti-asset-stripping and takeover provisions.

Mauritius was among the first few countries to receive ESMA's approval on the MOU at its meeting on 22 May 2013. ESMA negotiated the agreement on behalf of all 27 EU member state securities' regulators as well as the authorities from Croatia, Iceland, Liechtenstein and Norway. These arrangements include the exchange of information, cross-border onsite visits and mutual assistance in the enforcement of the respective supervisory laws. With the signature of the MoU, Mauritius has satisfied all the conditions under the AIFMD for Mauritius-regulated funds to continue to market in Europe under the private placement regimes of EU member states following the introduction of the AIFMD on 22 July 2013. The existence of cooperation arrangement is also an essential pre-requisite in non-EU alternative investment fund manager to be eligible for a 'passport' to be able to market non-EU alternative investment funds after 2015.

Guidelines for advertising and marketing of financial products
The FSC has, on 8 July 2013, issued draft guidelines for advertising and marketing of financial products (Guidelines) for consultation. The Guidelines aim to provide a better protection for consumers of financial services in Mauritius and to further promote responsible, ethical and professional conduct among persons who are involved in the chain of advertising and marketing of financial products, which are directed at consumers of financial services in Mauritius. As at date, the FSC has not indicated when these Guidelines will take effect.

The Netherlands

Oscar van Angeren, Harm-Paul Plas & Sylvia Dikmans
Houthoff Buruma

1. MARKET OVERVIEW
The investment fund market in the Netherlands is well established and developed. Funds are divided into two main types:
- Investment companies (*beleggingsmaatschappijen*). These are investment institutions (*beleggingsinstellingen*) with legal personality; and
- Investment funds (*beleggingsfondsen*). These are investment institutions without legal personality.

Unlike an investment fund, an investment company is not obliged to have a separate management company (*beheerder*). In this chapter, the term 'manager' refers to either the management company of an investment fund or investment company or the investment company itself where an investment company does not have its own management company.

No restrictions have been recently introduced on the participation by financial institutions in investment funds.

The Directive 2011/61/EU on alternative investment fund managers (AIFMD) must be implemented by EU Member States by 22 July 2013. The Netherlands has met this deadline.

The deadline for full authorisation of and compliance by pre-existing AIFMs is set for 22 July 2014. Accordingly, managers will in principle be able to benefit from a transitional period of one year until 22 July 2014 to become fully compliant with the new rules following from the AIFMD.

2. ALTERNATIVE INVESTMENT FUNDS
2.1. Common structures
The following legal vehicles are used for alternative investment funds:
- Private company (*besloten vennootschap met beperkte aansprakelijkheid*) (BV).
- Public company (*naamloze vennootschap*) (NV).
- Limited partnership (*commanditaire vennootschap*) (CV).
- Cooperative (*coöperatie*) (Coop).
- Fund for joint account (*fonds voor gemene rekening*) (FGR).

The BV and the NV are the main legal entities with legal personality used by commercial investors in the Netherlands. The statute law applicable to these companies is partly mandatory and include already basic corporate governance rules and a system of checks and balances. The standard corporate bodies in a BV or NV are the management board and the general meeting of shareholders. Optionally, a supervisory board may be established. A BV or NV is incorporated by means of a notarial deed executed before a civil law notary, and is registered in the commercial register of the Chamber of Commerce.

Similar to the BV and the NV, the Coop is a legal entity under Dutch law, having its own rights and obligations. Dutch company law provides for very little mandatory law on Coops. This creates a lot of flexibility to organise the bylaws (*statuten*) of the Coop according to the wishes of the members. Dutch law provides for three arrangements for liability of the members of a Coop: (i) statutory liability; (ii) excluded liability; and (iii) limited liability. The appropriate abbreviation must be added to the name of the Coop (WA, UA or BA).

The CV and the FGR do not have legal personality, these vehicles are rather agreements between parties. Therefore, these vehicles cannot be the holders of rights and obligations. In the case of a CV, a general partner usually holds the rights and obligations for the CV. The FGR has two legal entities which play an important role: the manager (*beheerder*) and the depositary (*bewaarder*) of the assets and liabilities of the FGR. The manager provides for the day-to-day management of the FGR. The role of the depositary is to hold the legal title to the assets of the FGR on behalf of the investors in the fund.

Advantages. Contractual forms such as the CV and the FGR are generally more flexible than the corporate forms. This is particularly relevant for tax purposes, but also for distribution mechanisms. The corporate forms usually involve common and preferred shares.

Disadvantages. Investors in CVs must avoid becoming involved in the management of the CV otherwise they assume liability. If the limited partner's name appears in the name of the CV, the limited partner assumes liability.

Except for the situation that a limited partner in a CV assumes liability, as mentioned above, the liability of an investor in each of the above mentioned fund vehicles (a shareholder in a BV or NV, a member of a Coop with excluded liability, a limited partner in a CV, or a participant in a FGR) is in principle limited to its agreed contribution to the fund.

The Financial Markets Supervision Act (*Wet op het financieel toezicht*) (FMSA) refers to participants' interests in funds as units or participation rights (*rechten van deelneming*).

The following legal vehicles are commonly used for investment managers and/or investment advisers of alternative investment funds:
- Private company (*besloten vennootschap met beperkte aansprakelijkheid*) (BV).
- Public company (*naamloze vennootschap*) (NV).
- Foundation (*stichting*).

2.2. Regulatory framework

The main Dutch laws that govern alternative investment funds are the FMSA, the Decree on the Supervision of Market Conduct of Financial Firms FMSA (*Besluit Gedragstoezicht financiële ondernemingen Wft, BGfo*) and the Decree on Supervision of Market Conduct Financial Firms FMSA (*Besluit prudentiële regels Wft*).

Only in case a fund (an investment company) does not have its own management company, the fund itself requires a licence from the Authority for the Financial Markets (*Stichting Autoriteit Financiële Markten*) (AFM).

The main Dutch laws that govern the investment manager or investment adviser are the FMSA, the Decree on the Supervision of Market Conduct of Financial Firms FMSA (*Besluit Gedragstoezicht financiële ondernemingen Wft, BGfo*) and the Decree on Supervision of Market Conduct Financial Firms FMSA (*Besluit prudentiële regels Wft*).

Before the implementation of the AIFMD, participation rights in an alternative investment fund could only be offered in the Netherlands if its manager had been licensed by the AFM, unless an exception or exemption applied (see below under vi.).

After the implementation of the AIFMD, a manager requires a licence from the AFM for the management of a Dutch alternative investment fund, the offering of participation rights in the Netherlands and, as Dutch manager, for the management of, or the offering of participation rights in an alternative investment fund, unless it falls under the light regime (see below).

If the investment manager/investment adviser would qualify as an investment firm (*beleggingsonderneming*) then it would of course be subject to a separate licence obligation under the EU Markets in Financial Instruments Directive (MiFID) as implemented in the Netherlands into the FMSA.

To qualify as a 'Dutch manager', the manager should have its seat in the Netherlands. The AFM may require that the persons that carry out the daily management of the fund are located in the Netherlands.

Before the implementation of the AIFMD, a licence was not required if one of the following exceptions or exemptions applied:
- Offerings of participation rights solely to qualified investors (as defined in FMSA) including pension funds, investment funds, banks and other institutional investors.
- Offerings of participation rights to fewer than 100 persons who are not qualified investors.
- Offerings of participation rights in an alternative investment fund with an individual denomination of at least EUR 100,000.
- Offerings of participation rights in an alternative investment fund which can only be acquired for a total consideration of at least EUR 100,000 per investor. The amounts of EUR 100,000 must be actually contributed to the fund, as committed capital does not qualify towards the relevant exemption.

Given the one year transition period, managers that offered participation rights in an alternative investment fund under an exception or exemption of the licence requirement in the FMSA, as mentioned above, can continue to do so until 22 July 2014.

As indicated, after the implementation of the AIFMD, the manager of an alternative investment fund does not require a licence from the AFM if it falls under the light regime. This light regime will apply if the manager, directly or indirectly through a company which the manager is linked by common management or control, or by a qualified direct or indirect interest, has assets under management:
- Not exceeding EUR 100 million; or
- If the alternative investment fund managed by the manager does not use leverage, not exceeding EUR 500 million, provided in the latter case that

the investors do not have any redemption rights for at least five years.

These exemptions to the licensing requirement of the manager are only available if the participation rights are offered:
- To professional investors only.
- To fewer than 150 investors.
- In consideration for at least EUR 100,000 per investor; and/or
- With a denomination of at least EUR 100,000.

If an exemption does apply, the manager will be subject to a registration requirement and also certain reporting requirements.

Other EU managers also do not require a licence from the AFM if they operate under a licence in another EU Member State (the 'passport regime'). The AIFMD provides 'maximum harmonization' for AIFMs that market AIFs to professional investors. However, for AIFMs that market AIFs to retail investors the AIFMD provides 'minimum harmonization'. This is because EU Member States are permitted to impose additional more restrictive and stringent national supervisory rules for such offerings. The Netherlands has decided to make use of the ability to impose additional rules ('top-up retail' rules) to protect investors. This does not apply to UCITS. As a result of EU Member States having the ability to impose these additional rules, the AIFMD passport regime will only be available in respect of AIFs that offer to professional investors and not to retail investors.

Before implementation of the AIFMD, offerings of units in retail non-UCITS funds from countries accredited by the Dutch Minister of Finance as having adequate supervision of investment funds did not need a licence from the AFM to offer units in the Netherlands, although they remained subject to certain (ongoing) disclosure requirements pursuant to the FMSA. However, these obligations are far less restrictive than those that apply to licensed retail funds. The Dutch legislator has decided to continue this 'adequate supervision regime' until at least 2018, provided that the AIFMD's minimum requirements are complied with. The relevant (from outside the EU) accredited countries are Guernsey, Jersey and the US (for SEC-registered funds). In certain circumstances, managers with a seat in another state may also be exempted.

The manager can submit a licence request by the AFM by filing a licence application form, including annexes, with the AFM. Requirements for such a licence relate to the suitability and reliability of policy makers and supervisors, integrity and structure of the business operations, control structure, the conflict of interest policy, solvability, solidity and liquidity.

The AFM will in principle decide on a licence application within 13 weeks of receipt thereof. This term may be extended by another 13 weeks.

2.3. Operational requirements

There are no specific limitations for an alternative investment funds to invest in certain asset classes. An alternative investment fund still should take adequate measures to prevent that they execute or procure transactions aimed at the acquiring or offering of a financial instrument that has been issued by a cluster munitions company, or extend loans to or acquire non-transferable shares in a cluster munitions company.

A manager of an alternative investment fund must ensure that a depositary is appointed for the fund which must be either an EU credit institution, an EU investment firm (MiFID) subject to the same capital requirements as credit institutions, or a prudentially regulated and supervised institution of a type that is eligible to be a depositary according to the UCITS Directive.

Where the investment fund's assets are held by a depositary, the manager must conclude a written management and custody agreement with the depositary. Rules enacted under the FMSA regulate the agreement's content.

A manager must provide the AFM and/or the Dutch Central Bank (De Nederlandsche Bank) information with regard to:
- the alternative investment funds it manages;
- the way it manages the alternative investment funds;
- the investments of the alternative investment funds;
- the markets on which the alternative investment funds are active;
- the principal exposures and most important concentrations of each of the funds it manages;
- the percentage of the fund's assets which are subject to special arrangements arising from their illiquid nature;
- any new arrangements for managing the liquidity of the fund;
- the current risk profile of the fund and the risk management systems employed by the manager to manage the market risk, liquidity risk, counterparty risk and other risks including operational risk;
- information on the main categories of assets in which the fund invested;
- the results of the stress tests performed; and
- any additional information on a periodic as well as on an ad-hoc basis, where necessary for the effective monitoring of systemic risk.

Furthermore, a manager of an alternative investment fund is required to submit to the AFM the annual accounts and annual reports of the alternative investment funds.

There are also specific reporting requirements for managers of alternative investment funds regarding obtaining control in companies.

Additional notification requirements apply if the manager intends to amend the conditions of the fund.

The manager of an alternative investment fund must publish its annual accounts, an annual report and certain other information listed in the Dutch Civil Code within four months of the end of the financial year. The semi-annual accounts must be published within nine weeks of the end of the financial year.

In case of alternative investment funds offering participation rights to retail customers, managers are obliged to publish on their website at least the prospectus, the conditions of the fund, the KIID, the most recent net asset value of the participation rights and the (semi-) annual accounts.

The use of side letters is not restricted.

Risk. a manager must have a permanent risk management function and certain conditions must be met to ensure that risk management is 'functionally and hierarchically' separated from operating units, including the portfolio management function. In practice, the impact on the fund will depend on the investment strategy and the existing risk management framework in place with respect to the fund.

Borrowing restrictions. The manager is required to observe a reasonable level of leverage. The Dutch Central Bank may impose limits to the level of leverage that a manager observes or otherwise impose restrictions on the management, in order to ensure the stability and integrity of the financial system.

Valuation and pricing. The FMSA contains specific rules on valuation and pricing. The Manager should have in place procedures to ensure accurate and independent valuation of the managed assets by an independent valuator (*taxateur*) or the manager itself, provided that the valuation task is functionally independent from the portfolio management and the remuneration policy and other measures ensure that conflicts of interest are mitigated and that undue influence upon the employees is prevented.

Insider dealing and market abuse. The FMSA contains extensive market abuse rules (for example, the prohibition of insider trading, tipping off and market manipulation).

Transparency. The conduct of business supervision by the AFM focuses on, among other things, orderly and transparent financial market processes and clear relations between market participants.

Money laundering. Alternative investment funds must verify the identity of any investors and check and monitor their risk profile for anti-money laundering purposes. Non-supervised funds must only verify the identity of their investors.

Short selling. New rules for the notification of short positions in listed companies apply in the Netherlands with effect from 1 November 2012. The new rules arise from the EU Regulation on short selling and certain aspects of credit default swaps.

In summary, notification must be made of any position attaining 0.2 per cent of the issued share capital, and of every subsequent 0.1 per cent above this threshold. Notifications starting at 0.5 per cent and every subsequent 0.1 per cent above this threshold will be made public via the short selling register. Notification must also be made of net short positions in sovereign debts that exceed or fall below specific threshold values, but these notifications will not be made public.

2.4. Marketing the fund

The production and offering of marketing materials for alternative investment funds which offer their participation rights in the Netherlands is governed by the FMSA, the BGfo, the Further Regulation on Supervision of Market Conduct Financial Firms FMSA (*Nadere Regeling gedragstoezicht financiële ondernemingen Wft, NRgfo*) and the Commission Regulation (EC) No.809/2004.

An alternative investment fund can be marketed by its manager or any person licensed as an investment firm (*beleggingsonderneming*) under Directive 2004/39/EC on markets in financial instruments (MiFID) as implemented in the FMSA or under an EU MiFID passport.

An alternative investment fund can be marketed to:
- Dutch public customers.
- Dutch institutional investors.
- Foreign public or institutional customers, provided that local laws are complied with.

Marketing in the Netherlands is generally subject to prospectus requirements.

The offering of transferable securities by a closed-ended fund is subject the requirements of the EU Prospectus Directive as implemented by the FMSA. However, a prospectus that meets the requirements of the EU Prospectus Directive is not required if one of the following exemptions applies:
- If the participation rights are offered solely to qualified investors (as defined in FMSA).
- If the participation rights are offered to fewer than 150 persons who are not qualified investors.
- If the participation rights are offered with an individual denomination of at least EUR 100,000 (or its foreign currency equivalent).
- If the participation rights offered can only be acquired for a total consideration of at least EUR 100,000 (or its foreign currency equivalent) per investor. The amounts of EUR 100,000 must be actually contributed to the investment institution, as committed capital does not qualify towards the relevant exemption.

In case one of the latter three exemptions apply, the marketing material must state that no prospectus that is approved by the AFM will be made generally available and that the offering will not be supervised by the AFM. The NRgfo contains detailed provisions on how this should be communicated.

If a manager is exempted from having a prospectus in place that meets the requirements of the Prospectus Directive, it should however still produce a prospectus if it offers participation rights in an alternative investment fund in the Netherlands under the rules of the AIFMD as implemented in the FMSA.

Only the prospectus of a closed-ended fund with transferable participation rights, which should meet the requirements of the Prospectus Directive, requires an approval from the AFM.

There are no additional requirements on marketing to public bodies such as government pension funds.

The marketing of an alternative investment fund by an intermediary on behalf of underlying clients would fall within the scope of, and should take place in compliance with, the requirements of MiFID, as implemented in the Netherlands into the FMSA.

2.5. Taxation

Two special corporate income tax regimes exist for alternative investment funds: the exempt investment fund and the fiscal investment fund. It also possible to use a tax transparent fund for joint account or a tax transparent limited partnership.
- Exempt investment fund (EIF). An exempt investment fund is fully

exempt from corporate income tax. Distributions are not subject to withholding tax. The main requirements are:
- the fund must be open-ended; for closed-ended alternative investment funds, the EIF cannot be used.
- the fund's activities must be limited to passive investment in financial instruments.
- The EIF-regime is therefore not open to direct investments in real estate. Moreover, it is not allowed for a EIF to indirectly invest in Dutch real estate.
- the fund must be a vehicle for collective investment (that is, it must have more than one investor/participant);
- the fund must have the legal form of an NV (corporation) or open fund for joint account (*fonds voor gemene rekening*) (unincorporated fund) or a similar type of foreign entity, established under the laws of an EU member state or a state that has concluded a double tax treaty with a non-discrimination clause with The Netherlands;
- the fund and/or its manager do not have to reside in The Netherlands;
- An EIF does not have specific shareholders, debt financing or profit distribution requirements.
- an EIF needs a licence from the Dutch tax authorities;
- an EIF cannot obtain a certificate of residence under a double tax treaty, unless a double tax treaty would explicitly grant treaty benefits to an EIF.

- Fiscal investment fund (FIF). A fiscal investment fund is subject to corporate income tax at a rate of 0 per cent. Distributions are subject to withholding tax (15 per cent unless reduced by a double tax treaty or reduced under the specific withholding tax rules). The main requirements are:
  - the fund must distribute its taxable profits within eight months of the year end;
  - the fund's activities must be limited to passive investment;
  - the fund must have the legal form of an NV (corporation), BV (company) or (*fonds voor gemene rekening*) (unincorporated fund) or a similar type of foreign entity established under the laws of an EU member state or a state that has concluded a double tax treaty with a non-discrimination clause with The Netherlands;
  - the fund must observe a 20 per cent borrowing limit (60 per cent for real estate);
  - detailed shareholders' requirements apply, which are different for licensed and unlicensed funds;
  - a FIF can only have one class of participations;
  - certain restrictions apply for appointing directors and supervisory directors;
  - the fund and/or its manager do not have to reside in The Netherlands;
  - a FIF does not need a licence from the Dutch tax authorities.
  - a FIF can obtain a certificate of residence under a double tax treaty.

- Tax transparent fund for joint account. A tax transparent fund is not seen as a person for corporate income tax and dividend withholding tax purposes. It is referred to as a closed fund for joint account.
  The closed fund for joint account is considered tax transparent if:
  - the fund issues participations/units without (prior) written consent of the participants; and
  - the transfer of participations/units in the fund requires the prior written consent of all participants/unit holders; and (under circumstances) ('Consent Mechanism'); and
  - the participations/units can only be redeemed by the fund itself ('Redemption Mechanism').

  Other requirements are:
  - it must be an unincorporated fund and not a limited partnership;
  - the fund and/or its manager do not have to reside in The Netherlands;
  - a tax transparent fund does not need a licence from the Dutch tax authorities;
  - a tax transparent fund cannot obtain a certificate of residence under a double tax treaty; and
  - in practice, tax transparent funds are less used for open-ended alternative investment funds.
- Tax transparent limited partnership. A tax transparent limited partnership is not seen as a person for corporate income tax and dividend withholding tax purposes. It is referred to as a closed CV. The main requirements are:
  - it must be a limited partnership;
  - a partnership interest can only be transferred with the prior consent of all partners;
  - new partners are only admitted with the prior consent of all partners;
  - a tax transparent limited partnership does not need a licence from the Dutch tax authorities. However, on request it can obtain a ruling confirming its tax transparent status;
  - the fund and/or its manager do not have to reside in The Netherlands;
  - a tax transparent limited partnership cannot obtain a certificate of residence under a double tax treaty; and
  - tax transparent limited partnerships are often used for closed-ended alternative investment funds.

Although there is no statutory requirement, it is advisable and common practice to obtain a tax ruling from the Dutch tax authorities confirming the tax treatment of respectively the EIF, FIF, Closed fund for joint account or closed CV.

Resident investors. The following regulations apply:
- General. A full credit applies for any resident withholding tax on dividends received for all types of Dutch resident investors (including Dutch tax-exempt investors), except for the EIF and the FIF. The FIF can apply a reduction rule of dividend withholding tax on distributions.

If an interest is held in a tax transparent fund (ie, closed fund for joint account or closed CV), the assets and liabilities are allocated pro rata to the participants and taxed accordingly. Certain entities, including qualifying pension funds and exempt investment funds, are exempt from corporate income tax and consequently do not pay tax on income and gains from their participations in alternative investment funds.
- Individuals. Individuals (unless they have a substantial interest or hold the fund participations as business assets) are taxed on their investments on the basis of a deemed return of 4 per cent of their net wealth at the beginning of the calendar year. This deemed return is taxed at 30 per cent, which means they effectively pay 1.2 per cent of the net wealth, irrespective of the actual income gains, losses and expenses.
Individuals holding a substantial interest are subject to 25 per cent on the actual net income from, and gains on, their fund participations.
If they hold a substantial interest in an exempt investment fund, the annual income is deemed to be at least 4 per cent. A substantial interest is held, if (together with certain family members) at least 5 per cent of the participations or a class of participations is held.
- Entities and businesses. Corporations, companies, other entities and individuals holding the interest as a business asset are generally taxed on the actual net income and gains. The general corporate income tax rate is 25 per cent and the highest income tax rate is 52 per cent. Certain entities (for example, pension funds) are exempt from, or not subject to, corporate income tax.

Non-resident investors. The following regulations apply:
- General. On distributions, including distributions to non-residents, by an FIF a 15 per cent withholding tax is applied. Generally there is no refund, but certain exempt entities can claim a refund on withholding tax paid.

Non-resident individuals, not having a permanent establishment in The Netherlands, are not subject to income tax on income and gains from a participation in an EIF or an FIF, unless they hold a substantial interest and that interest is not held as a business asset.

Non-resident entities, not having a permanent establishment in The Netherlands, are not subject to corporate income tax on income and gains from a participation in an FIF, unless they hold a substantial interest and that interest is not held as a business asset.

Non-resident entities, not having a permanent establishment in The Netherlands, are not subject to corporate income tax on income and gains from a participation in an EIF.

If an interest is held in a Dutch tax transparent fund, the assets and liabilities are pro rata allocated to the participants and taxed accordingly.
- Tax transparent fund. If a Dutch or foreign tax transparent fund holds Dutch real property directly, non-resident investors in that fund are liable to Dutch income tax or corporate income tax. Their tax treatment is similar to the tax treatment of Dutch residents.

In principle no establishment taxes or transfer taxes are due. If the alternative investment fund invests in Dutch real estate, the acquisition or expansion of a participation in a Dutch real estate fund, qualifying as Dutch real estate entity, can be subject to Dutch real estate transfer tax (RETT). An entity qualifies as a Dutch real estate entity in case its assets consist for 50 per cent or more of real estate assets and for 30 per cent or more of Dutch real estate assets and these assets are held with the purpose of exploitation or trading of these assets.

Under current law, RETT is only due if the interest acquired or expanded represents one-third or more in such an entity. This requirement is not limited to real estate entities with legal personality (ie, BV, NV etc). but also applies to entities without such personality. Please note that a new law proposal whereby the transfer of participations in real estate funds will incur RETT irrespective of the size of the interest in the real estate investment fund, is postponed for the time being.

In case the fund invests in real estate assets situated in the Netherlands, the EIF regime is not available (see main requirements EIF regime).

2.6. Customary or common terms
The terms of Dutch alternative investment funds do not substantially deviate from similar funds in other countries. Given that there are no statutory requirements with regard to the term of a fund, the term will mainly depend on the investment strategy of the fund.

Any terms on liquidity of interest will mainly depend on the tax treatment of the respective fund, as set out in section 2.5. above.

The terms of Dutch alternative investment funds regularly contain provisions that require key staff to devote a substantial part (a certain percentage) of their professional time to the management of the Fund. Failure to comply with this requirement may for example result in a reduction of the management fee.

In addition, terms of Dutch alternative investment funds often give investors the opportunity to remove the manager for 'cause', which may for example be fraud or an unremedied material breach of the conditions.

Also with regard to remuneration arrangements, Dutch alternative investment funds do not substantially deviate from similar funds in other countries. A remuneration arrangement usually consists of a fixed component (management fee) and a variable component (carried interest, performance fee). The terms often consist of clawback provisions.

3. RETAIL FUNDS
3.1. Common structures
This is the same as for alternative investment funds. Retail funds that qualify as UCITS are regulated by the UCITS Directive, as implemented in the FMSA.

3.2. Regulatory framework
This is the same as for alternative investment funds. Retail funds that qualify as UCITS are regulated by the UCITS Directive, as implemented in the FMSA.

3.3. Operational requirements
This is the same as for alternative investment funds. Retail funds that qualify

as UCITS are regulated by the UCITS Directive, as implemented in the FMSA.

3.4. Marketing the fund
This is the same as for alternative investment funds. Retail funds that qualify as UCITS are regulated by the UCITS Directive, as implemented in the FMSA.

3.5. Taxation
This is the same as for alternative investment funds.

3.6. Customary or common terms
This is the same as for alternative investment funds. Retail funds that qualify as UCITS are regulated by the UCITS Directive, as implemented in the FMSA.

4. PROPOSED CHANGES AND DEVELOPMENTS
As indicated above, on 22 July 2013 the AIFMD must be implemented in the Netherlands.

New Zealand

Alasdair McBeth **DLA Phillips Fox**

1. MARKET OVERVIEW

The New Zealand investment funds market is becoming increasingly dominated by KiwiSaver and the New Zealand Superannuation Fund. KiwiSaver is the New Zealand Government mandated voluntary long-term retirement savings scheme which came into operation in 2007. After six years there is now NZ$17.2 billion invested through KiwiSaver schemes and one in every two New Zealanders is a member.

The investment funds market is growing steadily, and total assets under management in New Zealand as at June 2013 were NZ$85.5 billion, an increase of NZ$10 billion from June 2012. KiwiSaver is a big part of this and will continue to be so. As New Zealand is a small market, just under 50 per cent of funds under management is invested in overseas assets.

The New Zealand Superannuation Fund was established by the New Zealand Government in 2003 to help pay for the increased cost of New Zealand's universal superannuation entitlements in the future. It now has more than NZ$22 billion in assets. Of that, NZ$3.4 billion is invested in New Zealand. This includes an exposure to alternate investments including property, forestry, infrastructure, rural property, private equity and other private markets.

Because the New Zealand market is small and the New Zealand Superannuation Fund is so large, it takes the lead in many alternative investments and frequently provides seed or cornerstone capital for alternative investment funds investing in New Zealand assets.

New Zealand is in the middle of the most significant review of, and increase in, financial services regulation the country has ever seen. This saw the introduction of a new regulatory body, the Financial Markets Authority, with extensive powers and responsibilities. In addition to seeing the review and replacement of all of our securities law, New Zealand has recently introduced a new regime for anti-money laundering and counter-financing of terrorism which came into full effect from 1 July 2013.

As a result of these regulatory changes, and also tax changes, non-New Zealand residents can invest into New Zealand funds without New Zealand tax liability as long as those funds meet certain conditions, including restrictions on investment in New Zealand assets. This initiative arose because of the New Zealand Government's wish to increase the level of offshore participation in the investment funds industry. It has also indicated a desire for New Zealand to be a credible international centre for domiciling and servicing investment funds.

New Zealand is a member of IOSCO, OECD and FATF.

2. ALTERNATIVE INVESTMENT FUNDS
2.1. Common structures
General comments
Traditionally, alternative investment funds were structured as limited liability companies, but since the passing of the Limited Partnerships Act 2008, New Zealand is increasingly seeing alternative funds structured as limited partnerships under this Act.

Alternative funds are available for both retail and wholesale clients in New Zealand, but they are predominantly marketed to wholesale clients.

Offers of securities to members of the public (being retail clients) must comply with the Securities Act 1978. Wholesale clients are investors who are not 'members of the public'. Securities are not offered to members of the public if the only persons to whom the securities are offered are:
- relatives or close business associates of the issuer or a director of the issuer;
- recognised professional investors;
- persons who are required to pay a minimum subscription of NZ$500,000; and
- any other person who has been selected other than a member of the public.

In addition to this, many provisions of the Securities Act 1978 do not apply if the only persons who are eligible to invest are experienced in investing and/or experienced in the business to which the offer of securities relates. Fund managers must use a process of verification on this basis.

Neither the Companies Act 1993 nor the Limited Partnerships Act 2008 distinguish between different investment activities. They are all treated the same.

Most alternative investment funds are established as closed-ended funds.

Limited partnerships
Limited partnerships are a relatively new concept in New Zealand, having only been introduced as a legal structure by the Limited Partnerships Act 2008. This legislation adopted what New Zealand considered to be international best practice, including parts of regimes from jurisdictions such as Delaware, California, New South Wales, Jersey, Guernsey and the United Kingdom.

Limited partnerships are not generally used for retail clients because of the additional governance and compliance requirements that are imposed under the Securities Act 1978.

One of the attractions of a limited partnership is that it is familiar to overseas investors. Because of the thin nature of the New Zealand market, alternative investment managers seek to attract overseas investment and structures with which they are familiar are an advantage. Other advantages of the limited partnership are its tax efficiency (see section 2.5.), and its privacy for investors.

To register a limited partnership there must be at least one general partner, at least one limited partner (who cannot be a general partner), and a limited partnership agreement. The identity of the limited partners and the contents of the limited partnership agreement must be notified to the Registrar but are not made publicly available. The identity of the general partner(s) is publicly disclosed on the Limited Partnerships Register. The general partner(s) are responsible for management of the partnership business whereas the limited partners are passive investors and not entitled to participate in management outside certain safe harbour activities. A partnership can be formed with a minimum of one general partner and one limited partner. Once registered, the limited partnership comes into existence and is a legal person in its own right, separate to its partners.

The liability of limited partners is limited to the capital contributions made or committed. The general partner has unlimited joint and several liability for the debt obligations of the partnership. As such, the general partner is usually structured as a company in order to quarantine the unlimited liability to which it is exposed by virtue of its management role.

The interests in a limited partnership are called partnership interests.

Companies

For retail clients, companies incorporated under the Companies Act 1993 are the principal vehicle for alternative investment. New Zealand companies are much like their overseas counterparts in that they have a separate legal personality to their shareholders, directors and employees. New Zealand companies do not have authorised share capital or par value for their shares. Creditor and shareholder protection mechanisms are instead built into requirements for the directors to certify corporate actions. Companies are registered on a public register with the New Zealand Companies Office where details of directors and, in some cases, shareholders and key documents such as the company's constitution are a matter of public record.

New Zealand companies are generally easy and cost effective to incorporate and maintain. Companies are generally unsuitable for open-ended funds as director approval and certifications are required for any redemption or issue of shares.

Shareholder liability is limited to the capital contribution including unpaid calls.

Investor interests in a New Zealand company are called shares.

Investment managers/investment advisers

Investment managers and/or investment advisers for New Zealand alternative investment funds are usually established as limited liability companies under the Companies Act 1993. In a limited partnership fund, the general partner is responsible for investment management and administration. A general partner has unlimited liability for the partnership, and is therefore generally a special purpose company. Investment management is frequently outsourced by the general partner to an investment manager.

If the fund is a company, the company will frequently outsource investment management to another company.

If the fund has been established by the investment manager then there will be an investment management agreement which sets out the obligations of the investment manager and the company or general partner.

2.2. Regulatory framework

Limited partnerships are governed by the Limited Partnerships Act 2008 and the rules of the limited partnership set out in a limited partnership agreement. Companies are governed by the Companies Act 1993 and the company's constitution (if any). If there is no constitution, the default provisions of the Companies Act will apply. Both companies and limited partnerships will be subject to financial reporting obligations under the Financial Reporting Act 1993. In the case of retail offerings, this will include filing of audited financial statements with the Companies Office as a matter of public record.

Retail offerings are also subject to the disclosure and governance requirements imposed by the Securities Act 1978 and associated regulations (see section 2.4.). The governance rules require funds that are not structured as companies to have an independent licensed statutory supervisor (see below). The effect of these rules is that alternative investment funds offered to retail clients are almost exclusively structured as companies rather than limited partnerships to avoid the cost of this independent supervision.

Neither wholesale nor retail alternative investment funds are currently licensed or authorised. However, new financial markets conduct rules that will come into effect over the next two to three years will require all retail funds to be registered on a register of managed investment schemes and regulated by the Financial Markets Authority (see section 4). Funds only offered to wholesale clients will have the option (but not the obligation) to register and become regulated.

Currently, investment managers are required to be registered on the Financial Service Providers Register under the Financial Service Providers (Registration and Dispute Resolution Act) 2008 and, if the funds they manage are offered to retail investors, join one of three government-approved dispute resolution schemes. However, this is merely a registration and dispute resolution regime. There is no licensing, authorisation or direct regulatory oversight of investment managers. This will soon change (see section 4).

There is indirect regulatory oversight of retail offerings and their managers by the Financial Markets Authority. Except where a retail offering is structured as a company, the fund must have an independent licensed statutory supervisor that oversees the manager's performance of its functions and oversees compliance with the terms of the offer. The statutory supervisor is subject to oversight by the Financial Markets Authority. The Financial Markets Authority also has regulatory oversight of the retail offering documents used to market the alternative investment fund and the manager's compliance with securities law requirements (such as the requirement to have an annually audited register of investors).

Registration on the Financial Service Providers Register and joining a dispute resolution scheme can be done online and is relatively straightforward. There are annual regulatory levies and dispute resolution membership fees payable based on funds under management.

Currently there are no local resident or other local qualification requirements. However, new rules are expected to pass into law soon that will require companies to have at least one New Zealand resident director and limited partnerships to have at least one New Zealand resident general partner (see section 4).

There are a number of exemptions from the Securities Act 1978 for retail offerings available based on such factors as territorial scope, the nature of the offer and recognition of offerings made under the regulatory frameworks of other jurisdictions, principally Australia.

2.3. Operational requirements

Other than not investing in investments which are prohibited under New Zealand law (such as cluster munitions), there are no legislative prohibitions on the types of activities or types of investment for either wholesale or retail alternative investment funds. However, the governing documents for the particular funds can impose prohibitions or restrictions. There are also disclosure requirements for retail offers.

Currently, there are no regulations in place that would, for example, require the appointment of a depository or custodian for either a limited partnership or a company for either retail or wholesale offers.

Once the new financial markets conduct rules take effect over the next two to three years, retail funds that are not structured as companies will need to have the assets of the fund held by an independent licenced supervisor or another independent entity that meets prescribed custodian requirements (see section 4). It is unclear whether retail funds structured as companies will be required to hold their assets in independent custody as this question is still being considered by policy makers and the Financial Markets Authority.

For retail offerings, audited financial statements need to be filed with the Companies Office as a matter of public record within a certain period after balance date.

For wholesale offerings, there is generally no requirement for audit or registration of financial statements except in the case of companies that have substantial overseas ownership and exceed certain size thresholds. Companies will generally need to have their financial statements audited unless its shareholders agree by unanimous resolution to dispense with the audit requirement.

Retail offers must be made pursuant to prescribed disclosure documents (see section 2.4.).

Wholesale offers are generally not subject to point of sale or periodic public disclosure requirements, although it is usual for an information memorandum to be provided to investors. However, companies are required to provide their shareholders with an annual report.

The use of side letters with individual investors is not restricted in New Zealand, subject to the obligations on the part of the general partner or company directors to act in the best interests of the limited partnership or company. However, for retail clients general disclosure will be required in the investment statement and prospectus (see section 1.4.).

All funds, regardless of structure, will be subject to domestic anti-money laundering and countering financing of terrorism regulation. This regime was recently upgraded to meet the latest FATF recommendations.

For retail offerings, the Financial Markets Authority expects disclosure documents to make clear disclosure of matters such as the principal or main risks associated with the offer, how the assets of the fund will be valued, the use of leverage in the fund and where the funds will be invested. However, there are no statutory rules imposing any specific restrictions on where funds can be invested or how much leverage can be used within a fund.

Once the new financial markets conduct rules take effect over the next two to three years, retail offerings of funds will need to comply with methodologies prescribed by the Financial Markets Authority as to the valuation of assets and the pricing of interests in the funds (see section 4).

Insider trading and false or misleading activity in respect of listed securities is prohibited.

There are no restrictions on short selling in New Zealand other than those imposed by NZX Limited for listed securities.

2.4. Marketing the fund

The marketing or production of offering or marketing materials is governed by the Securities Act 1978 and Securities Regulations 2009.

There are no restrictions on marketing materials for wholesale offers, except that any such documents must generally comply with the requirements of the Fair Trading Act 1986 (ie, not be misleading or deceptive).

The offering of a fund in New Zealand will be deemed to be the provision of a financial service requiring the entity to be registered on the Financial Service Providers Register.

Providing advice or making a recommendation in respect of a fund will be deemed to be the provision of a financial adviser service under the Financial Advisers Act 2008. For retail clients, generally the person providing the financial advice will need to be an Authorised Financial Adviser with the adviser required to comply with a series of conduct and disclosure obligations.

There are no legislative restrictions on the persons or entities that the fund can be marketed to, provided that relevant compliance requirements are satisfied depending on whether the person being marketed to is a retail or wholesale investor.

An offer of securities must generally only be marketed to retail clients in New Zealand using a registered prospectus and an investment statement. The prospectus must be registered with the Registrar of Companies at the time of the offer, with the investor required to have received the investment statement prior to subscription. There are some exemptions to this.

The prospectus and investment statement must meet prescribed content requirements. These disclosure documents are monitored and regulated by the Financial Markets Authority.

Offers to wholesale clients can be made without using a disclosure document. However, most wholesale offers have a form of information memorandum.

Advertisements including promotional material that indirectly or directly refers to an offer of securities to retail investors (for example, brochures, newsletters, marketing flyers, annual reports, letters to investors and electronic communications and presentations) must comply with the requirements of the Securities Act 1978 and Securities Regulations 2009. The content of advertisements is restricted. In some cases limited information is able to be given prior to an offer being made.

An advertisement may not be distributed to the public unless an appropriate certificate has also been completed at the time of distribution by the directors of the issuer.

Consumer law also governs the content of advertisements aimed at retail investors. This includes the Fair Trading Act 1986 and the Consumer Guarantees Act 1993, with various standards issued by the Advertising Standards Authority.

There are no additional marketing requirements when marketing to public bodies such as government pension funds as these bodies are generally deemed to be wholesale clients.

There are no restrictions on the use of intermediaries provided they are registered on the Financial Service Providers Register. If an intermediary is acting as a broker certain conduct obligations under the Financial Advisers Act 2008 will apply.

2.5. Taxation
Income tax
New Zealand has a highly developed tax system and imposes income tax on a dual basis of source and residence. Specific regimes exist for various entities, including limited partnerships and companies.

Limited partnerships
The tax rules for limited partnerships treat the partners as owning/holding their proportional share of the partnership's assets, liabilities income, losses and obligations for tax purposes. Generally this allows income, expenses, tax credits, gains and losses to flow through to the individual partners in proportion to that individual partner's partnership share. However, limitations on deductions exist (in simple terms, these cannot exceed the partner's basis in the limited partnership) with any excess that cannot be deducted in that income year being carried forward.

If the limited partnership has no New Zealand sourced income, then non-resident investors will have no New Zealand income tax liability in respect of their limited partnership interest.

The attribution of the limited partnership's assets, etc. to the individual partners can complicate transferring limited partnership interests, as this can crystallise a tax liability (for example, arising from the recapture of previously claimed depreciation or profits made on the sale of assets held on revenue account). However, there are carve-outs in some circumstances.

Companies
Companies pay tax at a rate of 28 per cent. This applies to both New Zealand resident companies and non-resident companies that derive New Zealand

sourced income (although there are some exceptions to this).

New Zealand operates an imputation credit system, which is designed to remove double taxation of income that would otherwise occur from income being taxed once at the company level and once at the shareholder level. When a company pays tax it generates imputation credits. Provided the company meets certain requirements, it can attach the imputation credits to the dividends distributed to its shareholders. The definition of a dividend for income tax purposes is extremely broad and includes any transfer of value from a company to its shareholders if referable to its shareholding. There are various exceptions to this broad definition (in particular, the return of paid up share capital).

Resident shareholders are assessed on gross dividends (ie, the dividend paid plus any attached imputation credit) but can use any attached imputation credit to satisfy their own tax liability. The company will be required to deduct resident withholding tax (RWT) on the dividend unless it is fully imputed (or credited).

If a company has non-resident shareholders, it is required to withhold non-resident withholding tax (NRWT) on dividends paid. The rate of NRWT will vary according to the type of dividend, the extent to which it is imputed and the nature of the recipient. In some situations the NRWT rate may be zero per cent.

If a company meets various requirements (including that it has no more than 5 shareholders under a specific count test) it can elect to be taxed under the look-through companies (LTC) regime. In simple terms, the LTC regime adopts a flow through tax treatment such that the shareholders in the LTC are regarded as holding their proportionate share of the assets, liabilities, income and losses of the LTC, and are taxed on that proportionate share (much as a partner in a partnership will be taxed). The regime includes anti avoidance type provisions (designed to stop excessive loss utilisation, and streaming to shareholders). The LTC regime came into effect on 1 April 2011 and replaced the qualifying company and loss attributing qualifying company regimes.

Alternatively, a company that meets various requirements may elect to be taxed as a form of portfolio investment entity (PIE). However, as the PIE regime is designed for widely-held investment vehicles (see section 3.5) it is unlikely to be an option for narrow range alternative investment funds.

Taxation of management company
A management company that is a limited liability company will be subject to company tax at 28 per cent (see above).

Other points
New Zealand tax residents who have investments in overseas companies, investment funds, pensions, and similar may need to consider these investments under the controlled foreign company (CFC) or foreign investment fund (FIF) regimes. The regimes operate to attribute CFC or FIF income to the New Zealand resident taxpayer so as to negate any attempt by the taxpayer to escape New Zealand income tax by accumulating wealth

offshore. Under these regimes, income may be attributed to the New Zealand investors irrespective of whether or not cash income has been received from the investment.

Goods and services tax
Goods and services tax (GST) is imposed under the Goods and Services Tax Act 1985 and is a consumption tax. It is imposed on the supply of goods and services in New Zealand by a registered person in the course of carrying on a taxable activity. Complex rules surround where the supply is made and where a person is regarded as being inside or outside New Zealand. GST can also be imposed on certain imported services under a reverse charge mechanism.

The standard rate of GST is 15 per cent of the value of the good or service being supplied. Certain suppliers are exempt from tax, in particular, unless certain elections are made, suppliers of financial services.

Funds need to be registered for GST, as do managers.

Tax Treaties
New Zealand is a party to a number of tax treaties that enable information sharing with other countries and, in some cases, provide relief from double taxation. At the end of August 2013, New Zealand has:
- double tax agreements with 37 countries (including its main trading partners) in force and another 3 either under negotiation or about to come into force;
- tax information exchange agreements with 10 countries in force and another 10 either under negotiation or about to come into force;
- signed the Multilateral Convention on Mutual Administrative Assistance in Tax Matters, although it has not bought this into effect as yet.

2.6. Customary or common terms
Alternative investment funds are usually closed end funds and have a five year term but do not have a finite life under law. Investors are not usually able to terminate the fund as of right. However, depending on the rules set out in the governing documents, a special majority of investors may be able to direct the manager or the company to terminate the fund.

Before a company or limited partnership can make a distribution to investors (this broad term typically covers any transfer of value from the entity to investors), the directors (in the case of a company) or general partner(s) (in the case of a limited partnership) must certify that the entity will satisfy the 'solvency test'. The solvency test is met if the entity, after payment of the distribution, is able to pay its debts as they become due in the normal course of business and the value of the entity's assets is greater than its liabilities (including contingent liability adjusted for the likelihood of the contingency arising). The requirement for the solvency test to be met before a distribution can be made is a creditor protection mechanism, but can limit the ability of the entity to make distributions, particular if they are leveraged and markets have turned against the investment strategy.

Generally, companies and limited partnerships will be structured as closed ended or relatively closely held vehicles and so there is generally no ability to redeem interests on demand.

There are currently no statutory rules requiring fund managers to invest their own money in the fund or requirements in respect of key individuals. For wholesale funds, key person provisions are usually included as a condition of side letters with individual investors. In respect of retail funds, once the new financial markets conduct regime comes into effect (see section 4), retail fund managers will need to obtain a licence from the Financial Markets Authority. This is likely to involve the fund manager satisfying the Financial Markets Authority that its key personnel are fit and proper, and capable of effectively performing their functions.

Investors may or may not be able to remove the fund manager by resolution, depending on how the governing documents are structured. Even if the manager can be removed by resolution, it may have rights to termination or there may be break fees.

Fees take a number of different formats. There will typically be a management fee paid for the management of the fund plus a performance fee payable where the performance exceeds a certain benchmark. The management fee typically ranges from 50 to 200 basis points depending on the type of fund involved. Performance fees will generally amount to 20 per cent of super-performance subject to beating the benchmark rate of return for the fund.

There are no statutory restrictions on leveraging a New Zealand fund. However, the governing document may impose internal restrictions on borrowing. In some cases borrowing will be completely prohibited, in others borrowing will be allowed for liquidity purposes only and in others borrowing may be allowed up to a certain proportion of the fund's value to enhance returns.

3. RETAIL FUNDS
3.1. Structures
Retail funds in New Zealand are almost exclusively structured as unit trusts and must comply with the Unit Trusts Act 1960. A unit trust fund is defined by the Unit Trusts Act 1960 as any scheme or arrangement, that is established under New Zealand law and that is made for the purpose, or has the effect of providing facilities for the participation, as beneficiaries under a trust, by subscribers or purchasers as members of the public and not as an association, in income and gains (whether in the nature of capital or income) arising from the money, investments and other property that are for the time being subject to the trust. There are a number of exclusions, including an exclusion for superannuation and KiwiSaver schemes. Unit trusts may be closed or open ended. Most unit trusts in New Zealand are open ended.

A unit trust is not a separate legal entity. It is created by a trust deed between the trustee and the manager.

Investors subscribe for units in a unit trust and are called unitholders. The liability of unitholders is limited to the unpaid amount on those units.

New Zealand investment managers and advisers are typically structured as companies due to the attractiveness of their limited liability nature.

3.2. Regulatory framework

The principal legislation for unit trusts is the Unit Trusts Act 1960. A trustee is appointed under the trust deed to hold the assets of the unit trust on trust for the benefit of the unit holders. The trustee is required to exercise due diligence in carrying out its functions under the trust deed. The trustee has the power to delegate its custodial obligations under the trust deed. It is usual for the trustee to delegate its custodial obligation to hold the assets to a custodian. The manager is appointed as administrator and investment manager of the unit trust and is required to use its best endeavours to ensure that the business of the unit trust is carried on in a proper and efficient manner. The manager also has the power to delegate the performance of its obligations under the trust deed.

Aside from general fair trading and conduct requirements, there are no specific rules and regulations that cover investment managers and investment advisers of retail funds in New Zealand. There are no prohibitions, for example, on the manager of a unit trust contracting with an investment manager or investment adviser domiciled outside of New Zealand, and those investment managers and advisers are not required to be licensed or registered in their home jurisdiction.

The Unit Trusts Act 1960 requires unit trusts to have a New Zealand domiciled company as manager and an independent trustee that is licensed under the Securities Trustees and Statutory Supervisors Act 2011.

Retail unit trusts are required to be registered on the register of unit trusts. This can be publicly searched through the Companies Office website. There are currently no licensing requirements for funds themselves. The manager is not required to be licensed but is required to be registered on the Financial Service Providers Register. This will soon change (see section 4).

In addition, the comments on retail offerings contained in section 2.2 will also apply to retail funds.

3.3. Operational requirements

The operational requirements relating to alternative funds set out in section 2.3. also apply to retail funds.

There is currently no regulatory requirement for a custodian, however retail unit trusts are required to have an independent licensed trustee. The independent licensed trustee may (and usually does) appoint a custodian. That custodian is not licensed.

The independent licensed trustee and custodian will both need to be registered on the Financial Services Providers Register. The manager of a retail unit trust is required to post a bond of NZ$40,000 to the Financial Markets Authority before the fund will be registered on the register of unit trusts by the Companies Office.

For retail funds, a copy of the financial statements needs to be registered with the Companies Office and the manager must report to unit holders on an annual basis.

Although there are no restrictions on side letters and there are no public disclosure requirements, they are rare in the retail unit trust business in New

Zealand. The comment under section 2.3 also applies to retail funds.

There are special financial reporting requirements which must be included in the prospectus for a retail unit trust each year. The prospectuses must be rolled over regularly and the date of rollover is linked to the date of the last audited financial statements. There are no special requirements imposed by regulation governing areas such as risk, borrowing restrictions, valuations and pricing the assets held by the fund. However, the Financial Markets Authority, through the use of guidance notes, requires clear and concise risk disclosures. Buying restrictions are normally imposed in a trust deed and are negotiated with the independent licensed trustee at the time the trust deed is agreed. Generally retail funds do not have high borrowing limits. Any borrowing rights must be clearly disclosed in the disclosure documents. Valuation and pricing of assets is agreed between the manager and the licensed trustee and is explained in the disclosure documents.

3.4. Marketing the fund
The regulatory regime governing retail funds is the same as the regulatory regime for alternative investment funds and is covered in section 2.4.

3.5. Taxation
See section 2.5 for general information on New Zealand tax.

Most retail funds established in New Zealand are a form of PIE known as a 'multi-rate PIE'. The PIE tax rules were introduced to remove a number of tax disincentives to investing through managed funds and to encourage investment.

This regime enables an eligible entity to elect to become a multi-rate PIE and pay tax on investment income based on a combination look-through/flow-through basis. In essence, the entity pays tax based on the aggregate of each investor's prescribed investor rate (PIR) applied to that investor's proportionate share of the entity's income. In very general terms, if the investor's PIR is:
(i) zero, then the investor accounts for its proportionate share of the entity's income in its own return; and
(ii) above zero, then the entity has accounted for the tax and the investor doesn't need to return that income. Consequences arise from applying the wrong PIR.

In broad terms, to qualify as a PIE an entity must be widely held and cannot hold more than a 20 per cent interest in any company it invests into. There are some exceptions to this. If the entity fails to meet the requirements to be a PIE, the normal tax rules will apply (generally, it will be taxed as a company (see section 2.5)).

An extension to the PIE regime has recently been introduced to encourage non-resident investors to invest in New Zealand managed funds. Non-resident investors into these 'foreign investment PIEs' pay no New Zealand income tax on income that is sourced from outside New Zealand.

3.6. Customary or common terms

There is no statutory term for a unit trust, although all unit trusts are subject to an 80 year perpetuity period. Unit trust deeds will generally provide for the unit trust to be terminated by either the manager or by a majority of unit holders.

There are generally no restrictions on the number of units able to be issued and redeemed, except as may be required to maintain the tax status of the trust. The Unit Trusts Act 1960 prohibits any restrictions on the transfer of units. The trust deed will typically prescribe circumstances in which the manager can suspend the redemption or issue of units in certain circumstances to protect the liquidity of the unit trust. The trust deed must also state whether the manager has an obligation to buy back units if requested to do so by a unitholder, and the conditions which will apply.

The assets of the unit trust are held separately from the assets of the manager in trust for the benefit of the unit holders. There are no requirements for the manager to invest in the unit trust, or for any key individuals to be involved in the management of the unit trust. Investments by and with related parties are permitted subject to the trust deed and disclosure to unitholders. The trustee can apply to the High Court for certain orders relating to the unit trust, including removal of the manager.

Fees payable to the manager, trustee and other third parties are set by agreement in the trust deed. Generally these are set by reference to a percentage of funds under management. Any limitations on the liability of the trustee and the manager are set out in the trust deed. The legislation prohibits the trust deed from exempting the trustee and manager from liability for breach of trust or negligence.

The trustee's and manager's powers and obligations are prescribed in detail in the trust deed, according to the particular nature of the unit trust and its objectives. There are no investment restrictions in the legislation. The trust deed will typically set out the range of authorised investments for the unit trust and the manager will operate within the parameters of an investment mandate agreed with the trustee.

The Unit Trusts Act 1960 implies into every trust deed a requirement that the trustee shall not act on any direction of the manager to acquire or dispose of any property of the unit trust if, in the trustee's opinion, the proposed acquisition or disposal of any property is not in the interests of the unit holders.

4. PROPOSED CHANGES AND DEVELOPMENTS

On 28 August 2013, the New Zealand Parliament passed the Financial Markets Conduct Act 2013. The Act is a complete re-write of New Zealand Securities laws. It replaces, consolidates and updates all of New Zealand's primary and secondary securities legislation, including the Securities Act 1978 and the Securities Markets Act 1988.

Key aspects of the new legislation as it relates to managed investment funds are as follows:
- The introduction of a unified regime of governance and reporting for all managed investment schemes, replacing the rules in the Unit Trusts Act 1960, the Superannuation Schemes Act 1989 and parts of the KiwiSaver

Act 2006.
- Managed investment schemes will have to be registered on a new schemes register.
- A new licensing regime for managers of managed investment schemes in addition to the existing requirement that supervisors of such schemes be licensed.
- Retail funds that are not structured as companies will need to have the assets of the fund held by the fund's independent supervisor or another independent entity that meets prescribed custodian requirements (although custodians will not be licensed).
- Augmentation of the regulation of market services in the Financial Advisers Act 2008 by providing a parallel licensing regime for 'discretionary investment management services'. This will require investment managers who manage assets on individual account for investors on a class basis (ie, without regard to investors' individual circumstances) to comply with compliance obligations similar to those applying to managed funds, including being licensed.
- Replacement of the current two-tiered retail offer documentation with a new disclosure regime based on the concept of a short, highly prescribed Product Disclosure Statement, supplemented by material placed on a public register and periodic disclosure of information that changes over time such as performance data.
- A shift in focus from criminal to civil liability for breaches of the new legislation, including introducing a new concept of 'accessory' liability and a presumption that certain breaches have caused loss unless the contrary is proven.

The New Zealand Parliament will also shortly pass the Companies and Limited Partnerships Bill into law. This aims to strengthen the rules around companies and limited partnerships upholding New Zealand's reputation as a safe place to do business. Notable changes include the requirement for both companies and limited partnerships to have at least one director or general partner that is New Zealand based, or is a director of a company in a country with which New Zealand has reciprocal arrangements for the enforcement of low-level criminal fines. The Bill also requires that, at registration, a company's ultimate holding company and the dates and places of birth of directors and general partners must be disclosed, and that those details must be kept up to date.

This Bill also looks to strengthen the powers of the Registrar of Companies, allowing better regulation and investigation where a company does not appear to be operating for legitimate purposes.

Criminalisation of breaches of directors' duties is another area which has been addressed, for which a director could be liable for a term of imprisonment not exceeding five years or a fine not exceeding NZ$200,000.

Portugal

Diogo Coutinho de Gouveia, Filipe Santos Barata
& Ana Paula Basílio **Gómez-Acebo & Pombo**

1. MARKET OVERVIEW

Undertakings for collective investment (UCIs) will soon be governed by Decree-Law No 63-A/2013 of 10 May 2013, which shall enter into force on 7 September 2013, and approved the new legal framework of undertakings for collective investment (LUCI). UCIs will until the aforementioned date be therefore subject to the rules laid down in Decree-Law No. 252/2003, of 17 November 2003, as amended (the old LUCI). Unless specified otherwise, reference will be made to the new LUCI, as it will enter into force soon.

UCIs are defined as institutions which have as their object the collective investment of capital raised from investors and whose operations are subject to a risk division principle and the defence of the exclusive interests of the investors. UCIs can be incorporated as:
- investment funds, ie, as a separate patrimony with no legal personality, which is divided into units belonging to the unit holders and is subject to the community property regime set forth in the LUCI. Investment funds are managed by a management company; or
- investment companies (under the form of a public limited company by shares) with legal personality. Investment companies can be either self-managed or managed by a management company.

UCIs may not be held liable in any circumstance by the debts of the unit holders or shareholders, the management entity, custodian, distributors or other UCIs.

UCIs investing in movable assets can be incorporated as securities investment funds (SIFs) or securities investment companies (SIMs). Both SIFs and SIMs can be open-ended or closed-ended. The share capital of open-ended SIMs (SICAVs) is variable, while the share capital of closed-ended SIMs (SICAFs) is fixed. SIFs and SIMs are essentially retail investment funds as opposed to private funds, since they typically will have as their object the investment of capital raised from the investors, by means of a public offer, even though they can be closed-ended or open-ended.

UCIs investing in movable assets include undertakings for collective investment in transferable securities (UCITS) which are UCIs that comply with the investment requirements set forth in the UCITS IV Directive, as amended. These are by excellence retails funds, as they must be open-ended UCIs exclusively targeting at least 100 non-qualified investors.

All other UCIs investing in securities or other financial assets (excluding immovable assets), whether they are open-ended or closed-ended, are included in a new categorisation of UCIs named Alternative Investment

Undertakings (AIUs). AIUs, which also include hedge funds, can also be incorporated as SIFs or SIMs.

Only UCIs set forth in the applicable law may be incorporated. To the best of our knowledge, no SIMs have yet been incorporated in Portugal at the time of this writing.

In May 2013, the value of assets managed by UCITS amounted to EUR 6,800.6 million-EUR 185.2 million (2.5 per cent) more than in April 2012.

The value of assets managed by the former special investment undertakings (which included hedge funds in accordance with the old LUCI) increased to EUR 6,641.1 million in May 2013 and were up 2.5 per cent from the preceding month.

The value of investments of SIFs in Portuguese public debt also increased 1.8 per cent as compared with May 2013 to EUR 400 million. Conversely, the amount of foreign public debt decreased by 2.5 per cent and amounted to EUR 644.7 million in May 2013.

As far as private debt is concerned, the amount invested in foreign bonds (which continues to be the most significant asset in the SIF portfolios – 26.2 per cent) increased by 2.1 per cent in May 2013 as compared to the preceding month and amounted to EUR 3,525.6 million. Investment in domestic bonds was reduced by 3.4 per cent to EUR 533.4 million in the same period.

Investment in shares in domestic companies decreased by 0.7 per cent to EUR 297.7 million and investment in shares of foreign companies was increased by 3.6 per cent to EUR 998.4 million in May 2013.

In May 2013, Espírito Santo Finantial Group securities were the most significant asset in the portfolio of SIFs (13.7 per cent) although there was a decrease of 0.8 per cent as compared with April 2013. In terms of significance, the Espírito Santo Finantial Group securities were followed by Zon Multimédia and Galp securities. Bankia securities were the most significant EU assets in SIF portfolios, and the most important non-EU assets in such portfolios were Tanzania Royalty Exploration securities.

Luxembourg continued to be the leading destination of SIF investments (22.2 per cent of the overall investment), followed by Portugal.

The management companies holding the highest market shares in May 2013 were ESAF (25.2 per cent), Caixagest (23.1 per cent) and BPI Gestão de Activos (14.7 per cent). Fundo Espírito Santo Liquidez managed by ESAF was the largest SIF recording an increase in its asset value of 7.2 per cent to EUR 1.69 billion.

Although the Portuguese financial entities have reached a satisfactory level of maturity in the management and distribution of UCIs, it must be noted that the Portuguese market is rather small compared with other countries where the investment funds industry is more developed.

2. PRIVATE FUNDS – CLOSED-ENDED
2.1. Common structures
UCIs can be open-ended or closed-ended, depending on whether the number of units is variable or fixed. Open-ended and closed-ended UCIs are typically not private funds, since they have as their object the collective investment of

capital raised from investors, usually by means of a public offer. It is deemed that capital is raised from the public whenever: (i) it is raised by targeting undetermined investors or at least 150 non-qualified investors; or (ii) capital raising is preceded by prospection or collecting investment intentions from undetermined investors or promotion by advertising. However, the LUCI now expressly provides that closed-ended UCIs, which are private funds, ie, that are not incorporated by means of a public offer, shall be only subject to the provisions of the LUCI that are adequate to such private funds, taking into account the subscription of such funds is of a particular kind, ie, is a private subscription. In particular, these closed-ended private funds are not subject to rules on the following issues:
- prospectus and key information for investors;
- minimum amount under management; and
- capital dissemination (minimum number of investors).

The aforementioned rules are also not applicable to UCIs whose capital is exclusively raised from qualified investors, which are subject to the operation rules set forth in the LUCI which are deemed adequate as far as qualified investors are concerned. The aforesaid closed-ended private funds and UCIs whose capital is exclusively raised from qualified investors are also not subject to certain rules concerning the authorisation application, the applicable incorporation documents and changes to such documents. This will be pointed out below. Such funds are also not subject to certain particular rules, notably concerning mergers, de-mergers, change of type of fund, liquidation and prohibited transactions, in case of conflict of interests.

However, since there are typically no closed-ended private funds in Portugal, this section will mostly refer to closed-ended UCIs (ie, closed-ended SIFs and SICAFs) pointing out the cases where such rules are not applicable to closed-ended private funds.

Closed-ended SIFs

SIFs are incorporated as investment funds that are separate patrimonies with no legal personality. The minimum net global value of the fund, ie, the aggregate of its assets less the aggregate of its liabilities, should be equal to EUR 1,250,000. The interests of the investors are called units and have no par value; the minimum number of investors is 30, but the public offer must be addressed to at least 150 non-qualified investors (as referred in the preamble of LUCI).

As mentioned above, the minimum number of investors' requirement is not applicable to closed-ended private funds.

SICAFs

SICAFs are incorporated as joint stock companies with a minimum share capital of EUR 300,000 (in case they are self-managed) divided into shares. The net global value of SICAFs ie, the aggregate of its assets less the aggregate of its liabilities should be also no less than EUR 1,250,000. The minimum number of investors of SICAFs is 30, but the public offer must be addressed to at least 150 non-qualified investors (as referred in the preamble of LUCI) and investors become shareholders of the company, being entitled to attend and vote at the shareholders' meetings.

No SICAFs have yet been incorporated in Portugal. Consequently, the rules concerning such entities will be exposed with less detail.

SICAFs are as a general rule subject to the provisions governing closed-ended SIFs and the Portuguese Corporate Code, unless the provisions of the code are inconsistent with this type of companies, its object or the LUCI. The share capital of SICAFs is divided into identical shares with no par value, which, unless otherwise provided, are subject to the rules governing units in closed-ended SIFs.

2.2. Regulatory framework

SICAFs and all management companies of closed-ended UCIs are subject to the supervision of the CMVM.

The most relevant laws and regulations applicable to closed-ended UCIs (closed-ended SIFs and SICAFs) are the following:
- Portuguese Securities Code;
- LUCI;
- CMVM Regulation on UCIs (RUCI), setting forth supplementary rules, notably on the terms of operation of UCIs; investment and risk management; asset management techniques; fees; asset valuation; closed-ended private funds; information requirements; distribution of units and terms of listing and merger, de-merger and liquidation. Reference shall be made to the draft regulation that is available at the time of this writing, which may be subject to amendments. However, it should be noted that until the definitive new RUCI is issued by the CMVM, Regulation No.15/2003 of the CMVM, as amended, shall be applicable;
- CMVM Regulation No.16/2003, of 18 December 2003, as amended, on accounting rules of UCIs.

The incorporation of any type of closed-ended UCI requires a prior authorisation of the CMVM after reviewing and verifying that all applicable legal requirements have been complied with. The main steps that will need to be observed in order to obtain the authorisation of the CMVM of closed-ended UCIs are those specified in section 4.2., as well as the time periods applicable to the authorisation procedure. Section 4.2. also contains a summary of the information to be included in general in the incorporation documents (in particular, the prospectus and the key investor information document (KIID). A prospectus of closed-ended UCIs, as well as a KIID must be drafted in case there is a public offer or the units are listed on a regulated market and the prospectus must comply with the model set forth in EC Regulation No.809/2004 of 29 April 2004.

As referred to above, the rules concerning the prospectus and the KIID are not applicable to close-ended private funds and UCIs whose capital is exclusively raised from qualified investors. The authorisation application does not need to include the grounds for setting out the minimum subscription amount, taking into account notably the complexity, risks and investors targeted by such funds.

Closed-ended UCIs must also set out in the incorporation documents the

following particular terms concerning:
- the conditions and the criteria relating to the initial subscription;
- the possibility of increasing or reducing the number of units to the extent certain conditions are met notably: (i) the approval by means of a resolution of units holders; and (ii) that the subscription and redemption prices are equal to the unit value on the day of financial settlement, subject to confirmation by an opinion issued by the auditor; and
- the possibility of carrying out partial amortisations of the value of the units.

A management regulation is required for all UCIs, including closed-ended SIFs and SICAFs.

Section 4.2. also contains a summary of the information to be included in the management regulation. Notwithstanding, the management regulation of closed-ended UCIs should also include the following information:
- the number of units or shares;
- the term of the UCI (if applicable);
- reference to the request to admission to trading on a regulated market (if any);
- the possibility and terms of extension of the duration of UCIs with a specified term;
- the duties and applicable rules to calling and operation of the meeting of unit holders;
- subscription periods, oversubscription and under-subscription rules, which are applicable to the incorporation of the UCI, as well as to the issue of new units;
- terms and conditions of guarantees of repayment of the capital or income payment given by third parties (if any); and
- terms of liquidation of the UCI.

Section 3.2. describes additional rules concerning information to be included in the authorisation application and the KIID of AIUs (which include closed-ended UCIs).

Management companies of closed-ended SIFs and SICAFs (where they are not self-managed) are SIF management companies or certain credit institutions, notably banks and credit financial institutions whose own funds are no less than EUR 7.5 million. In all cases, management companies are subject to prior authorisation and registration with the CMVM before they can carry out their activity. Management companies are subject in Portugal to the supervision of the CMVM and the Bank of Portugal. They can have their registered office in Portugal or in case they are authorised in an EU member state set up a branch in Portugal or act under the freedom to provide services.

It should be noted that regarding closed-ended UCIs, the following matters are subject to a resolution of the meeting of unit holders:
- overall increase of the management and custody fees;
- significant modification of the investment and income distributions policies and applicable time period for the calculation and disclosure of unit values;
- issuance or cancelation of units, respectively for the purposes of

subscription and redemption, and applicable terms;
- extension of the term of the UCI or modification of the duration of the UCI to an undetermined duration;
- merger, de-merger and change of the type of an UCI;
- replacement of the management entity, except within the same group;
- liquidation of the UCI before the expiration of its term or of UCIs of an undetermined duration; and
- any other matters provided in the applicable laws and management regulation.

The management company of closed-ended UCIs will have to comply with the resolutions taken by the unit holders' meeting on the aforementioned matters.

2.3. Operational requirements
Custodian
All closed-ended UCIs, including SIFs and SICAFs must have a custodian working in conjunction with the management company. Custodians may be credit institutions, notably banks and credit financial institutions, with a patrimony of no less than EUR 7.5 million, which are supervised by the CMVM and the Bank of Portugal. They can have their registered office in Portugal or in an EU member state and a branch in Portugal.

Please see section 4.3. 'Custodian', for details of the duties of custodians.

Reporting obligations
Changes to the incorporation documents of closed-ended UCIs are subject to notification to the CMVM, as described in section 4.3. 'Reporting obligations', for UCIs in general, including closed-ended UCIs.

Closed-ended private funds are not subject to the rules described in such section concerning changes that are qualified as relevant changes. Such changes are subject to the general regime concerning changes to the incorporation documents described in such section. In addition, changes to the incorporation documents of closed-ended UCIs whose capital is exclusively raised from qualified investors are subject to subsequent notice to the CMVM.

As regards periodic reporting, the obligations specified in section 4.3. 'Reporting obligations', apply equally to the management companies of closed-ended UCIs. Please see also section 3.3. which describes some particulars concerning reporting duties of the management companies of AIUs (which include closed-ended UCIs).

Closed-ended private funds and UCIs whose capital is exclusively raised from qualified investors do not have to prepare and disclose semi-annual reports and accounts.

Diversification
Closed-ended UCIs may invest in the assets described in section 3.3. 'Diversification'. Please also see the same section for information concerning the investment limits applicable to closed-ended UCIs.

2.4. Marketing the fund

The marketing of closed-ended UCIs may be carried out by the management company, by the custodian or by a financial intermediary (meaning notably credit institutions, such as banks and investment companies, eg, brokerage companies), duly authorised to execute placement activities of securities in public offers or to receive and transfer orders on behalf of third parties.

Please see section 4.4. for further information on the marketing of closed-ended UCIs.

2.5. Taxation

See section 4.5. for applicable taxation.

2.6. Customary or common terms

In accordance with the LUCI the term of a closed-ended UCIs should not exceed 10 years; the initial term of SIFs would not tend to exceed a couple of years.

The units of closed-ended funds are typically redeemed at the end of the term of the fund.

The management company does not invest its money in the entity and may not acquire shares on behalf of the management company in open-ended SIMs managed by such entities.

The typical rules applicable to the remuneration arrangements of open-ended SIFs are the following:

- The management company may receive a management fee from the retail fund. The fee may be equal to a percentage of the patrimony, but also a percentage of the patrimony and a percentage of the performance subject to certain requirements and whose maximum limit may not exceed 25 per cent of the performance, if positive). Performance fees are becoming much less frequent since the current financial crisis started.
- The custodian may receive a custodian fee.

3. HEDGE FUNDS

3.1. Common structures

The Portuguese hedge funds are now included in the categorisation of UCIs named AIUs, which can be divided in two sub-categories: (i) the Securities AIUs (open-ended or closed-ended) which exclusively invest in securities and other financial assets with exclusion of immovable assets; and (ii) other AIUs (ie, other closed-ended UCIs).

Within this new categorisation, Portuguese hedge funds can be incorporated as follows:

- Alternative investment fund, a separate patrimony with no legal personality; or
- SIMs, which can either be a 'SICAV – alternative investment' (with variable share capital) or a 'SICAF – alternative investment' (with fixed share capital, both corporate structures with legal personality).

For a description of these structures please see section 4.1. in what concerns open-ended Securities AIU. See section 2.1. for particulars concerning closed-ended AIUs (including hedge funds).

No corporate SIMs have been incorporated in Portugal at the time of writing.

3.2. Regulatory framework

Hedge funds (if they are companies) and the management companies of hedge funds are subject to the supervision of the CMVM.

The most relevant laws and regulations applicable to hedge funds and their management companies are the following:
- Portuguese Securities Code;
- LUCI;
- RUCI;
- CMVM Regulation No.16/2003, of 18 December 2003, as amended on accounting rules of UCIs.

The incorporation of a hedge fund requires a prior authorisation of the CMVM after reviewing and verifying that all applicable legal requirements have been complied with.

See sections 4.2. in what concerns the incorporation documents of AIUs. See also section 2.1. for such particulars concerning closed-ended AIUs.

An AIU shall unequivocally identify the respective investment policy. The incorporation documents of the AIU shall notably identify:
- the type of assets which may be included in its portfolio;
- the rules of operation (such as, subscription, redemption or reimbursement terms);
- the investment limits, ensuring a portfolio diversification in accordance with the risk diversification principle, taking into account the net global value of the AIU: (i) by asset or entity; (ii) of loan transactions and repo of financial instruments; (iii) of derivatives transactions; and (iv) short selling over financial instruments;
- the maximum limits of indebtedness.

In addition, the authorisation application of an AIU will include the following information:
- information evidencing that the management entity is capable of managing the AIU, taking into account its investment policy, its purposes, the management techniques used and the type of assets and markets in which the hedge fund will invest and the existing consultants, if applicable; and
- grounds for setting out the minimum subscription amount, taking into account notably the complexity, risks and targeted investors by the hedge fund.

The CMVM may refuse the authorisation to the trading of AIUs targeting specific investors to the extent the sufficient conditions to their adequate protection (in terms of complexity, liquidity of the assets and risk of the AIUs) are not met. Furthermore, the CMVM may refuse to grant the authorisation to closed-ended AIUs whenever the units of other closed-ended AIU managed by the same management entity are not fully subscribed.

The CMVM may request from the relevant applicants clarification, additional information or suggest amendments to the above referred documents.

Open-ended hedge funds may set forth a specific time period for the subscription and redemption of the units/shares.

In addition, the incorporation documents of AIUs and therefore hedge funds must also include the relevant KIID containing clear and objective information, in order to permit investors to understand the risks of the investment allowing them to take duly informed investment decisions and shall include information regarding the objectives and policy of the hedge fund, notably the main type of eligible assets, the limits of the investment, the maximum limits of indebtedness, as set forth in a schedule to the RUCI.

Section 4.2. specifies the main subsequent steps that will need to be observed in order to obtain the authorisation of the CMVM of UCIs in general, including AIUs that are hedge funds, and applicable time periods to the authorisation process.

Management companies of open-ended AIUs and SICAVs – alternative investment (when they are not self-managed) are SIF management companies. Management companies of closed-ended AIUs (including SICAFs – alternative investment when they are not self-managed) are SIF management companies or certain credit institutions (eg, banks and credit financial institutions). In all events, management companies are subject to prior authorisation and registration with the CMVM before they can carry out their activity. They must show that they are particularly capable of managing this particular sort of UCI, with regard to investment policy, management strategy and past experience.

3.3. Operational requirements
Custodian
All AIUs, including hedge funds, must have a custodian working in conjunction with the management company. Custodians may be credit institutions, notably banks and credit financial institutions, with a patrimony of no less than EUR 7.5 million, which are supervised by the CMVM and the Bank of Portugal. They can have their registered office in Portugal or in an EU member state and a branch in Portugal.

A description of the duties of the custodians is made in section 4.3. 'Custodian'.

Reporting obligations
Any changes to the incorporation documents of UCIs are subject to notification to the CMVM as described in section 4.3. 'Reporting obligations' for UCIs (including hedge funds).

As regards periodic reporting, the obligations specified in section 4.3. 'Reporting obligations' apply equally to the management companies of hedge funds.

In addition, the value of the units is calculated and disclosed at least monthly for open-ended Securities AIUs and monthly for closed-ended UCIs, with reference to the last day of the previous month, unless the CMVM authorises, in the case of closed-ended AIUSs which are not Securities AIU, that such calculation and disclosure be made less frequently up to a six month limit.

The managing entity shall adequately inform the unit holders at least every year of the evolution of the risk and valorisation of the AIUs, including a description of any relevant facts with impact on the value of the patrimony of the AIUs.

Diversification
Securities AIUs (open-ended or closed-ended) exclusively invest in securities and other financial assets with exclusion of immovable assets.

An AIU, which is not a Securities AIU, shall invest a minimum of 30 per cent of the respective global net value in non financial assets, as long as they are long lasting assets and have a determinable value and a maximum of 25 per cent of the respective global net value in real estate assets.

As referred above, an AIU shall unequivocally identify the respective investment policy and its incorporation documents of the AIU shall identity the type of assets which are included in its portfolio, the investment limits and the maximum limits of indebtedness.

CMVM may refuse certain assets for the incorporation of the AIU whenever the investor's protection and the regular operation of the market so determines, notably due to lack of transparency of the market where they are traded, the valorisation of the assets or of the units of the AIU.

4. RETAIL FUNDS
4.1. Common structures
SIFs
SIFs are incorporated as investment funds that are separate patrimonies with no legal personality. The minimum net global value of the fund, ie, the aggregate value of its assets less the aggregate of the liabilities of the fund should be equal to EUR 1,250,000. The interests of the investors are called units and have no par value; the minimum number of investors must be 100 in the case of UCITS (which must be open-ended investment funds) and 30 in the case of open-ended or closed-ended AIUs.

SIMs
SIMs are incorporated as joint stock companies with a minimum share capital of EUR 300,000 (in case they are self-managed) divided into shares. The net global value of SIMs must be at least equal to EUR 1,250,000. The minimum number of investors of SICAVs is 100 and of SICAFs is 30 (even if the public offer has to be addressed to 150 investors), and investors become shareholders of the company, being entitled to attend and vote at the shareholders' meetings.

SIFs and SIMs, can be open-ended or closed-ended, Even though they can be retail investment funds or companies, please see section 2 for information on closed-ended SIFs and closed-ended SIMs (SICAFs). Please also see section

3, which describes the particular terms applicable to retail funds that are AIUs, notably hedge funds. Consequently, this section shall mostly concern openended SIFs, and open-ended SIMs (SICAVs).

No SIMs have yet been incorporated in Portugal. Consequently, the rules concerning such entities will be exposed with less detail.

SICAVs are as a general rule subject to the provisions governing openended SIFs and the Portuguese Corporate Code unless the provisions of the code are inconsistent with this type of company, its object and the LUCI. The share capital of SICAVs is divided into identical nominative shares with no par value, which unless otherwise provided are subject to the rules governing units in open-ended SIFs.

4.2. Regulatory framework

All retail funds (if they are companies) and the management companies of retail funds are subject to the supervision of the CMVM.

The most relevant laws and regulations applicable to retail funds and their management companies are the following:
- Portuguese Securities Code;
- LUCI;
- RUCI;
- CMVM Regulation No.16/2003 of 18 December 2003, on accounting rules of UCIs.

The incorporation of any type of retail fund requires a prior authorisation of the CMVM after reviewing and verifying that all applicable legal requirements have been complied with. The main steps that will need to be observed in order to obtain the authorisation of the CMVM are the following:
a) Preparing an authorisation application by the management entity that must include at least the following information: (i) drafts of the incorporation documents; (ii) drafts of the agreements to be entered into with the custodian and with the distributors; (iii) drafts of any other agreements to be executed with service providers; (iv) documents evidencing that all entities involved in the operation of the UCI have accepted to perform their duties, in accordance with the aforementioned draft contracts; and (v) information on the suitability and experience of the directors of SIMs;

The incorporation documents include notably the following information:
- The management regulation contains the name of the UCI and the identification particulars (such as the name and registered office) of the management entity, the custodian, the subcontracted entities, and sets out: (i) their functions; (ii) the rights and obligations of the unit holders and of the management entity and custodian; (iii) the applicable terms as to the replacement of such entities; (iv) investment policies and objectives and assets that may be part of the investment portfolio and indebtedness levels; (v) the applicable income distribution policy; (vi) shareholder's voting rights policy with respect to the shares held by the UCI; (vii) applicable costs and fees; (viii) subscription and redemption unit values and frequency of disclosure of such values; (ix) terms and

means of payment, particularly in case of subscription and redemption; (x) the identification of the units, specifying different classes and voting rights, if applicable, and means of distribution; (xi) minimum subscription amounts; (xii) the maximum time periods for payment of redemption requests; (xiii) the initial value of units for incorporation purposes; (xiv) applicable terms as to the transfer of units; (xv) applicable terms as to the suspension of redemption and subscription; (xvi) applicable rules as to the calculation of the underlying assets and of the units; (xvii) a summary of the operations and transmission of orders policies, etc. In the case of management regulations of SIMs that are not self-managed, the management regulation also specifies the functions of such SIM and its coordination with the management entity.

- The prospectus (which comprises the information included in the management regulation) contains also amongst other information: (a) other information on the management company, including: (i) identification of the members of its corporate bodies and other functions performed by such members in other entities; (ii) information concerning the existence of a group including the management entity and other entities (custodian, distributors, consultants and other service providers and identification of the group; (iii) identification of other UCIs managed by the management company; and (iv) contact person for clarifying doubts; (b) information on other entities, in particular: (i) identification of the investment consultants and key terms of the applicable services agreement that might interest the participants; and (ii) identification of the auditor and the supervisory authority of the UCI; (c) data on disclosure of information, notably: (i) places, means and frequency of disclosure of the unit value and of the UCI's portfolio; and (ii) places and means of obtaining the reports and accounts, the auditor report and other documents concerning the UCI; and other information notably (d) historical evolution of the UCI results; (e) targeted investor profile; (f) information on the applicable tax regime.
- The key investor information document (KIID) includes appropriate and updated information about the essential characteristics of the UCI concerned, so that investors are able to understand the nature and the risks of the investment product that is being offered to them and, consequently, to take investment decisions on an informed basis. In particular, the KIID shall provide information on the following essential elements in respect of the UCI concerned:
  a) identification of the UCI;
  b) a short description of its investment objectives and investment policy;
  c) past-performance presentation or, where relevant, performance scenarios;
  d) costs and associated charges; and
  e) risk/reward profile of the investment, including appropriate guidance and warnings in relation to the risks associated with investment in the relevant UCI.

The detailed content of the KIID concerning UCITS is provided in the EU Regulation No.583/2010, of 1 July 2010 and in the RUCI.
- In addition, incorporation documents of SIMs must include: (a) its programme of activity setting out, inter alia, its organisational structure, as well as contemplated human, technical and material resources; (b) a list of the close links existing between the SIM and other natural or legal persons; (c) a statement made by the applicants with grounds certifying that the members of the management body meet the applicable independence requirements; (d) the notification made to the Bank of Portugal of the appointed management company of SIMs (in case they are not self-managed); and (e) an agreement be executed between the SIM and their management company which must be approved by the shareholders' meeting, in the case of SIMs that are not self-managed.

Section 3.2. describes the particular rules concerning incorporation documents of AIUs, including hedge funds, open-ended UCIs that are not UCITS, as well as closed-ended UCIs that are retail funds. Section 2.2. describes three particular rules concerning the incorporation documents of closed-ended funds.

b) filing of the authorisation application (which is signed by the management company, if any) with the CMVM;
c) the approval of the prospectus (which is required in case there is a public offer) is registered with the CMVM;
d) granting of the prior authorisation by the CMVM;
e) subscription of the units or shares within 12 months in the case of open-ended UCIs and 6 months in the case of closed-ended UCIs as of the notification of authorisation of the fund;
f) execution of the deed of incorporation if the retail fund is a company. The signature of the signatories of the incorporation deed must be recognised by a notary or by a person with similar powers to that effect, such as a lawyer;
g) registration with the commercial registry in the case of a company; and
h) registration with the CMVM of SIMs for the purposes of carrying out their activities, notably as financial intermediaries.

The CMVM shall notify the applicants of its decision within a 20-day time period (or 30-day period in case of self-managed SIMs) as of the date a complete application was received by the entity. This time period will be suspended for a maximum period of 10 days, in case the CMVM notifies the applicants that there are grounds for refusal, and notably should it notify them to provide outstanding documents or information within the aforementioned period. If the CMVM does not issue a decision within the 20 or 30-day period, the authorisation will be deemed as granted (implied approval).

Management companies of open-ended UCIs (UCITS and open-ended AIUs) and SICAVs (when they are not self-managed) are SIF management companies. In all cases, management companies are subject to prior authorisation and registration with the CMVM before they can carry out their activity. Management companies are subject in Portugal to the supervision of the CMVM and the Bank of Portugal. They can have their registered office in Portugal or in case they are authorised in an EU member state set up a branch in Portugal or act under the freedom to provide services.

4.3. Operational requirements
Custodian
All retail funds must have a custodian working in conjunction with the management company. The custodians may be credit institutions, notably banks and credit financial institutions, with a patrimony of no less than EUR 7.5 million, which are supervised by the CMVM and the Bank of Portugal. They can have their registered office in Portugal or in an EU member state and a branch in Portugal.

Amongst others, the duties of the custodians include the following:
- comply with the applicable law and regulations, with the incorporation documents of the UCI and with the agreements executed in connection with the UCI;
- custody of the assets of the UCI;
- deposit or registration of the assets of the UCI;
- execute the instructions of the management company, unless they are inconsistent with the applicable law or the incorporation documents;
- ensure that consideration is given in transactions concerning the assets of the UCI within time periods that are in accordance with market practice, and that such transactions comply with the applicable laws, regulations and incorporation documents of the UCI;
- promote the payment to the unit holders or shareholders of all income arising out of such units or shares and reimbursement or redemption values or liquidation proceeds;
- make and keep updated a chronological record of all transactions carried out for the UCI;
- carry out a monthly inventory of the assets and of the liabilities of the UCI;
- control and supervise the compliance, notably by the management company or the management of SIMs, of all laws and regulations and the incorporation documents of the UCI in the interest of the unit holders or shareholders;
- send annually to the CMVM a report on the supervision carried out during such year; and
- immediately inform the management company of SIMs that are not self-managed of changes of members of the management body.

Reporting obligations
Changes to the incorporation documents of UCIs are, as a general rule, subject to prior notification to the CMVM and shall be effective if the CMVM does not oppose to the notified amendments within a time period of 15 days as of the notice or an express decision of non-opposition is notified by the CMVM. However, certain amendments are subject to different rules as follows:

- Minor changes that require only notification to the CMVM to become immediately effectively, such as changes to the name, registered office and contact details of the management entity, the custodian, the distributor, the auditor or subcontracted entities; identification of the members of the corporate bodies of the management entity, change of the holders of the majority of the share capital of such entity or amendments concerning the control or entities of the same group of such management entity; the addition of new distributors; the reduction of the overall amount of several fees or setting out more favourable terms on such fees and other minor amendments, such as updating quantitative data or the adaptation to legal amendments;
- Relevant changes, ie, those resulting from: (i) a significant change of the investment or income distribution policies; or (ii) an overall increase of the management and custody fees and other fees in the case of UCIs. These amendments are only effective 40 days after the end of the 15-day time period given to the CMVM to oppose such amendments has elapsed or an express decision of non-opposition is notified by the CMVM;
- Change of the custodian or of the management entity, which are subject to approval of the CMVM.

As regards the periodic reporting obligations, the management companies of retail funds or SIMs are notably obliged to:

a) prepare an annual report. The annual report must be disclosed to the public and delivered to the CMVM within a period of four months as of the end of the period of time to which it refers;
b) prepare a semi-annual report. The semi-annual report must be disclosed to the public and delivered to the CMVM within a period of two months as of the end of the period of time to which it refers;
c) monthly disclose to the public and deliver to the CMVM the detailed composition of the portfolio of each UCI, the respective global net value, off-balance sheet liabilities and the number of units in circulation;
d) communicate to the CMVM any purchase or disposal of shares or securities giving the right to acquire shares carried out by directors of the management bodies or officers in charge of taking investment decisions of UCIs, which must be notified by such persons to the management entity;
e) send annually to the CMVM a report containing true and appropriate information on the type of derivatives financial instruments used, the underlying risks, quantitative limits and the elected risk assessment processes in relation to such derivative transactions and periodically report on execution of derivative transactions and compliance of rules governing exposure to derivatives;
f) calculate and disclose to the public on every business day the value of the units of UCITS; and
g) report on the number of voting rights attached to shares which are part of the UCI's portfolio, whenever such rights correspond to more than 2 per cent of the voting rights in a given issuer, including information with grounds justifying the exercise of such voting rights in a given manner.

The annual and semi-annual report referred to in (a) and (b) above must be disclosed to investors and unit holders, at no cost, in a durable medium other than paper, by means of a website or in paper format upon request of the investor. The financial information contained in the said reports must be subject to an auditing report issued by an auditor registered with the CMVM. Auditors also have the duty to promptly give notice to the CMVM of certain events relating to UCIs that they become aware during the performance of their duties, notably situations that may constitute an infringement to the applicable rules and regulations.

See section 3.3., 'Operational requirements – Reporting' for particulars applicable to AIUs.

Diversification and liquidity
As a general rule, UCITS may invest in the following liquid assets:
a) transferable securities and money market instruments that are:
   i. admitted to or dealt in on a regulated market in a EU member state, as defined in Article 4(1)(14) of Directive 2004/39/EC or, which operates regularly and is recognised and open to the public;
   ii. admitted to official listing on a stock exchange in a third country or dealt in on another regulated market in a third country which operates regularly and is recognised and open to the public provided that the choice of stock exchange or market has been approved by the CMVM or is provided in the incorporation documents;
b) recently issued transferable securities, provided that the terms of issue include an undertaking that an application will be made for admission to official listing on any of the stock exchange or other regulated market referred in the preceding sub-paragraphs (a) (i) and (ii) which operates regularly and is recognised and open to the public; and that the such admission is obtained within a year of issue;
c) units of UCITS authorised according to the LUCI;
d) units of other collective investment undertakings, whether or not established in a member state, provided that: (i) such other collective investment undertakings are authorised under such laws; and (ii) subject to a series of other requirements that, in general, aim to ensure that the level of protection for unit-holders in such other collective investment undertakings is equivalent to that provided for unit-holders in a UCITS; and that such UCIs may not invest more than 10 per cent of its assets in units of other UCIs;
e) deposits with credit institutions which are repayable on demand or maturing in no more than 12 months and that may be early withdrawn, provided that the credit institution has its registered office in a member state, or in a third country, provided in this event that it is subject to prudential rules that are deemed as equivalent to those laid down in Community law;
f) financial derivative instruments dealt in on a regulated market referred to in subparagraphs (a)(i) and (ii) or financial derivative instruments that are not dealt on regulated markets or multilateral negotiation systems,

provided that: (i) the underlying assets of the derivative consists of assets listed in these sub-paragraphs (a) to (g) or have at least one of such assets characteristics or that are financial indices, interest rates, foreign exchange rates or currencies, in which the UCITS may invest according to its incorporation documents; (ii) the counterparties to such derivative transactions are institutions subject to prudential supervision, in accordance with the Community law rules and criteria or subject to equivalent prudential supervision rules; and (iii) such derivatives are subject to reliable and verifiable valuation on a daily basis and can be sold, liquidated or closed at any time at their fair value at the UCITS' initiative; and

g) money market instruments other than those dealt on the regulated markets referred in subparagraphs (a)(i) and (ii) above, provided that its issuance or the issuer is subject to rules protecting investors or savings and provided that (i) they comply with certain precise rules either concerning its maturity or compliance with periodical profitability adjustments or a certain risk profile; (ii) they are liquid, in accordance with certain rules and their value may be accurately determined in any moment in time, in accordance with accurate valuation systems subject to certain specific requirements; (iii) adequate information on such instruments is available; and (iv) they are freely transferable.

In addition UCITS must comply with the following main general diversification rules and investment limits:

a) as a general rule, UCITS may not: (i) invest more than 10 per cent of its assets in transferable securities or money market instruments other than those referred to in sub-paragraphs (a) to (g) above; or (ii) acquire either precious metals or certificates representing them.
b) UCITS may also not acquire more than 10 per cent of shares with no voting rights, money market instruments or debt securities issued by the same issuer, as well as 25 per cent of the units issued by the same UCITS or Securities AIUs;
c) as a general rule, the investment in the securities and money market instruments issued by the same entity may not be higher than 10 per cent of the total net value of the UCI;
d) the investment in deposits held at the same entity may not be higher than 20 per cent of the total net value of the UCI;
e) in case both the securities and money market instruments issued by the same entity represent more than 5 per cent of the total net value of the UCITS, they may not be higher than 40 per cent of that value;
f) the investment in the shares/units in the UCIs referred to in point (d) of the preceding list of eligible assets may not exceed 30 per cent of the global net value of the UCITS;
g) the value of investment in securities, money market instruments, deposits or exposure to money market instruments traded outside regulated markets or system of multilateral negotiation may not be higher than 20 per cent of the net asset value of UCITS;
h) the investment in the securities and money market instruments issued

by entities that are part of the same group may not be higher than 20 per cent of the total net value of the UCITS.

The management entities may not carry out (including together with closed related entities) transactions on behalf of the aggregate of the UCIs managed by such entity that may give them a significant influence over any entity and, in particular, it may not acquire, on behalf of such UCIs, shares corresponding to more than 20 per cent of the voting rights in a given entity or enabling it to exercise a significant influence over the management of such entity. In addition, the aggregate of the UCITS and Securities AIUS managed by the same entity may not hold more than: (a) 20 per cent of shares with no voting rights in the same issuer; (b) 50 per cent of bonds issues by the same issuer or 60 per cent of the units of a given UCITS or Securities AIU.

In addition, the management entities may not, on behalf of the UCITS:
a) create liens or encumbrances, in any manner, over the assets, except in case of permitted financing operations or management instruments and techniques;
b) acquire any assets subject to real securities, seizures or interim measures;
c) short sell securities; money market instruments or certain other instruments; or
d) grant credit or give guarantees.

As a general rule, the management entity may also not carry out operations that may give rise to a conflict of interest (such as, the acquisition or disposal of assets), notably with the: (i) management entity; (ii) promoters of SIMs; (iii) SIMs that are not self-managed; (iv) entities holding more than 10 per cent of the capital or voting rights of SIMs that are not self-managed or the management company; (v) entities controlling or controlled or that are part of the same group of the management entity; (vi) entities in which the management company or an entity controlling or controlled or that is part of the same group of the management entity holds at least 20 per cent of the share capital or voting rights; (vii) the custodian or entities linked to the custodian by any of the manners referred in (iv) to (vi) above; (viii) the members of the management bodies of any of the aforementioned entities; and (ix) staff and other personnel of any of the aforementioned entities (except of the custodian) and that may give rise to a conflict of interest between the several UCIs managed by the management entity. The aforementioned rule is subject to exceptions, but, in any case, the value of assets held by the UCI that are issued or guaranteed by any of the entities listed in (i) up to (viii) of the preceding paragraph may not exceed 20 per cent of the net global value of the UCI.

4.4. Marketing the fund

The marketing of all UCIs may be carried out by the management company, by the custodian or by a financial intermediary (meaning notably credit institutions, such as banks and investment companies, eg, brokerage companies), duly authorised to execute placement activities of securities in public offers or to receive and transfer orders on behalf of third parties. Other entities may also be authorised by the CMVM to distribute UCIs provided that they have the adequate technical, human, material resources and expertise.

It must be noted that under the new LUCI marketing means the activity targeting investors, for the purposes of disclosing or offering the subscription of units or shares in UCIs, by means of any publicity or means of communication.

The KIID prospectus must be made available to any interested clients and investors in good time before the proposed subscription of any units or shares in UCIs.

The prospectus must be delivered together with the KIID to investors of open-ended UCIs (or close-ended UCIs in case of public offer) at no cost, in a durable medium other than paper, by means of a website or in paper format upon request of the investor. The disclosed version of the prospectus and KIID must be updated. Where the key investor information and the prospectus are to be provided in a durable medium other than paper or by means of a website, additional safety measures are provided in Regulation No.583/2010, of 1 July 2010, for investor protection reasons

Units or shares are subscribed and their redemption value is paid in accordance with the terms set out in the incorporation documents. The subscription and redemption value of units/shares is the value disclosed following the request. In the case of open-ended UCIs, subscriptions and redemptions are carried out with the same regularity as the disclosure of the unit's value (ie, typically every business day in case of UCITS, or at least monthly in the case of open-ended AIUs), regardless of the date of the respective request. Subscription, redemption and transfer fees may only be charged to the unit holders/shareholders in accordance with the terms and calculation methods set out in the incorporation documents.

The distributors of the units/shares must make available to the investors the information that must be provided to them by the management company for such purposes. All advertising materials relating to public offers of UCIs must be approved by the CMVM and refer to the existence of the prospectus and the KIID, the places where they can be obtained and the language in which they are written.

There are no particular restrictions concerning the distribution of retail funds to certain types of investors, once such funds are authorised by the CMVM.

4.5. Taxation
4.5.1. Taxation of UCIs
Taxation of SIFs

Taxation of income derived by SIFs varies according to the type and source of income. Capital gains, from both domestic and foreign sources, are subject to autonomous taxation at 25 per cent (as if they were derived by Portuguese-resident individuals) on the positive difference between capital gains and capital losses of the year.

Any other income derived from domestic sources, apart from capital gains, which is subject to withholding tax when derived by Portuguese resident individuals, is taxed by means of withholding at the same rates and other regime applicable to Portuguese resident individuals, or if tax, despite being due, is not withheld by the relevant entity, at the same rates that apply for withholding purposes. Where such income is not subject to withholding tax, taxation at 25 per cent on the net amount received each year applies.

Income other than capital gains derived from foreign sources is taxed autonomously at 20 per cent (income from treasury bonds, dividends or investment funds) or 25 per cent (remaining cases) on the net amount received each year. The SIF is generally entitled to deduct any foreign tax paid from tax due in Portugal.

4.5.2. Taxation of investors
Taxation applicable to investors in Portuguese UCIs will be different depending on whether the investor is an individual or a company and whether the same is resident in Portugal or abroad.

Individual investors resident in Portugal
Investors in UCIs who are considered Portuguese tax residents, according to the Portuguese domestic tax rules and the applicable tax treaties, are taxed for personal income tax purposes on income or capital gains derived from their investment in the relevant UCIs.

Portuguese resident individuals who invest in UCIs outside the scope of an agricultural, commercial or industrial activity are exempt from personal income tax on any income derived from units held in those UCIs (including income from the transfer or reimbursement of the units). Portuguese resident investors may, nonetheless, add such income to their global income of the year, in which case progressive tax rates up to 56.5 per cent will apply, depending on the global income of the investor. In the latter case, the investor is entitled to deduct from its taxable basis 50 per cent of the income derived by the UCIs from Portuguese resident companies and companies resident in other member states who meet the requirements of the Parent-Subsidiary Directive. On the other hand, tax paid by the UCI shall be considered a payment on account, being creditable against the investor tax liability.

The positive difference between capital gains and capital losses of the year derived from the sale of units in UCIs is autonomously taxed at 25 per cent. Portuguese resident investors may, nonetheless, add such income to their global income of the year, in which case progressive tax rates up to 56.5 per cent will apply, depending on the global income of the investor.

Income derived from units held in Portuguese UCIs by Portuguese resident individuals within an agricultural, commercial or industrial activity is not subject to withholding tax and shall be declared by the recipient as income under the general terms for PIT purposes. The relevant tax paid by the UCI shall be considered a payment on account, being creditable against the investor tax liability.

Individual investor's resident abroad
Under the PIT Code, individuals resident abroad are generally subject to Portuguese tax on any income derived from Portuguese sources. Depending

on the state of residence of the individual investor, international taxation rules or tax treaties may apply.

Income derived from units held in Portuguese UCIs by non-resident individual investors is exempt from PIT.

Corporate investors resident in Portugal
Generally speaking, companies are subject to corporate tax and to the Corporate Income Tax Code (CIT Code), approved by Decree-Law No.442-B/88 of 30 November, as amended. Portuguese companies investing in UCIs shall include any income or gain derived from the investment in their CIT taxable base, under the general terms of the domestic tax law.

Income derived from units held in Portuguese UCIs by companies resident in Portugal (or by a permanent establishment of a non-resident company) is not subject to withholding tax and shall be declared by the recipient as income under the general terms for CIT purposes. The relevant tax due or withheld shall be considered a payment on account.

Corporate investors' resident abroad
Portuguese taxation of non-resident companies differs depending on whether or not such companies have a permanent establishment in Portugal. In the former case, the general Portuguese CIT rules will apply. If the company is non-resident and does not have a permanent establishment in Portugal, it will only be subject to Portuguese taxation on any income derived from Portuguese sources.

Income derived from units held in Portuguese UCIs by non-resident corporate investors is exempt from tax for CIT purposes, as long as the income is not attributable to a permanent establishment in Portugal of the non-resident corporate entity.

4.6. Customary or common terms
The duration of an open-ended SIF is normally indefinite, save for guaranteed SIFs, which are normally wound up and liquidated after a fixed period of time.

Typically there are no duration restrictions as to the redemption of units of open-ended SIFs.

The management company does not invest its money in the entity and may not acquire shares on behalf of the management company in open-ended SIMs managed by such entities.

The typical rules applicable to the remuneration arrangements of open-ended SIFs are the following:
- The management company may receive a management fee from the retail fund. The fee may be equal to a percentage of the patrimony, but also a percentage of the patrimony and a percentage of the performance subject to certain requirements and whose maximum limit may not exceed 25 per cent of the performance, if positive. Performance fees are becoming much less frequent since the current financial crisis started.
- The custodian may receive a custodian fee.

See section 2 and section 3 for particulars applicable to each type of entity.

5. PROPOSED CHANGES AND DEVELOPMENTS
The implementation of UCITS IV Directive came with great expectation for the players in the Portuguese market, which is currently adapting to the new regulatory environment. UCIs will, for instance, now have to prepare and submit to the approval of the CMVM the standardised KIID. Further developments following the adoption of the Alternative Investment Funds Managers Directive are awaited by the market players, notably the European passport for European managers of alternative investment funds.

Singapore

Bill Jamieson, Amit Dhume & Manisha Rai
Colin Ng & Partners LLP

1. MARKET OVERVIEW

The Singapore fund management market is considered to be one of the leading asset management locations in Asia, with total assets under management of around S$1.6 trillion at the end of 2012. The Singapore funds market is constantly maturing in response to the growing demand for investments throughout the Asia-Pacific region.

There are currently over 500 participants in the asset management industry in Singapore operating under various licences/registration regimes.

Following the recent steps taken by Europe and the United States against tax evasion, Singapore has implemented international standards on fighting tax crimes. Thus, with effect from 1 July 2013, Singapore has criminalised the laundering of proceeds from serious tax offences. Singapore is also extending its Exchange of Information framework, in accordance with internationally agreed standards, to all of its existing tax agreement partners; signing the Convention on Mutual Administrative Assistance in Tax Matters; and allowing the Inland Revenue Authority of Singapore (IRAS) to obtain bank and trust information from financial institutions without the need for a court order.

In Singapore, the primary legislation regulating the investment funds industry is the Securities and Futures Act (Chapter 289) (SFA). The Monetary Authority of Singapore (MAS), which is Singapore's central bank, regulates all financial institutions in Singapore, including asset managers.

2. ALTERNATIVE INVESTMENT FUNDS

There is no separate regime for alternative investment funds in Singapore similar to the Alternative Investment Fund Managers Directive, however certain funds, for example money market funds, hedge funds, capital guaranteed funds, index funds, etc. are subject to additional requirements under the Code on Collective Investment Schemes issued by the MAS (CIS Code).

2.1. Common structures

While the structure of the fund would depend on the type of underlying investments and the nature of investors, etc., some common fund structures are mentioned below.

Private limited companies
There are no specific corporate structures available in Singapore which

are geared towards investment funds. A normal private limited company incorporated in Singapore can be used to establish a fund. Being a separate legal entity, liability for its debts and obligations lies on the company and the members are liable only to the extent of any amount unpaid on their shares. Members are entitled to a share of any dividends, when declared. Dividends can only be paid out of profits. A private limited company is generally subject to strict accounting and auditing requirements.

Private limited companies are subject to restrictions on the modes and methods of returning capital to an investor. Buybacks of ordinary shares are limited to 10 per cent of the issued ordinary capital of the company. These may be repurchased out of distributable profits or, if the company will still be solvent afterwards and looking forward 12 months, out of capital. Companies may otherwise only return capital to their shareholders if they follow one of the procedures in the Companies Act for companies to carry out a reduction of capital – either with approval of the Court or alternatively under a process that requires the directors to make a statutory solvency statement which looks forward 12 months and to file the statement and publicise the capital reduction by making a filing with the Accounting and Corporate Regulatory Authority (ACRA). Private equity funds, typically, issue redeemable preference shares to investors. Provided that the shares are fully paid they may be redeemed out of the capital of a company if all the directors have made a solvency statement in relation to the redemption and the company has lodged a copy of the statement with ACRA.

A separate private limited company is, typically, incorporated as a fund manager. This company enters into an investment management agreement with the fund and is paid management fees/receives carried interest.

Limited partnerships

A limited partnership (LP) consists of at least one general partner and one limited partner. An individual or a corporation may be a general partner or a limited partner. A limited partner has limited liability for the debts and obligations of the limited partnership, unless the limited partner takes part in the management of the limited partnership. The general partner is liable for all debts and obligations of the limited partnership incurred while it is a general partner. Usually in a fund structure, the general partner will be a limited liability entity formed by the fund's principals. A limited partnership is registered by the general partner with ACRA. The name of the limited partnership must contain the term 'Limited Partnership' or the acronym 'LP'. The full name and details of the general partner and the limited partners have to be registered at ACRA, although it is possible to maintain the particulars of the limited partners of the LP confidential from the general public if the manager of the fund is a person licensed to carry on fund management under the SFA or exempt from licensing and other requirements under the Limited Partnership Regulations are satisfied. An individual local manager must be appointed if the general partner is not ordinarily resident in Singapore. The local manager is responsible for statutory compliance and for filing relevant tax returns. LP interests are included in the definition of 'securities' in Section 239 (1) SFA, ie, for purposes of the prospectus provisions. The definition of 'securities' in Section 2 of the SFA, for purposes of the licensing provisions, includes shares in a body unincorporated, which would include an interest in a LP.

The advantages of structuring a fund as a LP include:
- the structure suits the different roles of the fund manager (the general partner) and investors (the limited partners) in a fund – in practice the general partner may delegate the investment management to a separate fund management company to help ring fence the fund manager from the liabilities of a general partner. Similarly the fund manager may use a limited partner vehicle to receive carried interest;
- a partnership agreement governs the relationship between the partners, the content of which is only lightly regulated and which means the structure is free from many of the legal constraints and formalities usually applicable to corporate entities, in particular regarding contribution and return of capital and distribution of profits;
- no solvency statement is required when returning capital;
- distribution of profit or capital can be made at any time as long as the general partner is solvent and would not become insolvent as a result of the distribution; and
- LPs can take advantage of some of the fiscal incentives offered to funds under Singapore law.

A disadvantage of structuring a fund as a LP is that it will not be treated by the IRAS as a legal person qualifying for tax treaty relief.

Unit trust
In Singapore, the most common Collective Investment Scheme (CIS) structure is a unit trust. The unit trust structure is also common in jurisdictions such as Australia, Ireland, New Zealand, South Africa and the United Kingdom. The unit trust industry in Singapore follows the English unit trust model, which may be distinguished from a company, an association or partnership.

A unit trust is a special form of trust constituted by a trust deed in which the trust property is vested in a trustee. In dealing with the trust property, the trustee agrees to abide by the directions of a manager for the benefit of the unitholders who collectively own the beneficial interests in the trust property.

The unit trust as an investment scheme provides investors with several benefits and is the preferred structure for retail funds. See below in section 3 on retail funds in Singapore.

Managers
The fund manager is usually structured as a private limited company and may be a subsidiary of a well-established asset management group or an associate formed by the principals of the fund. The fund manager is subject to licensing requirements unless it qualifies for an exemption. See below in section 2.2. for details.

2.2. Regulatory framework
Legislative framework
The establishment and operation of investment funds in Singapore are regulated under the SFA and rules and regulations made thereunder, including the Securities and Futures (Offers of Investments) (Collective Investment Schemes) Regulations (CIS Regulations). If the fund falls under the category of a CIS, it will need to comply with the requirements under the CIS Code (refer to section 3 for more information). The MAS has general and specific powers to supplement the statutory provisions and/or issue written directions to asset managers.

Collective investment scheme regime
As a general rule any collective investment scheme that is offered in Singapore is required to be authorised or recognised in Singapore by the MAS. CISs that are constituted in Singapore are referred to as authorised schemes and CISs that are constituted outside Singapore are referred to as recognised schemes. The CISs would need to comply with the requirements under the SFA and regulations made thereunder and make the necessary filings with the MAS. CISs that are offered to high net worth individuals and corporations are referred to as Restricted Singapore Schemes (if constituted in Singapore) and Restricted Foreign Schemes (if constituted outside Singapore) and are subject to fewer regulatory requirements than retail CISs. Where the offer in Singapore will be made to only a few investors, certain private placement exemptions may allow for a limited offer without the need for filing with the MAS.

Investment manager
The Investment manager/adviser is required to comply with, inter alia, the SFA, the Securities and Futures (Licensing and Conduct of Business) Regulations (Conduct of Business Regulations), Securities and Futures (Financial and Margin Requirements for Holders For Capital Markets Services Licenses) Regulations (Financial and Margin Regulations) and other guidelines and notices dealing with know your customer requirements, anti-money laundering and related matters.

Any person conducting fund management activity in Singapore is required to hold a Capital Markets Services Licence (CMS Licence) for fund management or be a Registered Fund Management Company (RFMC) or otherwise exempted from the requirements to hold a CMS Licence under the SFA. The MAS regulates fund managers in Singapore.

There are requirements for a minimum number of representatives, directors etc of a Singapore fund manager to be based in Singapore, depending whether the fund manager is a RFMC, limited to managing up to S$250 million for up to 30 qualified investors (essentially high net worth individuals and corporations) or 15 funds limited to qualified investors, or holder of a CMS Licence (either full or limited to managing investments for qualified investors or funds limited to them). At the minimum, there will need to be two professionals with five years' relevant experience based in Singapore to conduct fund management. Requirements for compliance and back office support will depend on the scale and nature of operations of the fund manager, as will capital requirements. At the minimum, an RFMC must have base capital of S$250,000 at all times.

There are exemptions from these licensing requirements available for certain financial institutions like banks and finance companies and for provision of fund management services to related corporations, etc. but these cannot be used by independent fund managers who want to manage third party monies.

A person who wishes to apply for a CMS Licence for fund management or to register itself as a RFMC is required to submit to MAS via its Corporate Electronic Lodgment (CEL) system the relevant form duly completed along with all supporting documents. The Guidelines on Licensing, Registration and Conduct of Business for Fund Management Companies issued by the MAS, which are to be read along with the SFA and related regulations, provide key details of the application process and requirements.

2.3. Operational requirements

Please see discussion on the 'Investment manager' in section 2.2. above. A fund management company is required to comply with all applicable business conduct requirements set out in the SFA, Business Conduct Regulations, Financial and Margin Regulations and related guidelines and notices issued by MAS relating to know your customer and anti-money laundering requirements etc.

Physical office and fit and proper guidelines
All CMS Licence holders and RFMCs are required to operate out of a physical office in Singapore. Directors, representatives, shareholders, etc. of the fund manager must satisfy the Guidelines on Fit and Proper Criteria issued by MAS, designed to help ensure the fund manager has the integrity and competence to discharge its duties.

Audit
Fund managers are expected to put in place adequate internal audit procedures and comply with annual external audit requirements.

Compliance and risk management
Fund management companies (FMCs) will be required to implement a compliance and risk management framework over their fund management operations, suited to the size and scale of their operations, to identify, address and monitor the risks associated with the assets that they manage. The risk management framework should take into account the key principles set out in the MAS Guidelines on Risk Management Practices and other relevant industry best practices. The Guidelines on Risk Management Practices cover responsibilities of directors and senior management, internal controls, credit risk, market risk, technology risk and operational risk, which includes business continuity management and controls on outsourced activities. In addition, the FMC will have to implement measures to mitigate

conflicts of interest. The fund manager may be required to procure a professional indemnity insurance policy and MAS may also require a letter of responsibility from the parent company.

Custody of AUM and valuation
In general, the MAS requires that assets under management (AUM) be held by an independent custodian; ie, a prime broker, depositories or banks which are properly registered or authorised in their home jurisdiction, although it recognises that private equity and wholesale real estate funds may adopt other methods, subject to appropriate disclosures and other safeguards. The AUM must be subject to an independent valuation carried out by a third party service provider or by an in-house fund valuation function under certain conditions.

Disclosure and AML/CFT
The FMC is also required by the MAS to disclose key information to its customers on both the AUM and the operations of the fund. Fund Managers will have to keep in mind Singapore's anti-money laundering and combating the financing of terrorism controls, which regard tax crimes as money laundering predicate offences. FMCs holding the proceeds of tax crime (as long as they are regarded as such in Singapore and in the foreign jurisdiction, if any) may face criminal prosecution for laundering the proceeds of criminal activities under the Corruption, Drug Trafficking and Other Serious Crimes (Confiscation of Benefits) Act.

2.4. Marketing the fund
General
Please see 'Collective investment scheme regime' in section 2.2. The SFA, the CIS Regulations, the 2013 Regulations mentioned below and guidelines issued by the MAS regulate the marketing of funds. The fund manager who holds a CMS Licence and a RFMC (or a person otherwise exempted from holding a licence) can market its own funds. A person licensed under the Financial Advisers Act (Chapter 110) (or exempted from holding such a licence) is also allowed to market a CIS. There are no restrictions on use of intermediaries for marketing of funds provided the intermediaries are properly licensed (or exempted from holding a licence).

The key requirements for Restricted Singapore Schemes and Restricted Foreign Schemes are stated below. For key requirements of retail CIS schemes, please see section 3.4.

Restricted Singapore schemes
- The fund manager must be licensed or regulated for fund management in the jurisdiction of its principal place of business (or be a public company that is exempted from the requirement to hold a CMS Licence for fund management) and be fit and proper.
- In the case of a scheme constituted as a unit trust, the trustee must be approved to act as trustee for a CIS.

Singapore

- Such schemes are not required to comply with any investment guidelines.
- Unlike offers to retail investors, a prospectus is not required, but an information memorandum will be required. The Securities and Futures (Offers of Investments) (Collective Investment Schemes) (Amendment) Regulations 2013 (2013 Regulations) came into force on 1 July 2013. The 2013 Regulations stipulate that a CIS that is offered to high net worth investors (ie, restricted Singapore and restricted foreign schemes) should be accompanied by an information memorandum that contains the information specified in the 2013 Regulations. This relates to disclosure with respect to investment risks, conditions and restrictions on redemption of units, preferential treatment to certain investors, track record of the CIS etc.

Restricted foreign schemes
- The fund manager must be licensed or regulated for fund management in the jurisdiction of its principal place of business and be fit and proper.
- Such schemes are not required to comply with any investment guidelines.
- Unlike offers to retail investors, a prospectus is not required, but an information memorandum will be required under the 2013 Regulations mentioned above.

Closed-ended funds – recent developments
With effect from 1 July 2013, new regulations have come into force that affect closed-ended funds. Previously, closed-ended funds were specifically excluded from the definition of 'Collective Investment Schemes' under the SFA. Closed-ended funds are funds that have the features of a collective investment scheme but under which units issued are exclusively or primarily non-redeemable at the election of the investors. Closed-ended funds were therefore not required to comply with the regulatory regime under the SFA that relates to CIS.

On 28 March 2013, the Securities and Futures (Closed-ended Funds) (Excluded Arrangements) Notification 2013 (2013 Notification) was promulgated. The 2013 Notification is issued under paragraph (b) of the definition of 'closed-ended fund' of the SFA, which gives MAS the power to issue a notification and deem certain arrangements not to be closed-ended funds. The 2013 Notification states that certain closed-ended funds, having the following characteristics, shall be considered to be CIS and shall be subject to the same regulatory regime as a CIS:
- the arrangement is constituted on or after 1 July 2013;
- all or most of the units issued under the arrangement cannot be redeemed at the election of the holders of the units;
- under the investment policy of the arrangement, investments are made for the purpose of giving participants in the arrangement the benefit of the results of the investments, and not for the purpose of operating a business; and
- the arrangement has one or more of the following characteristics:
  (i) the investment policy of the arrangement is clearly set out in a

document that is provided to each participant in the arrangement before, or at the time, the participant invests in the arrangement;
(ii) there is a contractual relationship between the entity in which the investments are made and every participant in the arrangement, which requires the entity to comply with the investment policy, as amended from time to time, of the arrangement; or
(iii) the investment policy of the arrangement sets out the types of authorised investments, and the investment guidelines or restrictions that apply to the arrangement.

The key practical impact of this for a fund manager is that it can no longer consider closed-ended funds to be outside the regulatory regime for CISs, which will require them to review their procedures for offers of closed-ended funds made to sophisticated investors. Previously closed-ended funds could be marketed under the prospectus safe harbours for offers of securities to high net worth individuals and corporations without filing with MAS as a CIS. Now, the exemption from the requirement to file with the MAS and comply with the Restricted Scheme regime applies only if the fund is marketed within the confines of the private placement or small offers safe harbours in the SFA.

There are no additional requirements for marketing to public bodies such as government pension funds. In fact there may be certain exemptions available from the prospectus requirements etc., as such pubic bodies may be 'institutional investors' (as defined under the SFA).

2.5. Taxation
Singapore has developed over the years several tax incentive schemes in order to attract fund managers and funds to the city state.

Offshore fund
A foreign fund managed by a Singapore based fund manager who holds a CMS Licence in Singapore or is exempted will be exempt from tax on specified income from designated investments if the fund is a 'prescribed person'. A fund will generally qualify as a prescribed person if it is not resident in Singapore and not 100 per cent owned by Singapore investors. In addition, Singapore resident non-individual investors are limited to holding 30 per cent/50 per cent (depending on whether the fund has less than 10 investors) of the fund or they face a penalty by the IRAS and will not enjoy tax exemption.

Singapore resident fund scheme
The Singapore Resident Fund Scheme essentially encourages the fund manager to base the fund in Singapore. The scheme grants tax exemption for 'specified income' from 'designated investments'. However, to avail of this scheme, the entity must be constituted as a Singapore tax resident company and must have its administration performed in Singapore.

The enhanced tier scheme
This scheme, that applies to both Singapore based funds and offshore funds,

offers a tax exemption for income and gains from designated investments. There are no restrictions on the percentage of Singapore investors in the fund and there are fewer restrictions on the choice of fund entity. The fund should have a minimum fund size of S$50 million to avail of this tax incentive.

The Singapore Resident Fund Scheme and the Enhanced Tier Scheme require MAS approval.

An investment fund may not make taxable supplies for Goods and Services Tax (GST) purposes and so its ability to recover input tax suffered on supplies made to it is very limited. Management fees payable to the manager will in principle attract GST. A MAS circular allows funds qualifying for income tax concessions managed or advised by a fund manager (as defined) to recover most of this GST.

An interesting development announced in the 2012 Singapore Budget was aimed at reducing concerns whether gains are capital in nature, and thus not taxable in Singapore, or taxable as trading income. In essence, where a company owns 20 per cent or more of the ordinary share capital of another company, and has held those shares at least 24 months prior to their disposal, then the gains will be exempt from tax. These provisions may be helpful for private equity funds that are not using the tax incentives mentioned above.

Tax Incentives for the fund management company

A Singapore based fund management company may apply for a 10 per cent concessionary income tax applying to the income deriving from the management of the fund, under the Financial Sector Incentive Scheme (FSI). This concessionary tax rate is awarded under certain conditions and at the MAS's discretion.

With effect from 28 June 2013, new applicants/companies seeking a renewal of the FSI-FM incentive will be subjected to having minimum net AUM of at least S$250 million, in addition to other qualitative and quantitative factors under the scheme.

Investors will want to keep in mind that even though the fund is based offshore, if most of the fund management activities are conducted in Singapore, the IRAS may regard the fund as a permanent establishment and thus subject its income to Singapore tax, unless it is covered by the relevant exemption under the Income Tax Act (Chapter 134) for foreign funds that are managed by Singapore fund managers.

2.6. Customary or common terms

Due to the private nature of alternative investment funds and the fact that they are offered mainly to sophisticated investors, there is flexibility in the terms that can be included in such structures. Generally speaking, private equity funds and wholesale real estate funds are constituted as fixed term closed-ended funds, and do not allow for prior redemption. Hedge funds are usually structured such that they may allow for redemptions once a quarter (quarterly dealing is required for retail CIS) or once in two quarters. Non-retail funds typically impose restrictions on the right of participants to transfer their interests to third parties to prevent any legal, fiscal, regulatory or administrative complications for the fund or the investors as a whole.

It is not uncommon for the investors in alternative investment funds to want to see a substantial investment by the management team in the fund to demonstrate their commitment to the fund. The MAS has also stated in the Guidelines on Licensing, Registration and Conduct of Business for Fund Management Companies that it attaches importance to the shareholders in the fund management company demonstrating commitment to the business and investing in the funds it manages.

Provisions regarding removal of the manager are negotiated on a case-by-case basis but it is becoming more common to see investors requiring provisions for no-fault removal, perhaps by a super-majority of investors. Key-man clauses are also often incorporated for the purpose of continuity. Related to these issues are provisions for escrow and clawback of the manager's carried interest (typically 20 per cent), which allow for adjustment of the manager's distribution of cumulative profits, as these fluctuate over the life of the fund.

Singapore places a high level of importance on investor protection and the manner in which assets are held. Even RFMCs that manage monies only on behalf of sophisticated investors are required to demonstrate to MAS that the assets are held by a third party custodian/trustee or otherwise custody risks are appropriately managed. In addition, the fund manager is required to demonstrate that there are proper compliance and risk management procedures in place.

3. RETAIL FUNDS
3.1. Common structures

Unlike alternative investment funds, retail funds are usually structured as a unit trust and are subject to the CIS regulatory regime, including the CIS Code. The participants' interests in the fund are referred to as units and the liability of the participants is limited to the investment made by the participant in the fund.

A unit trust is a special form of trust constituted by a trust deed in which the trust property is vested in a trustee. In dealing with the trust property, the trustee agrees to abide by the directions of a manager for the benefit of the unit holders who collectively own the beneficial interests in the trust property. For schemes constituted in Singapore, the manager must hold a Capital Markets Services Licence or be exempted from holding such a licence, and the manager is generally constituted as a private or a public company in Singapore as required. For a foreign fund, the manager would have to be licensed or regulated in the jurisdiction of its principal place of business and be fit and proper.

Types of unit trust schemes in Singapore
The majority of unit trusts in Singapore are structured as umbrella funds. An umbrella fund is a group of stand-alone sub-funds each having its own investment portfolio, with different investment objectives and strategies but all administered by the same manager. The purpose of this structure is to provide investment flexibility and widen investor choice. Investors in an

umbrella fund may invest in one or more of the sub-funds offered and may switch or exchange units of one sub-fund for those of another.

Other types of unit trust structure found in Singapore are single funds and feeder funds. The whole of the trust property of a single fund comprises one fund. The assets of a feeder fund are invested in another fund called the master fund, which may be a single fund, or a group of funds.

In the early 2000s, feeder funds were common in Singapore as foreign funds could not be offered directly to the public in Singapore. A foreign fund could only be offered through a Singapore based feeder fund with a Singapore manager and trustee investing in the foreign fund.

Foreign funds can now be offered directly to the public in Singapore provided they are approved by MAS as recognised schemes (if offered to retail investors) or as restricted foreign schemes (if offered to high net worth individuals and corporations).

The key benefits of the trust structure are that there no statutory rules on preservation of capital or distribution of profits, the trust can be structured as an umbrella fund with several sub-funds, giving the investors an opportunity to easily switch between sub-funds, and can avail of certain tax benefits (see section 3.5.).

Real Estate Investment Trusts (REITs)
REITs have been very successful in gathering assets and accessing the public capital markets in Singapore in recent years, driven in particular by the tax exemptions allowed for investment into income producing real estate assets in Singapore the structure affords. REITs are formed as unit trusts in Singapore, authorised as CISs and trade as listed securities on the Singapore Exchange (SGX). They are required to comply with the property fund guidelines in the CIS Code in addition to the SGX listing rules and the manager has to hold a CMS licence as a REIT manager.

Business Trusts
The Business Trust (BT) is another vehicle for investment in cash flow producing assets introduced in Singapore, modelled on the Australian managed investment trust. The Business Trust Act (BTA) provides the framework for the governance of BTs and regulates the rights of unitholders and creditors and the duties and accountability of the trustee-manager and its directors. The MAS registers BTs formed under the BTA and the SFA regulates public offers of units in BTs in the same way as offers of securities and of units in CIS.

BTs are business enterprises structured as trusts. They are hybrid structures with elements of both companies and trusts and several trade as listed securities on the SGX. There is also scope for using a private, unregistered investment vehicle modelled on the framework of a BT in certain circumstances.

A BT is created by a trust deed under which the trustee-manager has legal ownership of the assets of the underlying business and manages the business for the benefit of the beneficiaries of the trust. As dividends can be paid out of cash flows in a BT structure, BTs are particularly suited to businesses with high levels of capital investment and strong cash flows such as real estate, and other infrastructure/asset-backed businesses in sectors like hospitality, healthcare and shipping.

3.2. Regulatory framework
Please see section 2.2. In addition, for the authorisation/recognition requirements for retail funds, please see section 3.4.

CPF approved unit trusts
The Central Provident Fund (CPF) is the compulsory savings scheme in Singapore. CPF approved unit trusts are a special feature of the Singapore unit trust market. These are funds approved by the CPF Board under the CPF Investment Scheme. CPF members are permitted to use their retirement savings to purchase units in these approved trusts. Fund managers wishing to tap into this market must first have their funds approved by the CPF Board.

3.3. Operational requirements
Please see section 2.3. The manager of a retail CIS must prepare half-yearly financial statements and audited financial statements for the semi-annual report and annual report, in the manner prescribed by the Institute of Certified Public Accountants in its Statement of Recommended Accounting Practice 7: Reporting Framework for Unit Trusts. The manager must also prepare quarterly reports covering the information in Appendix 4 of the CIS Code. The trustee must send, or cause to be sent, to the investors the semi-annual accounts and semi-annual report relating to the CIS within two months from the end of the period covered by the accounts and report, and the annual accounts, report of the auditors on the annual accounts and annual report relating to the CIS within three months from the end of each financial year of the CIS. The semi-annual report and annual report contain a large amount of information.

Valuation guidelines apply to retail CIS under the CIS Code. Valuation of units is based on the fund's NAV. The NAV can be calculated in one of two ways: using market quotations and fair value. The manager of a CIS is responsible for determining whether the quoted price should be considered representative. The basis for determining the fair value of the asset must be documented. Except for quoted securities, all the assets of a CIS must be valued by a person approved by the trustee of the CIS as qualified to value such assets. When the fair value of a material portion of the assets of a CIS cannot be determined, the manager must suspend valuation and trading in the units of the CIS.

The price of units can be adjusted by adding or subtracting fees and charges, provided that those fees and charges are disclosed in the CIS's prospectus or trust deed.

3.4. Marketing the fund
Please see section 2.4. above. In addition, please note the following in relation to authorisation/recognition requirements for a retail fund before it can be offered to the public.

Schemes constituted in Singapore (authorised schemes)
The following are some of the key requirements to be complied with for retail schemes constituted in Singapore to be authorised by the MAS:
- the fund manager must hold a CMS Licence for fund management (or be exempted from holding a CMS Licence or be a public company in certain cases) and be 'fit and proper' as per MAS requirements;
- the trustee must be approved to act as trustee for the CIS if the CIS is constituted as a trust;
- the trust deed must comply with the prescribed requirements in the relevant regulations;
- the CIS must comply with the CIS Code; and
- a prospectus in compliance with the SFA must be lodged with the MAS.

Schemes constituted outside Singapore (recognised schemes)
The following are some of the key requirements to be complied with for retail schemes constituted outside Singapore to be recognised by the MAS:
- the fund manager must be licensed or regulated in the jurisdiction of its principal place of business and be fit and proper;
- the laws and practices of the jurisdiction in which the scheme is constituted should afford investors in Singapore protection at least equivalent to that provided by the SFA for comparable authorised schemes. The MAS would consider, for example, whether there is a legal requirement for the manager to manage the scheme in the interests of investors, whether there is independent adequate safekeeping of scheme assets, whether there is an independent party (such as an independent trustee in the case of a unit trust, or independent directors in the case of a mutual fund company) which exercises oversight over the fund manager;
- while the CIS is not subject to the investment guidelines set out in the CIS Code, the MAS would only recognise a foreign CIS if it is subject to investment guidelines in its home jurisdiction which are substantially similar to those in Singapore;
- there must be a representative for the scheme in Singapore to act as a liaison between investors and the foreign manager;
- a prospectus in compliance with the SFA must be registered with the MAS; and
- the fund manager of the fund (together with its related companies) should be managing at least S$500 million of discretionary funds in Singapore.

The information to be disclosed in relation to a retail CIS is specified in the prospectus requirements and additional information to be disclosed regarding the risks attaching to hedge funds is specified in the CIS Code and the CIS Regulations.

MAS indicated in its consultation paper on the changes to the treatment of closed-ended funds discussed in section 2.4. above that it would also expect a closed-ended retail fund to be listed on a securities exchange.

The 2013 Regulations came into force on 1 July 2013. The 2013 Regulations stipulate that a retail CIS prospectus will require additional disclosures that relate to, inter alia, methods of valuation, information on directors and key executives of the manager of the CIS, where the manager delegates any of its functions to a third party – the name of the delegate, the name of the financial supervisory authority which licenses or regulates the manager, etc., the names of trustees and custodians and custodial arrangements in respect of the assets.

3.5. Taxation

Most Singapore retail funds are structured as unit trusts. The trustee, being the legal owner of the income that accrues to the unit trust, is the party who is assessed to tax on the income of the unit trust.

However, if the unit trust avails of the Designated Unit Trust (DUT) scheme and is granted the DUT status by the IRAS, the income of the fund may not be subject to tax. The main qualifying criteria of the DUT scheme are as follows:
- the unit trust should be a CIS that is authorised by the MAS or exempted from authorisation under specified provisions;
- the unit trust should not be a REIT or property trust that invests directly in Singapore immovable properties;
- the trustee of the unit trust is a Singapore tax resident; and
- the fund manager of the unit trust holds a CMS Licence for fund management under the SFA or is exempt from holding such a licence.

If the DUT status is granted to a unit trust, certain income of the unit trust (designated income) will be excluded from the fund's statutory income and therefore not taxed on the trustee. The excluded income includes, inter alia:
- gains or profits derived from Singapore or elsewhere from the disposal of securities;
- interest (other than where Singapore withholding tax has been deducted);
- dividends derived from outside Singapore and received in Singapore;
- gains or profits derived from: (i) foreign exchange transactions; (ii) transactions in futures contracts; (iii) transactions in interest rate or currency forwards; (iv) swaps or options contracts; and (v) transactions in forwards, swaps or options contracts relating to any securities or financial index;
- distributions from foreign unit trusts derived from outside Singapore and received in Singapore;
- fees and compensatory payments (other than those where Singapore withholding tax has been deducted) from certain securities lending and repurchase arrangements with specified counterparties;
- rents and any other income derived from immovable property situated outside Singapore and received in Singapore;
- discount derived from outside Singapore and received in Singapore; and
- discount from qualifying debt securities (QDS).

Taxation of Investors
Provided certain conditions are satisfied, distributions made by a CIS that is authorised by the MAS to a Singapore investor or non-resident investor

will be exempt from Singapore income tax. This will however not apply to investors who hold units in the CIS as trading assets or through a partnership, and such investors will need to pay the necessary income tax.

3.6. Customary or common terms
Retail funds do not generally have a fixed term duration. Retail CISs are required to provide facilities for a holder of a unit to transfer the unit to a third party, in compliance with conditions the manager may impose.

Retail funds typically have daily dealing and the investor can redeem their investment out of the assets of the fund at a price based on net asset value. The manager can place restrictions on the issue and redemption of units in a CIS if this is provided for in the trust deed constituting the CIS.

The liquidity of units that are listed on the SGX will depend on the supply and demand for those shares in the secondary market.

The fund manager of a retail fund will typically levy an initial charge of up to 5 per cent of the investment amount from the investor and an annual management charge. The rate of annual management charge will vary depending on the investment proposition. Performance fees may be charged, which should conform to the requirements under the CIS Code.

In the case of BTs and REITs it is common for the trustee manager or the REIT manager to obtain units in the BT or REIT as management fee.

The CIS Code prescribes various requirements for retail funds with respect to permissible investments and borrowing. There are restrictions on the maximum amount of exposure to unlisted securities, listed and unlisted derivatives as well as maximum exposure to transferable securities and money market instruments issued by a single entity or related entities. The requirements will differ based on whether the fund is a non-specialised fund or a specialised fund like a currency fund, money market fund, hedge fund etc. As a general rule, a retail fund can borrow only to meet redemptions and short-term (not more than one month) bridging requirements. Aggregate borrowings for these purposes must not exceed 10 per cent of the deposited property at the time the borrowing is incurred.

4. PROPOSED CHANGES AND DEVELOPMENTS
The most recent changes are those in respect of closed-ended funds referred to in section 2.4. above and the 2013 Regulations referred to in section 3.4. above.

South Africa

David Anderson, Francisco Khoza, Mogola Makola
& Kirsten Kern   **Bowman Gilfillan**

1. MARKET OVERVIEW

The South African investment funds market can be broadly divided into two main areas, alternative investment funds (private equity funds, hedge funds, property loan stock companies (PLSs), property unit trusts (PUTs) and real estate investment trusts (REITs)), and retail funds (collective investment schemes).

The private equity funds market is well developed. Over the past 40 years, South Africa has seen a cycle of disinvestment followed by a cycle of re-investment by multinationals. Given this activity management buy-outs, management buy-ins and leveraged buy-outs have been prevalent for some time and private equity fund formation has increased steadily over the last 10 years. This trend is arguably set to continue given the strong continuing interest in investment in South Africa and its neighbouring countries. A number of the transactions concluded within the private equity sector in South Africa have a black economic empowerment (BEE) component. BEE is an important factor to consider when structuring private equity transactions in, inter alia, the mining sector and should be borne in mind generally in transactions within South Africa.

The South African hedge fund market is growing rapidly with investors able to take their pick of a number of funds offering hedge fund strategies. This despite the fact that the market is relatively new and small in size (estimated at R31 billion compared to US$2 trillion for the global hedge fund industry).

The important news in 2013 in the context of PLSs, PUTs and REITs has been the introduction of the REIT listed property structure to South Africa (effective 1 May 2013), which is internationally recognised. The Johannesburg Stock Exchange (JSE) has amended the JSE Listings Requirements to provide for the listing of REITs. According to the transitional arrangements under the JSE Listings Requirements, all PLSs, collective investment schemes (CISs) in property listed on the main board of the JSE in the financial real estate sector prior to 30 November 2012 to apply to the JSE for REIT status by no later than 1 July 2013.

If anything, restrictions on the participation in investment funds by financial institutions have been eased recently. In particular, pension funds registered under the Pension Fund Act 1956 may now invest up to 10 per cent of their assets in private equity funds which must have the following characteristics:
- a permissible structure (en commandite partnership, bewind trust or

company);
- fund managers must be members of the South African Venture Capital Association (SAVCA) and authorised as discretionary financial service providers under the Financial Advisory and Intermediary Services Act 2002 (FAIS);
- the fund must have valuation policies which comply with the International Private Equity Valuation Guidelines; and
- auditors must verify the private equity fund's assets every two years and the private equity fund must produce audited accounts within four months of year end.

Funds under management for the private equity industry as at 31 December 2012 were R126.4 billion (an increase of 10.4 per cent on the previous year's figure). Investment activity during 2012 was R10.6 billion which is significantly less than the figure for 2011 (R16.5 billion). Of this figure of R10.6 billion, R5 billion was for new investments. During 2012, R7 billion of funds were returned to investors, which once again is significantly less than the figure for 2011 (R25.7 billion). These figures are set out in the KPMG and SAVCA Venture Capital and Private Equity Industry Performance Survey of South Africa covering the 2012 calendar year (dated June 2013).

The hedge funds and REITs market has been active, particularly given the recent introduction of the South African REIT.

2. ALTERNATIVE INVESTMENT FUNDS
2.1. Common structures

The principal types of legal vehicles used to establish private equity (third party) funds are en commandite partnerships and bewind trusts. First, an en commandite partnership is a limited partnership where each partner en commandite (whose names are not disclosed) limits its liability to its co-partners for the losses of the partnership up to an agreed amount, on condition that it receives a fixed share of the profits. En commandite partners are not liable for partnership debts to partnership creditors, but they are liable to their co-partners. They lose their limited liability status if they actively participate in the partnership's business. The partnership's business is carried on by the general partner, whose name is disclosed. Second (and less common), a bewind trust where the beneficiaries of the trust (as opposed to the trustees of the trust) own the assets in undivided shares, and the trustees of the trust administer the assets.

The majority of hedge funds are structured as en commandite partnerships, with trusts and limited liability companies incorporated under the Companies Act 2008 ('Companies Act') being used too. A PLS must be a company listed on the JSE. A REIT can take the form of a company or a trust, and must also be listed on the JSE.

The advantages of en commandite partnerships and bewind (and other) trusts are that they offer investors limited liability and tax efficiency. Additionally en commandite partnerships are particularly easy to establish as they are not regulated. Bewind trusts must be registered with the Master of the High Court. There are no notable disadvantages in using either an en commandite partnership or a bewind trust save that while a partnership structure is easy to establish, it is not an easy structure to adapt in order to provide different segregated portfolios with investors' rights and liability limited to the segregated portfolio into which they are invested.

The advantage of a company is limited liability, the disadvantage is the compliance burden under the Companies Act.

Each investor in an en commandite partnership structure has limited liability in the sense that its losses are limited to the amount which it contributes (or agrees to contribute) to the partnership.

Each investor in a bewind (and other) trust has limited liability in the sense that its losses are limited to the amount which it contributes (or agrees to contribute) to the bewind (or other) trust.

A shareholder in a company is protected by the corporate veil of the company, and so has limited liability.

In the case of an en commandite partnership each participant's interest is referred to as a partnership interest. In the case of a bewind trust, each participant's interest is referred to as a beneficiary's interest. In the case of a company each participant's interest is referred to as a share. However, a PLS as a company is unique in the dual-linked nature of the interest held by investors. In this dual-linked structure, the investor holds a share and a debenture with 99 per cent of the value attributable to the debenture.

The principal legal vehicle for fund managers of alternative investment funds is a private company incorporated under the Companies Act which provides the shareholders with limited liability, save in exceptional circumstances.

2.2. Regulatory framework

Private equity funds and hedge funds are not subject to specific regulation however there are a number of statues which are relevant to the activities of private equity funds and hedge funds such as FAIS (fund managers have to be licensed for the purposes of FAIS), the Pensions Funds Act 1956 (which regulates investments by pension funds in private equity funds), the Exchange Control Regulations 1961 (which regulate the ability of private equity funds to attract investment from the non-resident investors and the ability to invest outside South Africa), the Trust Property Control Act 1988 and the Companies Act.

The Code of Conduct for Discretionary FSPs ('Code of Conduct') issued under FAIS refers specifically to the regulation of hedge fund managers. FAIS requires the managers to be approved as category IIA FSPs. A category IIA FSP is a financial service provider who provides intermediary services of a discretionary nature in relation to a particular hedge fund. A hedge fund manager must also apply to the FSB for a category II licence, which applies to discretionary financial services providers. The FSB issues the licence under the FAIS and supervises the activities of the managers.

PLS are subject to the supervision of the Companies and Intellectual Property Commission (CIPC) and the JSE.

REITs are subject to the South African taxation laws, the JSE Listings

Requirements and subject to the supervision of the JSE. Where the REIT is structured as a company it will also be subject to the Companies Act and supervised by the CIPC.

Private equity funds and hedge funds are not required to be licensed, authorised or regulated by a regulatory body. PLSs and REITs are subject to the authority of the JSE.

The principal statute is FAIS and the investment manager or investment adviser must be licensed as discretionary financial service providers for the purposes of FAIS.

There are no local residence qualification requirements to be met by an investment manager or an investment advisor. However an investment advisor or an investment manager has to meet certain fit and proper requirements applicable to all authorised financial services providers. The fit and proper requirements include, among others: requirements of honesty and integrity; experience and qualification requirements; and financial soundness.

There are general exemptions from some aspects of the fit and proper requirements (such as from certain examinations and continuous professional development requirements). In addition, an investment manager or investment advisor can always submit an application to the Registrar of Financial Services for a specific exemption.

In order to obtain authorisation a prospective manager (whether as a hedge fund/investment manager/investment advisor) has to complete and submit prescribed forms to the FSB. The relevant forms and guidance on how to complete the forms is available on the FSB website: *www.fsb.co.za*.

2.3. Operational requirements

There are no legal restrictions restricting the types of activity or the types of investment for private equity funds or hedge funds but the funds themselves commonly limit their ability to invest in listed companies, certain industry sectors and in certain countries. A PLS may only make investments in property shares and immovable property. A REIT entity must solely invest in immovable property assets and collateral debt investments and hedges used to reduce the risk associated with property related loans.

There are no statutory protections in place to protect the assets held by private equity funds. The relevant partnership agreement or trust deed will govern the relationship between the investors and the fund, to the extent that the specific protections are required these could be reflected in the partnership agreement or the trust deed (although that would be unusual).

In relation to hedge funds, the assets of the portfolio, together with any money or other assets received from an investor are protected under the money rules under FAIS. Also the assets and money invested in the hedge fund are considered 'trust property' for the purposes of the Financial Institutions (Protection of Funds) Act 2001 ('FI Act'). A manager and its authorised agent, trustee or custodian, must deal with trust money and assets in accordance with the constitutional document of the fund and in the best interests of investors.

In terms of the FI Act, the assets of a portfolio must be separated from the assets of the hedge fund manager, trustee or custodian, so that they are protected in the event of a claim against, or insolvency of the manager, trustee or custodian.

The assets invested in a PLS are protected by the Companies Act and the JSE. Similarly, the assets invested in REITs are protected under the JSE regulations.

On the assumption that the investment manager, investment adviser or general partnership is a limited liability company it must comply with the provisions of the Companies Act insofar as they relate to maintaining records, maintaining accounting records and producing financial statements.

Fund managers must provide investors with written reports on request. At a minimum, a written report must be supplied at least once every three months. The report must contain all information, which is reasonably necessary to enable the investor to produce a set of financial statements; determine the composition of the financial products comprising their investment and the change(s) over the reporting period; determine the market value of the financial products comprising the investment and the changes over the reporting period. There are no specific filing requirements for hedge funds.

In relation to the PLS and REIT the reporting requirements will be set out in the constitutional documents of the fund and will be subject to the filing requirements set out under the JSE Listings Requirements and the Companies Act.

There are no public disclosure requirements in relation to prospectuses or side letters, save as set out in the answer to section 2.3.

The use of side letters is not restricted and is not uncommon in the context of private equity funds.

There are no specific requirements of the type mentioned above imposed by regulation upon private equity funds or hedge funds. Parameters such as risk, borrowing restrictions and valuation are addressed in the relevant partnership agreement or trust deed. South Africa has legislation which is generally applicable addressing areas such as insider dealing, market abuse and money laundering, and private equity funds (and managers) will be subject to this legislation in the ordinary course.

Under the Code of Conduct applicable to hedge funds, the mandate between an investor and a hedge fund manager must contain a statement explaining the risks associated with investing in hedge funds. This statement is required in addition to the general risk disclosures that are required in mandates between financial service providers and their clients. The rules and regulations governing valuation and pricing, systems and controls are contained in the constitutive documents of the fund.

The Financial Markets Act 2012 regulates insider dealing and market abuse in relation to the REIT and PLS listed on the JSE. In relation to transparency, hedge fund managers are required to provide clients with written reports on request. At a minimum, a written report must be supplied at least once every three months. The client reporting requirements of PLSs and REITs will be set out in their constitutional documents.

2.4. Marketing the fund

FAIS governs the production and offering of marketing materials for private equity band hedge funds. The JSE Listings Requirements (and the Companies Act if the fund is a company) govern the production and offering of marketing materials in relation to PLSs and REITs.

Only an authorised financial services provider is permitted to market a private equity fund or a hedge fund. Only authorised sponsors or financial services providers are permitted to market a PLS or REIT.

Private equity funds and hedge funds should not be marketed to members of the public. Individual investors are typically introduced to the private equity fund by the fund manager.

Depending on the size of the fund, the level of investment and the relationship between the investor, the fund manager and the fund principals, some form of prospectus or memorandum will usually be made available summarising the relevant structure and investment terms. Investors should be made aware of the investment risks.

2.5. Taxation

Private equity funds (other than companies) are tax transparent in South Africa.

In some cases, there are establishment taxes levied in connection with an investor's participation in the fund or the transfer of the investor's interest. This depends on whether the fund is structured as a trust or a partnership and whether the investor is a resident or non-resident:

If, as a trust, any income that the fund receives is exempt from tax, provided that income is distributed to the beneficiaries during the tax year in which it is received. The fund is only subject to tax on any income it retains. If, as a partnership, the partnership is not a 'person' for tax purposes. The partners, in their individual capacities, are subject to tax on the income received by, or accruing to, the partnership according to their profit-sharing ratio.

Resident investors in a trust are taxed on the income distributed to them by the fund. Any fund income which is tax exempt retains that tax exempt status on distribution, provided it is distributed to the beneficiaries within the same tax year. Any tax deductions, or allowances, permitted by the fund can also be made by the beneficiaries where income is distributed (and can still be made by the fund where the amount is not distributed).

In a partnership, any income received by, or accrued to, the partnership is considered to pass to the partners on the same date (and in their profit-sharing ratio). The partners can deduct any permitted expenses and allowances. The ITA regulates the tax treatment of limited partners, provided that each limited partner is carrying on the trade or business of the partnership (whether or not it is a limited partnership). A limited partner is defined in the Income Tax Act 1962 (ITA) as any member of a partnership en commandite, an anonymous partnership or any similar partnership where a member's liability towards creditors is limited to their contributions. Partners must make a joint return to SARS, and each partner is separately and individually liable to SARS for their portion of the taxes due.

Non-resident investors can be taxed in South Africa on income received which is sourced from South Africa, unless the provisions of a specific DTA provide otherwise. Dividends and interest are now subject to withholding tax.

Insofar as REITs are concerned please see section 3.5.

2.6. Customary or common terms

The typical life of private equity funds in South Africa is generally between 7-11 years, and extensions of up to two years are common.

Liquidity of interests is increasingly becoming more available with new private equity funds offering flexibility to investors to redeem early.

Typically the fund manager will contribute roughly 2 per cent of the total funds raised by the fund.

Key man provisions are included as a matter of course.

Fund managers can typically be removed without cause by a 75 per cent majority of the limited partners and by a simple majority of the limited partners for cause.

The fund manager will charge a fee of around 2 per cent of committed funds and expect a 20 per cent carried interest after a hurdle rate of between 6 per cent-12 per cent has been cleared. Currently hurdle rates are the subject of debate in South Africa and as the given range indicates there is a lot of flexibility in respect of this point. Clawback and similar investor protection provisions are becoming increasingly common.

The partnership agreement or trust deed will contain comprehensive provisions setting out investment guidelines, requirements and prohibitions. These provisions will detail the minimum and maximum size of investments, the sectors in which the relevant portfolio companies should operate and/or the countries in which the relevant portfolio companies should operate.

3. RETAIL FUNDS

3.1. Common structures

Retail funds, in the South African context, are generally set up and classified as collective investment (unit trust) schemes. Where such funds do not qualify as collective investment schemes under South African law (in that such funds do not meet the prescribed legal definition of a 'collective investment scheme'), they may be established as companies.

While the closed-ended or open-ended nature of a fund is not a relevant consideration in the South African context, it may be said that open-ended funds would generally be set up as collective investment schemes, while closed-ended funds may be set up as collective investment schemes or as companies.

Where a fund is set up as a collective investment scheme, investors in that fund will own a portion of the fund's underlying assets and the fund will be regulated under the provisions of the Collective Investment Schemes Control Act, 2002 (CISCA). Where a fund is established as a company, on the other hand, fund investors will merely own shares in the company (and not the company's underlying assets) and the fund will be regulated by and under the

Companies Act.

In order to qualify (and be regulated) as a collective investment scheme, the structure of a fund will need to fall within the scope of the definition of a 'collective investment scheme' under CISCA. A 'collective investment scheme' is defined in CISCA as:

'a scheme, in whatever form, including an open-ended investment company, in pursuance of which members of the public are invited or permitted to invest money or other assets in a portfolio, and in terms of which:
(a) two or more investors contribute money or other assets to and hold a participatory interest in a portfolio of the scheme through shares, units or any other form of participatory interest; and
(b) the investors share the risk and the benefit of investment in proportion to their participatory interest in a portfolio of a scheme or on any other basis determined in the deed,
but not a collective investment scheme authorised by any other Act'.

Since the regulation applicable to funds under South African law differs markedly depending on whether such funds are established as collective investment schemes or as companies, it is important to distinguish between the two structures.

The rules and restrictions applicable to funds structured as collective investment schemes (including the rules and restrictions applicable to the marketing of such funds) differ materially from the rules applicable to funds that are structured as companies. A foreign (non-South African) fund that constitutes a company in the South African context may be marketed to members of the South African public, subject to certain requirements being met by the company (the issuer) under the provisions of the Companies Act. On the other hand, a foreign (non-South African) fund structured as a collective investment scheme in the South African context may not be marketed in or into South Africa unless such foreign fund itself has been formally approved under CISCA, a process which is lengthy and administratively burdensome.

As indicated, investors in a fund structured as a collective investment scheme own a portion of the fund's underlying assets. Investors in a fund structured as a company, on the other hand, merely own shares in that company and do not enjoy ownership over any of the company's (fund's) assets.

Where a fund constitutes a collective investment scheme, the participants' or investors' interests in such fund are known as participatory interests in such scheme.

Where a fund is established as a company, on the other hand, the participants' or investors' interests in such fund will be shares in such company.

Investment (asset) managers and/or investment advisers are generally established as private companies under South African law, in terms of the Companies Act. Some of the larger investment managers in South Africa are incorporated as public companies under the Companies Act.

It should be noted that investment managers and investment advisers, whether operating on a discretionary or a non-discretionary basis, are regarded as providing or rendering 'financial services' in the South African context (a term comprising financial advice and/or financial intermediary services). The provision of 'financial services' in or into South Africa will require portfolio managers and investment advisers to obtain a financial services provider (FSP) licence under FAIS. This licensing process has been dealt with in more detail in our response under section 3.2. below.

3.2. Regulatory framework

The provisions of CISCA and its subordinate legislation (including regulations) apply to collective investment schemes, while the provisions of the Companies Act and its subordinate legislation apply to funds structured as companies.

In either case, the rendering of financial advice and/or the performance of financial intermediary services to South African clients in relation to funds (whether foreign or domestic) will be governed by the provisions of FAIS and its subordinate legislation.

CISCA

CISCA provides for the formal approval of foreign (non-South African) collective investment schemes, and requires such approval to be attained prior to the solicitation of investments in the relevant fund or scheme from South African clients or investors. As such, an unapproved foreign scheme may not be promoted or marketed in or into South Africa (from offshore) or to South African investors.

In relation to domestic (South African) collective investment schemes, CISCA provides for the formal approval and registration of the manager of the scheme, but not of the scheme itself. The characteristics or attributes of the scheme itself would then be dealt with in the manager's application for registration.

Section 22 of CISCA provides the Registrar of Collective Investment Schemes with a general discretion to grant an exemption to any person from any provision of CISCA, where he considers such exemption to be in the public interest. Any such exemption (in relation to a foreign or a local collective investment scheme) would need to be formally applied for in the prescribed form and manner.

Foreign Scheme Approval

The approval process applicable to foreign collective investment schemes sought to be promoted or marketed in or into South Africa is an extensive and administratively burdensome one.

Formal application will need to be made on the forms prescribed for this purpose in the regulations promulgated under CISCA.

Local Scheme – Manager Approval

The process to secure registration as a manager is initiated by lodging certain documents with the Registrar of Collective Investment Schemes.

The Companies Act
Where a fund is established as a company, such company would need to be set up in accordance with the Companies Act and with reference to the practical rules of the Companies and Intellectual Property Commission in South Africa (CIPC). A fund structured as a company, therefore, would be required to be formally registered as a company, with the CIPC, in terms of the Companies Act.

Investment managers and investment advisers (whether discretionary or non-discretionary) operating in South Africa or into South Africa from offshore on a cross-border basis will be seen to be providing 'advice' or 'intermediary services' for the purposes of FAIS. Such investment managers and investment advisers will need to become formally licensed under FAIS and, post-licensing, will need to comply with the provisions of FAIS and its subordinate legislation (including with a mandatory code of business conduct).

Depending on the precise activities or functions of an investment manager/investment adviser, other South African statutes may also apply.

Investment managers and investment advisers providing financial services in or into South Africa are required to become licensed as FSPs under the provisions of FAIS. This entails the making of a formal application in South Africa, in the manner and form prescribed by the regulatory body charged with monitoring and policing compliance with the provisions of FAIS, the Financial Services Board (FSB). At present, there is no applicable distinction relevant to the type of client to whom financial services are provided for the purposes of licensing requirements under FAIS.

It may be noted that where the approved manager of a local scheme or the manager of an approved foreign scheme acts as investment manager or investment adviser in respect of that scheme, registration of such manager as an FSP under FAIS will not be required. This is in terms of a statutory exemption provided under FAIS.

An investment manager or investment adviser seeking to provide financial services from offshore without any office or physical presence in South Africa will be entitled to apply for and maintain an FSP licence under FAIS on a purely cross-border basis. As such, there is no physical presence requirement applicable to a foreign entity holding an FSP licence under FAIS.

Certain staff appointments will need to be made by an entity making application for an FSP licence. The persons fulfilling these roles or appointments under the entity's FSP licence need not be resident in South Africa and need not be South African citizens.

Where a fund is established under South African law using the structure of a company, the fund will need to be formally registered as a company with the CIPC and in accordance with the applicable rules. There are no exemptions from this formal registration requirement. Post-registration as a company, the ongoing compliance obligations imposed on companies under the Companies Act will also need to be complied with by the fund and its management.

As regards marketing or funds-raising in respect of funds established as companies, the Companies Act does provide for private placement offerings which, if applicable, will allow the fund in question to avoid complying with the requirements and rules imposed under the Companies Act on 'offers to the public'.

Under South African law, a company may be established through the purchase of an existing shelf company the details of which are then appropriately amended, or the company may be established from scratch. The process is a relatively simple one and entails the completion of various prescribed forms, which are then required to be lodged with the CIPC.

Matters such as shareholding and management of the intended company will be dealt with in accordance with the requirements on the various prescribed forms.

FAIS
An investment manager or investment adviser which is domiciled outside of South Africa and which has no physical presence in South Africa (such as a branch office) will qualify as a 'foreign FSP' for the purposes of Board Notice 166 of 2011 under FAIS, which Board Notice exempts foreign FSPs from compliance with certain of the provisions of FAIS.

Application for an FSP licence is required to be submitted to the FSB on a prescribed set of application forms, and must be accompanied by various prescribed supporting documents.

FAIS and its subordinate legislation require an applicant for an FSP licence to appoint or nominate certain persons to fulfil certain roles within the applicant for purposes of the licence ('Prescribed Roles').

The application form must be accompanied (inter alia) by information which satisfies the Registrar of Financial Services Providers (an official residing also under the auspices of the FSB) that the applicant complies with the FAIS-prescribed 'fit and proper' requirements for FSPs.

The Registrar of Financial Services Providers enjoys discretion to request additional information or documents necessary to enable him to meaningfully consider the application for an FSP licence.

3.3. Operational requirements
Foreign scheme
In terms of the Conditions, the Registrar of Collective Investment Schemes is empowered to refuse to grant approval to a foreign scheme under CISCA:
(a) where the applicant operator is unable to satisfy the Registrar that the investments the foreign scheme intends to promote in South Africa have a risk profile that is not significantly higher than the risk profiles of similar investments in participatory interests offered for sale in South Africa by local managers;
(b) if the foreign scheme invests in markets dissimilar to those qualifying for investment by local schemes;
(c) unless at least 90 per cent of the interest-bearing instruments included in

a particular fund enjoy a credit rating of 'investment grade' or higher by Moody's, Standard and Poor's or Fitch Ratings Limited;
(d) unless the borrowing of money is limited under the scheme rules to 10 per cent of the value of a fund and unless such borrowing is permitted only for the purpose of the redemption of participatory interests;
(e) if the inclusion in a fund of unlisted derivative instruments or uncovered exposures is allowed;
(f) if gearing, leveraging or margining by a fund of the scheme is permitted;
(g) if investments are offered for sale which may not, in terms of CISCA, be offered for sale by a local manager;
(h) if a fund of the foreign scheme invests in a fund of funds or in a feeder fund; or
(i) if a fund of funds of the foreign scheme is not invested in at least five other funds or is invested in another fund in excess of 20 per cent of the said fund of funds' market value.

Local scheme
These are set out in CISCA, Notes 15.03.

The trustee or custodian must be independent from the fund manager and the scheme itself.

3.4. Marketing the fund
FAIS and CISCA governs the production and offering of marketing materials. The manager of the fund (who need not be FAIS licensed) or an intermediary (who must be FAIS licensed).

The key content requirements for marketing materials are detailed in the South African Code of Advertising Practice (to which CISs are subject), as applicable.

Marketing materials do not require any licences or authorisations, but FAIS and CISCA must be complied with.

The provisions of the Public Finance Management Act 1999 should be considered when marketing to government pension funds and other government bodies.

3.5. Taxation
Funds. The tax treatment is determined by the type of fund.

CIS in Securities. Taxation of equity CIS is set out in section 25BA of the ITA, which was incorporated into the ITA in 2010. Section 25BA treats amounts, other amounts of a capital nature, received by or accrued to any portfolio of a CIS (other than a portfolio of a property CIS) as follows:
- if the amount is distributed to any person entitled to the distribution due to being the holder of a participatory interest in that portfolio within 12 months after its accrual to the portfolio, it is deemed to have directly accrued to the person on the date of distribution;
- if the amount is not distributed as set out above within 12 months of its accrual to the CIS, it is deemed to have accrued to the CIS on the last day of the 12-month period commencing on the date of its accrual to the CIS.

If the amount is attributable to a dividend received by or accrued to the portfolio, it must be deemed income of the portfolio (that is, the CIS will be subject to income tax on the dividends at the rate that applies to it).

Section 25BA of the ITA does not apply to:
- property CISs;
- capital amounts; and
- foreign CISs.

The effect of section 25BA is that revenue amounts received by or accrued to a CIS are either:
- taxed in the hands of the unit holders, if distributed to them within 12 months of their accrual to the CIS; or
- taxed in the hands of the CIS, if not distributed to the unit holders within 12 months of their accrual to the CIS.

If the revenue amounts are dividends, they are taxed in the hands of the CIS. Therefore, all dividends (which are ordinarily exempt from income tax) are treated as taxable ordinary revenue if retained beyond the 12-month period. Subsequent distributions to unit holders after the amount has been taxed in the CIS are tax free in the hands of the unit holders.

Property CIS. Property CISs are treated as persons and companies for tax purposes.

The taxation of property CISs changed on 1 April 2013 with the introduction of section 25BB into the ITA.

Section 25BB introduces the concept of Real Estate Investment Trusts (REITs) into the ITA and encompasses both the property CISs and PLS company regimes. Section 1 of the ITA defines a REIT as a resident company whose shares are both:
- listed on a stock exchange (as defined in section 1 of the Securities Services Act of 2004 and licensed under section 10 of that Act); and
- listed as shares in a REIT (as defined in the JSE Limited Listings Requirements).

The effect of this definition is that section 25BB only applies to listed companies.

Section 25BB primarily deals with the taxation of REITs themselves. It allows a REIT or controlled property company (CPC) (that is, a South African resident subsidiary of a REIT, as defined in International Financial Reporting Standard (IFRS) 10) to deduct the amount of any 'qualifying distribution' declared or incurred during any tax year by that REIT or CPC. A qualifying distribution is any dividend declared, or interest incurred, in respect of a debenture forming part of a property-linked unit during a tax year if:
- for REITs, CPCs or an associated property company incorporated, formed or established during that tax year: more than 75 per cent of the gross income received by or accrued to the REIT, CPC or associated property company until the date of declaration, consists of rental income; or
- in any other case: more than 75 per cent of the gross income received by or accrued to a REIT, CPC or associated company in the preceding tax year, consisted of rental income.

The aggregate amount of the deduction cannot be more than the taxable

income for that tax year of the REIT or CPC, before taking into account:
- the amount of taxable capital gains; and
- any deduction under section 25BB.

Any amount received or accrued to a REIT/CPC during a tax year in relation to a financial instrument (other than a share in a REIT, controlled property or associated property company) is treated as an amount of a revenue nature and included in the income of the REIT or CPC for that tax year.

REITs and CPCs are not subject to capital gains tax on the disposal of immovable property, shares in a REIT or a CPC.

Interest received by or accrued to a person during any tax year in respect of a debenture forming part of a property-linked unit in a REIT or a CPC held by that person is treated as a dividend in the hands of the recipients. In addition, interest paid in respect of a property-linked unit in a REIT or a CPC is treated as a dividend paid by that REIT or that CPC for the purposes of the withholding tax on dividends and not interest for the purposes of the withholding tax on interest.

REITs and CPCs are exempt from income tax on any gains realised on the disposal of immovable property, shareholding in RETTs and shares in CPCs.

It was announced in the 2013 budget speech that the REIT regime will be extended to unlisted REITs in specific circumstances.

Foreign CIS. Foreign CISs are treated as companies for tax purposes. The definition of a company is the ITA specifically includes a portfolio comprised in any investment scheme carried on outside South Africa that is comparable to a portfolio of a CIS in participation bonds or a portfolio of a CIS in securities where members of the public are invited or permitted to contribute to and hold participatory interests in that portfolio through shares, units or any other form of participatory interest. Although a foreign CIS is treated as a company for tax purposes, amounts paid to redeem participatory interests do not constitute dividends for tax purposes. Redemptions of participatory interests can trigger a capital gain or loss for the investor unless the participatory interests are held as trading stock.

Resident investors. Investors in CISs other than property CISs are taxed on any income received by, or accruing to, the CIS provided that it is distributed within a 12-month period. Any income which is exempt from income tax (or tax exempt dividend income) distributed by the CIS remains exempt from income tax once it is received by an investor.

Dividends distributed by a REIT to its resident shareholders are subject to income tax (and exempt from withholding tax on dividends), regardless of whether the REIT makes qualifying distributions during the tax year. The ordinary income tax treatment applies to any resident shareholder regardless of whether they are a company, trust or natural person. Interest forming part of a property linked unit is treated in a similar manner (as a dividend).

The acquisition of shares in REITs is exempt from securities transfer tax (STT).

Non-resident investors. Non-resident investors in CISs other than property CISs can be taxed in South Africa on the income received from a CIS or a PLS,

unless the provisions of a double taxation agreement (DTA) between South Africa and the non-resident's country of residence provides otherwise. As a general principle, South Africa taxes non-residents on income received or accrued to them from a South African source. To determine whether a non-resident is subject to tax in South Africa, regard must be had to the:
- Specific DTA applicable.
- Type of income.

Dividends distributed by a REIT to its foreign shareholders are exempt from income tax and withholding tax on dividends. Going forward, dividends distributed to foreign shareholders of REITs will be subject to withholding tax on dividends (and not be treated as ordinary revenue). This tax treatment is deferred until 1 January 2014. In the interim, all payments of this nature paid to foreign persons are exempt from withholding tax on dividends.

The acquisition of shares in REITs is exempt from STT.

3.6. Customary or common terms

Insofar as CISs are concerned it is usual to use the standard form documentation which is available on the FSB's website: www.fsb.co.za. Insofar as REITs are concerned they follow established international norms.

4. PROPOSED CHANGES AND DEVELOPMENTS

Insofar as private equity funds are concerned there are no significant proposals for reform of the private equity funds market in South Africa currently under discussion.

On 13 September 2012, the South African National Treasury released a paper setting out proposals for the regulation of hedge funds in South Africa. The paper proposes that the regulatory framework for hedge funds be set out as a declared scheme within the CISCA by the Minister of Finance and subsequently through the creation of a separate chapter for hedge funds within CISCA. This is still in the proposal stage.

In addition, it was proposed in the budget speech delivered on 27 February 2013 that hedge funds will fall under CIS legislation and will be regulated accordingly. While regulated hedge funds will be treated much like other CISs, unit holders will be required to treat their earnings as ordinary revenue when realised. It is stated that this should generate the intended tax result without interfering with daily operations.

Spain

Fernando de las Cuevas, Valentina Rodríguez & Remedios García **Gómez-Acebo & Pombo**

1. MARKET OVERVIEW

The investment funds market in Spain can be divided into two separate categories: those governed by Act 35/2003 of 4 November, on collective investment undertakings (LIIC) which include retail funds, real estate funds and hedge funds; and those governed by Act 25/2005 of 24 November, on private equity entities (LECR) which include private equity entities. Both the LIIC and the LECR allow these entities to be incorporated as:

- investment funds: separate patrimony with no legal personality, aimed at raising public funds to be managed and invested in different assets, depending on the investment policy, provided that the profit of the investor is collectively determined and managed by a management company.
- investment companies (joint stock companies): with legal personality, aimed at raising public funds to be managed and invested in different assets, depending on the investment policy, provided that the profit of the investor is collectively determined and can either be self-managed or managed by a management company.

The collective investment undertakings (IICs) covered by the LIIC can be divided into: (i) financial IICs, those that can only invest in financial instruments which include retail funds and hedge funds; and (ii) non-financial IICs, all those not considered financial IICs and non-categorised entities which include real estate IICs (no non-categorised entity has ever been registered in Spain).

The LECR applies to private equity funds and companies (ECRs) which are considered financial entities aimed at taking a stake in non-financial/non-real estate companies that carry out economic activities.

The patrimony of the Spanish financial investment funds industry was reduced by 6.3 per cent during 2012 to EUR 124,040 million and the patrimony of financial investment companies was reduced by 2.5 per cent to EUR 23,690 million (the recessive tendency of the last years seems to be stabilising). Also, during 2012 the patrimony of real estate IICs decreased by 6.7 per cent compared to 2011 reaching EUR 4,484 million and the patrimony of ECRs decreased to EUR 2,172 million (9 per cent less than in 2011).

In contrast, the patrimony of hedge funds increased by 12 per cent compared to 2011 reaching EUR 1,457 million.

Of the total 5,246 financial IICs registered at the end of 2012, 2,205 were investment funds, 2,981 were investment companies and only 60 were hedge funds. At the end of 2012, only 14 non-financial real estate IICs were registered with the Spanish Securities and Exchange Commission (SSEC).

Spain

With respect to the ECRs, 139 of the total 258 entities registered at the end of 2012 were private equity companies and 119 were private equity funds.

Even though the retail market in Spain has decreased these last years due to current financial market conditions, it has reached a satisfactory level of maturity that will set the foundations for future growth, bearing in mind that the Spanish market is small compared to other countries where the investment funds industry is more consolidated and has had more exposure. ECRs, hedge funds and real estate funds in particular, still have a lot more ground to cover before they achieve the level of maturity existing in other countries.

2. ALTERNATIVE INVESTMENT FUNDS
2.1. Common structures
Real estate funds
Spanish real estate IICs can be incorporated as:
- investment funds with a minimum patrimony equal to EUR 9,000,000 divided into units (if divided into sub-funds, each sub-fund shall have a minimum patrimony of at least EUR 2,400,000). The minimum number of investors is 100; or
- investment companies with a minimum share capital of EUR 9,000,000 divided into shares, and the investors become shareholders of the company, being entitled to attend and vote at the company's shareholders meetings regardless of whether the entity is managed by a management company. The minimum number of investors is 100. These are the only entities that can be incorporated as closed-ended entities (fixed share capital).

Real estate IICs must invest their patrimony in real estate property to be leased once acquired and real estate properties in the process of being built are subject to certain requirements.

Investing in a real estate company as opposed to investing in a fund will not afford any advantages or disadvantages since both entities are governed by the same laws and are subject to the same requirements and level of supervision.

Without prejudice to the above, investing in a real estate company will mean that in the case of changes in the investment policies, distribution of dividends, change of the management company or custodian, delegation of the management duties, change of control of the management company, merger, transformation, spin-off or changes in the fees, investors in an investment company will have to vote on these decisions at the shareholders meeting and accept the decisions of the majority of shareholders, while investors in an investment fund will have a separation right at no cost in case any of these changes are implemented.

Hedge funds
Spanish hedge funds are legally known as IICs *de inversión libre* (IICILs) and can be incorporated as:
- investment funds with a minimum patrimony equal to EUR 3,000,000

divided into units (if divided into sub-funds, each sub-fund shall have a minimum patrimony of at least EUR 600,000). The minimum number of investors is 25; or
- investment companies with a minimum share capital of EUR 2,400,000 divided into shares (if divided into sub-funds, each sub-fund shall have a minimum share capital of EUR 480,000), and the investors become shareholders of the company, being entitled to attend and vote at the shareholders meetings of the company. The minimum number of investors is 25.

IICILs can also be incorporated as funds of funds meaning an investment fund or company that must invest at least 60 per cent of its patrimony in the shares or units of other Spanish or foreign hedge funds.

Investing in IICILs incorporated as an investment company, as opposed to investing in an IICIL incorporated as an investment fund, will not afford any advantages or disadvantages since both entities are governed by the same laws and are subject to the same requirements and level of supervision.

Without prejudice to the above, investing in IICILs incorporated as investment companies will mean that in the case of changes in the investment policies, distribution of dividends, change of the management company or custodian, delegation of the management duties, change of control of the management company, merger, transformation, spin-off or changes in the fees, investors will have to vote on these decisions at the shareholders meeting and accept the decisions of the majority of shareholders, while investors in an investment fund will have a separation right at no cost.

Private equity funds
Spanish private equity funds can be incorporated as:
- funds with a minimum patrimony equal to EUR 1,650,000. The interests of the investors are called units; or
- companies with a minimum share capital of EUR 1,200,000 divided into shares. Investors become shareholders of the company, being entitled to attend and vote at the shareholders meetings of the company.

ECRs, regardless of whether they are incorporated as funds or companies, can be subject to the common regime or the simplified regime. Simplified regime ECRs must be offered without the use of any advertising, the minimum investment must be of at least EUR 500,000 (unless offered to institutional investors) and must not have more than 20 investors (excluding institutional clients, directors and officers, employees and the management company). Common regime ECRs are those that do not comply with one or more of the simplified regime conditions.

Investing in ECRs incorporated as companies as opposed to investing in ECRs incorporated as funds will not afford any advantages or disadvantages since both entities are governed by the same laws and are subject to the same requirements and level of supervision.

Subject to the wording of the articles of association and management regulations of the ECRs, in a company, shareholders normally have the power to approve any changes deemed appropriate, including replacing the management company with another entity, while in a fund, changes such as these are more limited.

2.2. Regulatory framework
Real estate funds

All real estate IICs and their management companies are subject to the supervision of both the SSEC and the Spanish Service for the Prevention of Money Laundering and Terrorist Financing (SSPMLTF).

The most relevant laws and regulations applicable to real estate IICs and their management companies are:
- LIIC;
- Royal Decree 1082/2012 which approves the regulations implementing the LIIC (RIIC);
- various SSEC circulars and orders from the Ministry of Economy on accounting, information obligations, risk diversification, economic reports and others; and
- the Royal Decree Law on capital companies.

The incorporation of real estate IICs requires the prior authorisation of the SSEC after review and verification that all legal requirements are complied with. To obtain the authorisation of the SSEC, the following are some of the main steps that will need to be followed:
- preparation of an authorisation project that must include at least: (i) name of the entity; (ii) share capital/patrimony; (iii) registered offices; (iv) if a company, names of the directors and information on whether the company will be self-managed or not (if managed by a management company, the name of the manager, and if self-managed, information on the accounting and administrative organisation, human resources, economic resources, internal company policies and procedures, risk assessment procedures, anti-money laundering procedures, etc. must be included) and if a fund, name of the manager; (v) prospectus; (vi) articles of association/management regulations; and (vii) investment objectives;
- filing of the authorisation project with the SSEC;
- granting of the prior authorisation by the SSEC;
- if a company, incorporation before a notary public and if a fund, signature of the incorporation agreement;
- if a company, registration with the Commercial Registry; and
- registration with the SSEC.

The SSEC has a period of two months, in the case of a fund, or three months, in the case of a company, from the date on which the project is filed to grant the authorisation, which is extendable if any additional information is requested by the SSEC. If a period of five months lapses from the date on which the authorisation project is filed without any written requests from the SSEC, the authorisation will be deemed to be granted (positive silence).

Also, management companies require the prior authorisation of the SSEC to be incorporated provided that all legal requirements are complied with, in particular, that the management company has sufficient economic, personal and operating resources to carry out the activity.

Hedge funds

IICILs and their management companies are subject to the supervision of both the SSEC and the SSPMLTF.

The most relevant laws and regulations applicable to hedge funds and their management companies are:
- LIIC;
- RIIC;
- Circular 1/2006 on hedge funds;
- various SSEC circulars and orders from the Ministry of Economy on accounting, information obligations, risk diversification, economic reports and others; and
- the Royal Decree Law on capital companies.

The incorporation of any type of IICILs requires the prior authorisation of the SSEC after review and verification that all the legal requirements are complied with. To obtain the authorisation of the SSEC the same main steps indicated above will need to be followed.

The SSEC has a period of three months from the date on which the project is filed to grant the authorisation, which is extendable if any additional documents or corrections are requested by the SSEC. If a period of five months lapses from the date on which the authorisation project is filed, the authorisation will be deemed to be granted (positive silence).

Also, the management companies of IICILs require the prior authorisation of the SSEC before they can be incorporated, provided all the legal requirements are complied with, in particular, that the management company has sufficient economic, personal and operating resources to carry out the activity, the directors have professional experience in the hedge funds industry and that the company has sufficient means to control the risks derived from the management of hedge funds.

Private equity funds

All ECRs and their management companies are subject to the supervision of both the SSEC and the SSPMLTF.

The most relevant laws and regulations applicable to ECRs and their management companies are:
- LECR;
- SSEC Circular 3/2010 on administrative proceedings, changes and modifications and authorisations of ECRs and their management companies;
- various SSEC circulars and orders from the Ministry of Economy on accounting, information obligations, risk diversification, economic reports and others; and
- the Royal Decree Law on capital companies.

The incorporation of any type of ECR requires the prior authorisation of the SSEC after review and verification that all the legal requirements are complied with. To obtain the authorisation of the SSEC, the following are some of the main steps that will need to be followed:
- preparation of the authorisation project of the entity that must include

at least the following information: (i) name of the entity; (ii) share capital/patrimony; (iii) registered offices; (iv) if a company, names of the directors and information on whether the company will be self-managed or not (if it is to be managed by a management company, the name of the manager must be included and if to be self-managed, information on the accounting and administrative organisation, human resources, economic resources, internal company policies and procedures, risk assessment procedures, anti-money laundering procedures, etc. must be included) and if a fund, name of the manager; (v) prospectus; (vi) articles of association/management regulations; (vii) investment objectives and investment decision process; and (viii) business plan;
- filing of the authorisation project with the SSEC;
- granting of the prior authorisation by the SSEC;
- if a company, incorporation before a notary public and if a fund, signature of the incorporation agreement;
- if a company, registration with the Commercial Registry; and
- registration with the SSEC.

The SSEC has a period of two months, for common regime entities, and one month, for simplified regime entities, from the date on which the project is filed to grant the authorisation. If the said periods lapse without any written communication from the SSEC, the authorisation request will be deemed to be denied (negative silence).

Also, the management companies of ECRs require the prior authorisation of the SSEC before they can be incorporated, provided all legal requirements are complied with, in particular, that the management company has sufficient economic, personal and operating resources to carry out the activity.

2.3. Operational requirements
Real estate funds
Control of the management company – the custodian
All real estate funds must have a custodian working in conjunction with the management company. The custodians may be brokers, in which case they are supervised by the SSEC, or banks, in which case they are supervised by the SSEC and the Bank of Spain. Custodians are also subject to the supervision of the SSPMLTF.

Among others, the duties of the custodian include:
- custody of the securities, cash and assets;
- control and supervision;
- issuance of unit certificates to investors;
- payment of share reimbursements to investors;
- receipt and transmission of purchase and sale orders; and
- any duty that may serve to improve its service.

Reporting obligations
Any changes in the authorisation project of the real estate IICs must be previously authorised by the SSEC. The SSEC has a period of two months, in the case of a fund, or three months, in the case of a company, from the

date on which the changes to the project are filed to grant the authorisation, which is extendable if any additional documents or corrections are requested by the SSEC. If a period of five months lapses from the date on which the changes to the project are filed without any written requests from the CSSEC, the authorisation will be deemed to be granted (positive silence).

As regards the periodic reporting obligations, real estate funds are obliged to:
- prepare a full prospectus which must be previously approved by the SSEC (and any changes thereto) and delivered to investors, if requested, before the initial subscription of any shares and in the case of any changes;
- prepare a key investors' information document which must be previously approved by the SSEC (and any changes thereto) and delivered to investors before the initial subscription of any shares and in the case of any changes;
- prepare an annual audited report which must be delivered to the SSEC and to investors within a period of one month from the end of the period of time to which it refers and to investors, if requested, before the initial subscription of any shares;
- prepare a semi-annual report which must be delivered to the SSEC and to investors before the initial subscription of any shares and within a period of one month from the end of the period of time to which it refers;
- prepare two quarterly reports which must be delivered to the SSEC and to investors, if requested, within a period of one month from the end of the period of time to which it refers and to investors, if requested, before the initial subscription of any shares;
- communicate to the SSEC the existence of any relevant facts that may affect the entity's performance, such as any event that may reasonably affect an investment decision of a client, any reduction in the entity's share capital equal to or higher than 20 per cent, any reimbursements that may affect 20 per cent or more of the entity's patrimony, any debt obligations *vis-à-vis* third parties exceeding 5 per cent of the entity's patrimony, changes in the management company or custodian and any other that may require changes to the entity's documents; and
- communicate to the SSEC the data of any investor directly or indirectly holding a significant participation in the entity, meaning an investor that reaches or falls below the following thresholds: 20 per cent, 40 per cent, 60 per cent, 80 per cent or 100 per cent of the entity's patrimony.

Assessment of the real estate property
Real estate IICs are obliged to appoint an official assessment company registered with the Bank of Spain. The assessment company shall make annual assessments of the properties following strict valuation rules that will serve to calculate the value of the patrimony and net asset value of the shares of the entity.

Diversification and liquidity
Real estate IICs must invest in properties that are already built or in the process of being built, in options allowing the purchase of properties or rights over the properties provided that these rights allow the properties to be rented, or in public concessions provided that these allow the properties to be rented.

Companies must invest at least 80 per cent of the annual average of their monthly assets in the said properties whilst funds must invest at least 70 per cent of the annual average of their monthly assets in the said properties and maintain liquidity equal to at least 10 per cent of the total assets of the preceding month (during the months when the redemption right is granted to investors). The rest of the entity's patrimony must be invested in securities listed on any stock exchange or on any other organised markets or trading systems.

Risk diversification rules prohibit the same asset from representing more than 35 per cent of the total patrimony of the entity.

Hedge funds
Control of the management company – the custodian
All IICILs must have a custodian working in conjunction with the management company or the investment company if self-managed. The custodians may be brokers, in which case they are supervised by the SSEC, or banks, in which case they are supervised by the SSEC and the Bank of Spain. Custodians are also subject to the supervision of the SSPMLTF.

Among others, the duties of the custodians include the following:
- custody of the securities, cash and assets;
- control and supervision;
- issuance of share/unit certificates to investors;
- payment of share reimbursements to investors;
- receipt and transmission of purchase and sale orders; and
- any duty that may serve to improve its service.

Reporting obligations
Any changes in the authorisation project of IICILs have to be previously authorised by the SSEC. The SSEC has a period of three months from the date on which the changes to the authorisation project are filed to grant the authorisation, which is extendable if any additional documents or corrections are requested by the SSEC. If a period of five months lapses from the date on which the changes to the project are filed, the authorisation will be deemed to be granted (positive silence).

As regards the periodic reporting obligations, IICILs and their management companies are obliged to:
- prepare a full prospectus which must be previously approved by the SSEC (and any changes thereto) and delivered to investors, if requested, before the initial subscription of any shares and in the case of any changes;
- prepare a key investor information document which must be previously approved by the SSEC (and any changes thereto) and delivered to investors before the initial subscription of any shares and in the case of any changes;
- prepare an annual audited report which must be delivered to the SSEC and to investors within a period of one month from the end of the period of time to which it refers;
- prepare a semi-annual report which must be delivered to the SSEC and to investors before the initial subscription of any shares and within a period

Spain

of one month from the end of the period of time to which it refers;
- prepare two quarterly reports which must be delivered to the SSEC and to investors, if requested, within a period of one month from the end of the period of time to which it refers;
- communicate to the SSEC the existence of any relevant facts that may affect the entity's performance, such as any event that may reasonably affect an investment decision of a client, any reduction in the entity's share capital or patrimony equal to or higher than 20 per cent, any reimbursements that may affect 20 per cent or more of the entity's patrimony, any debt obligations *vis-à-vis* third parties exceeding 5 per cent of the entity's patrimony, changes in the management company or custodian and any other that may require changes to the entity's documents;
- communicate to the SSEC the data of any investor directly or indirectly holding a significant participation in the entity, meaning an investor that reaches or falls below the following thresholds: 20 per cent, 40 per cent, 60 per cent, 80 per cent or 100 per cent of the entity's patrimony;
- carry out periodic stress tests and risk control and keep the reports obtained from such control on file for a period of five years; and
- prepare and send to the SSEC a monthly statistical report in the form approved by the SSEC.

Diversification and liquidity
IICILs may invest in any financial instruments although the general diversification and investment rules applicable to the rest of financial IICs are not applicable to these entities. IICILs may also invest in derivatives regardless of the nature of the underlying goods and obligations and may pledge their assets. The permitted debt ratio is five times the entity's patrimony.

IICILs incorporated as funds of funds are required to invest at least 60 per cent of their patrimony in other hedge funds (Spanish or foreign, provided that the foreign entities are similar to the IICILs or are domiciled in an OECD country), provided that no more than 10 per cent of the patrimony is invested in the same entity.

Private equity funds
Control of the management company – the custodian
ECRs are not required to have a custodian.

Reporting obligations
Any changes in the authorisation project of ECRs have to be previously authorised by the SSEC. The SSEC has a period of one month from the date on which the request for changes is filed to grant the authorisation or from the date in which the documents are deemed complete. If the said period lapses without a written communication from the SSEC, the authorisation will be deemed to be denied (negative silence).

As regards the periodic reporting obligations, ECRs subject to the common regime are obliged to:
- prepare a prospectus, unless it is subject to the simplified regime. The

prospectus and any changes thereto must be previously approved by the SSEC. Also, the prospectus must be delivered to investors;
- prepare an annual audited report. The annual report must be delivered to the SSEC and to investors;
- provide any information required by the shareholders according to the LECR; and
- communicate to the SSEC the data of any investor directly or indirectly holding a significant participation in the entity, meaning an investor that reaches or falls below the following thresholds: 20 per cent, 40 per cent, 60 per cent, 80 per cent or 100 per cent of the entity's patrimony.

ECRs must also inform the SSEC of any events that may affect the value of the shares or units of the ECRs, their business, performance and financial situation.

Diversification and liquidity
ECRs must invest at least 60 per cent of their assets in: (i) non-financial/non-real estate companies that, at the time of the investment, are not listed in any Spanish, European Union or OECD-regulated market; (ii) listed companies provided that these are excluded from listing within the 12 months following the date on which the stake is taken; and (iii) companies whose patrimony includes real estate properties (more than 50 per cent of the patrimony) provided that 85 per cent of the real estate properties of the patrimony are destined to an economic activity. Out of the said 60 per cent, up to 30 per cent of the assets may be dedicated to granting profit sharing loans and up to 20 per cent to granting other types of financing to non-participated companies and up to 20 per cent of their assets in other ECR. The rest of the assets may be invested in listed fixed income securities, shares and units of IICs, cash, loans or assets required for the exercise of its activities.

The main diversification rules limit the investment in the same company to 25 per cent of the assets of the ECR.

2.4. Marketing the fund
Real estate funds
The marketing (meaning any advertising activity aimed at obtaining clients which includes any type of communication sent to potential clients by any means, such as telephone calls, meetings, personalised letters and emails) of real estate IICs must be carried out with the assistance of a duly authorised financial intermediary (banks, brokers or management companies) and can be directed at any type of investors in Spain.

Hedge funds
The marketing (meaning any advertising activity aimed at obtaining clients which includes any type of communication sent to potential clients by any means, such as telephone calls, meetings, personalised letters and emails) of IICILs must be carried out with the assistance of a duly authorised financial intermediary (banks, brokers or management companies) and can be directed at any type of investors in Spain.

Spain

The marketing of the units or shares of IICILs is subject to certain rules which are: (i) the minimum subscription amount is EUR 50,000; (ii) the target clients can only be qualified investors (meaning banks, investment service companies, insurance companies, IICs and their management companies, pension schemes and their management companies; governmental entities; other legal entities not considered small and medium-sized companies; and individuals and legal entities who have requested to be treated as qualified investors provided they are approved and registered as such); and (iii) investors must sign a statement declaring that they are aware of the risks related to the investment. However, the marketing of IICILs incorporated as funds of funds is not subject to these rules and restrictions and can be directed at any investors although the statement whereby the client declares that it is aware of the risks involved in the investment is always required.

Private equity funds
The marketing of ECRs subject to the simplified regime must be done privately with no advertising activity (meaning any advertising activity aimed at obtaining clients which includes any type of communication sent to potential clients by any means, such as telephone calls, meetings, personalised letters and emails,) and can be directed at any type of investors.

The marketing of ECRs subject to the common regime can be directed at any type of investors. The marketing of ECRs is commonly carried out by the management company.

2.5. Taxation
IICs
The Spanish tax legislation does not differentiate between the different types of IICs except for the purposes of referring to certain conditions to be fulfilled in order to benefit from a more favourable tax regime, regarding the minimum number of investors and/or types of assets to be invested in. Therefore, we will refer herein to the taxation of IICs and their investors, globally, thus covering real estate funds, hedge funds and retail funds, as regulated in the LIIC.

Taxation of the fund
Spanish IICs (including real estate funds and hedge funds) are subject to the Spanish corporate income tax (CIT), as regulated in the consolidated text of the CIT Law, approved by Royal Legislative Decree 4/2004 and Royal Decree 1777/2004.

The calculation of the taxable income under CIT is made under the general CIT regime and, thus, takes as a starting point the profit or loss shown in the books of account, which is then modified by any adjustments imposed or permitted by the law.

The current general CIT rate is 30 per cent, but some Spanish IICs can benefit from a reduced 1 per cent tax rate upon compliance of some specific conditions and requirements. In particular, the IICs that can benefit from the reduced tax rate are: (i) financial investment companies and funds;

and (ii) real estate companies and funds, provided that the requirements established in Article 28, paragraph 5, of the CIT Law on number of investors and investment of the assets are complied with. These requirements are established in the CIT Law taking as a reference the corresponding regulation contained in the LIIC for each type of IIC.

Those IICs that benefit from the reduced tax rate cannot apply any CIT tax credits, nor the tax exemptions on income from foreign source.

Taxation of investors
The Spanish taxation applicable to investors in Spanish IICs may vary depending on whether the investor is a Spanish tax resident or not. Also, in the case of Spanish residents, their taxation differs for individuals and corporations.

(i) Spanish resident investors
Investors in IICs who are considered Spanish tax residents, according to Spanish internal tax legislation and applicable tax treaties, if any, are taxed under their corresponding personal tax in respect of income or capital gains resulting from their investment in the relevant IIC.

In general, individuals are subject to personal income tax (PIT), as regulated by Law 35/2006 and Royal Decree 439/2007. Companies, as well as other entities, are generally subject to the CIT according to the following rules:

Individuals
According to the provisions of the Spanish PIT Law, Spanish resident individuals are subject to the tax in respect of all their worldwide income and gains, including income and gains from IICs.

Generally, dividends from IICs and capital gains obtained as a consequence of the reimbursement or transfer of their units, do not benefit from a special tax treatment for the recipient. Instead, they will be taxed as savings income, being subject to a fixed rate of 21 per cent (up to EUR 6,000 per year), 24 per cent (for savings income between EUR 6,000 and EUR 24,000) and 27 per cent in respect of the excess over EUR 24,000 (these tax rates are temporarily applicable in 2012 and 2013). No tax credits or deductions for the avoidance of double taxation are available.

Please note, however, that as from 1 January 2013, capital gains made upon disposal of the units of an IIC are taxed at the general rates (up to 52 per cent) of the PIT if the disposal takes place within the first year after acquisition.

Notwithstanding the above, according to Article 94 of the PIT Law, investors in IICs that comply with some specific requirements can benefit from a deferral in the taxation of capital gains obtained as a consequence of the reimbursement or transfer of units or shares of IICs provided that: (i) the amount of such benefit is reinvested in the acquisition of units or shares of another IIC and the investor does have access to the funds before reinvestment; (ii) the number of unitholders or shareholders of the IIC whose shares or units are transferred exceeds 500; and (iii) the investor has not held more than a 5 per cent participation in the share capital of the relevant IIC during the 12 months prior to the transfer.

According to this special tax regime, the new shares or units received (upon reinvestment), will maintain the same date and acquisition cost of the former shares or units transferred or reimbursed, so that capital gains will be effectively taxed once the definitive transfer or reimbursement of the units or shares takes place.

Corporations
Spanish entities or corporations investing in IICs will include any income or gain obtained from such investment in their CIT taxable base, under the general rules of the tax.

In the case of investment in IICs benefiting from the reduced CIT rate, the investor will not be entitled to apply any tax credit on dividends or gains obtained from the IIC.

In the case of both individuals and corporations investing in IICs, if these are incorporated in a tax haven, the investor will include in its/his taxable base of each year the positive difference between the value of the units/ participations in the IIC at the end of the year and their acquisition cost. Such taxable difference will increase the acquisition cost for future years. In the absence of evidence, such difference will be presumed to be equivalent to 15 per cent of the acquisition cost of the shares/units. In addition, dividends distributed by the IIC will not be taxed at investor level but will reduce the acquisition cost for the purposes of determining the taxable amount each year.

(ii) Non-Spanish resident investors
Non-Spanish residents obtaining Spanish source income are subject to the non-residents' income tax (NRIT), as regulated in the consolidated text of the NRIT Law, approved by Royal Legislative Decree 5/2004 of 5 March, and in Royal Decree 1776/2004 of 30 July, which approved the regulations on the tax. Special attention shall also be paid to tax treaties entered into by Spain with other territories for the avoidance of double taxation, which could be of application depending on the residence of the investor.

Taxation of non-resident investors also differs depending on whether they operate in Spain through a permanent establishment or not. The concept of permanent establishment is contained in the NRIT Law, in the absence of an applicable tax treaty.

Foreign investors operating in Spain through a permanent establishment are taxed in similar terms to Spanish corporations, following the same rules of the CIT with some minor particularities.

Foreign investors who do not operate in Spain through a permanent establishment are taxed under the NRIT in respect of Spanish source income and gains. In general, income and gains obtained from an investment in Spanish IICs shall be subject to a reduced rate of 21 per cent (applicable rate in 2012 and 2013). However, a tax exemption is applicable in respect of gains obtained from the transfer or reimbursement of units or shares in investment funds, provided that such shares or units are listed on a Spanish official stock market, and that the investor resides in a territory with a tax treaty in force with Spain, which includes a provision for information exchange.

Private equity funds
Taxation of the ECR

The tax regime of ECRs is regulated by Article 55 of the CIT Law.

In general terms, gains obtained by ECRs upon disposal of qualifying investee companies (as defined in Article 2 of LECR) are 99 per cent exempt, provided the disposal takes place after the first year of holding and before the end of the fifteenth year. This term, however, can be extended under certain conditions. In contrast, the 99 per cent tax exemption shall not apply if the disposal takes place within the first year of shareholding or after the fifteenth year (except if the term is extended).

Neither shall this 99 per cent exemption apply if the transfer is made in of a party related to either the ECR, its shareholders or directors, or a resident in a tax haven, save if the transfer is made in favour of the investee company itself, any of the shareholders or directors of the investee company (provided he/she is not, and has not been, related to the ECR for a reason other than its relation to the investee company) or another ECR.

Finally, the 99 per cent does not apply if the shares of the investee company have been directly or indirectly acquired by the ECR from a related party, provided that prior to the acquisition the investee company and the shareholders of the ECR were also related parties.

If the ECR transfers its shares in the investee company to another related ECR, the original acquisition date and cost of the investments will be applied by the acquiring ECR for the purposes of determining the taxation applicable.

Regarding dividends received by the ECRs from their participating companies, the ECRs are entitled to a 100 per cent deduction (or exemption, under Article 21.2 of the CIT Law, in the case of non-Spanish investee companies), irrespective of the ECR's shareholding and duration of the investment.

Taxation of investors

As in the case of investors in IICs, the taxation of ECR's investors depend on their residence and status:

(i) In the case of Spanish resident investors subject to the Spanish CIT (or non-resident investors operating in Spain through a permanent establishment), they will be entitled to a 100 per cent tax credit, irrespective of their shareholding and duration of the investment, in respect of dividends received from the ECR and capital gains obtained upon disposal of their shares.

(ii) In the case of non-Spanish resident investors, (whether individuals or entities) who do not operate in Spain through a permanent establishment), income or gains obtained from their participation in the ECR shall not be considered to be obtained in Spain for NRIT purposes. The regime described in (i) and (ii) above shall not apply if the income is obtained through a tax haven.

(iii) In the case of Spanish individuals investing in ECRs, dividends or gains

Spain

obtained from their shareholding in the ECR shall be taxed in their PIT at the rates indicated in section 2.5., Taxation of investors, above.

2.6. Customary or common terms
Real estate funds

The duration of real estate funds is commonly indefinite whilst the duration of real estate companies is fixed between 10 to 20 years after which time the company is wound up and liquidated.

Investors in real estate funds must be allowed to redeem their shares at least once a year, although the SSEC may suspend the redemption for up to two years. In the case of real estate companies the shares cannot be redeemed until the duration date indicated in the prospectus and articles of association has lapsed although the shares may be transferred between investors provided that the transfer is communicated to the manager and to the custodian so that the shares registry can be updated.

There are no specific requirements as to the need to have the management company invest its money in the entity, although the seed money is normally provided by the manager.

Since real estate investment companies are incorporated as joint stock companies, the shareholders may vote at a shareholders meeting to change the management company while in the case of funds, the investors have a separation right in case of change of the management company.

The main rules applicable to the remuneration arrangements of real estate investment funds are:
- the management company may receive a management fee from the retail fund. The fee may be equal to a percentage of the patrimony (not higher than 4 per cent) or a percentage of the performance (not higher than 10 per cent) or both (not higher than 1.5 per cent of the patrimony and 5 per cent of the performance);
- the management company may receive a subscription fee and a reimbursement fee from the retail fund (not higher than 5 per cent of the net asset value of the units subscribed or redeemed);
- the custodian may receive a custodian fee from the retail fund (not higher than four times 1,000 of the annual patrimony); and
- the property assessment expenses shall be borne by the management company.

The LIIC and the RIIC do not establish any limitations regarding fees applicable to real estate companies since these can be controlled by the shareholders meeting.

As a further measure to protect investors, the properties of real estate funds are always held in the name of the fund, never in the name of the manager or custodian.

Hedge funds

The duration of IICILs is usually indefinite but this can change when they are incorporated as investment companies given that investors may take over the company and vote at the shareholders meeting to wind up and liquidate the company.

The net asset value of the shares or units of the IICILs must be calculated at least quarterly, although the shares or units will not be redeemable every time the net asset value is calculated. The shares or units may be transferred between investors provided that the transfer is communicated to the manager and to the custodian so that the shares registry can be updated.

There are no specific requirements as to the need to have the management company invest its money in the entity, although the seed money is normally provided by the manager.

Management companies managing IICILs are required to have additional measures for risk control, assessment and investment selection. Also, self-managed hedge IICILs or their managers are obliged to implement periodic risk control procedures including simulations of adverse conditions. In those cases where the IICILs are incorporated as investment companies, the shareholders may vote at the shareholders' meeting to change the management company.

The rules contained in the LIIC and the RIIC regarding the maximum fee limits and calculation methods (management fee, custodian fee, subscription and redemption fee) are not applicable to IICILs.

The assets of the IICILs are always held by the custodian in the name of the company or fund, never in the name of the manager or custodian.

Private equity funds

The duration of ECRs depends on the investment targets and objectives.

The diversification and investment ratios may be breached during the first three years from incorporation and during periods of 24 months after each divestment is made.

The shares or units may be redeemed according to the provisions of the articles of association or management regulations and will depend on the investment targets and objectives of the ECRs.

There are no specific requirements as to the need to have the management company invest its money in the entity, although it is common market practice that the seed money be provided by the manager.

The remuneration arrangements of private equity funds allow the management company to receive a management fee from the fund which may consist of a fixed or variable fee or a combination of both or carried interest. If the ECRs are self-managed companies then the directors of the entity may be entitled to remuneration as directors and in some cases to shares granting certain types of benefits.

3. RETAIL FUNDS
3.1. Common structures

Spanish retail funds can be incorporated as:
- investment funds with a minimum patrimony equal to EUR 3,000,000 divided into units (if divided into sub-funds, each sub-fund shall have a minimum patrimony of at least EUR 600,000). The minimum number of investors is 100; and

- investment companies with a minimum share capital of EUR 2,400,000 divided into shares (if divided into sub-funds, each sub-fund shall have a minimum share capital of EUR 480,000). The minimum number of investors is 100 and investors become shareholders of the company, being entitled to attend and vote at the shareholders meetings of the company.

As explained in sections 1 and 2, IICILs, real estate IICs and ECRs can also be offered to retail clients.

Investing in a retail fund incorporated as an investment fund as opposed to investing in an investment company will not afford any advantages or disadvantages since both entities are governed by the same laws and are subject to the same requirements and levels of supervision.

Without prejudice to the above, investing in a retail fund incorporated as an investment company will mean that in the case of changes in the investment policies, distribution of dividends, change of the management company or custodian, delegation of the management duties, change of control of the management company, merger, transformation, spin-off or changes in the fees, the investors in an investment company will have to vote on these decisions at the shareholders' meeting and accept the decisions of the majority of shareholders, while the investors in an investment fund will have a separation right at no cost.

3.2. Regulatory framework

All retail funds and their management companies are subject to the supervision of both the SSEC and the SSPMLTF.

The most relevant laws and regulations applicable to retail funds and their management companies are:
- LIIC;
- RIIC;
- various SSEC circulars and orders of the Ministry of Economy on accounting, information obligations, risk diversification, economic reports and others; and
- the Royal Decree Law on capital companies.

The incorporation of any type of retail fund requires the prior authorisation of the SSEC after review and verification that all the legal requirements are complied with. To obtain the authorisation of the SSEC the same main steps indicated in section 2.2., Real estate funds, will need to be followed.

The SSEC has a period of three months from the date on which the project is filed to grant the authorisation, which is extendable if any additional documents or corrections are requested by the SSEC. If a period of five months lapses from the date on which the authorisation project is filed, the authorisation will be deemed to be granted (positive silence).

Also, the management companies require the prior authorisation of the SSEC before they can be incorporated, provided all legal requirements are complied with, in particular, that the management company has sufficient economic, personal and operating resources to carry out the activity.

3.3. Operational requirements
Control of the management company – the custodian
All retail funds must have a custodian working in conjunction with the management company. The custodians may be brokers, in which case they are supervised by the SSEC, or banks, in which case they are supervised by the SSEP and the Bank of Spain. Custodians are also subject to the supervision of the SSPMLTF.

Among others, the duties of the custodians include:
- custody of the securities, cash and assets in safekeeping;
- control and supervision;
- issuance of shares/units certificates to investors;
- payment of share reimbursements to investors;
- receipt and transmission of purchase and sale orders; and
- any other duty that may serve to improve its service.

Reporting obligations
Any changes in the authorisation project of a retail fund have to be previously authorised by the SSEC. The SSEC has a period of three months from the date on which the changes to the creation project are filed to grant the authorisation, which is extendable if any additional documents or corrections are requested by the SSEC. If a period of five months lapses from the date on which the changes to the project are filed, the authorisation will be deemed to be granted (positive silence).

Regarding the periodic reporting obligations, retail funds (or their management companies) are obliged to:
- prepare a full prospectus which must be previously approved by the SSEC (and any changes thereto) and delivered to investors, if requested, before the initial subscription of any shares and in the case of any changes;
- prepare a key investor information document which must be previously approved by the SSEC (and any changes thereto) and delivered to investors before the initial subscription of any shares and in the case of any changes;
- prepare an annual audited report which must be delivered to the SSEC and to investors within a period of one month from the end of the period of time to which it refers;
- prepare a semi-annual report which must be delivered to the SSEC and to investors before the initial subscription of any shares and within a period of one month from the end of the period of time to which it refers;
- prepare two quarterly reports which must be delivered to the SSEC and to investors, if requested, within a period of one month from the end of the period of time to which it refers;
- communicate to the SSEC the existence of any relevant facts that may affect the entity's performance, such as any event that may reasonably affect an investment decision of a client, any reduction in the entity's share capital equal to or higher than 20 per cent, any reimbursements that may affect 20 per cent or more of the entity's patrimony, any debt obligations *vis-à-vis* third parties exceeding 5 per cent of the entity's

patrimony, changes in the management company or custodian and any other that may require changes to the entity's documents; and
- communicate to the SSEC the data of any investor directly or indirectly holding a significant participation in the entity, meaning an investor that reaches or falls below the following thresholds: 20 per cent, 40 per cent, 60 per cent, 80 per cent or 100 per cent of the entity's patrimony.

Diversification
Financial retail funds may invest in any listed securities and financial instruments; securities and financial instruments in the process of being listed; shares or units of UCITS; shares or units of non-UCITS; bank deposits; certain derivatives (provided, among others, that the underlying assets are listed securities and financial instruments or securities and financial instruments in relation to which the listing has been requested or shares of UCITS or non-UCITS); and certain non-listed securities provided that the following main diversification rules are complied with:
- the investment in listed securities and financial instruments and securities and financial instruments in the process of being listed and shares/units of UCITS and non-UCITS may not exceed 10 per cent of the total patrimony of the IIC; and
- the investment in the securities and financial instruments issued by the same entity may not be higher than 5 per cent of the total patrimony of the IIC, which may be increased up to 35 per cent in some cases.

In addition to the above diversification rules, any investments made in derivatives by the retail fund must be made with the utmost care, in accordance with strict risk control policies.

All retail funds must maintain a liquidity ratio of at least 3 per cent of the patrimony of the IIC during the existence of the entity.

3.4. Marketing the fund
The marketing (meaning any advertising activity aimed at obtaining clients which includes any type of communication sent to potential clients by any means, such as telephone calls, meetings, personalised letters and emails) of retail funds must be carried out with the assistance of a duly authorised financial intermediary (banks, brokers or management companies) and can be directed at any type of investors in Spain, once registered with the SSEC.

3.5. Taxation
See section 2.5. above.

3.6. Customary or common terms
The duration of retail funds is normally indefinite, save for two cases which are: (i) guaranteed funds, which are normally wound up and liquidated after a fixed period of time; and (ii) investment companies, when investors are not satisfied with the management and may take over the company and agree to wind it up and liquidate it (possible but not common practice).

The net asset value of the shares or units of retail funds must be calculated daily, although in some exceptional cases it may be calculated every 15 days. The shares or units may be redeemed at any time against the assets of the entity and may also be transferred between investors provided the transfer is communicated to the manager and to the custodian so that the shares registry can be updated.

There are no specific requirements as to the need to have the management company invest its money in the entity, although the seed money is usually provided by the manager.

In those cases where the retail fund is incorporated as an investment company, the shareholders may vote at the shareholders meeting to change the management company.

The main rules applicable to the remuneration arrangements of retail funds are:
- the management company may receive a management fee from the retail fund. The fee may be equal to a percentage of the patrimony (not higher than 2.25 per cent of the patrimony) or a percentage of the performance (not higher than 18 per cent) or both (not higher than 1.35 per cent of the patrimony and 9 per cent of the performance);
- the management company may receive a subscription fee and a reimbursement fee from the retail fund (not higher than 5 per cent of the net asset value of the units subscribed or redeemed); and
- the custodian may receive a custodian fee from the retail fund (not higher than two times 1,000 of the annual patrimony).

The LIIC and the RIIC do not establish any limitations regarding fees applicable to investment companies since these can be controlled at the shareholders' meeting.

A general principle applicable to all IICs in Spain is that the assets of the investment funds or companies are always held by the custodian in the name of the company or fund, never in the name of the manager or custodian.

4. PROPOSED CHANGES AND DEVELOPMENTS

The draft bill partially amending the LIIC is being discussed in the Spanish Parliament and will bring about the implementation of Directive 2011/61/EU on alternative investment fund managers (DAIFM), opening the door to non-UCITS in Spain which will significantly change the commercialisation regimes applicable to these entities.

Additionally, the LECR will be entirely amended to implement the DAIFM in Spain and also to update and give flexibility to the private equity industry. Although the draft bill revoking the LECR is in the early stages, we foresee that the main changes to come will be:
- a new type of ECR to be incorporated as a joint stock company will be created to cover collective investments not covered by the laws and regulations currently in force;
- ECRs will be obliged to appoint a custodian;
- the commercialisation regime of ECRs in Spain will be modified to provide more flexibility to the private equity markets; and
- the common and simplified regimes of the ECRs will disappear in accordance with the DAIFM.

Sweden

Niclas Rockborn & Olle Asplund **Gernandt & Danielsson**

1. MARKET OVERVIEW

Swedish investment fund savings plans date back to the 1950s. The Swedish fund market has since become home to a wide range of investment funds, offering various investment possibilities and risk levels.

In Sweden, fund saving is today a well-established type of saving. Approximately 98 per cent of the Swedish population (aged 18 to 74) currently save through various ways of fund savings. If premium pension savings are excluded, 74 per cent of the population own shares in funds. Approximately 67 per cent of all children also have fund savings. The percentage of the Swedish population that saves in funds has increased dramatically over time: in the mid-1990s, the figure was only about 50 per cent.

Net fund assets are equivalent to more than SEK2,200 billion (about EUR 256 billion). Many foreign fund management companies have established a presence in Sweden and the local banks' dominance of the fund market has declined. Over the last few years, independent players, banks and fund management companies have launched fund marketplaces where they offer a wide range of their own funds as well as external funds. The interest in so called special funds (as defined below) has particularly increased over the last 15 years. By the end of 1998, special funds accounted for 3 per cent of the total net fund assets. By the end of 2012, the corresponding number was 20 per cent.

One of the main principles of the Swedish fund legislation has been that funds should be open for subscription to the public and that unit holders shall have the right to redeem their units in the fund at any time (open-ended funds). Swedish legislation has not provided a regulatory framework for closed-ended funds. However, this has partly changed following the implementation of the Directive 2011/61/EU on Alternative Investment Fund Managers (the AIFM Directive) on 22 July 2013. The Swedish fund market has since become divided into two main categories of funds:

Undertakings for collective investments in transferable securities (UCITS)

These funds are regulated under the law implementing Directive 85/611/EEC on undertakings for collective investment in transferable securities (the UCITS Directive). The UCITS Directive has been implemented in Sweden through the Investment Funds Act (*lag (2004:46) om investeringsfonder*). With the implementation of the AIFM Directive, the Act changed its name to the Securities Funds Act.

Alternative investment funds (AIFs)

These funds are partly regulated under the law implementing the AIFM

Directive. The AIFM Directive was implemented in Sweden through a new domestic law on Managers of Alternative Investment Funds (*lag (2013:561) om förvaltare av alternativa investeringsfonder*) (the AIF Act), which entered into force on 22 July 2013. The new AIF Act covers the following two types of funds:
- Special funds: this fund type is currently regulated by the AIF Act, since it falls under the AIF Act's definition of AIF funds (corresponding to the definition in the AIFM Directive). Any requirements set out below for AIFs which are marketed to non-professional investors shall also apply to special funds, unless otherwise stated.
- Previously non-regulated funds: this fund type refers to funds, and so called fund-similar products (that is, funds which did not meet the requirements of the definition of 'fund' in the former Investment Securities Funds Act, for instance due to not fulfilling the requirement of risk spreading or being closed-ended), which previously were not subject to specific regulatory requirements in Sweden (with the exception of the rules for offering of securities under the Swedish Financial Instruments Trading Act, if applicable). Examples of such previously non-regulated funds are private equity funds, real estate funds, commodity funds and infrastructure funds. Following the implementation of the AIFM Directive, managers of these fund types are subject to the AIF Act, provided that the fund falls under the Act's definition of AIFs.

2. ALTERNATIVE INVESTMENT FUNDS
2.1. Common structures
The legal status of AIFs is not explicitly regulated in the AIF Act. AIFs may be formed on a contractual basis or as (limited liability) companies or partnerships (or in any other way).

The legal status of the AIF will not affect the application of the AIF Act. However, if a Swedish AIF will make regular purchases and redemptions of units, it is likely that it will be formed on a contractual basis, since Swedish law does not offer a framework with limited liabilities companies with variable share capital.

Swedish special funds, which must be open to purchase and redemption of units at least once a year, will consequently in practice be limited to the contractual form. This limitation with establishing an open-ended fund incorporated as a Swedish company is a competitive disadvantage.

The liability of an investor is typically limited to the amount they have contributed, or agreed to contribute, regardless of the legal status of the AIF. The participants' interest in an AIF is referred to as units when formed on a contractual basis, shares when formed as a company and interest when formed as a limited partnership.

The AIF Act does not regulate the legal status of investment managers, except for managers of special funds which must be limited liability companies. Also, an investment manager is assumed, according to the definition in the AIF Act, to be a legal entity.

2.2. Regulatory framework
Summary of principal statutes – AIFs

While the AIFM Directive mainly regulates the managers of AIFs, and not the actual AIFs themselves, the Swedish legislator decided to transfer all rules in the former Investment Funds Act that related to special funds into the new AIF Act, which then became the principal statue governing AIFs including special funds, and in particular, AIF managers.

In addition to the above, the Swedish Financial Supervisory Authority (*Finansinspektionen*) (the SFSA) has adopted regulations for AIF Managers (FFFS 2013:10). The regulations entered into force on 22 July 2013.

Another statue that may apply for AIFs is (for example) the Marketing Act (*marknadsföringslagen (2008:486)*), which provides that marketing measures must be compatible with good marketing by fund managers practice and must not be misleading.

The general rule is that AIFs themselves are not required to be licensed or authorised by any regulatory body. However, AIFs that are special funds are subject to approval of the fund rules by the SFSA. In particular, the SFSA will examine whether the special fund has a suitable diversification of investments taking into account the requirements which should be imposed in respect of risk spreading.

Summary of principal statutes – Investment advisors

First of all, an AIF manager authorised under the AIF Act will be able to provide discretionary management of investment portfolios pursuant to authorisation from the SFSA in accordance with the AIF Act. Such an AIF manager may also, inter alia, provide investment advice, pursuant to further authorisation.

Secondly, according to the Securities Market Act (*lag (SFS 2007:528) om värdepappersrörelse*), which implement Directive 2004/39/EC on markets in financial instruments (MiFID) (the MiFID Directive), authorisation may be granted by the SFSA to a securities company to conduct securities operation, including giving investment advice to clients in respect of financial instruments. For such securities companies, the SFSA regulations (FFFS 2007:16) governing investment services and activities will apply.

However, it should be noted that where an advisor is not providing advice to clients within the meaning of the Securities Market Act – for instance, where the advice is of general character and not related to specific financial instruments (for example allocations between different asset classes), addressed to a particular person nor based on an analysis of his or her abilities and needs – such activities are not subject to any authorisation from the SFSA.

Summary of principal statutes – Investment managers

The principle statutes applicable to AIFs are also applicable to AIF managers, as stated above.

Following the introduction of an authorisation requirement for managers of AIFs, the new AIF Act will have a major impact on managers of funds which fall under the definition of AIF funds, where such funds previously were not subject to any regulations.

The AIF Act does not apply to AIF managers who manage one or more AIFs whose only investors are the AIF manager or the parent undertakings or the subsidiaries of the AIF manager or other subsidiaries of those parent undertakings, provided that none of those investors are themselves AIF.

Furthermore, the Act is in accordance with Article 2.3 of the AIFM Directive, not applicable for the following:
- holding companies;
- institutions for occupational retirement provision;
- supranational institutions;
- national, regional and local governments and bodies or other institutions which manage funds supporting social security and pension systems;
- employee participation schemes or employee savings schemes; and
- securitisation special purpose entities.

In addition, the AIF Act provides for a partial exemption available to managers where the cumulative value of the alternative investment funds under management fall below a threshold of either EUR 100 million or, for managers that manage only unleveraged AIFs that do not grant investors redemption rights during a period of five years, a threshold of EUR 500 million. AIF managers who fall under this partial exemption will not be subject to full authorisation, but will have to register with the SFSA.

A Swedish AIF manager applying for a license to become a manager of an AIF fund shall be licensed by the SFSA if:
- the manager is headquartered in Sweden;
- the manager has sufficient initial capital and adequate capital base;
- shareholders or members of the manager who have, or are likely to get, qualifying holdings, are deemed suitable to exercise a significant influence of the management of the AIF manager;
- the persons involved in the management of the manager's activities have sufficient knowledge and experience and are otherwise suitable for such a task;
- there is reason to believe that the planned activities will be conducted under the provisions of the AIF Act and other regulations governing the manager's activities; and
- if the AIFM intends to manage a special fund, authorisation may only be granted if the manager is a limited liability company.

The application for a license to become a manager of an AIF fund shall contain:
- information on the persons effectively conducting the business of the manager;
- information on the identities of shareholders or members, whether direct or indirect, natural or legal persons, that have qualifying holdings and on the amounts of those holdings;
- a business plan setting out the organisational structure of the manager, including information on how the manager intends to comply with its obligations according to law;
- information on arrangements made for the delegation and sub-delegation to third parties of functions;

- information on the remuneration policies and practices;
- information on the investment strategies that will be used;
- information on where the master fund is established, if the managed AIF fund is a feeder fund;
- fund rules and instrument of incorporation or equivalent document;
- procedures for how the custodian shall be appointed;
- a draft prospectus; and
- a draft key investor information document (KIID), if the AIF fund that shall be managed is a special fund.

2.3. Operational requirements

The following restrictions on the types of activities for AIF funds and special funds apply.

AIFs

As a general rule, an AIF manager may not engage in any other activities than management of AIFs (certain exemptions apply, see Annex I of the AIFM Directive). There are no general restrictions on the type of investments AIF funds are allowed to do, provided that the requirements set out in the definition of an 'AIF' are met and – consequently – the investments are made in accordance with the investment policy. However, the license by the SFSA may be granted to a limited extent in terms of investment strategies. Restrictions should be applied when the AIF manager is deemed to lack sufficient resources or expertise to manage a particular type of investment strategy, such as investments in certain assets such as real estate and derivatives. From the license it shall also be made clear whether the AIF manager is authorised for discretionary management of investment portfolios or other ancillary services.

The AIF manager shall ensure that a single custodian is appointed for each AIF it manages. The appointed custodian must, whether it is a credit institution, an investment firm or another category of institution, be authorised by the SFSA.

The appointment of the custodian shall be evidenced by a written contract. The contract shall, inter alia, regulate the flow of information deemed necessary to allow the custodian to perform its functions for the AIF for which it has been appointed as custodian.

Where an AIF manager is appointed as external manager of an AIF, the AIF manager shall have an initial capital of at least EUR 125,000. For an internal manager of an AIF fund, this amount is set to at least EUR 300,000. Certain additional capital requirements apply if the AIF manager manages funds exceeding EUR 250 million, and also to cover potential liability risks, in accordance with Article 9 of the AIFM Directive.

Special funds

For operational requirements applicable to special funds, please see section 3.3. below regarding retail funds. However, it should be noted that the SFSA can authorise special funds to diverge from those investment restrictions.

Special funds must generally maintain an adequate spread of investments and diversification limits that are substantially similar to those of retail funds (unless the SFSA has approved specific exemptions).

Reporting requirements to investors

AIF managers shall for each of the AIFs that they manage and for each of the AIFs that they market in the EEA make available to investors a current prospectus. The prospectus shall contain the information set forth in Article 23 of the AIFM Directive.

For AIFs that an AIF manager markets in Sweden to non-professional investors, there must be a current KIID. The KIID shall in an easily understandable manner and in summary form provide the key information needed for investors to assess the AIF and the risk associated with investing in it. The contents of the KIID shall be fair and transparent and not misleading. It should be consistent with the relevant parts of the prospectus. The legal status of the AIF shall be evident from the KIID. It should also be stated if the AIF is a special fund.

For AIFs that are marketed to non-professional investors, the prospectus and the KIID shall be provided on request to investors free of charge. In due time before any agreement is entered into, investors must be provided with the KIID, even when not requested.

If the AIF manager through marketing offers to the public units or shares of an AIF, it shall from the offer be made clear that there is a prospectus and a KIID, and where these documents are available.

An AIF manager shall, for each of the AIFs it manages and for each of the AIFs it markets within the EEA, make available an annual report for each financial year no later than six months following the end of the financial year. The annual report shall be provided to investors on request. The annual report shall be made available to the competent authorities of the home member state of the AIF manager, and, where applicable, the home member state of the AIF. The annual report shall contain the information set forth in Article 22 of the AIFM Directive.

Specific requirements

The following specific requirements are imposed by the AIF Act.

An AIF manager shall have sound procedures for:
- management of the business and accounting;
- operation and management of their information systems; and
- internal control.

An AIF manager shall particularly:
- establish and implement policies for employees' own transactions;
- establish and implement policies for investments made for its own account;
- have procedures to ensure that each transaction carried out on an AIF fund account may be reconstructed retrospectively with respect to its origin, nature, parties, time and place; and
- have procedures to ensure that the assets of the AIF are invested in

accordance with the AIF Act and regulations governing the operations or the law of the country where the fund is established and the fund rules, instruments of incorporation or equivalent regulations.

Furthermore, AIF managers shall have:
- a system for liquidity management, in accordance with Article 16 of the AIFM Directive;
- a risk management function and risk management system in accordance with Article 15 of the AIFM Directive;
- a maximum level of leverage, in accordance with Article 15.4 of the AIFM Directive;
- procedures for the proper and independent valuation and a valuation function, in accordance with Article 19 of the AIFM Directive;
- agreement on outsourcing and sub-delegation, if applicable, in accordance with Article 20 of the AIFM Directive;
- systems to prevent conflicts of interest, in accordance with Article 14 of the AIFM Directive;
- agreements with prime brokers, if applicable, in accordance with Article 14.3 of the AIFM Directive;
- remuneration schemes, in accordance with Article 13 of the AIFM Directive; and
- rules on confidentiality and disclosure obligations.

In addition, a special fund shall have internal rules and procedures for handling complaints from investors in the fund and to manage ethical issues that arise in its operations.

Further, an AIFM manager must comply with: (i) the Money Laundering and Terrorist (Prevention) Act (*lag (2009:62) om åtgärder mot penningtvätt och finansiering av terrorism*), which implements Directive 2005/60/EC on the prevention of the use of financial system for the purpose of money laundering and terrorist financing, (ii) short-selling requirements, according to which the fund manager can sell securities that are held by the fund (for example, borrowed securities), that is, engage in short selling, but cannot sell securities which are not held by the fund (unless where an exemption applies to a special fund).

2.4. Marketing the fund

Marketing is defined in the AIF Act as a direct or indirect offering or placement at the initiative of the AIF manager or on behalf of the AIF manager of units or shares of an AIF fund it manages to or with investors domiciled or with a registered office in the EEA.

The production and offering of marketing material are governed by the AIF Act. Marketing of AIF funds may be conducted by AIF managers and MiFID-firms (investment advisors) in accordance with the below.

Marketing to non-professional investors

An AIF manager shall determine and adopt measures to prevent units or shares of the AIF fund being advertised to non-professional investors in Sweden when such marketing may not occur.

Swedish special funds may be marketed by an AIF manager (which has been licensed in accordance with the AIF Act) to non-professional investors without any particular license or authorisation. For all other AIFs, marketing to non-professional investors may only be conducted by AIF managers pursuant to a licence from the SFSA. Such a licence shall only be given for AIFs whose units or shares are admitted to trading on a regulated market or an equivalent market outside the EEA and for which there is a KIID.

AIFs where the unit or shareholder may not exercise its redemption rights at least five years from the initial investment, and which according to its investment policy generally invests in issuers or unlisted companies to acquire control of them, may be marketed to non-professional investors who commits to invest an amount equal to at least EUR 100,000 and in writing state that they are aware of the risks associated with the intended commitment or investment.

These marketing requirements apply to both Swedish and foreign AIF managers and for both Swedish and foreign AIFs.

Marketing to professional investors

Professional investors are defined in the AIF Act in accordance with the definition in the MiFID Directive.

A Swedish AIF manager who intends to market units or shares of an AIF within the EEA to professional investors in Sweden shall notify the SFSA in writing.

The notification must contain:
- a business plan with information on which AIF that will be marketed and where it is located;
- the fund rules for the AIF and its instruments of incorporation or equivalent document;
- information about the AIF's custodian;
- if the marketing concerns a feeder AIF, information on where the recipient AIF is established;
- a prospectus; and
- information on the measures adopted to prevent that marketing is made to non-professional investors.

The SFSA shall, within 20 working days after a complete notification was received, notify the AIF manager whether marketing may commence.

A Swedish AIF manager who intends to market units or shares on an AIF outside the EEA to professional investors in Sweden, must acquire a license from the SFSA pursuant to such marketing.

A foreign AIF manager may market units or shares of an AIF within the EEA to Swedish investors, following the notification to the SFSA by its home state regulator.

A foreign AIF manager who intends to market units or shares of an AIF outside the EEA to professional investors in Sweden, must acquire a license from the SFSA pursuant to such marketing.

An AIF manager outside the EEA who intends to market units or shares of an AIF fund to professional investors in Sweden, must acquire a license from the SFSA pursuant to such marketing.

2.5. Taxation
Different structures
Since AIFs are not considered to be a uniform category, no uniform rules regarding taxation of AIF funds apply. Instead, taxation is linked to the legal structure of the particular AIF.

For example, funds formed as limited liability companies and limited partnerships are taxed in accordance with the applicable rules for the particular legal entity. Swedish limited liability companies are not tax-transparent, which means that such companies are subject to a company tax at a rate of 22 per cent and that all capital gains its investors receive, as a general rule, are subject to capital gains tax. Swedish limited partnerships, on the other hand, are tax-transparent. Even so, non-domestic investors may be subject to tax in Sweden if the income is considered to be derived from a permanent establishment in Sweden. However, investors in Swedish limited partnerships may benefit from a certain exemption rules.

Taxation of special funds
Special funds are not considered to be legal persons (nor are retail funds), but nevertheless they are considered to be separate tax subjects in Sweden. According to current tax regulations, applicable as of 1 January 2012, special and retail funds are no longer tax liable for income from assets assignable to the funds. Instead, it is the unit holders that are subject to a standard taxation. The standard taxation is calculated based on the fund's value at the beginning of each calendar year and results in unit holders being tax liable for 0.12 per cent of the fund's value.

2.6. Customary or common terms
It is not possible to describe common terms and conditions which apply for all AIFs, due to their different structure and focus. It should also be noted that special funds are more equal to retail funds, please see section 3.6. below. However for other AIFs, in general, the following may be noted.

The typical life of an AIF varies between the funds' investment focus. For a general private equity fund it would typically be 7–10 years. It is common that there is a possibility for the investors to terminate the fund early or replace the fund manager, upon certain circumstances such as a material breach or gross negligence by the fund manager.

Further, an AIF is typically closed-ended, meaning that it is not possible to issue or redeem units or shares once the fund has been fully invested. However, it is usually possible to transfer or assign interests to third parties after having received permission from the fund manager.

Typically, an AIF has an investment period of 3–5 years, where the investors' capital commitments are invested in accordance with the AIF's investment policy.

3. RETAIL FUNDS
3.1. Common structures
Swedish UCITS (retail funds) are formed on a contractual basis and such

regulated funds cannot have any other legal form. A retail fund can be described as a multilateral contract between the: (i) unitholders, (ii) fund manager, and (iii) custodian. The liability of unitholders is limited to the amount they have contributed.

Swedish retail fund managers must be authorised by the SFSA to conduct fund operations. Only a Swedish limited liability company can be authorised for that purpose. The same restriction applies to Swedish securities companies providing investment services such as investment advice to clients in respect of financial instruments. Foreign fund managers and/or investment advisers are assumed to be legal entities.

3.2. Regulatory framework
Summary of principal statutes – Retail funds
The principal statues and regulations are the Securities Funds Act and the SFSA's Regulations Governing Securities Funds (FFFS 2013:9).

Summary of principal statutes – Investment managers
The principal statues and regulations for an investment manager are the same as applies to UCITS, please see above.

Domestic fund managers must be authorised by the SFSA to conduct fund operations in accordance with the Securities Funds Act. Such authorisation may only be given to a Swedish limited liability company.

The application for authorisation must, among other things, include a plan for the contemplated operations (business plan) containing a summary description of the fund management company's organisation. A business plan must further contain, among other things, the following information:
- the company's activities;
- the ownership list;
- the group description and organisation;
- the management list;
- a description of the economic situation;
- any outsourcing agreements;
- a description of the information system and any security issues;
- instructions for handling conflicts of interest;
- a description of compliance;
- a description of risk management;
- instructions for the internal audit;
- instructions for handling events of material significance;
- instructions for the management of ethical issues;
- instructions for the management of complaints; and
- measures taken to prevent money laundering and financing of terrorism.

Also, fund rules must be registered for all funds.

Foreign UCITS managers wishing to conduct business in Sweden must: (i) if domiciled within the EEA, notify the SFSA through its home state regulator before its activities commence, (ii) if domiciled outside the EEA, obtain authorisation from the SFSA.

Sweden

Summary of principal statutes – Investment advisors

Authorisation from the SFSA is required to conduct securities operations in accordance with the Securities Market Act. Authorisation may be granted for *inter alia* investment advice to clients in respect of financial instruments.

Authorisation to conduct securities operations shall be granted to a Swedish limited company where:
- the company's head office is in Sweden;
- the articles of association do not conflict with the Securities Market Act or any other statutory instrument;
- there is reason to believe that the envisaged operation will be conducted in accordance with the provisions of the Securities Market Act and other statutory instruments governing the company's operations;
- the holder or potential holder of a qualified holding in the undertaking is deemed suitable to exercise a material influence over the management of a credit institution;
- any person who is to serve on the undertaking's board of directors or serve as managing director, or be an alternate for any of the aforesaid, possesses sufficient insight and experience to participate in the management of a credit institution and is otherwise suitable for such duties; and
- the company otherwise fulfils the requirements set forth in the Securities Market Act.

A foreign company which is domiciled within the EEA and which is authorised to conduct securities operations in its home state does not need authorisation pursuant to the Securities Market Act. Such a company may conduct securities operations from a branch in Sweden or conduct securities operations, provided that the SFSA has received a notification from a competent authority in the company's home state.

3.3. Operational requirements
Retail funds

UCITS must maintain a suitable diversification of investments, taking into consideration the spreading of risk associated with the fund's investment focus as stated in the fund rules. UCITS can, subject to the limitations in the Securities Funds Act, invest in the following:
- Transferable securities and money market instruments: the value of transferable securities and money market instruments issued by any single issuer cannot exceed 5 per cent of the fund's value. The limit may be higher in certain cases, for example, when investing in government bills.
- Derivate instruments: An investment fund can invest in derivate instruments provided that: (i) they are traded on a regulated market, (ii) the underlying assets constitute or relate to money market instruments, interests rates, exchange rates or foreign currency, (iii) the underlying assets can be included in the fund according to the fund rules. An investment fund can also invest in derivative instruments that are traded directly between the parties, under certain circumstances.
- Units in a collective investment undertaking.
- Deposits with credit institutions.

- Liquid assets necessary for the investment fund's management.

In its investment operations, a fund manager cannot: (i) raise or grant cash loans, (ii) act as a guarantor, (iii) sell transferable securities, money market instruments, derivative instruments or units in collective investment undertakings that are not part of the fund. A fund manager can raise short-term loans that, collectively, do not exceed 10 per cent of its value. A fund cannot lend financial instruments (securities loans) that amount to more than 20 per cent of its net asset value (NAV).

A custodian holds the portfolio of the investment fund's assets. The name of the custodian must be stated in the fund rules which must be approved by the SFSA. A custodian must maintain its registered office in Sweden or, where a custodian is a Swedish branch of a foreign fund manager, in another state within the EEA.

The following institutions can act as custodian:
- supervised banks as defined in the Banking and Financing Business Act (*lag (2004:297) om bank- och finansieringsrörelse*);
- other credit institutions as defined in the Banking and Financing Business Act; and
- securities companies licensed to conduct specific ancillary operations under the Securities Market Act.

The custodian must conduct business independently of the fund manager and exclusively in the unitholders' interests. The custodian may be a company within the same group as the fund manager, provided that the companies are two separate legal entities.

Reporting requirements to investors

In relation to unitholders, a fund manager must regularly, and at least once a week, publish the value of the units of the relevant fund. A fund manager must further provide:
- an annual report within four months of the expiry of the financial year; and
- a half yearly report on the first six months of the financial year within two months following the expiry of the half-year.

The annual and half-yearly report must contain all information necessary to assess the investment fund's development and financial position.

Reporting requirements to regulators

A fund manager must:
- be able to present a list of each fund's asset holdings (as stated in the Securities Funds Act) at any time;
- submit certain information to the SFSA regarding its activities and each individual fund at the end of every quarter;
- prepare a list of each funds holding of financial instruments on the final banking day of each quarter; and
- submit a calculation of the total exposures for each fund at the end of every quarter.

Specific requirements
Risk: A fund manager must:
- identify, measure, control, internally report, and verify the risks associated with its business; and
- specifically ensure that its credit risks, market risks, operating risks and other risks do not, on aggregate, jeopardise its ability to fulfil its obligations to the investors, counterparties and so on.

Valuation and pricing: The value of a fund is the fund's value divided by the number of units in it. The fund's value is calculated by the fund manager in accordance with the principles stated in the fund rules. The fund's holdings must be valued on the basis of the applicable market value. Where investments are made in OTC-derivates the fund rules must state specifically how these assets are to be evaluated and what valuation principles will be used. Further, the Swedish Investment Fund Association (SIFA) provides guidelines for determining month-end values for performance measurement that must be considered in this respect.

Systems and controls: The fund manager is subject to various organisational requirements, including the following:
- current and appropriate internal control mechanisms that must ensure compliance with decisions and procedures at all levels of the fund manager;
- internal reporting and communication of information that is current and effective;
- current and documented decision-making procedures that clearly specify reporting lines, and an organisational structure that clearly allocates functions and areas of responsibility;
- permanent and effective compliance, risk management and internal audit functions; and
- systems and procedures for safeguarding the security, integrity and confidentiality of its information.

Insider dealing and market abuse: The fund manager must maintain current and adequate procedures to prevent, among other things, relevant persons from entering certain personal transactions (see below) where that relevant person either: (i) is involved in activities that can give risk to a conflict of interest, or (ii) has access to inside information within the meaning of the Financial Instruments Trading (Market Abuse Penalties) Act (*lag (2005:377) om straff för marknadsmissbruk vid handel med finansiella instrument*) or other confidential information relating to the fund manager's clients.

A relevant person includes: (i) a member of the senior management, a partner or a manager of the fund manager, (ii) an employee of the fund manager and any other natural person who either performs services for the company, is under the control of the company or who is involved on behalf of the company in conducting fund activities, and (iii) a natural person who, under an outsourcing agreement, is directly involved in conducting parts of the fund activities on behalf of the company.

The prohibited personal transactions are personal transactions that would:
- violate the Financial Instruments Trading (Market Abuse Penalties) Act;

- entail the misuse or improper disclosure of confidential information or a conflict of interest; and
- be likely to conflict with the fund manager's obligations under the Investments Funds Act.

A personal transaction is defined as a trade of a financial instrument, which is conducted by a relevant person or on a relevant person's behalf, where either:
- the relevant person is acting outside of the scope of the activities he carries out in his capacity as a relevant person; or
- the transaction is carried out on behalf of any of: (i) the relevant person himself, (ii) any other person with whom the relevant person has a family relationship, or with whom the relevant person has a close relationship, (iii) a person whose relationship with the relevant person is such that he has direct or indirect material interest in the outcome of the transaction, other than a fee or commission for the execution of the transaction.

Transparency: Subject to certain conditions, a fund manager must report in writing any change in the fund's holdings to the SFSA. A fund manager must:
- be able, at any given time, to present a list of each fund's holdings of all assets;
- prepare a list of each fund's holdings of financial instruments on the final banking day of each quarter; and
- calculate and report to the SFSA, on the last calendar day of every month, the fund's risk level in accordance with the 'standard deviation' (that is, performance of the fund), performance during the past month and the 'concentration risk' (that is, assets of the fund).

3.4. Marketing the fund

A UCITS which is domiciled within the EEA and has such license in its home state as set out in the UCITS Directive may only market units in Sweden after notification to its home state regulator pursuant to the UCITS Directive. There is no private placement exemption. The marketing of foreign UCITS in Sweden is governed by the Securities Funds Act.

Distribution of units in a UCITS in Sweden, as opposed to only marketing, is considered a regulated activity which requires a license pursuant to the Swedish Securities Market Act, the Swedish implementation of the MiFID. There is thus an additional requirement that may arise when units in a UCITS are marketed and distributed in Sweden. A license will be necessary for the distributor of the units in Sweden, unless the distribution is made by the UCITS itself.

Upon request, the full prospectus, the KIID, the most recent annual report and, where applicable, the half-yearly report published thereafter shall be provided or sent free of charge to any party intending to purchase units in a UCITS. Such parties shall, without request, be provided with the KIID in due time prior to the agreement to subscribe for units. In addition, any advertising made shall state that there exists a KIID and a full prospectus and also provide information on where the KIID and the full prospectus may be obtained.

The Swedish Marketing Act must furthermore be considered when marketing units of a UCITS in Sweden. In addition to the Swedish Marketing

Act, the Swedish Investment Fund Association has adopted guidelines for marketing and information by fund management companies which also should be taken into account. For an example, according to the guidelines, all marketing materials of units in a UCITS must include the following risk information in a position where it is readily visible:

'Past performance is no guarantee for future returns. The value of the money invested in the fund can increase or decrease and there is no guarantee that all of your invested capital can be redeemed.'

UCITS may be marketed to any investor, including professional and non-professional investors in Sweden. There are no differences between domestic and foreign funds.

According to the Securities Funds Act, a UCITS whose units are marketed in Sweden shall take necessary measures to enable it to provide to unit holders in Sweden any and all information which it must provide to unit holders pursuant to regulations applicable in its home state.

The marketing material does not require any licences or authorisations being obtained.

There are no additional requirements on marketing to public bodies such as government pension funds.

3.5. Taxation
As regards taxation, please see section 2.5. above in relation to special funds.

3.6. Customary or common terms
Retail funds are governed by the UCITS Directive, and consequently, the terms set out in that directive and the Implementing Directive and Implementing Regulations (583/2010 and 584/2010) are commonly used.

It should however be noted that the SFSA has published a template in Swedish regarding fund rules. The template forms a common framework for Swedish retail funds and includes information on what should be included in the provisions concerning, inter alia, the fund's character, investment focus, special investment objective, valuation subscription and redemption of units, fees and compensation, dividends and reporting.

4. PROPOSED CHANGES AND DEVELOPMENTS
As further described above, the AIFM Directive was implemented in Sweden on 22 July 2013. As regards to retail funds, Sweden is currently following the development of the UCITS V and UCITS VI Directives. For the upcoming UCITS V Directive it is inter alia expected that managers of UCITS funds will be subject to provisions on remuneration policies and practices in accordance with the AIFM Directive.

Furthermore, Sweden is also preparing the implementation of the forth money laundering directive (directive on the prevention of the use of the financial system for the purpose of money laundering and terrorist financing). The proposed changes are likely to be adopted at the end of 2013 or beginning of 2014 and will be implemented in Swedish law within two years thereafter.

The Swedish Government has decided to appoint a commission with the mandate to propose how the Swedish legislation shall be adapted to meet the requirements of the forthcoming EU legislations on the securities market, the so-called MiFID II (Markets in Financial Instruments Directive) and MiFIR (Markets in Financial Instruments Regulation). The commission shall also submit proposals for amendments to the Swedish legislation as a result of the on-going work within the EU on the amendments to the regulation on OTC derivatives, central counterparties and trade repositories (EMIR). The commission shall report to the Swedish Government by 30 June 2014.

Switzerland

Dr. Jasmin Ghandchi Schmid, LL.M.
Ghandchi Schmid Partners Ltd.

1. MARKET OVERVIEW

Switzerland is primarily a location for fund distribution. As of July 2013, 1,393 (12/2012: 1,383) domestic funds were authorised by the Swiss Financial Supervisory Market Authority FINMA (FINMA). At the same time 6,105 (12/2012: 6,118) foreign funds were authorised for distribution to retail clients in Switzerland, thereof approx. 5,873 (July 2013) were UCITS that enjoy a simplified authorisation procedure. The majority of the authorised foreign funds are domiciled in Luxemburg (07/2013: 4,121) and Ireland (07/2013: 1,030). The number of authorised foreign funds does not include foreign funds that were distributed exclusively to qualified investors that were not subject to authorisation/regulation until 28 February 2013 but are now regulated (see section 2.4.). It is estimated that the number of those funds may be substantial not only because of the former extensive definition of qualified investors that included investors (regardless of their total amount of assets) that concluded a written asset management agreement with a financial intermediary that meets certain requirements.

Switzerland plays a rather limited role as production location for (alternative investment) funds. Switzerland enacted as of 1 January 2007 the Federal Act on Collective Investment Schemes (CISA) that was a major step in Swiss legislation on collective investment schemes. CISA introduced in addition to the contractual fund three legal forms of collective investment schemes: the investment company with variable capital (SICAV), the limited partnership for collective investment schemes (LPCIS), and the investment company with fixed capital (SICAF). Any collective investment scheme, ie, assets raised from investors for the collective investment and managed for investors' account, has to organise itself in one of the legal forms provided by CISA unless it is exempt from the scope of the CISA, such as institutions for employee welfare (pension funds), social security institutions, corporate entities and institutions governed by public law, operational companies, holding companies, investment clubs, associations and foundations, investment companies that are listed at a Swiss stock exchange and meet certain requirements, in-house funds established by banks and securities dealers that meet certain requirements, structured products that have to meet certain requirements. Investment companies that are listed at a Swiss stock exchange or restricted to qualified investors are not governed by the Swiss legislation on collective investment schemes. Such structures are governed by the Swiss corporate law and possible listing regulations. These structures are not considered in the comments below. Swiss legislation on collective investment schemes distinguishes between open-ended and closed-ended collective investment schemes. The open-ended structures are further classified based on the type of investment, ie, securities funds, real estate funds, other funds for traditional investments, or other funds for alternative investments.

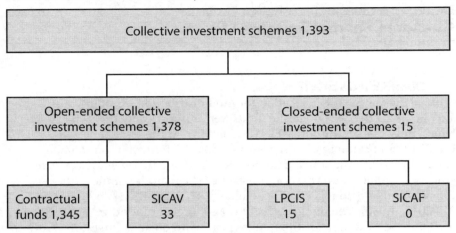

Above figures are based on the data provided by FINMA on its website as of 24 July 2013

All of these four legal forms of collective investment schemes are available for alternative investment funds. As of July 2013 60 contractual funds and 6 SICAVs were authorised as other funds for alternative investments and 43 contractual funds and 3 SICAVs were authorised as real estate funds.

The contractual funds and the SICAV are open to retail investors. However, the fund regulation may restrict the fund to qualified investors (see definition in section 2.4.) that would allow FINMA to exempt the collective investment schemes from certain legal requirements under certain conditions.

This article outlines the contractual fund, the SICAV and the LPCIS that are basically all available for alternative investment funds in section 2 highlighting the particularities for alternative investments. In section 3, retail funds, there will be mainly references to section 2. Since no SICAF has been authorised only the structure is outlined and no further comments are included.

The legislator's intention to promote Switzerland as a production location did not materialise. The quota of 4:1 between authorised foreign funds and domestic funds illustrates the predominance of foreign funds authorised for distribution. One key factor for the limited success as a fund production location is the uncompetitive tax regime. Another factor is that Switzerland focuses on asset management and private banking that are still the core competences in the financial services market. Fund distribution or asset management advice is more relevant than fund production. Considering the importance of distribution of foreign funds the marketing of foreign funds will be outlined in section 2.4.

Further, investment banks, including the two major Swiss banking institutions, play an important role as counterparties to alternative investment funds (hedge funds). Major foreign hedge funds managers (eg, Brevan Howard, Blue Crest) established branches in and moved operations to Switzerland.

Need of adaption to the new legislation in the EU, in particular the Directive on Alternative Investment Fund Managers (AIFM Directive), the financial crisis, and various financial scandals triggered a revision of the CISA and the Ordinance on CISA (CISO) that entered into force on 1 March 2013. The revised legislation contains substantial changes mainly in the areas of asset management, custody and distribution that have significant impact on the fund industry.

2. ALTERNATIVE INVESTMENT FUNDS
2.1. Common structures

All four legal forms for collective investment schemes are available for alternative investment funds, ie, open-ended structures in which the investors have a direct or an indirect claim for redemption of their units at net asset value at the expense of the collective assets (contractual fund and SICAV) and closed-ended structures in which the investors have neither a direct nor an indirect claim for redemption of their units at the net asset value at the expense of the collective assets (LPCIS and SICAF).

The contractual funds and the SICAVs are basically open for retail investors. However, if they are limited to qualified investors exemptions from certain regulatory requirements may be available if the protective purpose of the CISA is not impaired. The LPCIS is only available for qualified investors according to Article 10, paragraph 3 CISA. The SICAF is basically open for qualified and retail investors. The legislator intended to introduce the closed-ended structures for hedge funds and private equity investments. So far only 15 LPCIS are authorised and no SICAF is authorised.

The open-ended structures are further categorised based on the type of investment. Both types of open-ended collective investment schemes can be designed as securities funds, real estate funds, other funds for traditional investments, or other funds for alternative investments.

Most of the Swiss alternative investment funds are organised as contractual (open-ended) collective investment schemes for alternative investments. Many registered contractual funds are explicitly addressed to qualified investors.

Contractual fund

The contractual fund is the oldest type of regulated collective investment schemes and the most common fund structure in Switzerland (1,345 out of 1,393 authorised funds are contractual funds). A possible basic structure can be illustrated as follows:

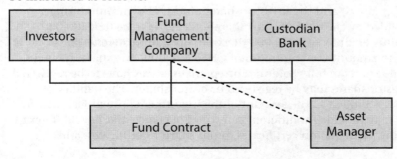

The contractual fund bases on a fund contract to which the fund management company, the custodian bank and the investors are parties. The assets of the fund (or the sub-fund of an umbrella fund) have to amount to a minimum of CHF5,000,000. The assets are owned by the fund management company on a fiduciary basis and shall be segregated for the benefit of the investors in case of bankruptcy of the fund management company. The investors hold fund units. Their liability is limited at the amount of their investment. Different classes of units can be established. The fund management company is a corporation with a minimum share capital of CHF1,000,000 and with domicile and administration head office in Switzerland. The main purpose of the fund management company has to be to conduct the fund business. However, the fund management company may also provide additional services in the area of asset management, investment advice, custodian services and technical administration of collective investment schemes. Asset management may be delegated under certain circumstances to authorised asset managers.

Investment company with variable capital (SICAV)

The SICAV was introduced 2007 and so far only 33 SICAVs are authorised. The SICAV is designed as a legal entity similar to the corporation although significant differences exist. A possible basic structure can be illustrated as follows:

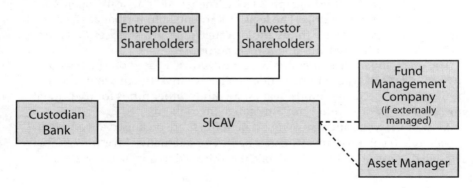

The exclusive purpose of the SICAV is the collective investment. The company name has to contain the designation of the legal form or the abbreviation SICAV. The share capital is not determined in advance. There are two types of shareholders: the entrepreneur shareholders (often the promoters/sponsors) and the investor shareholders. The minimum share capital provided by the entrepreneur shareholders has to be CHF500,000 (if self-administered) or CHF250,000 (if externally administered). The assets have to amount to a minimum of CHF5,000,000. The shares have no nominal value and are fully paid-in. Entrepreneur shares have to be registered shares. Investor shares may be registered or bearer shares. The liability of the investors is limited to the amount of the investment. The articles of association may provide for different categories of shares that have different rights. Issuing participation certificates, profit sharing certificates, and preferred shares is prohibited. The shares are basically transferable without restriction. Restrictions on transfer are only possible to a limited extent and only for non-listed SICAVs. Entrepreneur shareholders have the exclusive right to incorporate the SICAV and to decide about its dissolution. Each share has one vote. The corporate bodies are the shareholders' meeting, board of directors, and the auditors that have to be recognised by FINMA. The SICAV can be self-administered or externally administered. The externally administered SICAV delegates the administration to an authorised fund management company. The SICAV bases on the articles of association and the investment regulations. Asset management can be delegated under certain circumstances to authorised asset managers.

Limited partnership for collective investment schemes (LPCIS)
The limited partnership for collective investment schemes (LPCIS) is similar to the Anglo-American limited partnership structures. So far only 15 LPCIS were authorised. It is open only for qualified investors according to Article 10, paragraph 3 CISA and invests in venture capital but can also invest in real estate projects and alternative investments. The basic structure can be illustrated as follows:

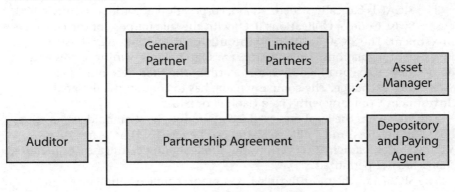

The LPCIS is based on a partnership agreement. The company name has to contain the designation of the legal form or the abbreviation KGK. The general partner with unlimited liability has to be a corporation, whose shareholders often are the sponsors/promoters with registered office in Switzerland and a share capital of at least CHF100,000. The general partner may only be active as general partner in one single LPCIS and cannot provide additional asset management services to third parties. The limited partners have to be qualified investors according to Article 10, paragraph 3 CISA.

Retail investors may have the possibility to invest through a vehicle that invests as limited partner and qualifies as such qualified investor. The liability of the limited partners is limited to the limited partners' contribution.

The auditor has to be recognised by FINMA.

The asset management may be delegated to an authorised asset manager.

The LPCIS has a flexible regulatory regime for investment regulations. The tax treatments may be considered as a disadvantage of this structure.

Investment company with fixed capital (SICAF)

So far no SICAF is authorised in Switzerland. One reason may be that certain investment companies are not governed by the Swiss legislation on collective investment schemes under certain circumstances, such as investment companies that are listed at a Swiss stock exchange, investment companies that have only qualified investors as shareholders or investment companies that meet the requirements of investment clubs. The basic structure can be illustrated as follows:

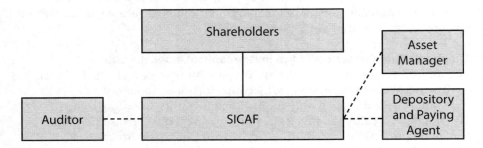

The SICAF is basically structured as a corporation according to Article 620 et seq. Swiss Code of Obligations (CO) with the sole purpose of the collective investment. The SICAF is based on the articles of association and issues investment regulations. The investors are shareholders owning shares and do not have to be qualified investors. Further, the shares are not listed at a Swiss stock exchange. The company name has to contain the designation 'Investment Company with Fixed Capital' or 'SICAF'.

The SICAF has the legal bodies of a corporation, ie, shareholders' meeting, board of directors, and auditors. Shares can be registered or bearer shares. Voting shares, participation certificates, profit sharing certificates, or preferred shares are not permitted.

The SICAF has the most flexible investment regime. Compliance costs compared to a listing at a Swiss stock exchange and the tax treatment may be considered as disadvantages of this structure. Structures including an offshore subsidiary of SICAF that holds the investments may be considered for tax purposes.

Asset managers

Swiss asset managers of collective investment schemes may be organised as a corporation (company limited by shares), corporation including partners with unlimited liability, limited liability company, general partnership, or limited partnership. The predominant legal form is the corporation. Foreign asset managers may establish a Swiss branch if certain requirements are met.

2.2. Regulatory framework

The regulatory framework for collective investment schemes in Switzerland includes the Federal Act on Collective Investment Schemes (CISA), the Ordinance on Collective Investment Schemes (CISO), the Ordinance

Switzerland

on Collective Investment Schemes issued by FINMA (CISO-FINMA), the Ordinance on Bankruptcy of Collective Investment Schemes issued by FINMA (CISO-FINMA Bankruptcy), and the Federal Act on Financial Market Supervision. The self-regulation of private representative industry associations is an important part of the regulatory framework. In the area of funds the Swiss Funds & Asset Management Association (SFAMA, formerly Swiss Funds Association, SFA) plays an important role, but also other representative industry associations are relevant, eg, the Swiss Association of Asset Managers, or the Swiss Structured Products Association. The FINMA declared various self-regulatory codes of conduct as minimum standard. The codes of conduct and guidelines issued by the SFAMA that are amended by various checklists, model documents (approved by FINMA) as well as the code of conduct of the Swiss Association of Asset Managers and Polyreg are recognised by FINMA as minimum standard. The SFAMA has issued the code of conduct for the Swiss Funds Industry, the code of conduct for asset managers of collective investment schemes and various guidelines (eg, valuation guidelines, total expense ratio (TER)/portfolio turnover rate (PTR) guidelines, performance guidelines, distribution guidelines, real estate guidelines, etc.). The codes of conduct, the guidelines as well as model documents are available on the website of the SFAMA (*www.sfama.ch*). Due to the revised legislation certain documents need to be revised. SFAMA and FINMA are currently in discussions and it is expected that most of the revised documents are available in the course of 2013.

Further, FINMA issues Circulars that provide guidance regarding its application of the legislation and guidelines mainly in relation to the application for authorisations. The Circulars and guidelines are available on the website of FINMA (*www.finma.ch*). FINMA is currently revising the Circular 08/8 on public marketing of collective investment schemes that is expected to enter into force in the 3rd or 4th quarter of 2013.

In addition, other special legislation may apply depending on the activity, status of the involved party, eg, money-laundering provisions for asset managers, banking provisions for the custodian banks, listing provisions for listed collective investment schemes, etc.

FINMA as supervisory authority executes a double supervision: FINMA on the one hand grants authorisations to the issuers and involved parties and on the other hand approves the products.

Contractual fund

The contractual fund is governed by Article 25 et seq. CISA and the regulatory framework as outlined above.

The fund management company and the custodian bank have to obtain authorisations from FINMA. The fund contract has to be approved by FINMA.

An authorisation granted to a fund management company covers also additional activities as fund management company for other collective investment schemes. The distribution of fund units by fund management company itself is covered by the authorisation as fund management company as well. The authorisation requirements contain general requirements for

all holders of authorisations under the CISA (Article 13 CISA) and certain special requirements for the specific holders of authorisations. The general requirements include (Article 14 CISA):
- persons responsible for the administration and the management enjoy a good reputation, guarantee proper management and have the required professional qualifications;
- qualified participants enjoy a good reputation and their influence does not have a damaging effect on prudent and solid business activities;
- performance of the duties according to CISA is ensured by internal regulations and an appropriate company organisation;
- sufficient financial guarantees are available.

FINMA may require compliance with codes of conduct of a representative business association.

Further, the specific requirements for the contractual funds have to be met, such as domicile and administration headquarter in Switzerland, main purpose has to be to conduct fund business, minimum share capital, type of shares, certain requirements regarding the board of directors, management, independency requirements between the fund management company and the custodian bank, separation of functions within the fund management company, detailed ratio requirements between own funds of the fund management company and the total assets of the collective investment schemes, etc. In relation to the application for an authorisation FINMA has published a guideline that is available on its website. In relation to the details of the authorisation of funds of hedge funds FINMA has developed certain practice.

The custodian bank has to obtain an authorisation from FINMA. It has to be a bank (with domicile or with a registered branch in Switzerland) within the meaning of Swiss banking legislation. An authorisation as custodian bank covers also additional activities as custodian bank for other collective investment schemes. Certain duties of the custodian bank may be delegated under certain circumstances. In relation to the application for an authorisation FINMA has published a guideline that is available on the website.

If an asset manager is appointed such asset manager has to obtain an authorisation from FINMA.

The fund contract and any changes require the consent of the custodian bank and have to be approved by FINMA. The change of the fund contract imposes additional requirements, such as publication requirements, etc.

The establishing, cancellation or merger of classes of units requires the consent of the custodian bank and the approval from FINMA. Other than the merger the establishing or cancellation of classes of units does not require compliance with the procedure/requirements of the change of a fund contract.

SICAV

The SICAV is governed by Article 36 et seq. CISA and the regulatory framework as outlined above.

The SICAV and the custodian bank have to obtain authorisations. The SICAV has to meet the general authorisation requirements as well as the specific requirements for SICAVs, eg, independency between management of SICAV and the custodian bank, etc. Regarding the authorisation for the custodian bank see comments above.

The articles of association and the investment regulations have to be approved by FINMA. In relation to the application for an authorisation FINMA has published a guideline that is available on the website.

Limited partnership for collective investment schemes (LPCIS)
The LPCIS is governed by Article 98 et seq. CISA and Article 594 et seq. CO and the regulatory framework outlined above.

The LPCIS has to be authorised by FINMA. The authorisation requirements contain general requirements and the specific requirements for the limited partnership, eg, the company name has to contain the legal form. The general authorisation requirements apply to the general partners accordingly. A detailed guideline regarding the details of an application for an authorisation for LPCIS is available on the FINMA website.

The partnership agreement has to be in writing and has to contain a minimum content. It has to be approved by FINMA. The SFAMA issued a model partnership agreement that is available on its website.

If an asset manager is appointed it has to obtain an authorisation.

Asset managers
Asset managers of Swiss collective investment schemes and asset managers that manage foreign collective investment schemes in or from Switzerland are subject to the regulatory framework outlined above. Further, Swiss asset managers and Swiss branches of foreign asset managers are governed by the corporate law provisions that apply to the respective legal form, ie, mainly corporations for Swiss asset managers. The asset managers are required to obtain an authorisation unless the asset manager has already an authorisation as a fund management company, a bank, a securities dealer or an insurance institution. If an asset manager manages the assets of a collective investment scheme that has exclusively qualified investors and the liquid assets (including leverage) amount to CHF100 million at maximum, or the illiquid assets amount to CHF500 million at maximum, or the investors are exclusively group companies of a group of which the asset manager is part of the legislation on collective investment schemes does not apply and no authorisation according to this legislation is required. These asset managers may opt-in under certain circumstances. Further exceptions may be available under certain circumstances.

The general authorisation requirements apply as well as a number of specific detailed requirements for asset managers, such as capital requirements (CHF200,000 or CHF500,000 depending on the specific circumstances) or specific requirements in case of branches of foreign asset managers, etc.

2.3. Operational requirements
Following the EU Regulation CISA provided for all holders of authorisations general provisions regarding the code of conduct, in particular the duty of loyalty, the duty of care and the reporting duty. These duties are specified

in more detail by CISA, its applicable ordinances and codes of conduct of representative industry associations that were recognised as minimum standard by FINMA.

Open-ended collective investment schemes are categorised by investment provisions as follows:
- securities funds;
- real estate funds;
- other funds for traditional investments; or
- other funds for alternative investments.

Statutory investment provisions are mainly set forth in CISA, CISO and CISO-FINMA. Umbrella funds may only cover sub-funds of the same type of fund and apply to each sub-fund individually. Collective investment schemes addressed exclusively to qualified investors may be exempted from certain investment provisions. The investment provisions for the different types of open-ended funds cover generally provisions regarding permitted investments, investment techniques, risk diversification, use of derivatives and special provisions for the specific fund (eg, valuation provisions or redemption rights for real estate funds), etc.

The securities funds invest in securities and correspond to the UCITS funds. Real estate funds invest in real property values. CISA and the applicable ordinances contain various special provisions for real estate funds, eg, regarding the permitted investments, risk diversification, use of derivatives, valuation, experts, redemption, etc. Other funds for traditional investments are funds that do not qualify as securities fund, real estate fund or other fund for alternative investments. Its investments, investment techniques, and investment restrictions have a risk profile that is typical for traditional investments. Other funds for alternative investments (typically hedge funds or funds of hedge funds) are defined in the legislation as funds with investments, investment techniques, and investment restrictions that have a risk profile that is typical for alternative investments.

Contractual funds that qualify as other (open-ended) collective investment schemes for alternative investments have more liberal investment possibilities but have to meet, in addition to the requirements for contractual (open-ended) funds, the requirements for other funds for alternative investments in order to meet higher investors' protection standards.

Permitted investments are all investments allowed for other funds for traditional investments, in particular investments in securities, precious metals, real estate, commodities, derivatives, units of other collective investment schemes as well as other property and rights. Investments that are marketable only to a limited extent, that are subject to large price fluctuations, that provide limited risk diversification, and for which valuation is difficult are permitted. In relation to funds of hedge funds additional special provisions apply. More liberal investment techniques, such as short selling, are possible but have to be mentioned in the fund regulations explicitly.

FINMA may allow additional investments and may allow deviations from the provisions regarding permitted investments, investment techniques, restrictions, or risk diversification in individual cases.

The special risks related to alternative investments have to be explicitly mentioned in the designation of the fund, in the prospectus and in any marketing material. Further, a warning clause that to be approved by FINMA has to be published on the first page of the fund regulations and the prospectus. The prospectus has to contain more detailed information and a glossary. Further, the prospectus with the warning clause has to be offered to interested parties free of charge prior to the conclusion of a contract or the subscription respectively.

Contractual fund

The involvement of a custodian bank is a mandatory requirement. It executes technical services (such as keeping of the fund's assets, issuance and redemption of fund units, etc.) as well as control duties (supervision of compliance of the fund management company with legislation, fund contract, etc.). The custodian bank has to be independent and has to have an appropriate organisation.

Delegation (and sub-delegation) of tasks by the fund management company to third parties that qualify for the delegated duties or the custodian bank is possible under certain circumstances. The delegation (and sub-delegation) of investment decisions to supervised asset managers is possible. Funds that are distributed in the EU shall not allow delegation of investment decisions to the custodian bank or other parties that may have potential conflicts of interests. The delegation of accounting to third parties domiciled in Switzerland is basically possible (support functions may be delegated to third parties domiciled abroad under certain circumstances). The fund management company remains liable as for its own actions. The details regarding the delegation are specified in FINMA Circular 2008/37 Delegation by Fund Management Company/SICAV (FINMA Circular 2008/37).

Each contractual fund has to publish a prospectus. It has to be adapted on an annual basis and/or if relevant changes occur. The content of the prospectus is set forth in detail in the CISA, the CISO and the annexes to CISO. A simplified prospectus has to be published for real estate funds. A key investor information document (KIID) has to be published for securities funds and other funds for traditional investments but not for other funds for alternative investments. The simplified prospectus or KIID have to be adapted on an annual basis or if relevant changes occur. The prospectus, simplified prospectus or KIID are not subject to approval by FINMA but have to be submitted to FINMA. The prospectus has to be made available to interested parties upon request prior to subscription free of charge. The prospectus, simplified prospectus, KIID and the source of supply have to be mentioned in any type of advertising. The simplified prospectus and KIID have to be offered to the interested parties free of charge.

The Net Asset Value (NAV) has to be calculated at the end of the financial year and on every day on which units are issued or redeemed. The fund management company has to publish the NAV at regular intervals.

For each open-ended collective investment scheme an annual report and a semi-annual report have to be published and submitted to FINMA.

Unless CISA or the applicable ordinances set forth otherwise the ordinary commercial accounting principles of the CO apply. Special provisions for real estate funds apply.

SICAV
The involvement of a custodian bank is a mandatory requirement. The custodian bank has to execute technical services (such as keeping of the fund's assets, issuance and redemption of fund units, etc.) as well as control duties (supervision of compliance of the fund management company with legislation, fund contract, etc.). The custodian bank has to be independent and has to have an appropriate organisation.

The SICAV has to appoint auditors recognised by FINMA.

The self-administered SICAV may delegate administration to the management. The externally managed SICAV delegates the administration to an authorised fund management company. Delegation of asset investment decisions are possible under certain circumstances and may be restricted. The details regarding the delegation are set forth in FINMA Circular 2008/37.

Regarding the NAV and the prospectus requirements see our comments above.

Regarding the accounting/reporting see our comments above.

Limited partnership for collective investment schemes (LPCIS)
The LPCIS invest in risk capital of enterprises and projects or other investments such as alternative investments or real estate projects.

The LPCIS has to appoint recognised auditors. It has to appoint a depositary and paying agent that are not subject to authorisation.

Although not explicitly requested it is assumed that a prospectus has to be issued annually and has to be updated if relevant issues change. It does not have to comply with the requirements of a prospectus set forth for open-ended collective investment schemes. However, it has to contain information regarding the investments, the investment policy, investment restrictions, risk diversification, risks related to the investments and investment techniques and in case of private equity investments the applied valuation principles have to be disclosed. The content list for prospectuses for open-ended funds is applicable only to a limited extent.

The accounting has to be in compliance with the ordinary accounting principles according to the CO. The provisions set forth for open-ended collective investment schemes are accordingly applicable in relation to reporting duties.

2.4. Marketing the fund
The marketing of Swiss and foreign collective investment is governed by CISA and its implementing ordinances. Further, other general marketing relevant legislation, such as unfair competition legislation, may apply. The term marketing is replaced in the revised legislation on collective investment schemes by the term distribution.

Distribution is defined as any offering (ie, effective offer to conclude an agreement) and advertising (ie, use of advertising means of any kind whose

content serves to offer or distribute collective investment schemes) for collective investment schemes that is:
- not exclusively addressed to investors listed in Article 10, paragraph 3, subparagraph a and b CISA, ie:
  - supervised financial intermediaries, such as banks, securities dealers, fund management companies and asset managers of collective investment schemes and central banks;
  - supervised insurance institutions;
- not covered by the exceptions set forth in Article 3, paragraph 2 CISA that do not qualify as distribution, ie:
  - reverse solicitation (including advisory situations and execution only situations);
  - written asset management agreements with certain supervised financial intermediaries or independent asset managers if certain requirements are met;
  - publication of prices, quotes, net asset values and control data by supervised financial intermediaries;
  - offering of employee participation plans in collective investment schemes.

If any of above exceptions apply the CISA and its ordinances do not apply regarding distribution.

Further, the distinction between qualified and non-qualified investors is relevant. The definition qualified investor was revised. According to Article 10, paragraph 3, 3bis and 3ter CISA (in connection with Article 6 and 6a CISO) qualified investors (Qualified Investors) are:
- supervised financial intermediaries such as banks, securities dealers, fund management companies and asset managers of collective investment schemes as well as central banks;
- supervised insurance institutions;
- public law corporate entities and employee welfare institutions with a professional treasury department;
- enterprises with a professional treasury department;
- high net worth individuals that have issued a written confirmation that they would like to qualify as qualified investor (opting-in). An investor is deemed to be a high net worth individual if he/she provides evidence that at the time of the acquisition:
  - he/she disposes of at least CHF500,000 and has the necessary market knowledge to understand the risks of the investment based on the personal education and the professional experience or comparable experience; or
  - he/she disposes of at least CHF5 million in assets.

Investors that have concluded a written asset management with a supervised financial intermediary or independent asset managers (see above exception from distribution) can declare in writing that they would not like to qualify as qualified investors (opting-out).

A distributor has to obtain an authorisation unless it is already holding an authorisation as bank, securities dealer, insurance institution, fund

Switzerland

management company, asset manager of collective investment schemes, or representative of foreign collective investment schemes.

Depending on whether the foreign collective investment scheme is distributed to non-qualified or Qualified Investors the following requirements apply:

The distribution of foreign collective investment schemes to non-qualified investors has to be approved by FINMA. Approval is granted if various requirements are met. A representative and a paying agent have to be appointed. The foreign collective investment scheme and the involved parties have to be supervised and governed by a legislation equivalent to the Swiss legislation and the name shall not give rise to deception or confusion. An agreement between FINMA and the foreign supervisory authority that is relevant for distribution regarding cooperation and exchange of information has to be concluded. The distributor has to be authorised.

In case of distribution of foreign collective investment schemes to Qualified Investors no approval is required but a representative and a paying agent have to be appointed and the designation of the collective investment scheme shall not give rise to deception or confusion. The distributor has to be authorised. A foreign distributor that only distributes to Qualified Investors may distribute without Swiss authorisation if it is adequately supervised in the country of its registered office/domicile.

The holders of authorisations (and called in third parties) have to comply with certain recording duties and information/disclosure duties.

FINMA issued a draft of a Circular on distribution of collective investment schemes that shall replace the FINMA Circular 2008/8 regarding Public Advertising on Collective Investment Schemes. This Circular shall provide more detailed guidance regarding the distribution. It is expected to enter into force in the 3rd or 4th quarter of 2013 and will be available on the FINMA website.

Swiss legislation on collective investment schemes does not provide for a general prohibition to market Swiss alternative investment funds to retail investors but protects investors by requiring more stringent transparency and information requirements.

In relation to foreign alternative investment funds that apply for approval/authorisation to publicly market in Switzerland FINMA requires that in addition to the general requirements the foreign alternative investment fund has to meet the same requirements as Swiss funds for alternative investments.

2.5. Taxation
Contractual fund/SICAV

The contractual fund and the SICAV are treated as tax transparent as long as they do not directly own real estate in Switzerland. Assets and earnings (retaining or distributing) are taxed at the investors' level.

If real estate is directly owned the open-ended funds are treated like legal entities and are subject to profit tax for earnings resulting from real estate. Further, capital taxes apply (cantonal/municipal level). Earnings and profits resulting from other investments are taxed at the investors' level.

If no real estate is directly owned taxation at the investors' level varies for private individuals owning the units directly, holding the units through a business, and legal entities. Private individuals owning the units directly are subject to income tax (only for earnings but not for capital gains generated by the fund), property tax and withholding tax. Private individuals holding the units through a business and legal entities are basically subject to profit or income tax respectively also for capital gains.

If the collective investment scheme directly owns real estate the income resulting from the collective investment scheme is subject to income and withholding tax at the investors' level to the extent that the total earnings of the collective investment exceed the earnings from direct real estate held by the collective investment scheme. Capital gains and already taxed income from real estate is not subject to income tax on the investors' level. For private individuals owning the units directly property tax is owed on the positive difference between total assets and real estate.

Capital gains resulting from the sale of units of the collective investment schemes are not subject to income tax for private individuals owning the units directly. However, transfers of units of Swiss collective investment schemes are subject to transfer stamp duty if a Swiss securities dealer is involved.

If a foreign investor invests in Swiss collective investment schemes this fact alone does not trigger income or profit tax in Switzerland but the investor will be subject to withholding taxes. Withholding taxes can be reclaimed based on a double taxation treaty. No withholding taxes are levied if at least 80 percent of the earnings of the collective investment schemes derive from foreign sources and the investor is an investor domiciled abroad.

Limited partnership for collective investment schemes (LPCIS)
The tax treatment of the LPCIS mainly corresponds to the tax treatment of open-ended collective investment schemes (see our comments above).

Tax rulings
In general, it is possible to obtain tax rulings in Switzerland. As the tax rules for the taxation at the level of the collective investment scheme are rather clear it is normally not necessary to obtain a tax ruling. However, under certain circumstances a tax ruling is advisable, such as in case of structures with foreign entities involved (allocation of profits), or regarding the tax treatment of carried interest or performance fee.

2.6. Customary or common terms
Contractual fund
The fund contract has to be approved by FINMA and contains provisions amongst others regarding the rights and duties of the investors, the fund management company, the custodian bank, and the asset manager, investment policy, risk diversification, calculation of the NAV and issue as well as redemption prices, allocation of income and profits, details of all remunerations, redemption commissions, ancillary costs, locations where the fund documentation is available, publication instruments, duration, division

into sub-funds, unit classes, investors' right to terminate, requirements for the deferral of repayment and forced redemption, restructuring, etc. The CISA and the applicable ordinances contain a detailed list of the minimum content and a model documentation is available on the website of the SFAMA.

SICAV
The articles of association and the investment regulations have to be approved by FINMA. The articles of association contain standard provisions for corporations such as company name, purpose, minimum contribution, convening of the shareholders' meeting corporate bodies, publication instruments and also provisions that are only applicable if included such as duration, limitation of the circle of shareholders to Qualified Investors, the transfer restrictions for shares, different categories of shares, delegation of management, voting by way of correspondence, different shareholders' meetings for different sub-funds, exception from the redemption rights, establishing, cancellation, merger of categories of shares by the board of directors. The investment regulations should cover basically the same content as the fund contract of a contractual fund except the provisions included in the articles of association. This may lead to duplications of content in the articles of association and the investment regulations. Core content is the investment policy, risk diversification, risks related to investments, costs and commissions.

The CISA and the applicable ordinances contain a detailed list of the minimum content and a model documentation is available on the website of the SFAMA.

Limited partnership for collective investment schemes (LPCIS)
The partnership agreement for the LPCIS has to be in writing and approved by FINMA. It has to contain a mandatory minimum content, eg, the company name and registered office, the purpose, the company name and the registered office of the general partners, the amount of the total of the limited partners' contribution, the duration, the conditions for the entry and exit of the limited partners, the maintenance of a register of the limited partners, the investments, the investment policy, the investment restrictions, the risk diversification, the risks related to investments, the investment techniques, the delegation of the management and representation, the engaging of a depository and paying agent. Further, it is recommended to include provisions regarding investment cycle, fee structure, allocation of profits, competences of the partners' meeting, information duties, exit of partners, details of the management and participation of the general partners, non-compete provisions for the general partners, reasons for dissolution of the partnership. A model partnership agreement is available on the website of the SFAMA.

The limited partnership does not have to issue investment regulations. Such provisions are included in the partnership agreement and the prospectus.

3. RETAIL FUNDS
3.1. Common structures
For retail funds the contractual fund, the SICAV and the SICAF are available.

Switzerland

The LPCIS is limited to qualified investors according to Article 10, paragraph 3 CISA. However, retail investors may have the possibility to invest through a vehicle that invests as limited partner and qualifies as qualified investor. Most of the retail funds are contractual funds. Please see comments under section 2.1. above.

3.2. Regulatory framework
Please see our comments on contractual funds/SICAVs under section 2.2. above.

3.3. Operational requirements
Please see our comments on contractual funds/SICAVs under section 2.3. above.

3.4. Marketing the fund
Please see our comments on contractual funds/SICAVs under section 2.4. above.

3.5. Taxation
Please see our comments on contractual funds/SICAVs under section 2.5. above.

3.6. Customary or common terms
Please see our comments on contractual funds/SICAVs under section 2.6. above.

4. PROPOSED CHANGES AND DEVELOPMENTS
As outlined above the legislation on collective investment schemes was revised and the revisions entered into force on 1 March 2013. Based on the revised legislation on collective investment schemes further ordinances and FINMA Circulars as well as various self-regulation and model documents issued by the SFAMA should adapted in the near future.

A new financial market legislation is being discussed. Based on a position paper issued by FINMA in February 2012 proposing measures to increase the client protection in the distribution sector, equaling the conditions for financial services providers and harmonising the Swiss financial market legislation to international standards. In March 2012 the Federal Council instructed the Federal Department of Finance to submit a consultation draft of a cross-sector law (Financial Services Act) (FSA) to the Federal Council by fall of this year. The Steering Group of the FSA published a hearing report in February 2013 outlining the possible strategic directions of such potential legislation. These directions covered issues relating to the scope of supervised entities, documentation of product characteristics, conduct and organisation of financial services providers, training of client advisors, enforcing claims of retail clients, and cross-border activity into Switzerland. Interested parties were invited to submit their comments in March 2013 and the draft of the FSA for consultation should be available in the autumn of this year.

United Kingdom

Sam Kay, Emily Clark & Phil Bartram **Travers Smith LLP**

1. MARKET OVERVIEW

The UK is regarded as one of the leading global asset management centres, with an investment funds industry covering both traditional and alternative asset classes. As well as having a sophisticated domestic market, this pre-eminence derives from having the experience and infrastructure to attract managers of overseas fund and clients.

The annual asset management survey of the UK's Investment Management Association (which, broadly, covers the UK retail funds market) found that, as at December 2012 total funds under management of UK-domiciled funds were £660 billion (up 14 per cent from a year earlier) and, including assets of overseas-domiciled funds managed in the UK, the figure increases to £1.4 trillion. Total assets managed in the UK by member firms of the IMA were £4.5 trillion, of which over a third (£1.8 trillion) was managed in the UK on behalf of overseas clients. Within the alternative asset classes, the UK's private equity industry group, the BVCA, found that whilst investment activity was down on the previous year (reflecting the challenging domestic economic environment) there was a marked increase in private equity fundraising from £4.2 billion in 2011 to £5.9 billion in 2012. Of that amount, around £1.6 billion was raised from overseas investors.

During 2012 and 2013, there has been a focus on the changing regulatory framework for the investment funds industry in the UK. The previous regulator of the financial services sector has been abolished and a new regulatory framework is in place. The new regime gives the Bank of England responsibility for financial stability, bringing together macro and micro prudential regulation, and has created a new regulatory body (the Financial Conduct Authority, or FCA) with a focus on the regulation of conduct by both retail and wholesale financial services firms. In addition, 2013 has seen the implementation of the pan-European directive, the Alternative Investment Fund Managers Directive (the 'AIFM Directive'), which has been implemented in the UK.

2. ALTERNATIVE INVESTMENT FUNDS
2.1. Common structures

Within the UK market, alternative investment funds can be, broadly, divided between closed-ended funds that focus on illiquid asset strategies (such as private equity, real estate and infrastructure funds) and open-ended funds that focus on liquid asset strategies (such as hedge funds). The common structures will be different between these two categorisations.

Closed-ended private funds

A private closed-ended fund in the UK will typically take one of two forms, although others are available.

Private closed-ended funds are often structured as limited partnerships. This is a form of partnership governed by statute: the Limited Partnerships Act 1907. Similar to other jurisdictions, the limited partnership will have one or more general partners and one or more limited partners. The general partner is responsible for the management of the limited partnership (although whether it fulfils this role will largely depend on the regulatory issues described below), but has unlimited liability for the debts and obligations of the partnership over and above the partnership assets. Conversely, the liability of a limited partner will be limited to the amount it contributes to the partnership, provided such limited partner takes no part in the management of the partnership: to the extent the limited partner does take part in management, it will be treated as a general partner and will lose the protection of limited liability. A limited partnership registered in England and Wales does not have any legal personality separate from its partners. By contrast, a limited partnership registered in Scotland is treated as having separate legal personality. Neither is a body corporate.

It is also possible for a private closed-ended fund in the UK to be structured as a unit trust. The English law concept of a trust has no equivalent in some other jurisdictions. It is a structure under which title to the fund's assets are held by a person with legal personality (the trustee) for the benefit of the fund's investors (the beneficiaries). The document constituting the trust (the Trust Deed) governs the relationship between the trustee and the beneficiaries and, in addition, strict fiduciary duties are owed by the trustee as a matter of law. A trust does not have separate legal personality: all legal relationships are entered into by or on behalf of the trustee. These vehicles are often used for certain real estate fund structures, though they may only be tax efficient for certain types of investor.

It would also be common for a UK-based private fund manager to establish its private closed-ended fund as an offshore vehicle (whether a partnership, a unit trust or a corporate entity). However, for the purposes of the description of closed-ended private funds in this chapter, the focus will be on English limited partnerships.

Open-ended private funds

A classic hedge fund structure in the UK would not include the actual hedge fund being domiciled in the UK. This is often because, to set up the fund onshore would lead to tax inefficiencies because the fund would be treated as 'trading' rather than 'investing' for UK tax purposes. Instead, hedge fund structures will invariably include an offshore company or offshore limited partnership established in a jurisdiction such as the Cayman Islands. A UK entity would then be appointed as the discretionary investment manager to, or investment adviser of, the hedge fund.

2.2. Regulatory framework

Financial services firms in the UK are subject to both domestic legislation and regional pan-European directives. The principal domestic legislation for the investment funds industry in the UK is the Financial Services and Markets Act 2000 (FSMA). Under FSMA, only appropriately authorised persons can carry on a regulated activity by way of business in the UK. It is a criminal offence to breach this requirement. Any agreement entered into by a person carrying on a regulated activity in contravention of this provision is unenforceable against the other party and the other party is entitled to recover any money paid and to compensation for any loss sustained.

To implement various provisions of the AIFM Directive, the Alternative Investment Fund Managers Regulations 2013 (SI 2013/1773) are now in force.

Closed-ended private funds

A limited partnership does not itself need to be authorised by any regulatory body in the UK. However, a limited partnership is likely to be an alternative investment fund (AIF) under the AIFM Directive, which is defined as a collective investment undertaking that raises capital from a number of investors, with a view to investing it in accordance with a defined investment policy for the benefit of those investors. Even if the limited partnership does not fall into the definition of an AIF, it is likely to be a collective investment scheme (CIS) under FSMA (a CIS is similar, but not identical, to the European concept of a collective investment undertaking). The FCA authorises and regulates the persons carrying out specific 'regulated activities' for the scheme in the UK, rather than the scheme itself. Acting as the manager of an AIF is a regulated activity, as is establishing, operating (which includes managing) and winding up an unregulated CIS. A suitably authorised person must therefore be appointed to carry out these activities on behalf of the limited partnership. This may be the general partner or, more usually, a separate affiliated entity is appointed. The FCA authorised entity will often provide services to a number of funds in the same group, although each will typically have a separate general partner in order to contain any liabilities which arise in the fund.

A regulated entity which conducts all of its activities in its capacity as operator/manager of the fund – whether an authorised AIFM or not – will be exempt from the EU Markets in Financial Instruments Directive.

Open-ended private funds

UK-resident managers or advisers of offshore hedge funds will be carrying on certain regulated activities such as discretionary investment management and/or giving investment advice, dealing as agent and arranging transactions on behalf of the fund. This means that they will need to be authorised and regulated by the FCA and will be subject to the FCA's rules. It is usually the case with offshore fund structures that the person regarded as the operator/manager of the fund will also be offshore and that the UK regulated entity is merely its delegate. This means that a UK manager will normally be subject to the EU Markets in Financial Instruments Directive (because it cannot

UK

benefit from the exemption for operator/managers of collective investment undertakings) and so its regulation will stem in part from EU requirements.

2.3. Operational requirements
Closed-ended private funds

One of the fundamental attractions in the UK of a limited partnership structure for private closed-ended funds is that the limited partnership is a flexible vehicle in terms of internal governance and control.

The statutory framework in the UK requires that a limited partnership is registered as such. This entails providing an application for registration to the Registrar for Limited Partnerships. The application must set out: the name of the partnership; the name of each general partner; the name of each limited partner; the amount of capital contributed by each limited partner; the address of the principal place of business of the partnership; and the term (if any) for which the limited partnership is to be entered into. Any changes to these details during the continuance of the limited partnership must be similarly registered within seven days of the relevant change. There are also formalities that must be followed on assignments of limited partnership interests, such as advertising the transfer in specific publications. Finally, it would be common for the limited partnership to produce annual audited accounts and these accounts may need to be publicly filed.

The FCA authorised manager must comply with applicable FCA rules, which have been supplemented by the requirements of the AIFM Directive. A key requirement is that the manager must maintain a minimum amount of capital. The amount of capital is likely to be greater if the manager operates under the AIFM Directive or the EU Markets in Financial Instruments Directive. Other requirements applicable to the typical manager in this structure include: prudential requirements, including relating to its governance, remuneration of key staff and internal systems and controls; FCA approvals of personnel in key positions; requirements relating to the conduct of the manager's business, including relating to disclosures to investors and the regulator; and anti-money laundering checks, including due diligence checks on new investors.

Historically, although the FCA authorised manager has had to comply with the rules set out above, there have been few operational requirements imposed on the fund itself. To the extent that the AIFM Directive applies, the manager must now ensure that certain requirements are imposed on the limited partnership, such as: the appointment of a depositary to have custody of certain assets and/or verify title to privately-held assets; organisational controls (relating to risk management, compliance, valuation for example), conduct of business rules (relating for example to due diligence, execution of orders and reporting) and rules relating to companies in which the fund has a substantial stake.

Open-ended private funds

For the hedge fund itself, the operational requirements will depend on the laws and regulations of the jurisdiction in which the fund has been

established. However, it would be usual for the fund to appoint the following service providers to assist with the operation of the fund:
- an administrator. The main roles of the administrator will be to calculate the NAV of the fund, deal with subscriptions and redemptions, calculate the fees that are payable to the fund manager and provide corporate and secretarial services;
- one or more prime brokers. The main roles of the prime broker will be to provide clearing and settlement facilities for the trades of the hedge fund, trade financing, securities lending, custody services, leverage and margin trading facilities;
- custodian. The custodian will take custody of the assets of the hedge fund. Whether an independent custodian is required may depend on the role being performed by the prime broker; it is possible for the prime broker to also act as custodian; and
- auditors. The auditors will need to be familiar with hedge fund accounting and should provide a level of independent oversight on the activities of the hedge fund. Some offshore jurisdictions require that the appointed auditors are physically based in that jurisdiction.

The FCA authorised manager must comply with applicable FCA rules. As a result, similar regulatory requirements will apply to those set out for closed-ended private funds such as limited partnerships, set out above.

Additional requirements of UK legislation particularly relevant to hedge funds include rules relating to market abuse and insider dealing; disclosures of interests in shares and related derivatives above certain levels; and disclosures of net economic short exposures to certain financial sector companies and companies subject to a rights issue.

2.4. Marketing the fund

The marketing of a private fund in the UK gives rise to four main considerations:
- the rules governing the communication of a financial promotion;
- the requirements of the AIFM Directive;
- the rules governing carrying on the regulated activities of arranging deals in investments; and
- the requirements relating to prospectuses.

The promotion of an interest in an unregulated CIS (such as a limited partnership interest) is restricted in the UK. It may not be promoted to the general public and, even for a private placement, there are broad restrictions on its promotion to different categories of recipients. The persons a limited partnership interest may be promoted to include: investment professional organisations; high net worth organisations; and, in limited circumstances, some certified high-net worth individuals and sophisticated individuals. There is some limited widening of the categories if the marketing is undertaken by an FCA regulated entity (as would be usual in the UK). Marketing documents need to meet UK standards and legends are customary.

As well as the domestic financial promotion rules, on a manager that is within the full-scope of the AIFM Directive, certain additional requirements are imposed under the terms of that directive. The manager must give the

UK

FCA one month's notice of the proposed marketing and must include certain pre-investment disclosures to investors, which are set out in the AIFM Directive. In the UK, the FCA permits the marketing of a private fund to wider group of recipients than the category of 'professional investors' referred to in the AIFM Directive, provided the financial promotion rules referred to above are complied with. It should also be noted that the FCA has implemented certain transitional rules to the marketing requirements under the AIFM Directive and these rules apply up to 22 July 2014, but only if the manager was in the business of managing AIFs before 22 July 2013.

A non-EEA manager of a non-EEA fund must give notice to the FCA under the AIFM Directive and conform to certain transparency obligations.

In practice, marketing activities in relation to a fund will also often involve the regulated activities of making arrangements with a view to another person buying or subscribing for interests in the fund. In view of this, fund marketing activities in the UK are generally conducted only by authorised persons. Any person conducting marketing activities in relation to a fund should consider whether authorisation is required and, if it is authorised, whether it has the appropriate permissions from the FCA to undertake these activities.

Onerous prospectus requirements, derived from the EU Prospectus Directive, apply if the marketing is treated as an 'offer to the public'. These requirements can be avoided if, broadly, the minimum subscription per investor is EUR 100,000 or if the fund is offered to fewer than 150 investors per EEA state. The EU Prospectus Directive does not apply to open-ended funds so, in the majority of cases, will not apply to hedge funds.

2.5. Taxation
Closed-ended private funds

A UK limited partnership (whether English or Scottish) is not a taxable entity for UK direct tax purposes and is instead fiscally transparent so that the partnership itself has no liability to tax on its profits or gains. This fiscal transparency means each limited partner is treated for UK tax purposes as owning his proportionate share of the assets of the partnership and is subject to tax on the income and gains allocated to it under the limited partnership agreement (whether or not distributed).

- Tax on gains – Where assets are held for long-term investment purposes, then when the partnership disposes of such assets UK tax resident limited partners will be treated as each having disposed of their proportionate share of the asset and will be deemed to have realised their proportionate share of any resulting gain or loss. A limited partner which is tax resident outside the UK will not be subject to UK tax on such a gain unless the partner holds their interest for the purposes of a UK trade (different rules may apply to holdings of residential property).
- Tax on investment income receipts – UK resident limited partners are subject to income tax on their share of the partnership's income returns whether these are interest income, dividends or, in the case of a real estate fund, rental income. The tax transparency of the partnership means that these payments retain their character as interest, dividend or

rent and are taxed accordingly. Most non-resident investors will only be subject to UK tax on this income to the extent withheld at source (the UK imposes withholding taxes on rental and interest income) but there are exceptions to this rule.
- Tax on trading income – If the limited partnership is carrying on a trade in the UK then limited partners will be subject to income tax (or corporation tax on trading income) on their share of trading profits and gains because the partnership will constitute a taxable presence in the UK through which the non-resident is carrying on a trade.

Where a UK limited partnership receives income from non-UK jurisdictions that levy withholding tax or receives capital proceeds from the sale of an asset situated in a jurisdiction which might tax that gain, then limited partners may seek to rely on the terms of a double tax treaty in order to obtain relief. Whether such relief is available will depend, in part, upon whether that non-UK jurisdiction treats a UK limited partnership as fiscally transparent.

A limited partnership operating as an investment fund which issues interests to investors and which makes investments may not make taxable supplies for VAT purposes and so its ability to recover input tax suffered on supplies made to it is very limited. Where the general partner appoints a manager to manage the partnership the fee payable to the manager will in principle attract VAT. This is most often managed by ensuring that the manager and the general partner are in the same VAT group.

Open-ended private funds
As noted above, the UK is not typically used as a domicile for hedge funds, but it is a popular location for investment managers of hedge funds and this is in part because of the Investment Manager Exemption (IME). Provided certain conditions are met, the IME ensures that a UK investment manager managing a non-UK hedge fund will not constitute a permanent establishment of the hedge fund in the UK. The IME enables a non-UK resident fund that is trading for UK tax purposes to appoint a UK-based investment manager without the risk of that part of the fund's profit that is attributable to the activity of the investment manager in the UK becoming subject UK tax.

The qualifying conditions for the IME are:
- the UK investment manager must be in the business of providing investment management services;
- the transactions carried out by the UK investment manager must be carried out in the ordinary course of that business;
- the investment manager must act in relation to the fund in an independent capacity. This will be met if the relationship between the manager and the non-resident fund (having regard to its legal, financial and commercial characteristics) is a relationship between persons carrying on independent businesses that deal with each other on arm's length terms. Broadly speaking, this will be deemed to be the case where the non-resident fund is a widely held collective fund or is being actively marketed with the intention that it becomes one or if the provision of

services to the non-resident and persons connected with him is not a substantial part of the manager's investment management business;
- the requirements of the 20 per cent rule must be met. Over a qualifying period, the investment manager and persons connected with it must not have a beneficial entitlement to more than 20 per cent of the non-resident fund's chargeable profit arising from transactions carried out through the investment manager. Where the 20 per cent threshold is exceeded, the part of the income of the non-resident to which the investment manager and connected persons are beneficially entitled is excluded from the benefit of the IME; and
- the investment manager must receive remuneration for the provision of services to the fund at not less than the rate that is customary for such business. For this, the UK tax authorities have stated that they will be guided by the OECD Transfer Pricing Guidelines and they also take the view that the fees payable must be brought into charge to UK tax when earned. A cash payment may be deferred or reinvested in the fund but this should not affect the recognition of the fee income for UK tax purposes.

2.6. Customary or common terms

To set out details of customary or common terms, the text below focuses on private equity funds structured as limited partnerships and offshore hedge funds.

Private equity funds
Term of the fund
This is typically 10 years, with a specific investment period of five to six years. It would be common for the overall term to be subject to extension, possibly requiring the consent of limited partners.

Commitment of investors
Under statute, the liability of a limited partner for the debts and obligations of a partnership is limited to the amount of capital it contributes to that partnership. Also, there is a restriction on the ability of limited partners to withdraw capital during the life of the partnership. To keep the capital element as small as possible, limited partners will typically split their commitments into a loan element (typically 99.99 per cent of total commitments) and a capital contribution element (typically 0.01 per cent of total commitments).

Drawdowns and default
The commitment of limited partners will usually be advanced in tranches and in such amounts as shall be determined by the manager and notified to that limited partner. The ability of the manager to draw down commitments after the end of the investment period will be limited to draw downs for certain specified matters, such as the payment of partnership expenses.

Because it would jeopardise the business of the partnership and, therefore, potentially adversely affect the investment made by other limited partners, there will be severe consequences on a limited partner who fails to comply with a drawdown notice. This could include causing such defaulting limited partner to forfeit its interest or forcing the sale of the interest on terms (including as to price) as the manager determines.

Management fee
The fee payable to the general partner will typically be structured as a priority profit share. From this priority profit share, the general partner will pay the manager its management fee.

During the investment period, the priority profit share is almost always calculated as a percentage fee (in the range of 1 per cent to 2.5 per cent per annum) applied to the total commitments made by the limited partners to the partnership.

The priority profit share is usually reduced after the end of the investment period to reflect the fact that further investment activity is not being undertaken. A common approach would be to calculate the priority profit share by reference to the aggregate acquisition cost of all investments held by the partnership, reduced by the acquisition cost of any investments which have been written off.

Economic terms
The limited partnership agreement constituting the fund will often contain a 'waterfall' of distribution payments to the partners. Following the repayment to limited partners of the amounts contributed by them to the partnership, the next available profits will be distributed to the limited partners in priority until they have received a certain minimum amount, known as the 'preferred return'. The preferred return is typically 8 per cent per annum. After this, the profit sharing ratio with the partnership is often changed so that a vehicle (the 'carried interest partner') owned by the management team becomes entitled to receive a share of the net investment gains. This is a form of incentive fee and is often called a 'carried interest'. The carried interest will typically be equal to 20 per cent of profits.

GP commitment
In order to improve alignment between the management team and the investors, there is normally a required for the management team to make a financial commitment to the partnership (or in parallel with the partnership). The amount of this commitment will vary, but it will need to be a substantial sum.

Investor protections
Because of the long-term nature of the investment made by limited partners, certain terms have become customary in order to provide investors with a level of protection.

Key-man terms: these provisions are designed to ensure that the partnership continues to be managed by the team who are considered key to the success of the fund, and to grant limited partners certain rights in the event that it does not. The key-man provisions usually stipulate that the key executives of the manager must devote a substantial amount of time to the business of the partnership. If this test is failed (for example, because certain individuals leave), the ability of the partnership to make new investments is would normally be suspended and may be terminated if adequate replacement key man are not appointed.

GP removal terms: a simple majority of limited partners may remove the general partner for no compensation if certain serious activity is carried out by the general partner, manager or affiliates. These 'cause' events would include fraud, wilful misconduct, bad faith and negligence. Similarly, it is becoming increasingly common to see terms whereby a super-majority of limited partners may remove the general partner when there has be no cause (sometimes called a 'no-fault divorce'). However, in these circumstances, compensation for removal of office may be required.

Successor fund provisions: a restriction is placed on the general partner/manager's ability to raise a successor fund before the investment period of the existing fund has come to an end.

Advisory committee
It is common for the partnership to establish an advisory committee comprising representatives of the limited partners. The tasks of the advisory committee will typically include reviewing material conflicts that arise. The function of the advisory committee is to consult with the manager and not to provide advice – and the manager is not typically required to follow any advice or recommendation of the advisory committee since the members of the advisory committee should not take part in the management of the partnership's business as this would jeopardise their limited liability status.

Offshore hedge funds
Subscriptions
As hedge funds are normally open-ended they will provide for regular dealing days (eg, monthly or quarterly) on which investors may subscribe for interests in the fund. A subscription fee may be payable.

Calculation of NAV
The fund will have a policy in place for the valuation of assets and the calculation of its net asset value (NAV) and the NAV per share of the fund, or a particular class of shares, as at each dealing day. The NAV per share will be the price at which subscriptions and redemptions may be made. It would be usual for the administrator to determine the NAV to ensure there is some independent oversight on the process. In certain circumstances, the calculation of NAV may be temporarily suspended if certain events occur (such as market turmoil or market illiquidity) which means the NAV cannot be accurately determined.

Management and performance fees

The amount of the management fee may vary (and may vary by different classes of shares within the same fund), but an annual fee in the range of 1 per cent to 2 per cent of the NAV (payable monthly or quarterly) would be common.

The performance fee will be a percentage (normally 20 per cent), paid annually, of the actual appreciation in NAV during the relevant calculation period. It is calculated by comparing the NAV at the end of the calculation period with the NAV at the start of same period. A 'high watermark' concept is often used to ensure any prior fall in NAV is taken into account before the performance fee is paid.

Equalisation and multi-series accounting

Where the frequency of subscriptions and redemptions differs from the period over which a performance fee is calculated (eg, investors can subscribe or redeem on a monthly basis, but the calculation period for the performance fee is annual) inequalities can arise for both investors and the manager if the performance fee charged simply takes account of the percentage increase in the fund's assets. There are two common approaches to deal with this:
- Equalisation attempts to make adjustments to the subscription amounts paid by investors, if the subscription takes place during a calculation period when a performance fee is accruing. It uses 'equalisation credits' and 'equalisation deposits' to ensure that the investor bears the correct amount of performance fee or has the correct amount at stake in the fund.
- Multi-series accounting creates a new series of shares on each subscription date. Any performance fee is then payable equally for all investors within a particular series.

Redemptions

The dealing days on which investors may redeem their shares may be subject to restrictions, such as:
- investors may be locked-in for a fixed period of time (eg, 12 months) before they are permitted to redeem (this is often referred to as a 'hard lock-up');
- investors may be required to pay a significant redemption fee in order to redeem within a fixed period from the time the shares were subscribed (this is often referred to as a 'soft lock-up');
- there may be a long period of notice required for a redemption;
- the proceeds (or part of the proceeds) payable on redemption may not be settled for a significant period of time after the redemption has been made.

Redemptions may be temporarily suspended if the calculation of NAV is itself suspended.

Gating

A specific restriction on redemptions is the ability of the fund to impose a 'gate'. This involves a ceiling on the number of shares in the fund that may be redeemed on any given dealing day. The gate is often calculated by reference to the amount of the NAV represented by the redemption requests.

Side pockets   The fund may have the ability to create a side pocket, which allows an amount of the hedge fund portfolio to be invested in illiquid assets and the fund to place limitations on the ability of the investor to redeem its shares, up to the value that has been invested in the illiquid assets. The side pocket is often created by transferring part of each investor's shareholding, equal to the aggregate cost of the illiquid investment, to a separate class of shares. The new class of shares may only be redeemed when the illiquid asset has been realised.

3.   RETAIL FUNDS
3.1. Common structures

The appropriate structure used by a retail fund in the UK will depend on whether the fund is open-ended or closed-ended.

For an open-ended structure, an open-ended investment company (OEIC) may be used. This is a collective investment scheme structured as a corporate vehicle which meets the following criteria:
- its purpose is the investment of its assets with the aim of spreading investment risk and giving its members the benefit of the results of the management of its assets; and
- it allows investors to realise their investments within a reasonable time at a price which reflects the value of the property held within the OEIC.

OEICs in the UK can be structured as a single fund or as an umbrella company with multiple sub-funds, each of which would have its own investment aims and objectives. The legal framework in the UK now provides for the ringfencing of the assets and liabilities of each sub-fund.

Also for an open-ended structure, an authorised unit trust (AUT) may be used. This is a type of unit trust authorised by the FCA, which is constituted by a trust deed made between the Trustee and the Manager of the fund. The property of the AUT is legally held by the Trustee but is managed by the Manager. The investors have beneficial ownership of the property of the fund. An AUT can have a single fund or an umbrella fund structure. In the latter case, each sub-fund is constituted under a separate trust and under UK law the assets and liabilities of each sub-fund are ringfenced.

For closed-ended structures, an investment trust company is used. This is a corporate fund vehicle (not a trust). Typically an investment trust company is an UK public limited company which has been approved by Her Majesty's Revenue & Customs as an investment trust for the purposes of section 842 of the Income and Corporation Taxes Act 1988. This gives the investment trust company a certain tax status. An investment trust issues shares to investors that are listed on the London Stock Exchange. It is possible to create share classes which have different characteristics. Many investment trusts will be regarded as AIFs under the AIFM Directive.

3.2. Regulatory framework
Categories of regulated fund

From a regulatory perspective, UK funds available for sale to the general public in the UK fall within one of the following categories: for openended funds, either an undertaking for collective investment in transferable securities (UCITS) or a non UCITS retail scheme (NURS); or for closed-ended funds, the investment trust company may be utilised.

UCITS and NURS can be structured either as OEICs or AUTs; the regulatory framework is substantially the same regardless of the legal form of the fund. Both are regulated funds which require authorisation from the FCA and must comply with detailed FCA rules.

UCITS funds are established and operate within the detailed regulatory framework contained within the UCITS Directive (2009/65/EC) (UCITS IV) and its associated implementing directives and regulations. UCITS offer a high degree of investor protection. One of the key advantages of a UCITS fund is that it can be marketed to investors throughout the EU without the need for additional, local authorisation in each country, known as the 'UCITS marketing passport'.

A NURS provides a similar level of investor protection to that of a UCITS and allows the manager more flexibility in terms of the investments the fund can make, for example, NURS can invest in real property and some types of commodities. However, a NURS does not benefit from the UCITS marketing passport. A NURS will be regarded as an AIF for the purposes of the AIFM Directive.

Authorisation of OEICs

OEICs are authorised by the FCA under the Open-Ended Investment Companies Regulations 2001. OEICs are governed by these regulations, FSMA and the FCA rules.

Market practice in the UK is that OEICs usually have only one director (commonly referred to as the authorised corporate director (ACD)), who must be a body corporate and an authorised person with the requisite permission under FSMA. In the context of a UCITS fund, the ACD may be an EEA firm operating as the manager of the fund under the UCITS management company passport.

An OEIC must have a depositary that is independent from the ACD. The depositary is responsible for the safekeeping of the property of the fund and also has certain oversight and monitoring functions in relation to the activities of the ACD. The Depositary must be a body corporate incorporated in the UK or another EEA state. Its affairs must be administered in the country in which it is incorporated and it must have a place of business in the UK. It must also be an authorised person with permission under FSMA to act as the depositary of the relevant type of OEIC.

Authorisation of AUTs

AUTs are governed by FSMA, the FCA rules and the general law of trusts.

The trustee and manager of an AUT must both be bodies corporate incorporated in the UK or another EEA state, each of their affairs must be administered in the country in which it is incorporated and they each must also be an authorised person with permission under FSMA to act as the trustee or manager (as applicable) of the relevant type of AUT. The trustee and manager must be independent of each other. The trustee is the legal owner of the assets of the AUT, holding them on trust for the investors, and will have certain oversight and monitoring functions. The manager is responsible for the day to day management and operation of the AUT. In the context of a UCITS fund, the manager may be an EEA firm operating as the manager of the fund under the UCITS management company passport.

Investment trust companies
Historically, investment trust companies were not regulated entities. Following the adoption of the AIFM Directive, some investment trust companies may regard themselves as AIFM and become authorised under the AIFM Directive. However, some investment trusts may have an external manager that is acting as the AIFM and will not, therefore, be regulated directly.

3.3. Operational requirements
UCITS and NURS
For both UCITS and NURS funds, whether structured as an OEIC or an AUT, there are very detailed operational requirements. FCA's rules contain comprehensive provisions governing the following:
- The fund's constitution.
- Pre-sale information for investors. This includes preparing a detailed prospectus, key investor information for UCITS funds and key features for NURS funds.
- The ongoing provision of information to investors. This includes a short report and a more detailed long report which are produced half yearly and annually.
- Procedures for making changes to the fund including the circumstances requiring prior investor approval, circumstances requiring prior notification to investors and post event notification obligations.
- The investment and borrowing powers of the fund. There are very detailed rules on the types of investment which can be held (which include transferable securities, most types of financial derivatives, regulated funds, money market instruments), the spread of investments, the limits on global exposure, counterparty risks and concentration. Physical, naked short selling of securities is not permitted although the use of financial derivatives to achieve the same economic exposure is permitted. For UCITS funds these rules are derived from the UCITS IV Directive and relevant implementing measures. For a NURS fund the requirements are similar but there is more investment flexibility. For example NURS can invest in real property, gold and unregulated funds.
- Dealing in shares or units. There are detailed rules governing the process through which investors buy and sell their shares or units. Daily dealing is normal market practice for retail funds, although UCITS funds can deal as infrequently as twice a month and for certain NURS funds eg, property funds dealing can be as infrequently as six monthly. Investors usually

deal at the next available price, rather than the last published price.
- The valuation of the fund and the pricing of shares or units is also covered by detailed regulations. The pricing of shares or units is based on the net asset value of the fund. Valuations are carried out by the ACD/manager and must be fair and accurate. Prices of shares or units must be made public.
- The maintenance of the share or unitholder register.
- The obligations of the ACD or manager.
- The obligations of the depositary or trustee.
- Procedure for changing the manager or the depositary or trustee.
- Payments which may be made from the fund's assets. The FCA rules restrict the types of payment that can be made by a fund out of its assets to those required for investment purposes, the administration of the fund and the remuneration of those operating the fund. Funds are not permitted, for example, to pay commission to intermediaries for the sale of shares or units.
- Accounting requirements including income allocation and distribution.
- Suspension of dealings in shares or units. There are procedures for emergency situations where a fund temporarily may not be able to value, price and deal.
- Termination of a fund.

The ACD or manager of the fund is also under various obligations to make notifications and provide information to FCA. FCA must be notified of significant changes to the fund in advance and provided with any revised prospectus, key investor information document, annual and half yearly reports. The depositary or trustee is also under obligations to make notifications and provide information to FCA. There is a specific requirement for the depositary or trustee to report on pricing errors and breaches of dealing rules on a quarterly basis. For a NURS fund the requirements of the AIFM Directive must also be met.

Investment trust company
As a public limited company the investment trust will have a board of directors who are responsible for managing its affairs. The board of directors will typically delegate the day to day operation of the investment trust. For example, investment management functions are usually delegated to a fund management company, a depositary/custodian will be appointed to be responsible for the safekeeping of the company's assets, a registrar will be responsible for the share register and a broker will advise on the listing of the company's shares. The fund manager, depositary/custodian and broker will usually be authorised and regulated by FCA.

An investment trust company's shares will be listed on the London Stock Exchange and it will therefore have to comply with FCA's Listing Rules and the continuing obligations on listed companies set out in FCA's Disclosure and Transparency Rules. Many investment trusts will be regarded as AIFs under the AIFM Directive. As a result either the investment trusts itself (if acting as the AIFM) or the appointed investment manager will be required to comply with the requirements of the AIFM Directive.

3.4. Marketing the fund
The marketing of a retail fund in the UK gives rise to two main considerations:
- the rules governing the communication of a financial promotion; and
- the rules governing carrying on the regulated activities of arranging deals in investments and giving investment advice in the UK.

Because the ACD or manager will be a FCA regulated entity, it may therefore issue financial promotions in relation to the fund. The FCA rules contain detailed requirements in the Conduct of Business Sourcebook which an authorised person should comply with when communicating a financial promotion and marketing a UCITS. These include a general obligation to ensure that the financial promotion is clear, fair and not misleading.

An unauthorised person should not make any financial promotion unless the financial promotion has been approved by an authorised person under FSMA.

In practice, marketing activities in relation to a fund will also often involve the regulated activities of making arrangements with a view to another person buying or subscribing for shares or units in the fund and giving investment advice. In view of this, fund marketing activities in the UK are generally conducted only by authorised persons.

Where the fund is a UCITS or NURS there are no restrictions on the types of investor to whom the fund can be marketed.

3.5. Taxation
For taxation purposes, a distinction needs to be made between OEICs and AUTs (referred to in this section as 'Authorised Investment Funds' or AIFs) and investment trust companies.

Taxation of the AIF
AIFs are within the charge to UK corporation tax but only subject to corporation tax at a reduced rate of 20 per cent. The AIF can claim deductions for management expenses and benefit from certain exemptions from corporation tax. In particular, AIFs are exempt from tax on capital gains from disposal of assets held by it. An AIF must determine the amount of income that is available for distribution as at each distribution date. The total amount of income available for distribution must be classified in the AIF's accounts as either yearly interest or dividend (not a combination of the two).

An AIF can only show its total income as interest income if it meets the Qualifying Investments Test. An AIF will satisfy the Qualifying Investments Test broadly if investments producing interest or a return similar to interest represent 60 per cent of the market value of its total investments. The AIF is, in principle, subject to 20 per cent corporation tax on such interest income, but if the Qualifying Investments Test is met, the AIF get a corresponding deduction for amounts distributed to investors. No such deduction is available if the AIF fails the Qualifying Investments Tests. If the Qualifying

Investments Test is not met then all of the income available for distribution must be classed as dividends. The AIF is likely to be exempt from corporation tax on its dividend income.

An AIF with a mixture of dividend and interest income but that does not pass the Qualifying Investments Test may apply to become a Tax Elected Fund (TEF) provided that it does not also have any income directly from a UK or overseas property business. The intention of the TEF regime is to move the point of taxation from the TEF to the investor so that the investor is taxed as though they had invested in the underlying assets directly. It does this by requiring the TEF to make two types of distribution, a dividend distribution and a non-dividend distribution. In general all dividend income received by the TEF will be distributed as a dividend distribution and all other income will be distributed as a non-dividend distribution. Investors are then taxed as though they have received a dividend (including the non-payable dividend tax credit) and a payment of yearly interest.

An AIF may also receive trading profits which will be subject to corporation tax. However if an AIF meets the 'Genuine Diversity of Ownership Condition' then amounts realised as gains on the disposal of certain investments (including shares and debt instruments) will be treated as exempt capital gains and not as trading income even if the AIF churns its portfolio in a way which suggests trading activity. Broadly, an AIF will meet the Genuine Diversity of Ownership Condition where the fund is marketed and made available sufficiently widely to reach a large number of the intended categories of (unconnected) investors.

Two new authorised funds have been established in the UK, created with the intention to be used as pooling vehicles for pension funds or as umbrella funds. These will either be in the form of a limited partnership or a co-ownership fund (the latter being a scheme constituted by contractual arrangements set out in a deed). Both of these vehicles would be regulated, but would have the advantage of being tax transparent.

Taxation of an investment trust company
In order for a company to be treated as an investment trust company it must make a one-off application for approval as such to HM Revenue & Customs and it must fulfil a number of conditions including: UK residency; listing on a regulated market (as defined by EU law); it must be widely held (this is a complex test); it must invest with the aim of spreading investment risk; and its income may derive from shares, land or other assets. Finally, the company must not retain more than 15 per cent of its income in any accounting period, ie, these returns must be distributed to investors.

Subject to certain exceptions, an investment trust is treated like any other UK resident company within the charge to corporation tax. The primary exception is that an investment trust is exempt from tax on chargeable gains although the investment trust also benefits from a relaxation of the rules governing loan relationships and derivative contracts.

Because, subject to the exceptions, an investment trust is treated like any other UK company for tax purposes, there is a tax inefficiency where it receives interest income. This is because the investment trust is subject to corporation tax on the interest it receives (by contrast dividends from most UK and overseas dividends are exempt from tax under general rules) which is then paid to investors by way of dividend for which no deduction is available and the dividend may taxed in the hands of investors.

To address this problem, an elective regime was introduced in 2009 which allows the investment trust a tax deduction for a dividend of interest income and treats the investor as if they had received interest rather than a dividend provided certain conditions are met. The UK Government is also looking to make investment trusts more flexible and attractive by relaxing some of the requirements described above.

3.6. Customary or common terms
Term of the fund
AUTs and OEICs do not generally have a fixed term duration.
Investment trusts can be unlimited in duration or have a fixed duration typically of between 5-10 years.

Liquidity of interests
AUTs and OEICs typically have daily dealing and the investor can redeem their investment out of the assets of the fund at a price based on net asset value.

For investment trusts the shares will be listed on the London Stock Exchange and the liquidity of the shares will depend on the supply and demand for those shares in the secondary market. Investment trust shares typically trade at a 10-15 per cent discount to net asset value.

Manager participation
In the context of retail funds there is no requirement for the manager to invest in the fund. For AUTs and OEICs the ACD/manager or its associates may invest in a fund but will not be able to exercise voting rights.

Remuneration arrangements
For AUTs and OEICs the ACD/manager will typically levy an initial charge of up to 5 per cent of the investment amount from the investor and an annual management charge is payable to the ACD/manager by the fund. The rate of annual management charge will vary depending on the investment proposition but will usually be in the range of 0.5 per cent to 1.75 per cent of the value of the fund. In addition the ACD/manager may also charge performance fees. These are not common market practice save for funds with complex investment or derivatives strategies. The regulatory framework permits exit fees to be charged but again this is not common market practice. For investment trusts, the investment manager appointed by the investment trust company will receive an annual management fee. The rate of the annual management fee will vary depending on the investment proposition but will usually be in the range of 1 per cent-2 per cent of the value of the fund. The investment manager may also receive performance fees if agreed with the investment trust company.

Investment and borrowing restrictions
For AUTs and OEICs detailed investment provisions apply depending on whether the fund is a UCITS or NURS. Borrowing capability is limited.

For investment trusts, the investment trust company will set its own investment objectives, policies and restrictions for the investment manager to adhere to. An investment trust company can borrow without restriction.

4. PROPOSED CHANGES AND DEVELOPMENTS
The AIFM Directive was only implemented in July 2013 and so there is still a process of bedding-in taking place. It should be expected that various changes occur in the medium term to the structure and operation of alternative investment funds as the market adjusts to the new regulatory framework.

More generally within the alternative asset classes, fundraising continues to be a challenge and there is a noticeable shift in the negotiating power between GPs/sponsors and investors. The investor-led guidelines on fund terms (such as the ILPA Private Equity Principles) are often being used by investors as a benchmark against which the commercial terms of the fund are tested.

The regulatory framework governing retail funds is continuously evolving.

In July 2012, the EU Commission presented a legislative proposal in relation to UCITS V. This focused on three areas, namely: (i) clarification of the UCITS depositary's functions and improvements to provisions governing their liability, should assets be lost in custody; (ii) the introduction of rules on remuneration policies that must be applied to key members of the UCITS managerial staff; and (iii) harmonisation of the minimum administrative sanctions that are to be available to supervisors in case of key violations of the UCITS rules. The UCITS V Directive, focusing on fund manager bonuses, is currently being negotiated between the EU Commission, EU Council and EU Parliament. It is expected that the Directive will be finalised in the fourth quarter of 2013 but it is unlikely to enter into force until 2015.

Also in July 2012, the EU Commission launched a consultation in relation to UCITS VI. This covered a variety of different areas including possible changes to the investment powers of UCITS (eg, eligible assets, use of OTC derivatives, efficient portfolio management), liquidity management issues, depositary passport and issues arising from UCITS IV implementation. In addition it also covered money market funds and long term investments which have both subsequently become the subject of separate EU Commission legislative proposals. We expect a legislative proposal on UCITS VI in the fourth quarter of 2013.

United States of America

Jay Milkes, Sarah Davidoff & Michael Doherty
Ropes & Gray LLP

1. MARKET OVERVIEW

The US retail funds market, both for open-ended and closed-ended funds, is well developed and very active. Open-ended retail funds, commonly referred to as mutual funds, are pooled investment vehicles that generally continuously offer shares to the public. Open-ended retail funds issue redeemable securities, which means that, except in extraordinary circumstances, on shareholder demand a fund must redeem its shares at net asset value (NAV) and pay redemption proceeds within seven days. Exchange-traded funds (ETFs) are typically organised as open-ended funds, although they are distinct in that their shares trade on an exchange throughout the trading day at prices that may differ from a fund's NAV. Closed-ended retail funds, which are often sold in underwritten public offerings, do not offer redeemable securities. Investors generally buy and sell shares of closed-ended funds in the secondary market on exchanges. Some 'retail' funds may be sold to institutional investors, which may be attracted to the liquidity, transparency or potential tax advantages of a registered product.

According to statistics from the Investment Company Institute website, as of March 2013, there were approximately 7,600 US open-ended funds with combined assets of over $13.5 trillion. Of this, about $2.6 trillion was invested in money market funds, which are a type of mutual fund required by law to invest in lower-risk securities. Investor interest in ETFs has also been strong; as of March 2013, the combined assets of the approximately 1,190 US ETFs were over $1.4 trillion, a 21 per cent increase in assets over the 12 trailing months. The closed-ended fund market is also robust; as of the end of March 2013, there were 602 US closed-ended funds with approximately $277 billion in assets under management (AUM).

The US hedge fund market is well-developed and actively populated by many managers, funds and high net worth and institutional investors. US hedge fund managers also manage significant assets of non-US investors. According to Hedge Fund Research, Inc., total industry assets reached an estimated $2.25 trillion as of 31 December 2012.

Hedge funds generally experienced a solid performance in 2012. The return of the AR Composite Index, a broad measure of hedge fund performance maintained by industry magazine AR, was estimated to be 6.48 per cent for the 2012 calendar year.

USA

The US private equity fund market is similarly populated by many managers, funds and a wide array of investors. Fundraising at US private equity firms remained relatively flat in 2012; however, conditions are promising for potential growth in deal-making by private equity funds in 2013, boosted by favourable credit conditions and attractive acquisition prospects. Short-term returns on private equity funds were relatively shaky in 2012, averaging just 5.5 per cent, the weakest performance since 2008, although long-term returns on such funds continued to outperform US and European public equity markets by a healthy margin over both the past five and 10 years (source: *Bain & Company*).

In addition to market growth for hedge funds and private equity funds, 2012 saw growth in the convergence of the two fund structures that spanned asset classes. Traits common to such 'hybrid' funds, which combine aspects traditionally limited to either hedge funds or private equity funds, include commitment-based structures, slow pay mechanics, side pockets of illiquid investments, lock-ins and limitations on the speed and manner in which investors may withdraw funds. In addition, hedge fund managers increased their focus in the retail fund space, resulting in the growth of registered fund of funds, business development companies (BDCs) and funds with a long-only investment strategy and lower fee structures.

2. ALTERNATIVE INVESTMENT FUNDS
2.1. Common structures

US private equity funds and hedge funds are typically structured as limited partnerships, which afford investors limited liability while providing the general partner with broad authority to oversee management of the fund. Generally, the fund enters into a separate management agreement with a manager which is an affiliate of the general partner. It is also possible for a private fund to be organised as a limited liability company (LLC), but this is less typical in the marketplace.

Typical structures include:
- A single Delaware limited partnership into which all investors (US and non-US) invest directly. This fund structure has the benefit of simplicity and generally permits pass-through tax treatment for US taxable investors. A primary disadvantage is that non-US and US tax-exempt investors may be subject to adverse tax consequences if the fund realises, respectively, income effectively connected with a US trade or business (ECI) or unrelated business taxable income (UBTI), which can give rise to certain US tax payment and filing obligations.
- A master-feeder structure where a non-US entity (generally organised in a tax efficient jurisdiction such as the Cayman Islands and which typically elects to be treated as a corporation for US tax purposes) invests into a Delaware limited partnership. The non-US entity generally will shield non-US investors from directly incurring ECI and US tax-exempt investors from incurring UBTI. Benefits include having a single pool of assets to manage; drawbacks include potential tax inefficiencies if the fund may generate significant amounts of ECI/UBTI.

- A parallel fund structure where a Delaware limited partnership and a second partnership (either Delaware or non-US) invest side by side, allowing the manager to make different investments for the US fund and the non-US fund based on tax or other considerations. However, it involves more complexity in organising and operating.
- A single Delaware limited partnership into which all investors, US and non-US, invest, and which contemplates that alternative investment vehicles (AIVs) may be established for particular investments to optimise US tax consequences for various groups of investors. This structure may be simpler to form at the outset but may present other complexities if multiple AIVs are used.

Investor interests in US funds are referred to as limited partnership or membership interests depending on whether the fund is a limited partnership or an LLC, respectively, and investor interests in non-US funds are referred to as limited partnership interests or shares, depending on whether the entity is organised as a limited partnership or corporation.

2.2. Regulatory framework

The Investment Advisers Act of 1940 (Advisers Act) is the primary source of law applicable to most hedge fund managers and private equity fund managers. The Advisers Act imposes substantive requirements on advisers and empowers the SEC to regulate adviser's activities. In addition, the effectiveness of the Dodd-Frank Wall Street Reform and Consumer Protection Act (Dodd-Frank), among other things, substantially altered the registration and reporting schemes under the Advisers Act, placed new restrictions on banks, and imposed new requirements on over-the-counter derivatives markets and transactions.

In addition to the Advisers Act, private funds and their managers may be subject to a number of other federal and state laws, including:
- The Investment Company Act of 1940 (ICA), which imposes substantive requirements on registered funds' organisation and operation and empowers the Securities and Exchange Commission (SEC) to regulate their activities.
- The Securities Act of 1933 (Securities Act), which governs the sale of fund interests and regulates the form and content of registration statements for sales to the public.
- The Internal Revenue Code of 1986 (IRC), which imposes requirements on funds wishing to take advantage of the favourable tax treatment afforded to entities classified as partnerships for US federal income tax purposes.
- Financial Industry Regulatory Authority (FINRA), which is a self-regulatory organisation overseeing securities firms doing business in the US. Regulations promulgated by FINRA govern FINRA members' sales and marketing of fund interests.
- Employee Retirement Income Security Act 1974 (ERISA), which governs the management of pension money.
- The Foreign Corrupt Practices Act (FCPA), which makes it unlawful

for any US company to offer, pay, promise or authorise (directly or indirectly) any bribe or kickback to any foreign official or political party for the purposes of assisting its business.
- The Securities Exchange Act of 1934 (Exchange Act), which governs the filings of ownership of public securities and regulates insider trading.
- Commodity Exchange Act of 1974 (CEA), which regulates hedge funds and their managers if the fund invests in futures, options and/or swaps. See also section 4 below.

Private equity funds and hedge funds are typically eligible for an exemption from certain federal securities laws, including the ICA and Securities Act (see section 2.4.). Similarly, private equity and hedge fund managers are generally required to register as investment advisers under the Advisers Act, absent an applicable exemption.

2.3. Operational requirements

All private equity and hedge fund managers are subject to Advisers Act anti-fraud provisions. US private fund managers with AUM above $150 million generally must register with the SEC as an investment adviser. Managers with separate account clients typically must register with the SEC if they have AUM above $100 million. Registration subjects an adviser to various requirements including those relating to custody, advertising, personal trading, record keeping and proxy voting.

Funds and their advisers must make governmental filings of the following, among other things:
- Ownership in public companies above certain specified thresholds set out in the Exchange Act.
- Form 13F under the Exchange Act (to report certain exchange traded equity securities, equity options/warrants, shares of closed-ended funds and convertible debt securities (only for advisers qualifying as institutional investment managers with discretion over $100 million in those securities).
- Form D filings to disclose initial and annual sales of fund interests in the US.
- Filings with states under Blue Sky laws.
- Filings with the Internal Revenue Service (IRS).
- Form ADV (see section 4).
- Form PQR must be filed with the NFA to disclose pool information.
- Certain large positions in US Treasury securities.
- Form S and Form SLT under the Treasury International Capital reporting system.

In addition, the SEC has adopted substantial new reporting obligations with respect to private funds under Form PF. These obligations are as follows:
- Advisers managing private funds (including certain separately managed accounts) with AUM between $150 million and $1.5 billion must file Form PF annually; those with AUM over $1.5 billion in AUM must file Form PF quarterly, and those with AUM under $150 million are not required to file but are subject to less comprehensive disclosure requirements.

- Form PF will require disclosure of the fund's investment strategy, gross and net assets, and investor and performance information, among other things.

Funds of funds are permitted to provide only a subset of the Form PF disclosure required of other private funds.

Offering memoranda and side letters are not required to be filed with the SEC but are subject to review by the SEC on examination.

Advisers not subject to registration under the Advisers Act may be subject to state registration requirements.

Advisers that engage in futures transactions may also be subject to registration under the CEA (see section 4).

Non-US advisers can manage assets of US investors. However, depending on the nature and extent of their US activities, non-US advisers may be required to register with the SEC or otherwise be subject to the Advisers Act in certain respects (see section 4).

The following areas are generally the most relevant areas of SEC emphasis, regulation or reporting for private equity and hedge fund managers:
- Valuation and pricing. Funds generally value securities in accordance with US generally accepted accounting principles (GAAP). All registered advisers must adopt and implement written policies and procedures reasonably designed to prevent violations of the Advisers Act and its rules.
- Money laundering. Most private equity fund managers maintain an anti-money laundering program and monitor compliance with the FCPA, rules promulgated by the Office of Foreign Assets Control (OFAC), and applicable CFTC and FINRA requirements regarding money laundering.
- ERISA. Special custody, fiduciary and other requirements apply under ERISA where a private equity fund is deemed to hold ERISA pension plan assets. Historically most private equity funds have sought to avoid these requirements either by limiting ERISA pension plan participation to under 25 per cent of each class of limited partner interests or by operating the fund as a venture capital operating company (VCOC). (See section 2.4.)
- Custody. Registered advisers must engage a qualified custodian (such as a bank, registered broker-dealer or other financial institution) to hold client assets. Managers are exempt from requirements to deliver quarterly account statements, provide notice of the qualified custodian or arrange for surprise audits, if they both:
  - engage an independent public accountant registered with, and subject to regular inspection by, the Public Company Account Oversight Board to perform an annual audit; and
  - distribute financial statements prepared in accordance with GAAP within 120 days (or 180 days for funds of funds) of the end of the fund's fiscal year.

Additional rules apply when an affiliate acts as qualified custodian.
- **Systemic risk**. Several federal regulators, including the Financial Stability Oversight Council, the Federal Reserve Board of Governors, the CFTC and the SEC monitor systemic risk of financial institutions including hedge funds (under Dodd-Frank). Fund offering documents typically list risk

factors related to an investment in the fund.
- **Insider dealing and market abuse**. Hedge fund managers must not engage in market manipulation and insider trading (Securities Act, Exchange Act and Dodd-Frank). Registered advisers must adopt and implement written policies and procedures designed to prevent insider trading.
- **Transparency**. For funds holding public securities, limited reporting of such holdings is required. The SEC can require additional reporting, including rules for the assessment of systemic risk (Dodd-Frank) (see below, 'Short selling') (see section 4, Dodd-Frank).
- **Short selling**. Rules regarding short sales are typically primarily applicable to hedge fund managers; Dodd-Frank prohibits 'a manipulative short sale of any security'. The SEC has also adopted a rule requiring stock exchanges to pause trading in certain stocks if the price moves 10 per cent or more in a five minute period. Separately, issuer's securities cannot be sold short within a restricted period before purchasing the same securities in the issuer's secondary public offering (Rule 105, Regulation M).

2.4. Marketing of the fund

Persons who sell interests in private equity funds must be registered as broker-dealers, subject to certain limited exemptions for issuers who market their own securities.

Persons who sell interests in hedge funds must be registered as broker-dealers, subject to certain limited exemptions for issuers who market their own securities; this is an area that has recently received increased SEC scrutiny.

Interests in private funds such as private equity and hedge funds are generally offered to US persons under a private placement exemption under the Securities Act.

In 2012, the 'Jumpstart Our Business Startups Act' (JOBS Act) was passed by Congress. Once signed into law and implemented, the JOBS Act would ease restrictions on advertising and other offering practices on fund managers conducting offerings in the US under Regulation D (see below), most notably by eliminating the prohibition against general solicitation.

Regulation D of the Securities Act

An offering may be exempt from registration if sales are restricted to accredited investors, generally defined as:
- persons with a net worth of $1 million (with spouse) or annual income of $200,000 ($300,000 with spouse); and
- businesses and other entity investors with total assets of $5 million.

The definition of accredited investor was recently amended to delete the 'value of the primary residence' from net worth.

Regulation S of the Securities Act

Interests in non-US private equity and hedge funds may be exempt from registration if offers and sales are made outside the US to non-US investors, even if those offers and sales are not made in a private placement.

Investment Company Act
Private equity and hedge funds typically operate under one of the following exemptions from ICA registration:
- interests are privately-offered to, and held by, fewer than 100 US beneficial owners qualifying as accredited investors.
- interests are only privately-offered to qualified purchasers, generally:
  - persons with $5 million in investments;
  - companies or other institutions with $25 million in investments; or
  - persons investing solely on behalf of qualified purchasers.

Commodity Exchange Act
Managers that engage in futures and commodities transactions or in other derivatives transactions may be required to register as commodity pool operators (CPOs) and commodity trading advisors with the CFTC, and become members of the National Futures Association (NFA).

CFTC registrants and NFA members must comply with various disclosure, record keeping and reporting requirements, as well as with other regulations.

ERISA
Under ERISA, funds may be restricted from accepting investments from the following:
- pensions and other employee benefit plans subject to ERISA; and
- entities whose assets are deemed to be 'plan assets' for purposes of ERISA.

Funds may place percentage restrictions on investments from such investors, or apply an outright ban. In order to permit unlimited investment by ERISA plans, funds are required to satisfy a series of operational rules, although many funds are not practicably able to comply with such rules. In addition, funds may become subject to ERISA by virtue of fund investments into equity securities.

2.5. Taxation
The US income tax treatment of private equity funds, as well as US and non-US investors in such funds, is similar in many respects to the US tax treatment applicable to hedge funds, as described below.

Funds
There is no entity level tax on US private equity or hedge funds, so long as they are not treated as publicly traded partnerships (which may be taxable as corporations in certain circumstances). A non-US fund formed as a non-US corporation or partnership that is taxed as a corporation for US income tax purposes may be subject to ECI and US withholding taxes (see section 2.1.). Neither private equity nor hedge funds are required to obtain any tax rulings prior to their establishment. However, a fund formed as a non-US partnership that intends to be taxed as corporation for US income tax purposes generally must file an entity classification election with the IRS to be so treated.

Resident investors
A taxable US investor reports on its own tax return its distributive share of the

USA

fund's annual taxable income or loss, regardless of whether distributions are received. The tax character of the income or loss also generally passes to the investor.

Non-resident and US tax-exempt investors
Non-US investors and US tax-exempt entities often invest through a non-US corporation, generally to avoid US tax on ECI and/or UBTI (see section 2.1.). In addition, as noted in section 2.1., private equity funds often utilise structures whereby non-US investors and US tax-exempt investors generally participate through a tax transparent partnership, but with particular investments being made through corporate structures to insulate these investors from incurring ECI or UBTI with respect to specific investments that raise a greater risk of generating such income.

See section 3.5. for current tax rates.

2.6. Customary or common terms
Private funds – closed-ended
Private equity funds are almost invariably organised as closed-end funds with limited marketing periods (ie, 12 to 18 months) followed by an investment period of four to seven years. The life of a fund varies, but often runs eight to ten years, with some extension ability by the general partner to provide for orderly liquidation. Such extension may require limited partner or advisory committee approval. Funds often can be terminated early upon a super majority vote of investors.

Fund interests do not carry general redemption rights, though limited partners usually do have a right to be redeemed where continued ownership could raise certain specified legal violations. A fairly substantial secondary market offers some liquidity to investors. Such transfers generally require general partner consent, but consent is typically granted absent any legal issues.

Funds typically are overseen by a general partner entity responsible for selecting and managing investments and overall fund operations. There is usually a separate management entity which receives a management fee for providing investment advice to the general partner. The general partner typically makes a relatively small capital contribution to the fund (eg, 0.2 per cent to 1 per cent of fund commitments) while principals and employees of the fund sponsor will commit to co-invest in portfolio company investments (typically from 2 per cent to 5 per cent of fund commitments). Such funding obligations may be deemed satisfied if the sponsor waives its right to management fees, providing certain US tax advantages to the sponsor.

Most funds impose a requirement that key personnel devote substantially all their business time to the fund, subject to certain specified exceptions. Limited partners usually have the right upon some majority vote to terminate the investment period or the fund if such key persons cease to devote such time or depart the manager. Limited partners also often have the ability to remove the general partner and manager for cause upon a simple majority vote, and sometimes they also have a no-fault removal right exercisable upon a super majority vote.

The fund manager is typically paid an annual management fee of 1 per cent to 2 per cent based on committed capital during the investment period, and based on invested capital less realised investments thereafter. The general partner typically receives a 20 per cent carried interest (though lower rates apply for certain funds). Often carry may be distributed based on returns from each particular deal, but ultimately may be subject to clawback based on performance of the portfolio as a whole. Sponsors often provide credit support for their clawback obligation through reserve accounts and individual guarantees.

Private equity funds generally do not face significant regulatory constraints as to their investments. However, their investment guidelines often contain restrictions, such as geographic and concentration limits.

Investors typically contribute capital periodically over the fund's life as called by the general partner. A majority of the capital is paid in during the investment period, but significant amounts may be paid in later for follow-on investments and expenses.

See section 2.3. for required reporting obligations to investors and regulatory authorities.

Private funds – open-ended
Hedge funds are typically formed as continuous offerings where investors have the ability to invest into the fund on an ongoing basis (generally, monthly or quarterly). Funds are dissolved pursuant to the provisions of their operating agreements.

Investors can usually redeem periodically (ie, monthly or quarterly) with prior notice. Redemptions may be subject to lockup periods, fees, gates, suspensions and reserves. Transfers are typically restricted and require prior approval by the general partner or manager.

For hedge funds structured as limited partnerships, the general partner may select the investments, manage the assets, and oversee the operations of the fund. In many cases, the fund manager is structured as a separate, though affiliated, entity.

Hedge funds structured as LLCs or non-US companies generally retain a fund manager pursuant to an advisory contract.

Hedge fund managers typically make significant investments into the fund with their own assets, alongside their clients, although it is not required.

In some cases, hedge funds impose time requirements upon members of management. Funds can include key man provisions in their operating agreements which can be triggered if, for example, key management individuals devote less than a specified amount of time to the fund, certain key management individuals depart from the fund, or redemptions by key management members exceed a specified level. Upon such a triggering event, the fund may be required to notify investors and/or allow investors to withdraw from the fund.

Hedge funds do not typically give investors the ability to remove the manager, except in limited circumstances due to accounting considerations.

Fees typically include both a base management fee (usually a percentage of

AUM) along with a performance component, which may be structured as a fee or as an allocation of profits.

Performance fees (generally calculated on realised and unrealised gains) may be subject to high water marks to make up prior losses and to ensure that fund managers only take fees on profits unique to an individual investment. The performance fee generally comprises a major portion of the fund manager's overall compensation.

Because hedge funds are not subject to the extensive regulatory scheme of registered funds, they have greater flexibility in the investments they can make and are not generally constrained or restricted in their investment activities, other than by their own guidelines. The fund manager generally has broad discretion in selecting investments and trading on behalf of the fund.

Some hedge funds may include investment limitations regarding region or concentration. However, most funds do not. Hedge funds may hold large cash positions when the fund manager deems it appropriate to remain uninvested, and may use both leverage and short selling as a part of their investment strategy.

See section 2.3. for required reporting obligations to investors and regulatory authorities.

Investors are usually required to fund their full investment upon being admitted to a hedge fund.

3. RETAIL FUNDS
3.1. Common structures
Open-ended retail funds, whether mutual funds or ETFs, can be organised as: (i) business or statutory trusts; (ii) corporations; (iii) limited partnerships; (iv) LLCs; or (v) another entity under the laws of any US state. Most open-ended funds are organised as Massachusetts business trusts, Delaware statutory trusts or Maryland corporations, each of which may qualify for beneficial tax treatment as described in section 2.5. These structures are attractive because they offer significant governance flexibility and do not require annual shareholder meetings. Liability and indemnification issues may also influence the choice of vehicle.

An open-ended fund can offer multiple classes of interests in a retail fund, or 'shares', with different expenses and offering different services, such as different shareholder servicing or distribution arrangements, although certain expenses, such as advisory and custodial fees, must be borne at the fund rather than the class level.

Closed-ended funds are typically organised in the same manner as open-ended funds. Unlike open-ended funds, however, closed-ended funds can issue preferred stock subject to certain conditions.

Another form of a closed-ended fund is a business development company (BDC), typically organised as a corporation; BDCs are essentially publicly-traded private equity or venture capital funds, investing primarily in non-public or small public companies.

3.2. Regulatory framework
The ICA is the primary source of applicable law for open-ended and closed-

ended funds. The ICA imposes substantive requirements on funds' organisation and operation, and empowers the SEC to regulate their activities. Retail funds are also subject to the statutes described in section 2.2., including the Securities Act, the Exchange Act, FINRA, the IRC and, for some funds, the CEA.

Open-ended funds
- Must register as an investment company under the ICA and most funds must register its offering of securities to the public under the Securities Act. Funds file their registration statement with the SEC on Form N-1A. Form N-1A includes disclosure regarding, among other things, the fund's investment objective(s), strategies and related risks, fees and annual fund operating expenses and how to purchase shares.
- Must annually update their registration statement.
- Most states require annual notice filings and charge fees if the fund's shares are sold in that state.
- Funds that invest beyond certain thresholds in non-hedge commodity interest positions and/or market themselves as a vehicle for commodity investing require that their advisors register as a CPO with the CFTC.

It is difficult and uncommon for a fund organised outside the US to register as an open-ended fund. The ICA prohibits a non-US fund from publically offering shares in the US except under an exemptive order. The SEC can grant an exemptive order if it is legally and practically feasible to effectively enforce the provisions of the ICA against the non-US fund and the order is otherwise consistent with the public interest and investor protection. The SEC has, however, issued exemptive rules that permit certain Canadian funds to register under the ICA without seeking exemptive relief.

ETFs
- Generally subject to the same regulatory regime as open-ended funds.
- Must comply with rules of the exchange(s) on which they trade, although they need to apply for and receive exemptive relief from the SEC for certain provisions of the ICA and, for some funds, certain provisions of the Exchange Act before offering shares.
- In 2008, the SEC proposed Rule 6c-11 under the ICA, which would significantly reduce the need for ETFs to first obtain exemptive relief; however, the timing for the adoption of this rule is currently uncertain. The SEC has given some indication that it intends to adopt a similar rule in the next few years.

Closed-ended funds
- Generally subject to the same regulatory regime as open-ended funds.
- Closed-ended funds with shares listed on an exchange are also subject to the exchange's rules and to the exchange's share listing requirements.
- BDCs elect to be treated as such and are subject to many provisions of the ICA, as well as certain requirements applicable only to BDCs.

The registration process for closed-ended funds is generally the same as for open-ended funds, with a few exceptions.

Advisers to both open-ended and closed-ended funds, including non-US advisers, are subject to the Advisers Act and the ICA.

3.3. Operational requirements

Under the ICA, retail funds must place and maintain their assets with a qualified custodian. If certain relatively onerous conditions are met, the fund can act as its own custodian. Funds may hold their non-US assets with government-regulated non-US banks, subsidiaries of US banks or bank holding companies, and may deposit non-US securities with non-US securities depositaries.

While shares of closed-ended funds and ETFs generally trade at market prices, open-ended retail funds must price the sale and redemption of its shares at NAV. The fund's NAV must reflect current market value of the fund's portfolio securities (less liabilities) where market quotations are readily available and fair value pricing, as determined by the fund's board of directors or designated advisor, when market quotations are not readily available.

Open-ended funds have ongoing reporting requirements to the SEC. Such filings include:
- annual updates to a fund's registration statement on Form N-1A;
- supplements to a fund's prospectus regarding material changes;
- periodic reports containing the fund's financial statements certified by the fund's CEO and CFO;
- semi-annual reports containing certain regulatory information;
- quarterly reports containing portfolio holdings information certified by the fund's CEO and CFO;
- annual reports on the fund's proxy voting record; and
- for money market funds, a monthly report regarding such money market fund's portfolio holdings.

Closed-ended funds must file substantially similar periodic reports with the SEC. ETFs generally follow the same regulatory reporting requirements as open-ended funds, although they are more transparent as some provide portfolio holdings information on a daily basis and others are based on publicly available indexes. Retail funds may also be required to make periodic filings with state securities regulators.

Retail funds also have ongoing reporting requirements to investors, including annual reports and a variety of additional disclosure documents.

3.4. Marketing the fund

Open-ended retail funds typically offer their shares to the public Exchange Act-registered broker-dealers. Distributors are subject to FINRA's rules and regulations. The distributor generally purchases shares from the fund and sells the shares to the public directly or indirectly through financial intermediaries.

ETFs sell and redeem shares in large blocks called 'creation units,' dealing only with brokerage firms and institutional investors designated as 'authorised participants.' Authorised participants act as marker makers. Fund shares are listed on an exchange, where they trade in smaller increments on the secondary market.

Closed-ended funds typically offer shares through an underwriting syndicate in a public offering. After the public offering, the shares of most closed-ended funds trade on exchanges.

Generally, open-ended funds can offer and sell their shares to any investor, although certain restrictions may be imposed. Additionally, broker-dealers recommending a fund's shares will generally be subject to FINRA requirements requiring them to analyse the 'suitability' of the fund's shares as an investment for their clients.

There are no general investor eligibility requirements for investors in closed-ended funds. There are requirements for authorised participants to purchase and redeem creation units of ETFs, but there are no general investor eligibility requirements for investors who trade ETFs in the secondary market.

3.5. Taxation

Retail funds typically seek to qualify as regulated investment companies (RICs) under the IRC to obtain beneficial tax treatment for themselves and their shareholders. A retail fund does not need to obtain a tax ruling prior to its formation in order to be treated as a RIC, provided it properly elects such treatment and meets certain ongoing qualification requirements.

A qualifying RIC is not subject to US federal income or excise tax at the fund level on income and gains from investments that are timely distributed to investors. Instead, the RIC's investors are taxed on RIC income and gains when dividends are actually paid to them. When a qualifying RIC pays dividends, it can pass through certain tax attributes of its income and gains, including net long-term capital gain, net tax-exempt interest and qualified dividend income, to its investors. Generally, all other dividends of RIC income and gains, including net short-term capital gain, are taxable to US resident investors as ordinary income. Any net gain resulting from a US resident investor's disposition of fund shares is generally taxable to the investor as capital gain.

The top marginal US federal income tax rates for individuals currently are: (i) 39.6 per cent for ordinary income and short-term capital gain; and (ii) 20 per cent for long-term capital gain and qualified dividend income. In addition, a 3.8 per cent tax is generally imposed on 'net investment income' of US resident individuals whose income exceeds certain thresholds. In the case of an investment in a RIC, net investment income generally includes: (i) dividends paid by the RIC; and (ii) any net gains resulting from the disposition of RIC shares.

Generally, dividends (other than specially designated dividends of net long-term capital gain and tax-exempt interest) paid to non-resident investors are subject to US federal income tax withholding at a 30 per cent rate (or a lower applicable treaty rate). However, under a special IRC exemption, dividends paid by a RIC to a non-resident investor of US source interest income or net short-term capital gain generally are exempt from withholding, provided the RIC reports them as such to investors. This special exemption will expire for taxable years of a RIC beginning after 31 December 2013, unless the US Congress extends the effective date, as it has done in the past.

Generally, non-resident investors are not subject to US federal income tax on gains realised on the disposition of RIC shares.

In general, US tax-exempt and non-resident investors can invest directly in a RIC without UBTI or ECI concerns.

3.6. Customary or common terms

The term of retails funds is typically perpetual, although a fund's board may decide to liquidate or merge a fund.

Many retail funds offer multiple classes of shares, each with different shareholder services and/or distribution arrangements. Each class generally has different fees and expenses, such as the level of fees allowed under ICA Rule 12b-1 and sales charges (or 'loads'), which, depending on the class of shares, may be charged upon initial purchase, upon the sale of shares, or not at all if shares are held for a sufficiently long period. For open-ended funds, an adviser of the fund can place certain restrictions on sales of fund shares. A fund can also establish minimum investment amounts, impose front-end, level or deferred sales charges, and limit the distribution channels through which shares are sold. It is also common for funds to limit the ability of frequent traders to purchase shares or otherwise limit the number of exchanges an investor can make within a specified period. A fund cannot suspend redemptions except under unusual circumstances. Funds may impose a redemption fee, generally up to 2 per cent, paid to the Fund as opposed to the distributor or broker. Although closed-ended fund shares are not redeemable at the shareholder's option, a closed-ended fund can repurchase its shares, including, in certain circumstances and subject to restrictions, at a price other than NAV.

Although there are no statutory restrictions on retail fund investors' rights to transfer or assign their rights to third parties, most open-ended fund investors seeking to dispose of their shares redeem them. In the case of ETFs and exchange-traded closed-ended funds, investors seeking to dispose of their shares typically sell them on an exchange.

The ICA requires a written investment advisory contract between a retail fund and its adviser(s). The contract must: (i) describe all compensation; (ii) be initially approved by shareholders, except for certain sub-advisers operating under exemption relief from the SEC; (iii) require annual approval, after an initial two-year period, of its continuance by a majority of the fund's board of directors or shareholders; (iv) provide that the fund may terminate the contract, without penalty, on 60 days' written notice; and (v) provide for automatic termination in the event of assignment. Although an asset-based fee is most common, some retail funds' advisory contracts include performance-based fees.

Funds wanting to classify as diversified are subject to certain requirements under the ICA. Funds that choose not to classify as a diversified companies remain subject to separate diversification rules under the IRC. Retail funds that concentrate in a certain industry or investments beyond 25 per cent of that fund's assets are also generally subject to certain additional disclosure requirements. Retail funds with names that point to certain types or categories or investments are also subject to certain investment requirements based on the name of the fund.

Retail funds are also subject to restrictions on transactions with affiliates and limitations on investments in other investment companies, securities-related businesses and, for open-ended funds, illiquid securities. With respect to money market funds, there are additional restrictions on portfolio quality, diversification, maturity and liquidity.

A fund must also disclose in its registration statement its investment policy in relation to certain matters, such as the purchase and sale of real estate and commodities. These investment policies cannot be changed without shareholder approval.

A fund is limited in its ability to borrow money. An open-ended fund can borrow money from a bank, but must maintain certain asset coverage in relation to these borrowings. The SEC is of the view that certain trading practices and derivative instruments that may cause a fund to be leveraged must be 'covered' either by asset segregation or offsetting transactions. Closed-ended funds are generally subject to the same restrictions as open-ended funds. However, a closed-ended fund can issue a senior debt security and a senior equity security, subject to asset coverage requirements, and can borrow from entities other than banks.

4. PROPOSED CHANGES AND DEVELOPMENTS
Retail funds
Recent legal developments potentially affecting retail funds include:
- proposed changes to the rules governing money market funds, which include floating NAVs for certain classes of funds that tend to cater to institutional investors and new rules and a fee relating to fund withdrawals in times of increased market stress;
- the still-pending proposal of a new rule and related amendments to replace Rule 12b-1 under the ICA, which would limit cumulative sales charges paid by an investor;
- the recently published rule pursuant to which financial companies, including retail funds, may be made subject to systemic regulation under Title I of Dodd-Frank;
- proposals by the CFTC designed to resolve or minimise certain conflicts between CFTC and SEC rules applicable to RICs whose trading subjects their advisers to regulation as CPOs;
- an increase in the use of social media and associated laws and regulation, which may require additional safeguards for retail fund employers to ensure regulatory compliance under the ICA and other applicable law;
- the likely development of valuation guidance and further development of derivatives guidance from the Division of Investment Management at the SEC, which may increase scrutiny on directors of retail funds;
- the possible development of an ETF exemptive rule; and
- pending applications using a variety of structures to limit portfolio transparency for active ETFs.

Alternative investment funds

Dodd-Frank was signed into law on 21 July 2010 for the purpose of preventing future financial crises. It effected sweeping changes to the overall US regulation of the financial services industry, including hedge funds and private equity funds. For example, Dodd-Frank required advisers with at least $150 million under management to register as investment advisers with the SEC by 30 March 2012. The SEC has informed newly-registered advisers that it intends to conduct focused examinations of their policies and practices.

Many other rules have been proposed under Dodd-Frank, but have not yet been adopted. These rules include the Volcker Rule, which will limit a bank's ability to trade its own capital and invest in hedge funds and private equity funds when adopted.

The SEC has also adopted changes to the disclosure requirements of Form ADV, the investment adviser registration form which provides key information regarding the advisory relationship to clients and to the regulatory bodies.

Under Dodd-Frank, the SEC has also enacted Rule 204(b)(1) which requires private fund advisers to periodically file Form PF, a comprehensive disclosure form requiring, among other things, details about the fund's strategy and trading practices.

Under Dodd-Frank, the SEC has also narrowed the available exemptions from registration as an adviser for certain 'foreign private advisers.' In order to qualify for the exemption, advisers must, among other things, not have a place of business in the US, and must have fewer than 15 clients and investors in the US who represent less than $25 million of AUM in private funds advised by it.

In a separate development, fund managers that engage in futures, options and/or swaps may be required to register as CPOs and/or CTAs with the CFTC and become members of the NFA. Effective 31 December 2012, the CFTC narrowed the applicability of the exemption from the CPO registration requirements, which was previously an exemption relied on by many hedge funds. As a result, general partners or managers of hedge funds that invest more than a *de minimis* portion of their assets in futures, options on futures, and certain derivatives must register with the CFTC as a CPO. Those subject to registration must comply with various disclosure, recordkeeping and reporting requirements, as well as with other regulations. However, CFTC Regulation 4.7 allows funds whose participants are limited to qualified eligible persons to claim relief from providing its investors with certain disclosure documents and other CFTC requirements.

All funds

Lastly, under the recently enacted FATCA rules, beginning in 2014, non-US funds, and certain US resident and non-resident investors in both US and non-US funds, may be subject to a 30 per cent US withholding tax generally on certain payments of US source income made to them unless the fund or investor, as applicable, satisfies relevant FATCA requirements, including under an inter-governmental agreement.

Contact details

GENERAL EDITOR
Samuel Kay
Travers Smith LLP
10 Snow Hill
London
EC1A 2AL
England
T: +44 20 7295 3000
E: samuel.kay@traverssmith.com
W: www.traverssmith.com

AUSTRALIA
Stephen Etkind, Karen Payne, Andrew Yik & Henry Wong
Minter Ellison Lawyers
88 Phillip Street
Sydney
NSW 2000
Australia
T: +61 2 9921 8888
F: +61 2 9921 8123
E: stephen.etkind@minterellison.com; karen.payne@minterellison.com; andrew.yik@minterellison.com and henry.wong@minterellison.com
W: www.minterellison.com

BRAZIL
Alexei Bonamin, Ana Claudia Akie Utumi & João Busin
TozziniFreire Advogados
Rua Borges Lagoa, 1328
São Paulo, SP
Brazil
04038-904
T: +55 11 5086-5000
F: +55 11 5086-5555
E: abonamin@tozzinifreire.com.br
autumi@tozzinifreire.com.br
jbusin@tozzinifreire.com.br
W: www.tozzinifreire.com.br

BRITISH VIRGIN ISLANDS
Tim Clipstone & Sophie Whitcombe*
Maples and Calder
Sea Meadow House
PO Box 173
Road Town
Tortola VG1110
British Virgin Islands
T: +1 284 852 3000
F: +1 284 852 3097
E: tim.clipstone@maplesandcalder.com
sophie.whitcombe@maplesandcalder.com
W: www.maplesandcalder.com
Tim is based in the BVI office and Sophie in London

CAYMAN ISLANDS
Paul Govier & Sophie Whitcombe
Maples and Calder
11th Floor
200 Aldersgate Street
London EC1A 4HD
United Kingdom
T: +44 20 7466 1600
F: +44 20 7466 1700
E: paul.govier@maplesandcalder.com
sophie.whitcombe@maplesandcalder.com
W: www.maplesandcalder.com

DENMARK
Claus Bennetsen
HORTEN Advokatpartnerselskab
Philip Heymans Allé 7
DK 2900 Hellerup
Copenhagen
Denmark
T: +45 33344000
F: +45 33344001
E: cbe@horten.dk
W: www.horten.dk

Contact details

FINLAND
Marcus Möller, Antti Lehtimaja,
Mirja Sikander & Pyry Somervuori
Krogerus
Unioninkatu 22
Helsinki 00130
Finland
T: +358 290 006200
F: +358 290 006201
E: marcus.moller@krogerus.com
W: www.krogerus.com

GERMANY
Uwe Bärenz & Dr Jens Steinmüller
P+P Pöllath + Partners
Potsdamer Platz 5
Berlin 10785
Germany
T: +49 (30) 25353-122
F: +49 (30) 25353-999
E: uwe.baerenz@pplaw.com
   jens.steinmueller@pplaw.com
W: www.pplaw.com

GIBRALTAR
Melo Triay, Robert Vasquez,
Javi Triay & Jay Gomez
Triay & Triay
28 Irish Town
Gibraltar
T: +350 200 72020
E: financial.services@triay.com.
W: www.triay.com

GUERNSEY
Gavin Farrell, Oliver Godwin, James
Haughton & Mandy Andrade
Mourant Ozannes, Guernsey
1 Le Marchant Street
St Peter Port
Guernsey GY1 4HP
T: +44 (0)1481 723466
F: +44 (0)1481 723935
E: guernsey@mourantozannes.com
W: www.mourantozannes.com

HONG KONG
Susan Gordon & Mary Nieto
Deacons
5th Floor Alexandra House
18 Chater Road
Hong Kong
T: +852 2825 9211
F: +852 2826 5375
E: susan.gordon@deacons.com.hk;
   mary.nieto@deacons.com.hk
W: www.deacons.com.hk

ICELAND
Gudmundur J Oddsson
LOGOS Legal Services
Efstaleiti 5
Reykjavik 103
Iceland
T: +354 5 400 300
E: gudmundur@logos.is
W: en.logos.is

IRELAND
Nollaig Greene, Elaine Keane,
Darragh Noone & Peter Maher
A&L Goodbody Solicitors
IFSC, North Wall Quay
Dublin 1
Ireland
T: +353 1 649 2000
E: dublin@algoodbody.com
W: www.algoodbody.com

ITALY
Raimondo Premonte & Marco
Zaccagnini
Gianni, Origoni, Grippo, Cappelli &
Partners
6-8 Tokenhouse Yard
London EC2R 7AS
England
T: +44-207 3971700
F: +44-207 3971701
E: rpremonte@gop.it
   mzaccagnini@gop.it
W: www.gop.it

JAPAN
Kazuhiro Yoshii, Ko Hanamizu, Anri Suzuki & Mariko Takashima
Anderson Mori & Tomotsune
Akasaka K-Tower
2-7, Motoakasaka 1-chome
Minato-ku
Tokyo 107-0051
Japan
T: +81-3-6888-1186
F: +81-3-6888-3186
E: kazuhiro.yoshii@amt-law.com
W: www.amt-law.com/en/

JERSEY
Niamh Lalor & Tim Morgan
Ogier
Ogier House
The Esplanade
St Helier
Jersey JE4 9WG
T: 01534 504000
F: 01534 504444
E: niamh.lalor@ogier.com
   tim.morgan@ogier.com
W: www.ogier.com

KOREA
Eui Jong Chung, Tongeun Kim, Dongwook Kang & David Ahn
Bae, Kim & Lee LLC
133 Teheran-ro, Gangnam-gu
Seoul 135-723
Republic of Korea
T: +822-3404-0000
F: +822-3404-0001
E: ej.chung@bkl.co.kr
   tongeun.kim@bkl.co.kr
   dongwook.kang@bkl.co.kr
   david.ahn@bkl.co.kr
W: www.bkl.co.kr

LUXEMBOURG
Jacques Elvinger
Elvinger, Hoss & Prussen
2, Place Winston Churchill
Luxembourg L-1340
T: +352 44 66 44 0
E: jacqueselvinger@ehp.lu
W: www.ehp.lu/

MALTA
Danièle Cop
Mamo TCV Advocates
Palazzo Pietro Stiges, 103 Strait Street
Valletta VLT1436
Malta
T: +356 212 32271
F: +356 212 44291
E: daniele.cop@mamotcv.com
W: www.mamotcv.com

MAURITIUS
Iqbal Rajahbalee, Shan Sonnagee & Bhavna Ramsurun
BLC Chambers
5th Floor, Unicorn Centre
18N Frère Félix de Valois Street
Port Louis Mauritius
T: +230 2137920
F: +230 2137921
E: iqbal.r@blc.mu
   shan.sonnagee@blc.mu
   bhavna.ramsurun@blc.mu
W: www.blc.mu

THE NETHERLANDS
Oscar van Angeren, Sylvia Dikmans & Harm-Paul Plas
Houthoff Buruma
Gustav Mahlerplein 50
Amsterdam 1082MA
The Netherlands
T: +31 (0)20 605 60 00
F: +31 (0)20 605 67 00
E: o.van.angeren@houthoff.com
   s.dikmans@houthoff.com
   h.plas@houthoff.com
W: www.houthoff.com

NEW ZEALAND
Alasdair McBeth
DLA Phillips Fox
TOWER Centre

Level 5,
50-64 Customhouse Quay,
Wellington 6011
New Zealand
T: +64 4 474 3257
E: alasdair.mcbeth@dlapf.com
W: www.dlapf.com

PORTUGAL
Diogo Coutinho de Gouveia & Filipe Santos Barata & Ana Paula Basílio
Gómez-Acebo & Pombo, S.L.P,
Sucursal em Portugal
Av. da Liberdade, 131
Lisbon 1250-140
Portugal
T: +351 213 408 600
F: +351 213 408 608
E: dgouveia@gomezacebo-pombo.com
W: www.gomezacebo-pombo.com

SINGAPORE
Bill Jamieson, Amit Dhume & Manisha Rai
Colin Ng & Partners LLP
36 Carpenter Street
Singapore 059915
Singapore
T: +65 63238383
F: +65 63238282
E: billjamieson@cnplaw.com
W: www.cnplaw.com

SOUTH AFRICA
David Anderson & Francisco Khoza
Bowman Gilfillan
165 West Street
Sandton, Johannesburg
South Africa
T: +27 11 669 9000
E: d.anderson@bowman.co.za
   f.khoza@bowman.co.za
W: www.bowman.co.za

SPAIN
Fernando de las Cuevas, Valentina Rodríguez & Taxation: Remedios García
Gómez-Acebo & Pombo Abogados, S.L.P.
Castellana 216
Madrid 28046
Spain
T: +915829132
F: +915829294
E: fcuevas@gomezacebo-pombo.com
   vrodriguez@gomezacebo-pombo.com
   rgarcia@gomezacebo-pombo.com
W: www.gomezacebo-pombo.com

SWEDEN
Niclas Rockborn & Olle Asplund
Gernandt & Danielsson Advokatbyrå KB
Box 5747
SE-114 87 Stockholm
Sweden
T: +46 (0) 8 670 66 00
F: +46 (0) 8 662 61 01
E: niclas.rockborn@gda.se
   olle.asplund@gda.se
W: www.gda.se

SWITZERLAND
Dr. Jasmin Ghandchi Schmid
Ghandchi Schmid Partners Ltd.
Tödistrasse 1
P.O. Box 1762
Zurich 8027
Switzerland
T: +41 44 289 91 00
F: +41 44 289 91 01
E: ghandchi@ghscp.com
W: www.ghscp.com

UNITED KINGDOM
Sam Kay, Emily Clark & Phil Bartram
Travers Smith LLP
10 Snow Hill
London EC1A 2AL
England
T: +44 20 7295 3000
E: samuel.kay@traverssmith.com
W: www.traverssmith.com

THE UNITED STATES OF AMERICA

Jay Milkes, Sarah Davidoff & Michael Doherty
Ropes & Gray LLP
1211 Avenue of the Americas
New York 10036
New York
USA
T: +(212) 596-9000
F: +(212) 596-9090
E: jay.milkes@ropesgray.com
   sarah.davidoff@ropesgray.com
   michael.doherty@ropesgray.com
W: www.ropesgray.com